D0919513

A GUIDE TO THE PAPERS OF BRITISH CABINET MINISTERS 1900–1964

Edited by Cameron Hazlehurst and Sally Whitehead with Christine Woodland

ROYAL HISTORICAL SOCIETY
GUIDES AND HANDBOOKS
No. 19

ROYAL HISTORICAL SOCIETY
GUIDES AND HANDBOOKS
No. 19

A GUIDE TO THE PAPERS OF
BRITISH CABINET MINISTERS
1900–1964

ROYAL HISTORICAL SOCIETY
GUIDES AND HANDBOOKS
ISSN 0080–4398

MAIN SERIES

1. *Guide to English Commercial Statistics, 1696–1782*. By G. N. Clark and Barbara M. Franks, 1938.
2. *Handbook of British Chronology*. Edited by F. M. Powicke, Charles Johnson and W. J. Harte. 1939. 2nd edition, edited by F. M. Powicke and E. B. Fryde, 1961. 3rd edition, edited by E. B. Fryde, D. E. Greenway, S. Porter and I. Roy, 1986.
3. *Medieval Libraries of Great Britain. A list of surviving books*. Edited by N. R. Ker. 1941. 2nd edition, 1964.
4. *Handbook of Dates for Students of English History*. Edited by C. R. Cheney. 1945. Reprinted, 1996.
5. *Guide to the National and Provincial Directories of England and Wales, excluding London, published before 1856*. By Jane E. Norton, 1950.
6. *Handbook of Oriental History*. Edited by C. H. Philips. 1951.
7. *Texts and Calendars. An analytical guide to serial publications*. By E. L. C. Mullins. 1958. Reprinted (with corrections), 1978.
8. *Anglo-Saxon Charters. An annotated list and bibliography*. By P. H. Sawyer. 1968.
9. *A Centenary Guide to the publications of the Royal Historical Society 1868–1968 and of the former Camden Society 1838–1897*. By Alexander Taylor Milne. 1968.
10. *Guide to the Local Administrative Units of England*. Volume I. *Southern England*. By Frederic A. Youngs, Jr. 1980. Reprinted, 1981.
11. *Guide to Bishops' Registers of England and Wales. A survey from the middle ages to the abolition of episcopacy in 1646*. By David M. Smith. 1981.
12. *Texts and Calendars II. An analytical guide to serial publications 1957–1982*. By E. L. C. Mullins. 1983.
13. *Handbook of Medieval Exchange*. By Peter Spufford, with the assistance of Wendy Wilkinson and Sarah Tolley. 1986.
14. *Scottish Texts and Calendars. An analytical guide to serial publications*. By David and Wendy Stevenson. 1987.
15. *Medieval Libraries of Great Britain*. Edited by N. R. Ker. *Supplement to the second edition*. Edited by Andrew G. Watson. 1987.
16. *A Handlist of British Diplomatic Representatives 1509–1688*. By Gary M. Bell. 1990.
17. *Guide to the Local Administrative Units of England. Volume II. Northern England*. By Frederic A. Youngs, Jr. 1991.
18. *Historians' Guide to Early British Maps*. Edited by Helen Wallis, assisted by Anita McConnell.

SUPPLEMENTARY SERIES

1. *A Guide to the papers of British Cabinet Ministers, 1900–1951*. Compiled by Cameron Hazlehurst and Christine Woodland. 1974.
2. *A Guide to the reports of the U.S. Strategic Bombing Survey. I Europe. II The Pacific*. Edited by Gordon Daniels. 1981.

A GUIDE
TO THE PAPERS OF
BRITISH CABINET MINISTERS
1900–1964

Cameron Hazlehurst
Sally Whitehead
and
Christine Woodland

CAMBRIDGE
UNIVERSITY PRESS

FOR THE ROYAL HISTORICAL SOCIETY

UNIVERSITY COLLEGE LONDON, GOWER STREET,

LONDON WC1E 6BT

PUBLISHED BY THE PRESS SYNDICATE OF THE UNIVERSITY OF CAMBRIDGE
The Pitt Building, Trumpington Street, Cambridge, CB2 1RP, United Kingdom

CAMBRIDGE UNIVERSITY PRESS
The Edinburgh Building, Cambridge CB2 2RU, United Kingdom
40 West 20th Street, New York, NY 10011–4211, USA
10 Stamford Road, Oakleigh, Melbourne 3166, Australia

© Royal Historical Society 1996

First published 1996

A catalogue record for this book is available from the British Library

Library of Congress cataloguing in publication data
Hazlehurst, Cameron, 1941–
A guide to the papers of British cabinet ministers, 1900–1964
Cameron Hazlehurst, Sally Whitehead and Christine Woodland.
p.   cm. – (Royal Historical Society guides and handbooks,
ISSN 0080–4398; no. 19)
Includes index.
ISBN 0–521–58743–3
1. Great Britain – Politics and government – 20th century – Archival
resources. 2. Cabinet officers – Great Britain – Archival resources.
I. Whitehead, Sally. II. Woodland, Christine. III. Title.
IV. Series: Guides and handbooks; no. 19.
Z2020.H39 1996
[DA566.7]
016.3544104′0922′0904–dc20   96–21151
CIP

ISBN 0 521 58743 3

SUBSCRIPTIONS. The serial publications of the Royal Historical Society, *Royal Historical Society Transactions* (ISSN 0080–4401), Camden Fifth Series volumes (ISSN 0960–1163) and volumes of the Guides and Handbooks Series (ISSN 0080–4398) may be purchased together on annual subscription. The 1997 subscription price (which includes postage but not VAT) is £50 (US$80 in the USA, Canada and Mexico) and includes Camden Fifth Series, volumes 9 and 10 (published in July and December) and Transactions Sixth Series, volume 7 (published in December) Guides and Handbooks No. 19. Japanese prices (including ASP delivery) are available from Kinokuniya Company Ltd, P.O. Box 55, Chitose, Tokyo 156, Japan. EU subscribers (outside the UK) who are not registered for VAT should add VAT at their country's rate. VAT registered subscribers should provide their VAT registration number.

Subscription orders, which must be accompanied by payment, may be sent to a bookseller, subscription agent or direct to the publisher: Cambridge University Press, The Edinburgh Building, Shaftesbury Road, Cambridge, CB2 2RU, UK; or in the USA, Canada and Mexico: Cambridge University Press, 40 West 20th Street, New York, NY 10011–4211, USA. Copies of the publications for subscribers in the USA, Canada and Mexico are sent by air to New York to arrive with minimum delay.

SINGLE VOLUMES AND BACK VOLUMES. A list of Royal Historical Society volumes available from Cambridge University Press may be obtained from the Humanities Marketing Department at the address above.

Printed and bound in the United Kingdom by Butler & Tanner Ltd, Frome and London

Contents

Acknowledgments

It is with great satisfaction that the work of 22 years is brought to a close with the publication of this revised edition. A work of reference such as this is not created without the assistance and advice of a large number of people and organisations; and it is more a pleasure than a duty to record our gratitude. First thanks must go to the bodies and institutions which have given support for this project over its twenty-year gestation: the Royal Historical Society, the Australian National University, the Australian Research Council, and the Queensland University of Technology. Trevelyan College and the Society of Fellows at the University of Durham made possible two research trips in Britain by electing Cameron Hazlehurst to Visiting Fellowships in 1990 and 1993.

As this revised edition relied heavily on the first edition, our thanks and acknowledgments for that edition still hold. Obviously, over a twenty-year period, we have made contact with many individuals and institutions who have made our task easier with their prompt and generous assistance. Regrettably, the hundreds of people who have helped us cannot all be named. But we would like to record our gratitude to all of the archivists, librarians, curators, and their assistants, who have advised us on the entries relating to collections in their care. We would also like to thank the former ministers and their families who have, in all but a tiny number of cases, provided us with information in a courteous and kind way. For those who have also provided warm hospitality and who have gone out of their way to assist us in our task, we offer our special thanks.

Acknowledgment is made in the main text of the *Guide* for advice and assistance in individual searches. But, in addition, we would like to thank a number of people upon whose time, skills, good nature, and patience we repeatedly drew: Dr Peter Beal at Sotheby's; Alan Bell and Clare Brown of the Rhodes House Library, Oxford; Dr B. S. Benedikz of the Birmingham University Library; Dr Richard Bingle of the Oriental and India Office Collections at the British Library; Dr Stephen Bird of the National Museum of Labour; Katharine Bligh of the House of Lords Record Office; Kathleen Cann of Cambridge University Library; J. Graham Jones of the National Library of Wales; Alan Kucia of the Churchill Archives Centre; Helen Langley of the Bodleian Library; Iain Maciver of the National Library of Scotland; John McLintock, C. C. Johnston, and Peter Vasey of the National Register of Archives (Scotland); Dr A. P. W. Malcomson of the Public Record Office of Northern Ireland; Dr Angela Raspin of the British Library of Political and Economic Science; Dr Stephen Roberts at the Royal

Commission for Historical Manuscripts; Dr Alison Rosie at the Scottish Record Office; Ian Sayer of the Sayer Archive; Dr Sarah Street of the Bodleian Library; Dr Roderick Suddaby of the Imperial War Museum; Dr Anne Summers of the British Library; and Eleanor Vallis of Nuffield College Library. In addition we are grateful to the various staff members with whom we have had contact at the Public Record Office.

We are also indebted to the following people for examining large sections of the manuscript and providing valuable assistance and suggestions: Dr Richard Davenport-Hines, Dr Roger Middleton, Professor Robin Moore, and Dr Anthony Seldon. Thanks are also extended to Professor George Egerton who allowed us access to his draft Bibliography of British Political Memoirs.

The enormous task of transferring the information from the first edition on to computer, and initiating inquiries for the second edition was performed by Dr Marion Stell at the Australian National University. At various times, particular queries have been pursued by Ms Anthea Bundock. But the greater part of the basic research work was performed by Sally Whitehead who also undertook the word processing and editing of the final manuscript.

Inevitably, our text will contain errors and omissions; and some of the information, especially that which relates to the custody of papers in private hands, will unavoidably become out-of-date (the bulk of the research for the *Guide* was completed by August 1995). We trust that users of the *Guide* will draw our attention to mistakes, changes in the ownership or location of papers, and discoveries of hitherto unknown collections by writing to us c/o: The School of Humanities, Queensland University of Technology, Carseldine Campus, Beams Road, Carseldine, Queensland 4034, Australia (email: C. Hazlehurst @ qut.edu.au).

Cameron Hazlehurst
Sally Whitehead
December 1995

Introduction

History of the *Guide*

This book is a revised and expanded edition of *A Guide to the Papers of British Cabinet Ministers 1900–1951* compiled by Cameron Hazlehurst and Christine Woodland and published by the Royal Historical Society in 1974.

Although almost all of the original entries have undergone revision, a great deal of the information in this volume has been drawn from the 1974 text and from research carried out in subsequent years by Christine Woodland. Accordingly, while responsibility for the text that follows is taken by Cameron Hazlehurst and Sally Whitehead, the inclusion of Christine Woodland's name on the title page recognises her invaluable contribution to the project as a collaborator over nearly 30 years and as the penultimate proof-reader.

The study of twentieth-century British political history was in its infancy in the mid-1960s. Embarking on a study of the Liberal Party in 1962 I had been struck by the very narrow range of sources used by the few scholars who had published works on Edwardian Britain, the First World War, and the 1920s. As a doctoral student in England from December 1965 onwards I began to pursue, as systematically as limited resources and other priorities allowed, information about the survival and location of papers relating to political parties and to the lives of people prominent in public life in the first quarter of the twentieth century.

Shortly after taking up a studentship at Nuffield College, Oxford in October 1966, I found in Dr Max Hartwell, a senior scholar who was warmly receptive to the suggestion of a properly funded large-scale 'political records project'. Though not himself a political historian, Dr Hartwell at once saw the potential inherent in a successful search for the surviving private papers of hundreds of politicians, civil servants, journalists, military and naval figures, and others who had played major roles in twentieth-century political life.

We set out therefore to identify and mobilise a group of historians, archivists, and others involved in the field of modern British history who would share our conviction that a compendium of details of the location, contents, and accessibility of the personal papers of politicians would be a major new research tool. It was not difficult to demonstrate that no systematic and comprehensive searches had been undertaken, and no single source of information on personal papers was available. The National Register of Archives contained extensive information about collections of papers in libraries and other public repositories, but its information on material in private hands was fragmentary and often out of date. Much time and money had been spent by individual researchers in their attempts to locate private papers. Even when their searches had led to a result, this was rarely recorded in such a way as to be generally available, and individual efforts were frequently duplicated.

With the support of the Warden of Nuffield, D. N. Chester, a small group of interested parties was brought together in 1967. The working party convened by Max Hartwell adopted recommendations early in 1968 to launch the Political Records Project as a pilot survey of Cabinet ministers' papers to test the feasibility of a wider-ranging survey of papers relating to twentieth-century politicians and political organisations. The Social Science Research Council agreed to finance the project from October 1968 until its completion. In October 1970, the Council extended its grant to permit the compilation of a guide for publication; and Nuffield College supplied both accommodation and supplementary financial assistance to enable Christine Woodland to continue her work on the project. The Council also agreed to sponsor a long term project based at the British Library of Political and Economic Science. The results of this substantial search for the papers of organisations as well as individuals were published in a series of volumes: Chris Cook, with Philip Jones, Josephine Sinclair, and Jeffrey Weeks, *Sources in British Political History 1900–1951* (6 vols, Macmillan 1975–85). Information in these volumes has been updated and augmented in *The Longman Guide to Sources in Contemporary British History*: Chris Cook and David Waller, eds, vol 1, *Organisations and Societies* (Longman 1994), and Chris Cook, Jane Leonard and Peter Leese, vol 2, *Individuals* (Longman 1994).

The first edition

The aim of the project which resulted in the first edition of the *Guide* was first to locate, and then briefly describe, the private papers of every person of Cabinet rank in the period 1900–1951. Rather than confine the survey to those individuals who actually served in the Cabinet, we included all of the holders of those government offices which were in the Cabinet at any time during the period. Holders of various *ad hoc* wartime ministries were included even though the conventional Cabinet was superseded by a War Cabinet for lengthy periods. We drew up a list of 323 names, covering the period between the general elections of 1900 and 1951. (We overlooked Edward Stanley, Lord Stanley, whose short tenure as Secretary of State for the Dominions, early death, and absence from some other reference works probably explains but does not excuse the error.) A considerable body of information already existed about some collections, particularly those in institutions. Our first task was to scour the indices at the National Register of Archives and to obtain detailed information from the national and local repositories. For some Cabinet ministers' papers, this was all that was needed. But even in these cases a useful centralisation of information was achieved.

The next step was to trace the families of the remaining Cabinet ministers. For many ministers, this was simply a matter of turning to the current edition of Burke's *Peerage* or *Who's Who*. But for others, who died unmarried, childless, or without title, we devised our own procedure. First, works of reference – such as the *Dictionary of National Biography* and *Who Was Who* – were checked for general information: dates of birth and death, details of origin, marriage, and children. Then, the catalogues of the British Library and Nuffield College Library were consulted for biographical and autobiographical works; any such works were read. If these searches failed to point to any obvious source of information we went to the Principal Probate Registry at Somerset House to read the ministers' wills and probate acts or letters of administration. Only a few wills specifically mentioned the disposal of papers or appointed a literary executor: but all gave the full names, addresses, and occupations of executors or administrators, and many gave detailed information such as names and relationships of a minister's family, as well as the name and address of the family solicitor. These names were checked in the postal, geographical, and professional directories; and where an individual could still be found, a letter, asking for help, was sent.

If the executors could not be found, we tried to contact the firm of solicitors, a feat often only achieved by searching through successive volumes of the annual *Law List*. If the solicitors could not be found or could not help, then we went back to Somerset House to search for a minister's widow or other relations and their executors. As their dates of death were not usually known to us, and the registers at Somerset House are arranged annually, this involved a good deal of physical exercise; but it was rewarding.

When this checking process failed to produce a lead, we used more oblique tactics – we wrote to the present constituency agent (if there was one), to the local library, to the local newspaper, or to some person or institution with which the minister had strong connections. Only when all these attempts failed, and we were unable to obtain leads from other interested scholars, was a file declared 'closed'. A description of our searches was compiled so that they need not be repeated by other researchers. It should be added, as a covering note, that in most cases it was thought neither necessary nor practicable to make exhaustive searches for any papers that may have been preserved by businesses, charities, or other institutions with which ministers were connected.

Where our letters elicited a positive result, we asked for permission to look at the papers. Sometimes historians who were expert in a particular field, and thus better able to explore and assess a collection quickly, examined the papers on our behalf. Sometimes we relied on detailed handlists of papers that had been professionally arranged and catalogued. But most of the collections were personally examined by either or both of the investigators. Obviously, the results of such searches can be little more than impressionistic; nevertheless, even this minimal examination and description represented a significant advance on what had previously been available.

We felt that information about access to a collection was as important as a description of its contents. This raised difficult problems since we could not expect all private individuals to try to cope with the flood of enquiries which the first edition might unleash. Owners of collections became aware of the possible results of announcing that a collection was available for research, and consequently more than 30 collections, some of them large and important, were deposited in libraries or record offices. In some cases, decisions were taken that papers would not be made available for specified periods of time. There were other cases where access was granted on an *ad hoc* basis to individual researchers although a collection remained formally 'not generally available'.

In a few cases no reply came to our letters. We wrote at least three times – and often sought to make contact through other channels – before we assumed that the person thus addressed was not going to reply. In such cases, our entry simply stated that we were unable to make contact with a particular individual. In a few cases, the reply was, in effect, that whatever survived was none of our business – a perfectly legitimate attitude – which we described in our entries as 'X was unable to help us'. All too often the reply came back that a minister's family had kept the papers for some years, usually until they moved house, and then 'as no one seemed to think the papers important . . .' they had been destroyed or thrown away. This was particularly true for the first Labour Cabinet ministers and is a sad reflection on the libraries and repositories which by the 1970s had become only too eager to collect whatever might have survived.

On the basis of our notes and discussions, a draft description was compiled and sent to the owners or custodians of the collections for their approval. Thus the first edition contained descriptions of the location, content, and accessibility of the papers, or of the searches which we unsuccessfully made for the papers, of 323 men and women: a unique, comprehensive source of information on the private papers of Cabinet ministers of the first half of the twentieth century.

The second edition

Revision of the *Guide* began almost immediately after the publication of the first edition in 1974. Our attention was soon drawn to several important additions or changes to the information given to us. We had hoped to publish a compendium of additions and alterations to the *Guide* at regular intervals in a scholarly journal, but unfortunately this proved beyond our resources and incompatible with other commitments. By the mid-1980s it seemed more sensible to produce a completely revised edition (especially on learning that people were still using the first edition with its ever-diminishing accuracy).

The Royal Historical Society commissioned the second edition in 1988. A small grant from the society supplemented the commitment of the Australian National University which made part-time secretarial and research assistance available. It was agreed that the revised edition would update the information provided on the 323 ministers in the first edition, and include all Cabinet ministers (or those who held positions included in a Cabinet during the period) until the resignation of Sir Alec Douglas-Home as Prime Minister in 1964. This incorporated those who held relevant positions in the Churchill, Eden, Macmillan, and Home governments. The total number of ministers was thus increased to 384 (60 'new' ministers and the previously omitted Lord Stanley).

Although the bulk of the research on the second edition was conducted from Australia – first in Canberra and from March 1992 in Brisbane where I had become Foundation Professor and Head of the School of Humanities at Queensland University of Technology – the methods remained much the same as for the first edition. Repositories and families listed in the first edition as holding papers were contacted again to confirm the continuing accuracy of our information or to advise of any changes to collections. New biographies and autobiographies were consulted for references, and letters were written to the 'additional' ministers or their families.

A small grant from the Australian Research Council brought Sally Whitehead to the project on a part-time basis in 1993. A Dean's Initiative Grant from successive Deans of Arts at the Queensland University of Technology made it possible to fund Ms Whitehead's collaboration on a full-time basis from mid-1994 to August 1995.

Working on the project from Australia has had obvious restrictions, not entirely alleviated by occasional trips to the UK. Where new collections have been discovered, it has not always been possible to inspect them personally, or to cajole an over-worked colleague in the UK to inspect them for us. In the case of collections in repositories, we have usually had to rely on the descriptions, catalogues, and lists compiled by or for the institutions themselves.

Tracing the relatives of our 'additional' ministers has not proved too difficult, mostly due to the obligingly large numbers of them who accepted peerages. We have, however, struck difficulty in re-establishing contact with some of the family members who held collections in the first edition. In many cases, these family members may have died in the interval since 1974, but we have not had the resources to conduct searches for the wills of these people. Where we have not been able to re-establish contact, we have tried to contact other family members (even some quite distant relations!), or have written to record offices and other repositories in the area to determine if they could help or knew of the fate of these collections. We have also asked colleagues with expertise in certain areas (such as agricultural history or the Conservative Party) if they knew of any other leads. Where none of these efforts has proved fruitful, we hope that interested scholars may have more success than us in tracking down these collections. It is some comfort to note that most of these 'missing' collections consisted only of press cuttings volumes; such material may be found in other sources. It may be that in our Antipodean quest to trace surviving relatives, we have missed obvious family or personal connections while diligently chasing second cousins once removed! Any advice on these connections would be gratefully received.

One noteworthy point we have struck in preparing the revised edition is the number of 'additional' ministers who are wary of admitting that they have kept any papers. Some of the information we have been given contradicts information provided to other researchers; we have tried to make this clear in our entries. Some family members now deny having papers which we saw and described in the first edition. Where this is the case, we have advised accordingly.

It is gratifying, though a little disturbing, to know that the first edition was still in use twenty years after its publication. In anticipation of the second edition having as lengthy a shelf-life, we have also asked family members or other private custodians with collections to allow us to indicate if they have made plans for the future of the papers. There is evidence that asking questions about the future has in a number of instances led to decisions that increase the likelihood that papers will survive and be accessible for research. It might have made our recent task easier if we had asked this question systematically when preparing the first edition.

The results of our survey may be summarised as follows. Obviously, fragmentation of many collections has meant that the total number of collections recorded far exceeds the number of ministers included in the Guide.

1. Individuals whose papers seem certain to have been totally lost or destroyed*: 58
2. Individuals for whom there are only very small collections in private hands and/or public repositories: 25
3. Individuals for whom there are collections in institutions and available for research: 205
4. Individuals for whom there are collections in institutions but not available for research: 13
5. Individuals for whom there are collections in private hands which are available for research: 58
6. Individuals for whom there are collections in private hands which are not available for research: 43
7. Individuals about whose papers we have no definitive information: 26
8. Ministers who have advised that they have kept no papers*: 11

(* but for whom we may have found small collections of non-private 'official papers' in repositories consisting of, for example, press cuttings, minutes, or letters in other people's collections).

We hope that a third edition of the *Guide* will not take twenty years to be produced. If funding can be secured, we propose to carry the search forward to 1979 in a supplementary volume which will include revisions and corrections for the 1900 to 1964 entries. In the meantime, some information about discoveries, institutional acquisitions, and sales of papers may be gleaned from the files and publications of the National Register of Archives and the Public Record Office (especially its annual reports which describe recent transfers and acquisitions in the category of 'Private Office' papers).

Cameron Hazlehurst
December 1995

How to Use the Guide

The entries for all ministers (including those who became peers) are arranged in alphabetical order of family name. Hyphenated names have been arranged by the name following the hyphen. Names beginning with 'Mac' or 'Mc' have all been treated as though they begin with 'Mac'. If a peer was the only holder of the title, the reference in the entry heading is Viscount X, not the 1st Viscount. The index of ministers is on p. 409 and includes cross-references from titles.

In the first edition of the *Guide*, we referred to ministers by their family names. In some instances this could have been confusing for readers – especially in relation to ministers who inherited or were granted titles which required a change of name. For this edition, we have referred to ministers by the name by which we believe they were most commonly known or remembered. There is obviously an element of arbitrariness about this procedure but it does avoid such disconcerting appearances as 'Fitzalan-Howard' for the 15th Duke of Norfolk and 'Robinson' for the 1st Marquess of Ripon.

The first paragraph of each entry is a brief biographical outline of the minister's parliamentary and ministerial career. Where we know that a minister used a particular given name or nick-name, we have indicated it. We have included details of constituencies held, junior ministries, ministries, and titles granted or inherited. We have only given details of the first and highest knighthoods granted. We have not included honours which do not involve a change in the style of address, or details of party offices except for party leaderships. As all of the ministers covered by the *Guide* were privy councillors, we have not given the date on which they were given that honour. Information in each category is provided chronologically, most often commencing with constituencies, then government posts held, and then honours. However, if honours were given or inherited before the person became an MP or minister, this information is provided first. Details of the public or private non-parliamentary careers of ministers are not listed but are often referred to in the body of the entry.

Details of constituency names and dates were taken from J. Vincent and M. Stenton, McCalmont's *Parliamentary Poll Book, British Election Results 1832–1918* (Harvester, Brighton 1971), and F. W. S. Craig, *British Parliamentary Election Results 1918–1949, 1950–1970* (Glasgow 1969; Chichester 1971). Dates of offices were taken from David Butler and Gareth Butler, *British Political Facts 1900–1994* (7th ed, Macmillan 1994), and Chris Cook and Brendan Keith, *British Historical Facts: 1830–1900* (Macmillan 1974). We have provided the month as well as the year on which ministers entered office, unless they went immediately to that office from the preceding office; the month and year of departure are always given.

In the second and succeeding paragraphs we have indicated where the papers are, whether or not they are available, under what conditions, and from whom permission to use the papers must be obtained. Reference numbers are supplied, if they exist, in brackets. Succeeding paragraphs elaborate on the content of a collection. As many collections have been split, we have described the main part of a minister's papers first.

There is an entry for each minister, even if our searches produced no result. We have described our searches and the answers we received. In many cases, a minister's relative or solicitor said that they did not know of the existence of any papers. We have passed on this 'negative' information so that historians will not need to repeat our searches and the informants concerned will not be troubled again unnecessarily. In the cases where we received no reply to several letters or inquiries through other channels, we have said that we were unable to contact the individual addressed. To maintain the privacy of those private individuals who were unable to help, or whose collections are closed, we have not given their addresses. In a small number of cases we have been asked not to publish addresses, even though the owner of a collection is happy to be identified.

The entries vary greatly in length. This is partly because of the varying size of the collections and partly because of the length of time we were able to spend on them. Where only a few papers survived, we are able to give a fairly full description. But many collections are vast and disorganised. To have done more than sample their contents would have required far more time and human resources than were available. Consequently, many descriptions of papers in private hands must be regarded as impressionistic. We deliberately concentrated our efforts on locating and describing collections that were not in institutions when we examined them. This has meant that collections in institutions, particularly those not yet listed, have had a much more cursory inspection. Usually, we have drawn up our descriptions of these papers by looking at whatever list or description was available, and by consulting the librarian and archivist concerned, rather than looking at the papers ourselves.

Readers of this edition who recall the first will note some innovations. Information about 'Private Office' papers held in the Public Record Office has been included wherever we have been able to gather it. For some ministers, especially those for whom there are insubstantial collections or who have not been prominently noticed in earlier historical writing, we have drawn attention to relevant biographical studies, monographs, theses, or articles. No attempt has been made to be exhaustive in the provision of bibliographical guidance; but it seemed sensible to refer especially to relatively obscure works which might otherwise have proved elusive. Publisher and date of publication appear in brackets after the biography or monograph reference; place of publication is London unless otherwise stated.

Details of the various libraries, record offices, and repositories are to be found in a list after the entries. This list is arranged alphabetically by the title of the various institutions; where the formal title of an institution is not generally used, we have given a cross-reference from the usual name. The Royal Commission on Historical Manuscripts produces *Record Repositories in Great Britain* which provides addresses, contact numbers, hours of operation, and facilities for repositories.

The list of ministers was drawn up from the holders of the following offices (Butler and Butler, op. cit.): Prime Minister; Lord President of the Council; Lord Chancellor; Lord Privy Seal; Chancellor of the Exchequer; Foreign and Commonwealth Affairs (including the Colonial and Dominion Offices); Home Office; Admiralty; Agriculture, Fisheries and Food; Aviation (including Air, Aircraft Production, and Civil Aviation); Attorney-General; Blockade; Defence (including Coordination of Defence); Education (including Science); Fuel and Power; Health; Housing and Local Government (including Local Government Board and Planning); India (and Burma); Information; Ireland; Labour (including National Service); Duchy of Lancaster; Materials; Paymaster-General; Pensions (including National Insurance); Minister without Portfolio; Postmaster-General; Reconstruction; Minister Resident; Scotland; Shipping; Supply (including Munitions); Technical Cooperation; Board of Trade; Transport (including War Transport); War; Welsh Affairs; Works (including Public Buildings).

We have not limited the *Guide* to the papers of ministers who actually were in the Cabinet – we have included all of the ministers who held certain offices such as the War Office which were traditionally of Cabinet status, even if a particular minister was not in the Cabinet. Students of administrative history may find this comprehensive coverage particularly useful. There are, in addition, five entries not covered by this brief: Baron Ashbourne, who was a member of the Cabinet as Lord Chancellor of Ireland; the 5th Earl Cadogan and the 1st Earl of Ypres, who were members of the Cabinet as Lords Lieutenant of Ireland; J. C. Smuts, the South African politician, who was a member of the War Cabinet 1917–19; and the 1st Lord Casey, a member of the War Cabinet 1942–43 as Minister of State Resident in the Middle East. For reasons that now seem less logical and compelling than they did originally, we decided not to include the position of Financial Secretary to the Treasury, although there were three occasions when holders of this position were in Cabinet: Edwin Montagu, Thomas McKinnon

Wood, and William Joynson-Hicks (who all held other positions which are included in our list of incorporated ministries). We also decided not to include ministers who held only the position of Minister without Portfolio, and who did not appear in the Cabinet while holding this position. This meant that William Deedes, Baron Deedes, is included, but the 11th Earl of Dundee and the 2nd Lord Mancroft are not.

Further Research Sources

This *Guide* has been compiled on the premise that it will provide only a starting point for potential researchers. The entries on each minister are not exhaustive in either sources or references. It has not been possible for us to peruse every monograph or thesis in which a minister or department features. But we have drawn attention to items that have come to our notice where they seem of particular interest or throw light on an otherwise obscure life. We have made no attempt to list every collection in which correspondence or papers *from* a minister may be found. In the case of ministers for whom we could find no significant collection or no papers at all we have sometimes listed stray correspondence in the collections of their colleagues.

The main sources for detailed material on ministers remain the National Register of Archives and the Public Record Office. Until recently the NRA published an annual guide which detailed collections which had been acquired or listed by repositories in the previous years. The Historical Manuscripts Commission has produced a series of *Guides to Sources for British History based on the National Register of Archives* focussing on Cabinet ministers 1782–1900, scientists, diplomats, colonial governors, churchmen, politicians, businessmen and industrialists, and a forthcoming guide *Principal Family and Estate Collections*. Users of the NRA are directed to Dick Sargent's article, 'The National Register of Archives' in the Special Supplement No. 13 of *Historical Research*, June 1995, pp 1–35, which has a useful section on current facilities and future plans to expand electronic access to NRA records.

As far as PRO holdings are concerned we have tried to obtain as much information as we can about relevant 'Private Office' papers. We have been able to add a good deal to what was known in 1974. But the information is not systematically recorded by the PRO, and there are many gaps in our knowledge. Researchers may find a great deal of useful information in the numerous handbooks which have been published by the PRO on the papers available in different departments. Details of these handbooks can be obtained from the HMSO.

Scholars familiar with the *Documents on British Foreign Policy* series and *The Transfer of Power* series sponsored by the Foreign and Commonwealth Office and also published by HMSO, will be aware of their value in relation to documents likely to have been seen by ministers at the Foreign and India Offices in particular. We have not attempted to indicate which volumes in these series are of relevance to particular ministers.

It is now possible to obtain entire series of public documents on microfilm from various microform and electronic publishers. Several which have come to our attention include Adam Matthew Publications (8 Oxford Street, Marlborough, Wiltshire SN8 1AP) who list in their 1995/96 catalogue the following items currently available or forthcoming: PREM 1 Papers of Prime Ministerial Advisors Outside Cabinet 1916–40; PREM 3 Papers concerning Defence and Operational Subjects 1940–45, Churchill Minister of Defence, Secretariat Papers; CAB 128 and 129 Cabinet minutes, conclusions, and memoranda 1945–64; T 171 Budget Papers 1943 and following; and British Labour Party Research Department memoranda and information papers 1941–79. Research Publications International (PO Box 45, Reading, RG1 8HF) list in their 1994/95 catalogue the following items: Home Intelligence Reports 1940–44; CO 904 Dublin Castle Record 1880–1921; Archives of the British Labour Party; Archives of the British Liberal Party; Archives of the British Conservative Party; Archives of the Independent Labour Party; Archives of the Fabian Society.

Another electronic research aid which may be helpful in tracking down papers is the National Inventory of Documentary Sources in the United Kingdom and Ireland (NIDS) which is published by Chadwyck-Healey (The Quorum, Barnwell Road, Cambridge CB5 8SW). NIDS details over 14, 000 finding aids to manuscript and archive collections from a large number of repositories across the UK and Ireland. NIDS also publishes microfiche of the registers and indexes of correspondence 1793–1919 from the Foreign Office at the PRO.

The Royal Commission on Historical Manuscripts (HMC) now has a World Wide Web page (http://www.hmc.gov.uk) which not only describes the work of the HMC but which also includes links to many British record offices and gives access to the National Register of Archives Database.

The PRO, HMSO, and the Institute of Contemporary British History are preparing selected government papers on CD-ROM. Sets currently available are Prime Ministers' and Cabinet Documents (selections from PREM 11, PREM 13, CAB 128, and CAB 129), Documents on External Affairs (from FO 371 and FO 370), and Cabinet Committees and Defence Documents (HMSO Electronic Publishing Sales, HMSO Publications Centre, PO Box 276, London SW8 5DT).

Institutional collections such as the Conservative Party Archives in the Bodleian Library, and the Labour Party Archives in the National Museum of Labour History, will also provide the researcher with abundant primary material. Much of these collections is available on microfilm (see above). The Conservative Party Archives are freely available up to 1964 with the exception of a few personal files. Those dated 1965–74 may be available with the permission of the Party

Chairman. Later papers are closed. A four volume list is available at the Bodleian.

We have not systematically searched for the institutional records relating to every minister. Guides to institutional and business records will be a good starting point for many inquiries. Business histories and other publications on the history of voluntary organisations, government agencies, municipalities, and a host of specialist interests and activities will no doubt yield a rich harvest for the scholar prepared to trace and read them all.

Unlike the early 1970s when the first edition was produced, there is now a plethora of guides to collections and compendiums of biographies available for the researcher. Some of the more helpful for students of modern British political history are: Chris Cook, *Sources in British Political History 1900–1951* (6 vols, Macmillan 1975–85); Joseph O. Baylen and Norbert J. Gossman (eds), *Biographical Dictionary of Modern British Radicals* (Harvester Wheatsheaf 1988), Joyce M. Bellamy and John Saville (eds), *Dictionary of Labour Biography* (9 vols, Macmillan 1972–93); Keith Robbins (ed), *The Blackwell Biographical Dictionary of British Political Life in the Twentieth Century* (Blackwell 1990); David Butler and Gareth Butler, *British Political Facts 1900–1994* (7th edition, Macmillan 1994), David J. Jeremy and Christine Shaw (eds), *Dictionary of Business Biography* (5 vols, Butterworth 1984–86); and *The Longman Guide to Sources in Contemporary British History*, Chris Cook and David Waller, vol 1, *Organisations and Societies* (Longman 1994), and Chris Cook, Jane Leonard and Peter Leese, vol 2, *Individuals* (Longman 1994).

A useful volume which came to hand too late to be referred to in individual entries is Ian Levitt (ed), *Scottish Office: depression and reconstruction, 1919–1959* (Scottish History Society 5th Ser., vol. 5, Edinburgh 1993).

Abbreviations

The following is a list of common abbreviations used throughout the *Guide*.

Adjusting to Democracy	Rodney Lowe, *Adjusting to Democracy: The Role of the Ministry of Labour in British Politics, 1916–1939* (Clarendon Press, Oxford 1986)
Blackwell	Keith Robbins (ed), *The Blackwell Biographical Dictionary of British Political Life in the Twentieth Century* (Blackwell, Oxford 1990)
BLPES	British Library of Political and Economic Science
Conservative Party Policy	John Ramsden, *The Making of Conservative Party Policy: The Conservative Research Department since 1929* (Longman 1980)
CRO	County Record Office
DBB	David J. Jeremy and Christine Shaw (eds), *Dictionary of Business Biography* (5 vols, Butterworth 1984–86)
DLB	Joyce M. Bellamy and John Saville (eds), *Dictionary of Labour Biography* (9 vols, Macmillan 1972–93)
DNB	*Dictionary of National Biography* (Oxford University Press)
	Sir Sydney Lee (ed), *DNB 1901–11* (1920)
	H.W.C. Davis and J.R.H. Weaver (eds), *DNB 1912–21* (1927)
	J.R.H. Weaver (ed), *DNB 1922–30* (1937)
	L.G. Wickham Legg (ed), *DNB 1931–40* (1949)
	L.G. Wickham Legg and E.T. Williams (eds), *DNB 1941–50* (1959)
	E.T. Williams and C.S. Nicholls (eds), *DNB 1961–70* (1981)
	Lord Blake and C.S. Nicholls (eds), *DNB 1971–80* (1986)
	Lord Blake and C.S. Nicholls (eds), *DNB 1981–85* (1990)
HLRO	House of Lords Record Office
IWM	Imperial War Museum
Lord Chancellors 1	R. F. V. Heuston, *Lives of the Lord Chancellors*

	1885–1940 (Clarendon Press, Oxford 1964)
Lord Chancellors 2	R. F. V. Heuston, *Lives of the Lord Chancellors 1940–1970* (Clarendon Press, Oxford 1987)
MBR	Joseph O. Baylen and Norbert J. Gossman, *Biographical Dictionary of Modern British Radicals* (Harvester Wheatsheaf 1988)
NLS	National Library of Scotland
NLW	National Library of Wales
NRA	National Register of Archives
NRA(S)	National Register of Archives (Scotland)
PRO	Public Record Office
PRONI	Public Record Office of Northern Ireland
RO	Record Office
Secretaries of State for Scotland	George Pottinger, *The Secretaries of State for Scotland 1926–76: Fifty Years of the Scottish Office* (Scottish Academic Press, Edinburgh 1979)
Sources	Chris Cook (ed), *Sources in British Political History 1900–1951* (6 vols, Macmillan 1975–85)
SRO	Scottish Record Office
UP	University Press

THE GUIDE

WILLIAM ADAMSON (1863–1936)

William Adamson was Labour MP for Fife (West) 1910–31. He was Secretary (later Secretary of State) for Scotland Jan-Nov 1924 and June 1929–Aug 1931. He was Chairman of the Labour Party 1917–21.

Adamson's son, Mr David M. Adamson, informed us that neither he nor his sisters had any papers. Mr Adamson thought that some papers were given by his father to a close friend some time before his death, so that the friend might write a biography. The friend is now dead. He had no family and Mr Adamson was unable to discover what happened to his father's papers. We were also advised by the NLS that the Secretary of the Scottish Labour History Society had searched without success for Adamson papers in the 1960s.

Adamson was elected General Secretary of the Fife and Kinross Miners' Association in Jan 1909. The privately printed minutes of the association's meetings 1901–13 were deposited in the NLS by the National Union of Mineworkers, Scottish Area (Dep 304). There are also Adamson's copies of the printed and typescript proceedings of conferences in March 1912 between ministers (Asquith, Grey, Lloyd George, and Sydney Buxton), the Consultative Committee of the Coalowners of Great Britain, and the Executive of the Miners' Federation of Great Britain relating to the miners' pay disputes.

Private Office papers relating to Adamson's periods at the Scottish Office are dispersed through the files of the five main Scottish Office departments held at the SRO: Agriculture and Fisheries (AF); Education (ED); Environment (formerly Scottish Development) (DD); Home and Health (HH); Industry (formerly Economic Planning/Industry) (SEP).

In *Secretaries of State for Scotland*, 38–45, Pottinger briefly recounts Adamson's political career, as do William Knox and John Saville in *DLB*, VII, 4–8. Reference should also be made to J. W. R. Mitchell, 'The emergence of Modern Scottish central administration 1885–1939' (DPhil, Oxford University 1987).

CHRISTOPHER ADDISON, 1st VISCOUNT ADDISON (1869–1951)

Dr Christopher Addison was Liberal MP for Shoreditch (Hoxton) 1910–22, and Labour MP for Wiltshire (Swindon) 1929–31 and 1934–35. He was Parliamentary Secretary to the Board of Education Aug 1914–May 1915, Parliamentary Secretary to the Ministry of Munitions 1915–Dec 1916, Minister of Munitions 1916–July 1917, Minister of Reconstruction 1917–Jan 1919, President of the Local Government Board Jan-June 1919, Minister of Health 1919–April 1921, Minister without Portfolio

April-July 1921, Parliamentary Secretary to the Ministry of Agriculture and Fisheries June 1929-June 1930, Minister of Agriculture and Fisheries 1930-Aug 1931, Secretary of State for Dominion Affairs Aug 1945-July 1947, Secretary of State for Commonwealth Relations July-Oct 1947, Lord Privy Seal 1947-March 1951, Paymaster-General July 1948-April 1949, and Lord President of the Council March-Oct 1951. He was created Baron Addison in 1937, Viscount Addison in 1945, and KG in 1946.

On being requested by the Cabinet Office in Sept 1934 to return all Cabinet minutes and papers issued to him while in office, Addison wrote 'declining to co-operate' (Recovery of Cabinet Documents Report, 29 Nov 1935, PRO, CAB 24/257).

Addison's surviving papers were deposited in the Bodleian Library in 1973 by his widow (Addison Papers) where they are currently being catalogued. They were arranged after his death by Lady Addison, and a box list was compiled. They fill 137 boxes. Additional Addison papers were deposited in the Bodleian in 1981-83 (MS Addison dep 138-44).

One of Addison's earliest political interests was the 1911 National Insurance Bill; he was a strong supporter of Lloyd George's policies at that time. There are several files relating to his work for this bill, showing his more general interest in local government reform, the poor law, and health. Addison first stood as Liberal candidate for Hoxton in 1907; there are files of papers on this and succeeding election campaigns.

The largest part of the papers relates to Addison's work at the Ministry of Munitions. All aspects of the ministry's work are represented: there are files on various aspects of the ministry's employment of women – their health, salaries, and labour relations; on the supply of particular materials, including files on the sinking of individual ships; on the development of particular weapons; and on the government's attempt to control liquor consumption (mainly printed papers).

Addison had a strong interest in encouraging scientific and industrial research. The collection includes papers from the Privy Council's committee on this problem and early papers on the establishment and organisation of the Medical Research Council 1918-20. There are files from Addison's work at the Ministries of Health and Agriculture. As well as subject files, for example, on Ireland, on the 1916-22 Coalition Government, and on the 1931 crisis, there are also files of correspondence with particular individuals, including letters to the King. There are only a few post-1945 papers. There are ten volumes of press cuttings. The collection also includes the typescript of Addison's diary June 1914-Feb 1919 with manuscript amendments and deletions. The diary was published by Addison, entitled *Four and a Half Years* (2 vols, Hutchinson 1934). Addison said in the published version that the diaries were usually dictated daily. Diary notes for the period April-July 1921 are also included in the papers. There are also proofs, correspondence, and reviews of Addison's memoirs, *Politics from Within, 1911–1918* (2 vols, Jenkins 1924). A small proportion of these papers was used in R. J. Minney, *Viscount Addison: Leader of the Lords* (Odhams 1958).

Additional Addison material deposited in the Bodleian Library in 1981–83 includes albums of press cuttings, framed photos, political cartoons and family correspondence, the latter closed to readers; miscellaneous letters 1930s-40s, an autograph letter from Clement Attlee 1949, and press cuttings and printed material; miscellaneous correspondence and papers 1925–73, including letters from Philip Snowden to Miss B. D. Low 1925–29, miscellaneous letters to Addison 1930–48, and press cuttings and printed material; and a tape made from an HMV gramophone recording of Addison giving a speech in 1950 when he was a guest of honour at the Diamond Jubilee dinner of the Shipping Federation. Addison, then Lord Privy Seal, refers to his time as Minister of Reconstruction at the end of the First World War, the work of the Shipowners' Committee led by Sir Alan Anderson, and the formation of the National Maritime Board. A copy of this tape is held by the British Library National Sound Archive.

The additional material, including the diaries 1900–31 of Mrs Isobel Addison, Addison's first wife, was used in Kenneth Morgan and Jane Morgan, *Portrait of a Progressive* (Clarendon Press, Oxford 1980). These diaries, now in the possession of Addison's grandson Mr William Ashcroft, include 'very little political comment'.

Records of the Leader of the House of Lords and Chief Whip 1945–94 are in the HLRO, but are subject to the 30 year rule (Addison was Leader of the House of Lords 1945–51).

A small quantity of material, mainly relating to Addison's early life, family background, and medical career remains in the care of his son, the 3rd Lord Addison. A small collection of letters of condolence on the death of her husband was given by Lady Addison to the Bodleian Library (MS Eng lett d 332–3).

Lady Addison also gave her own, very full, diaries comprising 27 volumes 1938–58, and including her unfinished autobiography, 'Looking Glass Land', to the British Library (Add MSS 71660–86). They are mostly a record of Lady Addison's own activities with occasional gossip and comments on the wives of public figures.

Fred R. van Hartesveldt contributed an entry on Addison to *MBR*, 3, 18–23, and Kenneth O. Morgan contributed an entry to *Blackwell*, 2–3.

SIR WILLIAM MAXWELL AITKEN, 1st Bt, 1st BARON BEAVERBROOK (1879–1964)

Max Aitken was Conservative MP for Ashton-under-Lyne 1910–16. He was Chancellor of the Duchy of Lancaster and Minister of Information Feb-Nov 1918, Minister of Aircraft Production May 1940–May 1941, Minister of State May-June 1941, Minister of Supply 1941–Feb 1942, Minister of War Production Feb 1942, and Lord Privy Seal Sept 1943–July 1945. He was knighted in 1911, created a baronet in 1916, and Baron Beaverbrook in 1917.

Some 900 boxes and 109 volumes of Beaverbrook's papers, originally deposited in the Beaverbrook Library, are now in the HLRO and available to researchers (NRA 19284). HLRO Memo No 54, 1975, is a guide to the collection. A full catalogue is in preparation and will be published in three separate volumes. Volume 1 is due to be published in 1996, *The Beaverbrook Papers: a Descriptive List*, Part 1, by Katherine Bligh. This volume details his Canadian papers, all business papers and correspondence, including the newspaper files.

There are 75 boxes of mainly Canadian business correspondence for 1903–10 and some political correspondence 1910–45, including correspondence with R. B. Bennett and W. L. Mackenzie King. General English correspondence 1910–64 fills 161 boxes. These boxes are arranged chronologically, then alphabetically within each year. At various stages during Beaverbrook's life, correspondence with particular individuals was withdrawn from the general series and kept separately; there are 86 boxes of this special series (C).

There are nine boxes of constituency papers for 1910–12, five boxes from Beaverbrook's work for the Canadian government in the First World War, and 12 boxes of papers from the Ministry of Information. During the Second World War Beaverbrook's private and civil service secretaries accumulated two sets of overlapping files; 14 boxes of the former, and 22 of the latter have survived. Beaverbrook kept only War Cabinet papers relating to aircraft production. In addition to these official papers there are 27 boxes of unofficial correspondence and eight boxes of correspondence on political topics. There are also 17 boxes concerning negotiations with the United States on the future of civil aviation, and four on oil supplies.

Beaverbrook's newspaper work and other business activities are amply represented, though most of what survives is post-Second World War. There is one box of papers concerning the *Daily Express* up to 1928; 62 boxes for 1928–64; one box concerning the *Evening Standard* up to 1928, 20 for 1928–64. There are over 20 boxes of office files of the Empire Crusade, including correspondence with possible parliamentary candidates. There is also material on Beaverbrook's involvement in campaigns relating to the Agricultural Party, the Co-operative Movement, and the Common Market.

The visitors' books for Cherkley 1911–64, and Beaverbrook's engagement diaries 1922–64, have survived. There are also private account books, 85 boxes relating to properties, 29 boxes of office memoranda, and 65 volumes of press cuttings. These include four volumes of articles by Beaverbrook and eight of reviews of his various books. Material for his books was gathered both from his own papers and elsewhere and has been kept together to fill 90 boxes; there are seven boxes of material for *Politicians and the War, 1914–1916* (2 vols, Thornton Butterworth 1928, Lane Publications 1932; revised one vol ed, Oldbourne 1960). Other books by Beaverbrook which contain either autobiographical material or quotations from original documents, are: *Politicians and the Press* (Hutchinson 1926); *Friends. Sixty years of intimate personal relations with Richard Bedford Bennett … A personal memoir with an appendix of letters* (Heinemann 1959); *Men and Power: 1917–1918* (Hutchinson 1956); *Courage. The story of Sir James Dunn* (Collins 1961); *The Decline and Fall of Lloyd George. And great was the fall thereof* (Collins 1963); *My Early Life* (Brunswick Press 1965); and *The Abdication of King Edward VIII* (Hamish Hamilton 1966, edited by A. J. P. Taylor).

The Harriet Irving Library, University of New Brunswick, holds 14.72 metres of Canadian correspondence 1928, 1939, 1946–64, and a collection of manuscripts 1827–1926, including letters of F. E. Smith, Lord Kitchener, and King Edward VII. The Library's R. B. Bennett Papers collection contains 398 pages of correspondence with Beaverbrook (vol 945). The National Archives of Canada have 10 centimetres of transcripts and original letters from Canadian public figures including R. B. Bennett 1902–46, R. L. Borden 1911–34, and W. L. Mackenzie King 1925–48 (MG 27 II G1). These letters have been listed by correspondent and date in Finding Aid No 15. A few family records are held by the Old Manse Library at Newcastle, New Brunswick.

The Sayer Archive holds c. 200 Beaverbrook letters, including one from Neville Chamberlain written on the day he resigned his premiership. These are available for research.

Twenty-four letters from Robert Horne to Beaverbrook were bought from a bookseller by the NLS after the closure of the Beaverbrook Library (Acc 8214).

In 1988 the 3rd Lord Beaverbrook advised that a report in the *Sunday Times*, 19 Feb 1978, which stated that '30,000 previously unseen memos' were in the possession of his father, Sir Max Aitken (Beaverbrook's elder son who disclaimed the barony) was erroneous. He reported that 'no further papers have come to light'.

There are 52 photos in the House of Lords' collection, and a small number of private photos and correspondence remain with the family.

John Wilson, autograph letters and historical documents dealer of Eynsham, Oxford, offered for sale in two parts a small collection of letters and telegrams from Churchill to Beaverbrook mostly dating in the late 1950s (Catalogues 49 and 50).

Some of Beaverbrook's Private Office papers are in the PRO at AVIA 11 and AVIA 9. Further Private Office papers can be found at CAB 127/239–580.

A. J. P. Taylor, *Beaverbrook* (Hamish Hamilton 1972) is based on the papers now in the HLRO and quotes copiously from them. It reveals Beaverbrook's involvement in previous biographical works. A more recent biography by Anne Chisholm and Michael Davie, *Lord Beaverbrook: A Life* (Hutchinson 1992) is based almost entirely on the papers supplemented by personal interviews. It has useful 'Source Notes' drawing attention to the destruction of some papers, and the retention of others by the family.

There is an entry by Katharine V. Bligh and Christine Shaw on Beaverbrook in *DBB*, 1, 23–9. Letters exchanged between Brendan Bracken and Beaverbrook are in Richard Cockett (ed), *My Dear Max: The Letters of Brendan Bracken to Lord Beaverbrook, 1925–1958* (The Historians' Press 1990) which, despite its title and sub-title, contains letters by Beaverbrook as well. Gregory P. Marchildon is authoritative in *Profit and Politics: Beaverbrook and the Gilded Age of Canadian Finance* (University of Toronto Press 1996).

ALBERT VICTOR ALEXANDER, EARL ALEXANDER OF HILLSBOROUGH (1885–1965)

Albert Alexander was Co-operative MP for Sheffield (Hillsborough) 1922–31 and 1935–50. He was Parliamentary Secretary to the Board of Trade Jan-Nov 1924, First Lord of the Admiralty June 1929–Aug 1931, May 1940–May 1945 and Aug 1945–Oct 1946, Minister without Portfolio Oct-Dec 1946, Minister of Defence 1946–Feb 1950, and Chancellor of the Duchy of Lancaster 1950–Oct 1951. He was created Viscount Alexander in 1950, Earl Alexander of Hillsborough in 1963, and KG in 1964.

A collection of 75 boxes of Alexander's papers was deposited at the Churchill Archives Centre in three deposits by his daughter, Lady Beatrix Evison (AVAR). The papers have been listed (NRA 12665); written application should be made to the Keeper of the Archives.

The listed papers include reports and correspondence on political matters 1924–51, but they are somewhat disappointing for information on the co-operative movement. There are no constituency letters. There are three fragments of diary: June 1942, March-June 1946 (concerning the Labour Party's Indian Mission), and April-Aug 1946. There are also press cuttings of articles by and about Alexander, and notes for speeches and broadcasts.

The papers of Alexander's local agent, Alderman Dr Albert Ballard, and of his constituency party have been deposited in the Sheffield Archives (Ballard papers and Co-operative Party Records). The papers have been listed (NRA 17108); copies of the lists are available at the Churchill Archives Centre. Both collections include many letters from Alexander and his wife about local and national issues. The party records include analyses of Alexander's voting record, correspondence about his appointments, and press cuttings.

There is a short biography: John Tilley, *Churchill's Favourite Socialist: A Life of A. V. Alexander* (Holyoake, Manchester 1995). The entry by H. F. Bing and John Saville in *DLB*, 1, 11–14, has a useful guide to relevant sources on the co-operative movement.

Defence ministry papers relating to Alexander's period as minister are usefully cited in Anthony Gorst, 'Facing facts? The Labour Government and defence policy 1945–1950', in Nick Tiratsoo (ed), *The Attlee Years* (Pinter Publishers 1991), 190–209.

SIR HAROLD RUPERT LEOFRIC GEORGE ALEXANDER, 1st EARL ALEXANDER OF TUNIS (1891–1969)

Field Marshal Sir Harold Alexander was Supreme Allied Commander, Mediterranean, 1944–45, and Minister of Defence March 1952–Oct 1954. He was created KG and Viscount Alexander of Errigal in 1946, and Earl Alexander of Tunis in 1952.

Alexander's official and semi-official correspondence and papers 1941–45 are in the PRO (WO 214/1–69; NRA 28825). His Private Office papers as Minister for Defence 1952–54 are also in the PRO (DEFE 13/25–69).

Most of Alexander's private papers, his letters to his family during the Second World War, and his diary of a visit to Korea in 1952 as Minister of Defence, are held by the 2nd Earl Alexander of Tunis.

In 1960 Alexander returned to the battlefields of North Africa and Italy and committed his memoirs of the war to paper with the help of Major John North. These were published as John North (ed), *The Alexander Memoirs 1940–1945* (Cassell 1962).

A biography of Alexander was written by Nigel Nicolson, *Alex* (Weidenfeld and Nicolson 1973). Nicolson used and quotes from the papers now in the PRO and the Korea diary, but did not have access to other family papers. Nicolson taped a number of interviews with Alexander's wartime and Canadian colleagues including Lord Rhyl, Field Marshals Harding and Templer, and US Generals Lemnitzer, Gruenther and Mark Clark. These tapes were copied by the IWM and are available there for research (Department of Sound Records, acc nos 3942–51). A tape of an interview with Lord Mountbatten is in the Mountbatten archives at Broadlands. Nicolson retained a number of letters from people connected with Alexander.

Letters quoted by Nicolson from Alexander's childhood, the First World War and the inter-war years are believed to remain at Caledon Castle, Alexander's family home in County Tyrone on the Irish border. Also in the care of Alexander's great-nephew Lord Caledon are Alexander's summaries of special incidents, such as an account of his childhood until he went to Harrow, a narrative of his experiences in Latvia in 1919, and his first campaign on the North West Frontier of India in 1935. These papers were kept with a substantial unsorted collection of Caledon family papers but have not been sighted in recent years.

There are 71 pieces of correspondence with Sir Basil Liddell Hart 1933–67 in the Liddell Hart Centre, King's College, London (LH 1/7).

The National Archives of Canada holds a set of seven volumes of reports of military campaigns in North Africa, Sicily, and Italy 1942–44, including maps and copies of directives (MG 27 III A). A file of correspondence and several scrap books relating to a trip by Alexander to Brazil in 1948 are also in the National Archives.

There are useful brief lives by David Hunt in *DNB 1961–1970*, 18–22, and by I. F. W. Beckett in *Blackwell*, 3–6.

JULIAN AMERY, BARON AMERY OF LUSTLEIGH (1919–1996)

Julian Amery was Conservative MP for Preston North 1950–66 and Brighton Pavilion 1969–92. He was Parliamentary Under-Secretary, War Office Jan 1957–Dec 1958, Parliamentary Under-Secretary, Colonial Office 1958–Oct 1960, Secretary of State for Air 1960–July 1962, Minister of Aviation 1962–Oct 1964, Minister of Public Building and Works June-Oct 1970, Minister for Housing and Construction 1970–Nov 1972, Minister of State, Foreign and Commonwealth Office 1972–March 1974. He was created Baron Amery of Lustleigh (a life peerage) in 1992.

Lord Amery's *Approach March: a venture in autobiography* (Hutchinson 1973) deals with his pre-parliamentary life. It is based on a substantial collection of personal papers: 'letters, diaries and diary notes. I had preserved almost all the letters sent to me during the years to which this book relates. My parents had done the same with mine to them. I had kept a diary of my visits to Spain during the Civil War and, though in breach of regulations, had done the same during my mission to the Albanian Resistance. I had also made notes, as leisure and security allowed, but usually within days or at most weeks of any talks or experiences that seemed of interest' (p. 17).

These papers, together with papers relating to his parliamentary and ministerial career, remained in Lord Amery's possession. A second volume of autobiography was being prepared.

Private Office papers from Lord Amery's period as Secretary of State for Air may be found at AIR 19 in the PRO.

Lord Amery contributed to the witness seminar on the 'Sandys Defence White Papers 1957' at the Institute of Contemporary British History.

LEOPOLD CHARLES MAURICE STENNETT AMERY (1873–1955)

Leo Amery was Conservative MP for Birmingham (South, later Sparkbrook) 1911–45. He was Parliamentary Under-Secretary for the Colonies Jan 1919–April 1921, Parliamentary and Financial Secretary to the Admiralty 1921–Oct 1922, First Lord of the Admiralty 1922–Jan 1924, Secretary of State for the Colonies Nov 1924–June 1929, Secretary of State for the Dominions (an office he was instrumental in establishing) June 1925–June 1929, and Secretary of State for India May 1940–Aug 1945.

His papers were in the possession of his son, the late Lord Amery of Lustleigh, 112 Eaton Square, London SW1 9AE. They are not generally available for research. Leo Amery had a very varied and active career and his large collection of papers (c.230 box-files and 40 volumes of diary) reflects many aspects of it. Although the present arrangement is not permanent, a brief list of the papers has been compiled; the numbers in brackets refer to the box numbers.

There are 17 box-files covering Amery's early life: family letters, as well as his Harrow notebooks, Oxford notes, and some of his early articles. From 1899–1909 he worked for *The Times*. A box of correspondence with Valentine Chirol, foreign editor, survives (18). A great deal of correspondence survives from his reporting of the South African war and his part in writing *The Times'* History (18–21). There are another 20 boxes of papers from this period, mostly correspondence (arranged alphabetically within years) with a few separate series of 'special' correspondents such as Lord Milner (25), and Violet Markham (26). There are also a few subject files – press cuttings, pamphlets, notes, etc., as well as correspondence – mainly about the Army, National Service, and Tariff Reform (22, 36), and also papers from Amery's earliest attempts to enter Parliament (27, 39): he stood for Wolverhampton (East) in 1906, 1908, and Jan 1910, and for Bow and Bromley in Dec 1910.

The period 1910–14 is covered by eight box-files. They include correspondence, speeches, articles and subject files on the Parliament Bill (47), Lloyd George's Insurance Act (47), the Army (52), Home Rule and the Curragh Crisis (49, 50, 53), and the Marconi Inquiry (51) (Amery was a member of the select committee).

Amery took both an administrative and military role in the First

World War. His brother-in-law, Hamar Greenwood, wrote (4 Sept 1914) to Amery's wife describing how Amery had been able to persuade Kitchener to accept a scheme for processing recruits which the staff officers had been afraid to press. He was later sent to Flanders, the Balkans, Gallipoli, and Salonika as an intelligence officer. There is a small amount of correspondence from his fellow officers, in particular several letters from Sir Ian Hamilton who commanded the Dardanelles Expedition. On his return to England (3 Nov 1915) Hamilton asked Amery to use his influence to stop attacks on Hamilton's direction of the expedition, at least until he could write his report and put his case (57). Amery's active service meant that he was abroad during several political crises of the war, in particular that of Dec 1916. Very little political correspondence seems to have survived from this period, possibly because the ship on which Amery was returning home was sunk by a submarine. During 1917–18 he served as an Assistant Secretary to the War Cabinet and took part in many of the conferences at Versailles. Memoranda, telegrams, and letters relating to his official work survive (69–72), as well as general correspondence, and various articles and speeches. There are two boxes (72, 73) of correspondence relating to his tenure of the Under-Secretaryship at the Colonial Office and at the Admiralty as well as material concerning his elections 1918–35 (79), memoranda and subject files on Overseas Settlement (i.e. emigration) (81), Malta (81), and on the currency question 1920–21 (81).

There are 30 box-files for the 1920s when Amery was Colonial and Dominions Secretary. In addition to general correspondence, there are 16 files of correspondence with governors and governors-general. There are also subject files on the League of Nations, the Irish Boundary Question, the General Strike, and finance, as well as papers concerning his Empire tour of 1927–28.

There are 30 box-files for the 1930s, when Amery was out of office. The subject files for that period include the 1931 crisis, disarmament, India, unemployment, the Abdication, Austria 1938, and Czechoslovakia.

During the Second World War Amery was Secretary of State for India and Burma. There are 20 boxes of telegrams, minutes to the Prime Minister, Cabinet memoranda, and correspondence with governors. There are also speeches and articles on India, as well as papers concerning Cripps's mission in 1942.

In 1945 Amery left office but 40 box-files reflect his continued and varied interests. There are several boxes of papers concerning the publication of his memoirs, including a draft for a fourth, unpublished volume (184, 185, 199, 200a, 200c), and also material for his *Thoughts on the Constitution* (Oxford UP 1947) (222). There are also files on the Empire Industries Association 1948–55, the Central Africa Federation 1952–54, correspondence with Chaim Weizmann 1930–55, and the Rhodes Trust 1939–55 (Amery was Senior Trustee 1933–55).

As well as these voluminous papers, Amery kept a diary 1917–55. It was dictated and then corrected by Amery. It is difficult to decide whether it was normally dictated daily, although on 5 March 1918 he talked of dictating arrears. The diary (as well as the other papers) is quoted extensively in Amery's memoirs, *My Political Life* (3 vols, Hutchinson 1953–55). Occasional annotations appear to have been added to the original text while the memoirs were being prepared. Against the entry for 16 July 1918, for example, he wrote: 'the omissions in my diary are often more vital than the inclusions!' There are, of course, gaps, eg in Sept 1918, when his secretary was on holiday. The entries for 1920, when his secretary was again away, are reminiscences and odd notes 'suggested by entries in my pocket book'. There are some notes for the period 1903–14 compiled on the same basis. The main diary, where it exists, is a very detailed political record. Each volume, which covers approximately a year, has about 250 pages. Selections were published in John Barnes and David Nicholson (eds), *The Leo Amery Diaries, 1, 1896–1929* (Hutchinson 1980) and *The Empire at Bay: The Leo Amery Diaries 1929–1945* (Hutchinson 1988), also edited by John Barnes and David Nicholson.

The National Archives of Canada (MG II G 3) holds photocopies of 28 pages of letters from G. R. Parkin to Amery, and one reply from Amery, spanning 1900–19, relating to Amery's literary activities, imperial federation, imperial defence, and the Canadian federal election of 1900.

There is a brief biography by Wm Roger Louis, *In the Name of God, Go!: Leo Amery and the British Empire in the Age of Churchill* (Norton, New York 1992). Amery's role in Indian affairs is discussed in Robin Moore's *Churchill, Cripps and India 1939–1945* (Clarendon Press, Oxford 1979), and *Escape from Empire. The Attlee government and the Indian Problem* (Clarendon Press, Oxford 1983). The HMSO series on the Transfer of Power 1942–47 contains much material on Amery.

John Barnes distils Amery's career in *Blackwell*, 9–12.

DERICK HEATHCOAT AMORY, 4th Bt, VISCOUNT AMORY (1899–1981)

Derick Amory was Conservative MP for Tiverton 1945–60. He was Minister of Pensions Nov 1951–Sept 1953, Minister of State, Board of Trade 1953–July 1954, Minister of Agriculture and Fisheries July-Oct 1954, Minister of Agriculture and Fisheries and Minister of Food 1954–Jan 1958, and Chancellor of the Exchequer 1958–July 1960. He was created Viscount Amory in 1960, GCMG in 1961, KG in 1968, and succeeded his brother as 4th baronet in 1972.

Lord Amory's nephew, Sir Ian Amory Bt, advised us that Amory 'kept no diaries or, it seems, papers of any consequence'.

An interview given by Amory in 1980 for the British Oral Archive of Political and Administrative History is available for consultation at the BLPES.

The PRO has identified Amory papers from the Ministry of Education (ED 136/694–898) and Ministry of Agriculture and Fisheries (MAF 236/13–23). Papers relating to Budgets are in T 171.

There is a sympathetic biography, *The Reluctant Politician: Derick Heathcoat Amory*, by W. Gore Allen (Christopher Johnson 1958). The book appears to be based in part on private information but it does not quote from documents. Amory's career is summarised by John Barnes in *Blackwell*, 12–14.

SIR JOHN ANDERSON, 1st VISCOUNT WAVERLEY (1882–1958)

John Anderson was created KCB in 1919, GCB in 1923, and Viscount Waverley in 1952. He was Independent National MP for the Scottish Universities 1938–50. He was Lord Privy Seal Oct 1938–Sept 1939, Secretary of State for Home Affairs 1939–Oct 1940, Lord President of the Council 1940–Sept 1943, and Chancellor of the Exchequer 1943–July 1945.

His biographer, Sir John Wheeler-Bennett, informed us that Anderson was 'extremely reluctant to commit himself to paper'. Neither Anderson's widow the late Ava, Viscountess Waverley, nor his son, the 2nd Viscount Waverley, had any papers. Such material as Wheeler-Bennett found was in the archives of the Home, India, and Irish Offices; no 'Anderson papers' survived with the family, although Sir John quoted from letters by Anderson to his first and second wife, and to his father, in his biography, *John Anderson, Viscount Waverley* (Macmillan 1962).

A few fragments on Anderson's work as Joint Under-Secretary of State for Ireland 1918–20 are available for research in the PRO (CO 904/188/1, 2). The first volume consists of papers, including witnesses' statements, connected with the attempted assassination of the Lord Lieutenant. There are also copies of several letters to Sir Hamar Greenwood and A. Bonar Law. Anderson's views on the negotiations with the Irish and the Irish situation are given in several memoranda. The second volume mainly consists of miscellaneous correspondence with General Macready May 1920–Sept 1921. There are several letters and memoranda clarifying the truce terms agreed in 1921.

Also available at the PRO is an incomplete set of papers of the Anderson Committee on pensions 1924 (PIN 1). The records of the Review Committee on the Export of Works of Art, chaired by Anderson, are in T 227/315–21.

Some of Anderson's papers as Lord President, previously in the keeping of the Cabinet Office, have been transferred to the PRO. They form the largest part of CAB 118 which contains Private Office papers of the Lords President 1938–47. Some files are closed for 50 years. Papers relating to Budgets are in T 171.

There are two collections of Anderson's papers in the Oriental and India Office Collections, British Library. The larger one (MSS Eur F 207) covers Anderson's period as Governor of Bengal 1932–37, and includes correspondence with successive viceroys, Lords Willingdon and Linlithgow; successive Secretaries of State for India, Sir Samuel Hoare and Lord Zetland; other officials and personal friends. There are also subject files on aspects of the political situation in Bengal. The collection has been listed. The smaller group (MSS Eur D 806) consists of two files, one containing miscellaneous personal correspondence 1937–41, and the other papers of the Royal Institute of International Affairs, Shanghai Study Group. Both collections are available for research.

A collection of papers preserved by Ava, Viscountess Waverley, was acquired on her death by Sophie Dupré, a dealer in autograph letters, manuscripts, and literary property. The collection, which Ms Dupré purchased over a considerable period, consisted mainly of correspondence of Lady Waverley but also included some letters to her husband. Much of this material has now been dispersed although some items remained unsold at the time we went to press. Details of items offered for sale may be found in the catalogues issued from time to time by Sophie Dupré, XIV The Green, Calne, Wiltshire SN11 8DQ.

SYDNEY ARNOLD, BARON ARNOLD (1878–1945)

Sydney Arnold was Liberal MP for West Riding of Yorkshire (Holmfirth, later Penistone) 1912–21; he joined the Labour Party in 1922. He was Under-Secretary of State for the Colonies Jan-Nov 1924, and Paymaster-General June 1929–March 1931. He was created Baron Arnold in 1924.

Arnold died unmarried. His estate passed to his two brothers, Frederick Octavius Arnold, who died in 1953, and Lawrence Septimus Arnold, who died in 1954. Arnold's nephew, Mr Gerald Arnold had a very small collection of papers relating to Arnold's political career, including a copy of his letter of resignation 5 March 1931, a copy of a letter to Ramsay MacDonald 27 Sept 1931 appealing to MacDonald not to go to the country as head of a national government, and the reply 29 Sept 1931, in which MacDonald reproached Arnold for not appreciating the necessity of his actions.

We have been unable to re-establish contact with Mr Arnold or to determine the fate of the papers he held in the early 1970s.

WILFRID WILLIAM ASHLEY, BARON MOUNT TEMPLE (1867–1939)

Wilfrid Ashley was Conservative MP for North Lancashire (Blackpool) 1906–18, Lancashire (Fylde) 1918–22 and Hampshire (New Forest) 1922–32. He was Parliamentary Secretary to the Ministry of Transport Oct 1922–Oct 1923, Under-Secretary of State for War 1923–Jan 1924, and Minister of Transport Nov 1924–June 1929. He was created Baron Mount Temple in 1932.

Twenty-six boxes of Ashley's papers form a very small part of the Broadlands estate archive, which was deposited by the Broadlands Trustees in the Hampshire RO. The Broadlands estate archive has now been transferred to the University of Southampton's Hartley Library. The Ashley material is dispersed through the Broadlands Archive. A catalogue is being prepared.

The bulk of the collection consists of correspondence. There is general correspondence for the years 1898–1912, 1914–23, 1926–38. This has been arranged alphabetically within years. Much correspondence with politicians has been separated from these letters and some of the letters from an individual put together in one bundle. For example, there are 90 letters from Sir William Joynson-Hicks for the period 1909–32; 35 from William Peel 1901–34; 26 from Bonar Law 1911–23; 36 from Sir Anderson Montague-Barlow 1916–30; 29 from Neville Chamberlain 1919–35; 33 from Herbert Morrison 1929–31 (mostly concerning the Road Traffic Bill); and 73 letters from Sir Arthur Steel-Maitland 1911–32. There is a further series of letters from politicians arranged alphabetically within years. Apart from this correspondence, Ashley's political career is represented only by such fragments as speech notes 1929–36, and a memo of a secret debate in the Commons in 1917.

Only a few papers have survived from Ashley's constituency work: there are printed election addresses for the 1906, 1910, and 1918 general elections, printed letters of thanks to canvassers, press cuttings, some photos of Ashley campaigning, and a blue silk handkerchief which he wore on all his campaigns. Ashley was private secretary to Sir Henry Campbell-Bannerman for a short time after he resigned from the Guards in 1898, and a fragment of diary 22 April–3 May 1899 and 29 letters 1899–1908 survive for this period. Ashley made tentative efforts to gain a Liberal seat but was stopped by his father's refusal of funds unless he stood as a Conservative.

The only ministerial papers in this collection are Foreign Office confidential prints of reports by Max Muller on the situation in Austria-Hungary in 1917. A few subject files represent Ashley's interests: Ireland (he acted as a Brigade-Major in the Ulster Volunteer Force) – mostly photos, passes, posters, and a few letters from Ashley's Irish tenants;

Germany (he was a member of the Anglo-German Fellowship but resigned the chair in the 1930s over the German treatment of Jews); and transport.

Ashley's remaining papers are miscellaneous bank account books, various commissions and certificates, photos, invitations, his letters to his first wife 1907–10, and diaries 1884–86, and for various trips abroad, eg to Morocco in 1894, and South Africa in 1898.

In addition to Ashley's own papers, the Broadlands Archive contains the papers of various members of his family. There are diaries, letters, and a press cutting book relating to his father, the Rt Hon Evelyn Ashley, and his mother Sybella. Two large bundles of Sir Ernest Cassel's correspondence 1886–1921, including a bundle of letters from the royal family, are included in the collection. Cassel was the father of Ashley's first wife. Also included in the archive are the papers of Ashley's daughter Edwina, Countess Mountbatten, and her husband, Earl Mountbatten of Burma.

Some of Ashley's Private Office papers from the Ministry of Transport are now available in the PRO (MT 62/1). The papers include a file on the 1928 Cabinet Policy Committee on railway rating and motor taxation.

Ashley's work as Minister of Transport is extensively covered in William Plowden, *The Motor Car and Politics 1896–1970* (Bodley Head 1971).

HERBERT HENRY ASQUITH, 1st EARL OF OXFORD AND ASQUITH (1852–1928)

H. H. Asquith was Liberal MP for Fife (East) 1886–1918 and Paisley 1920–24. He was Secretary of State for Home Affairs Aug 1892–June 1895, Chancellor of the Exchequer Dec 1905–April 1908, Prime Minister 1908–Dec 1916, and Secretary of State for War March-Aug 1914. He was Leader of the Liberal Party April 1908–Oct 1926. He was created KG and Earl of Oxford and Asquith in 1925.

One hundred and fifty-two volumes of Asquith's papers were given to Balliol College, Oxford, by his literary executors, his son, the Hon Arthur Asquith, and Sir Maurice Bonham Carter. The papers were later given to the Bodleian Library, where they are available for research (MSS Asquith 1–152, MS Asquith adds 1). The papers have been catalogued and an index compiled (NRA 12685). The collection is now read on microfilm.

Asquith is known to have destroyed a large quantity of his private correspondence. Nevertheless much of political importance remains including correspondence with King Edward VII and King George V; and drafts and copies of Cabinet letters to the kings, the main source for tracing Cabinet discussions and decisions until Lloyd George instituted Cabinet agenda and minutes in Dec 1916. This series of Cabinet letters is not complete; however, it does contain at least one letter not in the Royal Archives (MS Asquith 5, ff 86–7), dated 24 Feb 1909. There are letters, memoranda, and pamphlets on most of the political problems of Asquith's administration.

There are few papers from the period before Asquith became Prime Minister, and few constituency papers, except letters of congratulation on his victory at Paisley in 1920, and letters of condolence on his defeat in 1924. There are eight boxes of papers relating to the post-1918 Liberal Party, in particular, account books of party funds, and correspondence about the ownership of the *Westminster Gazette*.

The Bodleian Library also holds Asquith's engagement diary 1915 (MS Eng hist g 24).

The *Life of Lord Oxford and Asquith* by J. A. Spender and Cyril Asquith (2 vols, Hutchinson 1932), *Asquith* by Roy Jenkins (Collins 1964, 3rd ed 1986), and *Asquith* by Stephen Koss (Allen Lane 1976) all quote extensively from these papers, as does George H. Cassar, *Asquith as War Leader* (Hambledon 1994). There are few personal recollections or documentary quotations in Asquith's *The Genesis of the War* (Cassell 1923) and *Fifty Years of Parliament* (2 vols, Cassell 1926). Many personal letters, mostly by Asquith himself, are quoted in *Memories and Reflections 1857–1927* (2 vols, Cassell 1928); but these letters have not always been accurately transcribed, and, wherever possible, the originals should be consulted.

Certain private papers, including Margot Asquith's diaries, remain in private hands under the control of Lord Bonham Carter (13 Clarendon Rd, Holland Park, London W11 4JB).

A letter from Churchill to Asquith 11 Nov 1915 conveying his resignation from the Cabinet, is among a collection of 16 letters to Margot Asquith in the William R. Perkins Library, Duke University.

Asquith's own letters are rarely to be found in the Asquith collection, but may be found in other Bodleian collections. Some of his voluminous letters to female friends are now in public repositories: Sylvia Henley 1915–19 (Bodleian, MSS Eng lett c 542/1–5); Viola Tree 1909–13 (British Library, Add MS 59895, 61727); Lady Scott, later Lady Kennet (Churchill Archives Centre, NRA 12509).

Michael and Eleanor Brock edited *H. H. Asquith: Letters to Venetia Stanley* (Oxford UP 1982, 2nd ed 1985). The Brocks published approximately three-fifths of the collection which remains in the possession of Venetia Stanley's grand-daughter Anna Gendel. A typescript version of the Asquith-Venetia Stanley letters used by the official biographers of Churchill and in Cameron Hazlehurst, *Politicians at War July 1914 to May 1915* (Jonathan Cape and Basic Books, New York 1971) is available in the Bodleian Library among the uncatalogued papers of Martin Gilbert.

The collection of letters to Sylvia Henley in the Bodleian Library also includes single letters to Asquith from John Redmond 1915, Sir John Fisher 1915, and Sir Ian Standish Monteith (MSS Eng lett c 542/1–5).

CLEMENT RICHARD ATTLEE, 1st EARL ATTLEE (1883–1967)

Clement Attlee was Labour MP for Stepney (Limehouse) 1922–50 and Walthamstow (West) 1950–55. He was Under-Secretary of State for War Jan-Nov 1924, Chancellor of the Duchy of Lancaster May 1930–March 1931, Postmaster-General March-Aug 1931, Lord Privy Seal May 1940–Feb 1942, Secretary of State for Dominion Affairs 1942–Sept 1943, Deputy Prime Minister 1942–May 1945, Lord President of the Council 1943–May 1945, Minister of Defence July 1945–Dec 1946, and Prime Minister July 1945–Oct 1951. He was Leader of the Labour Party 1935–55. He was created Earl Attlee in 1955, and KG in 1956.

The main body of Attlee's papers was deposited in the Bodleian Library in 1978 by University College, Oxford, and a catalogue with index was produced in 1984 (NRA 27633). The papers are now divided into four sections, a total of 146 boxes. Section I, correspondence and papers arranged chronologically, covers the years 1945–51 and illustrates the way in which the machinery of government functions. It includes (Dep Attlee 13, fols 68–9) a memo by Attlee on the electoral truce in 1944. The bulk of this section which runs to 129 boxes consists of notes for the Prime Minister's speeches and broadcasts. Section II contains printed material and press cuttings 1937–51; Section III miscellaneous and personal papers 1924–57; and Section IV the correspondence and papers of Violet, Countess Attlee 1948–51.

In 1983 the Bodleian acquired from Patricia Beck the 82 letters Attlee wrote to her from 1957–67 (MS Eng lett c 571). In 1991 Lord Shawcross gave the Bodleian seven letters from Attlee dating from 1948–52 (MS Eng c 2720, fols 20–6). The papers of Lord Winterton, acquired in 1992, include three handwritten letters from Attlee 1950–55 (uncatalogued collection).

Attlee gave two files of his papers to the Bevin Library at Churchill College. These are now available to researchers at the Churchill Archives Centre (ATLE) after written application to the Keeper of the Archives. A list is available (NRA 12661). The first file contains an incomplete draft of Attlee's memoirs *As it Happened* (Heinemann 1955). The draft includes personal comments left out of the published version. There are also notes from the diaries of Margaret Attlee, daughter-in-law of Attlee's elder brother, Tom, and notes on Attlee's local government and parliamentary careers. The second file includes some correspondence with Churchill and Lady Megan Lloyd George, as well as miscellaneous notes on, for example, the organisation of the Cabinet (c.1932), and the making of appointments (mainly ecclesiastical) by the Prime Minister (c.1951).

Kenneth Harris was entrusted with a small collection of personal papers when preparing his authorised biography, *Attlee* (Weidenfeld and Nicolson 1982). These papers were later returned to Anne, Countess Attlee, 125 Hendon Lane, London N3 3PR. They include two boxes of genealogical papers and photos, miscellaneous correspondence with various members of the Attlee family, a box of press cuttings, six boxes of miscellaneous correspondence with old friends, constituents, and former colleagues, and two scrapbooks including press cuttings collected by Attlee's brother Bernard.

Mr Harris was also lent over 200 letters covering the years 1913-60 from Attlee to his brother Tom, who became a conscientious objector in the First World War while his brother served in Gallipoli, Mesopotamia, and the Western Front. These letters, previously in the possession of Tom's daughter-in-law, Mrs Margaret Attlee, have now been deposited in the Bodleian Library, where they will be available for research.

The late Lord Moyle, Attlee's literary executor, knew of no other surviving papers.

Some of Attlee's papers form the bulk of CAB 118 and some as Lord President in CAB 123 in the PRO (NRA 32908). Some files are closed for 50 years. Other papers relating to Attlee may be found in the files of the Military Secretariat of Cabinet 1938-47 (CAB 120); Cabinet Office registered files and Prime Minister minutes from Attlee (CAB 21) and Prime Minister's Office correspondence and papers 1945-51 are in PREM 8.

Mr Alick Fletcher, a cousin of the 2nd Lord Attlee, has the diaries of Margaret Attlee, notes from which are in the Attlee files in the Churchill Archives Centre. (There is very little mention of Attlee).

Francis Williams's *A Prime Minister Remembers: The War and Post-War Memories of the Rt. Hon. Earl Attlee* (Heinemann 1961) is based on Attlee's private papers and a series of recorded conversations with Williams. Recent biographies include Trevor Burridge's *Clement Attlee: A Political Biography* (Jonathan Cape 1985) and Jerry H. Brookshire, *Clement Attlee* (Manchester UP 1995). Reference should also be made to William Golant, 'The Political Development of C. R. Attlee to 1935' (BLitt thesis, Oxford University 1967), and Golant's articles 'The Early Political Thought of C. R. Attlee', *The Political Quarterly*, XXXX, 3, 1969, and 'The Emergence of C. R. Attlee as Leader of the Parliamentary Labour Party', *The Historical Journal*, XIII, 2, 1970. Roy Jenkins's *Mr Attlee: An*

Interim Biography (Heinemann 1948) does not draw on his subject's papers. The article by Raymond Smith and John Zametica, 'The Cold Warrior: Clement Attlee reconsidered, 1945–7', *International Affairs*, 61, 2, 1985, makes use of many of the PRO's files relating to Attlee. Sir Maurice Shock provides a concise and detailed sketch of Attlee's career in *DNB 1961–1970*, 46–55.

SIR JOHN LAWRENCE BAIRD, 2nd Bt, 1st VISCOUNT STONEHAVEN (1874–1941)

John Baird was Conservative MP for Warwickshire (Rugby) 1910–22 and Ayr Burghs 1922–25. He was Parliamentary Under-Secretary of State for Air Dec 1916–Jan 1919, Parliamentary Secretary to the Ministry of Munitions Jan 1919, Parliamentary Under-Secretary of State for Home Affairs April 1919–Oct 1922, Minister of Transport and First Commissioner of Works 1922–Jan 1924. He succeeded his father as 2nd baronet in 1920, and was created GCMG and Baron Stonehaven in 1925, and Viscount Stonehaven in 1938.

Lord Stonehaven's son, the 12th Earl of Kintore, informed us that he gave most of his father's papers to the National Library of Australia (MS 2127). He had retained only two large volumes of press cuttings 1925–30 and a printed diary of Stonehaven's travels in Abyssinia 1 Nov 1890–31 Jan 1891 and 24 April–20 May 1900.

The papers in the National Library of Australia (NRA 22806) relate mainly to Stonehaven's period as Governor-General of Australia 1925–30 and have been divided into nine series: general correspondence; royal correspondence; advice given on becoming Governor-General; correspondence on Stonehaven's resignation as Chairman of the Conservative Party; Committee of Imperial Defence Papers; papers on the powers of governors-general; diaries; press cuttings; and miscellaneous items.

The general correspondence has been arranged chronologically; it covers the period 1899–1940, but most of the letters are dated between 1926 and 1930. The series includes congratulations on the appointment as Governor-General of Australia, letters concerning the journey out to Australia, and comments on Australian politics, trade unionism, and socialism. The royal correspondence 1925–37, mainly letters from royal secretaries, is closed until it is 60 years old. The letters are arranged in chronological order. Subjects covered include the 1926 Imperial Conference, and the 1926 British General Strike, as well as comments on most aspects of Australian life.

The advice given on Stonehaven's becoming Governor-General was provided by his predecessor, Lord Forster. It ranges from dress appropriate for the Governor-General to laundry. The file also includes correspondence with Forster on the arrangements for a smooth succession. The file of papers on Stonehaven's resignation as Chairman of the Conservative Party mostly comprises letters and press cuttings dated after his resignation (3 March 1936).

The Committee of Imperial Defence papers are mostly printed papers advising the Australian government of information received by the British government and of the decisions reached in the light of this information. The papers on the powers of governors-general are mostly drafts or copies of cables 1926-27 exchanged between the United Kingdom, Australia, and New Zealand on the diminished powers resulting from the 1926 Imperial Conference.

There are diaries for 1919 and 1941. They include voluminous notes of conversations. The press cuttings cover 1892-1940 but mostly relate to the period as Governor-General. The miscellaneous papers include itineraries, seating plans, and other ephemera.

The Department of Special Collections, Aberdeen University Library, acquired a collection of papers of the Earls of Kintore in 1980 (MS 3064). This collection includes as volumes 129-43 and 145, diaries covering the years 1897-1915 (see NRA(S) 1318; NRA 10210). Copies of these diaries are held by the Royal Intelligence Corps Library.

At Rickarton House, Rickarton, Scotland, there are estate papers, and papers and correspondence on political affairs including intelligence reports on internal conditions in Austria-Hungary and Germany 1916, Irish affairs in the USA 1916 etc.; notes and letters on foreign affairs subjects 1924-37; speech notes and miscellaneous political correspondence 1919, 1935-36, 1939. These papers were previously held at Glenton House (NRA(S) 1130). Further estate papers are with Kinnear and Falconer Solicitors, Stonehaven. There is a list prepared by the NRA(S) (NRA 19342).

Stonehaven's period as Governor-General of Australia is discussed in Christopher Cunneen, *Kings' Men: Australia's Governor-Generals from Hopetoun to Isaacs* (George Allen & Unwin, Sydney 1983), 165-77.

PHILIP JOHN NOEL-BAKER, BARON NOEL-BAKER (1889-1982)

Philip Noel-Baker (he assumed the additional surname of Noel on his marriage in 1915) was Labour MP for Coventry 1929-31, Derby 1936-50 and Derby (South) 1950-70. He was Parliamentary Secretary to the Ministry of War Transport Feb 1942-May 1945, Minister of State at the Foreign Office Aug 1945-Oct 1946, Secretary of State for Air 1946-Oct 1947, Secretary of State for Commonwealth Relations 1947-Feb 1950, and Minister of Fuel and Power 1950-Oct 1951. He was awarded the Nobel Peace Prize in 1959. He was created Baron Noel-Baker (a life peerage) in 1977.

Lord Noel-Baker preserved a very considerable quantity of correspondence and other papers, particularly in relation to his work for the League of Nations and the United Nations. The collection was deposited in the Churchill Archives Centre in 1978 and 1982 (NBKR). There are 1044 boxes. A detailed list has been prepared (NRA 24828) and most of the papers are available for research.

A volume of Noel-Baker's correspondence concerning the League of Nations 1918–19 is to be found in the PRO (FO 800/249). Private Office papers as Secretary of State for Air are in AIR 19.

There is also relevant material relating to Noel-Baker's work in the League of Nations Archives. See *Guide to the Archives of the League of Nations 1919–1946* (UN Library, Geneva 1978).

David J. Whittaker's *Fighter for Peace: Philip Noel-Baker 1889–1982* (William Sessions, York 1989) makes extensive use of the papers at the Churchill Archives Centre.

A collection of 554 letters from Noel-Baker to Megan Lloyd George, and one letter (unposted) from her to him, formerly in the possession of Lady Megan's nephew David Lloyd Carey-Evans, is now in the NLW (MSS 23254–68). The letters, spanning the period 14 March 1940 to 5 Oct 1957, are quoted frequently in Mervyn Jones, *A Radical Life: The Biography of Megan Lloyd George 1902–66* (Hutchinson 1991).

STANLEY BALDWIN, 1st EARL BALDWIN OF BEWDLEY (1867–1947)

Stanley Baldwin was Conservative MP for Worcestershire (West or Bewdley till 1918, Bewdley from 1918) 1908–37; he took over the seat on the death of his father who had held it from 1892. Baldwin was Joint Financial Secretary to the Treasury June 1917–April 1921, President of the Board of Trade 1921–Oct 1922, Chancellor of the Exchequer 1922–May 1923, Prime Minister 1923–Jan 1924, Nov 1924–June 1929 and June 1935–May 1937, Lord President of the Council Aug 1931–June 1935, and Lord Privy Seal Sept 1932–Dec 1933. He was Leader of the Conservative Party May 1923–May 1937. He was created KG and Earl Baldwin of Bewdley in 1937.

Baldwin bequeathed 'all my political papers, memoranda and correspondence' to the Cambridge University Library, where they were bound into 233 volumes (Baldwin Papers). There is a 33 page *Handlist of the Political Papers of Stanley Baldwin, First Earl Baldwin of Bewdley* (1973) by A. E. B. Owen (NRA 16803). The papers were used by G. M. Young for his *Stanley Baldwin* (Hart-Davis 1952), by Keith Middlemas and John Barnes in *Baldwin* (Weidenfeld and Nicolson 1969), by H. Montgomery Hyde in *Baldwin, The Unexpected Prime Minister* (Hart-Davis 1973), and by Roy Jenkins, *Baldwin* (Collins 1987).

The Cambridge collection is open to researchers. The original arrangement of the papers – partly by subject, partly chronological –

has been retained. To emphasise the subject basis of the arrangement, the papers have been put into wide divisions: home affairs, empire affairs, foreign affairs, letters, personal, speeches, and papers withdrawn. This last division consists of papers marked as being the property of HM Government and which were set aside to be returned to the Cabinet Office. After the documents had been reviewed, it was decided that they could be retained by the Library but this decison was made too late for their return to their original places in the various files. Vols 176–8 contain correspondence with the royal family and their secretaries. They may be consulted only after the permission of HM's Private Secretary has been obtained. Application for this should be made to the Royal Librarian, Windsor Castle.

The Cambridge collection contains only Baldwin's 'political' papers. No family or personal papers are included. (The 'personal' section contains papers referring to the running of Chequers, the Prime Minister's country home, and the presentation of freedoms and honorary degrees). Baldwin kept no diary and rarely wrote a memo, or a 'political' letter, or kept a copy of those he did write. There is hardly any material before 1923. The papers mainly relate to his first two administrations; there is very little relating to his period in opposition in 1924, and no official or departmental papers 1935–37, but there is a considerable quantity of material for the period as Lord President of the Council 1931–35.

The late 3rd Earl held his father's personal papers, including a large box of Baldwin's letters to his mother 1889–1925. These letters are not at present available for research but Lord Baldwin quoted from them extensively in his biography *My Father: The True Story* (Allen & Unwin 1955). There are also some personal political papers which are not available for research. They include letters about Baldwin's gift to the Exchequer of £125,000 in 1919, Mrs Baldwin's account of the fall of the Coalition government in Oct 1922, copies of letters from Baldwin to his wife on the 1931 economic crisis and the formation of the National government, letters from J. C. C. Davidson on India (April 1932), and on a luncheon with Ribbentrop, the German Ambassador (Nov 1933), letters about the Abdication crisis, and letters from Neville Chamberlain May–Oct 1940.

The 3rd Earl's own papers (inherited by the 4th Earl in 1976) are of special interest to the student of Baldwin because he interviewed and corresponded with many of his father's contemporaries when he was writing his biography. He kept the correspondence and his notes of those interviews. These notes include a draft book on Baldwin and the rearmament question 1935–37 by Sir Harold Graham Vincent (private secretary to the Prime Minister), notes of interviews with Lord Citrine, Lord Davidson, Lord Hinchingbrooke, Lord Hankey, Lord Londonderry, Sir Horace Wilson, and James Stuart. There is also a collection of press cuttings, largely reviews or extracts from books by or about Baldwin and his contemporaries. Correspondence between the 3rd Earl, G. M. Young, and others 1946–54, was deposited at Cambridge University Library in 1973 (Add MS 7938).

Several other small collections relating to Baldwin have been acquired by Cambridge University Library: ten miscellaneous items deposited on permanent loan by Keith Middlemas, including five letters to Alan Dore (Add MS 8812); a collection of personal correspondence (Add MS 8770), and a slim volume of press cuttings (Add MS 8771) were bequeathed to the Library by D. Pepys Whiteley, a cousin; 48 letters from Baldwin to his son and heir Oliver 1916–47 (Add MS 8795) bought at Phillips Oct 1989. There are further miscellaneous letters from Baldwin scattered throughout the Library's other collections.

The papers referred to by Middlemas and Barnes as the 'J. P. Boyle manuscripts' were a few personal and family letters originally in the possession of Baldwin's eldest son, the 2nd Earl Baldwin. These manuscripts can no longer be found.

Some official papers still in Baldwin's possession at his death were returned to the Cabinet Office. Their fate is unknown. Papers of Prime Ministerial Advisors Outside Cabinet 1916–40 are held in the PRO at PREM 1.

Two volumes of notes of cases reviewed under Regulation 14 (B) by the Enemy Aliens Committee in the First World War, both of which belonged to Baldwin, are to be found in file 65 in the papers of J. C. C. Davidson.

Reference should also be made to the group of papers called 'Prime Ministers' (Class A) in the Thomas Jones papers at the NLW (NRA 30994). The Conservative Party Archives in the Bodleian Library should also be consulted.

SIR ARTHUR JAMES BALFOUR, 1st EARL OF BALFOUR (1848–1930)

Arthur Balfour was Conservative MP for Hertford 1874–85, Manchester (East) 1885–1906 and the City of London 1906–22. He was President of the Local Government Board June 1885–Feb 1886, Secretary for Scotland Aug 1886–March 1887, Chief Secretary for Ireland 1887–Nov 1891, First Lord of the Treasury 1891–Aug 1892 and June 1895–Dec 1905, Lord Privy Seal July 1902–Oct 1903, Prime Minister July 1902–Dec 1905, First Lord of the Admiralty May 1915–Dec 1916, Secretary of State for Foreign Affairs 1916–Oct 1919, and Lord President of the Council 1919–Oct 1922 and April 1925–June 1929. He was Leader of the Conservative Party July 1902–Nov 1911. He was created KG in 1922 and Earl of Balfour later in the same year.

Most of Balfour's political and philosophical papers have been deposited in the British Library (Add MSS 49683–962). The 280 volumes of papers have been divided into the following main groups: royal correspondence; correspondence with Prime Ministers; Cabinet; Committee of Imperial Defence and Foreign Affairs papers; papers as Lord President; Home Affairs papers; family correspondence; general correspondence; and literary manuscripts.

The five volumes of royal correspondence include foreign royalty and visiting heads of state. The ten volumes of correspondence with Prime Ministers include four volumes of correspondence with his uncle the 3rd Marquess of Salisbury 1872–1902 (Balfour was his private secretary 1878–80); one volume of correspondence with W. E. Gladstone, Lord Rosebery, Campbell-Bannerman, Asquith, and Lloyd George; one volume of correspondence with Bonar Law; and one volume of correspondence with Baldwin, Ramsay MacDonald, and Churchill.

The Cabinet and Committee of Imperial Defence papers include two volumes of Cabinet memoranda 1896–1928, three volumes of correspondence with Sir G. Clarke 1904–16, three volumes of correspondence with Maurice Hankey 1913–29, and three volumes of correspondence with Admiral Fisher 1902–16. There is one volume of correspondence and papers relating to Balfour's term as First Lord. There are seven volumes of Foreign Office papers 1878–1900, and 1902–29, including three volumes of papers on the 1918–19 Peace Conference. There are also five volumes of correspondence with Lord Lansdowne 1881–1922.

Four volumes of papers have survived from Balfour's term as Lord President of the Council. They include much material on the establishment of the scientific research councils, particularly the Medical Research Council.

Over 70 volumes of papers have survived relating to home affairs. They include six volumes of correspondence with Sir Bernard Mallet 1891–1915 on education reform, four volumes of correspondence with George Wyndham, and two volumes of memoranda on Ireland 1887–1902.

The six volumes of Balfour's family correspondence include four volumes of the Hon Mrs Dugdale's papers collected for her work on Balfour's biography. Balfour himself had begun his autobiography in 1928; Mrs Dugdale edited this as *Chapters of Autobiography* (Cassell 1930). She later published a two-volume biography *Arthur James Balfour* (Hutchinson 1936) which quotes extensively from the papers. Kenneth Young, *Arthur James Balfour* (G. Bell 1963), Sydney H. Zebel, *Balfour* (Cambridge UP 1973), and Ruddock Mackay, *Balfour: Intellectual Statesman* (Oxford UP 1985) are also based on these papers. Max Egremont's

Balfour (Collins 1980) draws on the material available in public repositories and also Balfour's correspondence with Lady Elcho, later the Countess of Wemyss, held by the Wemyss family at Gosford in East Lothian and Stanway in Gloucestershire. A collection of *The Letters of Arthur Balfour and Lady Elcho 1885–1917* has been edited by Jane Ridley and Clayre Percy (Hamish Hamilton 1992).

There are 32 volumes of general correspondence 1872–1929 and 20 volumes of letter books. Balfour's literary papers include his lectures, articles, books, and speeches, including the two volumes of autobiography mentioned above.

Balfour's personal papers, and some of his political papers, formerly kept at his family home, Whittingehame, in Scotland, were deposited in the SRO in 1986 (GD 433/2). The papers have been listed (NRA(S) 12). Intending researchers may consult the list at the NRA, the Institute of Historical Research, and the Scottish universities. The collection is open for research on condition that any proposed publication based on the papers must be submitted to Lord Balfour for approval. The more important papers are made available on microfilm. Photocopying is permitted only with Lord Balfour's written permission, requests for which must be made in writing to the SRO.

The Whittingehame papers cover Balfour's entire life and should clearly be used in conjunction with those in the British Library. There are papers relating to his candidature at Hertford and Manchester (East), speech notes, drafts for articles, and a good deal of correspondence. The latter includes correspondence with the 3rd Marquess of Salisbury on Lord Randolph Churchill's resignation in 1887, and correspondence on Ireland and the Empire with George Wyndham, Edward Grey, and Joseph Chamberlain. There is much correspondence with his political contemporaries from the 1920s; for example, with Lloyd George and Edward Grigg on closer union between the Coalition parties; with King George V and his secretaries, including a note by Balfour of an interview with Lord Stamfordham 21 May 1923 on the selection of Bonar Law's successor as Prime Minister; with Lord Derby on Anglo-French relations; and with the 4th Marquess of Salisbury and Maurice Hankey on Cabinet proceedings when Balfour was away from London in 1929. There is also some correspondence on Zionism 1919–23, including correspondence with Dr Weizmann, Philip Kerr, and Lord Rothschild. The collection includes some Cabinet and Committee of Imperial Defence memoranda, particularly from the latter's invasion Sub-Committee 1907–08.

Private Office papers relating to Balfour's period at the Scottish Office are dispersed through the files of the five main Scottish Office departments held at the SRO.

A further small collection of Balfour's papers is available at the PRO

(FO 800/199–217). The collection includes a volume of correspondence with the King and the Prime Minister 1917–18, two volumes of papers concerning the 1917 British War Mission to the USA, four volumes of miscellaneous correspondence 1917–19, and 12 volumes of correspondence 1916–22 arranged alphabetically by country. There is a typescript list (NRA 23627).

Balfour's papers as Chief Secretary for Ireland were transferred from the British Library to the PRO (PRO 30/60, 1–13). These papers are mainly concerned with the maintenance of law and order and include some registered files from the Royal Irish Constabulary Office in Dublin Castle. All are open for research with the exception of two pieces relating to Secret Service Papers. There are also Balfour's papers to Lord Northcote in PRO 30/56.

An album of letters to Balfour 1882–93 is available in the William R. Perkins Library, Duke University. Correspondents in this album include Joseph Chamberlain, Aretas Akers-Douglas, Lord Salisbury, and the Duke of Devonshire.

A bound volume of memoranda on education legislation 1906–08 mostly unsigned, but with two initialled 'A. J. B.', was acquired from the library of the Earl of Crawford by the Liverpool University Library (MS 24.30). No separate list of this is available.

The papers of John Satterfield Sandars, Balfour's private secretary 1892–1915, are in the Bodleian Library. These have been microfilmed and copies are issued to readers instead of the originals (X Films 2/1–16); they were used before Sandars's death, most notably by J. L. Garvin in his biography of Joseph Chamberlain, but were then closed for research until used by Max Egremont. The collection consists of 25 boxes of correspondence and memoranda, the greater part relating to the period of Balfour's premiership. The papers are particularly voluminous for 1903; they include a very considerable amount of material on the Cabinet crisis of that year. The collection is particularly important because of the extensive responsibilities given to Sandars by Balfour. Thus many letters, sent privately to Balfour, which might be expected to be found in his papers, were kept by Sandars. Moreover, much of Sandars's own correspondence relates to important questions of government and, after 1905, opposition policy and tactics. The collection includes letters from the King and his private secretaries to Balfour, together with copies of Balfour's Cabinet letters to the King. But the papers also reveal the extent to which the government's dealings with the Court were delegated to Sandars himself. Sandars's contacts with the Court persisted after the Conservatives had gone into opposition. These papers demonstrate how Sandars was used by various people, especially leading Conservatives, as an indirect approach to, and a means of gauging the opinion of, Balfour himself.

A catalogue, with a detailed list of correspondents is available (NRA 19043).

Reference should be made to Jason H. Tomes, 'A. J. Balfour and British Foreign Policy: the international thought of a Conservative statesman' (DPhil, Oxford University 1992).

GERALD WILLIAM BALFOUR, 2nd EARL OF BALFOUR (1853–1945)

Gerald Balfour was Conservative MP for Leeds (Central) 1885–1906. He was Chief Secretary for Ireland July 1895–Nov 1900, President of the Board of Trade 1900–March 1905, and President of the Local Government Board March-Dec 1905. He succeeded his brother as 2nd Earl of Balfour in 1930.

Balfour's papers formerly held at Whittingehame, his family home in Scotland, are now part of the Earl of Balfour Muniments at the SRO (GD 433/2). The papers have been listed (NRA(S) 12).

There are bundles and folders of letters and memoranda to Balfour, relating mostly to politics and public affairs 1895–1935, including correspondence with Joseph and Austen Chamberlain, Sir H. Plunkett, A. Bonar Law, T. M. Healy, Lord Milner, Keir Hardie, A. J. Balfour, Lady Betty Balfour, Lloyd George, the Marquess of Salisbury, and Lord Roberts. There are letters to Balfour concerning Irish political subjects 1895–98, and letters from Cecil Spring Rice 1905–18.

Private papers include several bundles of purely personal correspondence with Lady Frances and Lady Betty Balfour, and other miscellaneous correspondents. Balfour is frequently mentioned in letters from Lady Frances to A. J. Balfour 1894–1914, and his correspondence is included in the bundles of family letters 1878–1930.

Another collection of Balfour's papers was given to the PRO (PRO 30/60) (NRA 23635, pieces 36–54 only). Pieces 13–35 contain further papers for Balfour's term at the Irish Office. Pieces 36–44 contain Cabinet memoranda and Confidential Print 1897–1905. There are three volumes of Board of Trade papers 1901–05, containing correspondence, memoranda, and pamphlets and further volumes on subjects of particular interest to the Cabinet – India, the War Office and the Committee of Imperial Defence, South Africa, and the redistribution of parliamentary seats.

SIR HENRY CAMPBELL-BANNERMAN (1836–1908)

Henry Campbell-Bannerman (he assumed the additional surname of Bannerman in 1872) was Liberal MP for Stirling Burghs 1868–1908. He was Financial Secretary to the War Office Nov 1871–Feb 1874 and May 1880–May 1882, Parliamentary Secretary to the Admiralty 1882–Oct 1884, Chief Secretary for Ireland 1884–June 1885, Secretary of

State for War Feb-June 1886 and Aug 1892–June 1895, and Prime Minister Dec 1905–April 1908. He was Leader of the Liberal Party 1899–1908. He was created GCB in 1895.

Fifty-six volumes of his papers have been deposited in the British Library and classified in two series (Add MSS 41206–52 and 52512–21). Both series are open and have been divided under the following headings: (A) royal and special correspondence; (B) general correspondence; (C) notes and private correspondence; (D) journals and diaries; (E) letters and memoranda about Campbell-Bannerman. These papers were used by J. A. Spender for *The Life of the Right Hon. Sir Henry Campbell-Bannerman, G.C.B.* (2 vols, Hodder and Stoughton 1923). Spender stated (p. v) that Campbell-Bannerman never wrote much, particularly later in his life. The papers are also extensively quoted in John Wilson, *CB, A Life of Sir Henry Campbell-Bannerman* (Constable 1973) and John James McLean, 'Campbell-Bannerman: The New Imperialism and the Struggle for Leadership Within the Liberal Party, 1892–1906', (PhD thesis, University of Connecticut 1974).

Campbell-Bannerman's royal correspondence in the first series of papers includes letters from Queen Victoria and her secretaries 1886–1900, and two volumes of correspondence with King Edward VII and his secretaries. The 26 volumes of special correspondence include series of letters from the 1st Marquess of Aberdeen 1886–1908, H. H. Asquith 1893–1908, James Bryce 1886–1908, the Marquess of Lincolnshire 1899–1908, Lord Crewe 1905–08, W. E. Gladstone, H. J. Gladstone, and Sir William Harcourt. There are 11 volumes of general correspondence 1871–1908.

In section 'C' of the papers there are several notes for speeches and lectures, especially on South Africa. There is also some family correspondence 1884–1908, and his wife's correspondence 1884–1906. This section also includes Campbell-Bannerman's own letters to his cousin James Campbell 1881–1900.

Campbell-Bannerman's diaries take the form of pocket diaries for 1886–1908, excepting 1891. His journals record various tours abroad, such as his tour in Europe 1850–51, which he described in journal-letters to his sister Louisa, and which were published, edited by John Sinclair, Lord Pentland, *Early Letters of Sir Henry Campbell-Bannerman to his Sister Louisa* (Fisher Unwin 1925). Lady Campbell-Bannerman's notebooks of tours are also included in this section.

The last section of the papers – 'E' – was formed in answer to requests by Lord Pentland, Campbell-Bannerman's executor, for autograph letters from Campbell-Bannerman. Campbell-Bannerman's own letters were put in their relevant place in the preceding series but the letters to Lord Pentland and several brief memoirs about Campbell-Bannerman are included in this section.

The ten volumes of the second series include Campbell-Bannerman's drafts of his Cabinet letters to the King, as well as further correspondence with the King and his secretaries. There are many letters from Sir Edward Grey 1905–08, Lord Elgin 1906–08, and Winston Churchill, as well as three further volumes of general correspondence 1892–95. There is one volume of Campbell-Bannerman's letters to his wife 1892–95.

The NLS acquired in 1981 typescript copies of correspondence 1881–1908 collected by Lord Pentland (Acc 8049).

ANTHONY PERRINOTT LYSBERG BARBER, BARON BARBER (1920–)

Anthony Barber was Conservative MP for Doncaster 1951–64 and Altrincham and Sale 1965–74. He was a Junior Lord of the Treasury April 1957–Feb 1958, Economic Secretary to the Treasury Oct 1959–July 1962, Financial Secretary to the Treasury 1962–Oct 1963, Minister of Health 1963–Oct 1964, Chancellor of the Duchy of Lancaster June-July 1970, and Chancellor of the Exchequer 1970–March 1974. He was created Baron Barber (a life peerage) in 1974.

Lord Barber advised us that he kept no papers during his time as a Cabinet minister and that he has no papers which he considers would be of interest for the *Guide*.

The Conservative Party Archives in the Bodleian Library contain material (papers, correspondence, and speeches) from Barber's time as Party Chairman 1967–70. Permission to view the papers must be obtained by writing to the Chairman's Office, Conservative Political Centre, 32 Smith Square, London SW1P 3HH.

Papers relating to Budgets are in the PRO at T 171.

SIR (CLEMENT) ANDERSON MONTAGUE-BARLOW, Bt (1868–1951)

Anderson Montague-Barlow (he changed his name from Montague Barlow by deed-poll in 1946) was Conservative MP for Salford (South) 1910–23. He was Parliamentary Secretary to the Ministry of Labour April 1920–Oct 1922, and Minister of Labour 1922–Jan 1924. He was created KBE in 1918, and a baronet in 1924.

No papers have survived from the politically active period of Montague-Barlow's life. According to Lady Montague-Barlow, he destroyed a good deal of his own papers before his death and she herself destroyed his letters to her after she had read them. The only papers which have survived are the diaries Montague-Barlow kept on five foreign tours he made after 1924. These diaries have been placed in Rhodes House Library (MSS Brit Emp t 11–15). The diaries were kept in the form of letters to his sisters which were typed and bound up with photos, a few letters, press cuttings, and other souvenirs. The original letters do not seem to have survived. The diaries contain a great number of tourist's observations but because Montague-Barlow had been in the Cabinet, and, it may have been thought, might be a member of some future Cabinet, he met many of the leading politicians and administrators of the places he visited. It is for his impressions of these people and of the political, social and economic situation of the countries he visited, that the diaries are of special interest. There are also occasional retrospective references to Cabinet discussions on colonial business, such as the decision in 1923 to give political concessions to Kenya (Jan-April 1927 diary, p. 15): Montague-Barlow denies that the Cabinet were frightened by Lord Delamere's threats of secession.

The first diary (349pp) covers a tour mainly of India, though Iraq, Palestine, Turkey, and Greece were also visited, from Dec 1924 until April 1925. Lady Montague-Barlow described his political views as 'Left of Centre Conservative' and this view is borne out by his remarks on India, particularly by his fears that the new policies of Indianisation would be stultified by the old type of Indian Civil Service recruit. He met many of the leading Indians of the period and recorded his opinions of them.

The second diary (82pp) covers a tour of Malaya, Ceylon, India, and Egypt, made between Sept 1925 and March 1926. It is chiefly concerned with Malaya and seems in part to have been a business diary.

The third diary (222pp) covers a trip to East Africa made from Jan to April 1927. Again Montague-Barlow's conversations and impressions of local people and situations are recorded, including his fears of problems to come:

> ... the fine type of gentleman settler will make a splendid white-man's outpost in the Federation of E. Africa, which is bound to come ... but at the present I suspect they are rather conceited and contemptuous of many things, especially of native development and restrictions from home ... (p. 23).

Another trip to Tanganyika and Kenya was made from Dec 1927 to March 1928. The diary for this trip (100pp) indicates that Montague-Barlow was negotiating for some electoral scheme, though whether officially is not clear. He certainly met the Hilton Young Commission and discussed electoral projects and systems of land holding.

The last diary describes a trip to South America from Aug until Nov 1932. It seems to be more of a tourist's diary than the other four and includes more photos and press cuttings.

Montague-Barlow chaired the Royal Commission on the Location of Industry 1938. One hundred and twenty eight files of the commission's papers are available in the PRO (HLG 27). They are incomplete but it is not known if this is the result of contemporary weeding or of damage which may have occurred in the Second World War.

Adjusting to Democracy is a valuable guide to Montague-Barlow's work at the Ministry of Labour and to relevant PRO files.

ALFRED JOHN BARNES (1887–1974)

Alfred Barnes was Labour Co-operative MP for East Ham (South) 1922–31 and 1935–55. He was Minister of War Transport Aug 1945–March 1946, and Minister of Transport 1946–Oct 1951.

Mr Barnes informed us that he never kept any papers, press cuttings, speech notes or other records. However, some of his Private Office papers from the Ministry of Transport are now available at the PRO (MT 62/125–9). They include policy papers on shipping, ship-building, and road haulage. There is also a collection of press cuttings on Barnes 1922–74 in the National Museum of Labour History.

Joyce M. Bellamy contributed the brief entry on Barnes in *DNB 1971–1980*, 37–8.

GEORGE NICOLL BARNES (1859–1940)

George Barnes was Labour MP for Glasgow (Blackfriars; Glasgow Gorbals from 1918) 1906–22. He was Minister of Pensions Dec 1916–Aug 1917, and Minister without Portfolio 1917–Jan 1920. He was Chairman of the Labour Party 1910–11. He resigned from the Labour Party in 1918 when it withdrew from the Coalition so that he might take part in the Versailles negotiations.

According to Miss Jessie Barnes, his only daughter, all Barnes's papers were lost when his Herne Hill house was bombed during the Second World War. In the preface to his autobiography *From Workshop to War Cabinet* (Herbert Jenkins 1923), Barnes wrote that he never kept a diary and seldom kept letters.

A collection of 31 letters to Barnes was sold in three lots at Christie's on 16 April 1980. One lot was purchased by Ian Sayer for the Sayer Archive. It consists of 24 letters to Barnes from his colleagues c.1919–36 including Lloyd George (accepting Barnes's resignation from the government due to ill health), Baldwin, Robert Cecil, Neville Chamberlain and seven letters from Philip Snowden. Copies of these letters are available to *bona fide* scholars on a mail basis.

Six letters from J. C. Smuts c.1920–33 were acquired by the IWM in the same sale. It is not known who purchased the third lot of letters. A letter was forwarded by Christie's to the consignor of this collection but was returned as 'not known at this address'.

The files of the Labour Party hold c.276 items relating to Barnes 1900–07 (LP/GC). There is also material in the archives of the Labour Representation Committee (LP/LRC; NRA 14863). Both may be found at the National Museum of Labour History.

There are useful sketches of Barnes's life and career by Barbara Nield in *DLB*, IV, 7–15, and by David M. Head in *MBR*, 3, 63–8.

SIR MICHAEL EDWARD HICKS BEACH, 9th Bt, 1st EARL ST ALDWYN (1837–1916)

Michael Hicks Beach succeeded his father as 9th baronet in 1854, was created Viscount St Aldwyn in 1906, and Earl St Aldwyn in 1915. He was Conservative MP for Gloucester (East) 1864–85 and Bristol (West) 1885–1906. He was Parliamentary Secretary to the Poor Law Board Feb-Aug 1868, Under-Secretary of State for Home Affairs Aug-Dec 1868, Chief Secretary for Ireland Feb 1874–Feb 1878 and Aug 1886–March 1887, Secretary of State for the Colonies Feb 1878–April 1880, Chancellor of the Exchequer June 1885–Feb 1886 and June 1895–Aug 1902, and President of the Board of Trade Feb 1888–Aug 1892.

Hicks Beach's political papers have been deposited in the Gloucestershire CRO (D2455). These papers are described on pages 1–97 of the NRA Report 3526, which is the only list of the papers. There are papers concerning Ireland, with much material about Irish education, and the 1892 Irish Local Government Bill, as well as copies of Hicks Beach's letters to Disraeli 1874–81. The Colonial Office papers include copies of letters to Queen Victoria 1877–85 and correspondence with Sir Bartle Frere about South African affairs 1878–80. There is much material concerning the Zulu wars, including correspondence with Sir Garnet Wolseley 1879. There are also a few papers from the Board of Trade and many Cabinet memoranda. There are a large number of Treasury papers, mostly concerning departmental estimates, particularly the army. There is correspondence with Hicks Beach's political contemporaries including W. E. Gladstone on the Transvaal 1881, the Irish boycott campaign 1885, and the reform of procedure 1886, correspondence with Lord Randolph Churchill 1884–90, the Duke of Devonshire 1884–1905, Joseph and Austen Chamberlain, and the 3rd Marquess of Salisbury.

Some of Hicks Beach's estate and family papers are still in the possession of his grandson, the 3rd Earl St Aldwyn. These papers include the letters written by Hicks Beach to his wife and family on political matters which are quoted in Lady Victoria A. Hicks Beach, *Life of Sir Michael Hicks Beach, Earl St Aldwyn* (2 vols, Macmillan 1932). The remaining estate and family papers have been deposited in the Gloucestershire CRO (D2440).

There is a very small collection of letters to Hicks Beach in the Trinity College Library, Dublin.

(ISAAC) LESLIE HORE-BELISHA, BARON HORE-BELISHA (1893–1957)

Leslie Hore-Belisha (he assumed the additional surname Hore in 1912 when his mother re-married) was Liberal MP for Plymouth (Devonport) 1923–45. He became a Liberal National in 1931 and a Conservative in 1945. He was Parliamentary Secretary to the Board of Trade Nov 1931–Sept 1932, Financial Secretary to the Treasury 1932–June 1934, Minister of Transport 1934–May 1937, Secretary of State for War 1937–Jan 1940, and Minister of National Insurance May-July 1945. He was created Baron Hore-Belisha in 1954.

Hore-Belisha left his papers to his secretary and literary executor, Miss Hilde Sloane. Some use of them was made by R. J. Minney in *The Private Papers of Hore-Belisha* (Collins 1960, reprinted Gregg Revivals, Aldershot 1991). The papers appear to have been weeded after Miss Sloane's death with only 11 boxes of papers, mainly letters and diaries dealing with Hore-Belisha's period as a minister 1934–40, being deposited at the Churchill Archives Centre (HOBE; NRA 28241).

In the Liddell Hart papers at the Liddell Hart Centre there is a substantial collection of correspondence, notes of talks, and memoranda prepared for Hore-Belisha 1937–57 (Hore-Belisha Records). There are also obituaries, correspondence with James Minney and Hilde Sloane, articles by and about Hore-Belisha, and reviews and letters relating to Minney's book.

There is a small collection of material relating to Hore-Belisha in the papers of Major General Charles Haydon (Military Assistant to the Secretary of State for War 1938–39) at the IWM. It includes a handful of personal letters written by Hore-Belisha, as well as the holograph draft of part of Hore-Belisha's 1938 Army Estimates speech, his speech to the House of Commons on ceasing to be Secretary of State for War, seven folios of telegrams and manuscript notes from Hore-Belisha to Haydon, and an album of press cuttings and photos.

Secretary of State for War's Private Office papers are in the PRO at WO 259.

J. P. Harris, 'Two War Ministers: A Reassessment of Duff Cooper and Hore-Belisha', *War & Society*, 6, 1, May 1988, 65–78, draws on the papers at the Churchill Archives Centre. For Hore-Belisha's work at the War Office see Brian Bond, 'Leslie Hore-Belisha at the War Office' in Ian Beckett and John Gooch (eds), *Politicians and Defence: Studies in the Formulation of British Defence Policy 1845–1970* (Manchester UP 1981), 110–31. Brian Bond sketches Hore-Belisha's whole career in *Blackwell*, 213–14.

FREDERICK JOHN BELLENGER (1894-1968)

Captain Frederick Bellenger was Labour MP for Nottinghamshire (Bassetlaw) 1935-68. He was Financial Secretary to the War Office Aug 1945-Oct 1946, and Secretary of State for War 1946-Oct 1947.

For the first edition of the *Guide* Bellenger's eldest son, Mr R. C. Bellenger, informed us that he was unable to be of any assistance regarding his father's papers.

Three collections of Bellenger's papers were sold by Sotheby's in Dec 1992. The first collection consisted of over 30 letters to Bellenger. Correspondents included Clement Attlee, Ernest Bevin, Stafford Cripps, Anthony Eden, Hugh Gaitskell, and Liddell Hart. We have not been able to contact the purchaser of this collection.

The second and third collections, consisting of 21 letters from Lord Montgomery to Bellenger 1945-54 and 1946-47 respectively, were purchased by the IWM.

The provenance of these collections is unknown. Inquiries made at the Nottinghamshire RO and the University of Nottingham did not reveal any further Bellenger papers.

WILLIAM WEDGWOOD BENN, 1st VISCOUNT STANSGATE (1877-1960)

William Wedgwood Benn was Liberal MP for Tower Hamlets (St. George's) 1906-18 and Leith 1918-27. He was Labour MP for Aberdeen (North) 1928-31 and Manchester (Gorton) 1937-41. He was Secretary of State for India June 1929-Aug 1931, and Secretary of State for Air Aug 1945-Oct 1946. He was created Viscount Stansgate in 1942.

Most of Wedgwood Benn's papers were destroyed in a fire during the Second World War. Those which survived were very badly charred and affected by damp. They were deposited by his widow and his eldest son in the HLRO in 1973 (Stansgate Papers). A list of the papers has been compiled by S. K. Ellison (HLRO Memo 56, 1976; NRA 20882). Applications for access should be addressed to the Clerk of the Records.

The papers originally filled two rooms but the largest part of them consists of a unique collection of press cuttings. From 1920 onwards – if not before – Wedgwood Benn took copies of *The Times* in order to take cuttings. He purchased the 'Royal edition' which was printed on good quality rag paper so that his cuttings have survived in very good condition. As well as keeping the cuttings Wedgwood Benn devised a decimal subject classification. A very detailed conspectus gives an outline of the system. Thus files numbered 1050, 1051, 10511 contain cuttings about India, the North-west Frontier, and Pakistan. Almost every subject covered by *The Times* is represented. In addition, Wedgwood Benn made collections of the speeches and comments of his political contemporaries: there are four box-files of cuttings about Lloyd George 1908–33, a box-file of cuttings about Asquith 1919–22, a box-file of cuttings about Churchill 1904–14, and boxes of cuttings of Sir Edward Grey, Lord Rosebery, Lord Salisbury, Bonar Law, and Hamar Greenwood amongst many others.

Only a few boxes of more personal papers have survived. They include notes and rough drafts of a few chapters of autobiography: there is a chapter on Wedgwood Benn's early life, on parliament before 1914, and on being a whip. The chapter on his early life explains the history and purpose of his filing system. After reading Arnold Bennett, Wedgwood Benn kept a precise note of how he passed his time in a 'Job Book' and on various graphs; these have survived.

Probably the single most important item in this collection is Wedgwood Benn's diary. The surviving typed fragments cover Jan-May 1922, 1924, 1925, and 1926. They give a detailed account of Wedgwood Benn's activities in this period and show his increasing disillusion with Lloyd George. Later diaries have also survived, including a very detailed record of his period as President of the Inter-Parliamentary Union 1954–58.

As well as the diaries there are draft notes on the political situation in the 1920s and on the circumstances of Wedgwood Benn's transfer of allegiance from the Liberal to the Labour Party in 1927. A file of correspondence and notes survives from that period, including Wedgwood Benn's letter of resignation to the Leith Liberals, and letters from politicians such as Lord Oxford, Christopher Addison, Philip Snowden, and Charles Trevelyan. There is also a draft of Wedgwood Benn's letter of application for the Stewardship of the Chiltern Hundreds and the letter appointing him to that post.

Before Wedgwood Benn joined the Labour Party he had been a leader of the Radical Group of Liberal MPs. An annotated list of 'possible' Radicals invited to a dinner in Nov 1925 survives, as well as some miscellaneous correspondence, a note on the purpose of the group, and a 'Report of the Activities of the Parliamentary Radical Group, Easter to August 1926', which gives the dates of lunches held, their chief guests, and the subject discussed, as well as the group's division record and notes on points raised.

A few miscellaneous letters have survived including three from C. F. G. Masterman in 1920 – in a typescript note about Masterman, Wedgwood Benn describes him as an intimate friend. Wedgwood Benn's electoral addresses from 1918, Oct 1922, and Oct 1924, have also survived.

The papers were used and quoted by Sydney Higgins in *The Benn Inheritance: the Story of a Radical Family* (Weidenfeld and Nicolson 1984).

The collection includes no papers from Wedgwood Benn's tenure of office. Small fragments concerning his period at the Air Office are available at the PRO (AIR 19/551, 552); they concern the amalgamation of common services between the RAF, the Navy, and the Army, and the future of aircraft production.

The Oriental and India Office Collections, British Library, hold printed copies of Wedgwood Benn's correspondence with the Viceroy of India, the then Lord Irwin, in the Halifax collection (MSS Eur C 152/5–6; NRA 27436), and with the Governor of Bombay, Major-General Sir Frederick Sykes, in the Sykes Collection (MSS Eur F 150/1–3; NRA 27540).

Benn's role in Indian affairs is discussed in Robin Moore, *The Crisis of Indian Unity, 1917–1940* (Clarendon Press, Oxford 1974), and Carl Bridge, *Holding India to the Empire* (Sterling Publishers Private, New Delhi 1986).

SIR HENRY BUCKNALL BETTERTON, Bt, BARON RUSHCLIFFE (1872–1949)

Henry Betterton was Conservative MP for Nottinghamshire (Rushcliffe) 1918–34. He was Parliamentary Secretary to the Ministry of Labour March 1923–Jan 1924 and Nov 1924–June 1929, and Minister of Labour Aug 1931–June 1934. He was created a baronet in 1929, Baron Rushcliffe in 1935, and GBE in 1941.

Neither of Betterton's two daughters, nor the son and executor of his second wife, knew of any papers when the first edition of the *Guide* was being compiled.

The Hallward Library, University of Nottingham, holds some papers relating to Betterton's delivery of the Cust Foundation Lecture at University College, Nottingham in 1928 (UR 365), including letters from Betterton, and a copy of his lecture entitled 'Empire Migration'.

The Nottinghamshire Archives has only a letter from Betterton to F. L. Barker concerning disabled servicemen 1926 (M 24, 266).

Adjusting to Democracy is a valuable guide to Betterton's work at the Ministry of Labour and to relevant PRO files. Reference should also be made to Frederic M. Miller, 'National Assistance or Unemployment Assistance? The British Cabinet and Relief Policy, 1932–33', *Journal of Contemporary History*, 9, 2, April 1974, 163–84.

ANEURIN BEVAN (1897–1960)

Nye Bevan was Labour MP for Monmouthshire (Ebbw Vale) 1929–60. He was Minister of Health Aug 1945–Jan 1951, and Minister of Labour and National Service Jan-April 1951.

Bevan's papers were in the possession of Mr Michael Foot MP, while Mr Foot wrote a full-scale biography: *Aneurin Bevan, Volume I, 1897–1945* (McGibbon & Kee 1962); *Aneurin Bevan, Volume II, 1945–1960* (Davis-

Poynter 1973). Mr Foot informed us that the papers which survived are in great disorder and are not available for research. They will all eventually be deposited in the National Museum of Labour History, where a small amount is presently available (NMLH/MF/P1 and P5).

John Campbell, *Nye Bevan and the Mirage of British Socialism* (Weidenfeld & Nicolson 1987) is not based on Bevan's papers. Dai Smith, whose book *Aneurin Bevan and the World of South Wales* (University of Wales Press, Cardiff 1993) is more a 'cultural study' than a biography, has a small collection of Bevan material, including Bevan's agent's papers for the 1950s, which will be deposited in the South Wales Coalfield Archives at the University of Wales, Swansea.

The papers of Bevan's widow, Lady Lee, are to be housed at the Open University, Walton Hall, Milton Keynes, on the completion of her biography by Patricia Hollis (Lady Hollis of Heigham).

Shortly before his death Bevan was quoted in *The Guardian* (29 March 1960) as disapproving of people in active public life writing their memoirs. 'They do nothing but mischief. If they tell the truth it is hurtful, but usually they don't tell the truth'. Jennie Lee had published *Tomorrow is a New Day* (Cresset Press) in 1939. Revised and reissued as *This Great Journey* (McGibbon & Kee 1963) it remained for the author 'a useful aide-mémoire, more for what it does not say than for what it says' when she wrote *My Life with Nye* (Jonathan Cape 1980).

ERNEST BEVIN (1881–1951)

Ernest Bevin was Labour MP for Wandsworth (Central) 1940–50 and Woolwich (East) 1950–51. He was Minister of Labour and National Service May 1940–May 1945, Secretary of State for Foreign Affairs July 1945–March 1951, and Lord Privy Seal March-April 1951.

A collection of Bevin's wartime papers was deposited in 1967 by his daughter, Mrs S. E. R. Wynne, in the Churchill Archives Centre (BEVN). These papers have been listed (NRA 19698) and are generally available for research. The bulk of the papers consists of an alphabetically-arranged series of files. There are 33 boxes of 'Minister's Correspondence' but the series is incomplete. Bevin's political correspondents include Clement Attlee, Lord Beaverbrook, Brendan Bracken, and R. A. Butler. There are miscellaneous papers on various problems facing the War Cabinet, including the 1944 Education Act, and a memo on long term post-war policies. There are also papers relating to Bevin's Labour Party and trade union work. The latter include some papers from the 1930s on trade union attitudes to Fascism, Russia, and the League of Nations. There are three boxes of papers on Bevin's visits and tours 1940–41, two boxes of speech notes 1940–44, and six boxes of press cuttings 1940–45. A box of miscellaneous papers includes papers on post-war plans 1943, a file on the 1945 general election, and a file of notes of meetings with lobby correspondents in 1942.

In 1983 Bevin's biographer, Lord Bullock, deposited a further collection of Bevin papers in the Churchill Archives Centre. These papers have been listed. The papers, contained in 156 files, are arranged in 11 sections. There are 21 files of speeches; 18 files of papers and correspondence on visits; 13 files of general papers (mostly printed); and 13 files of miscellaneous correspondence (including a file of 'important' correspondence during 1944 with letters from Churchill, Attlee, Dalton, and Eden) all from Bevin's time as Minister of Labour and National Service 1940–45. There are 13 files of speeches as Foreign Secretary 1945–51; 19 files of Foreign Office papers and correspondence, including some personal correspondence 1945–51; 19 files of trade union papers 1889–1952; seven files of Labour Party correspondence 1940–45, and printed papers 1941–51; 14 files of personal and miscellaneous papers; nine files of photos and cuttings; and ten files containing letters of condolence on Bevin's death.

Bevin's pre-1940 union and political papers, formerly in the possession of the Transport and General Workers' Union, are now in the Modern Records Centre (MSS. 126), and have been listed (NRA 24096). There is a Modern Records Centre Information Leaflet (5) on 'Bevin TGWU Papers' which contains brief notes on the four groups of papers in the collection: trade unions and trade union bodies; official commissions and committees; non-governmental bodies and subject files; miscellaneous. Additions were made to the TGWU archive in 1995 which included previously undiscovered boxes of Bevin papers (MSS. 126/EB addits). They include two boxes of correspondence 1930s; two boxes of speeches and articles 1930s-40s; and notes of interviews conducted by the general secretary 1930s. These papers are not yet fully unpacked. Prior written permission to see the Bevin TGWU papers must be obtained from the Administrative Officer, Transport & General Workers' Union, Transport House, Palace St, Victoria, London SW1E 5JD, before application is made to the Modern Records Centre.

Bevin's Foreign Office papers, 37 bound volumes entitled 'Private Papers of Mr Ernest Bevin 1945–1951', were transferred to the FO 800 class in the PRO in 1982 (NRA 23627). The collection only concerns Bevin's Foreign Office work.

Alan Bullock, *The Life and Times of Ernest Bevin* (3 vols, Heinemann 1960–83) is based on all these papers, on material assembled from the organisations with which Bevin was connected, and from his friends. Francis Williams, *Ernest Bevin* (Hutchinson 1952) is largely based on Williams's own notes of his conversations with Bevin 1929–51. Peter Weiler, *Ernest Bevin* (Manchester UP 1993) has a useful bibliography which lists a range of PRO series relevant to the student of Bevin's ministerial career.

Material from the Bevin papers in the FO 800 series and relevant items from FO 371 and PREM files at the PRO are to be found in Roger Bullen and M. E. Pelly (eds), *Documents on British Policy Overseas*, series II, vols I to III, (HMSO 1986–89), and Ronald Hyam (ed), *British Documents on the End of Empire*, series A, vol two, *The Labour Government and the End of Empire 1945–1951* (HMSO 1992).

(JOHN) REGINALD BEVINS (1908–)

Reginald Bevins was Conservative MP for Toxteth 1950–64. He was Parliamentary Secretary, Ministry of Works Nov 1953–June 1957, Parliamentary Secretary, Ministry of Housing and Local Government 1957–Oct 1959, and Postmaster-General 1959–Oct 1964.

Mr Bevins was unwell when the *Guide* was being prepared and was unable to assist. His book, *The Greasy Pole: A Personal Account of the Realities of British Politics* (Hodder & Stoughton 1965) contains a few references to letters from political colleagues.

(EVELYN) NIGEL (CHETWODE) BIRCH, BARON RHYL (1906–1981)

Nigel Birch was Conservative MP for Flintshire 1945–50 and Flint West 1950–70. He was Parliamentary Under-Secretary of State, Air Ministry Nov 1951–Feb 1952, Parliamentary Secretary, Ministry of Defence 1952–Oct 1954, Minister of Works 1954–Dec 1955, Secretary of State for Air 1955–Jan 1957, and Economic Secretary to the Treasury 1957–Jan 1958. He was created Baron Rhyl (a life peerage) in 1970.

Lord Rhyl's widow, Lady Rhyl, died in 1991. Her nephew, the Earl of Clarendon, who was one of Lady Rhyl's executors, advised us that he did not think that Lord Rhyl left any papers as he was virtually blind in his later life. There were none of her husband's papers amongst Lady Rhyl's own papers.

Mr Enoch Powell, who contributed the entry on his former colleague in *DNB 1981–1985*, 37–8, also knew of no papers.

Lord Rhyl was Parliamentary Secretary when Lord Alexander of Tunis was Minister of Defence. A tape of the interview which he gave to Nigel Nicolson for his biography of Alexander is in the Department of Sound Records, IWM (3951/1).

AUGUSTINE BIRRELL (1850–1933)

Augustine Birrell was Liberal MP for Fifeshire (West) 1889–1900 and Bristol (North) 1906–18. He was President of the Board of Education Dec 1905–Jan 1907, and Chief Secretary for Ireland 1907–July 1916.

A small collection of Birrell's papers was deposited by his great-nephew and literary executor, Mr J. C. Medley in the Bodleian Library (Dep c 299–303). The written permission of Mrs Patricia Medley (Carlton Garth, West Burton, Leyburn, N Yorks DL8 4JY) must be sought before the papers may be read. The papers refer almost exclusively to Ireland. They include Cabinet memoranda about most aspects of Irish administration. There is a large collection of letters from Sir Matthew Nathan 1914–16 and a miscellaneous series of letters and memoranda, including suggestions for the exclusion of Ulster from the operation of any Home Rule bill, and the problems of administering the Defence of the Realm regulations in Ireland.

A small collection of the papers of Andrew Philip Magill, Birrell's secretary, 1914–23, is also in the Bodleian (MSS Eng c 2803–4). It includes several letters to Birrell from his contemporaries, as well as 29 letters from Birrell to Magill.

A further small collection of more personal Birrell papers was deposited by his step-son, Sir Charles Tennyson, in the Liverpool University Library (MS 10.1–3). There are three albums of approximately 250 letters to Birrell and his wife 1861–1912. An index of correspondents has been compiled. As well as letters, the albums contain some press cuttings, sketches, and other printed material. A copy of the 1906 Education Bill bound up with related memoranda is also available in the Library (MS 24.30). Sir Charles also deposited a small collection of letters from Birrell to various members of his step-family (MS 8.2–3). A few extracts are quoted in Sir Charles Tennyson, *Stars and Markets* (Chatto & Windus 1957).

Additions to the collections at the Liverpool University include a gift by Hallam Tennyson in 1986 of 82 items 1899–1976 (MS 8.4 (1–82)) consisting of 29 letters from Birrell to Sir Charles and Lady Tennyson, 30 from Sir Charles, with other letters from the family, some replies, three family photos, and a transcript from the diary of the Hon Cicely Tennyson which illustrates the close personal links between the Tennyson and Birrell families, and includes references to Eleanor Birrell's last illness and death. An autograph letter to Birrell from the 5th Marquess of Lansdowne c.1912 (MS 13.1(22)) and a series of nine letters from Birrell to his publisher Elliot Stock, notes of errata, etc., and corrected proof of title-page 1893–94, were purchased from Henry Bristow, autograph dealer, in 1987 (MS 8.5 (1–14)).

The British Library has letters to Mrs Maida Bernard 1876–1927 (Add MS 49372) and to H. G. Hutchinson (Add MS 49382). There is a collection of letters from Birrell to John Dillon in the Trinity College Library, Dublin (MSS 6455–909; NRA 23156).

Birrell's autobiography *Things Past Redress* (Faber & Faber 1937) appears to be based on personal reminiscence and does not quote from unpublished material. Many studies of Irish policy and administration discuss Birrell's role, notably Leon O'Broin, *The Chief Secretary: Augustine Birrell in Ireland* (Chatto & Windus 1969).

MARGARET GRACE BONDFIELD (1873–1953)

Margaret Bondfield was Labour MP for Northampton 1923–24 and Wallsend 1926–31. She was Parliamentary Secretary to the Ministry of Labour Jan-Nov 1924, and Minister of Labour (the first woman Cabinet minister) June 1929–Aug 1931.

In her autobiography *A Life's Work* (Hutchinson 1941) Miss Bondfield quoted frequently from letters and diaries. In compiling the first edition we were unable to trace any of Miss Bondfield's papers. She died unmarried, leaving her estate to the daughters of her sister, Mrs Harriet Farrant, and of her brother George Bondfield. Mr D. A. Kershaw, one of Miss Bondfield's executors, did not know of the existence of any papers and informed us that another of the executors, Miss Florence Farrant, a niece of Miss Bondfield, was dead. Administration of Miss Farrant's estate was granted to her widowed sister, Mrs Doris Knight, whom we were unable to contact.

The Bondfield papers had in fact crossed the Atlantic and were in the care of Professor Helen Lockwood of Vassar College who had been given full freedom to use the papers by Bondfield's executors. Professor Lockwood had intended to prepare an edition of some of the papers for publication. However, on her death in 1971 the Bondfield collection was deposited in the Vassar College Library (R 31 s 8). The existence of the Bondfield papers was brought to our attention early in 1992 by Dr Caroline Barron of Royal Holloway and Bedford New College.

The collection, inspected by Cameron Hazlehurst in May 1993, consists of 11 manuscript boxes, one smaller box, and 17 books. A very useful nine-page list is available, however some folders contain material which does not appear on the list. There are a number of pocket diaries covering the period 1898–1951, but incomplete on some years. The diaries mostly record engagements and in a few cases lists of books read. There are a few very brief entries in 1913, and a year end comment in 1921 about 'a year of spiritual darkness'.

The political papers in the collection include correspondence with colleagues such as Ramsay MacDonald, Clement Attlee, and Ernest Bevin; papers on the Labour Party and various election campaigns; papers on legislation (including the 1912 National Insurance Bill); congratulatory messages on her appointment as Minister of Labour and correspondence regarding her resignation in 1931. There are press cuttings 1898–1948, and copies of her articles, speeches, and broadcasts. There are also a few papers relating to her union interests, mostly dealing with working women.

Personal papers include correspondence, photos and miscellaneous papers relating to her many travels, as well as family papers. There is an original manuscript of 'American Diary' 1938–39, as well as papers relating to the publication of her autobiography.

Also included in the Bondfield papers is a copy of an unpublished 'senior essay' by Barbara Winkler, 'The Intractable Million: Margaret Bondfield and the Unemployment Insurance' (Vassar College 1974).

Following a request from the Acting Secretary to the Cabinet on 20 Sept 1934, Bondfield returned to the Cabinet Office 'any Cabinet Minutes and other Cabinet Papers and the Minutes and documents of Cabinet Committees and Sub-Committees which you may have retained when you vacated office'. A ten-page itemised 'receipt for Cabinet Documents surrendered ... to Colonel Ives on 1st February 1935' was sent by Sir Maurice Hankey on 5 Feb 1935. There is a separate list of 'Cabinet Memoranda Issued by Minister of Labour from June 1929–August 1931' (Bondfield MSS 4/8).

As is the case for many other key figures in the Labour Movement, the archives of the Labour Party in the National Museum of Labour History contain a good deal of relevant material. There are Bondfield letters 1909–31 (LP/JSM), as well as press cuttings (NRA 14863).

There is a biography of Bondfield's early life by M. Hamilton, *Margaret Bondfield* (Parsons 1924). Reference should also be made to S. Lewenhak, *Women and the Trade Unions* (Benn 1977).

Adjusting to Democracy is a valuable guide to Bondfield's work at the Ministry of Labour and to relevant PRO files. Marion Miliband's contribution on Bondfield in *DLB*, II, 39–45, has a comprehensive list of Bondfield's writings. There is further guidance to secondary sources and archival material in Fred C. Hunter's article in *MBR*, 3, 102–6. Bondfield's career is summarised by Kenneth D. Brown in *Blackwell*, 57–8.

SIR ARTHUR SACKVILLE TREVOR GRIFFITH-BOSCAWEN (1865–1946)

Arthur Griffith-Boscawen was Conservative MP for Kent (Tunbridge) 1892–1906, Dudley 1910–21 and Somerset (Taunton) 1921–22. He was Parliamentary Secretary to the Ministry of Pensions Dec 1916–Jan 1919, Parliamentary Secretary to the Ministry of Agriculture and Fisheries 1919–Feb 1921, Minister of Agriculture and Fisheries 1921–Oct 1922, and Minister of Health 1922–March 1923. He was knighted in 1911.

A small file of Griffith-Boscawen's papers was given by his widow to the Bodleian Library (MS Eng hist c 396, ff 88–139). Most of the papers date from 1922; they shed much light on the break-up of the Coalition government and on the feelings of the Conservatives working with Lloyd George. These papers are not quoted in Griffith-Boscawen's *Fourteen Years in Parliament* (John Murray 1907) or *Memories* (John Murray 1925).

The papers include a collection of six letters dated 10–19 Oct 1922 relating to Griffith-Boscawen's threatened resignation. In his original letter to Austen Chamberlain (dated 10 Oct), Griffith-Boscawen emphasised that he was resigning over the lack of governmental action on agriculture. At first he was restrained by the critical state of the Conservative Party, but eventually he felt forced to resign by the feeling in the party of alienation from the Coalition, despite his loyalty to Austen Chamberlain: '...I should have to support the Party against any individuals'. Griffith-Boscawen wrote a four-page memo on 'The Break Up of the Coalition – the Story of a Wonderful Week'. He also prepared a five-page, undated memo on policy for the new Bonar Law government.

Other papers are concerned with the Turkish crisis of Sept-Oct 1922. There are letters from Griffith-Boscawen to Curzon and Austen Chamberlain protesting that hostilities were being threatened before diplomacy had had a chance to do its job. Curzon's reply thanks Griffith-Boscawen for his support. Griffith-Boscawen had also protested that ministers who returned to London in Sept had been bewildered by the attitude of ministers who had been present during the summer. There are two letters from Sir Maurice Hankey, dated 2 and 7 Nov 1922, which state that there had been no delegation of powers by the Cabinet to a conference of ministers during the summer, but that these conferences had been called to advise the ministers concerned in the crisis. Hankey listed the Cabinet meetings and conferences of ministers which had considered the crisis.

The only other document is a seven-page memo by Griffith-Boscawen entitled 'Inland Transport After the War'. It is dated 21 Feb 1943.

ALAN TINDAL LENNOX-BOYD, 1st VISCOUNT BOYD OF MERTON (1904–1983)

Alan Lennox-Boyd (his father assumed the additional surname Lennox by deed poll in 1925) was Conservative MP for Mid Bedfordshire 1931–60. He was Parliamentary Secretary, Ministry of Labour Feb 1938–Sept 1939, Parliamentary Secretary, Ministry of Home Security Sept-Oct 1939, Parliamentary Secretary, Ministry of Food 1939–May 1940, Parliamentary Secretary, Ministry of Aircraft Production Nov 1943–Aug 1945, Minister of State for Colonial Affairs Nov 1951–May 1952, Minister of Transport and Civil Aviation 1952–July 1954, and Secretary of State for the Colonies 1954–Oct 1959. He was created Viscount Boyd of Merton in 1960.

Approximately 600 boxes of Boyd's papers, mostly dating from the period after 1959, have been deposited in the Bodleian Library and are currently being catalogued. A further 130 large photo albums/scrapbooks in family possession have been bequeathed to the

Bodleian by Viscountess Boyd. There are also extensive tape-recordings at Rhodes House Library relating to Boyd's career.

Private Office papers for Boyd's period at the Ministry of Aircraft Production are in the PRO at AVIA 9. Papers from the Colonial Office period are also available in the PRO at CO 967/277–8 (relating to Cyprus and Malta 1954) and PREM 11.

The Colonial Office periods are covered by D. J. Morgan, *The Official History of Colonial Development*, (5 vols, Macmillan 1980). Boyd's work as Colonial Secretary is discussed (without reference to private papers) in David Goldsworthy, *Colonial Issues in British Politics 1945–1961* (Clarendon Press, Oxford 1971), and A. N. Porter and A. J. Stockwell, *British Imperial Policy and Decolonization 1938–1964* (2 vols, Macmillan 1987–89).

SIR EDWARD CHARLES GURNEY BOYLE, 3rd Bt, BARON BOYLE OF HANDSWORTH (1923–1981)

Edward Boyle succeeded his father as 3rd baronet in 1945, and was created Baron Boyle of Handsworth (a life peerage) in 1970. He was Conservative MP for Handsworth 1950–70. He was Parliamentary Secretary, Ministry of Supply July 1954–April 1955, Economic Secretary to the Treasury 1955–Nov 1956, Parliamentary Secretary, Ministry of Education Jan 1957–Oct 1959, Financial Secretary to the Treasury 1959–July 1962, Minister of Education 1962–April 1964, and Minister of State, Department of Education and Science April-Oct 1964.

Boyle bequeathed his enormous collection of correspondence and papers, comprising nearly 55,000 items, to the Brotherton Library, University of Leeds (MS 660), where he was Vice-Chancellor from 1970 until his death. The collection has been catalogued and listed (NRA 30282). The list is in two parts, the second of which is an exceptionally thorough index of persons and subjects. Parts of the collection are closed until 2011 when their status will be reviewed. Other papers may be consulted before that date provided that the researcher produces a satisfactory reference.

The collection, which covers the period 1940–81, has been divided into 17 sections. They are: family papers; Boyle's domestic and financial papers 1945–81; appointment diaries 1964–80; general and personal correspondence 1940–81; constituency and west Midlands political papers; Birmingham and west Midlands non-political papers; Conservative party organisation and policy 1947–76; parliamentary and ministerial papers 1950–70; House of Lords papers 1970–81; miscellaneous political papers; University of Leeds papers; general university affairs; other non-party organisations; miscellaneous subject files; speeches; lectures and broadcasts; publications and personalia.

Boyle's 1980 interview for the British Oral Archive of Political and

Administrative History is available at the BLPES as well as in the collection at the Brotherton Library.

A collection of biographical essays on Boyle written by his friends, *Edward Boyle: His Life by his Friends* (Macmillan 1991) was edited by his sister Ann Gold. The essay which appears in this book by Jean Orr may be found in a fuller version entitled 'Lord Boyle and the Top Salaries Review Body' in the Brotherton Library collection (MS 958).

Boyle was extensively interviewed regarding the role of the Education minister in Maurice Kogan, *The Politics of Education: Edward Boyle and Anthony Crosland in conversation with Maurice Kogan* (Penguin, Harmondsworth 1971). Sir Edward Heath's brief life of Boyle in *DNB 1981–1985*, 49–51, draws on 'private information; personal knowledge'.

JOHN THEODORE CUTHBERT MOORE-BRABAZON, 1st BARON BRABAZON OF TARA (1884–1964)

John Moore-Brabazon was Conservative MP for Rochester (Chatham) 1918–29 and Wallasey 1931–42. He was Parliamentary Secretary to the Ministry of Transport Oct 1923–Jan 1924 and Nov 1924–Jan 1927, Minister of Transport Oct 1940–May 1941, and Minister of Aircraft Production 1941–Feb 1942. He was created Baron Brabazon of Tara in 1942, and GBE in 1953.

A collection of Brabazon's papers was deposited in the RAF Museum in 1970 (AC/71/3). The papers were partially listed in the late 1970s. The remaining papers have been box listed. The papers are all available for research.

The papers include pocket appointment diaries 1904–64 (1906–11, 1913–17, 1920 and 1941 missing). The political papers include correspondence and press cuttings concerning Brabazon's periods in office; correspondence with colleagues (including Neville Chamberlain, Lord Trenchard, and Lord Beaverbrook); some papers on the General Strike, Brabazon's constituency, and some House of Lords speeches.

The bulk of the papers consists of personal and sporting material, including letters from France during the First World War; papers relating to Brabazon's properties; general correspondence; and miscellaneous photos and cinefilm of the Brabazon family.

The sporting papers include material on Brabazon's hobbies, notably golf, yachting, and photography. There is also much material concerning different aspects of aviation. The collection also includes the personal papers of Lady Brabazon and material from other family members.

Private Office papers are available at the PRO in AVIA 9.

Moore-Brabazon's autobiography *The Brabazon Story* (Heinemann 1956) does not appear to quote from any papers.

BRENDAN RENDALL BRACKEN, VISCOUNT BRACKEN (1901-1958)

Brendan Bracken was Conservative MP for Paddington (North) 1929-45 and Bournemouth (Bournemouth East from Feb 1950) 1945-51. He was Minister of Information July 1941-May 1945, and First Lord of the Admiralty May-Aug 1945. He was created Viscount Bracken in 1952.

In his will Bracken directed that all of his privatate papers be destroyed. Mr Charles Lysaght, author of *Brendan Bracken* (Allen Lane 1979) informed us that Bracken systematically destroyed his papers during his life and that any remnants were destroyed, after his death, by his chauffeur. Bracken's books on English literary and political history were bequeathed to Sedbergh School.

Andrew Boyle, *Poor Dear Brendan. The Quest for Brendan Bracken* was published in 1974 by Hutchinson. Boyle's correspondence relating to the biography is in the Churchill Archives Centre, together with photocopies of letters to Lord Beaverbrook 1948-56 from the Beaverbrook Papers (BBKN; NRA 23365).

Correspondence between Bracken (23 letters) and Chaim Weizmann (38 letters) is in the Weizmann Archives, Israel.

There is an edition of letters exchanged between Bracken and Beaverbrook: Richard Cockett (ed), *My Dear Max: The Letters of Brendan Bracken to Lord Beaverbrook, 1925-1958* (The Historians' Press 1990) which, despite its title and sub-title, contains letters by Beaverbrook as well.

There is valuable material on different phases of Bracken's career in Ian McLaine, *Ministry of Morale* (George Allen and Unwin 1979), and David Kynaston, *The Financial Times: A Centenary History* (Viking Press 1988).

WILLIAM CLIVE BRIDGEMAN, 1st VISCOUNT BRIDGEMAN (1864-1935)

William Bridgeman was Conservative MP for Shropshire (Oswestry) 1906-29. He was Parliamentary Secretary to the Ministry of Labour Dec 1916-Jan 1919, Parliamentary Secretary to the Board of Trade 1919-Aug 1920, Parliamentary Secretary to the Board of Trade for the Mines Department 1920-Oct 1922, Secretary of State for Home Affairs 1922-Jan 1924, and First Lord of the Admiralty Nov 1924-June 1929. He was created Viscount Bridgeman in 1929.

Bridgeman's papers, formerly in the possession of his son, the late 2nd Viscount Bridgeman, are now in the Shropshire RO (SRO 4629; NRA 34743). There is a comprehensive catalogue of the papers and they are available for research.

The collection includes his personal and political papers, correspondence, diaries, press cuttings, and books, together with papers of his wife Caroline. There is also a small collection of printed election papers for 1906, 1910, and 1924, and photocopies of letters from Bridgeman to his third son Maurice 1923–35 (SRO 2225/1–40).

Churchill Archives Centre has copies of 100 letters received by Bridgeman when he was First Lord, his Geneva diary 1927, and a speech at Geneva 1928 (BGMN; NRA 18561).

Cambridge University Library has a small collection of letters from Stanley Baldwin to the 1st and 2nd Lords Bridgeman (Add 8781).

An edition of Bridgeman's diary and letters has been prepared by Philip Williamson, *The Modernisation of Conservative Politics: the Diaries and Letters of William Bridgeman 1904–1935* (The Historians' Press 1988). Dr Williamson also contributed the brief entry on Bridgeman in C. S. Nicholls (ed), *The Dictionary of National Biography Missing Persons* (Oxford UP 1993), 88–9.

Adjusting to Democracy refers only in passing to Bridgeman's work at the Ministry of Labour.

(WILLIAM) ST JOHN (FREMANTLE) BRODRICK, 1st EARL OF MIDLETON (1856–1942)

St John Brodrick was Conservative MP for Surrey (West) 1880–85 and Surrey (South West or Guildford) 1885–1906. He was Financial Secretary to the War Office Aug 1886–Aug 1892, Under-Secretary of State for War July 1895–Oct 1898, Under-Secretary of State for Foreign Affairs 1898–Nov 1900, Secretary of State for War 1900–Oct 1903, and Secretary of State for India 1903–Dec 1905. He succeeded his father as 9th Viscount Midleton in 1907, and was created KP in 1915, and Earl of Midleton in 1920.

For those interested in Brodrick's political and official career, the most important collection of his papers was deposited in the PRO in 1967 by his daughter, Lady Moira Loyd (PRO 30/67). The class list of this collection has been published in the List and Index Society, 70, *Public Record Office Gifts and Deposits. Supplementary List,* 1971; see also NRA 23461. A personal name index of correspondents and those mentioned in the papers has been compiled. The collection has been divided into two parts: papers concerning Brodrick's political career (PRO 30/67, 1–26) and papers concerning his interest in Ireland (PRO 30/67, 27–57).

Brodrick's political career is represented by papers from his term as Financial Secretary to the War Office. There are letters and minutes 1885–91, including a challenge to a duel from T. M. Healy in 1893. There are also papers from Brodrick's term as Under-Secretary of State at the War and Foreign Offices including correspondence on the Boer War and the Boxer Rebellion. Brodrick's papers as Secretary of State for War include correspondence on the conduct of the Boer War and the subsequent reorganisation of the War Office, and correspondence with the sovereign Nov 1900–Oct 1903. The papers relating to Brodrick's term as Secretary of State for India include correspondence with Lords Kitchener and Roberts, and papers concerning the dispute between Lord Curzon and Lord Kitchener. In addition there are a few miscellaneous papers, including memoranda on Haldane as Secretary of State for War, Lloyd George as an arbitrator, and on the maladministration of the War Office by Kitchener as Secretary of State.

Brodrick was one of the most important English landowners in Ireland and a leader of the Southern Irish Unionists. His Irish papers cover Sinn Fein, the Easter Rebellion, and later attempts to solve England's Irish problem. There are working papers of the Irish Convention, including printed papers, correspondence (including letters from Lloyd George), and a memo of an interview with the War Cabinet in 1918. There are papers concerning the split in the Southern Unionists, the offer to Brodrick of the viceroyalty in 1918, and the 1920–22 negotiations. There is also later correspondence about this period with historians, including Denis Gwynn.

None of Brodrick's papers were left to his son, the 2nd Earl of Midleton, but some were bequeathed to his second wife. Lord Midleton referred us to the family solicitors, Warrens in London, who had only retained a tin trunk of papers concerning Brodrick. The papers mostly related to the marriage settlements of Brodrick and his daughter, and to personal financial and legal affairs.

Twenty boxes of estate papers from Warrens have been deposited in the Guildford Muniment Room of the Surrey RO (145). They range from the 15th to the 20th century, but mostly date from the 18th and 19th centuries. They relate chiefly to the family's Surrey estates though there is material relating to Irish estates. A summary list of the collection has been made (NRA 11601 BK). The collection contains nothing relating to Brodrick's political career or personal life except for a few letters on estate and personal business. A further collection, comprising mainly volumes of correspondence and papers 1627–1903 (1248), contains a few letters to Brodrick 1901–03. Researchers wishing to look at these collections should make an appointment to visit the Muniment Room.

Papers concerning the Brodricks' Irish estates and earlier members of the Brodrick family were purchased by the National Library of Ireland in 1954 (MS 8899). A description of them can be seen in R. J. Hayes (ed), *Manuscript Sources for the History of Irish Civilisation* (G. K. Hall, Boston 1965), iii, 377–8.

Another small collection (one volume) of Brodrick's papers was purchased at Sotheby's in 1969 by the William R. Perkins Library, Duke University (Midleton papers). There are 88 letters 1890–1933 probably collected for their autographs. They include letters from Asquith on his 1918 parliamentary election defeat and on his opinion of the Kaiser's memoirs 1922. There are nine letters from Joseph Chamberlain including one giving Chamberlain's views on tariff reform 1903. There are 11 letters from Lord Cromer 1900–05; a letter from Lord Grey of Fallodon on Lloyd George's conduct of foreign affairs in 1922; and 11 letters from Lord Rosebery 1890–1916.

Six volumes of Brodrick's correspondence with Lord Curzon as Secretary of State for India 1903–06 have been deposited in the British Library (Add MSS 50072–7). The British Library also holds some of Brodrick's correspondence with A. J. Balfour 1885–1926 (Add MSS 49720–1), Arnold-Forster 1903–05 (Add MSS 50311, 50314) and Archbishop J. H. Bernard 1917–26 (Add MS 52781, ff 42–142v).

In May 1926 Brodrick wrote his version of the events leading up to Lord Curzon's removal from the viceroyalty in 1905, an account which was approved by A. J. Balfour and then printed by the India Office for limited circulation. This account is available in the Oriental and India Office Collections, British Library (MSS Eur B189).

Brodrick's memoirs, Lord Midleton, *Records and Reactions 1856–1939* (John Murray 1939) quote from letters and memoranda, including his own reports to King Edward VII on post-Boer War army reform.

HENRY BROOKE, BARON BROOKE OF CUMNOR (1903–1984)

Henry Brooke was Conservative MP for West Lewisham 1938–45 and Hampstead 1950–66. He was Financial Secretary to the Treasury July 1954–Jan 1957, Minister of Housing and Local Government and Minister for Welsh Affairs 1957–Oct 1961, Chief Secretary to the Treasury and Paymaster-General 1961–July 1962, and Home Secretary 1962–Oct 1964. He was created Baron Brooke of Cumnor (a life peerage) in 1966.

Lord Brooke advised Dr Cook (*Sources*, 3, p. 61) that he had not 'discovered any papers that would be of interest'. Brooke's son, the Rt Hon Peter Brooke, advised us that neither he nor his mother, Lady Brooke of Ystradfellte, knew of any papers which would be of interest.

An interview recorded in 1980 for the British Oral Archive of Political and Administrative History is available at the BLPES.

There is a brief biography of Brooke by Lord Blake in C. S. Nicholls (ed), *The Dictionary of National Biography Missing Persons* (Oxford UP 1993), 91–2.

(ALFRED) ERNEST BROWN (1881–1962)

Ernest Brown was Liberal MP for Warwickshire (Rugby) 1923–24 and Leith 1927–45 (he was a Liberal National from 1931). He was

Parliamentary Secretary to the Ministry of Health Nov 1931–Sept 1932, Secretary of the Mines Department 1932–June 1935, Minister of Labour (Labour and National Service from Sept 1939) 1935–May 1940, Secretary of State for Scotland 1940–Feb 1941, Minister of Health 1941–Nov 1943, Chancellor of the Duchy of Lancaster 1943–May 1945, and Minister of Aircraft Production May-July 1945.

We have been unable to trace any of Brown's papers. There were no children of his marriage. His executor, Mr C. R. Saunders, informed us that Brown requested that his papers be destroyed after his death; to the best of Mr Saunders's knowledge this request was carried out. Brown gave a collection of eight cartoons to the Mayor of Torquay in 1961; they are now housed in the Torre Abbey Mansion.

Private Office papers relating to Brown's period at the Scottish Office are dispersed through the files of the five main Scottish Office departments held at the SRO.

Adjusting to Democracy is a valuable guide to Brown's work at the Ministry of Labour and to relevant PRO files. Brown's ministerial career and especially his role in Scottish affairs is briefly surveyed in *Secretaries of State for Scotland*, 79–86.

GEORGE ALFRED BROWN, BARON GEORGE-BROWN (1914–1985)

George Brown was Labour MP for Derbyshire (Belper) 1945–70. He was Joint Parliamentary Secretary to the Ministry of Agriculture and Fisheries Oct 1947–April 1951, Minister of Works April-Oct 1951, First Secretary of State and Secretary of State for Economic Affairs Oct 1964–Aug 1966, and Secretary of State for Foreign Affairs 1966–March 1968. He was created Baron George-Brown (a life peerage) in 1970.

Lord George-Brown gave the bulk of his papers to the Bodleian Library in 1982. The collection consists of over 300 boxes of correspondence and papers, many of which are arranged by subject; appointment diaries for the 1960s and 1970s, photos, press cuttings, pamphlets, and annotated and inscribed books. Most of the material dates from the years 1952–81. The papers cover a wide variety of topics including defence, Israel and the Middle East, Northern Ireland, Africa, the Common Market, local government, education, housing, and elections. Certain sections of the papers are closed. There are several boxes relating to George-Brown's autobiography *In My Way* (Gollancz 1970).

A catalogue of the 1982 acquisition is nearing completion. Access to the papers requires the written permission of George-Brown's daughter, Mrs Frieda Warman-Brown, 34 Wellesley Road, Chiswick, London W4 4BN. Additional material donated in 1991 is closed until listed.

Transcripts of the journalist, J. R. L. Anderson's conversations with

George-Brown between April and Aug 1970 which formed the basis of *In My Way* are in the Anderson papers in the Bodleian (boxes 1–4).

A biography by Peter Paterson, *Tired and Emotional: The Life of Lord George-Brown* (Chatto and Windus 1993) is based on the papers. There are brief summaries of George-Brown's career by Michael Stewart in *DNB 1981–1985*, 54–6, and by Keith Robbins in *Blackwell*, 69–70.

ALEXANDER HUGH BRUCE, 6th BARON BALFOUR OF BURLEIGH (1849–1921)

Alexander Bruce became the 6th Baron Balfour of Burleigh in 1869 when the act of attainder on his family was removed. He was created KT in 1901. He was a representative peer for Scotland 1876–1921. He was Parliamentary Secretary to the Board of Trade Jan 1889–Aug 1892, and Secretary for Scotland June 1895–Oct 1903.

Balfour of Burleigh's papers are in the possession of his grandson, the 8th Lord Balfour of Burleigh. They have been listed (NRA(S) 923; NRA 18285). All enquiries about access to the papers should be addressed to the NRA(S) giving as much notice as possible.

The bulk of the papers concern the split in the Unionist ranks over tariff reform 1902–03. Perhaps the most important papers in the collection are Balfour of Burleigh's contemporary notes on the crisis for July-Sept 1903. He also wrote a nine-page memo on the events leading up to his resignation in Sept 1903, and a narrative of the preceding months. As well as Balfour of Burleigh's own impressions of these events, some of his correspondence with his Cabinet colleagues has survived. At a critical stage in the crisis, Balfour of Burleigh was Minister-in-Attendance at Balmoral, and thus isolated from his colleagues. There are several letters from the Duke of Devonshire, Lord James of Hereford, C. T. Ritchie, and A. J. Balfour. There are also Cabinet memoranda and manuscript notes of five '... questions put to Mr Chamberlain through A. J. B. in June 1903 by B. of B.'. Letters of regret at Balfour of Burleigh's resignation have survived, and also some correspondence with Lord George Hamilton in 1911 about Bernard Holland's account of the crisis in *The Life of Spencer Compton, 8th Duke of Devonshire* (2 vols, Longmans 1911).

There are few earlier papers, though there are some letters from W. E. Gladstone on the disestablishment of the Church of Scotland in 1889, and more letters about Church affairs from A. H. Charteris 1881–89. Balfour of Burleigh's continued interest in the Church is reflected in correspondence with A. V. Dicey in 1920 about the union of the Established and Free Churches of Scotland. The 8th Lord Balfour of Burleigh understood that more papers relating to church union in Scotland were given to the then Moderator of the Church of Scotland, Dr White. The Principal Clerk of the Church, the Rev D. F. M.

Macdonald, informed us that the Church had no such papers; however, the Church did deposit a small collection of the papers of Lord Sands with the SRO (CH1/10/1–6). The collection relates almost entirely to reunion matters; there are 73 letters from Balfour of Burleigh to Lord Sands 1911–21.

Balfour of Burleigh's own papers include miscellaneous correspondence with his political contemporaries, eg correspondence with the 3rd Marquess of Salisbury 1886–1902. There are also several memoranda, pamphlets, and letters on the reform of the House of Lords and the 1911 Parliament Act.

Balfour of Burleigh was Chairman of the Royal Commission on Trade Relations between the West Indies and Canada 1909–10. Some correspondence (including his letter of appointment 18 Aug 1909), reports, memoranda, and other submissions to the commission have survived.

From Oct 1915 to April 1916, Balfour of Burleigh investigated grievances among the Clyde munition workers. Correspondence, agenda, submissions from employers and employees, and transcripts of the inquiry have survived. Balfour of Burleigh also chaired a Board of Trade Committee to consider post-war commercial and industrial policy. The committee reported in 1918; reports, pamphlets, and memoranda survive.

Lady Frances Balfour, *A Memoir of Lord Balfour of Burleigh K.T.* (Hodder and Stoughton 1924) was based on papers put at her disposal by Balfour of Burleigh's widow and son. Some, at least, of those papers have survived, eg the narrative, written in 1911, about the events of 1903 (item 191).

Reference should also be made to J. W. R. Mitchell, 'The emergence of Modern Scottish central administration 1885–1939' (DPhil, Oxford University 1987).

VICTOR ALEXANDER BRUCE, 9th EARL OF ELGIN and 13th EARL OF KINCARDINE (1849–1917)

Victor Bruce was known as Lord Bruce until he succeeded his father as 9th and 13th Earl in 1863. He was created KG in 1899. He was Secretary of State for the Colonies Dec 1905–April 1908.

Most of Elgin's papers are in the possession of his grandson, the 11th Earl of Elgin, Broomhall, Dunfermline, Fife KY11 3DU (NRA 26223). The papers, which cover most of Elgin's life, were used and are frequently quoted in Ronald Hyam, *Elgin and Churchill at the Colonial Office 1905–1908: The Watershed of the Empire-Commonwealth* (Macmillan 1968). Applications from *bona fide* scholars and researchers to consult the papers must be made in advance to the Earl of Elgin and Kincardine, accompanied by covering letters from responsible sponsors.

The Broomhall collection is also the foundation of Sydney Checkland, *The Elgins, 1766–1917: A tale of aristocrats, proconsuls and their wives* (Aberdeen UP 1988).

Queen's University Archives, Canada, have microfilm copies of the Broomhall papers which relate to Canada, including correspondence with Earl Grey, Governor General of Canada, 1905–08; general correspondence to Elgin 1906–08; and miscellaneous printed material and memoranda.

Elgin's papers as Viceroy of India 1894–98 are in the Oriental and India Office Collections, British Library, having been deposited in 1956 by the 10th Lord Elgin (MSS Eur F 84; NRA 20533). There are 73 volumes of correspondence, including printed copies of correspondence with the Queen 1894–98, originals and printed copies (with an index) of correspondence and telegrams with the Secretary of State, and correspondence with persons in England and India. There are seven volumes of press cuttings. The collection also includes 44 volumes of Elgin's private secretary's correspondence, and 16 volumes of miscellaneous papers and photos.

A valuable guide to sources relevant to Elgin's period as Viceroy is Arnold P. Kaminsky, *The India Office, 1880–1910* (Greenwood Press, New York 1986).

JAMES BRYCE, VISCOUNT BRYCE (1838–1922)

James Bryce was Liberal MP for Tower Hamlets 1880–85 and Aberdeen (South) 1885–1906. He was Under-Secretary of State for Foreign Affairs Feb-May 1886, Chancellor of the Duchy of Lancaster Aug 1892–March 1894, President of the Board of Trade 1894–June 1895, and Chief Secretary for Ireland Dec 1905–Jan 1907. He was created Viscount Bryce in 1914, and GCVO in 1917.

The bulk of Bryce's papers were acquired by the Bodleian Library over a period of 40 years (Bryce papers). The first tranche was catalogued in great detail in the 1950s; it is divided into English and American papers ('Calendar of letters to and from English correspondents', MSS Bryce 1–20 and 'Calendar of papers relating to the United States of America', MSS Bryce USA 1–33). The papers have been listed (NRA 6716).

Brief entries for the two calendars were included in the 1993 catalogue of subsequent gifts and purchases of Bryce material. This catalogue, which includes a detailed index of correspondents, is arranged in the following way: general correspondence 1857–1922; literary papers 1864–1936; printed papers and press cuttings 1842–1922; personal and financial papers 1856–1921; family papers 1826–1958; and miscellaneous papers. The collection is now read on microfilm (X Films 8/1–167).

The general correspondence section includes Bryce's political papers, including constituency papers, and papers relating to Ireland, his Chancellorship of the Duchy of Lancaster, his Ambassadorship to Washington 1907-13, and papers relating to the First World War and education. The personal and financial papers include his diaries and notebooks 1858-c.1912.

Bryce's family gave his papers concerning Irish affairs to the National Library of Ireland (Add MSS 11009-16). This collection includes approximately 1000 documents dated 1878-1921 but most of the letters, memoranda, etc. are from 1906, and relate to the 1907 Irish Council Bill. The main correspondent is Sir Anthony MacDonnell. A further small collection of Bryce's papers has been deposited in the PRO (FO 800/331-5). It consists of four volumes of correspondence 1904-21, and population maps of Hungary.

H. A. L. Fisher's biography, *James Bryce* (2 vols, Macmillan 1927), quotes extensively from these papers and also from letters and rec-ollections given him by Bryce's friends. Edmund Ions, *James Bryce and American Democracy 1870-1922* (Macmillan 1968) is chiefly based on the Bodleian collection. John W. Brennan's contribution on Bryce to *MBR*, 3, 141-7, is a useful guide to specialist studies.

GEORGE BUCHANAN (1890-1955)

George Buchanan was Labour MP for Glasgow (Gorbals) 1922-48. He was Joint Parliamentary Under-Secretary of State for Scottish Affairs Aug 1945-Oct 1947, and Minister of Pensions 1947-July 1948.

Buchanan's widow, Annie, died in the early 1960s. They did not have any children. Buchanan's brother, Dr J. A. Buchanan, informed us that he had no papers belonging to Buchanan and that he could not suggest anyone else whom we might contact. Thus the small collection of papers, mainly relating to Buchanan's early life and personal affairs, that was used by R. K. Middlemas in *The Clydesiders* (Hutchinson 1965), does not appear to have survived.

Neither the Glasgow University Library nor the Mitchell Library, Glasgow, has any Buchanan papers.

The entry on Buchanan by William Knox in *DLB*, VII, 50-3, is based on published sources.

SIR STANLEY OWEN BUCKMASTER, 1st VISCOUNT BUCKMASTER (1861-1934)

Stanley Buckmaster was Liberal MP for Cambridge 1906-10 and Yorkshire (Keighley) 1911-15. He was Solicitor-General Oct 1913-May 1915, and Lord Chancellor 1915-Dec 1916. He was knighted in 1913, created Baron Buckmaster in 1915, GCVO in 1930, and Viscount Buckmaster in 1933.

Buckmaster's papers are in the possession of his grandson, Sir Hal

Miller. They are mainly in the form of letters covering most of his life.

Buckmaster's daughter, the Hon Mrs Barbara Miller, had intended to write a biography and she sorted the letters chronologically; the letters for each year have been put in a large envelope, and a list of contents, which includes the name of the correspondent and the subject of the letter, was sometimes written on the outside. Mrs Miller also began the compilation of a notebook on the events in Buckmaster's life and advertised in *The Times* for letters and recollections; a few replies are kept with Buckmaster's papers.

Most of the letters are 'political', though there are a few letters to his wife and daughter. The letters for 1914 include a typed note written in Oct 1914, justifying Buckmaster's activities as Press Censor in relation to Churchill's trip to Antwerp, and copies of a correspondence between Buckmaster and Edward Marsh, Churchill's secretary. There is also a memo justifying the suppression of the *Morning Post*'s references (18 Jan 1915) to the loss of the *Formidable*. Among the letters of congratulation written to Buckmaster in 1915 is a copy of his own letter to his predecessor as Lord Chancellor, Lord Haldane, expressing regret at the 'spite' which had led to Haldane's dismissal. There are no letters referring to the fall of Asquith's coalition government. There is, however, a typed memo, written by Buckmaster in Jan 1917, on those events; this is extensively quoted in *Lord Chancellors 1* as are many of the letters. The bundle of correspondence for 1917 includes a memo by Buckmaster on '. . . whether Asquith should come back. . .' which describes a meeting held by Asquith, Buckmaster, Samuel, McKenna, and Runciman c.21 Feb 1918 to discuss this question. There is also a memo for Asquith on war aims. The letters for 1918 include one from Austen Chamberlain on why he had joined the government, and a letter from Buckmaster to Harcourt describing Asquith's state of mind 22 April 1918.

Apart from the correspondence, there are other papers representing many facets of Buckmaster's life. There are school reports, and examination papers; Oxford battels and receipts; several printed election addresses; a book of press cuttings; pamphlets on birth control; evidence given before the Coal Mining inquiry of 1924; notes of Privy Council judgements 1928–30. There is also some correspondence of his father, J. C. Buckmaster.

James Johnston (ed), *An Orator of Justice: a speech biography of Viscount Buckmaster* (Ivor Nicholson and Watson 1932) is based entirely on speeches.

SIR REGINALD EDWARD MANNINGHAM-BULLER, 4th Bt, 1st VISCOUNT DILHORNE (1905–1980)

Reginald Manningham-Buller was Conservative MP for Daventry 1943–50 and Northamptonshire South 1950–62. He was Parliamentary

Secretary, Ministry of Works May-Aug 1945, Solicitor-General Nov 1951–Oct 1954, Attorney-General 1954–July 1962, and Lord Chancellor 1962–Oct 1964. He succeeded his father as 4th baronet in 1956 and was created Viscount Dilhorne in 1964.

R. F. V. Heuston, in *Lord Chancellors 2*, states that Lord Dilhorne had, before his death, advised that he had destroyed or would destroy all of his papers.

Dilhorne's son, the 2nd Lord Dilhorne, advised us that he believed his father did destroy all of his papers before his death. He had also declared his desire not to have a biography written.

In addition to the essay on Dilhorne in *Lord Chancellors 2*, Heuston also contributed the entry on him in *DNB 1971–1980*, 545–7.

(EDWARD) LESLIE BURGIN (1887–1945)

Leslie Burgin was Liberal MP for Bedfordshire (Luton) 1929–45 (he was a Liberal National from 1931). He was Parliamentary Secretary to the Board of Trade Sept 1932–May 1937, Minister of Transport 1937–April 1939, Minister without Portfolio April-July 1939, and Minister of Supply 1939–May 1940.

A very small collection of papers survived in the possession of his widow, Mrs Dorothy Burgin. Most of the papers concerned a goodwill speaking-tour which Burgin undertook to America in 1944. There were draft speeches, memoranda, photos, and press cuttings. There was a small collection of correspondence, mostly letters of sympathy to Burgin's widow, though also including six letters from Lord Simon, a close friend of Burgin. The beginnings of an autobiography, written during Burgin's last illness, also survived. We have not been able to determine the current location of this collection.

The Bedfordshire CRO holds only a few pieces relating to the 1935 general election in the papers of H. C. Janes, including a publicity leaflet and two letters from Burgin to Janes, one thanking him for messages of congratulations Nov 1935 (JN322). The Luton Central Library has no papers, nor does the Luton Museum.

Private Office papers may be found in the PRO at AVIA 11.

JOHN ELLIOT BURNS (1858–1943)

John Burns was 'independent labour' MP for Battersea 1892–95, and Liberal MP for the same constituency 1895–1918. He was President of the Local Government Board Dec 1905–Feb 1914, and President of the Board of Trade Feb-Aug 1914.

Burns died intestate and it seems clear that, in the confusion which followed his death, a large number of his papers were destroyed, many of them in the wartime salvage drives. A detailed account of what happened is to be found in a pamphlet by Yvonne Kapp 'John Burns's

Library', *Our History*, pamphlet 16, Winter 1959. Nonetheless a large collection of Burns's papers was retrieved and presented to the British Library by his family in 1946 (Add MSS 46281–345). The collection comprises 65 volumes which were divided into six main divisions: royal correspondence; special correspondence; general correspondence; speeches and memoranda; diaries; miscellaneous.

The single volume of royal correspondence includes letters from secretaries as well as various members of the royal family. The special correspondence includes series of correspondence from Asquith, Lloyd George, Churchill, and Ramsay MacDonald. There is an interesting series of letters from John Morley which includes a memo written by Burns about Morley in 1925. There is also correspondence reflecting Burns's trade union and labour activities, including letters from Keir Hardie and Robert Blatchford. There are 17 volumes of general correspondence. An index has been compiled for the correspondence divisions.

The speeches and memoranda division includes Burns's press contributions and what may be drafts and notes for an autobiography. There are also some miscellaneous notes in diary form 1888–1928. There are 33 volumes of diary for 1888–1920. The miscellaneous division includes Burns's various diplomas and his autograph collection.

A further, small, uncatalogued collection of Burns's papers was purchased in 1971 by the Battersea Library. They formed part of a collection of material on London made by Ernest Tyrrell. It is thought that Tyrrell, in his turn, acquired them from Burns's own library – certainly Burns collected such material. The collection in the local history collection of the Battersea Library includes printed speeches, illustrations, and news cuttings.

A bundle of 50 letters and a small collection of Burns's memorabilia lent by a Mrs Fuller, originally held at the Battersea Library, is now held at the Wandsworth Museum in the Putney Library. The letters are mostly from the period 1890–1912 but also include some letters from 1938 connected with Burns's work as a Trustee of the National Library of Wales. The letters are very miscellaneous in character: cases of injustice, etc., brought to Burns's attention; comments on speeches; Local Government Board private notices; invitations. There is a letter from James Bryce, then at the Local Government Board, dated 29 June 1894, asking for Burns's opinion on how to settle strikes; letters from Lord Thring 1895, on the use of prison labour; a letter from Sir Charles Dilke 24 June 1899 asking for Burns's cooperation in putting questions on labour and employment to Balfour in the debate on Home Office estimates; several letters 1902–12 from Frederick Rogers, organising secretary of the National Committee of Organised Labour, and other members of his executive, asking for help in their campaign for old age pensions. The memorabilia consist of ceremonial scrolls and keys, as well as a collection of pamphlets by Burns, his 1895 election address, some press cuttings, and several photos including one of his study at 106 Lavender Hill, and a press cutting showing Burns and Morley leaving 10 Downing Street after their last Cabinet meeting.

Burns's family gave a large collection of his books on working-class history to his union, now the Amalgamated Engineering and Electrical Union; these are housed in the library of the Trades Union Congress. As Burns appears to have kept many of his papers inside related books, a small collection of his papers is also to be found there. There are 25 manilla envelopes containing a very miscellaneous collection of papers. The papers include receipts, photos, and programmes for various ceremonial events, but the bulk of the papers are press cuttings 1894–1910, including cuttings on particular subjects such as the poor law and poverty. Rough notes by Burns include this comment on memoirs: 'I have read nearly all the memoirs, diaries, recollections, and revelations of the post-war period, and have found few worth remembrance, or even recognition ...'.

Burns's library on London was purchased by Lord Southwood for the London County Council in 1943. It is now part of the Greater London History Library and is available for research. It includes six boxes of pamphlets, press cuttings 1893–1936, copies of articles and of reports of speeches, handbills and papers about trades unions and strikes; none of the items dates from before 1888. Maps and prints relating to London which were part of the 1943 purchase now form part of the Greater London Map and Print Collections and have been catalogued in the map and print catalogues.

A further collection of 100 letters to Burns was purchased in 1972 by the Library of the California State University, Northridge (DA 530 A3 C6 Special Collections). These papers were purchased from the estate of the late Dona Torr, the Marxist historian. Many of the letters concern Burns's pre-1914 activities, including a visit to Australia in 1903, and his correspondence with Australian labour leaders.

William Kent, *John Burns: Labour's Lost Leader* (Williams & Norgate 1950) is based on the papers in the British Library and makes extensive quotations from them. Kenneth D. Brown has published several works on Burns including a biography, *John Burns* (Royal Historical Society 1977), the entry in *DLB*, V, 39–47, and the entry in *MBR*, 3, 148–53.

RICHARD AUSTEN BUTLER, BARON BUTLER OF SAFFRON WALDEN (1902–1982)

Richard Austen Butler ('Rab') was Conservative MP for Essex (Saffron Walden) 1929–65. He was Parliamentary Under-Secretary of State for India Sept 1932–May 1937, Parliamentary Secretary to the Ministry of

Labour 1937–Feb 1938, Under-Secretary of State for Foreign Affairs 1938–July 1941, President of the Board and Minister of Education 1941–May 1945, Minister of Labour May-July 1945, Chancellor of the Exchequer Oct 1951–Dec 1955, Lord Privy Seal 1955–Oct 1959, Secretary of State for Home Affairs Jan 1957–July 1962, First Secretary of State and Deputy Prime Minister 1962–Oct 1963, and Secretary of State for Foreign Affairs 1963–Oct 1964. He was created Baron Butler of Saffron Walden (a life peerage) in 1965, and KG in 1971.

A large collection of Butler's papers (approximately 150 boxes) was deposited in the Wren Library, Trinity College, Cambridge, upon his death in 1982. Access is controlled by trustees. A list is available (NRA 32443). The papers cover most aspects of Butler's personal and political life and are divided into 14 sections (A-P).

His political papers include official correspondence files 1933–64 (Section E) which also includes personal correspondence as Under-Secretary of State for India, Parliamentary Secretary, Ministry of Labour 1933–38, as well as Chancellor of the Exchequer, Home Secretary, Leader of the House, and Foreign Secretary 1956–64. Section F consists of 130 files of official papers 1932–68 concentrated mostly on Butler's position as Under-Secretary of State, India.

There are 46 general political files 1929–63 (Section G), including constituency and official papers, and a typed 'diary' for 1942–43. Section H consists of 118 files on the Conservative Party 1935–64 including conference papers, general correspondence, committee papers, and policy papers. In addition, there are his constituency correspondence 1935–64 (Section J), speeches and articles 1929–79 (Section K), and 117 files of press cuttings 1926–76 (Section L).

Other papers in the collection include personal and family correspondence and papers from 1916, and some family memorabilia dating from 1788. Butler's personal correspondence includes around 1000 letters on his failure to become Prime Minister in 1957 and 1963 (Section B). There are also 73 files of photos, and five files on Butler's funeral and memorial service in 1982.

The Conservative Party Archives in the Bodleian Library should also be consulted for files relating to the Education Act 1944; personal files on India 1940–45; and letter-books 1947–61. There are also papers and correspondence relating to Butler's chairmanship of the Conservative Research Department 1945–64, and of the Conservative Party 1959–61. The minutes of the Post-War Problems Central Committee 1941–45, which Butler chaired, are also in the Conservative Research Department Archives. *Conservative Party Policy* is important regarding the archives of the CRD which form an important part of the Conservative Party collection at the Bodleian.

Lady Butler's permission is required for access to the interview recorded by Butler in 1980 for the British Oral Archive of Political and Administrative History at the BLPES. Butler's covering note on the interview states 'it so happens I'd rather not refer to Lord Home till after his death.'

Papers relating to Budgets are in the PRO at T 171. Access to a transcript of a 1980 interview between Butler and Mr A. L. Teasdale concerning the Conservative leadership contest of Oct 1963 is available from Mr Teasdale, Nuffield College, Oxford OX1 1NF.

Butler quoted from his papers in his memoirs *The Art of the Possible* (Hamish Hamilton 1971). A second quasi-autobiographical volume, *The Art of Memory* (Hodder and Stoughton 1982) was published posthumously. The collection at Trinity College was the foundation of the authorised biography by Anthony Howard, *RAB: the Life of R. A. Butler* (Cape 1987). Howard's bibliography refers to some family documentary and photographic sources and provides a concise guide to previous books by and about his subject.

A diary kept by Lord Butler was disclosed to Martin Gilbert and quoted by him in *Winston S. Churchill*, VI, Finest Hour 1939–1941 (Heinemann 1983), 190, fn 3. The affirmations by Butler's widow and biographer, and by Sir Robert Rhodes James (*The Times Literary Supplement*, 4759, 17 June 1994, 36) that no diary ever existed cannot be reconciled with Gilbert's account in *In Search of Churchill: A historian's journey* (Harper Collins 1994), 224–5.

NOEL EDWARD BUXTON, 1st BARON NOEL-BUXTON (1869–1948)

Noel Buxton was Liberal MP for North Riding of Yorkshire (Whitby) 1905–06 and Norfolk (North) 1910–18; he was Labour MP for Norfolk (North) 1922–30. He was Minister of Agriculture and Fisheries Jan–Nov 1924 and June 1929–June 1930. He was created Baron Noel-Buxton in 1930.

Noel-Buxton's son, the 2nd Lord Noel-Buxton, informed us that his father's papers were in the possession of his sister, the Hon Mrs J. G. Hogg. Only a small collection, mainly of press cuttings, survives in her care. There are seven books of cuttings on the electoral activities of various members of the Buxton family 1847–1910 (including Lady Noel-Buxton's electoral addresses 1918–31), on the passage of the 1911 Parliament Act, on the first Labour government (including a note from Maurice Hankey on the procedure for taking the oath of Privy Councillor), on the 1929 election, the second Labour government and Noel-Buxton's resignation because of ill-health, and on Norwich MPs 1937–38. There is also a file of papers on Noel-Buxton's wife Lucy's 1931 election campaign – notes of expenses, speeches, meetings, model answers, questionnaires, and some correspondence.

A small collection of press cuttings on the Balkans 1903–07, and letters from Noel-Buxton's Liberal contemporaries in 1915 on the Balkans (apart from a life-long interest in the Balkans, Noel-Buxton was sent there to try to secure Balkan adherence to the Allied cause in 1914) was presented to the Bulgarian archives by Mrs Hogg. We have been unable to establish contact with the Bulgarian archival authorities.

Several American and Canadian universities have purchased substantial collections of Noel-Buxton's papers from dealers in England. The 2nd Lord Noel-Buxton told us that he did not know how these papers came to leave the family's possession.

One such collection is in the William R. Perkins Library, Duke University. The Duke collection (Noel-Buxton papers) consists of about 1000 miscellaneous letters 1896–1944. Noel-Buxton's correspondents include his brother, Charles Buxton, and other members of his family, as well as many political colleagues. There is also a collection of press cuttings 1905–44, particularly concerning Noel-Buxton's by-election at Whitby in 1905, the Balkans, women's suffrage, temperance, and some miscellaneous speech notes. There is a short description of this collection in the *National Union Catalog, Manuscript Collections, 1968* (Washington DC, 1969), entry no 1586.

In 1979 a further collection of Noel-Buxton's papers was acquired by Duke University. The addition has not been catalogued, but is available for research. It consists mostly of correspondence 1878–1947, including a long series to his parents, and various letters from politicians and other public personalities particularly relating to his efforts to avert the Second World War. There are also approximately 140 original photos taken in the Balkans in 1914, and a few corrected typescripts of speeches and parts of notebooks. In addition, the university acquired two letters to Noel-Buxton from Sidney Webb 1920.

A further collection is held in the Manuscript Collection of the Department of Rare Books and Special Collections at the McLennan Library, McGill University, Canada. This collection was purchased in 1961 from English dealers, but also includes papers given to Professor H. N. Fieldhouse by the 2nd Lord Noel-Buxton in 1968. The collection, and the circumstances in which it was assembled, is described in Robert Vogel's article, 'Noel-Buxton: The "Trouble-Maker" and his Papers', *Fontanus*, III, 1990, 131–50.

The collection covers four linear metres and access to this material is not restricted. The collection contains substantial amounts of material on the Balkans and the Balkan Committee 1896–1943, the Anti-Slavery Society, particularly in relation to Ethiopia 1932–45, attempts to secure a 'peace without victory' 1916–17, and attempts to secure a negotiated peace with Germany 1939–42. There is also material on the pre-1914 Liberal Foreign Affairs Group, various peace movements between the wars, and colonial problems. The collection also contains some of Lucy Buxton's papers, mainly on the Labour Party and domestic policy.

A collection of ten letters written to Noel-Buxton 1940–44 was purchased by the Wichita State University, Kansas, from Sotheby's in 1985 and is held in the Special Collections Department. The letters concern proposals for concluding peace with Germany. Correspondents include Lord Halifax and R. A. Butler.

Mosa Anderson, *Noel Buxton, A Life* (Allen & Unwin 1952) is based on the papers before their dispersal and quotes from autobiographical notes and reminiscences. T. P. Conwell-Evans, *Foreign Policy from a Back Bench 1904–1918* (Oxford UP 1932) also quotes fully from the papers, including a diary for 1914–15.

The entry by Margaret 'Espinasse and Bryan Sadler in *DLB*, V, 51–5, is based on published sources; but see also the life of Lady Noel-Buxton by Ann Holt in the same volume, 165–6, which draws on Mrs Hogg's collection of her father's papers.

SYDNEY CHARLES BUXTON, EARL BUXTON (1853–1934)

Sydney Buxton was Liberal MP for Peterborough 1883–85 and Tower Hamlets (Poplar) 1886–1914. He was Under-Secretary of State for Colonial Affairs Aug 1892–June 1895, Postmaster-General Dec 1905–Feb 1910, and President of the Board of Trade 1910–Feb 1914. He was created GCMG and Viscount Buxton in 1914, and Earl Buxton in 1920.

A large collection of Buxton's papers (formerly in the possession of his grand-daughter Mrs E. Clay) is not available while a biography of Buxton is being written by Dr Daniel Waley. Buxton's daughter, Lady Alethea Eliot, advised us that the family is considering depositing the collection in a library or museum once the biography is finished.

The bulk of the papers (which were examined for the first edition) relates to Buxton's official career. There are 50 folders, beginning with Buxton's work for the London Schools Board 1876–82, and including the 1886–89 Royal Commission on Education, the 1889 Conciliation Committee for the dock strike, and his terms of office at the Colonial Office, the Post Office, and the Board of Trade. Buxton seems to have kept a large number of departmental and Cabinet papers, as well as correspondence with civil servants. There is a subject file for each month of his term of office at the Board of Trade.

In addition to these subject files there is a large collection of correspondence, much of it arranged chronologically. Some of the earlier correspondence refers to Buxton's work on the 1889 Conciliation

Committee. There are letters from Campbell-Bannerman and Haldane in 1900 on party disunity, letters on fiscal policy 1904, and letters on various aspects of Buxton's official work, for example, a letter from Lloyd George in 1910 congratulating Buxton on his handling of a coal dispute in South Wales. There is a long series of letters (about 80) from Lord Ripon, Buxton's chief at the Colonial Office 1892–95. They cover the years 1893–1909 but most of them are from the period 1893–95 and they are in fact semi-official letters on Colonial Office daily business. Possibly of greatest interest are the letters from Buxton's friends during the period when he was Governor-General of the Union of South Africa 1914–20. Many of his friends wrote about the English political situation and the progress of the war. There is a series of letters from Sir Charles Hobhouse 1914–16 and a large number of letters from Sir Edward Grey 1888–1932. Grey's letters are disappointingly sparse in political commentary, except for the period in 1924 when the problem of Grey's succession as Liberal leader in the House of Lords was being discussed. There is also a file of letters from Sir George Barnes, mainly written in 1915, with detailed accounts of the progress of the war and the political situation.

Most of the papers relating to Buxton's term as Governor-General of South Africa fill a separate trunk. They have been arranged in approximately 25 folders and include some miscellaneous letters 1892–1913 and some relating to Buxton's term at the Colonial Office. The most important section of these South African papers contains 14 files arranged chronologically and includes Buxton's correspondence with successive Colonial Secretaries, Asquith, the King's secretaries, as well as officials and South African politicians such as Botha and Smuts. There is also a collection of press cuttings on Buxton's governor-generalship and three volumes of letters from his second wife to her mother. Some of this material was used in Earl Buxton, *General Botha* (John Murray 1924).

In addition to these papers there are several volumes of press cuttings 1878–88, 1896–1908, a volume of cuttings on the 1889 strike, two volumes of articles and pamphlets by Buxton, and a volume of reviews of these publications. The collection also includes the diary of Buxton's first wife, Constance – a typewritten transcript in six volumes which covers the years 1882–92.

A testimonial album, presented to Buxton in March 1912 in commemoration of his 25 years as MP for Poplar, was donated to the Borough of Poplar in 1957. It is now part of the Tower Hamlets Local History Library and Archives (Museum Piece 60), which is housed in the Bancroft Road Library.

Kenneth D. Brown's portrait of Buxton in *MBR*, 3, 162–7, is based on published sources.

GEORGE HENRY CADOGAN, 5th EARL CADOGAN (1840–1915)

George Cadogan was known as Viscount Chelsea from 1864 until he succeeded his father as 5th Earl Cadogan in 1873. He was created KG in 1891. He was Conservative MP for Bath 1873. He was Under-Secretary of State for War May 1875–March 1878, Under-Secretary of State for the Colonies 1878–April 1880, Lord Privy Seal Aug 1886–Aug 1892, and Lord Lieutenant of Ireland (with a seat in the Cabinet) June 1895–Aug 1902.

Many of Cadogan's papers were destroyed in a fire. But about 1750 letters previously in the possession of his grandson, the 7th Earl Cadogan, have been deposited in the HLRO. This collection has been listed by the Historical Manuscripts Commission (NRA 17340). A note about the contents of the collection appears in *Royal Commission on Historical Manuscripts. Report of the Secretary to the Commissioners 1970–1971*, 1971, 46–50.

There are very few letters in the collection covering Cadogan's early career, apart from his election campaign at Bath in 1873. The bulk of the papers dates from 1895–1900 and includes drafts of out-letters as well as memoranda. The letters reflect very fully the problems of Cadogan's term of office as Lord Lieutenant. They also include a series of letters from the Prince of Wales (with whom Cadogan was very friendly), and from Queen Victoria.

FREDERICK ARCHIBALD VAUGHAN CAMPBELL, 3rd EARL CAWDOR (1847–1911)

Frederick Campbell was known as Viscount Emlyn from 1860 until 1898 when he succeeded his father as 3rd Earl Cawdor. He was Conservative MP for Carmarthenshire 1874–85. He was First Lord of the Admiralty March-Dec 1905.

Over 800 boxes of Cawdor family papers were deposited in the Carmarthenshire Area RO (Cawdor papers). The collection mainly comprises family estate papers of the 17th-19th centuries but it does include six boxes of papers relating to Cawdor's political career (Cawdor 293–8). These boxes include correspondence with members of the Cabinet, the Admiralty Board, and officials in the Admiralty. There are Admiralty reports on coaling stations, submarines, Australian Naval Forces, and other subjects. There are three notebooks and various committee papers. There are also Cabinet memoranda. Cawdor 251 contains a notebook relating to some of Campbell's work as a director of the Great Western Railway (he was Chairman 1895–1905): there are notes on the costs of newspaper advertisements, a coal strike in South Wales, telegraph clerks, wages, and the costs of building locomotives.

A further bound volume of Cawdors's papers – mostly printed official documents – is currently in the Ministry of Defence Whitehall Library (Cawdor papers). However, the location of this collection is under review, and readers are advised to check with the Whitehall Library.

PETER ALEXANDER RUPERT CARINGTON, 6th BARON CARRINGTON (1919–)

Peter Carington succeeded his father as 6th Baron Carrington in 1938, and was created KCMG in 1958. He was Parliamentary Secretary, Ministry of Agriculture and Fisheries Nov 1951–Oct 1954, Parliamentary Secretary, Ministry of Defence 1954–May 1956, First Lord of the Admiralty Oct 1959–Oct 1963, Minister without Portfolio 1963–Oct 1964, Secretary of State for Defence June 1970–Jan 1974, Secretary of State for Energy Jan–March 1974, and Secretary of State for Foreign and Commonwealth Affairs May 1979–April 1982.

Lord Carrington told us, '...I don't really know what "private papers" are, and I don't think I have any. Certainly none which are in any order or which would be of any great interest to you. I was probably the only Minister who followed the rules and never took any papers out of my Department – and so the cupboard is bare!' Nevertheless, it would be prudent to consult Peter Carrington, *Reflect on Things Past: The Memoirs of Lord Carrington* (Collins 1988), noting the acknowledgement on p. vii of Joyce Smith 'who has, for years, struggled to bring some sort of order to my life and papers.' Lord Carrington now acknowledges that Joyce Smith had sorted out 'trunk loads of stuff'. However, he 'delved into one of the boxes and it seemed to consist entirely of bills!' (personal communication, 6 Dec 1993).

Records of the Leader of the House of Lords and Chief Whip 1945–94 are in the HLRO, but are subject to the 30 year rule (Carrington was Leader of the House of Lords 1963–64).

Patrick Cosgrave, *Carrington: A Life and a Policy* (Dent 1985) appears not to draw on private papers. There is a brief summary of Carrington's career by Patrick Cosgrave in *Blackwell*, 86–7.

SIR ARCHIBALD BOYD BOYD-CARPENTER (1873–1937)

Archibald Boyd-Carpenter was Conservative MP for Bradford (North) 1918–23, Coventry 1924–29 and Surrey (Chertsey) 1931–37. He was Parliamentary Secretary to the Ministry of Labour Nov 1922–March 1923, Financial Secretary to the Treasury March-May 1923, and Paymaster-General and Financial Secretary to the Admiralty 1923–Jan 1924. He was knighted in 1926.

His son, Lord Boyd-Carpenter, knows of no papers.

JOHN ARCHIBALD BOYD-CARPENTER, BARON BOYD-CARPENTER (1908–)

John Boyd-Carpenter was Conservative MP for Kingston-upon-Thames 1945–72. He was Financial Secretary to the Treasury Oct 1951–July 1954, Minister of Transport and Civil Aviation 1954–Dec 1955, Minister of Pensions and National Insurance 1955–July 1962, and Chief Secretary to the Treasury and Paymaster-General 1962–Oct 1964. He was created Baron Boyd-Carpenter (a life peerage) in 1972.

Lord Boyd-Carpenter advises that he proposes to deposit any surviving papers in the Bodleian Library.

His autobiography, *Way of Life: The Memoirs of John Boyd-Carpenter* (Sidgwick & Jackson 1980) does not quote directly from any papers.

CHARLES ROBERT WYNN-CARRINGTON, 3rd BARON CARRINGTON, MARQUESS OF LINCOLNSHIRE (1843–1928)

Charles Carrington (he obtained a royal licence to spell his surname with only one 'r' in 1880, but assumed the surname Wynn-Carrington in 1896) was Liberal MP for Wycombe 1865–68. He was President of the Board of Agriculture and Fisheries Dec 1905–Oct 1911, and Lord Privy Seal 1911–Feb 1912. He succeeded his father as 3rd Baron Carrington in 1868, and was created GCMG in 1886, Earl Carrington in 1895, KG in 1906, and Marquess of Lincolnshire in 1912.

A very large collection of Carrington's papers is in the care of his grandson's widow, the Hon Mrs Veronica Llewellen Palmer, Clos du Menage, Sark, Channel Islands, although they are actually owned by the nephew of Carrington's grandson, Mr Julien Llewellen Palmer, Hallyburton, Coupar Angus, Blairgowrie, Perthshire PH13 9JR (NRA 27389). The papers were very carefully sorted by Carrington's daughter, Lady Alexandra Palmer, in 1935. These papers have been microfilmed by the Bodleian Library (MSS Film 1097–153) and the National Library of Australia. The microfilm of the papers in the Bodleian is now open to scholars but a diary for the years 1914–18 (MS Film 1108) can only be seen with the written permission of Mr Llewellen Palmer and the Hon W. N. H. Legge-Bourke.

Possibly the most important items in the papers are Carrington's diaries. They cover the period 1877–1928. The entries vary in length and detail. Carrington himself used the diaries as the basis for volumes of unpublished memoirs: three volumes on *King Edward VII as I knew Him 1855–1910*, two volumes on *Lord Rosebery ... 1878–1912*, and a volume of general recollections. The first-mentioned were used by Sir Sidney Lee for his biography of the king. The volumes also include press cuttings, menu cards, photos, and transcripts of correspondence.

There are no official papers from Carrington's terms of office, but the collection includes a trunk of papers concerning his period as Governor of New South Wales 1885–90. There are bundles of letters from fellow Governors – Lords Carnarvon, Hopetoun, Kintore, Loch, and Onslow – as well as correspondence from Australian politicians and officials, in particular several bundles of letters 1877–94 from Sir Henry Parkes, Premier of New South Wales. There are manuscript and printed chapters by Carrington on different aspects of his governorship, including the problems of Australian federation and Chinese labour, and many notes for speeches, volumes of press cuttings, and presentation volumes on his departure from Sydney. There are also a few official files and some correspondence with the Colonial Office.

Carrington was on close terms with King Edward VII and with other members of the royal family. A considerable correspondence reflects this relationship. In some transcripts of this correspondence, the individuals mentioned are identified, for example, in the transcripts of letters from the Prince of Wales to Carrington 1880–85. As well as correspondence, there are scrapbooks and photo albums, for example from the 1875–76 Indian tour of the Prince, and from Carrington's mission in 1901 announcing the death of Queen Victoria in the capital cities of Europe. The latter includes Carrington's draft reports to both the King and to Lord Lansdowne. Carrington's relations with the court were strengthened by his position as Lord Great Chamberlain. There are several volumes relating to the coronation and funeral of King Edward VII, the marriage of the then Duke of York and Princess Mary, the coronation of King George V, and the investiture of the Prince of Wales. The volumes include not only press cuttings and souvenirs, but also Carrington's reminiscences, seating plans, rehearsal plans, and so forth. Telegrams from Queen Victoria for the period when Carrington was Lord Chamberlain of the Household (1892–95) have also survived.

There is much correspondence, both originals and transcripts. The bulk of it is arranged in alphabetical order. In particular there are two volumes of transcripts of some 'political' letters, letters of congratulation on being made a privy councillor, a Cabinet minister, and an earl, as well as congratulations on the birth of his son, and on his 80th birthday. There are transcripts of Carrington's letters to his wife 1879–1918 and other family correspondence. The collection also includes letters of condolence on the death of Carrington's son, Viscount Wendover, after the battle of Cambrai. There are press cuttings and a memorial book, as well as Wendover's letters from the front.

In addition to various domestic papers, such as a list of Carrington's wedding guests and their gifts, invitation, engagement, and visitors' books, hunting diaries, game and stud books, valuations of family plate and porcelain, the collection includes some papers of other members of the Carrington family: Lady Carrington's diaries and engagement books, letters to her from ladies-in-waiting to both Queen Alexandra and Queen Mary (Lady Carrington herself was a lady-in-waiting to Queen Alexandra), and also letters from her daughter Victoria, who was a Woman of the Bedchamber to Queen Mary. There are also some papers of Carrington's younger brother William, who was equerry to Queen Victoria 1881–1901, and to King Edward VII 1902–10, papers of his grandfather, the 1st Baron Carrington, and some papers of his mother. There are also some of Lady Alexandra Palmer's papers connected with the winding up of her mother's estate – including an inventory of the house contents.

The Mitchell Library, Sydney, holds a bound printed volume of contemporary notes by Carrington on Sir Henry Parkes's Federation Scheme 1889–90 (MLQ 342.901/L). The volume is in two parts. The first covers the period 15 June-29 Nov 1889 (23pp); the second covers the period 31 Dec 1889–24 Feb 1890 (12pp). Both parts are headed 'Most Strictly Confidential'.

Andrew Adonis's article, 'Aristocracy, Agriculture and Liberalism: The Politics, Finances and Estates of the Third Lord Carrington', *The Historical Journal*, 31, 4, 1988, 871–7, utilises the papers in Mrs Llewellen Palmer's care.

SIR EDWARD HENRY CARSON, BARON CARSON (1854–1935)

Edward Carson was Unionist MP for Dublin University 1892–1918 and Belfast (Duncairn) 1918–21. He was Irish Solicitor-General 1892, Solicitor-General May 1900–Dec 1905, Attorney-General May-Nov 1915, First Lord of the Admiralty Dec 1916–July 1917, and Minister without Portfolio 1917–Jan 1918. He was knighted in 1900, and created Baron Carson (a judicial life peerage) in 1921.

Many of Carson's papers were lost in the blitz so that, for example, nothing remains relating to his legal career. Such papers as survived, some 3000 documents, were purchased by the PRONI in 1962 (D1507; NRA 17985). A description of the papers is to be found in Appendix C of the *Report of the Deputy Keeper of the Records for the years 1960-1965*, Cmd 521 (Belfast 1968), 189–90. A catalogue and calendar of the papers was made in the 1960s (NRA 17985) but is regarded by the PRONI as unsatisfactory and the collection has therefore been rearranged in six sequences. The superseded calendar was comprehensively indexed by personal name, and these index cards are still usable as they record dates as well as the obsolete reference numbers.

The new arrangement of the collection is as follows: (A) letters and papers relating to Ireland 1896–1936; (B) letters and papers about non-Irish politics, Carson's legal career, the First World War, the Admiralty 1899–1935; (C) diaries of Ruby, Lady Carson 1915–29; (D) personal and personal financial letters and papers of Lord and Lady Carson 1891–1947; (E) obituary and biographical letters and papers; (F) miscellaneous printed and pictorial matter; (G) superseded calendar of the Carson Papers. Sections D, E and F are currently closed, and interested researchers should contact the PRONI for conditions of access.

When the first edition was being compiled, Carson's son, the late Hon Edward Carson, informed us that he had retained none of his father's papers but that he had placed them all in the PRONI.

Churchill Archives Centre holds copies of Cabinet papers 1915–17 and an index to the naval papers 1916–17 held at the PRONI (CARS; NRA 18561).

There is a small collection of correspondence to Carson, and various other miscellaneous papers, in the Trinity College Library, Dublin.

Edward Marjoribanks and Ian Colvin, *The Life of Lord Carson* (3 vols, V. Gollancz 1932–36) and H. Montgomery Hyde, *Carson, The Life of Sir Edward Carson, Lord Carson of Duncairn* (Heinemann 1953) were both based on Carson's papers and quote from them. So too do A. T. Q. Stewart, *Edward Carson* (Gill and Macmillan, Dublin 1981) and Alvin Jackson, *Sir Edward Carson* (Dundalgan Press for Historical Association of Ireland, Dundalk 1993).

RICHARD GARDINER CASEY, BARON CASEY (1890–1976)

Richard Casey, an Australian diplomat and Cabinet minister, was Minister of State Resident in the Middle East and a member of the War Cabinet March 1942–Dec 1943. He was created Baron Casey (a life peerage) in 1960, GCMG in 1965, and KG in 1969.

Lord Casey informed us that he had preserved a large number of papers relating to his career, including a diary kept for many years, his correspondence, bound files of his public statements, and volumes of press cuttings.

The papers, part of a larger Casey family collection, are now lodged in the National Library of Australia (MS 6150). The collection has been preliminarily listed and is generally available for research. However, there are restrictions on the originals and some of the photocopies of Casey's later diaries. The diaries cover the periods 1910–11, 1914–15, and 1939–76. The early diaries are open for research, and copies of parts of the later diaries are available for reference in the National Library of Australia and the Australian Archives. Otherwise the later diaries are closed. (In *The Age*, 2 Aug and 27 Nov 1989, William Pinwill reported that the Casey diaries which had been available in the National Library of Australia 'in unexpurgated form' since 1983, subject to a 30–year rule, had been temporarily withdrawn and returned with 62 deletions. The deletions related to comments of a personal nature (cuts requested by the Casey family); information that could prejudice

Australia's relations with foreign governments (as requested by the Department of Foreign Affairs and Trade); and the names of officers of the Australian Secret Intelligence Service (as requested by ASIS). Some of the deleted material had already been published in *Oyster: The Story of the ASIS*, by Brian Toohey and William Pinwill, Reed Books, Port Melbourne 1989).

The collection also includes 95 volumes of press cuttings 1924–78; and several hundred items of correspondence between Casey and a wide range of individuals. Most was written in the 1950s and 1960s. There are also drafts of several of his books, and a collection of general publications. There is also Casey's Order of the Garter and various war medals, as well as material concerning these.

A study of Lord Casey's father and grandfather, *Australian Father and Son* (Collins 1966), draws on voluminous family papers as well as Lord Casey's own recollections. There are some autobiographical passages relating to his period as Governor of Bengal in *An Australian in India* (Hollis and Carter 1947). A fuller account of Lord Casey's wartime career, drawing on diaries containing 'over 700,000 words', is in *Personal Experience 1939–1946* (Constable 1962).

Lord Casey's period as Australian Minister for External Affairs is covered by T. B. Millar (ed), *Australian Foreign Minister, the Diaries of R. G. Casey 1951–60* (Collins 1972). Millar explains in his preface that Casey's diary was 'his personal account of the day's events, those with which he was concerned and other happenings of importance or interest, dictated each day either to a Secretary or into a recording machine to be typed out later. For the period ... 26 April 1951 to 22 January 1960, his total diary entries come to well over a million words'.

In 1967, Lord Casey presented a bound photocopy of his diaries as Governor of Bengal to what became the Oriental and India Office Collections, British Library (Photo Eur 48); this is now available for research.

The Australian War Memorial holds a small collection of Casey papers including orders, messages, and maps relating to his work with the liaison force in France Aug 1918, containing orders to, and information on, movements of the 131st Infantry, American expeditionary forces (Acc No 3DRL/3710); a report on aerial patrol of the Pozières-Mouquet Farm sector made by Casey following the 2nd Australian Infantry Brigade advance on 19 Aug 1916, and a sketch of the trench position of the 1st Australian Division (Acc No EXDOC 129); and an account compiled by Casey on board HMAT *Orvieto* of the operations of SMS *Emden* July-Oct 1914 (Acc No 3DRL/3487). These items were donated by Casey between 1967 and 1970. There is also a typescript copy of Casey's diary April-June 1915 in the papers of C. E. W. Bean at the Australian War Memorial (3DRL6673, item 170).

W. J. Hudson's biography *Casey* (Oxford UP 1986) is based on official papers in the Australian Archives as well as family papers. The correspondence is also utilised in W. J. Hudson and Jane North (eds), *My Dear P.M.: R. G. Casey's letters to S. M. Bruce 1924–29* (Australian Government Publishing Service, Canberra 1980).

RICHARD KNIGHT CAUSTON, BARON SOUTHWARK (1843–1929)

Richard Causton was Liberal MP for Colchester 1880–85 and for Southwark (West) 1888–1910. He was Paymaster-General Dec 1905–Feb 1910. He was created Baron Southwark in 1910.

We have been unable to trace any of Causton's papers. Causton left all his estate to his widow who died in 1931; there were no children by the marriage. We have contacted three of Causton's great-nephews (Mr J. W. F. Causton, Mr G. L. C. Elliston, and Mr E. E. N. Causton) but none of them knew of the existence of any papers or what might have become of them. Lady Southwark, in *Social and Political Reminiscences* (Williams and Northgate 1913), did not quote from any of her husband's papers. She did quote from her own diaries and described her husband's electoral campaigns and their social and political life.

Lady Southwark left all her estate to her sister, Miss Evelyn Chambers. Miss Chambers died in 1946; she divided her estate between three of her nieces and appointed one, Miss Kathleen Chambers, as her sole executrix. We have not been able to trace Miss Chambers. The solicitors who acted for her were not able to give us a more recent address than 1948.

The Southwark Local Studies Library holds a small collection of press cuttings on Causton. The political press cuttings cover all of the general elections while Causton was an MP, but relate more to general issues than to Causton himself. The personal cuttings are mostly concerned with his golden wedding anniversary in 1921. The Library also holds microfilm runs of a number of local newspapers which contain material on Causton.

SIR GEORGE CAVE, VISCOUNT CAVE (1856–1928)

George Cave was Conservative MP for Surrey (Kingston) 1906–18. He was Solicitor-General Nov 1915–Dec 1916, Secretary of State for Home Affairs 1916–Jan 1919, and Lord Chancellor Oct 1922–Jan 1924 and Nov 1924–March 1928. He was knighted in 1915, and created GCMG in 1920, and Viscount Cave in 1919.

Sir Charles Mallet, *Lord Cave. A Memoir* (Murray 1931), was based on Cave's papers then in the possession of his widow, and quoted frequently from them. Unfortunately some at least of these papers have been destroyed. Cave's niece, Mrs Margaret Story, informed us that many were burnt after Cave's death by his brother when he was clearing out Cave's home. Neither Mrs Story nor Cave's secretary, Mr R. W. Bankes, knew of the existence of any surviving papers.

A large wooden box of papers (of which Mrs Story knew nothing) had been deposited in the British Library by Cave's widow in 1932 (Add MSS 62455–516). A list is available of the 62 volumes which are available for research.

The collection includes Cave's papers on Irish affairs 1914–25; prisoners of war 1915–19; the International Law Commission 1916–19; the Southern Rhodesian Commission 1919–21; and House of Lords reform 1923–27. It also includes his general correspondence 1878–1928, and family correspondence 1859–1910. There are copies of his speeches and press notices 1918 and photos. One volume contains a family history 1856–1929.

There are four volumes of condolence letters to Cave's widow, as well as one volume of Lady Cave's correspondence 1928–32. There is also a volume of correspondence 1928–32 to Sir Charles Mallet regarding his biography.

SPENCER COMPTON CAVENDISH, 8th DUKE OF DEVONSHIRE (1833–1908)

Spencer Cavendish was known as Lord Cavendish 1834–58, then as the Marquess of Hartington ('Harty-Tarty') until he succeeded his father as 8th Duke in 1891. He was created KG in 1892. He was Liberal MP for Lancashire (North) 1857–68, Radnor 1869–80, Lancashire (North-East) 1880–85 and North Lancashire (Rossendale) 1885–91 (Liberal Unionist from 1886). He joined in the coalition government with the Conservatives 1895–1903. He was Under-Secretary of State for War 1863–Feb 1866, Secretary of State for War Feb–July 1866 and Dec 1882–June 1885, Postmaster-General Dec 1868–Jan 1871, Chief Secretary for Ireland 1871–Feb 1874, Secretary of State for India April 1880–Dec 1882, Lord President of the Council June 1895–Oct 1903, and President of the Board of Education Jan 1900–Aug 1902. He was asked to form a government three times – in 1880 and twice in 1886 – but refused.

A large collection of his correspondence is in the possession of the present Duke of Devonshire. Applications to read the papers should be made to the Keeper of the Devonshire Collections, Chatsworth, Bakewell, Derbyshire DE45 1PP. Nearly 4000 letters have survived. They have been arranged in chronological order except for letters from John Tilly at the Post Office 1868–71, letters from Ireland 1870–74, Lord Ripon's letters from India 1880–83, 54 letters from the Duke to the Duchess of Manchester, whom he later married 1873–87, and 110 letters from Sir Henry James 1886–1908. The calendar of the series gives an indication of the contents of each letter. The letters, mostly to the

Duke, cover most of his political career; his correspondents include the prominent politicians of his day. There is a typescript list (NRA 20594/10).

Some of the Duke's papers as Secretary of State for India were deposited on permanent loan by the 11th Duke in the Oriental and India Office Collections, British Library (MSS Eur D 604). They are not listed. The collection includes bound volumes of telegrams exchanged with the Viceroy April 1880–Dec 1882, and six boxes of printed Cabinet papers 1880–85. Some of the latter are not included in the *List of Cabinet Papers 1880–1914* (PRO Handbook 4, 1964). Very few of the Cabinet papers concern Indian affairs.

Bernard Holland, *The Life of Spencer Compton, 8th Duke of Devonshire* (2 vols, Longmans 1911) was based on Devonshire's papers and quotes extensively from letters and other documents. Patrick Jackson, *The Last of the Whigs* (Fairleigh Dickinson UP, Cranbury, NJ 1994; distributed in the UK by Associated University Presses) was also based on the Devonshire papers as well as correspondence from the Duke in other collections. There is useful detail in David Cannadine, 'The Landowner as Millionaire: The Finances of the Dukes of Devonshire c1800–c1926', *Agricultural History Review*, 25, pt 2, 1977, and Cannadine's *Lords & Landlords: The Aristocracy and the Towns 1774–1967* (Leicester UP 1980). A brief sketch drawing on the papers at Chatsworth is in John Pearson, *Stags and Serpents: The Story of the House of Cavendish and the Dukes of Devonshire* (Macmillan 1983).

VICTOR CHRISTIAN WILLIAM CAVENDISH, 9th DUKE OF DEVONSHIRE (1868–1938)

Victor Cavendish was Liberal Unionist MP for Derbyshire (West) 1891–1908. He was Financial Secretary to the Treasury Oct 1903–Dec 1905, Civil Lord of the Admiralty June 1915–July 1916, and Secretary of State for the Colonies Oct 1922–Jan 1924. He succeeded his uncle as 9th Duke of Devonshire in 1908. He was created GCVO in 1912, and KG in 1916.

A small collection of the 9th Duke's papers, mainly concerning the period when he was Governor-General of Canada 1916–21, is in the possession of his grandson, the 11th Duke of Devonshire. Applications to read the papers should be made to the Keeper of the Devonshire Collections, Chatsworth, Bakewell, Derbyshire DE45 1PP. The papers have not been listed.

Included in the collection are the Duke's diaries, in 45 volumes, for the period 1899–1938. Applications to read the diaries should be made in the first instance to the Keeper, but are referred to the present Duke for his permission, due to their personal nature and relatively recent date. Microfilm copies of part of the diaries (3 Jan 1916–16 Oct

1921) are available in the National Archives of Canada (Reels A-653 and 654).

The Duke is referred to in David Cannadine, 'The Landowner as Millionaire: the Finances of the Dukes of Devonshire, c1800–c1926', *Agricultural History Review*, 25, pt 2, 1977, and Cannadine's, *Lords and Landlords: the Aristocracy and the Towns, 1774–1967* (Leicester UP 1980). John Pearson's *Stags and Serpents: the Story of the House of Cavendish and the Dukes of Devonshire* (Macmillan 1983), has a biographical chapter based on the collection at Chatsworth.

SIR FREDERICK CAWLEY, 1st Bt, 1st BARON CAWLEY (1850–1937)

Frederick Cawley was Liberal MP for South-East Lancashire (Prestwich) 1895–1918. He was Chancellor of the Duchy of Lancaster Dec 1916–Feb 1918. He was created a baronet in 1906, and Baron Cawley in 1918.

A small collection of Cawley's papers is in the possession of his grandson, the 3rd Baron Cawley, Bircher Hall, Leominster, Herefordshire HR6 0AX.

The collection is almost entirely composed of press cuttings, leaflets, and posters of Cawley's several election campaigns. There is nothing concerning his tenure of the Duchy. One of the earliest cuttings is from 1895; it describes Cawley's adoption meeting, and reports his speech giving his attitude to the topics of the day: he was in favour of Irish Home Rule, Welsh disestablishment, various electoral reforms, abolition of the Lords' veto, and an eight-hour day for the miners.

The 1900 general election produced a spate of leaflets accusing Cawley of being pro-Boer; apart from his criticism of Chamberlain he had sent £20 to a peace committee, which, his opponents claimed, helped to harden the Boers' attitude. In retaliation Cawley published a silk handkerchief depicting himself and his four sons, all in uniform, to show his contribution to the war. The same type of electioneering tactic is revealed in the 1905 campaign. There is a full collection of cuttings about Cawley's opponent, W. T. Hedges, as well as posters accusing Cawley of aiming to close public houses at 9pm and Cawley's emphatic denial. There is also a list of the questions Cawley was asked at different meetings. The list is analysed: out of 295 questions, 63 (the largest group) were described as 'Non Political'; 27 were asked on the fiscal question; 27 on working-class legislation; 26 on the land; and 21 on electoral and parliamentary reform. There are a few cuttings about the 1918 election campaign when his son, Oswald, succeeded him in the seat.

An undated 1000–word typescript memoir describes Cawley's career. Though this document is written in the third person, it was written by

Cawley himself. It refers to his role as chairman of the Liberal War Committee, the 'ginger group' of parliamentarians who pressed for a more vigorous prosecution of the war in 1916. But there is no mention of the Dardanelles Commission of which he was a member. (His son Harold, MP for Heywood Lancs, was killed in the Dardanelles in Sept 1915).

Two letters from Frederick Guest in Feb 1918 deal with Cawley's resignation from the government in order to make way for Lord Beaverbrook. A different version, in which his resignation is related to 'ill-health', is given in the typescript memoir.

(EDGAR ALGERNON) ROBERT GASCOYNE-CECIL, VISCOUNT CECIL OF CHELWOOD (1864–1958)

Robert Cecil was known as Lord Robert Cecil from 1868 when his father became 3rd Marquess of Salisbury, and was created Viscount Cecil of Chelwood in 1923. He was Conservative MP for Marylebone (East) 1906–10, and Independent Conservative MP for Hertfordshire (Hitchin) 1911–23. He was Minister of Blockade Dec 1916–July 1918, Parliamentary Under-Secretary of State for Foreign Affairs Dec 1916–Jan 1919, Lord Privy Seal May 1923–Jan 1924, and Chancellor of the Duchy of Lancaster Nov 1924–Oct 1927. He was awarded a Nobel Peace Prize in 1937.

Like his contemporaries, Cecil was requested in Sept 1934 by the Cabinet Office to return any Cabinet papers in his possession, and 'after the whole position had been fully explained to him in correspondence, Lord Cecil declined to co-operate' (Report to the Cabinet by Sir Maurice Hankey 29 Nov 1935, PRO, CAB 24/257).

Cecil himself presented 134 volumes of his papers to the British Library in 1954 (Add MSS 51071–204). A catalogue of the papers was published by the British Library in 1991. The papers have been divided into three main groups: special correspondence; general correspondence; and literary papers.

Cecil's special correspondents include A. J. Balfour 1906–29, Arthur Steel-Maitland 1911–21, Austen Chamberlain 1918–36, and Cecil's brother, the 4th Marquess of Salisbury 1906–43. A volume of memoranda about the 1907 Education Bill and another volume of general political memoranda are also included in this division of the papers. The special correspondence section includes some official correspondence on foreign affairs 1915–34. There are two volumes of Cabinet minutes 1917–27, Foreign Office memoranda 1915–18, and telegrams 1918–30. Cecil's League of Nations papers are also included in this section – he was in charge of League of Nations' business as Lord Privy Seal and Chancellor of the Duchy. There are eight volumes of League papers, including minutes of League meetings, papers concerning the 1927

Naval Disarmament conference and some memoranda produced by the League of Nations Union 1930–44. Cecil's diaries for the period 1917–37, largely concerning his work for the League, are included in this division.

The general correspondence is arranged chronologically. The literary papers (Add MSS 51193–204) are mainly correspondence concerning the publication of Cecil's numerous writings. Cecil published two volumes of memoirs, *A Great Experiment* (Jonathan Cape 1941), and *All the Way* (Hodder and Stoughton 1949), both of which quote from his papers. The former includes Cecil's '...Memorandum on Proposals for Diminishing the Occasion of Future Wars' (written in 1916, though not circulated to the Cabinet until 17 April 1917).

Further Cecil papers in the British Library include additional correspondence with A. J. Balfour 1876–1929 (Add MSS 49737–8) and James Chuter-Ede 1946–49 (Add MS 51192).

Four volumes of Cecil's miscellaneous Foreign Office correspondence 1915–19 are available at the PRO (FO 800/195–8; NRA 23627).

A further collection of some 20 boxes of Cecil's papers is in the possession of the 6th Marquess of Salisbury (CHE 1–118; NRA 10632). The collection includes correspondence, notes for speeches, memoranda, and articles by Cecil, mostly concerning League of Nations and international affairs 1876–1958. There are also family and personal letters, some of which are not available for research. The remainder of the papers in this collection will only be made available for research when they are at least 50 years old.

The Gascoyne-Cecil family and estate papers have been listed (NRA 32925). Written application for access should be made to the Librarian, Hatfield House, Hatfield, Herts AL9 5NF, stating the nature of the research being undertaken. Permission to read the papers is only granted on the condition that all references to, or extracts from, the papers will be submitted to Lord Salisbury for his permission to publish. No photographic reproduction of the papers is allowed.

There are other Cecil papers referred to in the *Guide to the Archives of the League of Nations* (UN Library, Geneva 1978).

JAMES EDWARD HUBERT GASCOYNE-CECIL, 4th MARQUESS OF SALISBURY (1861–1947)

James Cecil was known as Viscount Cranborne from 1868 until he succeeded his father as 4th Marquess of Salisbury in 1903. He was created GCVO in 1909, and KG in 1917. He was Conservative MP for North-East Lancashire (Darwen) 1885–92 and Rochester 1893–1903. He was Under-Secretary of State for Foreign Affairs Nov 1900–Oct 1903, Lord Privy Seal 1903–Dec 1905 and Nov 1924–June 1929, President of the Board of Trade March-Dec 1905, Chancellor of the

Duchy of Lancaster Oct 1922–May 1923, and Lord President of the Council Oct 1922–Jan 1924.

Salisbury's papers are in the possession of his grandson, the 6th Marquess of Salisbury. The papers are released progressively as they become 50 years old. The collection has been arranged chronologically within such major divisions as general correspondence, private family correspondence, estate papers, and some subject divisions such as India and honours. The general correspondence 1889–1947 is probably the most important part of the collection.

The Gascoyne-Cecil family and estate papers have been listed (NRA 32925). Applications to see them, stating the reason for wishing to read these papers, should be made in writing to the Librarian, Hatfield House, Hatfield, Herts AL9 5NF. Access will be granted on the condition that any reference to or quotation from the papers may only be made after Lord Salisbury's permission has been obtained.

The Earl of Selborne contributed the essay on Salisbury in *DNB 1941–1950*, 137–43.

ROBERT ARTHUR JAMES GASCOYNE-CECIL, BARON CECIL OF ESSENDON, 5th MARQUESS OF SALISBURY (1893–1972)

Robert Cecil ('Bobbety') was known as Viscount Cranborne from 1903 until he succeeded his father as 5th Marquess in 1947. He was created Baron Cecil of Essendon in 1941, and KG in 1946. He was Conservative MP for Dorset (South) 1929–41. He was Parliamentary Under-Secretary of State for Foreign Affairs Aug 1935–Feb 1938, Paymaster-General May–Oct 1940, Secretary of State for Dominion Affairs 1940–Feb 1942 and Sept 1943–July 1945, Secretary of State for Colonial Affairs Feb-Nov 1942, Lord Privy Seal 1942–Sept 1943 and Oct 1951–March 1952, Secretary of State for Commonwealth Relations March-Nov 1952, Lord President of the Council 1952–Jan 1957, and Acting Secretary of State for Foreign Affairs June-Oct 1953.

Salisbury's papers are in the possession of the 6th Marquess of Salisbury at Hatfield House. They are completely closed for research at present and no date for opening them is yet envisaged. None of his papers will be made available until they are 50 years old. There is however a list of the Gascoyne-Cecil family and estate papers (NRA 32925).

One volume of miscellaneous general correspondence 1935–38, from Salisbury's work at the Foreign Office (as Lord Cranborne), is available in the PRO (FO 800/296). Records of the Leader of the House of Lords and Chief Whip are in the HLRO, but are subject to the 30 year rule (Salisbury was Leader of the House of Lords 1951–57).

Lord Glendevon's brief entry on Salisbury in *DNB 1971-1980*, 130-1, is based mostly on 'personal knowledge'.

ROBERT ARTHUR TALBOT GASCOYNE-CECIL, 3rd MARQUESS OF SALISBURY (1830-1903)

Robert Cecil was known as Viscount Cranborne from 1865 until he succeeded his father as 3rd Marquess in 1868. He was created KG in 1878. He was Conservative MP for Stamford 1853-68. He was Secretary of State for India July 1866-March 1867 and Feb 1874-April 1878, Secretary of State for Foreign Affairs 1878-April 1880, June 1885-Jan 1886, Jan 1887-Aug 1892 and June 1895-Nov 1900, Prime Minister June 1885-Jan 1886, July 1886-Aug 1892 and June 1895-July 1902, and Lord Privy Seal Nov 1900-July 1902.

Salisbury's papers, previously held at Christ Church, Oxford, are in the possession of the 6th Marquess of Salisbury. Written application should be made to the Librarian, Hatfield House, Hatfield, Herts AL9 5NF, stating the nature of the research being undertaken. Permission to read the papers is only granted on condition that all proposed published references to or extracts from the papers will be submitted to the Marquess for his permission to publish.

The 3rd Marquess's papers have been divided into 27 classes, each of which is identified by a letter of the alphabet, and which fall into the following groups: (A) Foreign Office papers; (B) Cabinet papers; (C) letter books and copies of outgoing letters; (D) 20 volumes of copies of letters from Salisbury collected by Lady Gwendolen Cecil; (E-L) special correspondence; (M-Z) miscellaneous correspondence; (AA) Cinque Port papers; (BB) dinners, receptions etc.; and (CC) papers collected by Lady Gwendolen, including summaries and extracts from Salisbury's articles for the *Quarterly Review*.

As would be expected, one of the largest groups is the Foreign Office papers. There are 140 volumes, a two-volume calendar of which has been produced and distributed by the NRA (NRA 9226). Another major group is the special correspondence which fills 217 boxes. The main series of this correspondence (174 boxes) is arranged alphabetically by correspondent but there are also 20 volumes of correspondence with the royal family and its household, three volumes of foreign correspondence, seven volumes of ecclesiastical correspondence, three volumes of university correspondence, two volumes of Great Eastern Railway correspondence, and eight volumes of household and estate papers. This group of special correspondence is probably the most interesting for English political history. A card index of persons has been compiled.

Salisbury's period at the India Office is represented by four letter-books (C/1-4) and four boxes of papers (Q). A microfilm copy of some of these papers is available at the Oriental and India Office Collections, British Library (IOR NEG Reels 11671–88).

The miscellaneous correspondence has been divided into the following subgroups: 47 boxes of miscellaneous political correspondence 1866–1903 (M); 32 boxes of household, estate and county correspondence 1852, 1862, 1866–1903 (N); 35 boxes of personal correspondence 1852, 1860–1903 (O); one bundle of papers concerning Salisbury's constituency work at Stamford 1855–68 (P); three boxes of papers connected with the Great Eastern Railway mainly 1868–70 (R); three boxes of papers concerning universities 1869–1903 (S); five boxes of papers concerning Conservative Associations 1882–88 (T); six boxes of papers concerning ecclesiastical preferment (V); papers about parliamentary bills (W); deputations (W); honours (Y); and Lords Lieutenant (Z).

The 20 volumes of copies of letters from Salisbury collected by Lady Gwendolen Cecil (D) have been arranged alphabetically by correspondent. None of the copies is later than 1892. An index of correspondents has been compiled. Lady Gwendolen Cecil, *Life of Robert, Marquess of Salisbury* (4 vols, Hodder and Stoughton 1921–32) quotes from many of these papers but Lady Gwendolen deliberately excluded any work on the official papers.

The Gascoyne-Cecil family and estate papers have been listed (NRA 32925). In Hertfordshire Record Publications, IV, 1988, R. Harcourt Williams has edited *Salisbury-Balfour Correspondence: Letters exchanged between the Third Marquess of Salisbury and his nephew Arthur James Balfour, 1869–1892*. There is an authoritative essay on the Salisbury papers by J. F. A. Mason in Lord Blake and Hugh Cecil (eds), *Salisbury: The Man and His Politics* (Macmillan 1987), 10–29.

(ARTHUR) NEVILLE CHAMBERLAIN (1869–1940)

Neville Chamberlain was Conservative MP for Birmingham (Ladywood) 1918–29 and Birmingham (Edgbaston) 1929–40. He was Minister of National Service Aug 1916–Aug 1917, Postmaster-General Oct 1922–March 1923, Paymaster-General Feb-March 1923, Minister of Health March-Aug 1923, Nov 1924–June 1929 and Aug-Nov 1931, Chancellor of the Exchequer Aug 1923–Jan 1924 and Nov 1931–May 1937, Prime Minister 1937–May 1940, and Lord President of the Council May-Oct 1940. He was Leader of the Conservative Party May 1937–Oct 1940.

A large collection of Chamberlain's papers has been deposited by his family in the Birmingham University Library (Neville Chamberlain papers). The papers are open for research. Applications to read them should be made in writing to the Sub-Librarian (Special Collections) and should enclose a character reference. There is a list (NRA 12604) and a *Guide to the Chamberlain Collection* (1977). These papers were used in Keith Feiling, *The Life of Neville Chamberlain* (Macmillan 1946, reissued 1970), Iain Macleod, *Neville Chamberlain* (T. Muller 1961), and H. Montgomery Hyde, *Neville Chamberlain* (Weidenfeld & Nicolson 1976). These works are superseded by David Dilks, *Neville Chamberlain*, I, Pioneering and reform 1869-1929 (Cambridge UP 1984), and on Chamberlain as Minister for Health by Stephen Stacey, 'The Ministry of Health 1919-1929: Ideas and Practice in a Government Department' (DPhil thesis, Oxford University 1984). The Birmingham University Library will begin a three-year conservation microfilming and publication programme for the entire Chamberlain collection in 1996.

Perhaps the outstanding items in Chamberlain's papers are his political note-books 1913-40. There are also many diaries or journals of visits abroad, for example to India 1904-05. As well as 33 boxes of miscellaneous correspondence 1910-40, there is a great deal of family correspondence – not only letters to Neville but his letters to his brother Austen 1915-36, his sisters 1891-1940, his wife 1911-38, and his children 1927-39.

The collection includes various papers relating to Joseph Chamberlain: his birth and death certificates; some early family letters; letters of condolence on the death of his first wife in 1875; and various printed papers. There are also 128 letters from Neville to Joseph Chamberlain 1890-1914 and 36 from Joseph to Neville 1891-1904. There is correspondence to and from J. L. Garvin 1928-34 concerning his biography of Joseph Chamberlain, and correspondence between Neville Chamberlain and Sir Charles Petrie 1938-39 concerning the latter's *The Chamberlain Tradition* (Lovat Dickson 1938).

Apart from these diaries and correspondence, notes of speeches and broadcasts, and 41 boxes of press cuttings, the various stages of Chamberlain's life are well represented in other ways. There are several papers – including a diary, correspondence, and accounts – from his attempt to work a sisal plantation in the Bahamas. Chamberlain's municipal activities are well represented: as well as correspondence about the city's hospital, bank, and university, there are papers concerning Chamberlain's election as mayor 1916-17, the local Unionist Association, and Chamberlain's parliamentary elections, as well as constituency correspondence from the 1920s.

Chamberlain's official career at national level began in Dec 1916 when he was appointed director-general of the National Service Department. General correspondence, printed papers, and some letters of congratulation on his appointment and commiseration on his resignation have survived. Chamberlain's tenure of the Ministry of Health is amply represented by 11 bound volumes of the acts for which he was responsible and the speeches he made in their support which were presented by the ministry's officials in June 1929. The volumes include the 1925 Widows, Orphans and Old Age Contributory Pensions Bill, the 1925 Rating and Valuation Bill, and the 1928 Local Government Bill.

Chamberlain's terms of office as Chancellor of the Exchequer are represented by congratulations on his appointment in 1923, tables on defence expenditure 1920–34, papers on the 1931 financial crisis, and letters of congratulation on various budgets or particular bills. There are also files on more general political issues such as correspondence 1930–31 with Baldwin concerning Baldwin's conduct of the party, on Conservative party matters 1935–40, correspondence with Churchill 1927–40, on the 1931 political settlement, and on King Edward VIII's abdication.

Very little seems to have survived from Chamberlain's tenure of the premiership but that little is of great importance. There is a note by Chamberlain of his discussions with Hitler at Berchtesgaden in 1938, notes by Sir Horace Wilson of the same event, and a notebook of conversations between Hitler and Chamberlain in Sept 1938. Details of Chamberlain's itinerary and drafts of the messages Chamberlain sent to Hitler and Mussolini have also survived, and there are papers relating to Chamberlain's visits to Paris in 1938 and Italy in 1939. There is correspondence relating to the rumours about Chamberlain's shares in armaments firms 1939–40, the resignation of Leslie Hore-Belisha in 1940, and notes for the Norway debate in May 1940. There are guest lists and lunch books for 10 Downing Street 1937–40, and many letters of congratulation in 1937 and of support 1938–40.

The collection also includes the papers of Chamberlain's wife, Anne. There is some miscellaneous correspondence 1916–55, diaries for 1940, correspondence concerning various charities and functions, and correspondence 1941–46 with Keith Feiling concerning his biography. Obituary notices, and papers concerning Chamberlain's funeral and will, complete the collection.

Some of Chamberlain's papers as Lord President form part of CAB 118, which contains Private Office papers of the Lords President 1938–47, in the PRO. Papers of Prime Ministerial Advisors Outside Cabinet 1916–40 are in the PRO at PREM 1. Speeches of the Chancellor of the Exchequer 1925–37 are in the PRO at T 172/1520–9. The MH and HLG classes are also useful for Chamberlain's period at the Ministry of Health.

The Sayer Archive holds material on Chamberlain, including a letter to Beaverbrook on the day he resigned his premiership. The Conservative Party Archives in the Bodleian Library should also be consulted, in particular correspondence and speech notes from the Conservative Research Department (CRD 1/24; NRA 32908).

Chamberlain's only book, *Norman Chamberlain: A memoir* (John Murray 1923) reveals a good deal about its author.

JOSEPH CHAMBERLAIN (1836-1914)

Joseph Chamberlain was Liberal MP for Birmingham (Birmingham West from 1885) 1876-86; he became a Liberal Unionist in 1886 and held the seat till his death. He was President of the Board of Trade May 1880-June 1885, President of the Local Government Board Feb-March 1886, and Secretary of State for the Colonies June 1895-Oct 1903.

After Chamberlain left the Colonial Office in 1903 his assistant private secretary Edward Marsh was instructed to 'clear the files of redundant papers... The task involved examining and tearing up about twelve thousand old letters, a process punctuated with shrieks of laughter at some of the suggestions put forward by correspondents' (Christopher Hassall, *Edward Marsh: Patron of the Arts, A Biography*, Longmans, 1959, p. 116). Of the material which Chamberlain had chosen to preserve, a large collection (c.20,000 items) has been deposited in the Birmingham University Library (Joseph Chamberlain papers). A list of the papers is available (NRA 12604). The Library has also prepared a *Guide to the Chamberlain collection* (1977). Applications to see the papers should be made in writing to the Sub-Librarian (Special Collections) and should enclose a character reference. The entire Chamberlain collection will be included in a conservation microfilming and publication programme, expected to take three years from 1996.

The collection covers most aspects of Chamberlain's political career. There are family papers, including Chamberlain's letters to his various relations, typed extracts from the diary of Mary, his third wife, 1901-14, and some papers relating to his home and domestic finances. (Some correspondence with his sons Neville and Austen is to be found in their collections). There are papers and correspondence relating to Chamberlain's various election campaigns. Papers on most of the political problems of the time, domestic and foreign, have survived. There are, in particular, many papers and a great deal of correspondence on Ireland. There are letters, memoranda, and draft bills from Chamberlain's term of office at the Board of Trade: for example, on bankruptcy, Employers' Liability, and merchant shipping. There are many papers deriving from his part in the conference with the United States on the Newfoundland Fisheries 1887-88. An additional 700 letters between Chamberlain and Mary were deposited in 1981. Other papers including miscellaneous correspondence 1896-1913 are in the Austen Chamberlain collection also at Birmingham and are detailed in the following entry.

Chamberlain's role in Salisbury's government is fully represented by papers on colonial and imperial affairs, including papers on the Jameson raid, and on the reasons for his resignation in 1903. His entire political and official career is reflected in a general correspondence series and press cuttings. Chamberlain seems not to have kept a diary but there is a memo of events 1880–92 (JC 8/1/1) which was published as C. H. D. Howard (ed), *A Political Memoir 1880–1892* (Batchworth Press 1953). There are diaries he kept on various foreign tours. The collection also includes Sir Charles Dilke's diary 1880–85, and correspondence of the 1920s and 1930s when J. L. Garvin was writing the first three volumes of an official *Life*. The biography was completed by the Rt Hon Julian Amery and quotes extensively from the papers: *The Life of Joseph Chamberlain* (6 vols, Macmillan 1932–69). Peter Fraser, *Joseph Chamberlain: Radicalism and Empire* (Cassell 1966) also makes extensive use of the papers as does Denis Judd, *Radical Joe* (Hamilton 1977). The entry by Peter T. Marsh in *DBB*, I, 643–8, draws on business records in the GKN archives in its London headquarters and Smethwick, and Lloyds Bank archives in London and Colmore Row, Birmingham headquarters. Professor Marsh has also written a major biography based on Chamberlain's papers, *Joseph Chamberlain, Entrepreneur in Politics* (Yale UP 1994).

Original correspondence and a register of correspondence 1902–03 concerning Chamberlain's tour of South Africa while he was Secretary of State for the Colonies is in the PRO (CO 529 and 638). There are also papers to Lord Northcote in PRO 30/56.

The papers of J. W. Dodson, 2nd Baron Monk Bretton, in the Bodleian Library (Dep Monk Bretton), contain much material relating to Chamberlain. Monk Bretton was Chamberlain's secretary at the Colonial Office 1900–03. As well as letters addressed to Chamberlain, there are many Colonial Office papers annotated by him; in particular, there are many boxes of papers relating to Chamberlain's South African tour.

The papers of the Tariff Reform Commission set up by Chamberlain in 1903, and of the Tariff Reform League 1903–22, are in the BLPES and have been listed.

The National Archives, Canada, holds microfilm and photocopies of papers from Birmingham University which relate to Canada (MG 27 II A 2).

SIR (JOSEPH) AUSTEN CHAMBERLAIN (1863–1937)

Austen Chamberlain was Liberal Unionist MP for Worcestershire (East) 189292–1914, and Conservative MP for Birmingham (West) 1914–37. He was Civil Lord of the Admiralty July 1895–Nov 1900, Financial Secretary to the Treasury 1900–Aug 1902, Postmaster-General 1902–Oct 1903, Chancellor of the Exchequer 1903–Dec 1905 and Jan 1919–March 1921, Secretary of State for India May 1915–July 1917, Minister without Portfolio in the War Cabinet April 1918–Jan 1919, Lord Privy Seal March 1921–Oct 1922, Secretary of State for Foreign Affairs Nov 1924–June 1929, and First Lord of the Admiralty Aug-Oct 1931. He was Leader of the Conservative Party March 1921–Oct 1922. He was created KG in 1925.

Chamberlain's papers have been extensively quoted in print: in his autobiography, *Down the Years* (Cassell 1935), Chamberlain said that while he kept no diary, he had referred to occasional memoranda and letters. *Politics from Inside. An Epistolary Chronicle, 1906–1914* (Cassell 1936), was based on Chamberlain's letters to his step-mother, many of which were intended to be read to his father in order to keep him up to date with political events. Sir Charles Petrie, *The Life and Letters of the Right Hon. Sir Austen Chamberlain* (2 vols, Cassell 1939–40), includes substantial quotations. The most recent biography, drawing on the same personal collection, is David Dutton, *Austen Chamberlain: Gentleman in Politics* (Ross Anderson Publications, Bolton 1985). Robert C. Self (ed), *The Austen Chamberlain Diary Letters: The correspondence of Sir Austen Chamberlain with his sisters Hilda and Ida, 1916–1937* (Camden Fifth Series, vol. 5, Cambridge UP for Royal Historical Society 1995) has extensive political commentary.

Chamberlain's papers were deposited in the Birmingham University Library (Austen Chamberlain papers). Applications to see the collection should be made in writing to the Sub-Librarian (Special Collections) and should enclose a character reference. These papers have been listed (NRA 12604) and are described in the Library's *Guide to the Chamberlain collection* (1977). The Library will undertake a three year conservation microfilming and publication programme for the entire Chamberlain collection from 1996. All of Chamberlain's career is covered, and there is a good deal of family correspondence. As well as Chamberlain's letters to his wife and her replies, there are many letters to and from his sisters and his half-brother Neville. There is a series of letters from Chamberlain to his father 1908–12 and there are many of Joseph Chamberlain's papers in this collection: as well as papers concerning the Chamberlain family tree, there is Joseph Chamberlain's own marriage certificate, miscellaneous correspondence 1896–1913, a play by him entitled 'Politics, a political comedy', and other farces and miscellaneous papers.

Chamberlain's early political career is illustrated by correspondence 1892–1908 and papers concerning the 1906 general election. His role in Unionist affairs is reflected by papers on subjects such as Home Rule and Tariff Reform. There are also papers related to his candidature for the party leadership in 1911, his activities in July and Aug 1914, the formation of the May 1915 and Dec 1916 Coalition governments, the growth of Unionist discontent with the Coalition, the defeat of the Coalition in Oct 1922, and the reunification of the Conservative Party in 1923.

Chamberlain's official career is also represented: there are many Cabinet papers 1903–05 on various topics, and some correspondence, for example, with George Wyndham on Ireland. There are also many papers relating to India, including correspondence with Lords Chelmsford and Hardinge 1913–17, and also papers concerning Edwin Montagu's resignation in 1922. There is much concerning military operations in Mesopotamia during the First World War, the mis-management of which caused Chamberlain to resign. There seem to be few official papers for his tenure of the Foreign Office but there is a vast correspondence for the years 1920–37. There is also correspondence concerning the publication of his books. In 1981, 31 letters to Lord Beaverbrook 1911–36, part originals, part copies, were added to the collection.

Eight volumes of Chamberlain's miscellaneous correspondence as Secretary of State for Foreign Affairs have been deposited in the PRO (FO 800/256–63; NRA 23627). A list has been made.

Chamberlain's papers relating to the Genoa Conference April-May 1922 appear to have been left behind at Downing Street on the fall of the Lloyd George government. They are now to be found as files 126 and 128–30 in the papers of J. C. C. Davidson in the HLRO. The Davidson Papers also include a file (131) containing Chamberlain's copies of secretary's notes of conversations at 10 Downing St between Lloyd George, A. J. Balfour, and the Italian Minister for Foreign Affairs 26 June-7 July 1922.

HENRY CHAPLIN, 1st VISCOUNT CHAPLIN (1840–1923)

Henry Chaplin was Conservative MP for Mid-Lincolnshire (Lincolnshire, Sleaford from 1885) 1868–1906 and Surrey (Wimbledon) 1907–16. He was Chancellor of the Duchy of Lancaster June 1885–Feb 1886, President of the Board of Agriculture Sept 1889–July 1892, and President of the Local Government Board June 1895–Nov 1900. He was created Viscount Chaplin in 1916.

Chaplin's grandson, the 3rd Viscount Chaplin, informed us that he had no papers relating to Chaplin's life and career. However, a collection of Chaplin's papers was included in a deposit of family papers made by the 3rd Lord Chaplin's cousin, Lady Mairi Bury, in the PRONI (Londonderry Papers, D3099/1; NRA 19803).

Chaplin's papers relate mostly to his political career and his horse-racing interests. The political papers 1875–1928 include letters and other documents relating to Irish politics and Home Rule and con-stituency papers for Sleaford. There are also letters about miscellaneous political matters. Correspondents include Disraeli, A. J. Balfour, the

Duke of Northumberland, and Lord French. There is a letter from Lord Salisbury explaining that he is unable to offer Chaplin a seat in his Cabinet in 1900.

The personal papers include family letters, letters of congratulations on his peerage, and general correspondence with many members of the royal family, including Queen Victoria, the Prince of Wales (Edward VII), George V, and Princess Mary.

Other papers in the collection include material on the Blankney estate, Lincolnshire 1866-1925, press cuttings about Chaplin 1900-23, and a collection of photos 1860-1923. There are also a number of papers and letters on Chaplin's racing and hunting interests and the Blankney Stud Farm. Also included in the collection are the papers of Chaplin's wife, Lady Florence. These include letters to her from Chaplin and others 1873-81, and other accounts and personal papers 1874-81.

Lady Mairi's mother, Chaplin's elder daughter, published selections from Chaplin's papers in Edith H. Vane-Tempest-Stewart, Marchioness of Londonderry, *Henry Chaplin* (Macmillan 1926). Lady Londonderry said, in her introduction, that her father wanted some account of his political and sporting career to be published and, with this end in view, he prepared several letters and memoranda which she included in her book.

Some of Chaplin's papers are included in the Londonderry papers in the Durham CRO (D/Lo/F/626-32). A full description of the entire collection is to be found in S. C. Newton, *The Londonderry Papers* (Durham 1966) (NRA 11528). There are no personal or political papers apart from the papers used for Lady Londonderry's memoir. There are eight files of draft chapters, letters, and memoranda about Lady Londonderry's work, and press cuttings about Chaplin's 1907 election for Wimbledon.

Another small collection of Chaplin's papers is available in the Lincolnshire Archives (BS 13). The papers were included in a collection deposited by Messrs Burton & Co, solicitors. The papers almost all concern the management of Chaplin's Lincolnshire estates: audits, accounts, agreements, and draft contracts. But there are a few miscellaneous political papers: press cuttings about Chaplin's House of Commons activities; a printed speech on the 1881 Irish Land Bill; and letters and papers relating to the North Lincolnshire Conservative Registration and Election Association 1868-83. There is a list (NRA 5395).

Some letters 1875-90 from Chaplin and his children to his sister-in-law, Lady Alexandra Leveson-Gower, are available in the Sutherland collection in the Staffordshire RO (D 593/P/29/1/4,8). There is a list (NRA 10699).

Although it is based almost entirely on published sources, Henry Blyth's *The Pocket Venus* (Weidenfeld and Nicolson 1966) is a full account of the rivalry between Chaplin and the 4th Marquess of Hastings for the hand of Lady Florence Paget. For Chaplin's early political life the indispensable account is in R. J. Olney, *Lincolnshire Politics 1832–1885* (Oxford UP 1973).

SIR (ALFRED) ERNLE MONTACUTE CHATFIELD, 1st BARON CHATFIELD (1873–1967)

Ernle Chatfield was created KCMG in 1919, GCB in 1934, and Baron Chatfield in 1937. He was Minister for the Coordination of Defence Jan 1939–April 1940.

Chatfield's papers were deposited in the National Maritime Museum in 1973 (CHT/1–9; NRA 30121). A preliminary list of the papers is available.

The collection (it filled ten box-files) has been divided into seven groups: papers concerning Chatfield's early life; his Atlantic and Mediterranean commands; his term of office as First Sea Lord; his work on the Indian Defence Committee 1938–39; his term as minister; his later life; and photo albums.

The papers concerning Chatfield's early life consist of family genealogy. The Atlantic and Mediterranean command papers include some relating to the 1931 Invergordon mutiny. Chatfield's First Sea Lord papers include papers on the 1935 Naval Conference, a visit to the Combined Fleets, Gibraltar in 1938, and his promotion to Admiral of the Fleet. As well as general correspondence for the period, there is correspondence with Winston and Randolph Churchill 1936–42, Sir Robert Vansittart, Sir Warren Fisher, Lord Beatty, senior admirals, and other Commanders-in-Chief.

Chatfield's ministry papers do not reflect his activities particularly well. They have been divided into general papers (including correspondence with Winston Churchill) and papers concerning Anglo-American relations 1937–40.

Chatfield's later papers include three boxes of speech and broadcast notes, press cuttings, and correspondence with Professor Arthur Marder. They also include the manuscripts for Chatfield's two volumes of autobiography: *The Navy and Defence* (Heinemann 1942) and *It Might Happen Again* (Heinemann 1947). These are particularly interesting for they show the deletions made in the published version, for example, about the 1922 Washington Naval Conference.

A further deposit of papers was made to the National Maritime Museum by Chatfield's son, the 2nd Lord Chatfield, in 1993 (MS86/094; NRA 20623). They include letters from Chatfield to his wife 1910–40 (including letters from Washington 1921–22), letters from Chatfield to his son 1948–67, and letters of condolence to Lady Chatfield upon her husband's death.

There is a brief summary of Chatfield's naval and political career based on his papers by Peter Kemp in *DNB 1961–1970*, 185–8. Work on a biography of Chatfield commenced by Professor A. Temple Patterson is being continued by Eric Grove of the University of Hull.

CHARLES RICHARD JOHN SPENCER-CHURCHILL, 9th DUKE OF MARLBOROUGH (1871–1934)

Charles Spencer-Churchill ('Sunny') was known as Earl of Sunderland until 1883, then as Marquess of Blandford until he succeeded his father as 9th Duke in 1892. He was created KG in 1902. He was Paymaster-General 1899–March 1902, Under-Secretary of State for the Colonies July 1903–Dec 1905, and Joint Parliamentary Secretary to the Board of Agriculture and Fisheries Feb 1917–March 1918.

The Library at Blenheim Palace has only a small box of the 9th Duke's papers; it contains a fragment of diary written during the South African War and a few letters on family financial affairs. The only other surviving items are the Blenheim visitors' book, and some photo albums. None of these is generally available.

Marlborough's first wife Consuelo Vanderbilt Balsan described events surrounding their engagement, marriage, and divorce in *The Glitter and the Gold* (William Heinemann 1953). In the book Madame Balsan refers to her private photo collection which included photos of the Duke and their children, and quotes from some letters and a fragment of a 1908 journal, although she states at the beginning of the book that she had no journals, only 'meagre notes of engagements made' and press cuttings (p. xi).

The life of the Duke's long-time mistress and second wife, Gladys Deacon, is detailed in Hugo Vickers, *Gladys: Duchess of Marlborough* (Weidenfeld & Nicolson 1979; Hamish Hamilton paperback 1987). Throughout this biography, Mr Vickers quotes from the 'Gladys Deacon Papers' which he holds at his house, Wyeford, Ramsdell, Hampshire RG26 5QL. The collection contains correspondence to and from Gladys, including a long series of letters between her and Marlborough 1915–34, and the extensive correspondence between their lawyers during their divorce proceedings. There are also letters from Marlborough's mother Albertha, Lady Blandford, and a large number of photos and the Blenheim photo albums made by Gladys 1921–34. Mr Vickers is happy to allow *bona fide* researchers access to the collection, which has been catalogued.

Mr Vickers notes in *Gladys* that in 1929 'Sunny' sold some papers in the USA 'including letters from Winston Churchill, invitation cards and thank-you letters. Among this collection are a few letters from the Prince of Wales (later the Duke of Windsor) and the Duke of York (later King George VI)' (p. 285). This collection may now be found in the Manuscript Division, Library of Congress, Washington.

SIR WINSTON LEONARD SPENCER-CHURCHILL (1874–1965)

Winston Churchill was Conservative MP for Oldham 1900–04. He became a Liberal in 1904 and continued as MP for Oldham till 1906. He was Liberal MP for Manchester (North-West) 1906–08 and Dundee 1908–22. He was Conservative MP for Essex (Epping) 1924–45 and Woodford 1945–64. He was Under-Secretary of State for the Colonies Dec 1905–April 1908, President of the Board of Trade 1908–Feb 1910, Secretary of State for Home Affairs 1910–Oct 1911, First Lord of the Admiralty 1911–May 1915 and Sept 1939–May 1940, Chancellor of the Duchy of Lancaster May-Nov 1915, Minister of Munitions July 1917–Jan 1919, Secretary of State for War and Air 1919–Feb 1921, Secretary of State for the Colonies 1921–Oct 1922, Chancellor of the Exchequer Nov 1924–June 1929, Prime Minister May 1940–July 1945 and Oct 1951–April 1955, Minister of Defence May 1940–July 1945 and Oct 1951–March 1952. He was Leader of the Conservative Party Oct 1940–April 1955. He was created KG in 1953.

During his career Churchill accumulated an enormous collection of papers which provide a thorough and detailed history of his life. Before his death, Churchill settled the pre-July 1945 papers on the Chartwell Trust for the benefit of his family and descendants, and the post-July 1945 papers on his wife Lady Spencer-Churchill. The papers were sorted, arranged and microfilmed by the PRO between 1961–64, and a three volume list was produced. Volume I covered the papers up to 27 July 1945 (CHARTWELL), Volume II covered the papers after 27 July 1945 (CHURCHILL), and Volume III covered the papers of the Prime Minister's Private Office 1940–45 which were retained by the PRO and form part of the PREM class. The microfilm of the papers (PRO 31/19) is not available for research. The Chartwell and Churchill papers were eventually deposited at the Churchill Archives Centre, Cambridge.

The official biography was published in eight volumes by Heinemann: Randolph S. Churchill, *Winston S. Churchill, Vol I Youth 1874–1900* (1966); *Vol II Young Statesman 1901–1914* (1967); Martin Gilbert, *Vol III 1914–1916* (1971); *Vol IV 1917–1922* (1974); *Vol V 1922–1939* (1976); *Vol VI Finest Hour 1939–1941* (1983); *Vol VII Road to Victory* (1986); and *Vol VIII Never Despair 1945–1965* (1988). Relevant documents from the Churchill and other papers are extensively quoted in the *Companion Volumes* to the official biography.

Martin Gilbert has also published a one volume biography, *Churchill: A Life* (Heinemann 1991). Churchill's own numerous publications, including *The World Crisis* (6 vols, Thornton Butterworth 1923–31) and *The Second World War* (6 vols, Cassell 1948–54), also contain much documentary material. The unfinished biography by the 2nd Earl of Birkenhead published as *Churchill 1874–1922* (Harrap 1989) was also based on the collection.

The collection of Churchill papers at the Churchill Archives Centre is in six sections (NRA 20556). The first, and major, section is c.1210 boxes of the Chartwell Trust papers (CHAR) 1874–1945. The second section of the Churchill collection consists of c.850 boxes of 1945–65 papers bequeathed to the Churchill Archives Centre by Lady Spencer-Churchill (CHUR). The remaining four sections consist of: 106 boxes of various minor gifts and copies of Churchill papers (WCHL); 18 boxes of Churchill press photos purchased from a private vendor (CHPH); 82 boxes of Churchill press cuttings given to the Archives Centre by the Conservative Central Office (CHPC); and 8 boxes of uncatalogued, unedited video and audio tapes and transcripts of interviews for the BBC series *Churchill* 1992.

The future of the Chartwell Trust papers, and their continuing accommodation at the Churchill Archives Centre, was resolved in April 1995 when the British government purchased the trustees' interest in the papers on behalf of the nation through the National Heritage Memorial Fund. The papers will remain at the Churchill Archives Centre where a detailed computer catalogue and index listing each document and indexing it under author, recipient and subject, is hoped to be completed within the next five years. An outline catalogue of the collection is currently available. The papers are now fully available for research. Access is by appointment only and initial inquiries should be made in writing to the Archivist.

In addition to Churchill's own papers, the Churchill Archives Centre also holds 47 boxes of letters, diaries and albums of Lady Spencer-Churchill (CSCT).

Papers concerning defence and operational subjects 1940–45 of Churchill as Minister for Defence are in the PRO at PREM 3. Others may be found at CAB 120. Papers of Prime Ministerial Advisors Outside Cabinet 1916–40 may be found in PREM 1. Other war time official papers are in PREM 4 and papers relating to Churchill's 1951–55 administration are in PREM 11 (which covers 1951–64). Speeches of the Chancellor of the Exchequer 1925–37 are in the PRO at T 172/1520–9.

The Conservative Party Archives in the Bodleian Library should also be consulted.

Books about Churchill – and others with his name in the title – continue to proliferate. A review of recent Churchilliana is beyond the scope of this volume, but Paul Addison's *Churchill on the Home Front*

1900–1955 (Jonathan Cape 1992) has a valuable bibliographical guide on Churchill's domestic policies.

ROBERT GEORGE WINDSOR-CLIVE, 14th BARON WINDSOR, 1st EARL OF PLYMOUTH (1857–1923)

Robert Windsor-Clive succeeded his grandmother as 14th Baron Windsor in 1869, and was created Earl of Plymouth in 1905, and GBE in 1918. He was Paymaster-General 1891–July 1892, and First Commissioner of Works Aug 1902–Dec 1905.

Lord Plymouth's grandson, the 3rd Earl, had no papers, only a biography of his grandfather written by the 1st Earl's wife, *Robert George Earl of Plymouth 1857–1923* (privately printed, Cambridge UP 1932). The biography details Plymouth's political life and includes verbatim transcriptions of memoranda and correspondence sent by and to him relating to such matters as the completion of the Wellington monument in St Paul's Cathedral and the dispute between the government and the Dean and Chapter of Westminster in 1904 over alterations to the Chapel of the Pyx.

Miss Melissa Benton, his grand-daughter by his only daughter, did not know of any other papers in family possession. However, there are records relating to the Plymouth family estates in the NLW (NRA 34360), and the Hereford and Worcester, Shropshire, and Glamorgan ROs. The Glamorgan RO also has one bundle of papers 1911–15 relating to the appointment of magistrates and deputy lieutenants in Glamorgan in Plymouth's capacity as Lord Lieutenant of Glamorgan (D/D Pl 842). This is only available for inspection with special permission.

JOHN ROBERT CLYNES (1869–1949)

John Clynes was Labour MP for Manchester (North-East; Platting from 1918) 1906–31 and 1935–45. He was Parliamentary Secretary to the Ministry of Food July 1917–July 1918, Food Controller 1918–Jan 1919, Lord Privy Seal Jan–Nov 1924, and Secretary of State for Home Affairs June 1929–Aug 1931. He was Chairman of the Labour Party 1921–22.

When the first edition was prepared, Clynes's daughter-in-law, Mrs G. E. Clynes, had a very small collection of his papers; these papers were not generally available for research. Mrs Clynes thought that any other papers were probably destroyed during successive house-removals; she informed us that neither of Clynes's grand-children (then living in the USA) had any papers. We were unable to contact Mrs Clynes during preparation of the second edition.

The papers in Mrs Clynes's possession consisted almost entirely of press cuttings and printed material; the only other papers were invitations, short social notes, correspondence concerning Clynes's swearing-in as a Privy Councillor, and a letter from Clynes to his daughter describing the latter ceremony. A letter from Mrs Clynes to her daughter described her first visit to Windsor Castle. There was one album of press cuttings, almost all of which described speeches and social functions during the first Labour government of 1924. There were several loose cuttings of articles by Clynes, including one from the *News of the World*, 14 Sept 1947, describing the 1931 crisis, and many for the journal of the National Union of General and Municipal Workers. The collection also included two records of speeches for the 1929 general election campaign and Clynes's election addresses for his 1906, 1910, 1918, 1922, 1923, and 1935 election campaigns.

There are papers, press cuttings, and correspondence relating to Clynes 1900–30 in the Labour Party records in the National Museum of Labour History (LP/LRC, GC and JSM; NRA 14863). The Hoover Institution on War, Revolution and Peace at Stanford University holds 21 boxes of papers of the Inter-Allied Food Council records 1917–19 on which Clynes served with the representatives of France, Italy, and the USA.

Clynes's views of contemporary Labour politicians are to be found in short biographical articles in Herbert Tracey (ed), *The British Labour Party* (Caxton 1948). His own *Memoirs* (2 vols, Hutchinson 1937) quote from very few documents.

SIR GODFREY PATTISON COLLINS (1875–1936)

Godfrey Collins was Liberal MP for Greenock 1910–36; he was a Liberal National from 1931. He was Secretary of State for Scotland Sept 1932–Oct 1936. He was created KBE in 1919.

Collins's son, William Hope Collins (who died in 1967), informed us that Collins rarely kept any papers; his business habit was to write his decision or comment on whatever was sent to him and return the document to the sender. Mr W. H. Collins did have some personal papers about the break-up of the Liberal Party in the 1920s (Collins was Liberal Chief Whip 1924–26) and the work done by Collins on the Army Council. Unfortunately these papers could not be found and Mr James Collins, the son of W. H. Collins had only a volume of press cuttings. The cuttings were all from June-Dec 1935 and were taken from Scottish newspapers; they included coverage of the Nov 1935 general election when Collins was not expected to be returned. Collins's daughter, Mrs Elspeth Barry had a comprehensive collection of Collins's obituary notices made by his secretary. Mrs Barry also had cuttings concerning the 1929, 1931, and 1935 elections, Collins's becoming a privy councillor, and his appointment as a Cabinet minister in 1932. Her collection also included cuttings on a Scottish Education Bill, as well as numerous invitations and programmes for various functions.

Neither Mrs Barry nor Mr James Collins knew what became of the papers known to exist in 1966 nor of the existence of any other papers. David Keir, *The House of Collins* (Collins 1952), includes an account of Collins's career but it does not quote from documents.

The records of William Collins, Sons & Co have been deposited in the Glasgow University Archives (UGD 24343; NRA 31886). They appear to contain nothing directly related to Collins apart from the 'Report and Accounts of the Trustees of Sir Godfrey and Lady Collins' Marriage Settlement 1951' (UGD 243/1/12/8).

Private Office papers relating to Collins's period at the Scottish Office are dispersed through the files of the five main Scottish Office departments held at the SRO.

Pottinger's brief biographical chapter on Collins in *Secretaries of State for Scotland*, 54–62, draws on Scottish Office files (HH I/791) in the SRO. Reference should also be made to J. W. R. Mitchell, 'The emergence of Modern Scottish central administration 1885–1939' (DPhil, Oxford University 1987).

SIR (DAVID) JOHN COLVILLE, 1st BARON CLYDESMUIR (1894–1954)

John Colville was Conservative MP for Midlothian and Peebleshire (Northern) 1929–43. He was Parliamentary Secretary for the Overseas Trade Department of the Board of Trade Nov 1931–Nov 1935, Parliamentary Under-Secretary of State for Scotland 1935–Oct 1936, Financial Secretary to the Treasury 1936–May 1938, and Secretary of State for Scotland 1938–May 1940. He was created GCIE in 1943 and Baron Clydesmuir in 1948.

Colville's son, the 2nd Lord Clydesmuir, advised us that he had destroyed most of his family papers, only retaining those of especial interest to the family. He also advised that his father did not keep any papers on Cabinet meetings or from his period as Secretary of State for Scotland. Papers which were in the possession of Clydesmuir's daughter, the late Hon Mrs Dalrymple-Hamilton, were returned to her brother, and consisted mostly of old constituency papers. Colville's younger daughter, the Hon Mrs Whitcombe, had no papers relating to her father's career.

Private Office papers relating to Colville's periods at the Scottish Office are dispersed through the files of the five main Scottish Office departments held at the SRO.

There is a brief account of Colville's career, with special reference to Scottish affairs in *Secretaries of State for Scotland*, 74–9. Reference should also be made to J. W. R. Mitchell, 'The emergence of Modern Scottish central administration 1885–1939' (DPhil, Oxford University 1987).

SIR (ALFRED) DUFF COOPER, 1st VISCOUNT NORWICH (1890-1954)

Duff Cooper was Conservative MP for Oldham 1924-29, and for Westminster (St George's) 1931-45. He was Financial Secretary to the War Office Jan 1928-June 1929 and Sept 1931-June 1934, Financial Secretary to the Treasury 1934-Nov 1935, Secretary of State for War 1935-May 1937, First Lord of the Admiralty 1937-Oct 1938, Minister of Information May 1940-July 1941, and Chancellor of the Duchy of Lancaster 1941-Nov 1943. He was created GCMG in 1948 and Viscount Norwich in 1952.

Duff Cooper left his diaries, and other papers relating mainly to his period at the Paris embassy, to his literary executor, Sir Rupert Hart-Davis. Sir Rupert informed us that there were very few 'political' papers, except for the period when Duff Cooper was British Representative in Algiers. Most of the papers were of a personal, social, and literary nature. Sir Rupert gave all of the papers to his cousin, the 2nd Viscount Norwich; some of them, including diaries, some royal and personal letters, and material relating to the Paris Embassy period, remain in Viscount Norwich's possession.

Viscount Norwich deposited a large collection (39 boxes) of Duff Cooper's papers in the Churchill Archives Centre in 1986 (DUFC; NRA 31392). Application to view those papers available must be made in writing to the Archivist. The collection includes the personal and political papers found in the cellar of Lady Diana Cooper's London home by Dr John Charmley when writing *Duff Cooper: The Authorized Biography* (Macmillan 1986). These, as well as the papers then held by Sir Rupert Hart-Davis, were extensively cited by Charmley whose footnotes are also a useful guide to relevant PRO files.

The collection has been catalogued and divided into 13 sections, consisting of: correspondence between Duff and Diana Cooper; political career to 1939; political career 1939-43; Algiers and Paris 1944-47; literary papers; miscellaneous personal papers; correspondence with Hilaire Belloc; articles, speeches and pamphlets; Diana Cooper correspondence (mainly to Conrad Russell); correspondence with Rudolph (Kaetchen) Kommer; royal letters; private correspondence; and photocopied material collected by Dr Charmley. The correspondence between Duff and Diana Cooper was arranged by Artemis Cooper for her edition, *A Durable Fire: The Letters of Duff and Diana Cooper 1913-1950* (Collins 1983). It is arranged according to chronology and suitability for publication. The arrangement of the political papers, the literary papers, and the correspondence with Rudolph Kommer is that made by Duff Cooper himself. The miscellaneous personal papers and correspondence of Lady Diana were arranged by Dr Charmley. The royal correspondence is closed as is the private correspondence to Duff Cooper from a number of women friends.

Duff Cooper copied his diaries for 1952 and 1953 for Lady Caroline Duff, wife of Sir Michael Duff, 3rd Bt; he also returned to Lady Caroline her letters to him. She has presented the copies of the diaries and her correspondence 1931–51 (that is both her letters to Duff Cooper and his to her) to the British Library, but the papers will remain closed until 2009 or the death of Lady Caroline's son, whichever is the later (Reserved MS 94). The British Library also received in 1991 a collection of Lady Diana's correspondence c.1908–17, including Duff Cooper's First World War papers (Add MSS 70704–20). Evelyn Waugh's letters to Lady Diana 1932–66 may also be found in the British Library (Add MSS 69796–8).

Some papers concerning Duff Cooper's work with the French Committee of National Liberation in Algeria are available at the PRO (FO 660/106–99). They include reports on the political situation and the various resistance groups, as well as social papers connected with the Prime Minister's visit to Algeria.

In *Old Men Forget* (Hart-Davis 1953) Duff Cooper quoted from many letters and from his diaries. Lady Diana also quoted from his diaries and from his letters to her in her memoirs, *The Rainbow Comes and Goes* (Hart-Davis 1958), *The Light of Common Day* (Hart-Davis 1959), and *Trumpets from the Steep* (Hart-Davis 1960). Philip Ziegler, *Diana Cooper: The Biography of Lady Diana Cooper* (Hamish Hamilton 1981) should also be consulted. There is valuable material on Duff Cooper's term as Minister of Information in Ian McLaine, *Ministry of Morale* (George Allen & Unwin 1979).

SIR CHARLES ALFRED CRIPPS, 1st BARON PARMOOR (1852–1941)

Alfred Cripps was Conservative MP for Gloucestershire (Stroud) 1895–1900, South-East Lancashire (Stretford) 1901–06 and Buckinghamshire (Wycombe) 1910–14. He was Lord President of the Council Jan-Nov 1924 and June 1929–Aug 1931. He was created KCVO in 1908, and Baron Parmoor in 1914.

According to his son, the 2nd Baron Parmoor, all Parmoor's papers were given to his youngest son, Sir Stafford Cripps. Sir Stafford's widow, Dame Isobel Cripps, had no recollection of this nor did she know where any Parmoor papers might be found. The 4th Lord Parmoor has no idea where any surviving papers might be.

The house to which the papers may have been sent was burned down during the war and many valuable papers were certainly lost then, a loss which possibly included the Parmoor papers. Parmoor's grand-daughter, Lady Ricketts, advised us that she thought this to be the most likely fate of the papers.

In his autobiography, *A Retrospect* (Heinemann 1936), Parmoor quoted from several letters including correspondence with Ramsay MacDonald on the formation of the first Labour government in 1924.

SIR (RICHARD) STAFFORD CRIPPS (1889–1952)

Stafford Cripps was Labour MP for Bristol (East) 1931–50 and Bristol (South-East) Feb-Oct 1950. He was Solicitor-General Oct 1930–Aug 1931, Lord Privy Seal Feb-Nov 1942, Minister of Aircraft Production 1942–May 1945, President of the Board of Trade July 1945–Sept 1947, Minister of Economic Affairs Sept-Nov 1947, and Chancellor of the Exchequer 1947–Oct 1950. He was knighted in 1930.

A large collection of Cripps's papers was deposited in Nuffield College Library by his widow, Dame Isobel Cripps (Cripps papers). These papers fill three bays of shelving, and only a very rough, preliminary list has been compiled. The papers fall into two main types: subject files and speech files. This division is reflected by two series of descriptive entries, both arranged in approximate chronological order, and both ranging over Cripps's political life 1930–50.

The speech files include copies of speeches, notes, and information used for a particular speech. Articles for the press and broadcasts are included in this section. In many cases the speeches contain the only reference in the collection to particular events in Cripps's life: for example, the only official papers in the collection come from the Ministry of Aircraft Production and relate to Cripps's visits to factories and the speeches he made there. The only reflections of Cripps's period as British Ambassador in Moscow 1940–42 and his mission to India 1942 are in the text of several speeches and broadcasts made on his return.

The subject files include much material from Cripps's work in his constituency. There are files on the 1931 by-election, and the 1931, 1935, and 1945 general elections. There are several files of correspondence on constituency 'cases' – including many instances of constituents asking for help in revising their means test assessment. There are also several files on the Labour Party's annual conferences, particularly those at which the issues of membership in the Socialist League and the Popular Front were raised. Cripps's earlier, more harmonious, contacts within the party are represented by a file of papers on a proposal to market cigarettes to help the party's funds. There are a few papers on the founding of *Tribune* in 1936 but the collection is disappointing on the Socialist League and Popular Front. As well as Cripps's own activities there are files on such subjects as Spain, Germany, and the West Indies.

There are also 15 books of press cuttings, mostly post-1940. There are very few papers from the post-war period.

A further collection of Cripps's papers, formerly in the possession of Dame Isobel, is in the care of Sir Maurice Shock who is writing a biography. Sir Maurice plans to deposit the papers in Nuffield College Library by the end of 1996, to join the others which have already been deposited by Dame Isobel. Sir Maurice is making arrangements to make these papers available for use by researchers.

Some of Dame Isobel's papers are currently in the possession of Cripps's son's widow, Lady Cripps. Cripps's daughter, Lady Ricketts, advised us that these papers are mostly personal and are not likely to become available for public inspection. Any papers in this collection which are not personal will most probably be deposited in Nuffield College.

Cripps's Private Office papers from his period as Minister of Aircraft Production are in AVIA 9 at the PRO. Papers relating to Budgets are in T 171, and further papers may be found in CAB 127. There is correspondence 1934–36 with the Bristol SE Constituency Labour Party in the Bristol RO (39035; NRA 28401).

Colin Cooke, *The Life of Richard Stafford Cripps* (Hodder & Stoughton 1957) and Eric Estorick, *Stafford Cripps* (Heinemann 1949), were both based on all of Cripps's papers and contain many quotations from the diary Cripps began to keep in 1938, as well as some of Cripps's correspondence. Nicholas Mansergh (ed), *The Transfer of Power 1942–1947*, I, *The Cripps Mission January-April 1942* (HMSO 1970) prints a large number of documents concerning Cripps's first mission to India, including Cripps's own record of interviews with Indian leaders. These notes were deposited in the India Office in 1942 and are now available in the Oriental and India Office Collections, British Library (IOR:L/P, J/10/4). Further discussion of Cripps's role in Indian affairs is to be found in Robin Moore, *Churchill, Cripps and India 1939–1945* (Clarendon Press, Oxford 1979); *Escape from Empire. The Attlee Government and the Indian Problem* (Clarendon Press, Oxford 1983); and *Making the New Commonwealth* (Clarendon Press, Oxford 1987). Gabriel Gorodetsky's *Stafford Cripps' Mission to Moscow, 1940–42* (Cambridge UP 1984) was written with the cooperation of the family and is a good guide to relevant private papers and public records.

Sir Maurice Shock's forthcoming biography is foreshadowed in his contribution in *Blackwell*, 108–11.

HARRY FREDERICK COMFORT CROOKSHANK, VISCOUNT CROOKSHANK (1893–1961)

Captain Harry Crookshank was Conservative MP for Lincolnshire (Gainsborough) 1924–56. He was Parliamentary Under-Secretary of

State for Home Affairs June 1934–June 1935, Parliamentary Secretary for Mines 1935–April 1939, Financial Secretary to the Treasury 1939–Feb 1943, Postmaster-General 1943–Aug 1945, Minister of Health Oct 1951–May 1952, Lord Privy Seal 1952–Dec 1955. He was created Viscount Crookshank in 1956.

A small collection of his papers was given to the Bodleian Library (MSS Eng hist b 223; c 596–605; d 359–61) by the executors of his nephew, the late Lt Col P. R. H. Crookshank. The papers (15 boxes and volumes) are mainly notes for speeches covering the whole of Crookshank's political life, speeches made both in and out of Parliament. Topics include India, Home Office matters, financial policy, agriculture, coal-mining, wartime Cabinet committees, and the Ministry of Health.

One of the few letters in the collection is what appears to be a draft letter to the Prime Minister (5 Dec 1936) giving the reaction of Crookshank's constituents to the Abdication. Perhaps of greatest interest is a resignation speech drafted in Oct 1938 but marked 'not used'. A carbon of Crookshank's proposed letter of resignation is marked 'letter sent but afterwards "lay on the table"'. For his proposed speech Crookshank wrote that at Munich '. . . we did in fact yield to force and not to reason' and '. . . if he [the Prime Minister] can speak of what happened last week as peace with honour, then I can only say that in the realm of foreign affairs he is using a language I cannot understand'. As well as political speeches there are notes which show the religious aspect of Crookshank's character: a speech to Unitarians in 1938, and an address in St Mary's, Cambridge, in 1948 on 'My Faith and My Job'. There are a number of press cuttings on Crookshank's political activities. There are also appointment diaries for the years 1943–61.

The most important item in the collection is Crookshank's diary for July 1934–Oct 1951, and 1955–58. The diary was kept on loose-leaf notepaper, which has allowed considerable variation in the length of the entries. Most of the entries are purely social but there is some political comment, eg on the changes made in the government in 1942. The entries for this period include copies of letters written by Crookshank to Churchill when the Prime Minister offered him the Ministry of Works and a peerage, and Crookshank's letter to James Stuart, the Conservative Whip, and the latter's reply.

Two large scrap-books were given by Crookshank to the Lincolnshire Archives. They contain press cuttings and invitations mainly concerning Crookshank's political career.

SIR RICHARD ASSHETON CROSS, 1st VISCOUNT CROSS (1823–1914)

Richard Cross was Conservative MP for Preston 1857–62, Lancashire (South-West) 1868–85 and South-West Lancashire (Newton) 1885–86.

He was Secretary of State for Home Affairs Feb 1874–April 1880 and June 1885–Feb 1886, Secretary of State for India Aug 1886-Aug 1892, Chancellor of the Duchy of Lancaster June-July 1895, and Lord Privy Seal June 1895–Nov 1900. He was created GCB in 1880, and Viscount Cross in 1886.

Cross had stipulated in his will that his correspondence with the royal family, the viceroys, and the governors of Madras and Bombay should not be published but should be devolved with his title. His Foreign Office confidential prints were to be returned to the Permanent Under Secretary at the Foreign Office.

Fifty-seven volumes of Cross's papers as Secretary of State for India were deposited on permanent loan in what is now the Oriental and India Office Collections, British Library by his grandson, the 3rd Viscount Cross in 1959 (MSS Eur e 243; NRA 20535). They consist of correspondence with successive viceroys, governors of Madras and Bombay, and telegrams. Sixteen volumes of original index are included in the collection.

The remainder of Cross's papers were given to the British Library by the 3rd Viscount in 1962 (Add MSS 51263–89). A copy of the British Library list has been published by the List and Index Society, *Special Series*, vol 7, '*Rough Register*' of *Acquisitions in the Department of Manuscripts, British Library 1961–1965*, 1974, 62–3. The 27 volumes of papers have been divided into special correspondence, general correspondence, and family correspondence. The six volumes of special correspondence include two volumes of correspondence with the 3rd Marquess of Salisbury and his family 1874–1907, as well as correspondence with Disraeli and Northcote. The 13 volumes of general correspondence cover the years 1846–1913. There are five volumes of family correspondence including Cross's letters to his mother 1842–49, his letters to his wife 1859–81, and letters of condolence on the death of his wife and son.

A further small collection of papers has been deposited in the Lancashire RO (DDX 841). The collection includes letters on local politics 1857–62, 1868, 1871, some press cuttings, electoral addresses for 1857, and a letter to the Preston electors giving the reasons for his resignation in 1862. There are also some genealogical and estate papers. There is a list (NRA 17133).

In his *A Political History* (privately printed 1903) Cross described for his children his political and official career and quoted from a few letters, particularly from Queen Victoria.

D. J. Mitchell's PhD thesis, 'Richard Assheton Cross: a political biography' is available on microfilm (Ann Arbor 1976, DA 565.C85M57) and is published as *Cross and Tory Democracy: A Political Biography of Richard Assheton Cross* (Garland, Hamden CT 1991).

SIR RONALD HIBBERT CROSS, Bt (1896–1968)

Ronald Cross was Conservative MP for Rossendale 1931–45 and Lancashire (Ormskirk) 1950–51. He was Parliamentary Secretary to the Board of Trade May 1938–Sept 1939, Minister of Economic Warfare 1939–May 1940, and Minister of Shipping 1940–May 1941. He was created a baronet in 1941, KCVO in 1954, KCMG in 1955.

In the first edition we reported that Cross's daughter, the Hon Mrs N. D. Campbell, had been unable to find any papers relating to her father's political and official career.

However, in 1977, the IWM microfilmed copies of some of Cross's papers which were borrowed from his daughters (PP/MCR/164; NRA 28536). The bulk of the copies are of Cross's speeches and addresses to various bodies in England and Australia during the Second World War – Cross was UK High Commissioner in Australia 1941–45. There are papers, mostly press releases, relating to operations in Burma 1944. A group of letters, committee minutes, and publicity material deals with the Australian food parcels for Britain scheme 1947–50.

There is also some political and personal correspondence 1942–45 including two reports to Churchill about General Douglas MacArthur 1942 and 1944, a report on John Curtin, the Australian Prime Minister, 1944, and comments on Australian attitudes to Britain.

The IWM returned these papers to the family in 1981. This collection is in the possession of Cross's daughter, Mrs Karina Barton. It also includes a few other papers 'presumably of lesser interest' which were not microfilmed by the IWM, and some of her father's letters from the front in the First World War when he was in the Royal Flying Corps. These latter have recently been taken by the IWM for copying.

Sir John Colville relates a telling incident highlighting the relationship between Cross and his Prime Minister, Churchill:

> The P.M. had invited Cross, the Minister of Shipping, to lunch and was showing him great affability. Suddenly he charged back into the room at No. 10, where I was telephoning, and whispered hoarsely in my ear, 'What is the name of the Minister of Shipping?' 'Cross', I whispered back furtively, because the Minister was standing in the doorway. 'Oh', said the P.M. 'Well, what's his Christian name?' Cross must have heard the whole conversation. (Diary, 14 Nov 1940, in *The Fringes of Power*, I, Sceptre 1986, p. 349).

SIR SAVILE BRINTON CROSSLEY, 2nd Bt, 1st BARON SOMERLEYTON (1857–1935)

Savile Crossley succeeded his father as 2nd baronet in 1872, and was created KCVO in 1909, Baron Somerleyton in 1916, and GCVO in 1922. He was Liberal MP for Suffolk (North) 1885–92, and Liberal

Unionist MP for Halifax 1900–06. He was Paymaster-General March 1902–Dec 1905.

Crossley's grandson, the 3rd Lord Somerleyton, was unable to find any of his grandfather's papers. None of his other grandchildren whom we were able to contact knew of any papers.

GEORGE NATHANIEL CURZON, 5th BARON SCARSDALE, MARQUESS CURZON OF KEDLESTON (1859–1925)

George Curzon was Conservative MP for South-West Lancashire (Southport) 1886–98. He was Under-Secretary of State for India Nov 1891–Aug 1892, Under-Secretary of State for Foreign Affairs June 1895–Oct 1898, Lord Privy Seal May 1915–Dec 1916, President of the Air Board May-Dec 1916, Lord President of the Council 1916–Oct 1919 and Nov 1924–March 1925, a member of the War Cabinet Dec 1916–Oct 1919, and Secretary of State for Foreign Affairs 1919–Jan 1924. He was an Irish Representative Peer in the House of Lords 1908–16. He was created GCIE in 1898, Baron Curzon of Kedleston (an Irish peerage) in 1898, Earl Curzon of Kedleston in 1911, KG in 1916, and Marquess Curzon of Kedleston 1921; he succeeded his father as 5th Baron Scarsdale in 1916.

Sir Maurice Hankey reported to Cabinet in Nov 1935 that 'numerous reminders had been sent to Lady Curzon [to return any of her husband's Cabinet papers], but no reply has ever been received. This is a case in which it is very doubtful indeed whether the late Lord Curzon had in his possession at the time of his death any post-War Papers, and in all the circumstances it is suggested that no further action in this case be taken' (PRO, CAB 24/257).

A very large collection of Curzon's papers was deposited in what is now the Oriental and India Office Collections, British Library between 1962–77 by the Kedleston Trustees (MSS Eur F 111,112; NRA 20536). The collection covers the whole of Curzon's public career and much of his private life, and is available for research. A unified catalogue of the whole collection, arranged chronologically and divided into nine sections, is available.

The first section is concerned with Curzon's early life, education, and travels. It includes papers on his Under-Secretaryship at the India Office 1891–92, and at the Foreign Office 1895–98. Curzon travelled extensively during this period, and the section covers these journeys fully; there are diaries of his two world tours, correspondence, press cuttings, and pamphlets relating to the frontiers of India, Afghanistan, Persia, and the Far East, and letters from Abdur Rahman, Amir of Afghanistan 1894–98. The general correspondence 1869–98 includes letters from Curzon's personal and political friends, while the literary papers contain his reminiscences of meetings with famous men, such as H. M. Stanley, General Gordon, and W. E. Gladstone.

The second section comprises Curzon's papers as Viceroy of India 1898-1905 and later papers relating to India. As usual there are five series of viceregal correspondence: letters to and from the sovereign, the Secretary of State and other ministers, 'persons in England and abroad', 'persons in India', and telegrams. Curzon's private correspondence is divided into general correspondence, which is arranged chronologically, and correspondence with specific individuals arranged alphabetically, eg A. J. Balfour, and Lords Knollys and Selborne.

In addition Curzon kept papers, reports, correspondence, and his minutes on every aspect of Indian administration, with particular reference to the Indian princes, military administration, and foreign and frontier policy (notably Tibet, Persia, and the new North West Frontier Province). The printed official publications include material on these subjects, as well as summaries of Curzon's administration, archaeological and educational reports, some volumes of the census of India 1901, and Curzon's printed speeches.

Curzon maintained his interest in Indian affairs after his resignation (in 1905 following a dispute with Lord Kitchener about civil control of the military in India). This correspondence is arranged alphabetically, but there are also files on major topics, such as the building of the Victoria Memorial Hall in Calcutta, the removal of the capital to Delhi, the reversal of the partition of Bengal, and Indian constitutional reforms.

The third section consists of papers dating from 1906-14 when Curzon was out of office. The predominant political themes are Unionist party policy, the 1911 parliamentary crisis, the opposition to women's suffrage, and foreign policy. Curzon also exercised considerable influence as Chancellor of Oxford University, a trustee of the National Gallery, and as President of the Royal Geographical Society at the time of Captain Scott's 1911 Antarctic Expedition.

The fourth section covers the First World War and Curzon's return to office as Lord Privy Seal. His general correspondence is arranged chronologically, while the series of Cabinet notes and correspondence from 1915 is arranged alphabetically. There are also series of Cabinet and War Council papers and files on specific issues including the Dardanelles expedition, the debate about compulsory military service, the Air Board, Ireland, and foreign affairs.

Curzon's papers as Foreign Secretary form the fifth section of the collection. These include correspondence with the principal ambassadors (Paris, Berlin, Washington) and general correspondence arranged alphabetically within years. There are files on several major problems: Europe and North Africa, the Near and Middle East, Imperial Conferences 1921 and 1923, and the first Lausanne Peace Conference.

Political papers include memoranda on his relations with Lloyd George, the fall of the Coalition in Oct 1922, and the succession to Bonar Law in May 1923.

The sixth section consists of correspondence with the royal family, and the King and Queen of the Belgians; the seventh gathers together Curzon's scrapbooks of press cuttings relating to the whole of his career (18 volumes on home affairs and 17 volumes on Persia, Afghanistan, India, and the Far East); and the eighth is devoted to Curzon's own publications, including correspondence, background notes, drafts, and proofs. The final section consists of family papers, including Curzon's correspondence with his parents and his second wife, and papers on his various houses.

Much of the correspondence, including Curzon's letters to his contemporaries, is quoted in the authorised biography by the Earl of Ronaldshay, *The Life of Lord Curzon* (3 vols, Benn 1928). The Indian papers are extensively quoted in David Dilks, *Curzon in India* (2 vols, Hart-Davis 1969–70). Other biographical works based on the papers now in the India Office Collections include Leonard Mosley, *Curzon. The End of an Epoch* (Longmans 1960), and Kenneth Rose, *Superior Person, A Portrait of Curzon and his Circle in late Victorian England* (Weidenfeld & Nicolson 1969). Curzon himself wrote of his many travels in *Tales of Travel* (Hodder & Stoughton 1923).

Curzon's electoral address in June 1886 to the electors of Southport is in the Southport Public Library (942.72 Sa). That library also holds copies of speeches published by Curzon on general political matters 1891 (825.91 S) and on the fisheries question 1892 (629.2 Sa [Pamph]), and a collection of press cuttings and cartoons about Curzon (B.20. S).

A small collection relating to Curzon's terms of office as Under-Secretary and Secretary of State at the Foreign Office has been deposited in the PRO (FO 800/28, 147–58). It includes correspondence 1886–87 (FO 800/28), 1895–98 (FO 800/147–8), volumes 15–21 of Curzon's general correspondence 1919–24 (FO 800/152–1/*58), and three volumes of correspondence 1919–23 arranged by subject.

Curzon's correspondence with his first wife, *née* Mary Leiter, is in the possession of their youngest daughter, Lady Alexandra Metcalfe. These letters were used by David Gilmour, *Curzon* (John Murray 1994). Over 40 volumes of letters 1890–1906, about 90 per cent of which were exchanged between Curzon and Mary Curzon, and most of the rest were written by Mary from India to her family in Washington, have been bequeathed by Lady Alexandra to the Oriental and India Office Collections, British Library. On Curzon's first wife see Nigel Nicolson, *Mary Curzon* (Weidenfeld 1977) and John Bradley (ed), *Lady Curzon's India: letters of a Vicereine* (Weidenfeld and Nicolson 1985).

Curzon's nephew, the 2nd Viscount Scarsdale, had further personal papers, in particular Curzon's letters to his second wife. These papers are not available for research. They include Curzon's autobiographical notes on his early life; his correspondence with his mother 1869–75; letters from the royal family for the period of his official life; papers on financial matters; and papers on the management and history of Curzon's houses.

James G. Parker's *Lord Curzon 1859–1925: A Bibliography* (Greenwood, Westport 1991) deals with Curzon's private and offical papers as well as his published works and works about him. Nayania Goradia, *Lord Curzon: The last of the British Moghuls* (Oxford UP 1994) provides an Indian perspective on the viceroyalty. A new comprehensive biography is planned by Robin J. Moore.

(EDWARD) HUGH (JOHN NEALE) DALTON, BARON DALTON (1887–1962)

Hugh Dalton was Labour MP for Camberwell (Peckham) 1924–29 and Durham (Bishop Auckland) 1929–31 and 1935–59. He was Under-Secretary of State for Foreign Affairs June 1929–Aug 1931, Minister of Economic Warfare May 1940–Feb 1942, President of the Board of Trade 1942–May 1945, Chancellor of the Exchequer July 1945–Nov 1947, Chancellor of the Duchy of Lancaster May 1948–Feb 1950, Minister of Town and Country Planning 1950–Jan 1951, and Minister of Local Government and Planning Jan-Oct 1951. He was created Baron Dalton (a life peerage) in 1960.

Some 12 linear feet of Dalton's papers have been deposited in the BLPES (Dalton Papers). The papers were re-sorted and fully listed in 1977 (NRA 16530). Not all the papers mentioned in our earlier description have been found. It is also clear that Dalton's executors weeded the collection. They removed personal, defamatory, and Cabinet papers. For example, for Dalton's Chancellorship the only important item in the collection is his diary. The collection has been divided into three parts: diaries 1916–60; unpublished material; and printed material.

The unpublished material is sub-divided into four groups: (A) papers up to 1940; (B) 1940–45; (C) 1945–60; (D) business papers, drafts of books, cartoons, photos, etc. A fifth group (E) was formed from the Dalton MSS found in the A. G. Gardiner collection after the main part of the papers had been listed. Group A includes papers from Dalton's period in office at the Foreign Office, on economic reform, defence (especially the preparedness of the RAF for war in the 1930s), as well as Labour Party papers. The latter include a diary on the expulsion of Stafford Cripps from the Labour Party in 1939 (section 3/1). Group B includes papers from Dalton's terms of office in the

Ministry of Economic Warfare (7/2), his work with the Special Operations Executive (SOE) (7/3), and his term at the Board of Trade (7/4–7). Dalton's Principal Assistant Secretary at the Board of Trade was Hugh Gaitskell; the traces of Gaitskell in the Dalton MSS include two memoranda on the personnel and operations of the Board of Trade and its Mines Department, Feb 1942. There are also minutes to the Prime Minister on meetings with mine owners and miners' representatives in 1942. Dalton's political and general correspondence for this period (8) is arranged alphabetically. It includes ministerial correspondence with Attlee, Churchill, and other members of the wartime coalition.

Group C includes what remains of Dalton's papers from the third Labour government (9/1–3), letters of congratulation, and letters from his wife Ruth 1948–52.

Group E, section 18 is a box of papers found after the main list had been completed. It includes papers from the SOE 1940–41, the Ministry of Economic Warfare 1941, and the Board of Trade 1942–43.

The printed material in the collection (Part III) includes a large number of press cuttings 1926–58, chronologically arranged. There are also articles and book reviews by Dalton, a collection of Dalton's obituary notices, and reviews of Dalton's memoirs: *Call Back Yesterday: Memoirs 1887–1931* (Muller 1953), *The Fateful Years: Memoirs 1931–1945* (Muller 1957), and *High Tide and After: Memoirs 1945–1960* (Muller 1962).

There is an invaluable bibliography and guide to relevant private papers and public records in Ben Pimlott, *Hugh Dalton* (Jonathan Cape 1985), followed by Ben Pimlott (ed), *The Political Diary of Hugh Dalton 1918–40* (Jonathan Cape 1986) and *The Second World War Diary of Hugh Dalton 1940–45* (Jonathan Cape 1986). A revised edition of Pimlott's biography appeared under the Macmillan Papermac imprint in 1986.

There are six unpublished letters from Dalton in the First World War correspondence of Professor Edward Dent in the Cambridge University Library (Add MS 7973). They include five letters from Italy in 1918 which discuss politics and the war. There are also miscellaneous letters and notes in the National Museum of Labour History.

Further papers relating to Dalton's term as Minister of Economic Warfare can be found in the PRO at CAB 127/204–12 and 217/211–12 (NRA 32409). Papers relating to Budgets are at T 171.

SIR (JOHN) COLIN CAMPBELL DAVIDSON, 1st VISCOUNT DAVIDSON (1889–1970)

Colin Davidson was Conservative MP for Hertfordshire (Hemel Hempstead) 1920–23 and 1924–37. He was Chancellor of the Duchy of Lancaster May 1923–Jan 1924 and Nov 1931–May 1937, and Parliamentary and Financial Secretary to the Admiralty Nov 1924–Dec 1926. He was created GCVO in 1935 and Viscount Davidson in 1937.

Approximately 40 linear feet of Davidson's papers formerly in the Beaverbrook Library have been deposited in the HLRO (NRA 33872). Applications for access should be addressed to the Clerk of the Records. There are many boxes of general correspondence from 1911–60s, as well as series of correspondence with individuals, such as Bonar Law and Beaverbrook, and subject files. The latter best reflect Davidson's work: they begin in 1911, when he was private secretary to the Secretary of State for the Colonies, and include correspondence between Sydney Buxton and Bonar Law in 1915 about the political situation in South Africa. There are also two volumes of cases reviewed by the Enemy Aliens Committee under regulation 14(B) 1915–17 and some printed reports of Board of Trade Committees on the position of industries after the war. There are files on manpower and recruiting, railways, Poland and Russia 1917, reparations, the Genoa Conference, and coal reparations. There are 19 files of Cabinet papers, correspondence, departmental memoranda, and other papers from Davidson's period as Chancellor of the Duchy of Lancaster 1923–24 and a further 40 files relating to his second term at the Duchy of Lancaster. The small group of files collected during Davidson's brief Admiralty appointment includes one file dealing with his role as Deputy Chief Civil Commissioner during the General Strike. From 1926–30 he was Chairman of the Conservative Party; one box of papers represents this period. There is a full descriptive list of this collection by K. V. Bligh (HLRO Memo 78, 1990).

Selections from the Davidson papers were published by Robert Rhodes James in *Memoirs of a Conservative: J. C. C. Davidson's Memoirs and Papers* (Weidenfeld & Nicolson 1969). Sir Robert informed us that a few non-political papers were retained by Davidson's family. Copies of intercepted and decoded telegrams between various Russian leaders, quoted in R. H. Ullman, *Anglo-Soviet Relations,* iii (Princeton UP 1973), are now to be found in HLRO DAV/116.

In 1980, a collection of papers relating to Davidson's Latin-American activities was transferred to the HLRO from Canning House, home of the Hispanic and Luso Brazilian Councils. HLRO Memo 78, 1990, describes these papers as well as the main Davidson collection.

A further collection of Davidson's papers was given by his widow to the Bodleian Library in 1971 (MSS Eng hist b 219–22; c 557–87; d 344–56). A list and index of the papers have been compiled (NRA 17588). The papers relate almost entirely to the period 1931–39 when Davidson was Chairman of the Indian States Enquiry Committee (Financial) – a committee which was set up by the Round Table Conference. The papers have been divided into correspondence and general papers, miscellaneous files, files concerning particular Indian states, blue books, and miscellaneous papers (mostly photos).

The first section of the papers in the Bodleian includes correspondence with Davidson's contemporaries including Ramsay MacDonald and Lord Eustace Percy, as well as leading Indian politicians. There are also reports of the committee's meetings and papers which it prepared for the Cabinet Committee on India. The miscellaneous papers include diaries kept by Davidson and his wife on their Indian tour Jan-May 1932, notes of interviews and discussions, as well as printed memoranda on the various schemes put to the committee.

The files on particular Indian states include submissions to the committee by state governments and individuals, as well as committee minutes concerning these submissions. The Blue Books are nearly all concerned with Indian constitutional reform in the 1930s; some are annotated.

WILLIAM FRANCIS DEEDES, BARON DEEDES (1913–)

William Deedes was Conservative MP for Ashford 1950–1974. He was Parliamentary Secretary, Ministry of Housing and Local Government Oct 1954–Dec 1955, Parliamentary Under-Secretary, Home Office 1955–Jan 1957, and Minister without Portfolio July 1962–Oct 1964. He was created Baron Deedes (a life peerage) in 1986.

Lord Deedes has kept very few papers relating to his period as a Cabinet minister. However, he has retained a miscellaneous collection of papers including records of interviews, correspondence, files relating to his editorship of *The Daily Telegraph*, and files on his overseas travels both as a parliamentarian and foreign correspondent.

These papers were used in Duff Hart-Davis, *The House the Berrys Built: Inside the Telegraph 1925–1986* (Hodder & Stoughton 1990), and by Michael Cockerell, *Live from Number 10: The Inside Story of Prime Ministers and Television* (Faber and Faber 1988). Mr Cockerell was also given full access to Deedes's papers, and retains copies of some of these papers, when compiling the BBC portrait, 'Dear Bill – A Film Portrait of Lord Deedes' (transmitted BBC 2, Jan 1994).

ARETAS AKERS-DOUGLAS, 1st VISCOUNT CHILSTON (1851–1926)

Aretas Akers-Douglas (known as Aretas Akers until 1875) was Conservative MP for Kent (East; St Augustine's from 1885) 1880–1911. He was Patronage Secretary to the Treasury June 1885–Jan 1886, July 1886–Aug 1892 and July 1895, First Commissioner of Works 1895–Aug 1902, and Secretary of State for Home Affairs 1902–Dec 1905. He was created Viscount Chilston in 1911, and GBE in 1920.

A very large collection of his papers has been deposited in what is now the Centre for Kentish Studies (U.564). A two-volume catalogue of the papers has been compiled (NRA 9550). A brief description is included in Felix Hull (ed), *Guide to the Kent County Archives Office* (Maidstone 1958), 166–7. The papers are generally available.

The bulk of the collection consists of correspondence. There are almost 600 separate correspondence series with individuals; the most important are those with the 3rd Marquess of Salisbury (55 letters, 1885–1900), A. J. Balfour (25 letters, 1887–1911), and W. H. Smith (174 letters, 1885–91). Akers-Douglas's political letter books 1885–1911, and estate and personal letter books 1875–1911 have also survived. There are 15 volumes of press cuttings, and Akers-Douglas's diaries for 1873–1925, though these are mainly engagement diaries. One of the letter books of Richard Middleton, Conservative Chief Party Agent 1885–1902, has also survived in the collection.

Akers-Douglas told Lord Balcarres on 25 April 1910 that he had been 'recently overhauling his old correspondence and has just lately destroyed fifty-three letters addressed to him by Queen Victoria, and over sixty from Lord Salisbury' (John Vincent, ed, *The Crawford Papers, the journals of David Lindsay, 27th Earl of Crawford and 10th Earl of Balcarres 1871–1940 during the years 1892–1940*, Manchester UP 1984, 151–2). The Chilston papers contain only one letter from the Queen.

There are extensive quotations from the collection in *Chief Whip: The Political Life and Times of Aretas Akers-Douglas, 1st Viscount Chilston* by his grandson, Eric Alexander Akers-Douglas, 3rd Viscount Chilston (Routledge & Kegan Paul 1961).

SIR THOMAS LIONEL DUGDALE, 1st Bt, 1st BARON CRATHORNE (1897–1977)

Thomas Dugdale was Unionist MP for Richmond, Yorks 1929–59. He was Junior Lord of the Treasury May 1937–Feb 1940 and Feb 1941–Feb 1942, and Minister of Agriculture and Fisheries Oct 1951–July 1954. He was created baronet in 1945 and Baron Crathorne in 1959.

A substantial collection of papers has been preserved at Crathorne House, Yarm, Cleveland TS15 0AT. The papers are the property of the 2nd Lord Crathorne to whom enquiries about access should be addressed.

The collection covers family, business, and personal affairs. Among 56 boxes of correspondence, speeches, diaries, estate papers, and ephemera are: folders relating to Lady Crathorne's book *Tennants' Stalk* (Macmillan 1973); diaries of Lord and Lady Crathorne; files on the Abdication crisis, the Crichel Down case, and miscellaneous political matters.

There are separate volumes of press cuttings, mostly post-1927; photo albums; visitors' books from 1936 onwards; game books; catalogues of the library and the silver collection.

The Crathorne papers were used by Ian Nicolson for *The Mystery of Crichel Down* (Clarendon Press, Oxford 1986). Crichel Down is also illuminated by Edward Boyle, 'Ministers and the Administrative Process', *Public Administration*, 58, 1, Spring 1980, 1–11. Extracts and paraphrases from Lady Crathorne's diary of the Abdication crisis were published in *The Observer*, 7 Dec 1986.

The PRO holds material from Crathorne's period as Minister of Agriculture and Fisheries (MAF 236/12–23).

SIR HENRY EDWARD DUKE, 1st BARON MERRIVALE (1855–1939)

Henry Duke was Conservative MP for Plymouth 1900–06 and Exeter 1910–18. He was Chief Secretary for Ireland July 1916–May 1918. He was knighted in 1918, and created Baron Merrivale in 1925.

A collection of his papers, formerly in the possession of his grandson, the 3rd Baron Merrivale, was deposited in the Bodleian Library in 1986 (Dep b 242, c 714–17). There are four volumes and one portfolio. The collection consists of correspondence and papers 1915–17, including material relating to recruitment during the First World War, the Easter uprising, food production and the establishment of the Irish Convention; correspondence and papers June-Dec 1917, mainly relating to the proposed Ministry of Health, the Irish Convention and the rise of Sinn Fein; correspondence and papers Jan 1918–Jan 1919, mainly relating to the 1916 Military Service Bill and the Irish Convention, and letters to his daughter 1918; correspondence and papers, July 1917–April 1918, originally labelled 'Side Issues' relating to Sinn Fein and public order; and a copy of *Nationality*, 28 July 1917, with miscellaneous press cuttings, July 1917, April 1918.

The collection mainly consists of letters of congratulation to Duke on his election for Plymouth, on his appointment as a Lord of Appeal and as President of the Probate, Divorce and Admiralty Division, on his peerage, and on his retirement in 1933. There is, however, a small bundle of miscellaneous correspondence from his term of office as Chief Secretary, especially for 1916–17, including letters from Asquith, Walter Long, Lord Wimborne, and General Maxwell.

The papers were first used in D. G. Boyce and Cameron Hazlehurst, 'The Unknown Chief Secretary: H. E. Duke and Ireland, 1916–18', in *Irish Historical Studies*, xx, 79, March 1977, 286–311. There is a different perspective in Eunan O'Halpin, *The Decline of the Union: British Government in Ireland 1892–1920* (Gill and Macmillan, Dublin 1987), 118–56.

SIR ANDREW RAE DUNCAN (1884–1952)

Andrew Duncan was knighted in 1921, and created GBE in 1938. He was National MP for the City of London 1940–50. He was President of the Board of Trade Jan–Oct 1940 and June 1941–Feb 1942, and Minister of Supply Oct 1940–June 1941 and Feb 1942–July 1945.

The only papers in the possession of Duncan's surviving son, Mr Gordon Duncan, were copies of the reports of some of the Royal Commissions on which Duncan served, and a volume of obituary notices privately printed by the British Iron and Steel Federation.

Private Office papers as Minister of Supply are at AVIA 11 in the PRO.

There is an entry on Duncan by Aubrey Jones in *DBB*, 2, 196–200.

LAWRENCE JOHN LUMLEY DUNDAS, 2nd MARQUESS OF ZETLAND (1876–1961)

Lawrence Dundas was known as Lord Dundas until 1892, then as the Earl of Ronaldshay until he succeeded his father as 2nd Marquess of Zetland in 1929. He was created GCIE in 1917, and KG in 1942. He was Conservative MP for Middlesex (Hornsey) 1907–16. He was Secretary of State for India (and Burma from 1937) June 1935–May 1940.

A large collection of Zetland's papers has been deposited in the North Yorkshire CRO (ZNK X 10). Most of the papers have now been sorted and arranged but listing is not yet complete. The North Yorkshire CRO has microfilmed most of its holdings and the Zetland collection is normally available only on microfilm. Permission to quote from the collection must be obtained through the CRO.

The collection contains almost no papers relating to Zetland's term at the India Office or to his work on the Round Table Conference 1930–31 but it does contain a large number of papers relating to his long interest in Indian affairs and especially to his Governorship of Bengal 1917–22.

Long before his official interest in India began, Zetland (as Lord Ronaldshay) made several tours both of India, Persia, and the Far East. Notebooks and diaries survive from some of these tours, for example a tour of Ceylon in 1898, and of China and Japan in 1906. Ronaldshay was a member of the Royal Commission on Public Services in India 1912–14. His diary of a visit to India 12 Dec 1912 to 16 April 1913, his notebooks of evidence, and memoranda survive, as well as printed minutes of evidence, and papers on the recruitment, training, pay, and organisation of the various departments.

Ronaldshay's papers as Governor of Bengal include 120 letters to and from the successive viceroys, letters from the Secretaries of State for India, and copies of three letters to the King written in 1921, including a long account of Gandhi's non-cooperation movement.

There are also papers on the 1917–18 'outrages', memoranda on several Bengali revolutionary organisations, intelligence reports, translations of revolutionary literature, and statements made by persons questioned. There are also fortnightly reports on the Bengal political situation June 1920–Feb 1922. There are many official and unofficial printed papers including reports for 1916–20 on publications registered under Act XXV of 1867, on agriculture, and on the anti-malaria campaign. There is also a file – mainly of press cuttings – on Gandhi's activities. Ronaldshay's interests also ranged from a study of Islam and Eastern philosophy to the problems of the North West Frontier.

The collection contains the manuscripts of various publications and notes for speeches, lectures, and articles, many of which were about India. There is also a series of approximately 1000 'Selected Letters', mostly social and covering the 1900s-1950s, arranged by the Marquess himself in alphabetical order. These have now been listed and are generally available for consultation. The post-1945 Zetland papers have also been deposited with the CRO but they have not yet been sorted and are therefore closed to research. On preliminary inspection they did not appear to contain material of political interest; they are mainly about personal and estate finance and Zetland's private interests such as horse-racing.

Nineteen volumes of Zetland's papers were deposited in what is now the Oriental and India Office Collections, British Library in 1961 (MSS Eur D 609; NRA 20539). They consist of some correspondence and papers as Governor of Bengal, and more as Secretary of State for India and Burma, and as a member of the Round Table Conference. The collection in the India Office Collection includes diaries Feb 1917–March 1922. The diaries were kept at irregular intervals but contain fairly full descriptions of his activities and opinions.

A further collection of papers discovered by his family in 1973 has been added to the papers in the India Office Collection. The collection includes manuscript and typed drafts of Zetland's life of Curzon, a few miscellaneous letters, and about 20 photo albums covering his travels and his term of office in Bombay. The Zetland Collection in the India Office Collection now consists of 72 volumes, one box and 11 files.

Papers relating to the Zetland's Kerse estate are held by the SRO (NRA 10745).

In his volume of memoirs, *Essayez* (Murray 1957), Zetland quoted from many of his letters and from his diaries. Zetland's role in Indian affairs is discussed in Robin Moore, *The Crisis of Indian Unity, 1917–1940* (Clarendon Press, Oxford 1974), and *Churchill, Cripps and India 1939–1945* (Clarendon Press, Oxford 1979); and Carl Bridge, *Holding India to the Empire* (Sterling Publishers Private, New Delhi 1986).

SIR DAVID McADAM ECCLES, 1st VISCOUNT ECCLES (1904–)

David Eccles was Conservative MP for Chippenham 1943–62. He was Minister of Works Nov 1951–Oct 1954, Minister of Education 1954–Jan 1957, President of the Board of Trade 1957–Oct 1959, Minister of Education 1959–July 1962, and Paymaster-General and Minister for the Arts June 1970–Dec 1973. He was created KCVO in 1953, Baron Eccles in 1962, and Viscount Eccles in 1964.

Lord Eccles advised us that he has retained 'copies of my speeches, a letter or two from Churchill, and several from Macmillan, Rab Butler & others'. These papers, which are not available for research, will be bequeathed to Lord Eccles' son, the Hon John Eccles.

In 1979, Lord Eccles deposited two wallet files of his constituency papers in the Wiltshire CRO (WRO 1611). The papers consist of election papers and handbills for the Oct 1951 general election and miscellaneous notes and transcripts of speeches 1946–59. They have not been catalogued.

Eccles published *By Safe Hand: Letters of Sybil and David Eccles 1939–42* (Bodley Head 1983), a collection of correspondence with his first wife while he served overseas as a Counsellor in the Diplomatic Service. The edition contains less than half of the surviving five or six hundred letters and includes a few other documents.

There are autobiographical observations in other works by Eccles, notably: *Half-Way to Faith* (Geoffrey Bles 1966), *Life and Politics: A Moral Diagnosis* (Longmans 1967), and *On Collecting* (Longmans 1968).

Dennis Dean's article, 'Preservation or Renovation? The Dilemmas of Conservative Educational Policy 1955–1960', *Twentieth Century British History*, 3, 1, 1992, 3–31, is a valuable source on relevant PRO files.

JAMES CHUTER EDE, BARON CHUTER-EDE (1882–1965)

James Chuter Ede was Labour MP for Surrey (Mitcham) March–Nov 1923 and South Shields 1929–31 and 1935–64. He was Parliamentary Secretary to the Ministry of Education May 1940–May 1945, and Secretary of State for Home Affairs Aug 1945–Oct 1951. He was created Baron Chuter-Ede (a life peerage) in 1964.

After his death, Chuter Ede's papers were carefully examined and divided by his executors. A few papers were removed by the Cabinet Office; correspondence with the BBC, the British Museum, and the County Councils Association was returned to them. It seems probable that papers of an 'ultra-confidential' nature – such as correspondence with ex-prisoners – was destroyed. Certainly three Home Office files were destroyed.

Chuter Ede's library, literary writings, photos, and press cuttings were deposited in the Epsom Borough Library. The collection has not been catalogued, but is freely available for research. Prior notification of intent to consult the papers is, however, advised as space is limited. Some personal memorabilia are held at the Epsom and Ewell Museum, Bourne Hall, Ewell.

Fourteen volumes of Chuter Ede's diaries for 1941–45 and 1952 and a few other papers have been deposited in the British Library (Add MSS 59690–703). They contain a day-by-day description of the passage of the 1944 Education Act. They are available for research. The diaries were edited by Kevin Jeffreys as *Labour and the Wartime Coalition: From the Diary of James Chuter-Ede, 1941–45* (The Historians' Press 1987).

The British Library has received an addition to the collection, consisting of correspondence with Viscount Cecil of Chelwood 1946–49 (Add MS 51192).

Other papers relating to education were returned to the Department of Education and Science. They are now available at the PRO among the department's Private Office papers (ED 136). Some papers were also returned to the Home and Colonial Offices.

Chuter Ede was the Deputy Chairman of the BBC's General Advisory Council 1952–59 and the two files of correspondence returned to the BBC are available at the BBC's Written Archives Centre. The letters refer to Chuter Ede's participation in, and reactions to, radio and television programmes 1956–64. As well as Chuter Ede's own papers, the BBC has among its archives papers relating to Chuter Ede, including a series of press cuttings. There are also transcripts of his broadcasts including an interview, transmitted in 1960, with George Scott, Mrs D. Pickles, and Mrs J. Hubback, in which he answered questions relating to his career and beliefs.

His remaining papers were deposited in the Surrey RO in 1966 (390). A further deposit of papers was made by Chuter Ede's sister in 1971. The collection includes some South Shields constituency papers; papers relating to his work with the National Union of Teachers and with Surrey County Council; some general correspondence; diaries for 1946, 1–7 Jan 1948, and 1949; and some early personal papers – applications for teaching posts and testimonials 1903–10, and a letter written to his parents on the eve of his departure for France Sept 1914. There are letters from Hugh Dalton and Clement Attlee on the invasion of Czechoslovakia 1938–39. Some of the papers dealing with constituency business, police matters, religious affairs, and education are still restricted. The collection has been listed (NRA 20267). Permission to examine it must be obtained from the County Archivist, Surrey RO. Documents which are subject to restricted access may, at the discretion of the County Archivist, be made available to *bona fide* researchers who sign an undertaking not to identify individuals in any published work, and who provide a testimonial from a recognised authority.

SIR (ROBERT) ANTHONY EDEN, 1st EARL OF AVON (1897-1977)

Anthony Eden was Conservative MP for Warwickshire (Warwick and Leamington) 1923-57. He was Parliamentary Under-Secretary of State for Foreign Affairs Sept 1931-Dec 1933, Lord Privy Seal 1933-June 1935, Minister without Portfolio for League of Nations Affairs June-Dec 1935, Secretary of State for Foreign Affairs 1935-Feb 1938, Dec 1940-July 1945 and Oct 1951-April 1955, Secretary of State for Dominion Affairs Sept 1939-May 1940, Secretary of State for War May-Dec 1940, and Prime Minister and Leader of the Conservative Party April 1955-Jan 1957. He was created KG in 1954, and Earl of Avon in 1961.

Lord Avon's papers were formally deposited in the Birmingham University Library in 1990. They contain his personal and political papers, and are supplemented by the original Foreign Office papers for his periods as Foreign Secretary (FO 954), for which the University Library acts as a PRO Licensed Repository (microfilms are available at Kew). There is a handlist of the whole collection (NRA 28779). Access is by written application to the Librarian. The Avon Trustees have retained for the time being the right to grant access and permission to publish extracts from the Avon Papers, but these *must* be sought through the University Library. A number of personal files are withheld from consultation for the present time.

There are also Foreign Office papers in the PRO at FO 800/750-851 and War Office papers at WO 259.

In his three volumes of memoirs, *Full Circle, Facing the Dictators* and *The Reckoning* (Cassell 1960-65), Lord Avon quoted frequently from his notes, diaries, and correspondence. His *Another World, 1897-1917* (Allen Lane 1976) covers his war service years. Sir Robert Rhodes James was granted exclusive access to all of Eden's papers for his official biography *Anthony Eden* (Weidenfeld and Nicolson 1986).

David Carlton's *Anthony Eden: A Biography* (Allen Lane 1981) draws on the papers which are now at Birmingham as well as other PRO papers, as does A. R. Peters, *Anthony Eden at the Foreign Office 1931-1938* (Gower, Aldershot 1986). Victor Rothwell's *Anthony Eden: A political biography 1931-57* (Manchester UP 1992) makes some use of the Birmingham collection but is based mainly on published sources.

There are relevant documents from Foreign Office, Prime Minister, and Cabinet Office files in Roger Bullen and M. E. Pelly (eds), *Documents on British Policy Overseas*, Series II, vol I, (HMSO 1986). The Foreign Office files were used in David Goldsworthy (ed), *British Documents on the End of Empire, Series A*, vol III, *The Conservative Government and the End of Empire 1951-1957* (3 vols, HMSO 1994).

The Sayer Archive holds material on Eden. The Conservative Party

Archives in the Bodleian Library should also be consulted.

D. R. Thorpe has been commissioned by the Countess of Avon to write a new, authorised life of Eden. This is not expected to be published before 2000. In the meantime there is a comprehensive guide to archival and published sources in Alan Lawrence and Peter Dodd (eds), *Anthony Eden, 1897–1977: A Bibliography* (Greenwood Press, Westport 1995).

NESS EDWARDS (1897–1968)

Ness Edwards was Labour MP for Glamorganshire (Caerphilly) 1939–68. He was Parliamentary Secretary to the Ministry of Labour and National Service Aug 1945–Feb 1950, and Postmaster-General 1950–Oct 1951.

Edwards's son, Mr Rhys Edwards, advised us that his father had few papers because 'like most of the old students of the Central Labour College, they kept their records in their minds'.

The South Wales Coalfield Archive at the Main Library, University of Wales, Swansea, contains a very small collection of papers relating to Edwards including an undated pamphlet, 'Is this the road?'; a 1933 union application from Edwards to the SWMF; a High Court Order from Powell Duffryn Steam Coal Co Ltd of 6 Nov 1935 restraining Edwards and others from trespassing upon the Windsor Colliery, Abertridwr, and from holding a show of cards there; an open letter from Edwards at the SWMF to the Bedwas Workmen 3 June 1936; and an election handbill of Edwards as Labour candidate for Caerphilly parliamentary election March 1966 (SWCC: MND/17). There are also miscellaneous letters from Edwards amongst the constituency correspondence of D. J. Williams 1961–64 (SWCC: MNA/PP/127).

The Welsh Political Archive at the National Library of Wales holds only one stray letter from Edwards 1966 (James Griffiths papers C5/40). They do not know of any other material apart from miscellaneous papers relating to Edwards scattered throughout the records of the PRO and the National Museum of Labour History. The Glamorgan RO does not have any Edwards papers.

WALTER ELLIOT ELLIOT (1888–1958)

Walter Elliot was Conservative MP for Lanarkshire (Lanark) 1918–23, Glasgow (Kelvingrove) 1924–45 and 1950–58 and the Scottish Universities 1946–50. He was Parliamentary Secretary and Minister of Health for Scotland Jan 1923–Jan 1924 and Nov 1924–July 1926, Parliamentary Under-Secretary of State for Scotland 1926–July 1929, Financial Secretary to the Treasury Sept 1931–Sept 1932, Minister of Agriculture and Fisheries 1932–Oct 1936, Secretary of State for Scotland 1936–May 1938, and Minister of Health 1938–May 1940.

Almost all of Elliot's surviving papers were presented to the NLS (Acc 6721; NRA 29242) by his widow, the Baroness Elliot of Harwood, in 1976. The collection consists of ten boxes of letters, speeches, press cuttings, articles, photos, election addresses, a small quantity of official papers, and 38 volumes of press cuttings. A brief list is available.

Among Elliot's correspondents are Winston Churchill, Anthony Eden, R. A. Butler, Brendan Bracken, Harold Macmillan, and Chaim Weizmann. There are subject files dealing with Elliot's literary projects, Anglo-German relations 1946–57, foreign affairs (including the Suez crisis), the H-Bomb, overseas travel, and civil aviation in Scotland.

There is material relating to the biography by Sir Colin Coote, *A Companion of Honour* (Collins 1965) and a title index of Elliot's speeches. The press cutting volumes, some of which contain correspondence, notes, and memorabilia, cover the period 1920–58. Four files of papers dealing with Zionism and Israel were returned to Lady Elliot in 1975.

Private Office papers relating to Elliot's period at the Scottish Office are dispersed through the files of the five main Scottish Office departments held at the SRO.

There is a well documented chapter on 'Walter Elliot and the corporatist challenge' in Andrew Fenton Cooper, *British Agricultural Policy, 1912–36: A Study in Conservative Politics* (Manchester UP 1989).

Elliot's early life and ministerial career to 1936 are recounted in Elizabeth M. M. Taylor, 'The Politics of Walter Elliot 1929–1936' (PhD thesis, University of Edinburgh 1979). Taylor made use of the Elliot papers in the NLS and in the possession of Lady Elliot and provides a useful guide to relevant Dominion Office and Ministry of Agriculture and Fisheries files.

Reference should also be made to J. W. R. Mitchell, 'The emergence of Modern Scottish central administration 1885–1939' (DPhil thesis, Oxford University 1987).

ALFRED EMMOTT, BARON EMMOTT (1858–1926)

Alfred Emmott was Liberal MP for Oldham 1899–1911. He was Under-Secretary of State for the Colonies Oct 1911–Aug 1914, and First Commissioner of Works 1914–May 1915. He was created Baron Emmott in 1911, GCMG in 1914, and GBE in 1917.

A small collection of his papers was deposited in 1968 by his grand-daughter, Mrs J. Simon, in the Nuffield College Library (Emmott papers). The papers have been listed (NRA 17309). Mrs Simon informed us that many papers were probably destroyed when Lady Emmott moved house many years ago. The papers now in Nuffield were inherited by Emmott's elder daughter, Mrs Simon's mother.

The most important items in this collection are probably two volumes of diary for 24 Feb 1907–3 Oct 1915. Mrs Simon's permission must be obtained for quotations from the diaries. On 25 Oct 1908 Emmott wrote in his diary 'I am hoping now to keep a Parliamentary Diary, but must write it at the House. I began on a sheet of note paper the other day.' On 6 Dec 1908 he recorded 'I have made one or two notes at the House on how events there have struck me during the week'. No parliamentary diary can now be found.

The correspondence has been arranged in a single chronological series 1890–1927. The only exception to this arrangement is a file of papers from the Foreign Office Committee on the political situation in Russia which Emmott chaired 1920–21. The collection has some interesting correspondence on the discontent of some Liberals with Campbell-Bannerman's leadership of the party 1900–01, correspondence on the Congo Reform Association 1904–08, and on the War Trade Department which Emmott organised and ran 1915–19. There is also a considerable collection of press cuttings arranged in chronological order, and letters of condolence to Lady Emmott on his death. There are also notes by Mrs Simon on the provenance of these papers, on Emmott's family and early life, and extracts from some letters by Emmott to his elder daughter 1906–26 (the originals of these letters are not available for research).

A further five files of Emmott's papers, originally deposited in the House of Commons Library in 1965 by Mrs Simon, are now held in the HLRO (HC LIB MSS No 41). They include letters and memoranda concerning Winston Churchill 1900–11 (typed copies of some of these are included in the Nuffield collection), election manifestos, photos, press cuttings 1905–22, a note of Emmott's voting record in the House of Commons 1899 and 1900, and letters and memoranda concerning Emmott's work as Chairman of Ways and Means 1906–11. (See Maurice F. Bond, *Guide to the Records of Parliament*, HMSO 1971, p. 294).

The HLRO also holds copies of a few letters of condolence to Lady Emmott on the death of her husband. The originals, which were deposited in the Oldham Public Library in 1962, could not be traced in 1993 by the newly formed Archives Service in the Local Studies Library, Oldham.

Three letters between Emmott and Asquith in 1911 on the question of honours for women have been deposited in the Fawcett Library, London Guildhall University.

FREDERICK JAMES ERROLL, 1st BARON ERROLL OF HALE (1914–)

Frederick Erroll was Conservative MP for Altrincham and Sale 1945–64. He was Parliamentary Secretary, Ministry of Supply April 1955–Nov 1956, Parliamentary Secretary, Board of Trade 1956–Oct 1958, Economic Secretary to the Treasury 1958–Oct 1959, Minister of State,

Board of Trade 1959–Oct 1961, President of the Board of Trade 1961–Oct 1963, and Minister of Power 1963–Oct 1964. He was created Baron Erroll of Hale in 1964.

According to Cook (*Sources*, 3, p. 149) Lord Erroll 'retained his personal papers and has made arrangements for their safe keeping'. Lord Erroll advised us that he did not retain any correspondence or documentation referring to his time as a minister April 1955 to Oct 1964.

SIR LAMING WORTHINGTON-EVANS, 1st Bt (1868–1931)

Laming Worthington-Evans was Conservative MP for Colchester (Essex, Colchester from 1918) 1910–29 and Westminster (St George's) 1929–31. He was Parliamentary Secretary to the Ministry of Munitions Dec 1916–May 1918, Minister of Blockade July 1918–Jan 1919, Minister of Pensions 1919–April 1920, Minister without Portfolio 1920– Feb 1921, Secretary of State for War 1921–Oct 1922 and Nov 1924–June 1929, and Postmaster-General May 1923–Jan 1924. He was created a baronet in 1916 (at which time he assumed the additional surname of Worthington), and GBE in 1922.

Sixty-one boxes and volumes of his papers were given to the Bodleian Library by his son, the late Sir Shirley Worthington-Evans Bt, in 1972 (MSS Eng hist c 890–940, d 424–7, e 319–20, f 26). The papers have been listed (NRA 20696). A large number of Cabinet papers, some of which were annotated, were removed by the Cabinet Office in 1935. A list of these papers survives but the papers themselves have either been lost or destroyed, notwithstanding an undertaking given at the time to retain those which were annotated. The papers which remain are entirely political: there are no papers concerning Worthington-Evans's early life, his years as a solicitor, or any later personal papers.

Worthington-Evans first stood (unsuccessfully) for Parliament in 1906. A file of receipts and a return of expenses survive from this contest. Press cuttings, posters, buttons, election addresses, and other printed ephemera survive from his later election campaigns as well as some accounts, memoranda on the organisation of the constituency workers, canvass returns, and the reports of political 'missionaries', and some constituency correspondence.

Very little survives relating to Worthington-Evans's activities as a back-bencher. There are some press cuttings on state insurance and the National Insurance Act 1912–14. From 1915–16 some press cuttings survive, many concerning the commandeering of American securities and other aspects of war financing, such as the Women's War Loan scheme. There is also some correspondence dating from 1915–16. There are few papers relating to his term of office at the War and Foreign

Offices and the Ministry of Munitions; there are no papers relating to his terms of office as Minister of Blockade or Pensions.

There are several files concerning Ireland 1918–25. There is a list of contents to several of these files. They include Cabinet memoranda and, for 1921 and 1922, some weekly surveys of the situation by the Chief Secretary and by the General Officer Commanding. The papers include minutes of six meetings May-Nov 1920 of the Amendments Committee for the Government of Ireland Bill, minutes of conferences and notes of meetings with Irish leaders Oct-Nov 1921, a printed report of the proceedings of the Irish Convention, drafts of bills from 1914 to 1920, and the Articles of Agreement of the Irish Treaty. Much material exists relating to an Arbitration Committee to decide on the contributions and compensations of the English and Irish Governments. The committee appears to have sat from 1923 (at least) until 1925. Its papers include memoranda, correspondence, transcripts of meetings, reports, and a Final Report. There is also a copy of a drawing of Arthur Griffith by Paul Henry which was given to the Irish Free State in 1923. In a file of War Office papers there are several memoranda on the Irish military situation, the activities of Sinn Feiners after the 'truce', and the need to minimise the risk of misunderstanding about the terms of the truce.

There are many files on various aspects of finance and related problems for the period 1920–30; the Imperial Exchange and Currency, the Geddes committee's recommendations, a turnover tax, unemployment, various types of State Insurance, and political levies, are all considered in Cabinet memoranda, notes, articles, and correspondence. The problems of reparations and interallied indebtedness are also represented; these papers include a proposal by Worthington-Evans to neutralise the advantage to Germany of a depreciated mark by an exports tax. There are seven boxes relating to the Genoa Conference of 1922; they contain verbatim reports, notes on the delegates, Cabinet memoranda, and a letter from R. S. Horne, then Chancellor of the Exchequer, 23 April 1922, written in response to pressure from the King, urging that the negotiations with the Russians be conditional on an end to Bolshevik propaganda. There are also Cabinet memoranda on Iraq and Palestine 1921, 1922, and some correspondence with Lord Robert Cecil Aug 1922 on the implementation of the disarmament clauses of the peace treaties.

There are very few papers directly concerning Worthington-Evans's work at the War Office and the Post Office. There is a draft note on administering and accounting for expenditure at the War Office in 1923, and some Cabinet memoranda on attempts to reduce expenditure after the Geddes report. For a few days in March 1922 Worthington-Evans acted as Secretary of State for India. There is correspondence on Indian railways, copies of telegrams exchanged with the Viceroy, and some correspondence with the succeeding Secretary of State, Viscount Peel. There are two boxes of speeches from 1920 until 1930.

There are some papers concerning national politics, in particular Baldwin's election as leader of the Conservative Party and his decision to call a general election on tariff reform. There are letters from Austen Chamberlain in May 1923 and a memo on the events of May and June of that year. Worthington-Evans also wrote a 22–page memo on the events of Oct 1923. He was on various Unionist Party committees and, particularly for 1924, there are memoranda and minutes of meetings. In 1928 he was on the Cabinet committee which considered Conservative policy proposals, and some memoranda, minutes, and correspondence of this committee have been preserved.

Some of Worthington-Evans's papers as Parliamentary Secretary at the Ministry of Munitions have survived with official papers and are to be seen at the PRO (MUN 4/396–451). They include papers of the War Priorities Committee on commercial intelligence, supplies of various chemicals, and minutes of meetings with heads of departments 1917–18. These papers would appear to be those described in a list compiled at the Ministry in 1918 and now found in the PRO (MUN 5/25/262.1/25).

SIR AILWYN EDWARD FELLOWES, 1st BARON AILWYN (1855–1924)

Ailwyn Fellowes was Conservative MP for Huntingdonshire (North) 1887–1906. He was President of the Board of Agriculture March-Dec 1905. He was created KCVO in 1911, and Baron Ailwyn in 1921.

Neither Fellowes's son, the 3rd Lord Ailwyn, nor the widow of the 2nd Lord Ailwyn knew of any papers other than a volume of speeches made by Fellowes when he was President of the Board of Agriculture and a collection of invitations, royal commands, and tickets for parliamentary and state occasions 1897–1904 presented by Lord Ailwyn to the HLRO in 1981 (Hist Coll 287). The Hon Andrew Fellowes advised us that Fellowes's scrapbooks were cut up and distributed to several record offices.

Two of the scrapbooks were temporarily deposited in the Cambridgeshire RO, Huntingdon in 1974, where they were listed. The larger scrapbook contained press cuttings, correspondence, telegrams, photos, and miscellaneous social documents, including papers relating to the 1895, 1900, and 1906 general elections (1830, 1932, 1888–1907). The smaller scrapbook contained press cuttings and correspondence 1837–1911.

Mr Fellowes deposited part of the larger scrapbook in the Cambridgeshire RO, Huntingdon in late 1993. This deposit included a cartoon poster of the Huntingdonshire county election in 1830; some election propaganda; a letter from Fellowes to the press regarding the Devon Chamber of Agriculture; some reports of Fellowes's attendance at non-political and non-agricultural events; and a press report regarding some amateur theatricals from 1902. The Cambridgeshire RO, Huntingdon, also holds estate records.

The Norfolk CRO has a fragment of the smaller scrapbook relating to the 1911 Royal Norfolk Agricultural Show (Acc 20/2/74).

The fate of the remainder of the scrapbooks is unknown.

SIR RONALD CRAUFORD MUNRO-FERGUSON, VISCOUNT NOVAR (1860–1934)

Ronald Munro-Ferguson (his father assumed the additional surname of Munro in 1864) was Liberal MP for Ross and Cromarty 1884–85 and Leith Burghs 1886–1914. He was Secretary for Scotland Oct 1922– Jan 1924. He was created GCMG in 1914, Viscount Novar in 1920, and KT in 1926.

His nephew, Mr A. B. Munro-Ferguson holds three box-files of Novar's letters to his wife 1891–1913. The letters are full of uninhibited discussion of political affairs, particularly concerning relations between Lord Rosebery and Sir William Harcourt. Lord Rosebery's letters to Novar were returned to the Rosebery family and are part of the Rosebery collection. Mr Munro-Ferguson also holds his uncle's 1914–20 diaries, several photo albums and a large cutting book. Inquiries concerning access to these papers should be addressed to the NRA(S) (survey no 505).

A collection of Novar's papers (seven foot-run) relating to his term-of-office as Governor-General of Australia 1914–20 was deposited by his trustees in the Manuscript Section of the National Library of Australia in 1961 (MS 696). A detailed list and name index of the collection have been compiled (NRA 22805). The collection includes Novar's personal and official dispatches to the King, his personal and official correspondence with successive Secretaries of State for the Colonies, and his correspondence with Australian Prime Ministers, as well as correspondence with Australian politicians and officials. There are also a large number of subject files covering a wide range of subjects: from constitutional issues, and the question of channels of communication with England, to the visit in 1920 of the Prince of Wales. The NRA(S) has a copy of the list of these papers.

In 1935 Lady Novar presented three bundles of her husband's letters, totalling approximately nine shelf inches, to the Australian War Memorial (Acc No 3DRL/2574). The three groups are copies of letters from Novar to the King 1914–20; copies of letters from Novar to Sir William Birdwood 1915–20; and letters from Sir William Birdwood to

Novar 1915–20. The Novar/Birdwood correspondence is open for research, but readers must sign an agreement indemnifying the Australian War Memorial against any legal action that may arise as a result of publication of material in the collection.

We were advised by Professor John Poynter of the University of Melbourne, who is working on an edition of selections from Novar's papers and diaries in his Australian years, that a transcript of the diaries for 1915 and 1917–20, currently held by Mr Munro-Ferguson, will be deposited in the National Library of Australia with the other Novar papers.

Private Office papers relating to Novar's period at the Scottish Office are dispersed through the files of the five main Scottish Office departments held at the SRO.

Reference should be made to J. W. R. Mitchell, 'The emergence of Modern Scottish central administration 1885–1939' (DPhil thesis, Oxford University 1987).

SIR ROBERT BANNATYNE FINLAY, 1st VISCOUNT FINLAY (1842–1929)

Robert Finlay was Liberal MP for Inverness Burghs 1885–86; he became a Liberal Unionist in 1886 and held the seat 1886–92 and 1895–1906; he was Conservative MP for Edinburgh and St Andrews Universities 1910–16. He was Solicitor-General Aug 1895–May 1900, Attorney-General 1900–Dec 1905, and Lord Chancellor Dec 1916–Jan 1919. He was knighted in 1895, and created GCMG in 1904, Baron Finlay in 1916, and Viscount Finlay in 1919.

At the time our first edition was published it was understood that Lord Finlay's grand-daughter, the Hon Lady Hayes, of Wemyss House, Nigg, Ross & Cromarty, Scotland, had a very small collection of papers. It included press cuttings, menu cards, and a few letters commiserating with Finlay when he was not appointed Lord Chancellor in May 1915 and congratulating him when he was appointed in Dec 1916. Some of the latter had been quoted in *Lord Chancellors 1*.

We were also advised that a further collection of papers, formerly in the possession of Finlay's solicitors, had been added to the collection held by Lady Hayes. Most of these papers were said to concern Finlay's various estates and property but there were also some papers of legal and political interest. There was a memo written by Finlay in Dec 1910, describing the negotiations between government and opposition over the Parliament Bill. A copy of this memo is available in Austen Chamberlain's papers (AC 10/2/57); it is quoted in Chamberlain's *Politics from Inside. An Epistolary Chronicle, 1906–1914* (Cassell 1936), 295–7. There were also some papers relating to Finlay's work on the 1903 Alaskan boundary dispute, his views on how to deal with the 1912 strikers, and his opinion on the need for re-election of ministers brought into the government or given new portfolios 1915–16.

However, Lady Hayes now advises that she has never had 'anything relevant in my possession here or in our previous home, Arabella House'.

The only exception is a collection of letters exchanged between Finlay and his wife before their marriage. These letters were previously in the possession of Finlay's nephew, the late David Thomson. They are not available for research.

HERBERT ALBERT LAURENS FISHER (1865–1940)

Herbert Fisher was Liberal MP for Sheffield (Hallam) 1916–18 and for the English Universities 1918–26. He was President of the Board of Education Dec 1916–Oct 1922.

Two hundred and fifty-six boxes and volumes of his papers are held by the Bodleian Library (MSS Fisher 1–251, MS Fisher adds 1). A detailed catalogue has been prepared which includes an index (NRA 16446).

Most of Fisher's life was spent in the academic, rather than the political, world and his papers reflect this balance: there are lecture notes, bibliographies, articles, reviews, manuscripts, and reviews of Fisher's books. These include the manuscript of his memoirs, *An Unfinished Autobiography* (Oxford UP 1940). There are, however, several boxes of papers derived from his official career. These include Board of Education memoranda, and papers relating to the 1918 Education Act. There are also Cabinet papers on various topics, including liquor control 1920, gas warfare, the League of Nations, and Ireland. Fisher kept a diary for part of his term in office 21 Nov 1917–14 Dec 1922 and subsequently, from 8 Feb 1923 to 8 Dec 1924; this is included in the collection. There are diaries for various tours he made, for example to Holland in 1910, and to the USA in 1930. There are also notes made by Fisher of conversations with Lord Rosebery in 1909, with Lord Morley in 1911, and with Lloyd George in 1916.

Apart from his work at the Board of Education, Fisher served on several committees and commissions. There is correspondence on the 1912 Royal Commission on Indian Public Services, and memoranda on alleged German war atrocities.

There are several boxes of general correspondence covering Fisher's entire life, including letters to his wife 1907–40 (some of which are only available with the written permission of their daughter Mary Bennett), and letters to Gilbert and Lady Mary Murray 1890–1939. There is also a collection of correspondence between Fisher and Margaret Woods 1897–1934 (MS Eng lett e 26).

MS Fisher adds 1 consists of the Fishers' household accounts 1899–1942.

At New College, Oxford, of which Fisher was Warden from 1925 until his death, there are 19 files of correspondence written by and to him by students and parents relating to the 1926 General Strike (2802). The collection is available to *bona fide* scholars who should write to the Archivist, The Library, New College, Oxford OX1 3BN.

David Ogg, *Herbert Fisher* (Edward Arnold 1947), quotes from the papers in the Bodleian.

WILLIAM HAYES FISHER, BARON DOWNHAM (1853–1920)

William Hayes Fisher was Conservative MP for Fulham 1885–1906 and 1910–18. He was Financial Secretary to the Treasury Aug 1902–April 1903, Parliamentary Secretary to the Local Government Board May 1915–June 1917, President of the Local Government Board 1917–Nov 1918, and Chancellor of the Duchy of Lancaster and Minister of Information 1918–Jan 1919. He was created Baron Downham in 1918.

A small bundle of Hayes Fisher's letters has survived in the possession of his grandson, Mr Peter Hayes Fisher.

There are few papers relating to Hayes Fisher's official career. There is a letter from A. J. Balfour in Nov 1905, explaining why Hayes Fisher could not be offered a Privy Councillorship (see *Lord Chancellors 1*, 254–5 and 366). Hayes Fisher was finally created a Privy Councillor in July 1911; Asquith's letter informing him that the King had approved the granting of the honour, and the official notice of his taking the oath, with a covering letter from the Privy Council's clerk, have all survived. There is also a three-page typed memo about Hayes Fisher's appointment as Parliamentary Secretary to the Local Government Board with some relevant telegrams.

The remaining papers are miscellaneous letters, including three letters from Princess Louise about charity work, 1903 and 1916, a summons to attend Parliament 1886, and a letter from Balfour about the Royal Patriotic Fund Corporation Dec 1903.

GEOFFREY WILLIAM RICHARD HUGH FITZCLARENCE, 5th EARL OF MUNSTER (1906–1975)

Geoffrey FitzClarence succeeded his uncle as 5th Earl of Munster in 1928. He was made KBE in 1957. He was Paymaster-General June 1938–Jan 1939, Parliamentary Under-Secretary of State for War Jan–Sept 1939, Parliamentary Under-Secretary of State for India and Burma Jan 1943–Oct 1944, Under-Secretary of State for Home Affairs 1944–July 1945, Under-Secretary of State for Colonial Affairs Oct 1951–Oct 1954, and Minister Without Portfolio 1954–Jan 1957.

For the first edition the Earl of Munster informed us that he had no papers of interest.

Munster's nephew, John Birkbeck, Litcham Hall, King's Lynn, Norfolk PE32 2QQ, has his uncle's surviving papers. They are available for research, although they are not indexed and Mr Birkbeck doubts they are of much interest. The papers include the diary of General Lord Gort; the despatches of the operations of the British Expeditionary Force; the second despatch of the Commander in Chief BEF France Feb 1st–May 31st 1940; and a report of Lord Munster's welfare tour of India. There are also a few boxes of letters, many of which are congratulatory on Munster becoming a Minister, and many of which concern his relationship with King William IV, of whom he was a direct descendant.

LORD EDMOND GEORGE PETTY-FITZMAURICE, BARON FITZMAURICE (1846–1935)

Lord Edmond Fitzmaurice was created Baron Fitzmaurice in 1905. He was Liberal MP for Calne 1868–85 and Wiltshire (Cricklade) 1898–1905. He was Under-Secretary of State for Foreign Affairs Jan 1883–June 1885 and Dec 1905–Oct 1908, and Chancellor of the Duchy of Lancaster 1908–June 1909. Eleven box-files of his papers are in the possession of the Trustees of the Bowood Collection, Bowood Estate Office, Bowood, Calne, Wiltshire SN11 0LZ.

Fitzmaurice had himself sorted through his papers – as an historical biographer he was clearly well aware of the problems of historians – and some of his papers have explanatory notes or comments by him. He arranged the papers, most of which take the form of correspondence, by writer and then in date order, with a few subject and miscellaneous files. This original arrangement has been retained.

There is one box-file of 'general correspondence', that is, correspondence consisting of fewer than five letters to or from an individual. This general correspondence is arranged alphabetically by the writers' names; it was not possible to check whether a particular writer occurs under his family name, courtesy title, or last title so all these names should be checked. The exception to this is the Fitzmaurice or Lansdowne family itself who are all grouped together under Fitzmaurice rather than being scattered between the two names. It is remarkable that the collection includes only four letters to Fitzmaurice from his brother, the 5th Marquess of Lansdowne, despite their overlapping and long political lives. The four, which are in the general correspondence in this collection, were written in June 1909, when Fitzmaurice resigned because of his ill-health, and they bear witness to a close personal relationship. The outside of each file in this section gives the names of the correspondents and the dates of their letters.

Fitzmaurice's 'Special', or extensive, correspondence fills seven box-files. A list of the dates of the letters is on the outside of the file for each correspondent. There are long series of correspondence with Sir Henry Campbell-Bannerman 1900–07, James Bryce 1900–21, Lord Crewe 1906–33, Sir Charles Dilke 1876–1908, Lord Eversley 1912–28, W. E. Gladstone 1874–98, Lord Granville 1880–98, Sir Edward Grey 1905–08, Lord Ripon 1905–09, the 6th Earl Spencer 1910–22, and J. A. Spender 1905–35. The last two series in particular are full of political discussion.

The three box-files of subject files include correspondence 1876–77 to Frank H. Hill, Political Editor of the *Daily News*, on the Balkan situation, a few Foreign Office printed memoranda and correspondence, some drafts of Foreign Office letters and memoranda by Fitzmaurice, and correspondence 1907–08 about Congo Reform with Lord Cromer, E. D. Morel, and John Harris. The miscellaneous files include press cuttings, 1898 election leaflets, and some verses by Fitzmaurice.

Following Fitzmaurice's death, his family returned to Brigadier-General J. H. Morgan a large group of letters which he had written to Fitzmaurice (J. H. Morgan, *Assize of Arms, Being the Story of the Disarmament of Germany and her Rearmament* [*1919–1939*], 2 vols, Methuen 1945, i, p. 34). It has not been possible to determine whether these letters have survived, as the whereabouts of Morgan's own papers are now uncertain.

HENRY CHARLES KEITH PETTY-FITZMAURICE, 5th MARQUESS OF LANSDOWNE (1845–1927)

Henry Petty-Fitzmaurice was known as Viscount Clanmaurice until 1863, then as the Earl of Kerry until 1866 when he succeeded his father as 5th Marquess of Lansdowne. He was created GCMG in 1884, and KG in 1895. He was Under-Secretary of State for War April 1872–Feb 1874, Under-Secretary of State for India April-July 1880, Secretary of State for War June 1895–Nov 1900, Secretary of State for Foreign Affairs 1900–Dec 1905, and Minister without Portfolio May 1915–Dec 1916.

A large collection of Lansdowne's papers, previously in the possession of the Trustees of the Bowood Collection, has been acquired by the British Library. The papers were extensively used and quoted in Lord Newton, *Lord Lansdowne, A Biography* (Macmillan 1929). Lansdowne's great-grandson, the Earl of Shelburne, advised us that these papers have not been calendared. But listing by the British Library has begun and the collection may be consulted by prior arrangement with the Department of Manuscripts.

Lansdowne's papers as Viceroy of India 1888–94, presented to the

India Office in 1929 by the 7th Marquess, are now in the Oriental and India Office Collections, British Library (MSS Eur D 558; NRA 8657). They consist of 26 volumes of correspondence and telegrams, as well as summaries of Lansdowne's actions as Viceroy, arranged by department, and two volumes of speeches. The correspondence has been arranged in the usual viceregal order: correspondence with the Queen (one volume), correspondence and telegrams with the Secretary of State for India (nine volumes), correspondence with persons in England (five volumes), and correspondence with persons in India (11 volumes). Printed copies of this correspondence are also to be found in the Printed Books Department of the British Library.

Some of Lansdowne's papers as Secretary of State for Foreign Affairs are available in the PRO (FO 800/115–46). The papers include two files of general correspondence 1898–1905. The remainder of the papers are arranged alphabetically by country and cover the years 1900–06, although the box of papers concerning Germany includes some for 1920–24. A subject index has been compiled (NRA 23627).

Microfilm copies of those of Lansdowne's papers which relate to his term of office as Governor-General of Canada 1883–88 have been made by the National Archives of Canada (MG 27 I B6).

REGINALD THOMAS HERBERT FLETCHER, BARON WINSTER (1885–1961)

Reginald Fletcher was Liberal MP for Hampshire (Basingstoke) 1923–24, and Labour MP for Warwickshire (Nuneaton) 1935–42. He was Minister of Civil Aviation Aug 1945–Oct 1946. He was created Baron Winster in 1942, and KCMG in 1948.

Lord Winster left most of his estate to his widow; she died shortly after him. She left Winster Lodge, their home in Crowborough, and its contents to the Bishop of Chichester for the benefit of Anglican clergy. In the first edition we noted that only five volumes of press cuttings had survived in the house, in the charge of a management committee. Most of the volumes covered Winster's post-1945 activities but one volume was solely devoted to the Gallipoli campaign of 1915 (in which Winster fought). One volume contained cuttings relating to Winster's term as Governor of Cyprus 1946–48. As well as reports on social activities and tours there were several pages of cuttings from the British and Cypriot press on the British proposals for limited self-government in Cyprus. The rejection of these terms led to Winster's resignation. A log-book kept by midshipman Fletcher Sept 1901–July 1903 was included in this collection, as well as the visitors' book for his homes from 1910 onwards.

We have now been advised by the Bishop of Chichester that Winster Lodge no longer belongs to the diocese and that the person responsible for clearing out the house has no recollection of these volumes of press cuttings. They have not been deposited in either the East or West Sussex Archives offices.

Winster's surviving executor, the National Westminster Bank, did not know of the existence of any papers. Winster left some books and prints to the Royal Naval College, Greenwich, but his bequest did not include any papers. The National Maritime Museum did not know of the existence of any papers.

Winster's involvement with the Secret Intelligence Service is briefly discussed in Christopher Andrew, *Secret Service: The Making of the British Intelligence Community* (Heinemann 1985), 345, 350, 379, 549. Ivor Bulmer-Thomas drew on personal knowledge for his entry on Winster in *DNB 1961–1970*, 366–8.

HUGH OAKELEY ARNOLD-FORSTER (1855–1909)

Hugh Oakeley Arnold-Forster (he assumed the additional surname Forster in 1877) was Liberal Unionist MP for Belfast (West) 1892–1906, and Conservative MP for Croydon 1906–09. He was Parliamentary Secretary to the Admiralty Nov 1900–Oct 1903, and Secretary of State for War 1903–Dec 1905.

Eighty-three volumes of Arnold-Forster's papers were presented by his son to the British Library in 1960 (Add MSS 50275–357). They have been divided into four main groups: Admiralty papers; War Office papers; diaries; and miscellaneous.

Arnold-Forster's Admiralty papers include printed, typed, and manuscript papers on staff appointments and salaries, ships' boilers, consumption of water and coal, education, and annual estimates 1901/2–1904/5. An original index to these papers has survived.

Arnold-Forster's War Office papers cover such topics as the Committee of Imperial Defence 1903–04, and the Esher Committee. There are also submissions to the King 1904–05. Again, an original index survives.

Arnold-Forster's diaries cover 1903–08. According to a note by Arnold-Forster himself, they were dictated daily; when he was away from home he wrote the entries himself and forwarded them for transcribing. The diaries exist both in typescript and manuscript. The miscellaneous papers include various pamphlets and the 1901 report and press cuttings of the Lands Settlement Committee which Arnold-Forster had chaired.

The British Library also holds correspondence between Arnold-Forster and A. J. Balfour 1888–1909 (Add MSS 49722–3) and Arnold-Forster's letters to Lt-Col R. J. Marker 1905–09 (Add MSS 52277 A, ff 40–112).

Family and estate records dating to the 16th century and three boxes of political papers relating to Arnold-Forster's period in the War Office 1903–05 which are mentioned but not listed in NRA 23462, formerly in the possession of N. M. Arnold-Forster, have been deposited in the Wiltshire CRO (WRO 1390). The War Office papers include correspondence with many of the key political figures of the period.

Trinity College Library, Dublin, holds a substantial collection of family correspondence 1859–1921, including Arnold-Forster's own correspondence (MSS 5000–1), miscellaneous papers concerning Arnold-Forster, and letters from him (MSS 5002 and 5002a respectively). Also included in the collection is the correspondence of his sister, F. E. Arnold-Forster (MSS 5004–6) and his adoptive father (MS 4986). A list of the authors, address and addressee with dates of the letters is available (NRA 22032 and 30476).

Arnold-Forster's wife Mary, in *The Rt. Hon. H. O. Arnold-Forster: a Memoir by his Wife* (Edward Arnold 1910), quoted from many letters especially to his mother, and also compiled a list of his books and articles.

For Arnold-Forster's work at the War Office see Ian Beckett, 'H. O. Arnold-Forster and the Volunteers' in Ian Beckett and John Gooch (eds), *Politicians and Defence: Studies in the Formulation of British Defence Policy 1845–1970* (Manchester UP 1981), 47–68, and J. Bertie, 'H. O Arnold-Forster at the War Office, 1903–5' (PhD thesis, Liverpool University 1974).

SIR HENRY HARTLEY FOWLER, 1st VISCOUNT WOLVERHAMPTON (1830–1911)

Henry Fowler was Liberal MP for Wolverhampton (Wolverhampton East from 1885) 1880–1908. He was Under-Secretary of State at the Home Office Dec 1884–June 1885, Financial Secretary to the Treasury Feb–July 1886, President of the Local Government Board Aug 1892–March 1894, Secretary of State for India 1894–June 1895, Chancellor of the Duchy of Lancaster Dec 1905–Oct 1908, and Lord President of the Council 1908–June 1910. He was created GCSI in 1895, and Viscount Wolverhampton in 1908.

Fowler had one son and two daughters. His son, the 2nd Viscount Wolverhampton, died in 1943 leaving no issue. The widow of the 2nd Viscount died in 1947; her family knew of no papers. Fowler's elder daughter, Ellen, married Alfred L. Felkin who wrote the biography of Fowler in *DNB*, Supplement Jan 1901–Dec 1911, II, 49–52. Mrs Felkin died in 1929, her husband in 1942. He appointed the Fowler family law firm and his brother-in-law as executors. The younger daughter, Edith, married the Rev William R. Hamilton. In *The Life of Henry Hartley Fowler, 1st Viscount Wolverhampton* (Hutchinson 1912) she quoted from several letters. Mr and Mrs Hamilton had two sons. Neither of them knew of any papers, nor did the family law-firm, Messrs Fowler, Langley and Wright of Wolverhampton.

Over 30 years ago the Oriental and India Office Collections, British Library purchased three volumes of correspondence from Mr Edward Hall, the antiquarian, but he was unable to give any details of the provenance of these volumes. The volumes (MSS Eur C 145) consist of printed and manuscript correspondence 1894-95 with the Viceroy, Lord Elgin.

Publications, theses, and archival sources relevant to Fowler's India Office years are usefully listed in Arnold P. Kaminsky, *The India Office 1880-1910* (Greenwood Press, New York 1986).

SIR HUGH CHARLES PATRICK JOSEPH FRASER (1918-1984)

Hugh Fraser was Conservative MP for Stone 1945-50 and Stafford and Stone 1950-84. He was Parliamentary Under-Secretary of State and Financial Secretary, War Office Nov 1958-Oct 1960, Parliamentary Under-Secretary of State for the Colonies 1960-July 1962, Secretary of State for Air 1962-April 1964, and Minister of Defence for the Air Force April-Oct 1964. He was knighted in 1980.

Fraser's former wife, Lady Antonia Fraser, advised us that any surviving papers would be in the possession of their son, Benjamin Fraser. However Mr Fraser recently advised Lord Jellicoe (who inquired on our behalf) that 'unfortunately Poppa was not a record keeper by inclination and therefore no family papers of this type have ever been traced'.

There is a brief biography of Fraser by John Biggs-Davison in *DNB 1981-1985*, 148-9.

SIR JOHN DENTON PINKSTONE FRENCH, 1st EARL OF YPRES (1852-1925)

John French was created KCB in 1900, Viscount French in 1916, KP in 1917, and Earl of Ypres in 1922. He was Lord Lieutenant of Ireland May 1918-April 1921.

The IWM holds 14 boxes of French's papers acquired from several sources by deposit and purchase (75/46/1-14; NRA 29546), most notably his diaries March 1900-June 1902, and Aug 1914-April 1921. There is also his correspondence with George V and other leading political and military figures. The collection contains official records 1914-15; Irish papers 1918-21; and letters to his mistress, Mrs Bennett, and her sister Mrs Hood 1918-20. There are 25 letters to French and his son 1904-36; as well as a volume of telegrams received by his widow following his death. There are also three volumes of press cuttings. French's papers are only available to *bona fide* scholars. Anyone wishing to consult the diaries is required to sign an undertaking not to infringe copyright.

In the Lovat Fraser papers in the IWM (Spec Misc N3) there are letters from Asquith to French 3 Oct 1914 and 3 June 1915 sent by French to Fraser in June 1919 with other material relating to his wartime relations with Asquith.

The Museum also holds a microfilm copy of the papers of Lt-Col B. J. H. Fitzgerald (NRA 28542), who was French's ADC in South Africa and his private secretary in France in 1915. These include personal letters from and concerning French.

A small fragment of French's diary for June 1919–Aug 1920 was bought by the National Library of Ireland in 1955 (MS 2269). There are 76 pages of manuscript entries, some of which are badly torn. French's diary 1899–1900 is held by the Brenthurst Library, 44 Main St, Johannesburg, 2000, South Africa.

Long selections from French's papers, in particular his almost daily diary entries, were published by French himself and by his son, the Hon E. Gerald French. French's account of the first months of the First World War and the effectiveness of British military preparations are to be found in his *1914* (Constable 1919). Gerald French wrote *The Life of F.M. Sir John French, 1st Earl of Ypres* (Cassell 1931), *French Replies to Haig* (Hutchinson 1936), *Some War Diaries, Addresses, and Correspondence... the Earl of Ypres* (Herbert Jenkins 1937) and *The Kitchener-French Dispute. A Last Word* (Maclellan, Glasgow 1960); all of these were based on his father's papers. Richard Holmes's *The Little Field-Marshal* (Jonathan Cape 1981) draws extensively on the papers held in the IWM as does George H. Cassar, *The Tragedy of Lord French* (Associated University Presses 1985).

SIR DAVID PATRICK MAXWELL-FYFE, EARL OF KILMUIR (1900–1967)

David Maxwell-Fyfe was Conservative MP for Liverpool (West Derby) 1935–54. He was Solicitor-General March 1942–May 1945, Attorney-General May–Aug 1945, Secretary of State for Home Affairs and Minister of State for Welsh Affairs Oct 1951–Oct 1954, and Lord Chancellor 1954–July 1962. He was knighted in 1942, and created GCVO in 1953, Viscount Kilmuir in 1954, and Earl of Kilmuir in 1962.

Lord Kilmuir's literary trustees deposited a collection of his papers in the Churchill Archives Centre (KLMR). A list has been compiled (NRA 14286) but not all of the papers are open, particularly the most recent. The papers are almost all post-1942 – some of Kilmuir's papers were destroyed by the bombing of both his house and his chambers in the Second World War. In the preface to his memoirs, *Political Adventure* (Weidenfeld & Nicolson 1964), Kilmuir stated that he had never 'harboured' documents but that he had written memoranda after what he considered were important events in which he had taken part. These memoranda or notes were used as the basis of his book but they are not in the collection deposited in the Churchill Archives Centre. A few letters are also quoted in the book. Kilmuir's widow, the Countess De La Warr, informed us that she did not know what became of the notes.

The papers deposited at Churchill have been divided into six groups: diaries; press cuttings; speeches; photos; correspondence; miscellaneous. The diaries cover 1954-61 but they are only engagement diaries except for 1/5, which describes the events of July-Dec 1956. The press cuttings cover 1942-51. They include cuttings made during his tenure of the Solicitor-Generalship, as well as his period in opposition 1945-51, and his part in the Nuremberg War Criminal trials (he was Deputy Chief Prosecutor). The correspondence is mainly from the periods 1949-52 and 1955-62, including letters relating to his memoirs. There are also letters concerning his legal activities, his wartime services, the Nuremberg trials and a few papers relating to his unsuccessful candidacy at Wigan in 1924.

There is a useful biography in *Lord Chancellors 2*, 161-80. Professor Heuston also contributed the brief essay on Kilmuir in *DNB 1961-1970*, 408-9.

HUGH TODD NAYLOR GAITSKELL (1906-1963)

Hugh Gaitskell was Labour MP for Leeds (South) 1945-63. He was Parliamentary Under-Secretary to the Ministry of Fuel and Power May 1946-Oct 1947, Minister of Fuel and Power 1947-Feb 1950, Minister of State for Economic Affairs Feb-Oct 1950, and Chancellor of the Exchequer 1950-Oct 1951. He was Leader of the Labour Party 1955-63.

Gaitskell's diaries are in the possession of his family. They are not available for research, but his diary for 1945-56 was edited by Philip Williams and published in 1983 by Jonathan Cape.

In 1980, a collection of 181 boxes of Gaitskell's papers was deposited in the Library, University College, London. They are not available for research while they are being catalogued.

Most of the surviving papers are post-war but there are a few papers from Gaitskell's unsuccessful attempts to win a seat at Chatham in the 1930s. There are also papers from Gaitskell's pre-war political activities in Leeds, including a long series of correspondence with his political agent. There are also lecture notes and drafts for articles and books on economics. There are very few official papers apart from some Ministry of Fuel papers, and congratulations on his various appointments and on his budget. The bulk of the collection − in the form of letters, committee papers, speech notes, memoranda, pamphlets, and press cuttings – derives from the 1950s.

There are 12 box-files of constituency papers, including correspondence about visits, party meetings, particular cases, and a long correspondence with Gaitskell's agent. Gaitskell's Labour Party papers include drafts of party publications and material from the party's conferences, meetings, and general elections. There are also several boxes of correspondence with MPs and politicians, especially Sir Stafford Cripps and Hugh Dalton. There are many subject files of press cuttings, memoranda, and pamphlets.

The archives of the South Leeds Labour Party, which contain five bundles of correspondence between Gaitskell and George Murray, his constituency secretary, concerning arrangements for visits to the constituency and meetings 1952–63, are to be found in the Leeds District Archives (SLLP 13; NRA 31009).

The Institute of Contemporary British History has included in its oral history programme a witness seminar on 'The Campaign for Democratic Socialism 1960–64' which was chaired by Professor David Marquand and included Lords Jay, Mayhew, and Rodgers, and the Rt Hon Dick Taverne as witnesses. The archives of the Campaign for Democratic Socialism, collected by Lord Rodgers, are expected to be deposited at Nuffield College Library.

Papers relating to Budgets are in the PRO at T 171.

The major biography by Philip Williams *Hugh Gaitskell: A Political Biography* (Jonathan Cape 1979) is based on the papers. There is a volume of collected biographical essays by his contemporaries: William T. Rodgers (ed), *Hugh Gaitskell* (Thames and Hudson 1964).

Dr Brian Brivati, Institute of Contemporary British History, is writing a biography which is due to be published by Hodder Headline in 1996.

SIR (AUCKLAND) CAMPBELL GEDDES, 1st BARON GEDDES (1879–1954)

Professor Campbell Geddes was created KCB in 1917, GCMG in 1922, and Baron Geddes in 1942. He was Unionist MP for Hampshire (Basingstoke) 1917–20. He was Minister of Reconstruction July 1917–Jan 1919, Minister of National Service Aug 1917–Aug 1919, President of the Local Government Board Nov 1918–Jan 1919, and President of the Board of Trade 1919–March 1920.

According to his eldest son, the late 2nd Baron Geddes, Geddes was very methodical in destroying both official and business papers and after his death none were found.

However, a substantial collection of Geddes's correspondence, speeches, and press cuttings, together with copies of material garnered from the PRO and other repositories as well as reminiscences from 60 friends gathered shortly after his death collected by his surviving son, the Hon Dr David Geddes, has been deposited in the Churchill Archives Centre (GEDD).

These papers are currently being catalogued. A preliminary grouping of the papers includes: military career 1906–58 (published works, 1 file); medical career 1909–50 (published works and correspondence, 4 files); minister 1916–24 (published works, correspondence, press cuttings, research collected by David Geddes, 14 files); ambassador 1920–24 (press cuttings and correspondence, 8 files); business career 1924–48 (correspondence and press cuttings, 1 file); civil defence 1938–45 (correspondence, published works, speeches, 7 files); speeches 1918–23 (3 files). There is also a substantial amount of family and personal material.

The minutes of private meetings and circulars of the Royal Commission on Food Prices 1924–25, of which Geddes was the Chairman, may be found in the PRO at MAF 69/1–5. There is some correspondence with Sir Basil Liddell Hart 1938–53 in the Liddell Hart Centre (LH 1/311).

Dr Geddes has written an unpublished monograph, 'Auckland Geddes in Washington: A biographical study' (1991) which briefly covers his father's early life as well as his period as Ambassador to Washington 1920–24.

In his book, *The Forging of a Family* (Faber & Faber 1952), Geddes devoted some 50 pages to his own career, written in the third person; conversations are quoted, but very few letters are mentioned. There are valuable chapters on Geddes's work as Minister of National Service in Keith Grieves, *The Politics of Manpower, 1914–18* (Manchester UP 1988).

SIR ERIC CAMPBELL GEDDES (1875–1937)

Eric Geddes was knighted in 1916, and created GBE in 1919. He was Unionist MP for Cambridge 1917–22. He was First Lord of the Admiralty July 1917–Jan 1919, Minister without Portfolio Jan-May 1919, and Minister of Transport 1919–Nov 1921.

Geddes's son, Sir Reay Geddes, believed that his father kept no papers. However, Dr Lawrence Roe Buchanan, 'The Governmental Career of Sir Eric Campbell Geddes', (PhD thesis, University of Virginia 1979) has established that Geddes kept papers which he classified and indexed. On his death they were divided by his executors into official and private categories. In 1940 the official papers were sent to the Secretary of the War Cabinet. It seems likely that the private group went to his brother Lord Geddes. As they do not appear to have survived they were presumably destroyed by Lord Geddes along with some of his own papers.

The papers of Geddes for July 1915–Aug 1916 when he was Deputy Director-General Munitions Supply are in the PRO (SUPP 12/1; NRA 32916). A list of Geddes's own papers from the Ministry of Munitions period, drawn up in 1919, is also to be found in the PRO (MUN 5/26/262 1/49). These munitions papers are now lost, though they were used by the official historians of the Ministry of Munitions. Geddes's Private Office papers as Controller (May-Sept 1917) and First Lord of the Admiralty are available at the PRO (ref ADM 116/1804–10). ADM 116/1804 is an index of the correspondence. His Ministry of Transport papers are also at the PRO (MT 49). The bulk of these papers is concerned with the drawing up and passage of the 1921 Railways Act which amalgamated 123 separate railway companies. There are notes of meetings, proposals, and deputations from the different groups. There is also much material on railway administration, the revision of the 1921 season ticket rates for the Underground, and the 1919 strike. There are also papers concerning canals, ferries, ports, roads, and traffic – for example on the use of road works to alleviate unemployment. Relevant material is also to be found at the PRO in RAIL 527 (North Eastern Railway) and AIR 19 (Private Office papers at the Air ministry).

In *The Forging of a Family* (Faber & Faber 1952), Lord Geddes devoted 30 pages to Eric Geddes's career; only a few letters are quoted but there are also occasional descriptions of conversations. Some of the text is a verbatim reproduction of a manuscript written by Eric Geddes in 1920 which was partly copied by A. J. Sylvester in 1932 and may now be found in the Lloyd George Papers.

Keith Grieves, *Sir Eric Geddes: Business and government in war and peace* (Manchester UP 1989) is a useful brief biography which appears not to have drawn on Dr Buchanan's thesis. Grieves has an excellent bibliographical note and guide to selected reading. He draws attention to important correspondence and press cuttings in the Lloyd George and Bonar Law papers, and to documentation of Geddes' connection with the Dunlop Rubber Company in the records of BTR plc.

Geddes's career as a transport company executive and industrialist is the subject of an excellent entry by R. J. Irving and R. P. T. Davenport-Hines in *DBB*, 507–16. Geddes's work at the Ministry of Transport is discussed in William Plowden, *The Motor Car and Politics 1896–1970* (Bodley Head 1971).

Andrew McDonald's 'The Geddes Committee and the Formulation of Public Expenditure Policy, 1921–1922', *The Historical Journal*, 32, 2, 1989, 643–74, is a good guide to sources on the context of the Geddes axe.

EDWARD GIBSON, 1st BARON ASHBOURNE (1837–1913)

Edward Gibson was Conservative MP for Dublin University 1875–85. He was Irish Attorney-General 1877–80, and Lord Chancellor of Ireland (with a seat in the Cabinet) 1885–86, 1886–92 and June 1895–Dec 1905. He was created Baron Ashbourne in 1885.

A considerable collection of Lord Ashbourne's papers was deposited by his grandson, the 3rd Baron Ashbourne, in the HLRO (Ashbourne Papers). Photocopies of the bulk of the collection are available in the PRONI. A calendar of the papers has been published by the PRONI (NRA 18808): A. B. Cooke and A. P. W. Malcomson, *The Ashbourne Papers, 1869–1913* (HMSO, Belfast 1974). As well as personal and legal papers, there are papers referring to his election campaigns, including letters of support and Gibson's election address for Waterford in 1874. The bulk of the papers is composed of correspondence from Ashbourne's terms of office. His correspondents included Salisbury 1884–1907, Hartington, A. J. Balfour 1887–1902, and the various viceroys of Ireland.

There are some printed Cabinet memoranda and draft bills and also a few fragments of notes on Cabinet meetings. There are volumes of press cuttings, photos, and speeches; and notes and correspondence concerning Ashbourne's biography of Pitt.

Three volumes of diaries cover the years 1884, 1890–91, 1894, 1898, 1902, and 1912 but most of the entries are disjointed jottings mainly written in 1912, and one volume concerns journeys abroad in 1872. There are also ten notebooks whose subjects range from the establishment of a life peerage to quotations from politicians on various questions.

SIR HARDINGE STANLEY GIFFARD, 1st EARL OF HALSBURY (1823–1921)

Hardinge Giffard was knighted in 1875, created Baron Halsbury in 1885, and Earl of Halsbury in 1898. He was Conservative MP for Launceston 1877–85. He was Solicitor-General Nov 1875–April 1880, and Lord Chancellor June 1885–Feb 1886, Aug 1886–Aug 1892 and June 1895–Dec 1905.

Eight volumes of Lord Halsbury's papers were given to the British Library by his grandson, the 3rd Lord Halsbury, in 1970 (Add MSS 56367–77). These papers had previously been described in NRA 6238. An outline of the papers' arrangement can be seen in List and Index Society, *Special Series, Vol 8, 'Rough Register' of Acquisitions to the Department of Manuscripts, British Library 1965–1970*, 1975, 323–4.

There are three volumes of general correspondence 1867–1921 and three volumes of special correspondence, including letters from the 3rd

Marquess of Salisbury 1885–1903, the 4th Marquess of Salisbury 1904–17, W. H. Smith 1886–91, the 8th Duke of Devonshire 1894–1902, Joseph Chamberlain 1895–1914, the 5th Marquess of Lansdowne 1896–1915, and Lord James of Hereford 1897–1906. In addition, there are two volumes of drafts and notes for speeches and memoranda on Halsbury's career. Amongst the topics covered by these papers is the 1911 Parliament Act – Halsbury was a leader of the Tory 'Die-hard' peers – as well as some of his more famous legal cases.

Alice Wilson Fox, *The Earl of Halsbury, Lord High Chancellor (1823–1921)* (Chapman Hall 1929), quotes from many of these papers as does Heuston in *Lord Chancellors 1*, 3–82. Richard A. Cosgrove, 'Lord Halsbury: Conservatism and Law' in J. A. Thompson and Arthur Mejia (eds), *Edwardian Conservatism: Five Studies in Adaptation* (Croom Helm 1988) is essentially based on published sources.

SIR JOHN GILMOUR, 2nd Bt (1876–1940)

John Gilmour was Conservative MP for Renfrewshire (East) 1910–18 and Glasgow (Pollok) 1918–40. He was Secretary of State for Scotland Nov 1924–June 1929, Minister of Agriculture and Fisheries Aug 1931–Sept 1932, Secretary of State for Home Affairs 1932–June 1935, and Minister of Shipping Oct 1939–April 1940. He succeeded his father as 2nd baronet in 1920, and was created GCVO in 1935.

Gilmour's papers, formerly in the possession of his son, the Rt Hon Col Sir John Gilmour, Bt, DSO, MP, have been deposited in the SRO (GD.383; NRA 37640). Readers may consult the papers on condition that they sign an undertaking to submit the relevant parts of any proposed publication based on them for the approval of Sir John Gilmour.

The papers mostly consist of personal and political correspondence 1903–25, with various people including Bonar Law, Lloyd George, Viscount Novar, Austen Chamberlain, David Lindsay, Leo Amery, and Archibald Sinclair. There is also a typescript of Gilmour's 'war diary' 1914–22 (based on his correspondence from Lemnos, Gallipoli, Egypt, and Palestine), and election addresses to electors of the Pollok division of Glasgow 1918–31.

Private Office papers relating to Gilmour's period at the Scottish Office are dispersed through the files of the five main Scottish Office departments held at the SRO.

Gilmour's political career, with special reference to Scottish affairs is briefly sketched in *Secretaries of State for Scotland*, 29–37. Reference should also be made to J. W. R. Mitchell, 'The emergence of Modern Scottish central administration 1885–1939' (DPhil thesis, Oxford University 1987).

HERBERT JOHN GLADSTONE, VISCOUNT GLADSTONE (1854–1930)

Herbert Gladstone was Liberal MP for Leeds 1880–85 and for Leeds (West) 1885–1910. He was Financial Secretary to the War Office Feb-July 1886, Under-Secretary of State for Home Affairs Aug 1892–March 1894, First Commissioner of Works 1894–June 1895, and Secretary of State for Home Affairs Dec 1905–Feb 1910. He was created GCMG and Viscount Gladstone in 1910.

The greater part of Gladstone's papers – 134 volumes – was deposited by his widow in the British Library in 1935 (Add MSS 45985–6118; NRA 14174). They have been divided into eight main divisions: royal correspondence; special correspondence; family correspondence; general correspondence; official papers; notes; diaries; literary papers. An index of correspondents has been compiled.

There is one volume of correspondence with successive sovereigns and their secretaries. There are 57 volumes of special correspondence including two volumes of correspondence with Sir Henry Campbell-Bannerman 1886–1908, one volume with Asquith 1892–1922, one volume with Lord Crewe 1886–1928, six volumes with Lewis Harcourt 1894–1920 (mainly for the period when Harcourt was Colonial Secretary and Gladstone Governor-General of South Africa 1910–14), two volumes with General Botha 1910–14, one volume with J. C. Smuts 1910–28, and one volume with Lord Buxton (Gladstone's successor in South Africa). There is considerable correspondence with more of Gladstone's political contemporaries and with Liberal whips (Gladstone was Liberal Chief Whip 1899–1905). There is also correspondence with his constituents, including three volumes 1880–1923 with Joseph Henry, Lord Mayor of Leeds in 1918. There are only three volumes of family correspondence including correspondence with his father 1881–84. There are 39 volumes of general correspondence 1880–1930.

Gladstone's official papers have been sub-divided by his various terms of office. There are three volumes of papers as First Commissioner of Works and two volumes as Under-Secretary at the Home Office. The five volumes for Gladstone's period as Secretary of State at the Home Office cover some of the most difficult problems of his department: the 1906–08 Licensing Bill; the passage of the 1908 Coal Mines (Eight Hours) Act; and the 1907–08 Prevention of Crime Act. There are four volumes of papers as Governor-General of South Africa. An additional three books of press cuttings mainly for this period are available in the Printed Books department of the British Library (1899.b.11). There are five volumes of Gladstone's papers as Liberal Chief Whip, including two notebooks of lists of possible Liberal candidates. Gladstone's later activities are also represented, for example, his work for Belgian war refugees.

There are two volumes of notes for speeches 1881–1929. The diary in this collection is for 1910–13. Gladstone's literary manuscripts include his Oxford lecture notes and the typescript of an unpublished autobiography.

A further 13 volumes of Gladstone's papers were opened for research in 1960 (Add MSS 46474–86). They are arranged on the same principles as the preceding collection. They include Gladstone's diaries – mainly notes of interviews – for 1899–1905 and 1922–24. An original name index for these diaries survives. There are more papers concerning parliamentary constituencies and candidates, including papers on the administration of the Liberal Party and two volumes of correspondence with Sir Donald Maclean 1921–29.

Most of the Gladstone family's personal papers have been deposited in St Deiniol's Library, Hawarden (Glynne-Gladstone MSS). Access to these papers is granted by the Clwyd RO, to which all applications should be addressed. Researchers wishing to see these papers are advised to give several days' notice of their visits so that the papers may be transferred to the RO. For a list of the collection see C. J. Williams, *Handlist of the Glynne-Gladstone MSS in St Deiniol's Library, Hawarden* (List & Index Society Special Series, 24, 1990). There are a few fragments of Gladstone's papers in this collection, including his political diary 1880–85. There is some correspondence with various members of his family and with political contemporaries 1866–1930. Of considerable interest for any study of Gladstone is his correspondence with his brother H. N. Gladstone, Baron Gladstone 1865–1930. There are 1642 letters from Herbert including many written when at the Home Office and in South Africa.

Sir Charles Mallet, *Herbert Gladstone. A Memoir* (Hutchinson 1932) is based on Gladstone's papers and quotes from the draft autobiography. Gladstone's own *After Thirty Years* (Macmillan 1928), though ostensibly about his father, has many glimpses of his own observations and activities. There are valuable studies of Gladstone as Chief Whip in H. W. McCready, 'Chief Whip and Party Funds: the Work of Herbert Gladstone in the Edwardian Liberal Party, 1899 to 1906' *Canadian Journal of History*, 6, 3, Dec 1971, 285–303, and T. O. Lloyd, 'The whip as paymaster: Herbert Gladstone and party organisation', *English Historical Review*, LXXXIX (1974), 785–813.

The 1978 Ohio State University PhD thesis by Carol Anne Sainey, 'Viscount Gladstone and British Policy Towards South Africa 1910–1914', is based on the Gladstone papers and the relevant Colonial Office original correspondence files in CO 551.

JOSEPH BRADSHAW GODBER, BARON GODBER OF WILLINGTON (1914–1980)

Joseph Godber was Conservative MP for Grantham 1951–79. He was Joint Parliamentary Secretary, Ministry of Agriculture, Fisheries and Food Jan 1957–Oct 1960, Parliamentary Under-Secretary of State, Foreign Office 1960–June 1961, Minister of State, Foreign Office 1961–June 1963, Secretary of State for War June-Oct 1963, Minister of Labour 1963–Oct 1964, Minister of State, Foreign and Commonwealth Office June 1970–Nov 1972, and Minister of Agriculture, Fisheries and Food 1972–March 1974. He was created Baron Godber of Willington (a life peerage) in 1979.

Lord Godber's son, the Hon Richard Godber, advised us that he has in his possession very few personal papers of his father's but no Cabinet papers. Lord Godber himself had told Dr John Gooch in 1979 that he had not retained any papers relating to his brief period as Secretary of State for War.

WILLIAM GEORGE ARTHUR ORMSBY-GORE, 4th BARON HARLECH (1885–1964)

William Ormsby-Gore was Conservative MP for Denbigh 1910–18 and Staffordshire (Stafford) 1918–38. He was Under-Secretary of State for the Colonies Oct 1922–Jan 1924 and Nov 1924–June 1929, Postmaster-General Sept-Nov 1931, First Commissioner of Works 1931-May 1936, and Secretary of State for the Colonies 1936–May 1938. He succeeded his father as the 4th Baron Harlech in 1938, and was created GCMG in 1938 and KG in 1948.

His son, the 5th Lord Harlech, informed us that a thorough search had not revealed any private papers and that it is to be feared that his father destroyed his papers before he died. Philip Jones, *Britain and Palestine 1914–1948, Archival Sources for the History of the British Mandate*, 1979, 57–8, reports Lord Harlech as stating that 'the family archives are unsorted and closed'.

There are some Harlech papers in the Brogyntyn Collection in the NLW. They include letters to Harlech from friends, colleagues, and relatives, including a series written by his wife during the Royal Tour of South Africa in 1947. Other correspondents include Frank Weston, Bishop of Zanzibar; Sir Herbert Stanley; Sir Patrick Duncan, Governor-General of South Africa; and Clement Attlee. The collection also contains copies of papers and of addresses, relating mostly to the colonies, delivered by Harlech; and correspondence and accounts relating to the renovation of the grave of Captain Owen Arthur Ormsby-Gore.

A collection of some 20 letters written by Harlech as an undergraduate

1905 were offered for sale by Henry Bristow Ltd, Ringwood, Hants, in 1980.

The NRA advised us that there is Harlech correspondence with P. V. Emrys-Evans 1942–48 (British Library, Add MS 58244); Arthur Creech Jones 1936–39 (Rhodes House Library, MSS Brit emp s 332); Lord Lothian 1929–39 (SRO, GD40); and J. H. Oldham 1924–31 (Rhodes House Library, MSS Afr s 1829).

There is a brief biography of Harlech by K. E. Robinson in *DNB 1961–1970*, 812–14.

GEORGE JOACHIM GOSCHEN, 1st VISCOUNT GOSCHEN (1831–1907)

George Goschen was Liberal MP for the City of London 1863–80, Ripon 1880–85 and Edinburgh (East) 1885–86. He became Liberal Unionist MP for St George's, Hanover Square 1887–1900. He was Paymaster-General Nov 1865–March 1866, Chancellor of the Duchy of Lancaster Jan-July 1866, President of the Poor Law Board (and in the Cabinet) Dec 1868–March 1871, First Lord of the Admiralty 1871–Feb 1874 and June 1895–Nov 1900, and Chancellor of the Exchequer Jan 1887–Aug 1892. He was created Viscount Goschen in 1900.

A small collection of Goschen's papers was deposited in the Bodleian Library (Dep c 182–3) by his grand-daughter, the Hon Mrs F. Balfour. There is a list (NRA 5677).

There are 33 letters from A. J. Balfour 1887–95, mainly about Ireland; 16 typed copies of letters to Queen Victoria 1885–86 (the originals are in the Royal Archives); and three packets of letters from Goschen, writing in his capacity as Chancellor of Oxford University, to Percy Matheson 1904–07. The Bodleian Library has also acquired several miscellaneous letters including a register of some of Goschen's letters as First Lord of the Admiralty (MS Eng hist c 386) and a guardbook including letters of Goschen 1873–1906 (MS Eng lett e 123).

The small size of this collection is something of a mystery since the Hon Arthur D. Elliot, in his biography *The Life of George Joachim Goschen, 1st Viscount Goschen 1831–1907* (2 vols, Longmans, Green & Co 1911), quoted from diaries, letters, and an autobiographical fragment concerning Goschen's childhood and early years. These papers seem to have been used as late as 1946 by Percy Colson in his *Lord Goschen and his friends: The Goschen Letters* (Hutchinson 1946). But when the 2nd Viscount died in 1952 his daughter, Mrs Balfour, found only those papers which she has deposited in the Bodleian. Mrs Balfour inquired at that time amongst other members of her family but discovered no other papers. It is possible that the 2nd Viscount destroyed them when he moved from his old house. The 3rd Viscount Goschen knew of no papers other than those in the Bodleian. Arthur Elliot's papers have now been deposited in the NLS but there are no Goschen papers among them nor is there any indication there of what became of them.

About 80 letters to Goschen and his brother Charles are owned by Goschen's great-nephew, Mr D. C. Goschen, Mukonde, PO Box 69488, Bryanston 2021, Republic of South Africa. They are held for Mr Goschen by his sister-in-law, Mrs E. M. Goschen, Silvester's Farm, Lower Froyle, Alton, Hants. Most of the letters, which cover the years 1846–66, are from Goschen's father. They particularly concern Goschen's work for the family firm, Fruhling and Goschen; there are some 30 letters for the years 1854–56, when Goschen was supervising the firm's interests in South America. There are also letters from Charles Goschen in Feb 1890 on Goschen's financial position, and several letters from Goschen's mother.

Among the papers of Goschen's youngest brother Edward are a few letters from Lord Goschen as First Lord of the Admiralty in the later 1890s. Some of these are quoted in Christopher H. D. Howard (ed), *The Diary of Edward Goschen 1900–1914* (Camden Fourth Series, 25, Royal Historical Society, 1980, 8–9). The papers of Sir Edward Goschen Bt are in the care of his grandson, Sir Edward Goschen Bt, Lower Farm House, Hampstead Norreys, Newbury, Berkshire RG16 0SG.

There are letters to and from Goschen on financial questions 1887–97 in the Welby papers at the BLPES (SR 1017; NRA 7538). There is also a small collection of letters from Goschen (undated) in the John Dillon Collection, Trinity College Library, Dublin.

T. J. Spinner, *George Joachim Goschen. The Transformation of a Victorian Liberal* (Cambridge UP 1973), used all the available papers, including those belonging to Mr D. C. Goschen. Professor Spinner also informed us that he was able to contact most of the Goschen family, but found no papers, other than those mentioned above.

HARRY GOSLING (1861–1930)

Harry Gosling was Labour MP for Stepney, Whitechapel and St George's 1923–30. He was Minister of Transport Jan-Nov 1924, and Paymaster-General May-Nov 1924.

Gosling's adopted daughter, Mrs Christina Mann, informed us that she believed that her father's papers were all destroyed. She had only press cuttings of his obituary notices. Gosling's autobiography, *Up and Down Stream* (Methuen 1927), does not appear to quote from any papers.

There is material on Gosling in the Labour Party archives in the National Museum of Labour History (LR/LRC and GC; NRA 14863).

The brief biography by W. S. Sanders in *DNB 1922–1930*, 352–3, is based on Gosling's autobiography as well as 'private information; personal knowledge'. John Lovell contributes the useful sketch of Gosling's life in *DLB*, IV, 83–9.

GEORGE GRANVILLE SUTHERLAND-LEVESON-GOWER, 5th DUKE OF SUTHERLAND (1888–1963)

George Sutherland-Leveson-Gower was known as Earl Gower until 1892, and then as Marquess of Stafford until he succeeded his father as 5th Duke of Sutherland in 1913. He was created KT in 1929. He was Under-Secretary of State for Air Oct 1922–Jan 1924, Paymaster-General July 1925–Dec 1928, and Parliamentary Under-Secretary of State for War 1928–June 1929.

Neither Sutherland's widow, Clare, Duchess of Sutherland, nor his kinsman, the 6th Duke of Sutherland, knew what became of the Duke's papers. There are none in the Muniment Room at Dunrobin Castle, nor are there any in the Sutherland Papers in the Staffordshire RO.

Sutherland's niece, the 24th Countess of Sutherland, advised us that she has various press cuttings books, but that any other papers and books were left to Sutherland's widow. She advised that her uncle had moved house just before his death, and believed that a lot of letters were thrown away at this time. We have not been successful in our attempts to contact Sutherland's step-son Mr Michael Dunkerly.

The NLS holds Sutherland estate papers 1861–1920, and the Shropshire RO holds Leveson-Gower Lilleshall estate deeds (NRA 33433).

The Duke's memoirs, *Looking Back* (Odhams Press 1958) do not appear to quote from any papers.

WILLIAM GRAHAM (1887–1932)

Willie Graham was Labour MP for Edinburgh (Central) 1918–31. He was Financial Secretary to the Treasury Jan-Nov 1924, and President of the Board of Trade June 1929–Aug 1931.

We were unable to trace any Graham papers. There was no issue of his marriage. His wife, Ethel, to whom he left all his property, died in 1947. The solicitors who acted for her executrixes were unable to put us in touch with them and we were unable to trace them.

Graham's brother, Thomas Newton Graham, wrote a biography *Willie Graham* (Hutchinson 1948). He quoted from several articles by Graham and a few letters. Mr Graham died in 1965 but his sister, Lady Mathers, informed us that the papers on which the book was based were returned to Graham's widow when the book was finished and that no one in the family knew what became of these papers.

The NLS has one letter from Graham in the Mathers Papers collection, relating to the Adoption of Children (Scotland) Bill which was sponsored by Lord Mathers 1930 (Acc 4826, Box 1/3). There is no other material relating to Graham in the Mathers collection (Lord Mathers married Graham's sister Jessie in 1940, long after Graham's death).

J. S. Middleton contributed the brief entry on Graham in *DNB 1931–1940*, 856–7.

ARTHUR GREENWOOD (1880–1954)

Arthur Greenwood was Labour MP for Nelson and Colne 1922–31 and Wakefield 1932–54. He was Parliamentary Secretary to the Ministry of Health Jan-Nov 1924, Minister of Health June 1929–Aug 1931, Minister without Portfolio in charge of economic affairs May 1940–Feb 1942, Lord Privy Seal July 1945–April 1947, Paymaster-General July 1946–March 1947, and Minister without Portfolio April-Sept 1947.

Like other ex-ministers, Greenwood was requested in Sept 1934 by the Cabinet Office to return any Cabinet papers. In 1935 the Cabinet was informed that 'no reply has been received to the original circular or to the reminders which have been sent to him. It is inferred that he is unwilling to co-operate' (report presented to Cabinet by Sir Maurice Hankey, 29 Nov 1935, PRO, CAB 24/257).

Greenwood's papers were given to the Bodleian Library in 1982 (NRA 17232). Very few papers relating to his early life have survived. Most of the material presently stored in the original box-files relates to First World War reconstruction policy and Greenwood's ministerial career during the 1920s. The topics covered in the latter include the Labour Government 1924; housing 1920–24; the Ministry of Health 1924; and government papers on insurance and pension schemes 1929–31.

Greenwood was also concerned with reconstruction policy during the Second World War and there are boxes labelled Chairman of the Reconstruction Problems Committee 1940–42; War Cabinet 1940–42; and manuscripts and notes for speeches 1939–40. (The files of the Reconstruction Secretariat which Greenwood organised are in the PRO at CAB 21/1584).

There are only five boxes for the post-war period. Two of these contain correspondence and papers relating to the Labour Party, the National Executive Committee, and party conferences 1940s-50s. Most of Greenwood's appointment diaries for these years have survived.

The collection contains a large amount of printed material, including 16 boxes of printed pamphlets, several books on the history of the Labour Party, and miscellaneous press cuttings.

Both Greenwood and his son Anthony (later Lord Greenwood of Rossendale 1911–82) were the subjects of projected biographies. Arthur Greenwood's papers include an undated and possibly ghosted draft autobiography, 'By Labour we live', and the outline of Geoffrey McDermott's, 'He spoke for England, the life of Arthur Greenwood'. Correspondence relating to biographies of the Greenwoods and letters of condolence on the death of Arthur can be found in the papers of

Lord Greenwood, also in the Bodleian Library. Both collections have brief descriptions.

Researchers who wish to consult Lord Greenwood's papers must first obtain the written permission of his widow, Lady Greenwood.

Cabinet Office ministerial correspondence and papers as Lord Privy Seal 1945–47 are in the PRO at CAB 118 (NRA 32908).

SIR (THOMAS) HAMAR GREENWOOD, 1st Bt, 1st VISCOUNT GREENWOOD (1870–1948)

Hamar Greenwood (he was christened Thomas Hubbard) was Liberal MP for York 1906–10, Sunderland 1910–22 and Conservative MP for Walthamstow (East) 1924–29. He was Under-Secretary of State for Home Affairs Jan-April 1919, Secretary for Overseas Trade 1919–April 1920, and Chief Secretary for Ireland 1920–Oct 1922. He was created a baronet in 1915, Baron Greenwood in 1929, and Viscount Greenwood in 1937.

Greenwood's daughter, the Hon Mrs D. R. de Lazlo, informed us that her father's papers were stored in a cellar in a part of Gray's Inn which was destroyed by an incendiary bomb in the Second World War. Mr Richard Miller, who was asked by the 2nd Lord Greenwood to write a biography of his father, was unable to find any papers, and therefore abandoned the project.

Several studies provide valuable assessments of Greenwood's Irish administration and references to relevant sources: John McColgan, *British Policy and the Irish Administration, 1920–22* (George Allen & Unwin 1983), Charles Townshend, *The British Campaign in Ireland 1919–1921: The Development of Political and Military Policies* (Oxford UP 1975), and Sheila Lawlor, *Britain and Ireland 1914–23* (Gill and Macmillan, Dublin 1983). Michael Foot contributed the brief summary of Greenwood's life to *DNB 1941–1950*, 324–5.

SIR EDWARD GREY, 3rd Bt, VISCOUNT GREY OF FALLODON (1862–1933)

Edward Grey succeeded his grandfather as 3rd baronet in 1882, and was created KG in 1912, and Viscount Grey of Fallodon in 1916. He was Liberal MP for Northumberland (Berwick-on-Tweed) 1885–1916. He was Parliamentary Under-Secretary of State for Foreign Affairs Aug 1892–June 1895, and Secretary of State for Foreign Affairs Dec 1905–Dec 1916. He was Liberal Leader in the House of Lords 1923–24.

In his memoirs, *Twenty-Five Years* (2 vols, Hodder & Stoughton 1925), Grey said that all his private papers, with two unspecified exceptions, were at the Foreign Office. These papers are now available in the PRO at FO 800/35–113 (NRA 23627). There are five volumes of general papers from his period as Under-Secretary; the remaining papers derive from his term as Secretary of State. They include 46 boxes of papers arranged by country – eg three boxes about Egypt 1905–16, 12 about France, and two about Germany. There are also 16 boxes of correspondence with other departments of state, and correspondence with King Edward VII, King George V, and Queen Alexandra. The remaining eight boxes are miscellaneous papers including some concerning Sir Roger Casement. An original index survives.

Grey himself quoted extensively from these papers in his memoirs, though they were selected for him from the Foreign Office archives by J. A. Spender because of Grey's failing eyesight. Other official papers are cited in G. P. Gooch and H. W. V. Temperley (eds), *British Documents on the Origins of the War 1898–1914* (11 vols, HMSO 1926–38).

Some personal papers, for example, Grey's correspondence with his first wife, are quoted in G. M. Trevelyan, *Grey of Fallodon* (Longmans, Green 1937); Trevelyan also quoted from an unpublished autobiography, but the fate of these private papers is not known for certain, and they cannot now be found.

Grey had no children. His two wives died before him and their families had no knowledge of the existence of any papers other than those in the PRO. Grey's will contains no reference to his papers, nor did he appoint literary executors. For his biography, *Sir Edward Grey* (Cassell 1971), Professor Keith Robbins pursued two possible sources of information: the Grey family and the Trevelyan family. Grey's estate was inherited by his nephew, Sir Cecil Graves. Neither his widow, Lady Graves who owned the copyright of Grey's letters, nor his son knew of the existence of any papers.

Grey himself may have contributed to the destruction of whatever he retained after leaving office. In a speech to the Whitefriars Club in 1905 he spoke of 'the quantities of clippings, the drawers' full of opponents' speeches, kept in the hope of being able to produce a quotation at an inconvenient moment; pamphlets and magazines by the hundred-weight; blue books and Hansards by the ton ... I think of the splendid time I shall have making a bonfire of them all. How I will stir the fire, and how I will mulch my roses with the ashes' (Aaron Watson, *A Newspaper Man's Memories*, Hutchinson, n.d., p. 266). It is of course likely that not many papers survived the two house fires suffered by Grey. The owners of Fallodon at the time of the first edition had no knowledge of any papers and a personal inspection by Professor Robbins failed to discover them. Trevelyan's family and friends were unable to give any positive information but all assumed that he would have returned the papers to the family. Professor Robbins is willing to give more detailed information about his searches to interested scholars.

On 18 Dec 1986 Sotheby's offered for sale a collection of about 190 letters and memoranda from Grey to John Morley including autograph notes by Morley. The 400 pages of documents covered the period 15 Dec 1905 to 29 June 1910. They were accompanied by a copy of Trevelyan's life of Grey. Trevelyan had apparently enjoyed access to the 'letters that passed between Grey and Morley' in 1906 'and for years afterwards' (Trevelyan, *Grey of Fallodon*, 185, 223). We have been unable to determine the provenance or fate of this collection.

There are letters from Grey to Louise Creighton 1901–10 and 1911–31 in the Bodleian Library (MS Eng lett e 73/1–2). Ten letters from Grey, nine of them to Siegfried Sassoon 1930–32, regarding the health of his stepson Stephen Tennant, are in the Cambridge University Library (Add MS 8889/3/154–63). Ornithological papers are in the Edward Grey Institute, Dept of Zoology, Oxford University, South Parks Rd, Oxford.

JAMES GRIFFITHS (1890–1975)

James Griffiths was Labour MP for Carmarthenshire (Llanelli) 1936–70. He was Minister of National Insurance Aug 1945–Feb 1950, Secretary of State for the Colonies 1950–Oct 1951, and Secretary of State for Wales Oct 1964–April 1966.

There are two principal collections of Griffiths papers, one at Coleg Harlech and the other in the NLW.

Mr Griffiths himself deposited three suitcases of papers in the Library of Coleg Harlech (James Griffiths papers). The papers are not yet listed but they are available for research.

The bulk of the papers refer to Griffiths's Welsh activities. From 1925–36 he was Miners' Agent to the Anthracite Miners' Association. His 1925 election address for this position survives, as do press cuttings on the coal industry, notes of meetings with officials of the Mines Department, and many papers on compensation for accidents in general and for silicosis in particular. Griffiths's work on behalf of the miners he represented is reflected by correspondence on particular cases and copies of the major legal judgements of the period. No papers relating to Griffiths's work as President of the South Wales Miners' Federation are included in this collection.

Many papers have survived from Griffiths's parliamentary election campaigns, including all his election addresses 1936–64, as well as press cuttings, posters, and typescripts of the many election broadcasts Griffiths made. In addition, for the 1936 by-election, when Griffiths first stood for Llanelli, there are many letters encouraging him to stand and wishing him well. They include a letter from Sir Stafford Cripps 10 Feb 1936 saying '. . . it is so important to have real Socialists in the House of Commons now, there are so many reformists'.

Griffiths's constituency work is represented by correspondence on particular cases and on matters of general interest to Llanelli, especially economic matters such as the location of new strip mills and the suggested closure of the ordnance factory at Penby. There are also papers dealing with a suggested new town for mid-Wales.

Griffiths's parliamentary activities are represented by the manuscript of his maiden speech (delivered 23 April 1936 on the effects of the tariff on the Welsh economy), a note of congratulation for the speech from Clement Attlee, and papers relating to an attempt in 1969 to amend the Workmens' Compensation and Benefit Act by a private member's bill. There are also a few Parliamentary Labour Party papers: the report of a questionnaire on House of Commons' services conducted in 1968; a declaration on how the party would elect a prime minister if similar circumstances to those arising on the resignation of Sir Anthony Eden occurred while the Labour Party was in office; and the party's code of conduct adopted in 1968.

There are drafts and press cuttings of articles by or about Griffiths, including biographical articles, articles about the Ammanford White House Society in 1925, Griffiths's 'Westminster Commentary' written for the *Llanelly Mercury* 1959–60, and many press cuttings on Welsh nationalism. There is a manuscript draft of Griffiths's *Glo* (H. Evans & Sons, Liverpool 1945) and the typescript of his memoirs, *Pages from Memory* (Dent 1969). The latter includes some of the original typed notes described by Griffiths in his memoirs as his substitute for a diary.

A few papers survive relating to Griffiths's work as a Governor of the BBC in Wales. There are also manuscript notes for speeches, for example nominating Dr H. King as Speaker 1966, and commemorative addresses on Lloyd George and Vernon Hartshorn.

Griffiths kept more papers until his death and these were deposited by his widow in the NLW (NRA 23695). Unfortunately Griffiths had destroyed most of the contemporary notes or diaries he kept because at that time, he said, he felt that they would be of no future interest. But the collection that remained was substantial. It has been catalogued and divided into five groups: early career 1890–1936; political career 1936–75; Welsh affairs 1938–75; papers relating to Griffiths's auto-biography 1961–69; and a final group of speeches, addresses, broadcasts, etc. 1919–75.

The early career group includes papers relating to his activities in the South Wales Miners' Federation 1920–36 and the Labour Party 1919–26. The political career group includes papers on his activities in the Labour Party 1940–75; papers as Minister of National Insurance 1945–50; and material on colonial affairs 1939–72. There are also papers on Czechoslovakia and Spain 1936–39; the visit of Bulganin and Khrushchev 1956; the Suez Crisis; the death of Nye Bevan 1960; the

Nigeria-Biafra War 1968–70; and on National Superannuation and Social Insurance 1969.

The Welsh Affairs group includes papers on the Welsh Reconstruction Advisory Council 1942–44; devolution of Wales 1938–55 and 1963–75; education 1959–66; and miscellaneous Welsh affairs 1960–75. This group also includes Griffiths's papers as Secretary of State for Wales 1964–66; constituency papers 1956–69; and local government reorganisation 1961–70.

The papers relating to Griffiths's memoirs include correspondence, notebooks, typescripts, and reviews. The final group of papers includes reminiscences 1955–74; broadcasts 1937–67; lectures 1942–71; speeches and addresses 1943–69; articles and reviews 1941–74; press cuttings 1919–74; and miscellaneous personalia 1930s–75.

A transcript of an interview with Griffiths is held at the South Wales Coalfield Archives, University of Wales, Swansea.

Griffiths's work as Colonial Secretary is discussed in David Goldsworthy, *Colonial Issues in British Politics 1945–1961* (Clarendon Press, Oxford 1971), which draws on the records of the Fabian Colonial Bureau. *The Official History of Colonial Development* (5 vols, Macmillan 1980) by D. J. Morgan is a useful guide to sources relating to Griffiths's period at the Colonial Office.

James Griffiths and his Times (Labour Party Wales and the Llanelli's Constituency Labour Party 1978) includes an essay by Griffiths on 'Welsh Politics in my lifetime' and a 60 page 'Appreciation' by J. Beverley Smith which makes use of the collections at Coleg Harlech and the NLW and includes a valuable guide to other sources, notably David B. Smith, 'The Rebuilding of the South Wales Miners' Federation, 1927–1939' (PhD thesis, University of Wales 1976). Griffiths's wife Winnie privately published *One Woman's Story* in 1979.

SIR EDWARD WILLIAM MACLEAY GRIGG, 1st BARON ALTRINCHAM (1879–1955)

Edward Grigg was created KCVO in 1920, KCMG in 1928, and Baron Altrincham in 1945. He was Liberal MP for Oldham 1922–25, and National Conservative MP for Cheshire (Altrincham) 1933–45. He was Parliamentary Secretary to the Ministry of Information Sept 1939–April 1940, Financial Secretary to the War Office April-May 1940, Joint-Under-Secretary to the War Office 1940–March 1942, and Minister Resident in the Middle East Nov 1944–May 1945.

Grigg's papers are in the possession of his son, Mr John Grigg, 32 Dartmouth Row, London SE10 8AW. A microfilm of the greater part of the papers was made by the Queen's University Archives, Canada; copies are now available in the Bodleian Library (MSS film 999–1013), as well as at Harvard University and Duke University.

Except for a few miscellaneous letters and press cuttings, no papers appear to have survived from Grigg's terms of ministerial office. However, much has survived which relates to his other activities: military secretary to the Prince of Wales 1919–20; private secretary to Lloyd George 1920–22; Governor of Kenya 1925–30; and Chairman of the Milk Reorganisation Commission 1932. These papers, which cover the years 1919–46, and fill 30 boxes, have been divided into six main sections: general correspondence; subject files; printed material; speeches and publications; personal; duplicates.

The general correspondence series consists of private correspondence and official correspondence which has no subject file. The series is arranged chronologically by year and within each year alphabetically by correspondent. An index has been compiled for this section; it too is arranged chronologically by year and then by correspondent. Each entry for a particular individual gives the number of letters, their outside dates, and sometimes an indication of the content of the letter(s).

The subject files have been arranged into 12 main divisions: First World War schemes 1916–18; the Prince of Wales's tours 1919–20; foreign affairs 1919–22; imperial relations 1918–22; India 1920–22 – which has a considerable amount of material on the resignation of Edwin Montagu; Ireland 1920–21; (these last four sub-sections relate to Grigg's years as secretary to Lloyd George); East Africa 1925–30; Lady Grigg's Welfare League; Milk Reorganisation Commission; election material 1923 and 1933 (many letters which would have been put in this category have been destroyed); defence 1932–45 (many letters which for the most part expressed agreement with the national register proposals or suggested alternatives have been destroyed); *The Observer* tribunal 1941–42 – Grigg was a member of the tribunal appointed to settle the differences between J. L. Garvin and W. Astor when the former resigned.

The printed material is divided into seven sections: press cuttings 1919–25: these were arranged by Grigg's secretary and cross-referenced (not microfilmed); a scrapbook for the 1933 Altrincham by-election; press cuttings for 1940–45 (not microfilmed); reviews of *Faith of an Englishman* (Macmillan 1936), *The British Commonwealth* (Hutchinson 1943), *British Foreign Policy* (Hutchinson 1944); and various pamphlets.

Grigg's speeches have been divided into speeches and broadcasts. The section including his articles does not include his letters to *The Times* – they are to be found in the general correspondence series.

The personal papers consist of family correspondence arranged alphabetically and miscellaneous items – bills, statements, etc., which were not microfilmed. The final section of duplicates was also not microfilmed.

The Conservative Party Archives in the Bodleian Library should also be consulted. Grigg's papers as 'Imperial editor' of *The Times* are at the News International RO, PO Box 49, Virginia St, London E1 9XY (NRA 19359).

SIR (PERCY) JAMES GRIGG (1890–1964)

James Grigg was created KCB in 1932. He was National MP for Cardiff (East) 1942–45. He was Secretary of State for War Feb 1942–Aug 1945.

Grigg's papers were deposited by his executors in the Churchill Archives Centre (PJGG). A list is available (NRA 15458). The post-1945 papers are now open to research including a few files from 1963–66 previously closed under the 30–year rule. Grigg wrote in the preface to his autobiography *Prejudice and Judgment* (Jonathan Cape 1948): 'From none of my jobs have I brought away more than a handful of papers and at no time have I ever kept a diary' (p. 8); nevertheless some interesting papers have survived.

The only material relating to Grigg's early life came from his father's papers; it includes a speech day address by his headmaster, Grigg's school-certificate, the order of service for his wedding and an early photo. Only a few letters from the various Chancellors he served have survived.

Most of the papers derive from Grigg's Indian service: he was Financial Member of the Government of India 1934–39. Correspondence with Neville Chamberlain, Churchill, Montagu Norman, Lords Linlithgow and Lothian, and others has survived. It includes several long and blunt letters from Philip Snowden 1935–36 (3/12). There are files on Indian Federation, the Indian political situation, on the Reserve Bank, and on a financial enquiry. There are also ten albums compiled by Lady Grigg which include not only programmes, photos and souvenirs, but also her letters to her husband 1934–36, and to Thomas Jones 1934–39. Grigg's own attitude to Indian affairs and later events is revealed in his letters to his father 1937–53.

Only a few papers have survived from Grigg's term of office as Secretary of State and as an MP. They include congratulations, correspondence about the loss of his pension, and correspondence inviting Grigg to stand as National MP for Cambridge University in April 1945. The miscellaneous correspondence includes many letters from soldiers, including Sir Bernard Paget and especially from Field Marshal Lord Montgomery. The latter seems to have sent Grigg drafts of speeches for comment as well as frequently corresponding with him, particularly in 1949–58 and 1962–63.

There is a good deal of material concerned with the publication of Grigg's memoirs; it includes permissions to quote from letters, and reviews by Churchill and others. There are also cuttings of reviews by Grigg and related letters, correspondence with Sir James Butler on the official history of the Second World War, and several draft obituaries of Churchill, Lord Montgomery, Lord Alanbrooke, Sir John Dill, Sir Bernard Paget, and Lord Wavell. A few papers have survived from Grigg's other postwar activities, in particular a file of correspondence relating to his chairmanship of the Commission of Inquiry into the preservation of departmental records, and the proposal in 1957 that he be chairman of the Independent Television Authority.

Private Office papers of the Secretary of State for War are in the PRO at WO 259.

FREDERICK EDWARD GUEST (1875–1937)

Freddie Guest was Liberal MP for Dorset (East) 1910–22, Gloucestershire (Stroud) 1923–24 and Bristol (North) 1924–29. In 1930 he became a Conservative and was MP for Plymouth (Drake) 1931–37. He was Secretary of State for Air April 1921–Oct 1922.

Neither Guest's son, Raymond R. Guest, nor his great-nephew, the 3rd Lord Wimborne, knew of any papers.

We were not successful in our attempt to contact Guest's daughter Mrs Diana Manning before her death in 1994. Mrs Manning's daughter, Lorraine de la Valdène Odasso, did not know of any papers. We were not able to contact his grandchildren in the USA, Raymond, Winston and Frederick Guest.

Alfred Cochrane's entry on Guest in *DNB 1931–1940*, 379–80, is based on published sources.

IVOR CHURCHILL GUEST, 1st BARON ASHBY ST LEDGERS, 3rd Bt, 2nd BARON WIMBORNE, 1st VISCOUNT WIMBORNE (1873–1939)

Ivor Guest was Conservative MP for Plymouth 1900–04. He became a Liberal in 1904 and sat for Plymouth until 1906 when he became Liberal MP for Cardiff 1906–10. He was Paymaster-General Feb 1910–May 1912. He was created Baron Ashby St Ledgers in 1910, succeeded his father as 3rd baronet and 2nd Baron Wimborne in 1914, and was created Viscount Wimborne in 1918.

His grandson, the 3rd Viscount Wimborne, knew of no papers relating to Guest's career.

Mr David Satinoff has a collection of 16 letters from Churchill to his cousin Guest mostly in 'a characteristically advisory vein, mainly discussing political issues of mutual interest', spanning the years 1898–1912.

At a July sale at Sotheby's in 1967 several other letters from Churchill to Guest were offered individually for sale, including Churchill's announcement to his cousin of his forthcoming marriage in 1908 headed 'Secret till Saturday', and a letter 28 May 1915 discussing the Dardanelles campaign ('my great enterprise'), and stating 'the new cabinet is interesting and formidable; – I am very well received and regarded in it'.

Alfred Cochrane's entry on Guest in *DNB 1931–1940*, 380–1, is based on published sources.

WALTER EDWARD GUINNESS, 1st BARON MOYNE (1880–1944)

Walter Guinness was Conservative MP for Bury St Edmunds (Suffolk West, Bury St Edmunds from 1918) 1907–31. He was Under-Secretary of State for War Oct 1922–Oct 1923, Financial Secretary to the Treasury 1923–Jan 1924 and Nov 1924–Nov 1925, Minister of Agriculture and Fisheries 1925–June 1929, Joint Parliamentary Secretary to the Ministry of Agriculture May 1940–Feb 1941, Secretary of State for the Colonies 1941–Feb 1942, Deputy Minister of State, Middle East Aug 1942–Jan 1944, and Minister Resident in the Middle East Jan-Nov 1944. He was created Baron Moyne in 1932.

Julian Amery, who knew Moyne in the Middle East in the Second World War, records: 'It was said that he once asked his secretary, "I want to give a party. Please type out a list of my friends." When she asked who they were, he had replied: "I don't really know, but have a look at my letters and diaries and invite the people you think I'd like to see" ...!' (Julian Amery, *Approach March: a venture in autobiography*, Hutchinson 1973, p. 315).

In the early 1970s the 2nd Lord Moyne, knew of no surviving papers relating to his father's career nor did his secretary, Miss D. Osmond.

Subsequently large batches of Moyne's daily letters to his wife 1914–18, and pencilled notes enclosed with them, came to light. These had formed the basis of a 'diary' of the war which Moyne composed in 1919. An edition of this work, supplemented by extracts from the original material on which it was based, was edited by Brian Bond and Simon Robbins under the title *Staff Officer, The Diaries of Walter Guinness (First Lord Moyne), 1914–1918* (Leo Cooper 1987). The 2nd Lord Moyne's papers are in the care of his literary executor, his daughter the Hon Rosaleen Mulji. Mrs Mulji has not yet sorted her father's papers and cannot confirm the existence of these letters or any other surviving papers of her grandfather's.

Moyne's daughter, the Marchioness of Normanby, confirmed in 1994 that no further papers have since come to light.

Evidence that other papers were held by Moyne before his death is found in his refusal 'to give up his [Cabinet] Papers' in reply to the request of Sept 1934 by the Cabinet Office to return them (report to Cabinet by Sir Maurice Hankey, 29 Nov 1935, PRO, CAB 24/257).

RICHARD BURDON HALDANE, VISCOUNT HALDANE (1856–1928)

Richard Haldane was Liberal MP for Haddingtonshire or Lothian (East) 1885–1911. He was Secretary of State for War Dec 1905–June 1912, and Lord Chancellor 1912–May 1915 and Jan-Nov 1924. He was created Viscount Haldane in 1911 and KT in 1913.

Haldane's papers form the greater part of a large deposit of Haldane family papers in the NLS (MSS 5901–6109). There is a list (NRA 11618). As well as a considerable body of correspondence 1882–1928, there are several drafts and memoranda, eg on Haldane's role in Anglo-German negotiations before 1914, and his impressions of several of his contemporaries – Asquith, Grey, Rosebery, A. J. Balfour, and John Morley. Though not strictly a part of Haldane's own papers, his almost daily letters to his mother 1866–1924 are a vital source for historians. Haldane himself seems to have regarded these letters as his diary. His letters to his sister Elizabeth 1874–1928 (MSS 6010–13) are also an important source because they are often more detailed though less frequent than the letters to his mother. Elizabeth Haldane's diary (MSS 20240–4) is also part of the collection.

A further deposit of Haldane family papers made by Dr T. G. N. Haldane in 1974 (Haldane Papers Add MSS 20034–230) includes volumes of press cuttings, family correspondence, fee-books, drafts and typescripts of Haldane's autobiography, notebooks, drafts of articles, speech notes, and obituaries.

The papers of Haldane's biographer Sir Frederick Maurice at the Liddell Hart Centre contain five stray letters dated between 1894 and 1928, including one from Joseph Chamberlain on South African financiers and provincial universities Sept 1902, and Haldane to Lord Crewe on opposition front bench arrangements Dec 1916 (Maurice Papers 3/3/1–6).

There are photocopies of correspondence with Sir Ernest Cassel in the Cassel collection in the Churchill Archives Centre (EJCL).

It is clear from Haldane's posthumously published *An Autobiography* (Hodder & Stoughton 1929) that he himself sorted through and destroyed a large part of his papers. What survives has been used and is frequently quoted in Sir Frederick Maurice KCMG, *Haldane* (2 vols, Faber & Faber 1937–39), Dudley Sommer, *Haldane of Cloan* (Allen & Unwin 1960), Stephen Koss, *Lord Haldane: Scapegoat for Liberalism* (Columbia UP, New York and London 1969), Edward M. Spiers, *Haldane: An Army Reformer* (Edinburgh UP 1980), Eric Ashby and Mary Anderson, *Portrait of Haldane at Work on Education* (Macmillan 1974), and

Lord Chancellors 1. For Haldane's work at the War Office see John Gooch, 'Haldane and the "National Army"' in Ian Beckett and John Gooch (eds), *Politicians and Defence: Studies in the Formulation of British Defence Policy 1845–1970* (Manchester UP 1981), 69–86, and E. M. Teagarden, *Haldane at the War Office: a study in organisation and management* (Garden Press, New York 1976).

GEORGE HENRY HALL, 1st VISCOUNT HALL (1881–1965)

George Hall was Labour MP for Merthyr Tydfil (Aberdare) 1922–46. He was Civil Lord of the Admiralty June 1929–Aug 1931, Parliamentary Under-Secretary of State for the Colonies May 1940–Feb 1942, Financial Secretary to the Admiralty 1942–Sept 1943, Parliamentary Under-Secretary of State for Foreign Affairs 1943–May 1945, Secretary of State for the Colonies Aug 1945–Oct 1946, and First Lord of the Admiralty 1946–May 1951. He was created Viscount Hall in 1946.

A small collection of Lord Hall's papers, formerly in the possession of his son the 2nd Viscount, is now, we believe, in the possession of his daughter-in-law, Lady Hall, and not held at Nuffield College, where it was only held briefly during the 1970s. Copies of significant items from these papers have been deposited in the Brynmor Jones Library, University of Hull (DX/84/1.12).

Hall's local political activities are mainly represented by printed papers and press cuttings. There is a cuttings book 1916–56, copies of the *Aberdare Division Labour News* 1922, and the 1929 election issue of the *Aberdare Leader*. There are also copies of the ILP's 'Notes for Speakers' March 1929, mainly concerned with Lloyd George's promises and performance, and 'Bullets for Baldwinism', n.d. There is a stencilled copy of voting in the various miners' lodges for a miners' parliamentary candidate 12 July 1920. There is a copy of Hall's 1929 election address. There are also photos and press cuttings of a visit to Aberdare of the then Duchess of York.

Hall's parliamentary activities are, again, mainly covered by press cuttings – one book covers 1929–56 and includes some of Hall's campaign literature. Hall seems to have particularly interested himself in the 1924 Miners' Bill (there is a letter from Thomas Richards congratulating him on a speech, 30 May 1924), on nystagmus, the miners' disease, and the 1934 Unemployment Bill. There is a typescript entitled *The Coordination of the Social Services*, n.d. A file marked 'letters important' includes letters from Churchill, the Attlees, and Eden but they are mainly concerned with Hall's appointment to office or his retirement.

A very small number of papers has survived from Hall's terms of office. His first and last acts as Civil Lord to the Admiralty were to write to his son. In his last letter, 24 Aug 1931, he described the Cabinet held before Ramsay MacDonald went to Buckingham Palace to hand in his resignation. There is also a typed letter from MacDonald explaining the need for a National Government. Apart from press cuttings, only fragments survive from his wartime positions, for example a page in Hall's writing recording the War Cabinet's approval of his discussions with the American Ambassador 16 Aug 1944 – no subject is mentioned. Hall's tenure of the Colonial Office is represented by a file on the Brooke family of Sarawak – their tax liabilities and their administration in 1946. There is also a 'Diary of Negotiations with the Jewish Agency on Jewish Participation in the Conference' 27 July-30 Sept 1946. Hall's tenure of the Admiralty is covered by press cuttings, photos of a visit to the Fleet by the royal family, and of the Admiralty Board in session, as well as letters from naval personnel on his retirement.

There are various miscellaneous papers from the last period in Hall's political life: memoranda on free trade in Europe 1957 and 1959; notes and diaries from trips abroad – to Northern Rhodesia in 1954, Australia 1956, and the USA and Canada 1958; notes for a speech in the House of Lords on (?) Wales, n.d.; a collection of press cuttings about political leaders, including reviews of Attlee's memoirs. There are several copies of *Punch* 19 Sept 1947 with Illingworth's cartoon featuring Hall.

A small collection of more personal papers has survived. There are address books and pocket diaries for 1930, 1941, 1944, 1947–61. Several copies of Hall's will survive, as well as letters of condolence to his son. There are also cuttings of obituaries in the local and national press.

A biography based on the Hall papers was contributed by the editors to *DLB*, II, 145–8. Hall's work as Colonial Secretary is examined in D. J. Morgan, *The Official History of Colonial Development* (5 vols, Macmillan 1980).

GEORGE NIGEL DOUGLAS-HAMILTON, 10th EARL OF SELKIRK (1906–1994)

George Douglas-Hamilton succeeded his father (under terms of special remainder) as 10th Earl of Selkirk in 1940. He was created GCMG in 1959, GBE in 1963 and KT in 1976. He was Paymaster-General Nov 1953–Dec 1955, Chancellor of the Duchy of Lancaster 1955-Jan 1957, and First Lord of the Admiralty 1957–Oct 1959.

Lord Selkirk retained some private papers. A file of papers relating to his period as UK Commissioner for Singapore and Commissioner-General for South East Asia 1959–63 was placed in the care of the Foreign and Commonwealth Office.

Lord Selkirk contributed to the witness seminar on 'The Sandys

Defence White Papers 1957' at the Institute of Contemporary British History.

A dispute over succession to the Earldom (Selkirk had no children) was settled in March 1996 in favour of Lord James Douglas-Hamilton, who will disclaim the title to retain his seat in the Commons.

LORD GEORGE FRANCIS HAMILTON (1845–1927)

Lord George Hamilton (son of the 1st Duke of Abercorn) was Conservative MP for Middlesex 1868–85 and for Middlesex (Ealing) 1885–1906. He was Under-Secretary of State for India Feb 1874–April 1878, Vice-President of the Council (responsible for education) 1878–April 1880, First Lord of the Admiralty June 1885–Feb 1886 and Aug 1886–Aug 1892, and Secretary of State for India July 1895–Oct 1903. He was created GCSI in 1903.

Hamilton's son, Ronald Hamilton, OBE, presented 34 volumes of his papers relating to India to what is now the Oriental and India Office Collections, British Library in 1951 (MSS Eur C 125–6, D 508–10; NRA 10867) This collection consists of 15 volumes of correspondence and papers 1895–98 between Hamilton and the then Viceroy, Lord Elgin, and 18 volumes of correspondence 1899–1903 between Hamilton and Lord Curzon, Elgin's successor. There is also one volume of printed telegrams 1895–98. Hamilton left behind him in the India Office his correspondence with members of the royal family and governors, as well as files on special cases. These are also available for research at the India Office Collection (MSS Eur F 123). Two volumes of printed correspondence 1896–98 between Hamilton and Lord Sandhurst, Governor of Bombay, were purchased by the Indian Institute, part of the Bodleian Library, in 1940 (93 C 69, 70).

There is correspondence written by and relating to Hamilton in the personal and political correspondence of the 1st Duke of Abercorn (D.623A/251–64), and the papers of Dr W. E. Ball, a Secretary of the Non-Conformist Unionist Association 1885–89 (D.2396), both to be found in the PRONI.

We were unable to contact Hamilton's grand-daughter, the Countess Czernin. However, Hamilton's great-nephew, Sir Rupert Buchanan-Jardine Bt, did not know of any other papers.

In his two volumes of memoirs, *Parliamentary Reminiscences and Reflections 1868–1885*, and *1886–1906* (John Murray 1917, 1922), Hamilton quoted from a few letters and papers. Hamilton's tenure of the India Office is placed in context in Arnold P. Kaminsky, *The India Office, 1880–1910* (Greenwood Press, New York 1986). Kaminsky's bibliography is an excellent guide to relevant public records, private papers, and unpublished theses.

ROBERT WILLIAM HANBURY (1845–1903)

Robert Hanbury was Conservative MP for Tamworth 1872–78, Staffordshire (North) 1878–80 and Preston 1885–1903. He was Financial Secretary to the Treasury June 1895–Nov 1900, and President of the Board of Agriculture and Fisheries 1900–May 1903.

We have been unable to trace Hanbury's papers. Hanbury was married twice but had no children. His second wife remarried; there was no issue of this marriage. She died in 1931, her second husband in 1944; his executor did not know of the existence of any papers. In his will, Hanbury had particularly mentioned his eight nieces, the daughters of his sister. We were able to trace one of his nieces, Mrs Margaret Swann-Mason. She died in 1955 but her daughter, Hanbury's great-niece, informed us that his sister destroyed practically all the papers she had before her death and certainly nothing survived with either Miss Swann-Mason or her cousins relating to Hanbury.

Hanbury lived and was buried at Ilam Hall, Ashbourne, then in Derbyshire, but now in Staffordshire. Neither of the two CROs knew of any papers. The house is now owned by the National Trust but the Trust had no records concerning Hanbury.

Hanbury's death, Sir Henry Lucy wrote, 'keenly felt in the House of Commons, irreparable to the agricultural community, is a heavy blow to the Government' (Henry W. Lucy, *The Balfourian Parliament 1900–1905*, Hodder and Stoughton 1906, p. 253). Modern historians of the Conservative Party have ignored Hanbury's career. The brief biographical sketch by Ernest Clarke in *DNB 1901–1911*, 195, is based only on published sources.

SIR MAURICE PASCAL ALERS HANKEY, 1st BARON HANKEY (1877–1963)

Maurice Hankey was created KCB in 1916, GCB in 1919, and Baron Hankey in 1939. He was Minister without Portfolio Sept 1939–May 1940, Chancellor of the Duchy of Lancaster 1940–July 1941, and Paymaster-General 1941–March 1942.

Five hundred and thirty-eight files of Hankey's papers were deposited in the Churchill Archives Centre (HNKY; NRA 31396), where Captain Stephen Roskill produced a biography in three volumes: *Hankey, Man of Secrets*, vol i *1877–1918*, vol ii *1919–1931*, vol iii *1931–1963* (Collins 1970, 1972, 1974). The diaries and general correspondence for these periods are open to research. Applications should be made through the Keeper of the Archives. Hankey's personal papers are closed to research.

Captain Roskill quoted extensively from Hankey's diary (begun in March 1915) and from Hankey's many letters to his wife. Hankey himself quoted from his diary and papers in his *The Supreme Command*

(2 vols, George Allen & Unwin 1961) and in *The Supreme Control: at the Paris Peace Conference 1919* (George Allen & Unwin 1963).

A further collection of Hankey's papers is available in the PRO (CAB 63; NRA 28775). The collection includes what Hankey called his 'Magnum Opus' files which may possibly have been used by him in writing *The Supreme Command* and were certainly drawn on for his *Diplomacy By Conference: Studies in Public Affairs 1920–1946* (Ernest Benn 1946). They include memoranda prepared by Hankey for the Prime Minister and the War Cabinet, notes, and correspondence. In particular there is much material about the Gallipoli campaign and the Dardanelles Commission, including correspondence Jan-May 1915 between Churchill and Admiral Fisher about the Dardanelles, Hankey's own letters from Gallipoli July-Aug 1915, and the memoranda he submitted as evidence to the Dardanelles Commission. There are also pre-war memoranda on the organisation of the expeditionary force, and appreciations of the war situation. But most of this collection is concerned with Hankey's role between the wars and in the Second World War. There are papers relating to his visits abroad; from the 1921–22 Washington Conference (Hankey was British Secretary) which includes letters from Tom Jones describing negotiations with the Sinn Fein leaders, some personal correspondence which includes requests for help, congratulations for various honours and appointments, and papers concerning the Suez Canal Company (Hankey was a director 1938–39 and 1945–58). CAB 63/83–119 are Second World War papers and are now all available. As Hankey was government spokesman in the House of Lords on Economic Warfare there are many papers from this department, especially on oil. There are also papers concerning refugees, and contingencies for the invasion of Britain. There is correspondence with W. Beveridge in Feb 1940 on the composition of the 1916 War Cabinet.

The papers of John Bickersteth, a Canadian academic, also at Churchill Archives Centre, include reports to Hankey on Canadian affairs 1932–40 (BICK).

John F. Naylor, *A Man and an Institution: Sir Maurice Hankey, the Cabinet Secretariat and the custody of Cabinet secrecy* (Cambridge UP 1984) contains a valuable guide to official 'documentary collections and other related works'.

LEWIS HARCOURT, 1st VISCOUNT HARCOURT (1863–1922)

Lewis ('Loulou') Harcourt was Liberal MP for North-East Lancashire (Rossendale) 1904–16. He was First Commissioner of Works Dec 1905–Nov 1910 and May 1915–Dec 1916, and Secretary of State for the

Colonies Nov 1910–May 1915. He was created Viscount Harcourt in 1916.

A large collection of papers (253 boxes and volumes) was deposited in the Bodleian Library in 1972 by his son, the 2nd Viscount Harcourt (MSS Harcourt dep 347–600). The collection contains the papers of both Harcourt and his father, Sir William Harcourt, as well as many family papers relating to both men. The papers of father and son are inextricably related, as Harcourt was for many years his father's private secretary. An extensive political correspondence, in which Harcourt was engaged on his father's behalf, and both sides of the correspondence between father and son, are to be found as part of the papers of Sir William. The whole collection has been sorted, catalogued, and indexed by P. J. Bull and others (NRA 3679).

An additional collection of papers (221 boxes and volumes) was acquired by the Bodleian in 1984–86 (MSS Harcourt dep adds 69–267). It includes correspondence with Harcourt's wife, and with his step-mother, and political correspondence with Asquith, Lloyd George, Sir Edward Grey, and other prominent politicians.

The diaries kept by Harcourt, mainly while his father was in office, are among the more interesting items in his papers. They cover the years 1880–87 and 1892–95. There are typed copies of these diaries, although the typescripts are not an exact transcription of the originals. These diaries are available for research. Manuscript diaries for the years 1905–15 were in the possession of Lord Harcourt in the early 1970s, but his daughter the Hon Mrs Crispin Gascoigne advises that they cannot now be found.

The papers relating to Harcourt's term of office as First Commissioner of Works include printed estimates 1906–11 and files on various matters in which the Office of Works was involved, including the allocation of rooms in the Palace of Westminster, extensions to the Tate Gallery, and alternatives for the Latin inscription above Admiralty Arch.

The papers which represent much of Harcourt's activity as Colonial Secretary were neatly sorted and labelled in 1916 under the supervision of Harcourt's assistant private secretary, J. C. C. Davidson, later 1st Viscount Davidson. Davidson had arranged for 'private' letters which had been attached to registered departmental papers to be returned to Harcourt. Colonial Office officials pointed out that previous Secretaries of State had 'always left any private letters which had got attached to the papers with the department'. But, as Davidson recorded, the practice of attaching private letters in this way had 'greatly increased since Lord Crewe's day' (Davidson to Harcourt, 1 March 1916, Harcourt MSS, dep 446). There are files of correspondence with various governors, such as Lords Gladstone, Liverpool, Islington, and Buxton. The latter reported secret interviews with Botha and Smuts Oct 1914–May

1915. There are also volumes of official correspondence 1911–16, and of private correspondence for the same dates. These volumes are arranged alphabetically by correspondent; lists at the front of each volume give the names of the correspondents and the dates and subjects of their letters. Similar lists are to be found in the correspondence files. Scattered throughout both series are Colonial Office memoranda and correspondence with Davidson 1915–16 on 'office news'.

There is a box of papers 1915–16 when Harcourt was Acting President of the Board of Trade. The papers cover such problems as the supply of petrol, the quantity of beef available from South America, and the wages of South Wales' miners. Harcourt received several deputations at this time. To one, from the miners, on 19 June 1916, which demanded the nationalisation of the mines, Harcourt replied: 'This is not the time, but they can at least show that nationalisation would be a success. From this point of view, now is their chance'.

Harcourt's membership of the Cabinet is represented by printed Cabinet memoranda and Foreign Office telegrams (some annotated) 1908–16. There are also some pages of pencilled notes taken at Cabinet meetings. Two issues stand out as being of special interest to Harcourt: the 1909–10 Budget and the negotiations with Germany. In the budget, Harcourt was mainly concerned with Lloyd George's proposals for a succession duty; he used information from his Oxfordshire estates in several memoranda written for the Cabinet. Distrust for Lloyd George is demonstrated in his correspondence with Sir A. Thring, the First Parliamentary Counsel. Harcourt was deeply involved in the negotiations with Germany 1911–14. As Colonial Secretary he took part in the attempts to revise the secret treaty of 1898, especially in reference to Portuguese Africa. He was also concerned in the attempts to reach a more general understanding with the Germans, as his interviews and correspondence with von Kühlmann, Admiral Eisendecher, and Sir Edward Grey demonstrate.

There is much material from his terms of office as First Commissioner of Works and Secretary of State for the Colonies.

Also held at the Bodleian are 86 boxes of Harcourt family correspondence and papers (MSS Harcourt dep 601–87), which include the papers of Mary, Viscountess Harcourt relating to the First World War and the Red Cross. These papers are mostly uncatalogued.

THE HON JOHN HUGH HARE, 1st VISCOUNT BLAKENHAM (1911–1982)

John Hare was Conservative MP for Woodbridge 1945–50 and Sudbury and Woodbridge 1950–63. He was Minister of State for Colonial Affairs Dec 1955–Oct 1956, Secretary of State for War 1956–Jan 1958, Minister of Agriculture, Fisheries and Food 1958–July 1960, Minister of Labour

1960–Oct 1963, and Chancellor of the Duchy of Lancaster 1963–Oct 1964. He was created Viscount Blakenham in 1963.

Lord Blakenham advised Dr Chris Cook that he had kept no papers (*Sources*, 3, p. 47). Blakenham's brother, the 5th Earl of Listowel, advised us that he did not know of any surviving papers.

The Conservative Party Archives at the Bodleian Library have many papers produced by the chairman's office when Blakenham held that position (CCO 20). A handlist is available. The papers include correspondence with party members; general election memoranda; files on various issues such as local government, housing, pensions, public opinion and Europe; and correspondence with the Leader of the Party, as well as Blakenham's appointment diaries and notes for speeches in 1964. Permission to view the papers must be obtained by writing to the Chairman's Office, Conservative Political Centre, 32 Smith Square, London SW1P 3HH.

The brief biography of Blakenham by William Whitelaw in *DNB 1981–1985*, 180–1, is based on personal knowledge.

WILLIAM FRANCIS HARE, 5th EARL OF LISTOWEL (1906–)

William Hare was known as Viscount Ennismore from 1924 until he succeeded his father as 5th Earl of Listowel in 1931, and was created GCMG in 1957. He was Parliamentary Under-Secretary of State for India Oct 1944–May 1945, Postmaster-General Aug 1945–April 1947, Minister of Information Feb-March 1946, Secretary of State for India and Burma 1947–Jan 1948, Minister of State for the Colonies 1948– Feb 1950, and Parliamentary Secretary to the Ministry for Agriculture and Fisheries Nov 1950–Oct 1951.

Lord Listowel has only a very small collection of papers relating to his political career. Most of these papers concern his appointment as Governor-General of Ghana 1957–60. They include correspondence with President Nkrumah and with the Queen's secretaries, as well as correspondence with the Foreign and Commonwealth Office on domestic arrangements. There are also some letters concerning Harold Macmillan's visit to Ghana in Jan 1960, and some notes of Mr Macmillan's conversations with Ghanaian leaders.

Only a few fragments survive from Lord Listowel's earlier periods in office. There is a postcard from George Bernard Shaw advocating a return to the penny post, a copy of a long letter from General Wavell to Winston Churchill 24 Oct 1944, giving Wavell's views on the situation in India, some letters from the Governor of Burma 1947, a long letter from John Freeman on the negotiations with Burma in 1947, a letter of thanks for his work at the India and Burma Office from Clement Attlee, and some papers concerning the work of the Molson committee in 1961 on the boundary dispute between the Buganda and the Bunyoro.

Lord Listowel was Chairman of Committees in the House of Lords 1965–75 and has in his possession the letters he exchanged with the Lord Chancellors during this period (Elwyn-Jones, Hailsham, and Gardiner).

An important collection of weekly letters between Lord Listowel and Lord Mountbatten 25 April–9 Aug 1947 about the transfer of power from Britain to India and Pakistan was presented by Lord Listowel to the Oriental and India Office Collections, British Library (MSS Eur C 357). However, Lord Listowel's last two letters from Lord Mountbatten, dated 1978, remain in his possession.

Lady Listowel's papers relating to Rhodesia and Tanzania 1968–71 are in the Centre for South African Studies, University of York.

Lord Listowel is writing an autobiography. He published an article on the independence of India, 'The Whitehall Dimension of the Transfer of Power', *Indo-British Review*, VII, 3 and 4, 1978, 22–31.

Lord Listowel's role in Indian affairs is discussed in Robin Moore, *Escape from Empire: The Attlee Government and the Indian Problem* (Clarendon Press, Oxford 1983) and *Making the New Commonwealth* (Clarendon Press, Oxford 1987). The HMSO series on the Transfer of Power 1942–47 contains much material on him.

SIR HAROLD SIDNEY HARMSWORTH, 1st Bt, 1st VISCOUNT ROTHERMERE (1868–1940)

Harold Harmsworth was created a baronet in 1910, Baron Rothermere in 1914, and Viscount Rothermere in 1919. He was President of the Air Council Nov 1917–April 1918.

Lord Rothermere bequeathed all his papers to William Collin Brooks. Brooks died in 1959 and his widow died in 1972. Shortly before Mrs Brooks's death, she returned Harmsworth's papers to his son, the 2nd Viscount Rothermere. The late Lord Rothermere informed us that there were only a very small number of papers; most of his father's papers were destroyed during his lifetime. The few papers which survived were of a purely personal and family nature and were not available for research.

Rothermere is prominent in Stephen Koss, *The Rise and Fall of the Political Press in Britain*, vol 2, *The Twentieth Century* (University of North Carolina Press, Chapel Hill 1984). There is an informative brief biography and bibliography by Christine Shaw in *DBB*, 3, 57–65.

VERNON HARTSHORN (1872–1931)

Vernon Hartshorn was Labour MP for Glamorganshire (Ogmore) 1918–31. He was Postmaster-General Jan–Nov 1924, and Lord Privy Seal with special responsibility for unemployment June 1930–March 1931.

Hartshorn's son, Mr V. I. Hartshorn, had until the 1960s a large collection of press cuttings 1910–30 relating to his father's political career, but these were sent for salvage. Only one volume of press cuttings survived. It included some letters of sympathy sent to Mrs Hartshorn after her husband's death, including one from Ramsay MacDonald. The volume formed the basis of an article by Peter Stead, 'Vernon Hartshorn: Miners' Agent and Cabinet Minister', *Glamorgan Historian*, vi, 1969, 83–94.

The NLW holds one letter from Hartshorn in 1906 to Samuel T. Evans (Samuel T. Evans papers 24). There are also a few letters in the National Museum of Labour History. There are no Hartshorn papers in the Glamorgan RO.

There is a brief entry on Hartshorn by the editors in *DLB*, I, 150–2.

SIR PATRICK GARDINER HASTINGS (1880–1952)

Patrick Hastings was Labour MP for Wallsend 1922–26. He was Attorney-General Jan–Nov 1924. He was knighted in 1924.

In preparing the first edition, we were told that neither of Hastings's daughters, Mrs Patricia Hastings and Mrs N. Bentley, had any papers relating to their father's political career. Hastings's widow told Dr H. Montgomery Hyde, when he was writing his biography, that Hastings used to throw everything away.

None of the various books on Hastings's life appears to quote from unpublished material: *The Autobiography of Sir Patrick Hastings* (Heinemann 1948); Patricia Hastings, *The Life of Patrick Hastings* (Cresset Press 1959); H. Montgomery Hyde, *Sir Patrick Hastings. His Life and Cases* (Heinemann 1960).

ANTONY HENRY HEAD, 1st VISCOUNT HEAD (1906–1983)

Antony Head was Conservative MP for Carshalton 1945–60. He was Secretary of State for War Oct 1951–Oct 1956, and Minister of Defence 1956–Jan 1957. He was created Viscount Head in 1960, KCMG in 1961, and GCMG in 1963.

Head's son, the 2nd Viscount Head, advised that his father was not in the habit of keeping papers. The few papers which exist are held by the family, who have asked that they remain private.

The PRO has identified papers from Head's period as Minister of Defence 1956–57 (DEFE 13/4–70).

There is an informed sketch by Sir John Colville in *DNB 1981–1985*, 186–8.

SIR LIONEL FREDERICK HEALD (1897–1981)

Lionel Heald was Conservative MP for Chertsey 1950–70. He was Attorney-General Nov 1951–Oct 1954. He was created KT in 1951.

Heald's son, Mr Mervyn Heald, QC, advised us that his father did not keep an archive and that there are no surviving papers of interest.

SIR EDWARD RICHARD GEORGE HEATH (1916–)

Edward Heath was Conservative MP for Bexley 1950–74, Bexley Sidcup 1974–83 and Old Bexley and Sidcup 1983–present. He was Lord Commissioner of the Treasury Nov 1951–Dec 1955, Parliamentary Secretary to the Treasury 1955–Oct 1959, Minister of Labour 1959– July 1960, Lord Privy Seal 1960–Oct 1963, Secretary of State for Industry, Trade, Regional Development and President of the Board of Trade 1963–Oct 1964, and Prime Minister and First Lord of the Treasury and Minister for the Civil Service June 1970–March 1974. He was Leader of the Conservative Party Aug 1965–Feb 1975. He was created KG in 1992.

Sir Edward advised us that he holds 'an extremely comprehensive archive of all my personal papers (several hundred boxes)' which covers the whole of his political life. These papers, which are stored at his home in Salisbury, are not available for research as he is presently engaged in writing his memoirs.

The Conservative Party Archives in the Bodleian Library contain Chairman's office correspondence at the time when Heath was Chief Whip 1955–59 as well as other correspondence and papers in the Chairman's papers and in the Conservative Research Department collection relating to Heath.

Heath's books *Sailing: a Course in My Life* (Sidgwick & Jackson 1975), *Music: a Joy for Life* (Sidgwick & Jackson 1975) and *Travels: People and Places in My Life* (Sidgwick & Jackson 1977) all contain autobiographical material.

John Campbell did not have access to the private papers in preparing *Edward Heath: A biography* (Jonathan Cape 1993).

ARTHUR HENDERSON (1863–1935)

Arthur Henderson was Labour MP for Durham (Barnard Castle) 1903– 18, Lancashire (Widnes) 1919–22, Newcastle (East) 1923, Burnley 1924– 31 and Derbyshire (Clay Cross) 1933–35. He was President of the Board of Education May 1915–Aug 1916, Paymaster-General with special responsibility for labour Aug–Dec 1916, Minister without Portfolio and Member of the War Cabinet 1916–Aug 1917, Home Secretary Jan–Nov 1924, and Secretary of State for Foreign Affairs June 1929–Aug 1931. He was Chairman of the Labour Party 1908–10 and 1914–17, and Leader of the Party 1931–32. He presided over the World Disarmament Conference 1932–35 and was awarded the Nobel Prize for Peace in 1934.

Mary Agnes Hamilton, in her biography *Arthur Henderson* (Heinemann

1938) quoted occasionally from letters by Henderson. But in her preface she said that once Henderson had answered a letter or finished with a document, he put it into the wastepaper basket and that only a small amount of written material survived him. According to Raymond Postgate, *The Life of George Lansbury* (Longmans, Green 1951), 'a long and intimate' correspondence between Henderson and Lansbury existed when Miss Hamilton was writing her book but it had since been 'wantonly destroyed' (p. 279).

Henderson's sons did not retain any of their father's papers. But, although it seems that many of Henderson's personal papers have been destroyed, much of his political correspondence has survived. Most of the letters, files, reports, and memoranda that he wrote and received in his capacity as Secretary of the Labour Party are preserved in the archives of the Labour Party. Application to see these papers should be made to the librarian at the National Museum of Labour History. Lists are available (NRA 14863).

The Labour Party records can be divided into two broad categories. There are, first, the minutes of the National Executive Committee; they include not only formal minutes of meetings, but also appended reports, memoranda, and circulated correspondence. As Henderson was secretary of the Party from 1911–34, much of this material was written by him. Secondly, the correspondence files of the Party are also preserved. Again, in his secretarial capacity, much of this is Henderson's work, and for the period 1911–24 the files are very extensive. Much of the correspondence is catalogued and indexed. Until 1907 correspondence is filed by year; after then (loosely) by subject or by individual. The biggest single classification is correspondence boxed under the name of the assistant secretary, J. S. Middleton.

There are several lacunae. The period 1915–17 is not well covered and correspondence becomes thin after 1924. On the other hand, more material is constantly appearing and these gaps may be filled slowly.

Separate from the archives of the National Executive are four boxes of papers catalogued as 'Henderson Papers'. There is some political correspondence for the years 1917 and 1929–31; a box of Cabinet papers 1915–17; and some press cuttings and private letters.

A further small collection of Henderson papers has been deposited in the PRO. It consists of miscellaneous correspondence for June 1929–Aug 1931 (FO 800/280–4). A list is available.

John Saville's short entry on Henderson in *DLB*, I, 161–7, has a valuable bibliography. More recent literature is evaluated in Bernard A. Cook's article on Henderson in *MBR*, 3, 402–9. There is also a useful bibliographical note, including details of manuscript collections containing material relevant to Henderson's life, in F. M. Leventhal's *Arthur Henderson* (Manchester UP 1989) which 'does not profess to be either exhaustive or notably revisionist... [but] seeks to update Ms Hamilton's version and to incorporate the important and mostly quite recent scholarship' (p. ix).

Chris Wrigley's *Arthur Henderson* (GPC Books, Cardiff 1990) demonstrates the value of the national records of Henderson's union, the Friendly Society of Iron Founders. These are held in the Modern Records Centre, University of Warwick (MSS. 41/FSIF). For Henderson's period as Secretary of Party, the Labour Party National Executive 1912–35, the Executive Minutes and correspondence files 'give an impression of not only his day-to-day life at work, but often personal details as well' (Wrigley, p. 204). The Ministry of Munitions records cited by Wrigley are important for Henderson's role in industrial relations in 1915–16.

ARTHUR HENDERSON, BARON ROWLEY (1893–1968)

Arthur Henderson was Labour MP for Cardiff (South) 1923–24 and 1929–31, Staffordshire (Kingswinford) 1935–50 and Rowley Regis and Tipton 1950–66. He was Joint Parliamentary Under-Secretary of State for War March-Dec 1942, Financial Secretary to the War Office Feb 1943–May 1945, Under-Secretary of State for India and Burma Aug 1945–Aug 1947, Minister of State for Commonwealth Relations Aug-Oct 1947, and Secretary of State for Air 1947–Oct 1951. He was created Baron Rowley (a life peerage) in 1966.

For the first edition, Lord Rowley's brother, Lord Henderson, informed us that Rowley did not keep official papers in his private files and that, unfortunately, the latter were all destroyed after Rowley's death by his secretary. We have been unable to contact Rowley's widow.

There are Private Office papers as Secretary of State for Air at the PRO in AIR 19.

PATRICK GEORGE THOMAS BUCHAN-HEPBURN, BARON HAILES (1901–1974)

Patrick Buchan-Hepburn was Conservative MP for Liverpool East Toxteth 1931–50 and Beckenham 1950–57. He was Junior Lord of the Treasury Nov 1939–June 1940 and Dec 1944–May 1945, Parliamentary Secretary to the Treasury Oct 1951–Dec 1955, and Minister of Works 1955–Jan 1957. He was created Baron Hailes in 1957.

Fifty boxes of Hailes's papers have been deposited at the Churchill Archives Centre (HAIS). A list is available (NRA 24830).

The collection includes 19 files of constituency correspondence 1928–57; 14 files from Hailes's time in the Whips' Office 1939 and 1944–55; six files of notes and papers on political speeches 1932–56; 38 files of general correspondence 1929–61; and 184 files of correspondence, papers, and speeches on Hailes's time as Governor-General of the Federation of the West Indies 1958–62.

AUBERON THOMAS HERBERT, 8th BARON LUCAS, 11th BARON DINGWALL (1876–1916)

Auberon Herbert succeeded his uncle as 8th Baron Lucas and 11th Baron Dingwall in 1905. He was Under-Secretary of State for War April 1908–March 1911, Under-Secretary of State for the Colonies March-Oct 1911, Parliamentary Secretary to the Board of Agriculture and Fisheries 1911–Aug 1914, and President of the Board of Agriculture and Fisheries 1914 until May 1915 when he resigned to go on active service.

A small collection of Herbert's papers formerly in the possession of his niece, the 10th Baroness Lucas and 13th Baroness Dingwall, is now with his great-nephew, the Hon Timothy Palmer, West Woodyates Manor, Salisbury, Wilts SP5 5QS.

There are several papers connected with Herbert's taking his seat in the House of Lords and with his maiden speech, 24 and 25 June 1907. At that time Herbert was private secretary to R. B. Haldane and his speech was in support of the Territorial Army Bill. As well as the *Hansard* reports and letters of congratulation, there is a letter written by Herbert describing his own feelings and reactions. There are also press cuttings on the King's speech to Lords Lieutenant about the bill Oct 1907, and a memo of Aug 1906 on the formation of territorial associations.

Some correspondence and a pamphlet 1907–08 demonstrate Herbert's interest in the New Forest ponies. His interest in agriculture is represented by correspondence on the formation of a Southern Counties Agricultural Cooperative Sept-Nov 1910.

There are no papers referring to Herbert's terms of office. When he resigned in 1915, he joined the Royal Flying Corps. There is a photo of him in uniform. Among other contributions to the war effort, he offered land for a land settlement scheme for servicemen. Correspondence July 1916 explains that the land was geologically unsuited for small-holdings. There are also obituary notices and extracts from the *DNB* and *The Balliol War Memorial Book*. He was posted missing, presumed dead, in Nov 1916.

Mr Palmer also has some 50 volumes of folio scrapbooks containing diary entries, correspondence, press cuttings, photos, and other ephemera of Herbert's sister Nan, Baroness Lucas and Dingwall, covering the years 1897–1940.

SIR GORDON HEWART, 1st VISCOUNT HEWART (1870–1943)

Gordon Hewart was Liberal MP for Leicester (Leicester East from 1918) 1913–22. He was Solicitor-General Dec 1916–Jan 1919, and Attorney-General 1919–March 1922. He was knighted in 1916, and created Baron Hewart in 1922, and Viscount Hewart in 1940.

Hewart's widow, Lady Hewart, informed us when the first edition was being prepared that no papers survived. Her flat had been burgled and a deed box was stolen, presumably in the hope that it contained jewellery; in fact it contained Lord Hewart's private and official papers. The box was not recovered.

Hewart's grandson, Sir Howard Hodgkin, confirmed in 1994 that none of his grandfather's papers has since come to light.

Robert Jackson, *The Chief: The Biography of Gordon Hewart, Lord Chief Justice of England 1922–1940* (Harrap 1959) was based on Hewart's papers, and quotes extensively from a memo Hewart wrote about his appointment as Lord Chief Justice.

SIR WILLIAM JOYNSON-HICKS, 1st Bt, 1st VISCOUNT BRENTFORD (1865–1932)

William Joynson-Hicks ('Jix') (he assumed the additional surname Joynson in 1895 on his marriage) was Conservative MP for Manchester (North-West) 1908–10, Middlesex (Brentford) 1911–18, and Middlesex (Twickenham) 1918–29. He was Parliamentary Secretary to the Overseas Trade Department Oct 1922–March 1923, Postmaster and Paymaster-General March-May 1923, Financial Secretary to the Treasury (with a seat in the Cabinet) May-Oct 1923, Minister of Health Aug 1923–Jan 1924, and Secretary of State for Home Affairs Nov 1924–June 1929. He was created a baronet in 1919 and Viscount Brentford in 1929.

Joynson-Hick's grandson, the 4th Lord Brentford, advised us that he had a couple of boxes of papers which are currently in the keeping of Mr Jonathon Hopkins who has prepared a preliminary catalogue of the collection. Mr Hopkins is preparing a fuller and annotated catalogue, which will in due course be submitted to meet the requirements of an MPhil degree at the University of Westminster.

The collection consists of two boxes of papers. The first box contains typescripts of autobiographical fragments including: an untitled introduction on family upbringing (5pp), 'Early Manhood and Early Ambitions' (5pp), 'The Beginning of my Legal Career' (3pp), 'The Legal Business of the [London and General Omnibus Company]' (10pp), 'Early Parliamentary Career' (5pp), 'My Visit to the Front' (9pp), 'The General Strike' (12pp), 'A Day in the Life of a Cabinet Minister' (4pp), 'A curious instance of the pressure put upon the Home

Secretary ... by Members of Parliament' (1p), 'The Home Office' (9pp), 'Law and Order' (9pp), 'The King's Illness' (9pp), 'The King and the Queen' (10pp), 'Princess Elizabeth' (3pp), 'The Royal Residences' (10pp), 'Relinquishing the Seals of Office' (2pp), and 'Votes for Women' (3pp). There are various biographical pieces collected by H. A. Taylor in 1933 (see below); correspondence regarding Joynson-Hicks's viscountcy; and pamphlets and miscellanies including a book of press cuttings and articles written by Joynson-Hicks. This box also contains some file-bound personal papers which have been arranged under the headings: Home Office – general; royal correspondence and peerage; prayer book and religion; letters re agriculture and the nationalisation of land plan of the Labour Party initiated by Mr Steed 9/2/28; police matters including bribery; Soviet activities, bolshevism, ARCO etc.; and private correspondence. There are also three packets of letters from Joynson-Hicks to his wife 1895–1925, mostly from the Home Office.

The second box contains papers on Joynson-Hicks's election defeat of Churchill 1908. There is also a collection of personal letters to Joynson-Hicks which were bundled up for H. A. Taylor and are arranged under the headings: political (including one from Churchill 1904 expressing his sorrow that they are to be political opponents); Air Ministry business 1917–18; prayer book and religious letters; royal letters 1915–30 (mainly from Lord Stamfordham); telegrams on elevation to the peerage; miscellaneous correspondence; and two press cuttings books; Lady Joynson-Hicks's notebook and various miscellaneous cards, election postcards and addresses.

The papers were used in the biography by H. A. Taylor, *Jix: Viscount Brentford* (Stanley Paul 1933). The memoranda and draft chapters for a volume of memoirs are quoted in the book, eg, Joynson-Hicks's feelings on being 'Minister in attendance'.

Discussion of the extent of Joynson-Hicks's anti-semitism, particularly as Secretary of State for Home Affairs, may be found in the following related articles: David Cesarani, 'The Anti-Jewish Career of Sir William Joynson-Hicks, Cabinet Minister', *Journal of Contemporary History*, 24, 1989, 461–82; W. D. Rubinstein, 'Recent Anglo-Jewish Historiography and the Myth of Jix's Antisemitism', pt I, *Australian Journal of Jewish Studies*, 7, 1, 1993, 41–70, and pt II, *Australian Journal of Jewish Studies*, 7, 2, 1993, 24–45; Geoffrey Alderman, 'Recent Anglo-Jewish Historiography and the Myth of Jix's anti-Semitism: A Response', *Australian Journal of Jewish Studies*, 8, 1, 1994, 112–21; and W. D. Rubinstein, 'Professor Alderman and Jix: A Response', *Australian Journal of Jewish Studies*, 8, 2, 1994, 192–201.

Joynson-Hicks's long interest in the automobile industry and related policy issues is well covered in William Plowden, *The Motor Car and Politics*

1896–1970 (Bodley Head 1971). John Ramsden's sketch in *Blackwell*, 235–7, is the best short introduction.

CHARLES HILL, BARON HILL OF LUTON (1904–1989)

Dr Charles Hill was Liberal-Conservative MP for Luton 1950–63. He was Parliamentary Secretary, Ministry of Food 1951–April 1955, Postmaster-General 1955–Jan 1957, Chancellor of the Duchy of Lancaster 1957–Oct 1961, and Minister of Housing and Local Government and Minister for Welsh Affairs 1961–July 1962. He was created Baron Hill of Luton (a life peerage) in 1963.

Shortly before his death, Lord Hill's daughter, the Hon Mrs Susan Fairbairn, advised us that he was too ill to provide any assistance. In *Sources* (3, p. 220), Dr Cook notes Lord Hill's advice that 'he has no important papers'.

In *Both Sides of the Hill* (Heinemann 1964), Lord Hill quoted speeches and broadcasts, but did not quote from any letters or diaries. In *Behind the Scenes* (Sidgwick & Jackson 1974) he provided an account of his work at the ITA and BBC, and 'includes many extracts from his diaries' (preface), which he kept during his years at the BBC. The surviving diaries are in the care of Lord Briggs.

The BBC Written Archives Centre holds papers concerning Hill's work as the 'Radio Doctor' and official records generated during his Chairmanship of the BBC, (which are not open beyond 1969), but do not have any of his diaries. The only private document held by the BBC Written Archives Centre is the manuscript of his autobiography.

The Wellcome Institute for the History of Medicine does not have any Hill papers, and advises that the British Medical Association holds only a few miscellaneous letters.

For Hill's association with broadcasting see Asa Briggs, *The History of Broadcasting in the United Kingdom*, III, *The War of Words* and IV, *Sound and Vision* (Oxford UP 1970, 1979), and Bernard Sendall, *Independent Television in Britain*, 1, *Origin and Foundation*, 1946–62 and 2, *Expansion and Change, 1958–68* (Macmillan 1982, 1983).

SIR SAMUEL JOHN GURNEY HOARE, 2nd Bt, VISCOUNT TEMPLEWOOD (1880–1959)

Samuel Hoare was Conservative MP for Chelsea 1910–44. He was Secretary of State for Air Oct 1922–Jan 1924, Nov 1924–June 1929 and April–May 1940, Secretary of State for India Aug 1931–June 1935, Secretary of State for Foreign Affairs June–Dec 1935, First Lord of the Admiralty June 1936–May 1937, Secretary of State for Home Affairs 1937–Sept 1939, and Lord Privy Seal and a Member of the War Cabinet 1939–April 1940. Hoare succeeded his father as 2nd baronet in 1915, and was created GBE in 1927, GCSI in 1934, and Viscount Templewood in 1944.

One hundred and fifteen boxes of Lord Templewood's papers were deposited by his executors (his widow and his nephew) in the Cambridge University Library (Templewood papers). The papers are generally available, but exceptions include some First World War files (for example, papers of the British Intelligence Mission to Petrograd 1915-17), and some royal correspondence. A detailed list of the papers has been made with subject and correspondent indices.

There are very few official papers, most of them presumably having been left in his respective ministries. Nevertheless there are 28 boxes of general political papers. In addition there are volumes of Cabinet ministers' and other papers, press cuttings, and scrapbooks. There is also an extensive collection of correspondence and other material concerning his early life: his letters from school and college, and various notes and reports from 1905, when Templewood was assistant private secretary to Alfred Lyttelton, then Colonial Secretary. There are many drafts and notes relating to Templewood's various publications including his study, *Empire of the Air: The Advent of the Air Age 1922-1929* (Collins 1957), and his memoirs for the years 1931-40, *Nine Troubled Years* (Collins 1954). Templewood wrote that the latter book was based on his own contemporary notes and papers; he also acknowledged the help of Anne and Hilda Chamberlain. Copies of Neville Chamberlain's letters to his sisters 1938-39 have been deposited with this collection and are available for consultation.

Templewood deposited some of his India Office papers with what is now the Oriental and India Office Collections, British Library in 1958 (MSS Eur E 240); a list of the papers is available (NRA 20540). They include 32 volumes, 55 files, 16 pamphlets, and an album compiled to commemorate his visit to India in 1927. These papers include eight volumes of correspondence with the 1st Marquess of Willingdon, Viscount Waverley, the 1st Earl of Halifax, Lord Erskine, W. Malcolm, Lord Hailey, Gandhi, and others, as well as speeches by Willingdon and Templewood himself, and selections from *Hansard*.

One volume of miscellaneous general correspondence relating to his tenure of the Foreign Office has been deposited in the PRO (FO 800/295; NRA 23627).

John A. Cross's biography, *Sir Samuel Hoare: a political biography* (Jonathan Cape 1977) made use of the Cambridge collection. Sir Samuel Hoare, *The Fourth Seal: The End of a Russian Chapter* (Heinemann 1930) is an account of secret service work and other experiences in the First World War. It incorporates contemporary letters and reports.

SIR CHARLES EDWARD HENRY HOBHOUSE, 4th Bt (1862–1941)

Charles Hobhouse was Liberal MP for Wiltshire (East or Devizes) 1892–95 and Bristol (East) 1900–18. He was Under-Secretary of State for India Jan 1907–April 1908, Financial Secretary to the Treasury 1908–Oct 1911, Chancellor of the Duchy of Lancaster 1911–Feb 1914, and Postmaster-General 1914–May 1915. He succeeded his father as 4th baronet in 1916.

As there were no children of his marriages, Hobhouse was succeeded by his half-brother, the father of the 6th baronet, Sir Charles Hobhouse. Sir Charles told us when we were preparing the first edition that he had been unable to discover any of his uncle's papers. The family home was used by a school and by the army during the last war and much seems to have disappeared at that time. Moreover some papers were pulped in salvage drives. Sir Charles's father deposited some family papers in the Wiltshire CRO but these deposits do not include any of Hobhouse's papers. Mrs W. D. C. Trotter, Hobhouse's step-daughter, advised us that she did not know of the existence of any papers.

In our first edition, although we were aware of, and had seen, a number of Hobhouse diaries, selections from which were published as Edward David (ed), *Inside Asquith's Cabinet: From the Diaries of Charles Hobhouse* (John Murray 1977), we were refused permission to refer to them. Mr David's book does not reveal the location of the sources on which it is based, although the 'enthusiasm and encouragement' of Sir Charles Hobhouse, Bt are acknowledged. These diaries have since been purchased by the British Library (Add MSS 60504–07). They consist of travel journals, including one of a world tour, July 1890 to May 1891, and three volumes of political journals, 1893–98 and 1904–15. Approximately ten percent of the political journals was not included in the published version.

There is a brief biography of Hobhouse by Trevor Wilson in C. S. Nicholls (ed), *The Dictionary of National Biography Missing Persons*, (Oxford UP 1993), 316–17.

SIR JOHN (GARDINER SUMNER) HOBSON (1912–1967)

John Hobson was Conservative MP for Warwick and Leamington 1957–67. He was Solicitor-General Feb–July 1962, and Attorney-General 1962–Oct 1964. He was knighted in 1962.

We have not been able to contact Lady Hobson or their three daughters.

There were no Hobson papers at the Warwickshire RO, only the minute book of the Warwick and Leamington Conservative Association 1885–1959 (CR 1392).

The brief essay on Hobson by Charles Fletcher-Cooke in *DNB 1961–1970*, p. 523, is based on 'private information; personal knowledge'.

JOHN HODGE (1855–1937)

John Hodge was Labour MP for South-East Lancashire (Gorton; Manchester Gorton from 1918) 1906–23. He was Minister of Labour Dec 1916–Aug 1917, and Minister of Pensions 1917–Jan 1919.

No papers survived in the possession of Hodge's family, except for a photo album owned by his daughter, Miss Wilhelmina Hodge. As well as photos of Hodge during the period in which he held office, there were four press cuttings. Two of these reported a visit paid by Hodge to the Hepworth Studios where a scheme for retraining and employing disabled soldiers was being organised by Cecil Harmsworth. While there Hodge acted as Minister of Pensions in a film about the problems of the wounded soldier. There was a typed copy of a poem (anon) entitled 'The Staying of Arthur' which condemned Arthur Henderson for remaining in office after the introduction of conscription (Jan 1916). We were not able to contact Miss Hodge during preparation of the second edition.

The Labour Representation Committee records among the Labour Party archives in the National Museum of Labour History contain material relating to Hodge's work (LP/LRC).

The Modern Records Centre holds some of the archives of the Iron and Steel Trades Confederation (MSS. 36) of which Hodge was founding president. As well as files relating to Hodge's union activities, the confederation's correspondence files include some miscellaneous speech notes about the Boer War (MSS. 36/H25), and about the causes of the First World War (MSS. 36/M64). There are letters and memoranda from Gorton Trades Council about Hodge's support for the war (MSS. 36/H25) and material from the 1922 election (MSS. 36/L41).

Hodge's *Workman's Cottage to Windsor Castle* (Sampson & Low 1931) quotes verbatim conversations, but appears to be based on Hodge's reminiscences.

There is a brief life and comprehensive list of sources in David Howell and John Saville's entry on Hodge in *DLB*, III, 109–15. *Adjusting to Democracy* is a valuable guide to Hodge's work at the Ministry of Labour and to relevant PRO files.

SIR DOUGLAS McGAREL HOGG, 1st VISCOUNT HAILSHAM (1872–1950)

Douglas Hogg was knighted in 1922, created Baron Hailsham in 1928, and Viscount Hailsham in 1929. He was Conservative MP for St Marylebone 1922–28. He was Attorney-General Oct 1922–Jan 1924 and Nov 1924–March 1928, Lord Chancellor 1928–June 1929 and June 1935–March 1938, Secretary of State for War Nov 1931–June 1935, and Lord President of the Council March-Oct 1938.

His son, Lord Hailsham of St Marylebone, informed us that his father systematically destroyed his papers. All that was thought to survive when the first edition was compiled were fee books and letters of congratulation and condolence, sometimes with replies. As these papers were in store they were not readily available. They were used and frequently quoted in *Lord Chancellors 1*.

Thirty-two boxes of Hailsham's papers have since been deposited in the Churchill Archives Centre (HAIL). The papers have been catalogued but remain closed indefinitely. The collection has been arranged in four sections: correspondence; political papers; other interests; and family and business papers.

The 75 files of correspondence 1924–39 include letters from Baldwin, Kipling, Neville Chamberlain, Churchill, Halifax, Lord Londonderry, and Hailsham's son Quintin Hogg. The seven files of political papers 1924–36 include two files of Cabinet conclusions 1924–25; one file on constituency meetings March-Oct 1925; and four files of political and parliamentary notes on various matters.

The collection also includes three files of papers on the Polytechnic 1934–38; one file on the British Empire Cancer Campaign 1937–39; and 17 files of family and business files 1931–39.

The Conservative Party Archives in the Bodleian Library should also be consulted.

QUINTIN McGAREL HOGG, BARON HAILSHAM OF SAINT MARYLEBONE (1907–)

Quintin Hogg was Conservative MP for Oxford City 1938–50 and St Marylebone 1963–70. He was Joint Parliamentary Under-Secretary of State for Air April-May 1945, First Lord of the Admiralty Sept 1956–Jan 1957, Minister of Education Jan-Sept 1957, Lord President of the Council 1957–Oct 1959, Lord Privy Seal 1959–July 1960, Minister for Science Oct 1959–April 1964, Lord President of the Council July 1960–Oct 1964, Minister with special responsibility for sport 1962–April 1964, Minister with special responsibility for dealing with unemployment in the North-East 1963–64, Minister with special responsibility for higher education Dec 1963–Feb 1964, Secretary of State for Education and Science April-Oct 1964, and Lord Chancellor June 1970–March 1974 and May 1979–June 1987. He succeeded his father as 2nd Viscount Hailsham in 1950 but disclaimed his peerages for life on 20 Nov 1963. He was created Baron Hailsham of Saint Marylebone (a life peerage) in 1970.

Around 600 boxes of Hailsham's papers and diaries were deposited in the Churchill Archives Centre (HLSM; NRA 18561). The papers have been listed but are closed indefinitely. The collection does not include any personal diaries.

Among the Conservative Party Archives in the Bodleian Library there is a small collection of Hailsham's papers including Chairman's office correspondence and papers 1957-59; Steering Committee minutes 1957-59; and drafts of 'Conservative Statement of Policy' 1949.

The PRO has identified some Ministry of Education papers relating to Hailsham 1957 (ED 136/884-901). Records of the Leader of the House of Lords and Chief Whip 1945-94 are in the HLRO, but are subject to the 30 year rule (Hailsham was Leader of the House of Lords 1960-63).

In *The Door Wherein I Went* (Collins 1975), Lord Hailsham said that any autobiography he wrote would 'inevitably be lacking alike in spice and ardour'. Although it reveals few secrets and quotes no documents, *The Door Wherein I Went* contains much more on Hailsham's political life and less on 'philosophy and religion' than its introductory chapter promises.

A Sparrow's Flight: the memoirs of Lord Hailsham of St Marylebone (Collins 1990), as Hailsham noted in the last chapter, was written from memory. Chris Cook, Jane Leonard and Peter Leese, *The Longman Guide to Sources in Contemporary British History*, 2, *Individuals* (Longman 1994) note that Geoffrey Lewis is preparing an official biography (p. 145).

Michael Cockerell was given full access to Hailsham's public and private papers, and retains copies of some of them, in compiling the BBC portrait, 'The Passionate Peer – A Film Portrait of Lord Hailsham' (transmitted BBC 2, June 1990).

SIR ALEXANDER FREDERICK DOUGLAS-HOME, BARON HOME OF THE HIRSEL (1903-1995)

Alec Douglas-Home was known as Lord Dunglass from 1918 until he succeeded his father as 14th Earl of Home in 1951. He disclaimed his peerages for life on 23 Oct 1963. He was knighted in 1962 and created Baron Home of the Hirsel (a life peerage) in 1974. He was Unionist MP for South Lanark 1931-45, Conservative MP for Lanark 1950-51, and Unionist MP for Kinross and West Perthshire 1963-74. He was Joint Parliamentary Under-Secretary, Foreign Office May-July 1945, Minister of State, Scottish Office Nov 1951-April 1955, Secretary of State for Commonwealth Relations 1955-July 1960, Lord President of the Council March-Sept 1957 and Oct 1959-July 1960, Secretary of State for Foreign Affairs 1960-Oct 1963, Prime Minister and First Lord of the Treasury 1963-Oct 1964, and Secretary of State for Foreign and Commonwealth Affairs June 1970-March 1974. He was Leader of the Conservative Party Nov 1963-Aug 1965.

Lord Home advised us: 'My papers, such as they are, are all here', at his home, The Hirsel in Berwickshire.

D. R. Thorpe is currently preparing an official biography of Lord Home which is expected to be published in 1996 by Sinclair-Stevenson of London, under the putative title, *Alec Home: a Prime Minister and His Times*. Mr Thorpe, who had access to the large collection of papers at The Hirsel, provided us with a brief description of them.

There are 111 boxes of private and political papers together with some loose and uncatalogued material, mostly relating to the post-war period, especially 1960–74. These papers will be fully catalogued in the future. There are 108 substantial scrapbooks collected by Lady Home and covering the period 1928–90. These provide 'a unique insight into Lord Home's family and public life'. There are 185 boxes of estate papers, of which a full catalogue is available at the NRA(S). There are also volumes of family memorabilia, including photos and draft manuscripts and proofs of Lord Home's books.

The transcript of an interview with Lord Home made in 1980 is now available in the British Oral Archive of Political and Administrative History at the BLPES. Records of the Leader of the House of Lords and Chief Whip 1945–94 are in the HLRO, but are subject to the 30 year rule (Home was Leader of the House of Lords 1957–60).

Lord Home's autobiography, *The Way the Wind Blows* (Collins 1976) and his *Letters to a Grandson* (Collins 1983) contain a few quotations from his papers. In *Sir Alec Douglas-Home* (J. M. Dent & Sons 1970), Kenneth Young quotes directly from tape-recorded conversations and draws on 'a number of documents, notes, photographs and letters' made available by Lord Home and former colleagues (p. xi). Anthony Seldon's contribution on Home in *Blackwell*, 209–13, is a valuable interim assessment.

LORD JOHN ADRIAN HOPE, 1st BARON GLENDEVON (1912–1996)

Lord John Hope (younger twin son of the 2nd Marquess of Linlithgow) was Conservative MP for Midlothian North and Peebles 1945–50 and Edinburgh Pentlands 1950–64. He was Joint Parliamentary Under-Secretary of State for Foreign Affairs Oct 1954–Nov 1956, Parliamentary Under-Secretary of State for Commonwealth Relations 1956–Jan 1957, Joint Parliamentary Under-Secretary of State for Scotland 1957–Oct 1959, and Minister of Works 1959–July 1962. He was created Baron Glendevon in 1964.

Lord Glendevon retained only a series of scrapbooks which consist mainly of press cuttings, but also include a few letters and messages. The scrapbooks were kept at Lord Glendevon's Guernsey home but were not available for research.

At the time of his death Lord Glendevon was writing an autobiography. There are a few glimpses of him in Ted Morgan's *Maugham* (Simon and Schuster, New York 1980). Lord Glendevon married Somerset Maugham's daughter Elizabeth Mary ('Liza') in 1948.

JOHN ADRIAN LOUIS HOPE, 1st MARQUESS OF LINLITHGOW (1860-1908)

John Hope was known as Lord Hope until he succeeded his father as the 7th Earl of Hopetoun in 1873. He was created GCMG in 1889, KT in 1900, and Marquess of Linlithgow in 1902. He was Paymaster-General 1895-98, and Secretary for Scotland Feb-Dec 1905.

Very few of Linlithgow's papers appear to have survived; those that do have been listed by the NRA(S) as part of the very large collection of Hopetoun MSS (NRA 17684). The papers are controlled by the Hopetoun Papers Trust, but enquiries should be directed to the NRA(S). The Hopetoun archivist is, however, prepared to answer postal enquiries of a limited and specific nature.

Almost all of the papers which have survived relate to Linlithgow's term of office as first Governor-General and Commander-in-Chief of Australia 1900-02. There is a wooden chest of formal addresses of welcome and a dispatch case of official papers. The papers cover such topics as the various schemes for Australian federation, the defence of Australia, arrangements for the opening of the first Parliament, and proposals for the design of a Commonwealth of Australia flag. There is also some miscellaneous correspondence with Australian and British politicians, including the Secretary of State for the Colonies, Joseph Chamberlain, letters to Linlithgow's private secretary, and the letter (30 Jan 1905) in which A. J. Balfour invited him to take over the Scottish Office. The collection also includes Australian account books, some from 1889-95 when Linlithgow was Governor of Victoria. This earlier period is also represented by two volumes of press cuttings 1888-89 and 1892-95. A further volume for 1881-87 also survives. Apart from papers concerning honours conferred on Linlithgow – such as the Knighthood of the Thistle – the only other surviving papers appear to be printed order papers and bills from the House of Lords 1883. There are several photo albums. Microfilm copies of his Australian papers are available in the National Library of Australia (M936-7, M1154-6, M1584).

Private Office papers relating to Linlithgow's period at the Scottish Office are dispersed through the files of the five main Scottish Office departments held at the SRO.

For a study of Lord Hopetoun as Australia's first Governor-General, together with extensive source references to British and Australian publications, archives, and private papers, see Christopher Cunneen, *Kings' Men: Australia's Governors-General from Hopetoun to Isaacs* (George

Allen & Unwin, Sydney 1983). Reference should also be made to J. W.
R. Mitchell, 'The emergence of Modern Scottish central administration
1885–1939' (DPhil, Oxford University 1987).

SIR ROBERT STEVENSON HORNE, VISCOUNT HORNE OF SLAMANNAN (1871–1940)

Robert Horne was created KBE in 1918, GBE in 1920, and Viscount
Horne of Slamannan in 1937. He was Conservative MP for Glasgow
(Hillhead) 1918–37. He was Minister of Labour Jan 1919–March 1920,
President of the Board of Trade 1920–April 1921, and Chancellor of
the Exchequer 1921–Oct 1922.

Horne died unmarried. His nephew, Mr J. R. Lamberton, was one
of his executors, and he received all of Horne's chattels. In the first
edition we reported that Mr Lamberton informed us that he had only
Horne's personal and family papers and that these papers were not
available for research. Mr Lamberton had no knowledge of any political
papers.

This collection was deposited by Mr Lamberton's widow in the
Glasgow University Archives in 1981 (DC89). It consists of 27 folders
of material on Horne, consisting mostly of press cuttings, newspaper
articles, speeches and correspondence on business and political matters.
The press cuttings include material on Horne's political career 1908–
38; his term in office as Minister of Labour 1919–24; and his speeches
during the general election of 1922. There are papers and correspondence relating to his electorate, and political topics including the
Suez Canal; trade and finance; the National Health Insurance scheme;
the coal industry, including the 1928 World Fuel Conference; and the
remonetarisation of silver. Business papers include material on his
involvement with the Great Western Railway and Baldwin & Co Ltd.
There are three folders of papers on Horne's titles and congratulatory
messages on his elevation to the peerage. There is a folder of obituaries
on Horne from national and provincial newspapers and an inventory
of his library at the time of his death. Mrs Lamberton advised the
University Archivist that most of Horne's original papers were destroyed
before he died.

The NLS purchased a small collection of 24 political letters from
Horne to Lord Beaverbrook (Acc 8214). The letters, which the Library
thinks were probably originally part of the dispersal of the Beaverbrook
Library, were purchased from a bookseller.

Adjusting to Democracy is a valuable guide to Horne's work at the
Ministry of Labour and to relevant PRO files. Geoffrey Channon's
entry in *DBB*, 3, 349–54, is an informed account of Horne's business
and railway interests. Horne's career is outlined by John Ramsden in
Blackwell, 215–17.

DAME FLORENCE GERTRUDE HORSBRUGH, BARONESS HORSBRUGH (1899–1969)

Florence Horsbrugh was Conservative MP for Dundee 1931–45 and Manchester Moss Side 1950–59. She was Parliamentary Secretary, Ministry of Health July 1939–June 1945, Parliamentary Secretary, Ministry of Food 1945, and Minister of Education Nov 1951–Oct 1954. She was created GBE in 1954 and Baroness Horsbrugh (a life peerage) in 1959.

The Churchill Archives Centre holds 11 boxes of Lady Horsbrugh's papers (HRSB; NRA 21966). Researchers should apply in writing to the Archivist to view the papers.

The collection has been divided into six sections. The political papers consist of six files 1931–54, including speech notes, correspondence with Halifax and Churchill on the United Nations 1945, and 12 letters addressed to Lady Horsbrugh as Minister of Education. The correspondence consists of 14 files. Correspondents include Anne Chamberlain, Churchill, Edward Heath, Macmillan, Sir John Simon and Lords Avon, Haig, and Hailsham. The press cuttings comprise 12 volumes mainly for 1931–39. In addition there are nine files of photos; six files on Lady Horsbrugh's honours and awards; and ten files on souvenirs, programmes, and the Horsbrugh family tree.

The PRO holds papers for Horsbrugh's period as Minister of Education, 1953–54 (ED 136/694–892).

The brief essay on her by Baroness Elliot of Harwood in *DNB 1961–1970*, p. 541, is based on 'private information; personal knowledge'.

HENRY FITZALAN-HOWARD, 15th DUKE OF NORFOLK (1847–1917)

Henry Fitzalan-Howard was known as Lord Maltravers until 1856, then as the Earl of Arundel until he succeeded his father as 15th Duke of Norfolk in 1860. He was created KG in 1886. He was Postmaster-General July 1895–April 1900 when he resigned to go to South Africa on active service.

The Duke's papers are at Arundel Castle, Sussex. They are listed in F. W. Steer (ed), *Arundel Castle Archives*, I (Chichester 1968).

The collection is extensive, amounting to several thousand letters. The Duke saved almost all of his correspondence, and the collection covers every aspect of his life and interests, including his political career, between 1860 and 1917. The collection has been described as 'religious and educational correspondence and papers 1860–1917 (40 bundles and items) including letters from F. W. Faber and J. H. Newman, general and charitable correspondence including correspondence of his private secretaries (in 500 bundles) with other political, family and estate correspondence and papers' (Royal Commission on Historical Manuscripts, *Papers of British Churchmen 1780–1940* [Guide to Sources for British History based on the National Register of Archives, 6, HMSO, London, 1987], p. 28).

Also held at Arundel Castle is a compilation of obituaries of the Duke, *Henry Fitzalan-Howard, 15th Duke of Norfolk*, edited by Gwendolen, Duchess of Norfolk (1917), and the manuscript of an incomplete and unpublished biography of the Duke by Bernard Holland.

Application to read the papers should be made in writing to the Librarian of the Duke of Norfolk, Dr J. M. Robinson, Arundel Castle, West Sussex BN18 9AB. (A charge of £10 a day is made for access to the muniment room).

The collection is utilised in John Martin Robinson, *The Dukes of Norfolk: A Quincentennial History* (Oxford UP 1982). There is a brief entry on the Duke in *DNB 1912–1921*, 273–4.

ROBERT SPEAR HUDSON, 1st VISCOUNT HUDSON (1886–1957)

Robert Hudson was Conservative MP for Cumberland (Whitehaven) 1924–29 and Southport 1931–52. He was Parliamentary Secretary to the Ministry of Labour Nov 1931–June 1935, Minister of Pensions 1935–July 1936, Parliamentary Secretary to the Ministry of Health 1936–May 1937, Parliamentary Secretary, Department of Overseas Trade, Board of Trade 1937–April 1940, Minister of Shipping April-May 1940, and Minister of Agriculture and Fisheries 1940–July 1945. He was created Viscount Hudson in 1952.

Hudson left all his personal effects to his son, the 2nd Viscount Hudson, who died in 1963. The widow of the 2nd Viscount, now Lady Duncan-Sandys, had none of her father-in-law's papers and thought that what papers there were went to Hudson's sister, Miss Violet Hudson. Hudson's widow died in 1969 and Mrs Maclean, a close friend of Lady Hudson, who helped to dispose of her effects knew of no papers.

At the time of preparing the first edition, Violet Hudson had a small collection of papers. Miss Hudson stated that her brother kept very few papers and much of what he kept was destroyed during the bombing of the Second World War. The papers Miss Hudson had included press cuttings 1929–49, a few personal family letters, and correspondence on financial and legal matters. There was also a visitors' book for the 1930s and some photo albums. Miss Hudson has since died. The press cuttings which she had are now in the possession of Hudson's grand-daughter, the Hon Mrs Annabel Garton. Neither Mrs Garton nor Lady Duncan-Sandys knew what had become of the remainder of the papers previously with Miss Hudson.

Scattered correspondence and papers relating to Hudson can be found in the CAB and MAF files at the PRO.

Adjusting to Democracy refers only in passing to Hudson's work at the Ministry of Labour. Hudson's work at the Ministry of Agriculture and Fisheries is examined in Roger Middleton, 'The Formulation and Implementation of British Agricultural Policy 1945–1951' (PhD thesis, University of Bristol 1992).

SIR ROBERT HUTCHISON, BARON HUTCHISON OF MONTROSE (1873–1950)

Major-General Robert Hutchison was created KCMG in 1919, and Baron Hutchison in 1932. He was Liberal MP for Kirkcaldy Burghs 1922–23 and Montrose Burghs 1924–32; he became a Liberal National in 1931. He was Paymaster-General Dec 1935–June 1938.

For the first edition, Hutchison's widow, Mrs Alma Laurie, (whose first husband was Hutchison's first wife's brother), who died in 1992, advised us that she knew of no papers. Her son, Mr John Drysdale, did not know of any official papers either, but has some private family papers at his home.

JOHN BURNS HYND (1902–1971)

John Hynd was Labour MP for Sheffield (Attercliffe) 1944–70. He was Chancellor of the Duchy of Lancaster and Minister for Germany and Austria Aug 1945–April 1947, and Minister of Pensions April-Oct 1947.

Hynd's papers formerly in the possession of his widow, were deposited at the Churchill Archives Centre in 1986, by his daughter Mrs Sheila Young (HYND: NRA 31391). The collection had been kept very methodically by Hynd in four filing cabinet drawers and about 20 box-files.

Hynd did not keep a diary, nor has much correspondence survived. His constituency work is represented by two box-files and three files. They include correspondence with the National Union of Railwaymen about getting on their panel of prospective candidates, his selection for Sheffield in 1938, and later correspondence about election expenses. Hynd was an NUR clerk 1924–45 but there is little material about this early career. There is printed election material for all the general elections 1945–66, including some of Hynd's opponents' material. There are some local party pamphlets from the 1920s, press cuttings about local politics, a small amount of correspondence with his agent, his monthly letters to his local party 1966–68, lists of rules and members of the local party, and some correspondence on the grant of the freedom of Sheffield to Hynd in 1970.

The chief source for Hynd's pre-parliamentary activities is a volume of press cuttings beginning in the 1930s. Hynd kept further cuttings but these were not arranged in a volume. There is also a volume of cuttings of articles by him for the earlier period as well as two box-files of later articles. There are two slim volumes of political cartoons which Hynd drew in the 1930s under the name 'Hynder'.

Very little material has survived from Hynd's period in office. He was a keen photographer and there are four albums containing photos he took while in Germany; there is also volume one of the *British Zone Review* (1945).

The remaining boxes and files may be described as 'subject' files: leaflets, press cuttings, etc. on particular topics or geographical areas, for example housing, race, prices and incomes, Latin America, Central Africa. Hynd continued his interest in German affairs and there is a great deal of material about many aspects of Germany including Command Papers on the various treaties and the wider problems of disarmament. Hynd was a firm supporter of European unity and the Common Market, an interest reflected by many files: for example he was a founder of the Anglo-Australian Society, and of the Parliamentary Council of the European Movement. As well as these subject files, there are two boxes of speeches and a box-file of broadcasts made by Hynd. Many of the latter were on the overseas network of the BBC or for foreign networks.

There is very little Labour Party material: a box of Parliamentary Labour Party standing orders, a file of speeches at various local meetings, and a box of various leaflets. Hynd's appointment diaries 1944–71 (except 1945) have survived. Mrs Hynd also had an interesting file of letters of condolence, many of which describe him at work, particularly in Germany. Hynd wrote a biography of his friend *Willy Brandt* (Lincolns-Prager 1966); the typescript and correspondence concerning publication have survived.

There are also several tape recordings of speeches made by Hynd, including the speech he made on receiving the freedom of Sheffield and radio broadcasts made during a visit to Latin America in 1965.

In the first edition we reported our understanding that a collection of Hynd's constituency papers was in the care of Alderman S. I. Dyson of Sheffield; but we were unable to make contact with Alderman Dyson. The Sheffield Archives has advised us that Alderman Dyson died in 1978, but the only papers he deposited were his diaries as Lord Mayor. There are no constituency papers for Hynd.

ALBERT HOLDEN ILLINGWORTH, BARON ILLINGWORTH (1865–1942)

Albert Illingworth was Coalition Liberal MP for Lancashire (Heywood) 1915–18 and Lancashire (Heywood and Radcliffe) 1918–21. He was

Postmaster-General Dec 1916–April 1921. He was created Baron Illingworth in 1921.

In the first edition we noted that Illingworth's widow, Lady Illingworth, had his papers. Most of the papers were in store and inaccessible. We were only able to see two files of correspondence. All the letters and memoranda dated from the period 1916–21 and dealt with such diverse topics as national service schemes in 1915, oil supplies in 1916, government policy on Irish Home Rule in Nov 1918, and the proposed excess profits duty of 1921. There were several League of Nations Union papers 1921 about disarmament and the Hungarian monarchy; several papers related to Illingworth's work on the War Office Committee advising the Director of Army Contracts; and several War Cabinet memoranda and agenda concerning rationing and the Whitley Council civil service reform proposals, and the civil service's pay rise in 1920.

We have since learned from Lady Illingworth's nephew, Mr W. J. A. Wilberforce, that after her death in 1986 all of Lord Illingworth's papers were destroyed. This occurred during the fraudulent conversion of Lady Illingworth's estate orchestrated by her niece, Baroness de Stempel. Lady Illingworth, who died in an old people's home at Hereford, was left penniless by her niece's fraudulent actions. Evidence was given in Baroness de Stempel's trial that the Illingworth papers and other property were removed illegally from a London bank and never seen again. Civil litigation was expected by Lady Illingworth's executors to recover pictures and any other surviving items to honour her original 1975 will which left most of her property to two (unnamed) beneficiaries (*The Times*, 23 April 1990).

Mr Wilberforce further advised that as far as he knew there were no other papers.

PHILIP ALBERT INMAN, BARON INMAN (1892–1979)
Philip Inman was created Baron Inman in 1946. He was Lord Privy Seal April-Oct 1947.

Lord Inman informed us that he kept very few papers from the period when he was in office, a time when he was under great stress (his son was gravely ill and he himself was not well) and without much secretarial help. Moreover, Lord Inman sorted much of his correspondence and destroyed a large number of letters. All that survived from that period was a collection of more than 500 letters of congratulation (including letters from Sir Stafford Cripps and Lord Longford), a letter concerning his swearing in as a Privy Councillor, some correspondence about the appointment of his successor as Chairman of the BBC, and a list of the many Cabinet Committees on which Inman served. There were also a large number of press cuttings including some dating from Inman's entry and departure from office.

Lord Inman's autobiography, *No Going Back* (Williams & Northgate 1952), quotes only from press cuttings. The correspondence mentioned there with George Lansbury has since been destroyed. Nor did Inman systematically keep correspondence with such friends as Arthur Henderson and Ellen Wilkinson and other Labour figures, though odd letters may still survive.

Inman did have three large boxes of papers, mostly press cuttings. They consisted mainly of his own articles or reviews and reviews of his many books. There were also papers related to Lord Inman's long connection with Charing Cross Hospital.

The fate of these papers is not known. We have not been successful in our attempts to contact Inman's daughter, the Hon Rosemary Eban. His son Philip died in 1968; we have not been able to contact his widow Mrs Judith Wingfield.

SIR THOMAS WALKER HOBART INSKIP, 1st VISCOUNT CALDECOTE (1876–1947)

Thomas Inskip was Conservative MP for Bristol (Central) 1918–29 and Hampshire (Fareham) 1931–39. He was Solicitor-General Oct 1922–Jan 1924, Nov 1924–March 1928 and Sept 1931–Jan 1932, Attorney-General March 1928–June 1929 and Jan 1932–March 1936, Minister for the Coordination of Defence 1936–Jan 1939, Secretary of State for Dominion Affairs Jan-Sept 1939 and May-Oct 1940, and Lord Chancellor September 1939–May 1940. He was knighted in 1922, and created Viscount Caldecote in 1939.

Inskip's son, the 2nd Viscount Caldecote, informed us that his father kept very few papers and amongst these the only item of any importance is his diary. A copy of this diary for 26 Aug-19 Sept 1938 and Jan 1939–20 April 1940 has been deposited at the Churchill Archives Centre (INKP). A few omissions have been made. It is now open to general inspection; but Lord Caldecote's permission is required for any proposed quotations of passages bearing on personal relationships or communications with colleagues.

In *Lord Chancellors 1*, 590–602, Heuston quoted extensively from these sections of Inskip's diary. Professor Heuston also quoted from earlier sections of Inskip's diary and from several letters, most of them letters of appreciation written after Inskip's death. Lord Caldecote thinks that these earlier diaries may survive amongst his mother's papers. If he finds them he will probably deposit them with the other diaries at Churchill. The report, NRA 16049, contains no further information.

GEORGE ALFRED ISAACS (1883–1979)

George Isaacs was Labour MP for Kent (Gravesend) 1923–24, Southwark (North) 1929–31 and 1939–50 and Southwark 1950–59. He was

Minister of Labour and National Service Aug 1945–Jan 1951, and Minister of Pensions Jan-Oct 1951.

For the first edition, Mr Isaacs told us that he had no papers of any kind relating to his political career and that it was always his intention to ensure this state of affairs.

Southwark Local Studies Library has a small collection of material on Isaacs including biographical press cuttings, some photos, and a copy of the order of proceedings in 1957 when Isaacs was made freeman of the borough. The library also has the *South London Press* (from 1865 onwards) which has many references to Isaacs's activities, as well as short biographical notes from *Over the Bridge* (Southwark Cathedral's magazine) 1952 and the *South London Observer* 1958.

George Eastwood's biography, *George Isaacs* (Odhams Press 1952) was partly based on information supplied by Isaacs but it does not quote from any documents.

Isaacs' period as General Secretary of NATSOPA (1909–48) is covered in James Moran, *NATSOPA Seventy-five Years* (Heinemann on behalf of NATSOPA 1964), and R. B. Suther, *The Story of NATSOPA* (National Society of Operative Printers and Assistants 1929).

Isaacs's role as Minister of Labour is discussed in Justin Davis Smith, *The Attlee and Churchill Administrations and Industrial Unrest 1945–55: A Study in Consensus* (Pinter Publishers 1990).

SIR RUFUS DANIEL ISAACS, 1st MARQUESS OF READING (1860–1935)

Rufus Isaacs was Liberal MP for Reading 1904–13. He was Solicitor-General March-Oct 1910, Attorney-General 1910–Oct 1913, and Secretary of State for Foreign Affairs Aug-Nov 1931. He was knighted in 1910, and created Baron Reading in 1914, GCB in 1915, Viscount Reading in 1916, Earl of Reading in 1917, and Marquess of Reading in 1926. He was Liberal Leader in the House of Lords 1931–35.

A considerable collection of papers concerning Reading's term of office as Viceroy of India 1921–26 was deposited by his widow in the India Office, now the Oriental and India Office Collections, British Library. This collection was deposited in two parts (MSS Eur E 238 and MSS Eur F 118; NRA 20531). The first part contains Reading's official Indian papers, the second (which was opened for research in 1972) contains personal papers. In his biography, *Rufus Isaacs, 1st Marquess of Reading* (2 vols, Hutchinson 1943–45), Reading's son, the 2nd Marquess, said that his father wrote very few letters and kept even fewer.

MSS Eur E 238 includes several volumes of printed correspondence, some of which were indexed. The Viceroy's correspondence was traditionally divided into letters and telegrams to the sovereign, letters and telegrams to the Secretary of State, correspondence with persons in England, and correspondence with persons in India. There are also several volumes of speeches by Reading, the printed 'Summary' of his administration, and volumes of Legislative Assembly decisions. The collection includes many files related to Reading's membership of the Joint Committee for Indian Constitutional Reform 1933–34 and his activities during the Round Table Conference and the Simon Commission. There are also several departmental files.

MSS Eur F 118 consists of more personal correspondence though there are more papers on Indian affairs. There are 90 files of correspondence arranged alphabetically, generally covering the period 1910–35 but with some earlier letters. There are also further correspondence files with prominent politicians such as Lloyd George 1919–29, Edwin Montagu 1904–23, the then Lord Irwin 1926–30, and Sir John Simon 1916–35. In addition there are Cabinet papers 1913–19, peace negotiations papers, papers concerning Reading's mission to the USA 1917, papers concerning land taxes 1909, correspondence with Lloyd George and Lord Grey of Fallodon about political funds 1929, correspondence about the 1931 political crisis, and press cuttings 1901–23.

An additional deposit in 1975 comprises the financial records of Reading's legal practice including fee-books, ledgers and cash books (14 volumes, 1888–1913) with diaries for 1914 and 1915, and a few pages for 1917.

The Indian papers of Reading's first wife Alice, consisting of letters to her family in England 1921–25, were also deposited in the India Office Collection in 1972 and 1975 (MSS Eur E 316). They were used in Iris Butler, *The Viceroy's Wife: letters of Alice, Countess of Reading from India 1921–5* (Hodder 1969). The papers of Yvonne Fitzroy, private secretary to the Marchioness while she was vicereine, are also available at the India Office Collection (MSS Eur E 312).

A small collection of papers has also been deposited in the PRO (FO 800/222–6). They include three indexed volumes of miscellaneous correspondence 1918–19, and a volume of telegrams to and from Sir W. Wiseman, all concerned with Reading's special mission to the USA in 1918–19, and one volume of miscellaneous correspondence from his tenure of the Foreign Office in 1931.

It is known that Reading sometimes made notes, in a personal code, relating to contemporary events. These notes do not appear to have survived.

But one tin box of letters and scrapbooks, including documents relating to the Marconi affair, remains in the possession of the 4th Marquess of Reading. These papers were used in Denis Judd, *Lord*

Reading (Weidenfeld and Nicolson 1982). There is also a biography by H. Montgomery Hyde, *Lord Reading: the Life of Rufus Isaacs, First Marquess of Reading* (Heinemann 1967).

HASTINGS LIONEL ISMAY, BARON ISMAY (1887–1965)

General Hastings Ismay was created KCB in 1940, GCB in 1946, Baron Ismay in 1947, and KG in 1957. He was Secretary of State for Commonwealth Relations Oct 1951–March 1952.

A collection of Ismay's papers is held at the Liddell Hart Centre (ISMAY papers). The papers have been listed (NRA 12103), but access to the list is restricted. Ismay's daughter, Lady Allendale, does not know of any other papers.

The papers in the Liddell Hart Centre have been divided into five broad categories: personal; Churchill; subject correspondence; special personal correspondence; and general and miscellaneous personal correspondence. The personal papers include Ismay's diaries for the years 1945, 1947–56. There are also copies of speeches 1943–52; press cuttings 1943–57; personal and family (mainly from his mother) correspondence 1893–1920; and papers relating to his autobiography, *The Memoirs of Lord Ismay* (Heinemann 1960).

The Churchill papers consist of personal and miscellaneous correspondence with Churchill 1940–64; correspondence with Clementine, Lady Churchill and Mary Churchill 1941–65; and correspondence and galleys relating to the Churchill memoirs 1946–56.

The subject correspondence includes papers on the Somaliland operations; the General Strike; various defence issues 1936–63; India 1946–57 (including letters written to Lady Ismay 1947–48); and NATO 1952–57.

Correspondents in the special personal correspondence include Lord Alanbrooke, Attlee, Eden, Lord Casey, Dwight Eisenhower, the 1st and 2nd Lords Hankey, Lord Mountbatten, and Lord Salisbury.

The general and miscellaneous personal correspondence consists of mostly Second World War material including the Prime Minister's personal telegrams 1941 and 1942; and notes on War Cabinet meetings 1943–45.

Further miscellaneous papers 1922–49, previously in the Cabinet Office, are now at the PRO (CAB 127/1–56; NRA 32409). There are also papers relating to Ismay in CAB 120 which are the Secretariat files of Churchill as Minister of Defence.

There is a biography by Sir Ronald Wingate, *Lord Ismay: a biography* (Hutchinson 1970). See also Robert S. Jordan, *The NATO International Staff/Secretariat 1952–1957: A Study of International Administration* (Oxford UP 1967).

SIR HENRY JAMES, BARON JAMES OF HEREFORD (1828–1911)

Henry James was Liberal MP for Taunton 1869–85 and Bury 1885–95. He became a Liberal Unionist in 1886. He was Solicitor-General Sept-Nov 1873, Attorney-General 1873–Feb 1874 and May 1880–June 1885, and Chancellor of the Duchy of Lancaster July 1895–Aug 1902. He was knighted in 1873, and created Baron James of Hereford in 1895.

An important collection of his papers was deposited by his nephew, Mr Philip Gwynne James, in the Hereford and Worcester CRO (M45). A calendar of the papers has been compiled (NRA 19716); access to the papers is allowed. The collection relates almost entirely to the years 1880–1909. It was used by Lord Askwith in *Lord James of Hereford* (Ernest Benn 1930); and there is some correspondence to Askwith from the families of James's contemporaries about the difficulties of finding James's letters in their own family papers.

The correspondence was originally arranged in bundles for each year, each bundle being further sub-divided into political, professional, social, and royal sections. Letters from prominent individuals have been put into separate bundles though this arrangement is not entirely consistent. As might be expected, the letters are an important source for a study of late Victorian politics. Askwith pointed out that the Marquess of Hartington, later 8th Duke of Devonshire, the Liberal Unionist leader, wrote frequently to James, sometimes twice a week; and Hartington's letters form a large part of this correspondence. There are also series of letters from Sir Charles Dilke, G. J. Goschen, Lord Salisbury, Lord Randolph Churchill, and W.E. Gladstone. A list of the contents of the trunk made in 1912 states that correspondence covered the years 1840–1911 and that an index and notes about their contents existed; these cannot now be found, and only the correspondence for 1880–1909 appears to have survived.

As well as the correspondence, there is a memoir for 1886–1909 (a typed copy fills 152 pages), which was written by James possibly with the aim of interesting someone in writing a biography. There is also a manuscript diary for 1894, notes on the framing of the Corrupt Practices Act 1883, unflattering press cuttings on James's role in the Parnell Commission (he acted for *The Times* with Sir Richard Webster), and a scrapbook of obituaries and tributes on James's death.

The Hereford and Worcester CRO also purchased a further small collection of papers, consisting of a bundle of letters 1899–1901 from James to H. Cunynghame, concerning the Railway Accidents Commission (AK96/1–34). These are also available for consultation.

GEORGE PATRICK JOHN RUSHWORTH JELLICOE, 2nd EARL JELLICOE (1918-)

George Jellicoe succeeded his father as 2nd Earl Jellicoe in 1935, and was created KBE in 1986. He was Joint Parliamentary Secretary, Ministry of Housing and Local Government June 1961-July 1962, Minister of State, Home Office 1962-Oct 1963, First Lord of the Admiralty 1963-April 1964, Minister of Defence for the Royal Navy April-Oct 1964, and Lord Privy Seal and Minister in Charge, Civil Service Department June 1970-June 1973.

Lord Jellicoe advised us 'I really do not think that I have any papers which would be worth noting'. However, he plans to have those papers which he holds examined and listed with a view to identifying material that may be of interest to historians.

Records of the Leader of the House of Lords and Chief Whip 1945-94 are in the HLRO, but are subject to the 30 year rule (Jellicoe was Leader of the House of Lords 1970-73).

THOMAS JOHNSTON (1881-1965)

Thomas Johnston was Labour MP for Stirlingshire (West) 1922-24, 1929-31 and 1935-45 and Dundee 1924-29. He was Parliamentary Under-Secretary of State for Scotland June 1929-March 1931, Lord Privy Seal March-Aug 1931, and Secretary of State for Scotland Feb 1941-May 1945.

When we enquired for the first edition of the *Guide*, Johnston's widow did not know of the existence of any papers. In his *Memories* (Collins 1952) Johnston described much of his career but only quoted from published sources.

However, in 1973, the NLS bought one box of notebooks, addresses, correspondence, and papers 1904-57 (Acc 5862). The correspondents include Keir Hardie and Sidney and Beatrice Webb. The papers relating to Scotland include material on Scottish trade unionism, Scottish Home Rule 1941-49, and the Scottish Rights of Way Society 1952.

There is also a small collection of papers at the Mitchell Library, Glasgow which was donated anonymously in 1966 (Donation number 27604). Nothing is known of their provenance. The papers have not been listed and appear to be a collection of miscellaneous papers 1928-57, including correspondence from George Dallas of the Workers Union, Joseph Duncan of the Scottish Farm Servants' Union (4), R. Burnett (Canadian MP), J. J. Cargill of the North of Scotland Hydro-Electric Board, Philip Noel-Baker MP (2), and Robert Murray MP (2). There are also many scribbled notes on land, crofting, titles, pollution, etc. and related press cuttings; Labour Party press releases; a typescript 'National Dividends in Food'; correspondence, etc. on fisheries. The main subjects of the collection appear to be land ownership, forestry, agriculture, and the Hydro-Electric Boards.

Graham Walker, *Thomas Johnston* (Manchester UP 1988) is a good guide to relevant material in the public records at Kew and in Edinburgh, and to apposite journal articles and books.

Private Office papers relating to Johnston's periods at the Scottish Office are dispersed through the files of the five main Scottish Office departments held at the SRO.

ARTHUR CREECH JONES (1891–1964)

Arthur Creech Jones was Labour MP for West Riding of Yorkshire (Shipley) 1935–50 and Wakefield 1954–64. He was Under-Secretary of State for the Colonies Aug 1945–Oct 1946, and Secretary of State for the Colonies 1946–Feb 1950.

Sixty-one boxes of Creech Jones's papers were deposited by his widow in the Rhodes House Library (MSS Brit Emp s 332). The papers have been catalogued in great detail and an index of names and subjects has been compiled (NRA 14026). The papers have been divided into six main groups: biographical material; personal correspondence; speeches and writings; visits; Labour Party; colonial work. The papers are available for research.

There are five boxes of biographical papers. They include personal correspondence 1904–20, election pamphlets, papers relating to Creech Jones's conscientious objections (he was imprisoned 1916–19), papers relating to the Workers' Travel Association 1929–59, notes on Creech Jones's parliamentary work as Colonial Secretary, as well as cartoons, photos, and honours.

The three boxes of personal correspondence include many letters from R. H. Tawney 1929–62, as well as letters of congratulations for Creech Jones's various achievements, and letters of condolence to his widow on his death. The miscellaneous correspondence 1913–61 is arranged alphabetically.

There are two boxes of papers relating to Creech Jones's visits to British dependencies and four boxes of Labour Party material. The latter is almost entirely concerned with colonial policy and with the New Fabian Research Bureau.

The material relating to Creech Jones's colonial work is the most extensive. It has been subdivided into five groups: papers concerning specific territories (there are, for example, four boxes of papers concerning Palestine); ten boxes of papers concerning the Colonial Office's Advisory Committee on Education in the Colonies (Creech Jones was a member of the committee 1936–45); papers concerning colonial development and welfare; printed material; and seven boxes of official papers. The latter were closed until 1994 under the 30–year rule since they include Colonial Office internal reports and minutes, dispatches, correspondence, and a few Cabinet papers. No papers relating to Creech Jones's work as parliamentary private secretary to Ernest Bevin seem to have survived.

There are also two boxes of Creech Jones correspondence and memoranda in the papers of the Fabian Colonial Bureau at Rhodes House Library (MSS Brit Emp s 365). Other material relating to his work with the Fabian Society is to be found in the Society's papers in the Nuffield College Library.

Creech Jones's work as Colonial Secretary is discussed in David Goldsworthy, *Colonial Issues in British Politics 1945-1961* (Clarendon Press, Oxford 1971), which draws on the records of the Fabian Colonial Bureau.

D. J. Morgan, *The Official History of Colonial Development* (5 vols, Macmillan 1980) deals with Creech Jones's tenure of the Colonial Office.

Patricia Pugh is currently completing a biography of Creech Jones based on a wide variety of institutional and personal papers; it will be published by the British Academic Press.

AUBREY JONES (1911-)

Aubrey Jones was Conservative MP for Birmingham Hall Green 1950-65. He was Minister of Fuel and Power Dec 1955-Jan 1957, and Minister of Supply 1957-Oct 1959.

Mr Jones's papers, consisting of 170 boxes, have been deposited in the Churchill Archives Centre (AUJO). The papers include diaries, correspondence, and newspaper cuttings. They have been listed (NRA 18561), but cannot be fully catalogued as Mr Jones is still adding to the collection. The collection is closed at present.

Mr Jones described his book *Britain's Economy: The Roots of Stagnation* (Cambridge UP 1985) as 'part autobiographical' (p. viii). He also states that while he was able to access papers from the Cabinet Office relating to his activities in the Departments of Energy, Defence, and Employment, the Department of Trade and Industry was unable to find any papers relating to his period as Minister of Supply (p. viii).

SIR KEITH (SINJOHN) JOSEPH, 2nd Bt, BARON JOSEPH (1918-1994)

Keith Joseph succeeded his father as 2nd baronet in 1944, and was created Baron Joseph (a life peerage) in 1987. He was Conservative MP for Leeds NE 1956-87. He was Parliamentary Secretary, Ministry of Housing and Local Government Oct 1959-Oct 1961, Minister of State, Board of Trade 1961-July 1962, Minister of Housing and Local Government and Minister for Welsh Affairs 1962-Oct 1964, Secretary of State for Social Services June 1970–March 1974, Secretary of State for Industry May 1979–Sept 1981, and Secretary of State for Education and Science 1981–May 1986.

Lord Joseph advised us in 1993 that he had not kept any papers.

There are some Joseph papers 1975–79 in the Conservative Research Department collection of the Conservative Party Archives in the Bodleian Library.

Julian Critchley's short study in *Blackwell*, 233–5, is informed but undocumented. The bulk of the information in Morrison Halcrow, *Keith Joseph: A Single Mind* (Macmillan 1989) comes from interviews with contemporaries. But Joseph himself is thanked for 'time and patience and memory and political analysis, always characteristically and properly meticulous, almost to a fault, in trying to be fair to all the actors in the political drama, and equally properly meticulous in protecting the privacy of his home life'.

There is a long interview with Lord Joseph on his political career in *Contemporary Record*, 1, 1, Spring 1987, 26–31.

FREDERICK WILLIAM JOWETT (1864–1944)

Frederick Jowett was Labour MP for Bradford (West) 1906–18 and Bradford (East) 1922–24 and 1929–31. He was First Commissioner of Works Jan-Nov 1924.

Jowett's papers are extensively quoted in A. Fenner Brockway, *Socialism over Sixty Years. The Life of Jowett of Bradford* (for National Labour Press by Allen & Unwin 1946). This book was planned as an autobiography and the author attempted to let Jowett speak for himself wherever possible. Lord Brockway informed us that after using Jowett's papers he sent them for deposit in Bradford City Library. Unfortunately the papers were 'intercepted' by Jowett's literary executor, Alderman Brown, who kept them in his own home. Alderman Brown died in 1952 and, before anyone could intervene, his sister destroyed all the papers in his care including the early minute books of the Bradford ILP as well as Jowett's papers.

The only surviving Jowett papers in the Bradford District Archives are letters exchanged with Philip Snowden and Sir Rupert Howorth in Sept and Oct 1934 in which Jowett undertook to return two pouches of Cabinet documents in his possession to the Cabinet Office (5D87/3/2 5/1–2; NRA 31982). In a letter to Snowden 21 Sept 1934 asking for advice about how to respond to the Cabinet Office request to return Cabinet documents Jowett wrote: 'Would you mind telling me what you are doing about it for my guidance? I have not many and would not think of publishing any of them but I had much rather keep what [I have] to help my memory in case of need for any legitimate purpose'. Noting that the letter from the Cabinet Office was 'a request not a demand' Snowden advised him to keep those he thought useful and to return the rest.

There is Jowett correspondence in the Labour Party archives in the National Museum of Labour History (Labour Representation Committee 1901–06; Labour Party General Correspondence 1906–07; War Emergency Workers' National Committee; Parliamentary files 1929), as well as some press cuttings (LP/LRC, GC, and WNC).

There is a short biography by James A. Filkins in *MBR*, 3, 492–6. It contains a useful guide to Jowett's own publications and to the locations of relevant archival material in the Labour Party Archives and the ILP Archive at the London School of Economics.

Aspects of Jowett's career are covered in J. Reynolds and K. Laybourn, 'The Emergence of the Independent Labour Party in Bradford', *International Review of Social History*, XX, pt 3, 1975, 313–46; Keith Laybourn, ' "The Defence of the Bottom Dog": The Independent Labour Party in Local Politics' in D. G. Wright and J. A. Jowitt (eds), *Victorian Bradford*, (Bradford Metro 1982), 223–44; J. A. Jowitt and K. Laybourn, 'War and Socialism: The Experience of the Bradford Independent Labour Party 1914–1918', *The Journal of Regional and Local Studies*, 4, 2, Autumn 1984, 57–72; Keith Laybourn and Jack Reynolds, *Liberalism and the Rise of Labour 1890–1918* (Croom Helm 1984); W. D. Ross, 'Bradford Politics 1880–1906' (PhD thesis, University of Bradford 1977).

SIR WILLIAM ALLEN JOWITT, EARL JOWITT (1885–1957)

William Jowitt was Liberal MP for the Hartlepools 1922–24 and Preston 1929. He resigned to become Labour MP for Preston 1929–31 (National Labour MP Aug-Oct 1931), and Labour MP for Ashton-under-Lyne 1939–45. He was Attorney-General June 1929–Jan 1932, Solicitor-General May 1940–March 1942, Paymaster-General March-Dec 1942, Minister without Portfolio 1942–Oct 1944, Minister of National Insurance 1944–May 1945, and Lord Chancellor July 1945–Oct 1951. He was knighted in 1929, created Baron Jowitt in 1945, Viscount Jowitt in 1947, and Earl Jowitt in 1951.

Jowitt's papers are in the possession of his only child, Lady Penelope Wynn-Williams. The collection includes over 50 volumes of press cuttings covering most of Jowitt's life, and some letters and files.

Some of his papers can be found in the PRO at CAB 127/159–93. Files of the Reconstruction Secretariat which served Jowitt as Paymaster-General and Minister without Portfolio can be found in the PRO at CAB 21/1584.

An authorised biography by R. F. V. Heuston was completed in the late 1960s but remains unpublished. An abbreviated version was included in Professor Heuston's *Lord Chancellors 2*. There is a brief sketch of his career by John S. Peart-Binns in *DLB*, VII, 130–3, which provides a comprehensive list of Jowitt's writings.

SIR HUDSON EWBANKE KEARLEY, 1st Bt, 1st VISCOUNT DEVONPORT (1856–1934)

Hudson Kearley was Liberal MP for Devonport 1892–1910. He was Parliamentary Secretary to the President of the Board of Trade Dec 1905–Jan 1909, and Food Controller Dec 1916–June 1917. He was created a baronet in 1908, Baron Devonport in 1910, and Viscount Devonport in 1917.

Kearley's son, the 2nd Viscount Devonport, informed us that no papers survived relating to his father's life or political career.

Correspondence as Food Controller is in the PRO at PRO 30/68.

Kearley's *The Travelled Road – Some Memories of a Busy Life* (Rochester: for private circulation 1935) does not quote from any papers. His role as Food Controller is well documented in L. Margaret Barnett, *British Food Policy During the First World War* (George Allen and Unwin 1985).

FREDERICK GEORGE KELLAWAY (1870–1933)

Frederick Kellaway was Liberal MP for Bedford (Bedfordshire, Bedford from 1918) 1910–22. He was Parliamentary Secretary to the Ministry of Munitions Dec 1916–April 1921, Deputy Minister of Munitions Jan 1919–April 1921, Secretary of the Department of Overseas Trade, an Additional Under-Secretary of State for Foreign Affairs, and an Additional Parliamentary Secretary to the Board of Trade April 1920–April 1921, and Postmaster-General 1921–Oct 1922.

Kellaway's papers passed to his two daughters. None were held by his son.

Kellaway's younger daughter, Mrs Helen Beckley, 12 Rother View, Burwash, Etchingham, E Sussex TN19 7BN, has a small collection of letters and press cuttings. Most of the letters are collected in an album; they are mainly letters of congratulation and appreciation. But there is also, for example, a letter 20 July 1908 from J. A. Pease, then Liberal Chief Whip, asking Kellaway to stand as Liberal candidate for Northamptonshire (South), and a letter from Viscount Althorp commiserating with Kellaway on his defeat in that constituency in 1910. The letters of congratulation include several from Lloyd George and Churchill.

Possibly the most interesting items in this collection are six letters 1914–17 from Kellaway to his wife, mostly describing his work at the Ministry of Munitions under Lloyd George and how Lloyd George conducted the Ministry: Kellaway quotes Lloyd George's welcome to him at Munitions: 'another Pacifist come to make shells...'.

The collection also includes a few press cuttings, the *Bedford Liberal Searchlight* for Nov 1921, some cartoons of Kellaway as Postmaster-General, and Kellaway's 1922 election manifesto.

Most of the collection is currently in the care of Mrs Beckley's son, Mr R. C. Beckley, 114 Kings Road, Kingston, Surrey KT2 5HT, to whom all of the papers will be bequeathed.

A small collection of press cuttings, formerly in the possession of Kellaway's elder daughter, are now held by her widower, Mr King, Hunts Green, Bradford Road, Sherborne, Dorset. The collection includes Kellaway's election addresses for the 1907 London County Council elections as well as for the Jan 1910, 1918, and 1922 parliamentary elections. There are reports of Kellaway's withdrawal as Liberal candidate for South Northamptonshire, and of his victory in Bedford. There are also reports of a speech he made in 1919 defending the work of the Munitions Ministry, and reports of his activities as Postmaster-General.

PHILIP HENRY KERR, 11th MARQUESS OF LOTHIAN (1882–1940)

Philip Kerr succeeded his cousin as 11th Marquess of Lothian in 1930, and was created KT in 1940. He was Chancellor of the Duchy of Lancaster Aug–Nov 1931, and Parliamentary Under-Secretary of State for India 1931–Sept 1932.

A large collection of Kerr's papers, deposited by his cousin, the 12th Marquess of Lothian in the SRO, was purchased by the SRO in 1992 (GD40/17). The papers have been listed (NRA 10737) and are open for research.

The original deposit was divided into six main groups: Round Table papers; papers as private secretary to Lloyd George; subject files; general correspondence; papers as Ambassador to the USA; and articles and speeches.

There are 879 pages of papers concerning the Round Table 1897–1931, including pamphlets, articles, memoranda, and correspondence. The 55 files of papers as private secretary to Lloyd George 1917–21 range from Russia, India, the Middle East, the peace negotiations, reparations, European frontiers, Germany, and Ireland. There are 125 subject files 1921–39. They include Kerr's correspondence as editor of the *Daily Chronicle* 1921–22, papers on East Africa 1927–30, the control of naval armaments 1927–30, and the formation of the National Government 1931 (including letters from Ramsay MacDonald and Herbert Samuel). There are many papers on India 1931–37, particularly concerning constitutional reforms. Files on Germany 1935–38 include memoranda of a visit there, and of conversations with Hitler and Goering. The 192 volumes of general correspondence 1918–39 are arranged by year and then alphabetically. There are 13 volumes of Kerr's private correspondence as Ambassador to the USA 1939–40. They are arranged alphabetically by writer or by subject. There are 34 volumes of articles and speeches.

The second deposit in 1972 included 600 letters from Kerr to his family 1903–40, press cuttings, articles, two notebooks concerning the Indian Franchise Committee 1932, and material collected by Sir James Butler for his biography of Kerr (see below). The bulk of this deposit concerns Kerr's work as private secretary to Lloyd George. There are letters, memoranda, and minutes on India, economic affairs, conscientious objectors, the Dardanelles 1916–17, Kerr's mission to Switzerland 1918, war aims, reparations, Ireland, Russia, and Turkey. There are also correspondence files of letters between the two men, reporting on the Peace Conferences, reparations, and European relations.

Private Office papers relating to Kerr's period as Ambassador to the USA 1939–40 are in the PRO.

Sir James R. M. Butler, *Lord Lothian, Philip Kerr 1882–1940* (Macmillan 1960), was based on the papers and quotes from a large number of letters, memoranda, and press cuttings. *The American Speeches of Lord Lothian July 1939 to December 1940* (Oxford UP 1941) includes a memoir of Kerr by Sir Edward Grigg. There are two Italian publications, *Lord Lothian: Una Vita per la pace*, a collection of essays edited by Giulio Guderzo (The University of Pavia 1986), and A. Bosco, *Lord Lothian: Un pioniere del federalismo, 1882–1940* (1988) of which an English edition is currently being prepared. John Pinder and Andrea Bosco edited *Pacifism is not enough: collected lectures and speeches of Lord Lothian* (Lothian Foundation 1990).

CHARLES WILLIAM KEY (1883–1964)

Charles Key was Labour MP for Poplar, Bow and Bromley 1940–50 and Poplar 1950–64. He was Parliamentary Secretary to the Ministry of Health Aug 1945–Feb 1947, and Minister of Works 1947–Feb 1950.

Key had no children and on the death of his widow in 1965 a small suitcase of papers and photos was inherited by his cousin, Mr W. A. Ankerson, who deposited the collection in the Bodleian Library in 1972 (Dep a 51, c 475–6, d 369–73, e 172). There is a catalogue (NRA 18262).

The greater part of the collection consists of photos. Perhaps most interesting of these is an album of photos of the Poplar rates strike presented to Key on 9 Nov 1922. There are photos of the council passing its resolution, of the march to answer the High Court summons, and of the arrest and release of the councillors. Most of the photos are identified. Key's own version of the rates strike is to be found in his pamphlet *Red Poplar* (1925). Another album has photos of Key at various functions as Minister of Works: from lighting the Christmas tree in Trafalgar Square 1947, to laying the foundation stone of the new House of Commons in May 1948. There is also a collection of photos showing Key's work during the Second World War as Regional Commissioner for the London Civil Defence Region.

A slim volume of press cuttings has survived for the period 1940–41. It covers Key's election; there are copies of his electoral address and photos of him arriving at Westminster to take his seat. There are also reports of his maiden speech, and other speeches in which he was particularly concerned about the supply of milk for mothers and infants. There are some press cuttings about Key's work for the provision of air-raid shelters (Poplar, partly through his efforts, had the lowest death rate in London from the raids) and the script of a broadcast he made on the same subject. There is also a copy of Cmd 7616, *The Report of the Tribunal appointed to inquire into Allegations reflecting on the Official Conduct of Ministers of the Crown and other Public Servants, 1948–49*: the report of the Lynskey Tribunal, to which Key gave evidence and from which he emerged completely cleared of any misconduct. The collection includes some letters of condolence to Key's widow, including a tribute from Clement Attlee, obituary notices, and Key's birth certificate. There is also a meticulously arranged notebook on a wide range of subjects, from agriculture to war pensions.

SIR (HORATIO) HERBERT KITCHENER, 1st EARL KITCHENER OF KHARTOUM (1850–1916)

Herbert Kitchener was created KGMG in 1894, Baron Kitchener in 1898, Viscount Kitchener in 1902, Earl Kitchener of Khartoum in 1914, and KG in 1915. He was Secretary of State for War Aug 1914–June 1916.

On Kitchener's death, his trustee Arthur Renshaw and Herbert Creedy of the War Office went through the papers at York House. 'Such as are of historical or state importance are to be sealed and deposited at the Bank so that the family will not get immediate possession of them' (Creedy to Esher, 10 June 1916, Esher MSS 4/6). They found the papers 'in rather a chaotic condition and where the records of the past are is difficult to say. We are having the Residency at Cairo searched' (Creedy to Esher, 25 June 1916, Esher MSS 4/6).

Sir Philip Magnus, in the introduction to his biography, *Kitchener. Portrait of an Imperialist* (Murray 1958), said that from the age of 34 Kitchener diligently kept what he regarded as important papers, including copies of telegrams and reports sent, as well as those received, and that while Kitchener was at the War Office he removed papers which would now be regarded as official papers. Sir Philip went on to say that with regard to his personal papers Kitchener was very chaotic and that chance played a large part in determining what survived and what did not. Sir Philip frequently quoted from Kitchener's papers, as did Sir George Arthur in his *Life of Lord Kitchener* (3 vols, Macmillan 1920).

Kitchener's great-nephew, the 3rd Earl, deposited the collection Sir Philip used in the PRO (PRO 30/57). The papers have been divided into four sections: papers up to 1914; 1914–16 papers; personal and estate papers; and papers collected by Sir George Arthur for his biography. There is a list (NRA 7283).

The papers up to 1914 reflect Kitchener's military career: there are papers connected with the Palestine and Cyprus Surveys 1874–78; the 1884–85 Sudan Expedition (including Kitchener's own notes); the conquest of the Sudan (including telegrams, intelligence reports, and Kitchener's correspondence with Lord Cromer 1897–99); the Boer War (including Kitchener's correspondence with Queen Victoria 1899–1901, with Lord Roberts 1901–02, and with Lord Midleton); Kitchener's term of office as Commander-in-Chief in India 1902–09 (including correspondence with Lord Curzon 1900–05 especially on their dispute about control of the Indian army); and his term as Minister Plenipotentiary in Egypt 1911–14.

The First World War papers include a complete series of dispatches from Sir John French and Sir Douglas Haig in France, Sir Ian Hamilton and General Birdwood in Gallipoli, and Sir John Hanbury Williams in Moscow. There is also Kitchener's correspondence with his Cabinet colleagues, correspondence about munitions, and about his fateful journey to Russia.

The personal and estate papers are very disconnected and miscellaneous but they do include some royal letters, letters from Margot Asquith, and an engagement diary for 1913–14.

The papers collected by Sir George Arthur include letters of condolence sent on Kitchener's death and Sir George's own correspondence with people who knew Kitchener, arranged alphabetically.

A small collection (23 pieces) of Kitchener's War Office Private Office papers 1914–16 is also available at the PRO (WO 159). WO 159/1 is an index to the collection and was contemporaneously described as a general catalogue of 'The Creedy (Kitchener) Papers'. Sir Herbert Creedy was Private Secretary to successive Secretaries of State at the War Office including Kitchener. The collection has been divided into three sections: strategical and political papers; miscellaneous papers; and letters from Colonel (later Brigadier-General) the Hon Sir H. Yarde Buller 1914–16, the British Military Attaché to the French Army Headquarters 1914–17.

The strategic and political papers include Cabinet memoranda and drafts of Cabinet memoranda. There are also four letters from Sir Edward Grey 24-26 Sept 1914 warning Kitchener about indiscreet articles on the war in *The Times*. The miscellaneous papers include notes by Sir Henry Wilson and an undated paper on the risk of a gas scandal which describes Lloyd George as not having a grasp of the seriousness of the situation.

A further collection of Kitchener's papers is available at the Oriental and India Office Collections, British Library among a collection of the papers of his Military Secretary in India, General Lord Birdwood (MSS Eur D 686/1-52; NRA 27457). As well as correspondence with Lords Curzon and Roberts on the dual military control dispute, there are official documents on the defence of India, and relations with Afghanistan and Persia. The British Library holds working papers 1872-77 relating to the survey of western Palestine conducted by Kitchener and Claude Conder (Add MS 69848).

Another small collection was purchased by the British Library at Sotheby's in 1963 (Add MSS 52276-8). The collection consists of three volumes of the papers of Kitchener's ADC in India, Lt-Col R. J. Marker, but some of Kitchener's own papers are included, for instance in the correspondence between Kitchener and Marker 1902-11. As well as some general correspondence, there are letters from H. O. Arnold-Forster 1905-09, and Lt Col C. à Court Repington 1904-11. A copy of the British Library list has been published by the List and Index Society, *Special Series vol 7, 'Rough Register' of Acquisitions of the Department of Manuscripts, British Library, 1961-1965*, 1974, p. 111.

The papers of H. A. Gwynne, editor of the *Morning Post*, at the IWM include some letters to and replies from Kitchener, mostly for 1914 (HAG/13).

There are several recent studies including George H. Cassar, *Kitchener: architect of victory* (William Kimber 1977); Peter King, *The Viceroy's Fall: how Kitchener destroyed Curzon* (Sidgwick and Jackson 1984); Trevor Royle *The Kitchener Enigma* (Michael Joseph 1985); and Philip Warner, *Kitchener: the man behind the legend* (Atheneum Publishers, New York 1986).

For Kitchener's work at the War Office see Peter Simkins, 'Kitchener and the Expansion of the Army' in Ian Beckett and John Gooch (eds), *Politicians and Defence: Studies in the Formulation of British Defence Policy 1845-1970* (Manchester UP 1981), 87-109.

SIR ERNEST HENRY LAMB, 1st BARON ROCHESTER (1876-1955)

Ernest Lamb was Liberal MP for Rochester 1906-Jan 1910 and Dec 1910-18. He was Paymaster-General Nov 1931-Dec 1935. He was knighted in 1914, and created Baron Rochester in 1931.

Lamb's elder son, the 2nd Baron Rochester, informed us that he knew of no surviving papers relating to his father's political and official career. Lord Rochester did not think any other family member had any papers either.

GEORGE LANSBURY (1859–1940)

George Lansbury was Labour MP for Tower Hamlets (Bow and Bromley) 1910–12 and for Poplar, Bow and Bromley 1922–40. He was First Commissioner of Works June 1929–Aug 1931. He was Leader of the Labour Party 1932–35.

Along with his contemporaries, Lansbury was requested in Sept 1934 by the Cabinet Office to return any Cabinet papers which he had retained. The Cabinet was later told that 'Apart from a bare acknowledgement no reply has been received, but statements have appeared in the newspapers to the effect that he has no intention of returning his papers' (report by Sir Maurice Hankey, 29 Nov 1935, PRO, CAB 24/257).

Twenty-six bound volumes of Lansbury's papers were eventually deposited by his son-in-law Raymond Postgate in the BLPES (Lansbury papers). A list and index of the papers is available (NRA 7528).

These are all that remain after more than 30 boxes of both official and personal papers were taken and seized by the Cabinet Office in 1944 (see Postgate's foreword to *The Life of George Lansbury*, Longmans, Green 1951). Postgate averred that 'nothing whatever was returned. I was sent, it is true, a set of signed applications to subscribe to the *Labour Gazette* in 1893; but if this was an official's jest or what I have never fathomed' (p. viii). According to the Cabinet Office, only Cabinet papers were removed from the collection and the 'few items of correspondence' were returned to Postgate. The Cabinet papers were 'not retained' by the Cabinet Office. John Shepherd of the Anglia Polytechnic University in Cambridge advised us that the increasingly acrimonious correspondence between Postgate and the Cabinet Office over his abortive attempts to secure the return of his father-in-law's papers is in the PRO at CAB 21/2393.

The papers at the BLPES were divided by Postgate into five main divisions when he was writing the biography: 17 volumes of correspondence and papers arranged chronologically 1877–1940; Postgate's own correspondence about Lansbury arranged alphabetically 1940–50; memoranda, correspondence, and pamphlets arranged by subject – eg voluntary schools 1928–31, unemployment and the means test, India, the Labour Party manifesto and programme of 1929, and a memo by Lansbury on 'The Cabinet Crisis of 1931'; photos; and press cuttings about books by Lansbury.

The Borthwick Institute of Historical Research has a small collection of the papers of Major David Graham Pole (UL 5), which includes many letters from Lansbury and papers concerning him. A list of the papers is available. The papers mainly refer to Indian affairs (Pole was vice-chairman and honorary secretary of the British Commission on Indian and Burma affairs 1918–39) and financial matters; but they also include Lansbury's guarantee of one issue of the *Daily Herald* (July 1912), some notes probably written by Lansbury in the 1929 election campaign, and correspondence about Lansbury's proposed visit to Hitler April 1937.

Three box-files of press cuttings about Lansbury are available at the Tower Hamlets Local History Library and Archives (100). There are over 2000 cuttings 1894–1940 including cartoons 1920–36. The collection includes a few letters as well as his manuscript of 'The Principles of the English Poor Law'.

Lansbury wrote several volumes of memoirs including *My Life* (Constable 1928) and *Looking Backwards and Forwards* (Blackie 1935). Lansbury's son Edgar wrote a biography entitled *George Lansbury My Father* (Sampson Low, Marston 1934) which quotes from private correspondence as well as public speeches and articles. The biography also quoted from memoranda submitted to the Cabinet by Lansbury as First Commissioner of Works. As a result of these disclosures, the Prime Minister sanctioned action by officials to persuade the publishers to withdraw all unsold copies of the book. Edgar Lansbury was prosecuted under the Official Secrets Act for having received information 'with reasonable ground to believe when he received it' that it had been given to him in contravention of the Act. He was fined £20 and ordered to pay costs of 20 guineas (John F. Naylor, *A Man and an Institution: Sir Maurice Hankey, the Cabinet Secretariat and the custody of Cabinet secrecy*, Cambridge UP 1984, 212–14). George Lansbury, who had made the papers available to his son, was not prosecuted.

An extensive bibibliography accompanies Margaret Cole's biography of Lansbury in *DLB*, II, 214–27. Two biographies were published in 1990: Bob Holman's *Good Old George: The Life of George Lansbury* (Lion) and Jonathan Schneer's *George Lansbury* (Manchester UP) which 'focusses upon George Lansbury's efforts as a socialist, feminist and pacifist' and draws on the files of the Independent Labour Party and the Fellowship of Reconciliation at the BLPES; the Labour Party collection at the National Museum of Labour History; the Social Democratic Federation collection at the Marx Memorial Library, London; and the records of the Peace Pledge Union, Dick Sheppard House, London.

The footnotes to Noreen Branson, *Poplarism, 1919–1925: George Lansbury and the Councillors' Revolt* (Lawrence and Wishart 1979) are a good guide to relevant material on Lansbury in the minutes of the Poplar Board of Guardians and Poplar Borough Council.

Gerald Studdert-Kennedy brings a fresh perspective to Lansbury in his entry in *Blackwell*, 250–4. John Shepherd examines the 1935 crisis in his article 'Labour and the Trade Unions: George Lansbury, Ernest Bevin and the Leadership Crisis of 1935' in Chris Wrigley and John Shepherd, *On the Move: Essays in Labour and Transport History* (Hambledon Press 1991), 204–30. Dr Shepherd is completing a book on Lansbury with the support of the family. It will be published by Oxford UP.

ANDREW BONAR LAW (1858–1923)

Andrew Bonar Law was Conservative MP for Glasgow (Blackfriars) 1900–06, Camberwell (Dulwich) 1906–10, Lancashire (Bootle) 1911–18 and Glasgow (Central) 1918–23. He was Parliamentary Secretary to the Board of Trade Aug 1902–Dec 1905, Secretary of State for Colonial Affairs May 1915–Dec 1916, Chancellor of the Exchequer 1916–Jan 1919, member of the War Cabinet Dec 1916–Oct 1919, Lord Privy Seal Jan 1919–March 1921, and Prime Minister Oct 1922–May 1923. He was Leader of the Conservative Party Nov 1911–Mar 1921 and Oct 1922–May 1923.

One hundred and seventeen boxes of Bonar Law's papers were bequeathed to his close friend, Lord Beaverbrook, and are now in the HLRO; they have been listed and thoroughly indexed (NRA 19286). The card index and catalogue is available in the HLRO and also on microfiche (copies obtainable from Chadwyck-Healey, The Quorum, Barnwell Road, Cambridge CB5 8SW). Only 17 boxes concern his personal and business life; the rest reflect his political and ministerial career. They have been arranged under the following headings: papers as an MP; as Parliamentary Secretary to the Board of Trade; leader of the Conservative Party; Colonial Secretary; Chancellor; Leader of the House of Commons; Lord Privy Seal; 1921–22 papers; and papers as Prime Minister.

Bonar Law's papers as an MP have been divided into correspondence 1900–11 (one box), general papers (including press cuttings, papers on the 1908 Licensing Bill, trade unionism, and tariff reform), and constituency correspondence (one box). There is a single box of papers as Parliamentary Secretary to the Board of Trade. Boxes 24–37 are filled with his correspondence as Leader of the Conservative Party. Boxes 38–49 contain other papers – memoranda and press cuttings – on such topics as elections, finance, foreign affairs, Ireland, House of Lords' reforms, and the Marconi inquiry. There are also some papers from the Committee of Imperial Defence's Subcommittee on Invasion 1907–14 and papers of the Diverted Cargoes Committee Aug 1914–Jan 1915. Boxes 50–64 cover Bonar Law's term of office as Secretary of State for the Colonies. As well as Cabinet papers, correspondence, and memoranda (including political as well as official), arranged chronologically, there are press cuttings, suggestions for honours, papers on

Ireland, and post-war reconstruction. There is also some political correspondence and Bonar Law's own account of the events of Dec 1916. Boxes 65–76 contain Law's papers as Chancellor of the Exchequer, including his warrant to act as Chancellor. The many official papers include draft Cabinet minutes for 5 April 1917–15 Aug 1919 which were so secret that they were not printed. Boxes 77–80, his papers as Leader of the House, include a box of letters to the King 22 March 1916–21 Nov 1918 describing the House's proceedings. There is also an index to Bonar Law's speeches in the House. His papers as Lord Privy Seal (boxes 86–106) include papers on the peace conference as well as papers on Cabinet conclusions and ministerial conferences. There are letters to the King 4 Feb 1919–23 Dec 1920, notes for debates, and correspondence. Boxes 95 and 96 contain his papers as Leader of the Party 1918–21 and are mostly memoranda and correspondence about the Coalition. One box of correspondence covers the period in 1921–22 after he resigned all his offices because of ill-health. Boxes 108–117 contain his papers as Prime Minister. There are both general and special correspondence series including papers on appointments and the Nov 1922 general election. There are also many subject files.

A further collection of papers was deposited in the HLRO in 1992 by Bonar Law's grandson, Bonar Sykes. This consists of two packets of letters and telegrams of sympathy to Bonar Law and a small packet of press cuttings on the death of his wife in 1909; one album of photos 1909–15; and three volumes of press cuttings, including reports of Bonar Law's speeches 1911–14, a number of cartoons 1917–22 and cuttings on his becoming Prime Minister, his resignation, and on his final illness and death. This volume also includes letters of sympathy to Frederick Sykes on Bonar Law's death.

Lord Blake's biography, *The Unknown Prime Minister. The Life and Times of Andrew Bonar Law 1858–1923* (Eyre & Spottiswoode 1955), quotes substantially from these papers. A new biography is being prepared by Prof R. J. Q. Adams from the Texas A&M University.

There is evidence that some of Bonar Law's papers were returned to official keeping: for example in the PRO (FO 899), a miscellaneous collection of printed Cabinet papers 1900–18, there are two volumes of papers for 1915–16 which were returned by Bonar Law's secretary in May 1923.

It should be noted that the papers of J. C. C. Davidson contain a number of files of Bonar Law's correspondence and official documents which were evidently kept by Davidson when he served as Bonar Law's private secretary at the Colonial Office. Details may be found in HLRO Memo 78.

Reference should also be made to the 'Prime Ministers' group of papers in the Thomas Jones collection (Class A) in the NLW (NRA 30994).

The National Archives of Canada holds photocopies of correspondence between Bonar Law and Sir Robert Borden and others concerning matters of interest to Canada (MG 27 II A1).

Papers of Prime Ministerial Advisors Outside Cabinet 1916–40 are in the PRO at PREM 1.

RICHARD KIDSTON LAW, 1st BARON COLERAINE (1901–1980)

Richard Law was Conservative MP for Kingston-upon-Hull (South-West) 1931–45, Kensington (South) 1945–50 and Kingston-on-Hull (Haltemprice) 1950–54. He was Financial Secretary to the War Office May 1940–July 1941, Parliamentary Under-Secretary of State for Foreign Affairs 1941–Sept 1943, Minister of State at the Foreign Office 1943–May 1945, and Minister of Education May-July 1945. He was created Baron Coleraine in 1954.

Lord Coleraine informed us that he had never systematically kept papers though some did survive. He never kept a diary nor subscribed to a press cuttings agency. Lord Coleraine added that the most important papers concerning his period as Minister of State will be in the public records since he personally drafted most of the Cabinet papers circulated in his name.

Coleraine's son, the 2nd Lord Coleraine, holds his father's surviving papers, although they have not been arranged and are not accessible.

Private Office papers related to Lord Coleraine's period at the Foreign Office are in the PRO at FO 800/430.

J. Enoch Powell contributed the entry on Coleraine to *DNB 1971–1980*, 485–6.

FREDERICK WILLIAM PETHICK-LAWRENCE, BARON PETHICK-LAWRENCE (1871–1961)

Frederick Pethick-Lawrence (he assumed the additional surname Pethick in 1901 on his marriage) was Labour MP for Leicester (West) 1923–31 and Edinburgh (East) 1935–45. He was Financial Secretary to the Treasury June 1929–Aug 1931, and Secretary of State for India and Burma Aug 1945–April 1947. He was created Baron Pethick-Lawrence in 1945.

Pethick-Lawrence's literary executrixes were his two secretaries, Miss Esther Knowles and Mrs Gladys Groom-Smith. Miss Knowles presented a collection of papers to the library of Pethick-Lawrence's old college, Trinity College, Cambridge (Pethick-Lawrence MSS). The collection consists of nine boxes (some 1800 letters in all), mainly of correspondence to and from Pethick-Lawrence. Correspondents include many of

Pethick-Lawrence's Cabinet colleagues and British and Indian political and literary figures. A list of names of correspondents and numbers of letters is available.

Pethick-Lawrence himself presented a small collection of papers concerning India and Burma to the Oriental and India Office Collections, British Library in 1958 (MSS Eur D 540; NRA 25125). They include correspondence and memoranda between the Financial Secretary and the Secretary of State for India on the 'Financial Safeguards' 1931, and press cuttings, cartoons, and photos from the British and Indian press on the 1946 British Cabinet Mission to India.

Pethick-Lawrence's autobiography *Fate Has Been Kind* (Hutchinson 1943) quotes from only a few papers but Vera Brittain, *Pethick-Lawrence: A Portrait* (George Allen and Unwin 1963), was based on all of the papers and quotes frequently from them, particularly Pethick-Lawrence's letters to his first wife Emmeline, which had been left to Miss Knowles.

Pethick-Lawrence's role in Indian affairs is discussed in Robin Moore, *Escape from Empire. The Attlee Government and the Indian Problem* (Clarendon Press, Oxford 1983), and *Making the New Commonwealth* (Clarendon Press, Oxford 1987). The HMSO series on the Transfer of Power 1942-47 contains much material on Pethick-Lawrence.

JOHN JAMES LAWSON, BARON LAWSON (1881-1965)

Jack Lawson was Labour MP for Durham (Chester-le-Street) 1919-49. He was Financial Secretary to the War Office Jan-Nov 1924, Parliamentary Secretary to the Ministry of Labour June 1929-Aug 1931, and Secretary of State for War Aug 1945-Oct 1946. He was created Baron Lawson in 1950.

The small collection of Lawson's papers held by his daughter, the Hon Mrs Irene Lawson, described in the first edition, was deposited in the University of Durham Library in 1992. A summary list has been produced (NRA 37246).

The collection, which consists of 15 boxes, includes a journal of loose sheets Jan-May 1937 and another, written in pencil and kept only intermittently, for 27 Aug 1941-25 Aug 1945. This latter journal contains lengthy reflections on contemporary problems and on his own life. There are also 13 volumes of pocket diaries, recording appointments and addresses 1934-35, 1942-45, 1950-54, and 1958-59.

Very little appears to have survived from Lawson's terms of office at the War Office; all that has been found is a draft letter of resignation 26 Nov 1945 when doctors were being released from military service out of turn. No contemporary document survives from Lawson's time as Financial Secretary to the War Office but there is an article by Lawson published about 1950 describing the 1924 Labour government Lawson was appointed Lord Lieutenant of Durham in 1949. Some correspondence about a visit by the Queen Mother in 1956 survives. The bulk of the papers relates to Lawson's interests in mining and his constituency and also to his various books, articles, and radio programmes.

There are many surviving papers which relate to Lawson's activities on behalf of the miners among whom he began his life. There are pit agreements (including one dated 1897), arbitration agreements, and notes on conditions in the mines culled from royal commissions and other sources. There are also photos of the mines, press cuttings largely concerned with accidents, and a 14–page manuscript, entitled 'The Monster', about accidents underground.

Lawson published several books and many articles during his lifetime, for example, his own autobiography *A Man's Life* (Hodder & Stoughton 1932) which does not appear to quote from any papers. Some correspondence and other papers concerning these publications survive. There is a typescript of an autobiographical account of his life from c.1933. There is also a typescript and some correspondence concerning a radio broadcast entitled 'Something of My Philosophy' 28 March 1954. There are notes or memoirs of several of his colleagues, including George Lansbury and Clement Attlee, an eight-page memo of Lawson's visit to Spain in 1936, and a 62–page memo on his visit to the Near East in 1937.

A considerable amount of miscellaneous correspondence survives especially from the late 1950s and early 1960s; and there are also three letters 1915 from Lawson's brother William, who was killed later in the First World War. There is a letter from Hore-Belisha 15 March 1938 congratulating Lawson on a speech. Congratulations on his peerage have also survived. There are many notes for speeches and sermons. Fourteen pocket diaries for the years 1933–59 have addresses and appointments.

One file of constituency correspondence has survived, mainly dating from 1926, and this relates to unemployment and the general strike. The file contains Lawson's notes to ministers and civil servants as well as the original complaints and his replies.

The Durham University Library received a second instalment of Lawson papers in Aug 1994 from Lawson's grand-daughter, Mrs Elaine Smith (1994/5 Lawson papers). This additional collection was also in the possession of Mrs Lawson, stored in inaccessible parts of her loft and garage, and given to the Library when she moved into a nursing home. The Library estimates that the second instalment is twice as large as the first; but as it is in complete disorder, it will be some time before it is sorted and listed.

Joyce Bellamy and Daniel E. Martin used the Lawson papers in their entry in *DLB*, II, 227–30.

Lawson himself wrote biographies of contemporary miners' leaders, *Peter Lee* (Epworth Press 1936, revised ed 1949), and *The Man in the Cap: The Life of Herbert Smith* (Methuen 1941).

FREDERICK JAMES LEATHERS, 1st VISCOUNT LEATHERS (1883–1965)

Frederick Leathers was created Baron Leathers in 1941, and Viscount Leathers in 1954. He was Minister of War Transport May 1941–July 1945, and Secretary of State for the Coordination of Transport, Fuel, and Power Oct 1951–Sept 1953.

Lord Leathers's son, the 2nd Viscount Leathers, informed us that he had no papers of consequence relating to his father's political or ministerial career.

Some of Leathers's Private Office papers from the Ministry of War Transport are now available in the PRO (MT 62/3–95). As well as papers concerning various conferences, there are copies of telegrams between Churchill and F. D. Roosevelt about American assistance. There are many papers on shipping, including files of meetings with the seamen's trade union leaders and the ship owners. Also available are papers from Co-ordination of Transport Fuel and Power 1951–53 (MT 62/130–46).

There is a brief essay on Leathers by Francis Keenlyside in *DNB 1961–1970*, 640–2.

SIR ARTHUR HAMILTON LEE, VISCOUNT LEE OF FAREHAM (1868–1947)

Arthur Lee was Conservative MP for Hampshire (Fareham) 1900–18. He was Civil Lord of the Admiralty Oct 1903–Dec 1905, Parliamentary Secretary to the Ministry of Munitions Nov 1915–July 1916, Minister of Agriculture and Fisheries Aug 1919–Feb 1921, and First Lord of the Admiralty 1921–Oct 1922. He was created KCB in 1916, GCB in 1929, Baron Lee of Fareham in 1918 and Viscount Lee of Fareham in 1922.

A miscellaneous collection of approximately 17 box-files of Lee's papers, which was held at the Beaverbrook Library, is now held at the Courtauld Institute of Art. It has been listed.

The collection has been arranged into 12 sections. The first contains a copy of Lee's memoirs, *A Good Innings and a Great Partnership* (3 vols, privately printed 1939) which frequently quote from his correspondence and his wife's diaries, none of which appear to have survived. An abbreviated edition of these memoirs has been published: Alan Clark (ed), *A Good Innings: The Private Papers of Viscount Lee of Fareham* (John Murray 1974). Lee also privately published *Letters that Remain (friendly or otherwise) from the Postbag of Arthur and Ruth Lee 1891–1941* (1941) of which originals and typescript copies of the letters (many from Lee's political colleagues) may be found in section two (one box-file). Some of the letters to be found in this section were not included in the book. Section three contains printed proof sheets of letters included in *Letters that Remain*.

Section four (one box-file) contains miscellaneous speech notes; copies of Lee's miscellaneous speeches and speeches as Minister of Agriculture and Fisheries; assorted correspondence from Prime Ministers and their wives, including Violet Attlee, Anne and Neville Chamberlain, Lucy and Stanley Baldwin, Clementine Churchill, and Ramsay MacDonald; and the pen used in signing the 1921 Naval Treaty in Washington.

Section five (four box-files) includes wartime letters, various photos and other miscellanea. Section six (five box-files) contains original and typescript copies of letters from a variety of people, divided alphabetically. Section seven (one box-file) relates to the Chequers estate, while section eight (three box-files) contains Lee's correspondence regarding art matters. Section nine (one box-file) contains original typescript and manuscript correspondence with Theodore Roosevelt 1897–1918 and Edith Roosevelt 1913–41. Sections ten and eleven contain a miscellaneous collection of photos and letters. Section 12 consists of two black cylinders containing certification of Lord and Lady Lee's entry into the Order of the Hospital of St John of Jerusalem.

THOMAS WODEHOUSE LEGH, 2nd BARON NEWTON (1857–1942)

Thomas Legh was Conservative MP for South-West Lancashire (Newton) 1886–98 when he succeeded his father as 2nd Baron Newton. He was Paymaster-General June 1915–Aug 1916, and Assistant Under-Secretary of State for Foreign Affairs 1916–Jan 1919.

Newton's grandson, the 4th Lord Newton, informed us that his grandfather left only voluminous diaries, beginning in 1883, but these are not generally available for research. The diaries are extensively quoted and paraphrased in Lord Newton's *Retrospection* (John Murray 1941). They are now in the care of Newton's great-grandson, the 5th Lord Newton.

Newton's role in the 1911 constitutional crisis is discussed in D. B. Southern, 'Lord Newton, the Conservative Peers and the Parliament Act of 1911', *English Historical Review*, 96, 1981, 834–40, and Patricia Kelvin and Corinne Comstock Weston, 'The "Judas Group" and the Parliament Bill of 1911', *English Historical Review*, 99, 1984, 551–63. The articles are reprinted in Clyve Jones and David Lewis Jones (eds), *Peers, Politics and Power: The House of Lords 1603–1911* (Hambledon Press 1986).

FREDERICK ALEXANDER LINDEMANN, VISCOUNT CHERWELL (1886–1957)

Professor Frederick Lindemann was created Baron Cherwell in 1941, and Viscount Cherwell in 1956. He was Paymaster-General Dec 1942–Aug 1945 and Oct 1951–Nov 1953.

A large collection of Cherwell's papers has been deposited in the Nuffield College Library (Cherwell papers). The papers were rearranged and listed in 1981, and only two files remain closed. A list of the files is available at both Nuffield and the NRA (NRA 16447). Researchers wishing to read the open papers should complete the application forms available in the library; the forms will then be sent by the library to the Cabinet Office for approval, a process taking approximately ten days.

The main body of the papers has been divided into the following sections: personal and biographical; Oxford University; scientific research, writings, conferences; scientific correspondence; publications, lectures, speeches; Second World War, preparations and statistical section, general papers; Second World War, statistical section, military and scientific topics; Second World War, statistical section, economic topics; politics and the Conservative Party; personal and social correspondence.

There is a two volume catalogue of these papers which includes an index of correspondents. A supplementary catalogue describes a small quantity of documents mainly written on patents in German, and inventions, research and publications, and shorter notes. Most of this material, which was discovered in 1982, relates to Lindemann's early scientific career in Germany 1910–14.

Some Private Office papers can be found in the PRO at CAB 127/194–203 (NRA 32409).

These papers are extensively quoted in Lord Birkenhead's biography *The Prof. in Two Worlds* (Collins 1961). Sir Roy Harrod, *The Prof* (Macmillan 1959) is a personal memoir not based on these papers.

DAVID ALEXANDER EDWARD LINDSAY, 27th EARL OF CRAWFORD and 10th EARL OF BALCARRES (1871–1940)

David Lindsay was known as Lord Balcarres from 1880 until he succeeded his father as 27th Earl of Crawford and 10th Earl of Balcarres in 1913. He was created KT in 1921. He was Conservative MP for North Lancashire (Chorley) 1895–1913. He was President of the Board of Agriculture and Fisheries July-Dec 1916, Lord Privy Seal 1916–Jan 1919, Chancellor of the Duchy of Lancaster 1919–April 1921, First Commissioner of Works 1921–Oct 1922, and Minister of Transport April-Oct 1922.

A large collection of Lord Crawford's papers, previously deposited in John Rylands University Library, Manchester, is now held by the Department of Manuscripts, NLS (Acc 9769). A summary box list of the political and personal correspondence and papers has been prepared. There are 45 boxes, including papers relating to the National Art Collections Fund, HM Office of Works, and the National Gallery.

The general political correspondence and papers 1896–1931 is contained in five boxes, and there are a further three boxes of correspondence 1924–40 with individual personal or political friends including Lords Halifax, Linlithgow, Lloyd, and Tweedsmuir (John Buchan); one box of correspondence with Crawford's brother, Sir Ronald Lindsay, diplomatist 1923–40; and two boxes of correspondence 1905–37 with his son, Lord Balniel, later 28th Earl of Crawford.

For access to the Crawford Papers in the NLS researchers must obtain prior permission from Crawford's grandson, the 29th Earl of Crawford and Balcarres. Any photography or other form of reprography may be limited, and also requires the permission of Lord Crawford.

Other papers remain in the possession of the present Lord Crawford: a diary which covers general, social, political, and artistic matters; and papers relating to his period as Chief Whip and as First Commissioner of Works. Limited access to these papers may be allowed to senior researchers.

A selection from the papers retained by Lord Crawford has been published in John Vincent (ed), *The Crawford Papers: The journals of David Lindsay twenty-seventh Earl of Crawford and tenth Earl of Balcarres 1871–1940 during the years 1892 to 1940* (Manchester UP 1984).

Liverpool University Library holds a bound volume on educational legislation 1906–08 acquired from Crawford's library. Most of the documents are unsigned; but two are initialled 'A.J.B.' (MS 24.30).

SIR PHILIP CUNLIFFE-LISTER, 1st EARL OF SWINTON (1884–1972)

Philip Cunliffe-Lister (he changed his name from Lloyd-Greame in 1924) was Conservative MP for Middlesex (Hendon) 1918–35. He was Parliamentary Secretary to the Board of Trade Aug 1920–April 1921, Secretary to the Overseas Trade Department and Additional Parliamentary Secretary to the Board of Trade 1921–Oct 1922, President of the Board of Trade 1922–Jan 1924, Nov 1924–June 1929 and Aug-Nov 1931, Secretary of State for the Colonies 1931–June 1935, Secretary of State for Air 1935–May 1938, Cabinet Minister Resident in West Africa June 1942–Oct 1944, Minister of Civil Aviation 1944–July 1945, Chancellor of the Duchy of Lancaster and Minister of Materials Oct 1951–Nov 1952, and Secretary of State for Commonwealth Relations 1952–April 1955. He was created KBE in 1920, GBE in 1929, Viscount Swinton in 1935, and Earl of Swinton in 1955.

Lord Swinton bequeathed 42 boxes of his papers to the Churchill Archives Centre (SWIN). The papers are subject to the 30-year rule operated by the Churchill Archives Centre. A catalogue is available (NRA 21107).

The collection has been divided into three sections. Section I (Acc No 174) contains First World War papers including letters from Swinton (then Lloyd-Greame) to his wife from France c.May-Oct 1916, and selected Cabinet papers relating to manpower 1917–18. Papers 1919–39 include correspondence with Neville Chamberlain 1925–38; a letter from Geoffrey Lloyd re the formation of the National Government 14 Aug 1931, and Swinton's appointment as President of the Board of Trade Aug 1931; letters to Lady Swinton from Swinton and others. There is also a collection of Cabinet papers, and letters of sympathy on Swinton's resignation from the Air Ministry May-June 1938. Papers 1940–45 include Swinton's West African letters to Lady Swinton 1942–44, and correspondence on the death of his son John, who was killed in action in 1943. There is also a collection of War Cabinet papers on civil aviation 1944–45. There are memoranda, correspondence, and letters on the House of Lords Leaders' Conference 1948 and House of Lords Parliamentary bill 1947–49.

Papers from Swinton's term as Secretary of State for Commonwealth Relations include mostly personal correspondence, but there is also material relating to a Commonwealth tour and Swinton's own notes of a Commonwealth Prime Ministers' meeting June 1953. There is a collection of personal letters 1956–70, including letters on Macmillan's retirement from the premiership 1963. There are papers relating to reform and procedure in the House of Lords and Rhodesia 1956–71. There are drafts of and correspondence relating to *Sixty Years in Power*, including comments by Harold Macmillan on the section concerning his resignation. There are papers on the Anglo-Belgian Union; and financial correspondence, tax papers, and dividend warrants 1966–71. There are also press cuttings relating to Swinton kept by Conservative Central Office 1965–73.

Section II (Acc No 270) contains early papers including pre-war letters 1901–13, Swinton's letters to his father 1916–17; miscellaneous papers 1920–29 and 1930–39; and index and minutes of proceedings of Secretary of State's progress meetings about RAF expansion measures 1935–38. Papers 1940–45 include letters as Secretary of State 1942–43 and intelligence service telegrams from the Foreign Office regarding Governor-General Dakar 1943. The papers 1945–59 include engagement diaries 1951, 1954, 1957; copies of speeches 1946–59, and material for speeches 1941–56.

Section III (Acc No 313) contains papers and letters 1919–79 including material on negotiations with Russia; papers relating to *I Remember;* and

Indian affairs 1949. Papers 1950–62 include a closed file of correspondence with Attlee and John Maud regarding security services 1950–51; and correspondence with Selwyn Lloyd on Conservative Party organisation. There are copies of speeches 1958–61 and engagement diaries 1958, 1961, 1962, 1964, 1966.

Swinton's memoirs, *I Remember* (Hutchinson 1948), quote frequently from his correspondence and in his further volume, *Sixty Years of Power: Some Memories of the Men who Wielded it* (Hutchinson 1966), he gave his views on the Prime Ministers he had known and on the working of the Cabinet system. Alan Earl, 'The Political Life of Viscount [sic] Swinton 1918–38' (MA thesis, Manchester University 1960) was written with the subject's help and quotes from many letters, mainly before 1932. J. A. Cross, *Lord Swinton* (Clarendon Press, Oxford 1982) uses the Swinton papers at the Churchill Archives Centre but notes (p. 301 fn. 15) the disappearance of some of the documents cited in Earl's thesis, notably the 'voluminous correspondence' with Lord Derby in Aug 1923.

A small collection of Swinton's Air Ministry papers is available at the PRO (AIR 19/23–4). The collection includes documents on the Inskip inquiry into the relationship between the Fleet Air Arm and shore-based aircraft 1936–39, papers on the state of air preparedness 1937–38, and minutes and reports of the Nursing Service Committee.

JOHN JESTYN LLEWELLIN, BARON LLEWELLIN (1893–1957)

Jay Llewellin was Conservative MP for Middlesex (Uxbridge) 1929–45. He was Civil Lord of the Admiralty May 1937–July 1939, Parliamentary Secretary to the Ministry of Supply 1939–May 1940, Parliamentary Secretary to the Ministry of Aircraft Production 1940-May 1941, Parliamentary Secretary to the Ministry of Transport (later War Transport) 1941–Feb 1942, President of the Board of Trade Feb 1942, Minister of Aircraft Production Feb-Nov 1942, Minister for Supply Resident in Washington DC 1942–Nov 1943, and Minister of Food 1943–Aug 1945. He was created GBE in 1953, and Baron Llewellin in 1945.

In the first edition we reported that Llewellin's sister, Miss Mary Llewellin had a small collection of her brother's papers.

Possibly of greatest interest was a long (47pp) note by Llewellin on his work at the Ministry of Aircraft Production under Lord Beaverbrook and at the Board of Trade. The note described Llewellin's first meeting with Beaverbrook and the formation of the ministry. Llewellin gives Beaverbrook warm praise for his work: 'It was his drive and initiative which did the trick...'. There was also a file of speech notes and carbon copies of letters written to Miss Llewellin in 1943 when Llewellin was Minister Resident in Washington.

The remainder of the collection consisted of 15 volumes of press cuttings and photos. The first, covering the years 1889-1919, included cuttings on his parents' wedding, his days at Eton, rowing at Oxford, and fighting in the First World War (his commission as second lieutenant in 1916 had also survived). Other volumes covered his election campaigns and public activities. A very full volume of cuttings survived from Llewellin's tenure of the Ministry of Food; it included reports of the first experiments with frozen and dehydrated food as well as the resumption of the distilling of whisky (Aug 1944). The bulk of the volumes covered Llewellin's term of office as first Governor-General of the Federation of Rhodesia and Nyasaland 1953-57, the formation of the federation, Llewellin's arrival, and his varied activities. Llewellin died suddenly, while still in office, and a number of obituaries and tributes from both England and Rhodesia survived.

In addition to these papers, Miss Llewellin had a large collection of her brother's letters to herself and to their elder brother William. Although these letters mainly concerned family matters, there was also some political content. Gilbert Thomas, *Llewellin* (Barker 1961), frequently quoted from these letters. Thomas also gave long quotations from Llewellin's diaries; these could not be found, and indeed Miss Llewellin had no recollection of diaries being kept.

Mary Llewellin has since died and we have been advised by Mr F. W. W. Bernard, who was one of Miss Llewellin's executors, that neither he nor the other executors knows what became of this collection. He believed that it was possible that Miss Llewellin gave the collection to the National Archives of Zimbabwe before her death; but unfortunately they have advised us that they do not have the papers. Mr Bernard did not know of any other family member who may have received the papers.

We have also been advised by Llewellin's step-sister, Mrs C. W. Douie, that she cleared up Mary Llewellin's house after her death, and had no knowledge of the papers. However, she was able to buy back four albums at the sale of Miss Llewellin's goods. The albums include one of press cuttings on the Wartime Ministry of Food, and the other three are mostly photos.

Papers collected in Llewellin's Private Office at the Ministries of Supply and Aircraft Production are at the PRO (AVIA 9 and AVIA 11). Private Office papers from the Ministry of Food are at MAF 286.

GEOFFREY WILLIAM LLOYD, BARON GEOFFREY-LLOYD (1902-1984)

Geoffrey Lloyd was Unionist MP for Birmingham Ladywood 1931-45, and Conservative MP for Birmingham King's Norton 1950-55 and Sutton Coldfield 1955-74. He was Parliamentary Under-Secretary,

Home Office Nov 1935–April 1939, Parliamentary Secretary for Mines 1939–May 1940, Parliamentary Secretary for Petroleum 1940–June 1942, Parliamentary Secretary (Petroleum), Ministry of Fuel and Power 1942–May 1945, Minister of Information May–Aug 1945, Minister of Fuel and Power Oct 1951–Dec 1955, and Minister of Education Sept 1957–Oct 1959. He was created Baron Geoffrey-Lloyd (a life peerage) in 1974.

Lord Geoffrey-Lloyd advised Dr Cook that he did not keep a diary or 'make a habit of retaining official correspondence'. He destroyed all his constituency correspondence after he retired from Parliament (Cook, *Sources*, 3, p. 171).

In 1985 Geoffrey-Lloyd's executors deposited a large collection of files in the IWM (85/46/1–32). The collection contains correspondence, reports, minutes, and committee papers etc., relating to Geoffrey-Lloyd's work as Parliamentary Secretary for Mines at the Board of Trade and the Ministry of Fuel, Light and Power, and particularly concerning the Petroleum Warfare Department and the development of FIDO and PLUTO. A full list of the contents of the 33 boxes is available.

The PRO has a small collection of papers from Geoffrey-Lloyd's period as Minister of Education (ED 136/884–901).

Dennis Dean, 'Preservation or Renovation? The Dilemmas of Conservative Educational Policy 1955–1960', *Twentieth Century British History*, 3, 1, 1992, 3–31, is a valuable source on relevant PRO files.

SIR GEORGE AMBROSE LLOYD, 1st BARON LLOYD (1879–1941)

George Lloyd was Conservative MP for Staffordshire (West) 1910–18 and East Sussex (Eastbourne) 1924–25. He was Secretary of State for the Colonies May 1940–Feb 1941. He was created GCIE in 1918, GCSI in 1924, and Baron Lloyd in 1925.

The 2nd Lord Lloyd deposited most of his father's papers in the Churchill Archives Centre (GLLD). The papers have been listed (NRA 12663), but they are not generally available. Applications should be made to the Keeper of the Archives. The papers have been divided into seven main groups: personal; eastern affairs; India; Egypt; public and political; literary; business. This arrangement was largely Lloyd's own, his main interest being to use the papers for reference for speeches and articles. This has led to the letters not being arranged in chronological order and to there being some overlap between divisions.

The personal papers include Lloyd's birth certificate, school reports, passports, car and aeroplane log books, as well as a large collection of press cuttings and photos, correspondence concerning his various appointments, letters from his father and other members of his family, and several letters 1929-36 from T. E. Lawrence. The section includes copies of letters from Lloyd to his wife written in 1939.

The eastern affairs papers include correspondence and reports compiled by Lloyd when he was attaché in Constantinople 1905-07 and special commissioner for British trade to the area 1907-08. They include 62 volumes of telegrams between the Porte and its ambassadors 1889-1908 which Lloyd acquired in 1908. There is also war correspondence concerning this area, Lloyd's diary for Gallipoli March-Oct 1915, and for a journey with T. E. Lawrence probably made in 1917.

The Indian papers derive from Lloyd's governorship of the Bombay Presidency 1918-23 and from his later continued interest in the area. They include papers concerning his arrival and departure, various administrative problems, and correspondence with princes and chiefs. Lloyd's Egyptian papers (he was High Commissioner for Egypt and the Sudan 1925-29) are of the same type but include a considerable correspondence with Sir Austen Chamberlain and Sir William Tyrrell, as well as copies of official telegrams and Cabinet papers on the Middle East.

Lloyd's political papers include about 130 subject files on the domestic, colonial, and foreign problems of his day. There are also papers concerning his West Staffordshire constituency, including receipts and general correspondence. There are no papers relating to Eastbourne. Lloyd's political correspondence is mainly for 1930-40, arranged alphabetically within each year. There is a great deal of material concerning Lloyd's work for the British Council, including correspondence, and papers from his many tours on the Council's behalf. There are also six files from the Colonial Office in this section – two files of 1940 correspondence and four subject files.

Lloyd's literary papers are mainly typed notes for speeches and articles written after 1921 though a few notes from 1909-11 have survived. There are 18 files on Lloyd's personal financial affairs.

The Middle Eastern Centre, St Antony's College has some of Lloyd's letters to his sister 1900-11 as well as some other miscellaneous papers.

Lloyd himself described his Egyptian career in *Egypt since Cromer* (2 vols, Macmillan 1933-34).

Colin Forbes Adam, *Life of Lord Lloyd* (Macmillan 1948) draws on both Lloyd's own papers and those of Lady Lloyd whose diaries and letters are now also deposited at the Churchill Archives Centre. John Charmley, *Lord Lloyd and the Decline of the British Empire* (Weidenfeld and Nicolson 1987), is based on the papers at the Churchill Archives Centre as well as a wide range of official records of Lloyd's career.

(JOHN) SELWYN BROOKE LLOYD, BARON SELWYN-LLOYD (1904–1978)

Selwyn Lloyd was Conservative MP for Wirral 1945–76. He was Minister of State, Foreign Office Oct 1951–Oct 1954, Minister of Supply 1954–April 1955, Minister of Defence April-Dec 1955, Secretary of State for Foreign Affairs 1955–July 1960, Chancellor of the Exchequer 1960–July 1962, and Lord Privy Seal Oct 1963–Oct 1964. He was created Baron Selwyn-Lloyd (a life peerage) in 1976.

The Churchill Archives Centre holds 495 boxes of Selwyn-Lloyd's papers (SELO; NRA 23627) deposited by the trustee of his estate. Readers wishing to use the papers should write to the Archivist. Selwyn-Lloyd had advised Cook (*Sources*, 4, p. 160) that his collection consisted of 'a mass of papers, including letters, press cuttings, diaries, speech notes, records of interviews, etc'.

The PRO has identified papers from Selwyn-Lloyd's periods as Secretary of State for Foreign Affairs and Minister of Defence. The Foreign Affairs papers (FO 800/691–749) 1955–56 include personal diaries of engagements and general correspondence. The Defence papers (DEFE 13/25–73) relate to 1955. Papers relating to Budgets are in T 171.

The Conservative Party Archives in the Bodleian Library contain material relating to the Enquiry into Party Organisation 1962–63 and drafts of 'Britain Strong and Free' 1951. Records of the Leader of the House of Commons 1961–91 are in the HLRO, but are subject to the 30 year rule (Selwyn-Lloyd was Leader of the House of Commons 1963–64).

Selwyn-Lloyd detailed his time as Speaker in *Mr Speaker, Sir* (Jonathan Cape 1976) and his observations on the Suez Crisis in *Suez, 1956: A Personal Account* (Jonathan Cape 1978).

A biography by D. R. Thorpe, *Selwyn Lloyd* (Jonathan Cape 1989) was based on exclusive access to Selwyn-Lloyd's papers supported by extensive research in private papers and public records which are listed in a valuable select bibliography.

DAVID LLOYD GEORGE, 1st EARL LLOYD GEORGE OF DWYFOR (1863–1945)

David Lloyd George was Liberal MP for Caernarvon Boroughs 1890–1945; he styled himself an Independent Liberal from 1931. He was President of the Board of Trade Dec 1905–April 1908, Chancellor of the Exchequer 1908–May 1915, Minister of Munitions 1915–July 1916, Secretary of State for War July-Dec 1916, and Prime Minister 1916–Oct 1922. He was Leader of the Liberal Party in the House of Commons Oct 1926–Nov 1931. He was created Earl Lloyd George of Dwyfor in 1945.

The Cabinet was informed in Nov 1935 that 'at an interview with Mr. Lloyd George's Private Secretary some months ago it was learned that, while Mr. Lloyd George was willing that his [Cabinet] Papers should be returned after his death, he was not prepared to surrender them during his lifetime. There is no reason to think that Mr. Lloyd George will reconsider this decision' (Cabinet Procedure...Recovery of Cabinet Papers Report, 29 Nov 1935, PRO, CAB 24/257).

One thousand and forty-one boxes of Lloyd George's papers and photos, bequeathed to his widow, were purchased by Lord Beaverbrook in 1949. They are now owned by the Beaverbrook Foundation and housed in the HLRO. The papers have been listed (NRA 15700) and are divided into the following series: (A) papers as an MP to 1905, 13 boxes; (B) papers as President of the Board of Trade, five boxes; (C) papers as Chancellor, 36 boxes; (D) papers as Minister of Munitions, 27 boxes; (E) papers as Secretary of State for War, ten boxes; (F) papers as Prime Minister, 254 boxes; (G) papers for 1922–45, 264 boxes; (H) press cuttings, arranged in alphabetical order and mostly after 1922, 390 boxes; (I) personal papers, 42 boxes.

Series A-G have been divided into correspondence and papers. The correspondence has been subdivided into semi-official, special (that is, with particular individuals), foreign (arranged by country), general, and Cabinet notes. The papers have been divided into semi-official, Cabinet, and general. They include speech notes, briefs for speeches made during his premiership, and notes on deputations. Series F and G have 'secretarial' sections, that is papers produced by Lloyd George's secretaries. They include notes on the political situation 1939–45 made by A. J. Sylvester, Lloyd George's secretary, when Lloyd George was away from Westminster. Series G includes articles and books by Lloyd George, correspondence about their publication, and material used in them – including papers removed from Lloyd George's own and other people's papers.

A card index of every reference to any person or subject (except in the printed papers) has been made for series A-E, and partly for F and G. The index and catalogues are available in the HLRO and are also on microfiche (copies obtainable from Chadwyck-Healey, The Quorum, Barnwell Road, Cambridge CB5 8SW).

Large portions of Lloyd George's papers have been published, initially in his own *War Memoirs* (6 vols, Odhams Press 1935–36), and *The Truth About the Peace Treaties* (2 vols, Gollancz 1938). Two early biographies were based on the papers: *David Lloyd George* by Malcolm Thomson (Hutchinson 1948); and *Tempestuous Journey* by Frank Owen (Hutchinson 1954). John Grigg, *The Young Lloyd George* (Eyre Methuen 1973), *Lloyd*

George, The People's Champion, 1902–1911 (Eyre Methuen 1978) and *Lloyd George, From Peace To War, 1912–1916* (Methuen 1985), are based on the papers now in the HLRO and those in the NLW (see below). So too are Bentley Brinkerhoff Gilbert, *David Lloyd George, a political life: the Architect of Change 1863–1912* (Ohio State UP, Columbus 1987) and its sequel *David Lloyd George, a political life: Organizer of Victory 1912–1916* (Ohio State UP, Columbus 1992). Other books utilising the papers include John Campbell, *Lloyd George: the Goat in the Wilderness 1922–1931* (Jonathan Cape 1977); John Turner, *Lloyd George's Secretariat* (Cambridge UP 1980); and Chris Wrigley *Lloyd George and the Challenge of Labour* (Harvester 1990). Chris Wrigley, *David Lloyd George and the British Labour Movement: Peace and War* (The Harvester Press, Hassocks 1976), p. 272, fn. 26, refers to some documents relating to Lloyd George's tenure of the Ministry of Munitions now to be found in the Munitions papers at the PRO (MUN 5/73/324), as 'a folder of files removed from Lloyd George's Papers'.

The papers of Frances Stevenson, Lloyd George's secretary, mistress, and second wife relate almost entirely to Lloyd George and have also been deposited in the HLRO. As well as photos and some personal letters, they consist of a draft of her autobiography (*The Years that are Past*, Hutchinson 1967), her correspondence with Lloyd George, and diaries 1914–44. The diaries and letters have been edited by A. J. P. Taylor in *Lloyd George: a Diary by Frances Stevenson* (Hutchinson 1971) and *My Darling Pussy: the Letters of Lloyd George and Frances Stevenson, 1913–41* (Weidenfeld and Nicolson 1975).

A collection of over 3500 letters to Lloyd George's first wife and other members of his family was purchased by the NLW in 1969 (NLW MSS 20403–93). A selection has been edited by Kenneth O. Morgan: *Lloyd George, Family Letters 1885–1936* (University of Wales Press & Oxford UP 1973).

A large collection of early letters and diaries of Lloyd George previously in the possession of his nephew, Dr W. R. P. George of Criccieth, is now also in the NLW (The William George Papers). The collection contains about 4000 letters written to his brother William George 1890–1916; 12 of Lloyd George's diaries 1878–88; notes for speeches; letters from prominent politicians including Asquith, Churchill, Bonar Law, Keir Hardie, T. E. Ellis and Herbert Lewis; and family letters and diaries. The papers were used in Herbert du Parcq, *Life of David Lloyd George* (4 vols, Eyre & Spottiswoode 1912–14), and William George, *My Brother and I* (Gomer, Llandysul, Dyfed 1958), and Dr George himself wrote *Lloyd George, Backbencher* (Gomer 1983) and *The Making of Lloyd George* (Faber 1976).

The NLW purchased two groups of papers, previously in the possession of Lloyd George's grandson, the 3rd Earl Lloyd George. The first group (NLW MSS 21787–92) includes correspondence and papers relating to Welsh Disestablishment. The second group (NLW MSS 22514–37) comprises general correspondence 1906–15; correspondence 1920s-30s, including a series of letters on the Liberal Party; Lloyd George's correspondence with Ramsay MacDonald 1930–35; as well as notebooks and notes for speeches (see D. Ifans, *Lloyd George Papers, a catalogue of MSS 22514–22537 in the National Library of Wales*). The Library believes that other papers in this collection were auctioned.

In 1991 the NLW also acquired the family papers of Lloyd George's daughter Lady Olwen Carey-Evans, including correspondence from and with her parents 1890–1942, and speech notes of Lloyd George 1904–21 (NRA 28941). What is believed to be 'the last Lloyd George archive remaining in private hands' – some 300 letters to Lloyd George and his secretaries, speech notes, and family photographs – was bought by the NLW from Viscount Tenby in 1996. There are groups of letters on National Insurance 1911 and Ireland 1917, and four from Frances Stevenson May 1922. The NLW has also acquired the papers of A. J. Sylvester (Lloyd George's secretary 1923–45) including diaries, transcriptions, and correspondence 1923–45.

Some of the documentation sent to Lloyd George as Prime Minister is now to be found in the papers of Edward Grigg, Philip Kerr, and Maurice Hankey. Reference should also be made to the group of papers called 'Prime Ministers' (Class A) in the Thomas Jones collection in the NLW (NRA 30994).

Papers of Prime Ministerial Advisors Outside Cabinet 1916–40 are in the PRO at PREM 1. The Caernarfon Area RO holds material relating to Lloyd George including some of his speech notes and a few letters 1912–16; also sound recordings of some of Lloyd George's speeches and interviews with Lady Olwen Carey-Evans (XD/33, XS/2009; NRA 33161).

The Sayer Archive also holds material on Lloyd George.

GWILYM LLOYD GEORGE, 1st VISCOUNT TENBY (1894–1967)

Major Gwilym Lloyd George was Liberal MP for Pembrokeshire 1922–24 and 1929–50, and Conservative MP for Newcastle-upon-Tyne (North) 1951–57. He was Parliamentary Secretary to the Board of Trade Sept–Nov 1931 and Sept 1939–Feb 1941, Parliamentary Secretary to the Ministry of Food Oct 1940–June 1942, Minister of Fuel and Power 1942–Aug 1945, Minister of Food Oct 1951–Oct 1954, and Secretary of State for Home Affairs and Minister of State for Welsh Affairs 1954–Jan 1957. He was created Viscount Tenby in 1957.

A small, miscellaneous collection of his papers formerly in the possession of his younger son, the 3rd Lord Tenby, has been purchased by the NLW. The bulk of the collection consists of congratulations on entering office and on Lloyd George's various honours. These have been weeded and only those from prominent individuals or of personal importance retained. There are a few notes for speeches: on capital punishment; on Suez (3 Dec 1956); and on being given the freedom of Cardiff in 1956. There are a few letters from Churchill, most of them simply offering posts in the government. There is a file of papers relating to the First World War and some papers concerning the 1951 election campaign, including campaign material and letters of support from Churchill and Lord Beaverbrook. Perhaps of greatest interest is a note on the visit made by Lloyd George with his father to Hitler in 1936. Lloyd George says that the visit was made solely to study what the Germans were doing to meet their unemployment problem. There are also a few pages of typed notes which were the beginnings of a volume of memoirs never completed. They include Lloyd George's impressions of political contemporaries, such as Stanley Baldwin, Neville Chamberlain, and Sir John Simon, as well as childhood, family, and parliamentary reminiscences.

Lord Tenby informed us that the previously reported large file of papers relating to a law suit brought against Lloyd George in 1957 by a Mr Marrinan, for granting authorisation (as Secretary of State for Home Affairs) to the police in 1956 to tap Marrinan's telephone, has now been destroyed.

There is a brief biography of Lloyd George by Kenneth O. Morgan in *DNB 1961–1970*, 664–6.

WALTER HUME LONG, 1st VISCOUNT LONG (1854–1924)

Walter Long was Conservative MP for Wiltshire (North) 1880–85, Wiltshire (East or Devizes) 1885–92, Liverpool (West Derby) 1893–1900, Bristol (South) 1900–06, County Dublin (South) 1906–10, Strand 1910–18 and Westminster (St. George's) 1918–21. He was Parliamentary Secretary to the Local Government Board 1886–92, President of the Board of Agriculture July 1895–Nov 1900, President of the Local Government Board 1900–March 1905 and May 1915–Dec 1916, Chief Secretary for Ireland March-Dec 1905, Secretary of State for Colonial Affairs Dec 1916–Jan 1919, and First Lord of the Admiralty 1919–Feb 1921. He was created Viscount Long in 1921.

According to Long's own *Memories* (Hutchinson 1923), he 'faithfully kept' records though he did not, for instance, record conversations in his diaries. His book is based only on his recollections. Sir Charles Petrie, Bt, in *Walter Long and His Times* (Hutchinson 1936) said that shortly before his death Long destroyed many of his papers. There are letters from Long's grandson in Austen Chamberlain's papers which also mention specifically that Long seems to have destroyed papers concerning the formation of the 1916 coalition.

A substantial collection of Long's papers has been deposited in the Wiltshire RO (WRO 947). A full list of the papers has been prepared (NRA 15883); the papers have been arranged as far as possible according to the offices Long held.

Long's work as Parliamentary Secretary to the Local Government Board is reflected by copies of bills with civil servants' memoranda 1889–92, papers concerning the administration of the poor law 1887–92, and papers concerning the Labourers' Allotments Bill 1886–87. Long's work at the Board of Agriculture is represented by papers, including correspondence with the Treasury, on grants for agricultural training centres 1896–97, papers on the salaries and rank of the Board's staff 1897–98, papers concerning the appointment of the Director-General of the Ordnance Survey 1898, and delays to the survey's work because of lack of accommodation 1899. There are no papers concerning Long's unpopular attempts to eradicate rabies. Long's Irish Office papers cover education, nationalist societies 1903–05, recruitment to the Royal Irish Constabulary 1904–06, the working of the 1903 Land Act, land congestion, the state of the west and south-west of the country 1905, and the position of Sir A. P. MacDonnell, the Permanent Under-Secretary 1905. In addition there are a large number of draft bills and Cabinet memoranda on a variety of subjects 1895–1905.

A gap occurs in the papers and the later (1915–24) papers are more miscellaneous. As well as Cabinet papers on the war and on peace negotiations, and a report by Sir Basil Thomson on communist activities in Britain 1921, there is a memo of the discussions leading up to the formation of the 1916 coalition and letters from political contemporaries 1915–16. There are a few memoranda on Admiralty business, on Ireland, and the Turko-Greek war. In addition, there is material on Conservative party affairs 1922–24. This includes a memo by Long on the break up of the Coalition, which gives details of some of the various meetings and interviews which occurred. There is also a letter from Long to Sir George Younger 22 Oct 1922 on the end of the Coalition.

Long's grandson, the 4th Viscount Long, discovered some more of Long's papers in June 1973. They were added to the collection in the Wiltshire RO. They appear to have been sent to Long by his civil servants when he finally left office in 1921.

This additional collection consists of: papers relating to Long's term of office at the Irish Office in 1905, most of which relate to the dispute with Sir A. P. MacDonnell; files on various parliamentary measures 1910–12, including reform of the House of Lords, land policy, and poor law reform; papers on the Unionist party's reorganisation 1910–11, with memoranda from local parties on how they were organised and how they selected their candidates; and a great deal of genealogical material, a file on Colonial Office administration, and a file of correspondence with Lord Derby Jan 1917–July 1918. The later letters in this file are particularly interesting as they were written when Derby was at the Paris Embassy and Long was describing the political situation to him. There are also a great number of papers from the Irish Office, the Colonial Office, and the Admiralty, as well as some personal investment papers, and reports and memoranda of the Unionist reorganisation committee. There are files of correspondence with Sir John French, A. J. Balfour, Lloyd George, Bonar Law, Hamar Greenwood, and others concerning the various attempts to settle the Irish problem 1916–22. Most of the files contain copies of Long's letters; there are very few replies.

An additional volume of Long's papers is available for research in the PRO (ADM 116/3623). The contents are miscellaneous and range from correspondence found when Bloemfontein was captured in 1901, and Long's trusteeship of the Wiltshire Yeomanry, to minutes of the War Cabinet's Raw Materials Board. There is also some correspondence with Sir Maurice Hankey 6 Dec 1920 on leaks to the press of Cabinet discussions, and correspondence with Sir F. E. Smith on the Sex Disqualification Bill 1919–20.

The British Library also holds 41 volumes of Long's papers (BL Add MSS 62403–43) which were purchased at Sotheby's on 20 July 1981. Prominent correspondents include Arthur Balfour 1905–22; the 5th Marquess of Lansdowne 1906–19; Bonar Law 1907–22; Asquith and his wife Margot 1907–23; Arthur Bigge, Lord Stamfordham 1911–22; Austen Chamberlain 1907–23; the 17th Earl of Derby 1908–23; the 1st Viscount Chaplin 1906–16; Professor Albert Dicey 1908–15; and Lord and Lady Beresford 1908–15. There are also 22 volumes of general correspondence, partly in French, 1873–1924.

Also included in the collection are 13 volumes of press cuttings, invitations, programmes, photos of personal and political interest, c.1853–1924; and one volume of correspondence etc., of members of the Long and Dick families 1775–1881.

The IWM has letters from Long's son 1914–15.

WILLIAM LYGON, 7th EARL BEAUCHAMP (1872–1938)

William Lygon was known as Viscount Elmley until he succeeded his father as 7th Earl Beauchamp in 1891. He was created KCMG in 1899, and KG in 1914. He was Lord President of the Council June-Nov 1910 and Aug 1914–May 1915, and First Commissioner of Works Nov 1910–Aug 1914. He was Liberal Leader in the House of Lords 1924–31.

In the first edition we reported the advice of Lord Beauchamp's son, the 8th Earl Beauchamp, that he knew of no letters or papers and that his father did not keep a diary. The only papers we saw were some 20 scrapbooks for the years 1891–1938 which covered his father's career. As well as mementos, such as menus, programmes, and photos, the scrapbooks included press cuttings which, in particular, illustrate Beauchamp's strong support for free trade.

It is now known that a collection of Beauchamp's papers has survived at the family home, Madresfield Court, Malvern, Worcestershire. But the papers are neither sorted nor listed and their present owner, the Hon Lady Morrison, advised that they will remain closed for at least the next 15 years.

In the Mitchell Library, Sydney, there are three volumes of correspondence relating to Beauchamp's period as Governor of New South Wales 1899–1900 (A 1828–29, 3012); a short 'diary' – mostly written several months later than the events described – covering his appointment and various incidents in New South Wales (A 3295); a visitors' book and two volumes listing menus and dinner guests May 1899–Oct 1900 (A 5016, B 1516, 1517).

The Gloucestershire RO has correspondence and papers for Beauchamp as Lord Lieutenant of Gloucestershire 1911–20 (D551; NRA 11510).

There is a brief biography by Cameron Hazlehurst based on the available Beauchamp papers, as well as Colonial Office and New South Wales government archives, in Bede Nairn and Geoffrey Serle (eds), *Australian Dictionary of Biography* (Melbourne UP 1979), 7, 235–6.

THE HON ALFRED LYTTELTON (1857–1913)

Alfred Lyttelton was Liberal Unionist MP for Warwick and Leamington 1895–1905, and Conservative MP for St George's, Hanover Square 1906–13. He was Secretary of State for the Colonies Oct 1903–Dec 1905.

Most of Lyttelton's own papers, with those of other members of his family, including his wife, were deposited in 1970 by their son, Lord Chandos, in the Churchill Archives Centre (CHAN). The papers have been listed (NRA 19700). Applications for access should be made to the Keeper of the Archives.

The whole collection comprises 70 boxes of papers, of which about a third are Alfred Lyttelton's papers. The collection has been divided into the papers of the several individuals represented; each division is arranged in alphabetical order of correspondents. Lyttelton's papers are to be found in sections two and three. Most of the papers are family letters. The only political papers are several boxes of correspondence with governors and others when Lyttelton was Colonial Secretary. For example, there are several letters from Joseph Chamberlain 1899–1909, Lord Grey 1903–11, Lord Milner 1903–05, and Lord

Selborne 1905–09. There are also a few miscellaneous Colonial Office files, speech notes, and press cuttings.

Additional Lyttelton family papers were deposited in 1974 and 1975 and are also listed, including 21 boxes of Lyttelton's wife, Dame Edith Lyttelton's papers. These include correspondence and memoirs including letters from G. B. Shaw and W. B. Yeats 1888–1945.

Many of Lyttelton's letters to his wife Edith are quoted in her biography, *Alfred Lyttelton. An Account of his Life* (Longmans, Green 1917). His brother, the Hon Edward Lyttelton, published privately an account of Lyttelton's early background: *Alfred Lyttelton, His Home-Training and Earlier Life* (1915).

OLIVER LYTTELTON, 1st VISCOUNT CHANDOS (1893–1972)

Oliver Lyttelton was Conservative MP for Hampshire (Aldershot) 1940–54. He was President of the Board of Trade Oct 1940–June 1941 and May-July 1945, Minister of State June 1941–March 1942, Minister Resident in the Middle East Feb-March 1942, Minister of Production 1942–Aug 1945, and Secretary of State for the Colonies Oct 1951–July 1954. He was created Viscount Chandos in 1954, and KG in 1970.

Lord Chandos deposited his family's papers, including his own, in the Churchill Archives Centre (CHAN). The papers have been listed (NRA 19700); applications for access should be made to the Keeper of the Archives. Papers relating to Lord Chandos himself are very few in number. They consist almost entirely of his letters to his mother from the front 1915–18. He informed us that he had never kept a diary or copies of his own letters.

The Churchill Archives Centre received three further deposits of Chandos papers between 1974 and 1978. These comprise 16 files of correspondence 1900–71 (correspondents include Churchill, Eden, Lady Violet Bonham Carter and Edward Heath), and 30 files of speeches 1942–71. These additional papers have also been catalogued.

The Memoirs of Lord Chandos (Bodley Head 1962) appear to be based on the author's reminiscences and do not quote from any papers. In *From Peace to War: A Study in Contrast 1857–1918* (Bodley Head 1965) Chandos quoted from his family papers, and included selections from his own letters from the front.

A small collection of papers relating to Chandos's work as Minister of Production is available for research at the PRO (BT 87). It includes papers relating to his visit to the USA in 1942, and notes for speeches and broadcasts. Also available are some papers from the Colonial Office 1952 (CO 967/239–76; NRA 28778).

Chandos's work as Colonial Secretary is discussed (without reference to private papers) in David Goldsworthy, *Colonial Issues in British Politics*

1945–1961 (Clarendon Press, Oxford 1971). Chandos's period at the Colonial Office is covered in D. J. Morgan, *The Official History of Colonial Development* (5 vols, Macmillan 1980).

CHARLES ALBERT McCURDY (1870–1941)

Charles McCurdy was Liberal MP for Northampton 1910–23. He was Parliamentary Secretary to the Ministry of Food Jan 1919–March 1920, Food Controller 1920–March 1921, and Joint Parliamentary Secretary to the Treasury 1921–Oct 1922.

Because McCurdy's chambers were bombed, only a small collection of papers survived in the possession of Mr C. J. Brook, the adopted son of McCurdy's late secretary, Miss Brook. Apart from obituary notices and a letter of condolence sent to Miss Brook, the collection included a press cutting on the end of the *Daily Chronicle* with a note by McCurdy giving his version of events, a letter from Lord Beaverbrook 1941 thanking McCurdy for his support for the Empire Crusade, and a carbon copy of a letter to *The Times* on the duty of citizens to intervene in crimes of violence. The collection also included a note by Miss Brook that (in 1958) she had 'no papers at all'.

McCurdy's niece, Mrs G. G. Wingfield, had only a copy of her uncle's 1910 election address.

SIR GORDON MACDONALD, 1st BARON MACDONALD OF GWAENYSGOR (1888–1966)

Gordon Macdonald was Labour MP for Lancashire (Ince) 1929–42. He was Paymaster-General April 1949–Oct 1951. He was created KCMG in 1946, and Baron Macdonald of Gwaenysgor in 1949.

His son, the 2nd Lord Macdonald of Gwaenysgor, knew of no papers. His younger daughter, the Hon Mrs Fullard, had some papers but they were not available for research as they included some personal papers. We were not able to contact Macdonald's other children.

Macdonald published *Atgofion Seneddol* [*Parliamentary Reminiscences*] (W. Griffiths, di Frodyr 1949).

(JAMES) RAMSAY MacDONALD (1866–1937)

Ramsay MacDonald was Labour MP for Leicester 1906–18, Glamorganshire (Aberavon) 1922–29 and Durham (Seaham) 1929–31 and National Labour MP for Durham (Seaham) 1931–35 and the Scottish Universities 1936–37. He was Prime Minister and Secretary of State for Foreign Affairs Jan-Nov 1924, Prime Minister June 1929–June 1935, and Lord President of the Council 1935–May 1937. He was Chairman of the Labour Party 1911–14 and Leader of the Party 1922–31.

The great bulk of the MacDonald papers has been deposited at the PRO (PRO 30/69; NRA 23368). The collection contains 1669 pieces, some of which contain several files. It includes the papers of MacDonald, his wife Margaret (d. 1911), and papers given by MacDonald to his secretary, Mrs Rosenberg (Rose Hoenig). The latter are only on loan to the PRO and are designated by the letter 'R' throughout the list. The papers have been listed under three main headings: personal; political; and official. Portions of the list relating to 'political-party matters 1890–1937' and correspondence with 'members of the public, parliamentary and party colleagues, professional advisers, friends and acquaintances' have been published as List and Index Society, 199, *Ramsay MacDonald Correspondence 1890–1937* (PRO 30/69), and distributed to subscribers in 1983.

Both MacDonald and his wife appear to have been very methodical in keeping their papers: Mrs MacDonald made an index to her personal correspondence. But their original order was disturbed, partly by MacDonald himself (possibly with a view of writing an autobiography), by Sir Frank Markham, by Ishbel MacDonald, by a thief, and a fire! Nevertheless, there are no obvious gaps in the papers, apart from the possible destruction of 'crank' letters after 1931. There are, however, very few letters for the period 1916–23, possibly because MacDonald had no private secretary at that time.

MacDonald's personal papers include 45 files of correspondence from 1890 onwards, as well as earlier papers relating to his mother, aunt, and maternal grandparents. There is correspondence between Mac-Donald and his wife, and with their children. There is a school diary, five pages of a diary for 1912, and two larger bound volumes of diary from 1910 to 1937. There is also an engagement diary for 1911, an appointments diary for 1917, and MacDonald's official diary as Lord President. There are several notebooks: on his South African tour 1902; and on the labour unrest of 1911 and the part MacDonald played in this. His wife's papers include some 20 volumes of diary and notebooks for 1883–1906, as well as a considerable amount of correspondence and papers concerning her own family. There are 132 files of papers concerning MacDonald's literary activities.

A short biography and guide to sources concerning Margaret Mac-Donald was contributed by John Saville and James A. Schmiechen to *DLB*, VI, 181–5.

MacDonald's political papers cover a wide range in both time and scope. They include his activities in the Fabian Society, the Independent Labour Party, the Social Democratic Federation, the Labour Party, and the National Labour Party, as well as his pacifist activities, and his work for the Fellowship of the New Life. They include long runs of socialist newspapers 1892–1937 and a large number of pamphlets. There are over 100 boxes of general correspondence as well as subject files. There are also notes for speeches, interviews with the press, and press cuttings. There are a few memoranda by MacDonald on, for example, Labour-Liberal relations 1906–07, and on the possibility of socialists joining the coalition government, both in May 1915 and Dec 1916. For the period of MacDonald's term of office as Secretary to the Labour Representation Committee (LRC) 1900–06, the papers are not very revealing; but for the period 1906–14, when he was Chairman of the LRC 1906–09 and was struggling to become Leader of the Parliamentary Labour Party (PLP), the papers illuminate the internal struggles of the PLP, and MacDonald's increasingly close relationship with the Liberal Party. The papers for 1914 are of great value; but thereafter their volume and interest declines sharply. There are 66 files of constituency papers. There are also a few, very interesting, papers related to MacDonald's candidature at Dover and Southampton in the 1890s.

The last but greatest part of the collection (nearly 700 files) relates to MacDonald's terms in office. The main series of Cabinet papers have been returned to the Cabinet Office. The Private Office files of the 1924 government were found to be in great chaos and it appears that no successful filing system was devised at the time. For example, a collection of correspondence to be filed by Miss Cracknell was filed under the heading 'Miss Cracknell'. Some attempt at subject division has been made, as well as separating purely Foreign Office papers from the Prime Minister's own. By 1929 a proper system had been devised and this has been reconstructed. Running parallel to these papers are some 50 files of more private correspondence on official matters, particularly on such problems as honours and appointments. The papers of Rose Rosenberg, MacDonald's private secretary, form a basis of this group. These papers are very full and throw a good deal of light on MacDonald himself, the Labour Party, national and international politics.

A small collection (two pieces) of Foreign Office general correspondence 1923–24 arranged alphabetically by country is also available at the PRO (FO 800/218, 219) while Papers of Prime Ministerial Advisors Outside Cabinet 1916–40 are in PREM 1.

The John Rylands University Library, University of Manchester, has a significant collection of MacDonald papers which appears to have become separated from the main collection when it was deposited in the PRO. The collection is unlisted, but is available for research. Its provenance and content is detailed in David Howell, 'The Ramsay MacDonald Papers in the John Rylands University Library of Manchester: An Initial Discussion', *Bulletin of the John Rylands University Library of Manchester*, 72, 2, Summer 1990, 101–20.

The collection consists mostly of correspondence to MacDonald with some draft and some carbon copy replies. There are over 80 letters for 1907, including correspondence from Keir Hardie, Philip Snowden, and Bruce Glasier. Other correspondents include Charles Trevelyan, whose resignation from the Cabinet in Feb 1931 is well covered; Lady Londonderry; and Sir Samuel Hoare commenting on the Abyssinian problem Aug 1935. There are only a few letters from Arthur Henderson.

There is little material for the post-war decade, but there are some significant papers on Labour politics in the 1920s, including two letters written by miners' leaders during the General Strike 1926. The collection is most detailed on the second Labour government, and contains valuable material on MacDonald's activities after 1931, including Cabinet papers from the 1930s, and MacDonald's hand written diary for the 1933 London World Economic Conference. There are many personal appointment diaries, in addition to pamphlets, minutes, and notes relating to specific organisations and issues. There is also material relating to MacDonald's activities in Dover and Southampton.

A further eight volumes of MacDonald papers are deposited in the BLPES (MacDonald papers; NRA 7529). Five of the volumes contain Mrs MacDonald's papers 1895–1912 on various social issues such as the employment of women, factory and shop legislation, the 1901–02 Licensing bill, and housing. The three volumes of MacDonald's papers 1896–1923 have been arranged chronologically. They include much printed material, press cuttings, and some correspondence. The papers have been indexed.

There is a substantial body of routine Labour Party correspondence 1905–14 to and from MacDonald in the Labour Party Archives available at the National Museum of Labour History (LP/MAC/08,09).

Reference should also be made to the group of MacDonald letters to Sir Alexander Grant and others 1894–1935, and the files of telegrams and letters received by MacDonald on the death of his wife, in the NLS (MSS 25274–5). The NLS also has c.650 books from MacDonald's library mainly relating to Scottish history and literature (JRM 649–54).

The official biography is David Marquand, *Ramsay MacDonald* (Jonathan Cape 1977). Austen J. Morgan, *James Ramsay MacDonald* (Manchester UP 1987) is a brief account also based on the major collections. Jane Cox (ed), *A Singular Marriage: A Labour Love Story in Letters and Diaries: Ramsay and Margaret MacDonald* (Harrap 1988) is based substantially on correspondence in the PRO collection. It should be read in conjunction with J. Ramsay MacDonald, *Margaret Ethel MacDonald* (Allen & Unwin 1912).

MALCOLM JOHN MacDONALD (1901-1981)

Malcolm MacDonald was Labour MP for Nottinghamshire (Bassetlaw) 1929-35, and National Labour MP for Inverness-shire, Ross and Cromarty 1936-45. He was Parliamentary Under-Secretary of State for Dominion Affairs Sept 1931-June 1935, Secretary of State for Colonial Affairs June-Nov 1935 and May 1938-May 1940, Secretary of State for Dominion Affairs Nov 1935-May 1938 and Oct 1938-Jan 1939, and Minister of Health May 1940-Feb 1941.

After his death, MacDonald's papers were deposited by his family with the Royal Commonwealth Society where they were catalogued. The papers were then transferred to the Durham University Library where they are now located in the Archives and Special Collections section. They are available for research (NRA 30832). Some additional papers with related material from the papers of his sister Mrs Sheila Lochhead are catalogued as Misc 1994/5:20 MacDonald papers.

The introduction to the list of the collection details its history as well as advising that a 'substantial number of documents' was removed by the Foreign and Commonwealth Office because they fell under the 30-year rule, or they were regarded as being 'sensitive'. The introduction advises that some purely private material was also withdrawn by the family.

The collection has been arranged in a broad chronological manner. The general political papers include sections on the Labour Party (correspondence 1924-28 and League of Nations papers 1927); Mac-Donald's parliamentary career (papers on elections 1929-36, official and semi-official correspondence 1929-40, papers on his various constituencies, the formation of the National government and Labour Party, and later papers relating to his parliamentary career 1969-80). There is material relating to his period in the Dominions and Colonial Offices, including official papers on Australia, New Zealand, Africa, Palestine, India, Ireland, and later papers on the Commonwealth; and official correspondence relating to the Ministry of Health 1940-41.

MacDonald's international activities are reflected in the sections of material (correspondence, research papers, telegrams, despatches, articles, etc.) on Canada, South-East Asia, India, Laos, China, and Africa. These include material from his periods as Governor-General of Malaya, Commissioner General of South East Asia, and as Governor, Governor-General and High Commissioner of Kenya.

The personal papers include private correspondence (including some relating to his father's death), and material relating to his properties 1935-58, and personal finances 1929-68. Other material includes papers on his early years and education; his retirement; his writings (including his speeches, books, articles, interviews, and his general diaries 1925 and 1929–43, and other notebooks 1931–68), and printed material including press cuttings on him 1932–76, and other topics of interest.

A collection of photos by and relating to MacDonald was kept by the Royal Commonwealth Society for its library in London.

There are various papers relating to MacDonald's activities at the Colonial and Dominions Offices at the PRO. Professor Mary Turnbull who is working on a study of MacDonald and the transition from Empire to Commonwealth, advised us that his papers as wartime High Commissioner in Canada were brought back to the PRO, but that papers relating to his time as Governor-General and then Commissioner General in South-East Asia were almost certainly destroyed.

In the introduction to *People and Places: Random Reminiscences* (Collins 1969), MacDonald stated that he had never kept a diary or notes or reflections on current events for his own use. In *Titans and Others* (Collins 1972) he gave his impressions of political figures he had known.

A recent study is Clyde Sanger, *Malcolm MacDonald: Bringing an End to Empire* (Queens UP, McGill 1995).

REGINALD McKENNA (1863–1943)

Reggie McKenna was Liberal MP for Monmouthshire (North) 1895–1918. He was Financial Secretary to the Treasury Dec 1905–Jan 1907, President of the Board of Education 1907–April 1908, First Lord of the Admiralty 1908–Oct 1911, Secretary of State for Home Affairs 1911–May 1915, and Chancellor of the Exchequer 1915–Dec 1916.

A small collection of McKenna's papers was deposited by his son in the Churchill Archives Centre in 1966 (MCKN). A list of the papers is available (NRA 12034). The description of the papers as very large and 'very nearly complete' by McKenna's nephew, Stephen McKenna, in the preface of his *Reginald McKenna* (Eyre & Spottiswoode 1948) appears to have been exaggerated, although it is possible that some of the papers used by Stephen McKenna have not survived.

The collection deposited at the Churchill Archives Centre contains a few personal letters 1908–11, and some miscellaneous Board of Education correspondence 1906–08. The major part of the collection derives from McKenna's term of office at the Admiralty. In 1913 some of these papers were listed, probably by the Admiralty Historical Section. McKenna's correspondents include the King, the Prime Minister, members of the Cabinet, especially Lloyd George and Churchill, members of the Admiralty Board, naval officers, and MPs. Particularly outstanding is the correspondence of both McKenna and his wife with Lord Fisher 1908–20. There are, in addition, some printed papers and press cuttings.

McKenna's tenure of the Home Office is represented by correspondence with Asquith about the move from the Admiralty Sept-

Oct 1911, notes of a conversation with Asquith 20 Oct 1911, correspondence with Churchill 1911–12, and miscellaneous correspondence.

McKenna's Letters Patent for the Exchequer have survived, as well as his budget speech notes for 1915 and 1916, correspondence about the mission to the United States Aug-Sept 1915, correspondence with the Prime Minister 1915–16, and miscellaneous correspondence.

McKenna's son, Mr David McKenna has advised that there are no other papers in family possession. Attempts to trace papers that may have been in Stephen McKenna's possession have been unsuccessful.

Edwin Green's essay on McKenna in *DBB*, 4, 33–7, draws on the archives of the Midland Bank of which McKenna was chairman from 1919 until his death.

SIR WILLIAM WARRENDER MACKENZIE, 1st BARON AMULREE (1860–1942)

William Mackenzie was created KBE in 1918, GBE in 1926, and Baron Amulree in 1929. He was Secretary of State for Air Oct 1930–Nov 1931.

His son, the 2nd Lord Amulree, deposited a small collection of Amulree's papers in the Bodleian Library in 1970 (translated into gift in 1990 and re-shelfmarked as MSS Eng c 2361–8, MS Eng d 2101). The collection comprises nine boxes of miscellaneous correspondence 1925–37, and papers relating to the 1933 Royal Commission on the future of Newfoundland.

Amulree's correspondents include the leading Labour politicians of his day – Ramsay MacDonald, J. H. Thomas, Margaret Bondfield, Lord Parmoor, and Willie Graham. There are also a few drafts of letters and memoranda by him on industrial rationalisation 1928, colonial development 1929, and notes of the conclusions of a Cabinet meeting 24 Aug 1931.

The papers on Newfoundland include correspondence, telegrams to the Dominions Office, and memoranda. There is also a desk diary containing notes of evidence and interviews, and some conclusions by Amulree.

There is a brief biography by Sir Horace Wilson in *DNB 1941–1950*, 555–6.

SIR JOSEPH PATON MACLAY, 1st Bt, 1st BARON MACLAY (1857–1951)

Joseph Maclay was created a baronet in 1914, and Baron Maclay in 1922. He was Minister of Shipping Dec 1916–March 1921.

When we were preparing the first edition, the 3rd Lord Maclay advised us that all his grandfather's papers had been destroyed.

The NRA(S) has two surveys oif Maclay papers (NRA(S) 2667 and 2668). All enquiries about access shɔuld be directed to the Registrar, NRA(S). The papers described in survey 2667 include correspondence with Asquith, Lloyd George, Baldwin, Austen Chamberlain and Montague Norman 1909–32; press cuttings on the Ministry of Shipping 1916–22; and letters on church matters 1916–22.

The papers described in survey 2668 are mainly Ministry of Shipping papers including a report on the position of shipping and shipbuilding industries after the war 1916; a memo on the result of a standard ship programme (nd); the standard contract between the shipping controller and ship builder 1917; correspondence and papers on the sale of ex-enemy tonnage, with a list of the vessels, purchasers, and price 1920–22; a memo on the British tonnage service 1921; and correspondence with Lloyd George on convoys 1933. There are also statements of tonnage owned by Maclay & MacIntyre 1915–16.

A collection of six letters from Churchill to Maclay 1917–18 was offered for sale by Phillips, Son & Neale in June 1993. The letters were to Maclay in his capacity as Minister of Shipping and are concerned with supplies and munitions during the First World War. The collection also included miscellaneous letters, mostly wartime, to Sir Maurice Hankey and Lord Robert Cecil. Lord Maclay did not know the provenance of these papers, but did not believe that it was his family.

JOHN SCOTT MACLAY, 1st VISCOUNT MUIRSHIEL (1905–1992)

John Maclay was National Liberal and Conservative MP for Montrose Burghs 1940–50 and Renfrewshire West 1950–64. He was Parliamentary Secretary, Ministry of Production May–July 1945, Minister of Transport and Civil Aviation Oct 1951–May 1952, Minister of State for Colonial Affairs Oct 1956–Jan 1957, and Secretary of State for Scotland 1957–July 1962. He was created Viscount Muirshiel in 1964 and KT in 1973.

Lord Muirshiel advised us in 1990 that he held 'many papers connected with various parts of my life'. After his death his niece, Mrs Martha Steedman, dispersed his papers. Mrs Steedman advised us that all family papers went to Lord Maclay, as did all correspondence and photos concerning Muirshiel's work as Lord Lieutenant of Renfrewshire, and 'the many books of press cuttings'. All government papers were sent to the Glasgow University Archives, where they have yet to be listed (DC 371).

Papers relating to the Civic Trust, of which Muirshiel was chairman for many years, were sent to The Scottish Civic Trust, 24 George

Square, Glasgow G2 1EF. They do not include any personal papers. Papers relating to the Burnell Collection were sent to The Burnell Collection, Pollok Country Park, Glasgow G43 1AT.

Mrs Steedman advised that she destroyed the copies of minutes of Quarriers Homes, of which Muirshiel was chairman.

The transcript of an interview made in 1980 for the British Oral Archive of Political and Administrative History is now available in the BLPES.

Private Office papers relating to Maclay's period at the Scottish Office are dispersed through the files of the five main Scottish Office departments held at the SRO.

There is a brief biography of Lord Muirshiel in *Secretaries of State for Scotland*, 146–55.

SIR DONALD MACLEAN (1864–1932)

Donald Maclean was Liberal MP for Bath 1906–10, Selkirkshire and Peebles-shire (Midlothian and Peebles-shire, Peebles and Southern from 1918) 1910–22 and Cornwall (North) 1929–32. He was President of the Board of Education Aug 1931–June 1932. He was created KBE in 1917.

A small collection of Maclean's papers was deposited by his family in the Bodleian Library in 1972 (Dep a 49–50, c 465–71, 473, e 171). The papers have been catalogued (NRA 17784). There are two boxes of correspondence which have been arranged in two chronological series: early letters to his wife 1905–07, and general papers 1906–31. There are also appointment diaries for 1909–13, 1916, 1920–21, 1923–24, and 1926–30.

The general papers mostly concern Liberal Party affairs. There is correspondence on the financing of the *Westminster Gazette* 1912–16; letters and memoranda on the organisation of the Asquithian Liberals 1918–19; several memoranda of meetings with Lloyd George 1919–24, and notes on Liberal reunion 1924; and notes on the position of the party at the various general elections. There are a few papers about Maclean's appointment as President of the Board of Education. Maclean's letters to his wife are full of accounts of his political activities and comments on current issues.

IAIN NORMAN MACLEOD (1913–1970)

Iain Macleod was Conservative MP for Enfield West 1950–70. He was Minister of Health May 1952–Dec 1955, Minister of Labour and National Service 1955–Oct 1959, Secretary of State for the Colonies 1959–Oct 1961, Chancellor of the Duchy of Lancaster 1961–Oct 1963, and Chancellor of the Exchequer June 1970.

Macleod's widow, Lady Macleod, advised us that her husband had left no personal papers and that 'even the entries in his engagement book were made illegible'. Lady Macleod added that had her husband written an autobiography, he would have used his 'prodigious memory' as his source.

There are two biographies: Nigel Fisher, *Iain Macleod* (Deutsch 1973), and Robert Shepherd, *Iain Macleod* (Hutchinson 1994).

Macleod's work as Colonial Secretary is discussed (without reference to private papers) in David Goldsworthy, *Colonial Issues in British Politics 1945–1961* (Clarendon Press, Oxford 1971). There are brief sketches of Macleod's career by Ian Gilmour in *DNB 1961–1970*, 700–4, and by Michael Bentley in *Blackwell*, 286–7.

Papers relating to Budgets are in the PRO at T 171. The Conservative Party Archives in the Bodleian Library should also be consulted for papers from Macleod's Chairmanship of the Conservative Party 1961–63. Records of the Leader of the House of Commons 1961–91 are in the HLRO, but are subject to the 30 year rule (Macleod was Leader of the House of Commons 1961–63). *Conservative Party Policy* is important regarding the archives of the CRD.

HUGH PATTISON MACMILLAN, BARON MACMILLAN (1873–1952)

Hugh Macmillan was Lord Advocate Feb-Nov 1924, and Minister of Information Sept 1939–Jan 1940. He was created GCVO in 1937, and Baron Macmillan (a judicial life peerage) in 1930.

About 400 miscellaneous letters were deposited by Macmillan's niece, Mrs H. P. Dyson, in the NLS (MSS 25260–5; NRA 29056). Most of the letters are 'ceremonial', that is letters on his entering or leaving office. However, there are about 100 letters from Ramsay MacDonald with copies of Macmillan's letters to MacDonald. This correspondence covers the period 1924–37 and includes such topics as Scottish legal business, the royal commission on lunacy, Macmillan's appointment to the Honours Committee, and the Oscar Slater appeal. Oscar Slater had been convicted of murder in 1909 but in 1928, after 19 years of imprisonment and much agitation on his behalf, the conviction was quashed and he was released (see William Roughhead, *The Trial of Oscar Slater*, 3rd ed, Sweet & Maxwell 1929). The Library also has a box of papers presented by Lady Macmillan concerning the foundation of the NLS, with which Macmillan was closely involved (MSS 25266–73).

Mrs Dyson deposited four additional boxes of her uncle's papers in the British Library (Add MSS 54575–8). These papers cover the years 1934–49 and largely relate to Macmillan's work as a Trustee of the British Museum.

Macmillan's *A Man of Law's Tale* (Macmillan 1952) quotes from a few letters, for example his letter of resignation as Minister of Information in 1940. Ian McLaine's *Ministry of Morale* (Allen & Unwin 1979) has valuable material on Macmillan's short term as Minister of Information.

(MAURICE) HAROLD MACMILLAN, 1st EARL OF STOCKTON (1894–1986)

Harold Macmillan was Conservative MP for Stockton-on-Tees 1924–29 and 1931–45 and Bromley 1945–64. He was Parliamentary Secretary to the Ministry of Supply May 1940–Feb 1942, Parliamentary Under-Secretary of State for the Colonies 1942–Dec 1942, Minister Resident in North West Africa 1942–May 1945, Secretary of State for Air May-Aug 1945, Minister for Housing and Local Government Oct 1951–Oct 1954, Minister of Defence 1954–April 1955, Secretary of State for Foreign Affairs April-Dec 1955, Chancellor of the Exchequer 1955–Jan 1957, and Prime Minister 1957–Oct 1963. He was Leader of the Conservative Party Jan 1957–Nov 1963. He was created Earl of Stockton in 1984.

Macmillan's personal papers were deposited in the Bodleian Library in 1994. The papers are not accessible without specific permission from the family and the Trustees of the Macmillan Archive. The Bodleian Library expected cataloguing of the collection to take some time; it was to commence with Macmillan's diaries.

The Macmillan Archive was inspected in March 1994 before it was transferred to the Bodleian. The archive was housed in a former meat store in a number of steel filing cabinets. The papers were arranged thematically, an order established by Macmillan when writing his memoirs. Among the papers examined were a vast amount of 'official' papers including documents marked 'top secret', 'secret', and 'most secret', and a number of 'top secret' Prime Minister's personal telegrams. There were also papers on the establishment of the Macmillan Archive Trust, on which Macmillan wrote, 'I have, no doubt, got papers (especially from war time) which strictly I should not have...' (letter to Mr Moir, Fladgates, 28 Jan 1964). Settlement was made on 27 July 1964 between Macmillan and the Trustees for 'records, memoranda, diaries, letters, official or unofficial papers relating to the life of the settlor from his early days to the present time...'. It appears, however, that Macmillan did return some Cabinet conclusions to the Cabinet Office in the early 1970s.

Macmillan quoted extensively from his papers in his memoirs: *Winds of Change 1919–1939* (Macmillan 1966); *The Blast of War 1939–1945* (Macmillan 1967); *Tides of Fortune 1945–1955* (Macmillan 1969); *Riding the Storm 1956–1959* (Macmillan 1971); *Pointing the Way 1959–1961* (Macmillan 1972); *The End of the Day 1961–1963* (Macmillan 1973). See also *War Diaries: Politics and War in the Mediterranean, January 1943–May 1945*

(Macmillan 1984). Macmillan also reflected on *The Past Masters: Politics and Politicians* (Macmillan 1975)

The official biography by Alistair Horne, *Macmillan* (2 vols, Macmillan 1988–89; revised Papermac edition 1990–91) relies principally on the private papers, supplemented by interviews with Macmillan and his contemporaries. Professor John Turner's biography, *Macmillan* (Longmans 1994) makes considerable use of PRO material on the Macmillan premiership. Dr Peter Catterall has been commissioned by the family to edit Macmillan's diary.

A collection of papers relating to the work of the various Ministers Resident has been opened in the PRO (FO 660). It includes papers derived from Macmillan's work as Minister Resident in North West Africa 1943–44 (FO 660/12–105 and 200–343). There are memoranda on the political situation in the Mediterranean and in North West Africa, and on General de Gaulle and the Free French. There are also many press cuttings.

Papers of Prime Ministerial Advisors Outside Cabinet 1916–40 are in the PRO at PREM 1. Papers relating to Budgets are in T 171. AVIA 11 contains material relevant to Macmillan's brief tenure of the Air Ministry. FO 800/663–90 relates to Macmillan in the Foreign Office 1955, while DEFE 13/25–73 relates to his term as Minister of Defence. Prime Ministerial correspondence is in PREM 11.

Correspondence with Macmillan & Co Ltd authors up to 1969 may be found in the British Library; Reading University Library holds other Macmillan publishing correspondence. These collections include only an insignificant amount of Harold Macmillan material.

Macmillan's involvement in foreign affairs in the early 1950s is documented in Roger Bullen and M. E. Pelly (eds), *Documents on British Policy Overseas* (HMSO 1986), series II, vol I.

THOMAS JAMES MACNAMARA (1861–1931)

Thomas Macnamara was Liberal MP for Camberwell (North) 1900–24 (the division became North-West Camberwell in 1918 when he became a Coalition Liberal). He was Parliamentary Secretary to the Local Government Board Jan 1907–April 1908, Parliamentary and Financial Secretary to the Admiralty 1908–March 1920, and Minister of Labour 1920–Oct 1922.

We have been unable to trace Macnamara's papers. His widow died in 1955. They had three sons and one daughter. The eldest son, Neil Cameron Macnamara, died in 1967; his widow had never heard him mention anything about his father's papers and did not know of the existence of any papers. We were unable to trace the second son. The youngest son, Terence Macnamara, had no idea of what may have happened to his father's papers but thought that as his only sister was very interested in politics she may have had them. However, Macnamara's only daughter, Mrs Elsie Cameron Scott, died in 1965 and her husband knew of no papers.

Adjusting to Democracy is a valuable guide to Macnamara's work at the Ministry of Labour and to relevant PRO files. Dr Robin Betts of the Department of Education, University of Liverpool, relies mainly on published sources for his study of 'Dr Macnamara and the Education Act of 1902', *Journal of Educational Administration and History*, 25, 2, 1993, 111–21. Dr Betts has also completed a biography of Macnamara which remains unpublished.

HECTOR McNEIL (1907-1955)

Hector McNeil was Labour MP for Greenock 1941–55. He was Parliamentary Under-Secretary of State for Foreign Affairs Aug 1945–Oct 1946, Minister of State for Foreign Affairs 1946–Feb 1950, and Secretary of State for Scotland 1950–Oct 1951.

McNeil's widow, Sheila McNeil, informed us that he kept no personal papers and that apart from film and tape recordings of three speeches he made at the United Nations, she had only his letters to her, and an incomplete rough draft of a biography she began writing. None of these items is available for research.

Private Office papers relating to McNeil's period at the Scottish Office are dispersed through the files of the five main Scottish Office departments held at the SRO.

McNeil's career is covered by George Pottinger in *Secretaries of State for Scotland*, 117–29. Pottinger was McNeil's private secretary at the Scottish Office.

RONALD JOHN McNEILL, BARON CUSHENDUN (1861-1934)

Ronald McNeill was Conservative MP for Kent (St Augustine's; Canterbury from 1918) 1911–27. He was Parliamentary Under-Secretary of State for Foreign Affairs Oct 1922–Jan 1924 and Nov 1924–Nov 1925, Financial Secretary to the Treasury 1925–Oct 1927, and Chancellor of the Duchy of Lancaster 1927–June 1929. He was created Baron Cushendun in 1927.

A selection was copied from McNeill's papers by the PRONI in 1961 (T 1829 and Mic 63). A description of this selection may be seen in PRONI, *The Report of the Deputy Keeper of the Records for the Years 1960–1965*, Cmd 521, Belfast 1968, p. 134.

Most of the papers copied concern McNeill's earlier life. There are letters to him as editor of the *St. James's Gazette* 1900–04, including one from Lord Milner on the labour question in the Transvaal Nov 1903.

There are also some autobiographical notes, compiled about 1910. There are several letters about McNeill's unsuccessful attempts to enter Parliament, and letters of congratulation on his Privy Councillorship 1924, and on his entry to the Cabinet 1927. There is a particularly interesting letter from McNeill to his family Aug 1928 explaining the circumstances of his being Acting Secretary of State for Foreign Affairs Aug-Dec 1928, when Sir Austen Chamberlain was ill. A small file of estate papers for Cushendun, Co Antrim, has also been deposited in the PRONI (D 971).

The original papers from which the selection was made were in the possession of McNeill's elder daughter, the Hon Mrs Esther McNeill-Moss. She died in 1968 and we were not able to contact her son, Mr G. M. McNeill-Moss, to ascertain whether he had the papers, and whether they were available for research.

A further collection of McNeill's papers is available at the PRO (FO 800/227-8). It consists of two volumes of miscellaneous correspondence 1922-23 and 1927-29.

McNeill's *Ulster's Stand for the Union* (John Murray 1922) is semi-autobiographical.

SIR (JAMES) IAN MACPHERSON, 1st Bt, 1st BARON STRATHCARRON (1880-1937)

Ian Macpherson was Liberal MP for Ross and Cromarty (Inverness-shire, Ross and Cromarty from 1918) 1911-35. He was Under-Secretary of State for War Dec 1916-Jan 1919, Chief Secretary for Ireland 1919-April 1920, and Minister of Pensions 1920-Oct 1922. He was created a baronet in 1933, and Baron Strathcarron in 1936.

Most of Macpherson's papers were destroyed by bombing during the Second World War. He had written his autobiography, but while going to deliver the manuscript to his publishers, he lost it by leaving it on the seat of a taxi. The manuscript was never recovered; it was the only copy. Until 1970 Macpherson's family believed that no papers had survived. But a small suitcase of papers was then discovered and these were given by Macpherson's son, the 2nd Lord Strathcarron, and his daughter, Lady Runge, to the Bodleian Library (MSS Eng hist c 490-2, d 309; NRA 16872).

Almost all of the papers refer to Ireland. As well as the printed *Intelligence Reports* for 1913 and 1914, and Horace Plunkett's printed *Report to the King on the Irish Convention* (1918), there is a stencilled Report of Censorship December 1918 by Lord Decies, the Irish Press Censor, and a file on the effect of demobilisation on Irish unemployment. This includes memoranda by E. Shortt and Sir S. Kent, as well as suggestions for remedies. There is also a draft Administration of Justice (Ireland) Bill Nov 1919, with a stencilled memo by the Home Secretary on the imprisonment of Sinn Fein prisoners in England and drafts of the Government of Ireland Bill with a commentary by 'F. F. L.' Sept 1918. There are also a number of letters to Macpherson from Lord French, then Lord Lieutenant of Ireland. The letters are full of the problems French had to face: whether or not to use discharged servicemen to fill the ranks of the RIC (25 May 1919); the problems of martial law and of a curfew (20 Oct 1919); the number of troops needed (8 Nov 1919); and the infiltration of spies into Dublin Castle (11 Dec 1919). There are several memoranda: on the possibility of enlisting ex-servicemen as special constables Aug 1919; on the difficulties of the Three Judges Bill (by Walter Long) Dec 1919; on the raising of a loan by Sinn Fein; on the activities of such prominent individuals as Michael Collins; and (by Macpherson) describing Lloyd George's reactions to Irish events 20–22 Dec 1919.

The only papers relating to Macpherson's tenure of the Ministry of Pensions are a press cutting and a pamphlet by Macpherson entitled *The Nation's Debt to the Disabled, Widowed and Fatherless. How it has been met* (June 1922).

There are a few constituency papers for the period 1920–22 including agents' letters and reports, as well as constituents' problems. The agents reported on the opinions of 'Important People' and their views on Coalition Liberals. There are also a few press cuttings and several anti-Asquith leaflets. A few miscellaneous letters have survived, for example, R. S. Horne to Mrs Macpherson approving Macpherson's planned transfer to the Scottish Office 28 Sept 1922.

NIALL MALCOLM STEWART MACPHERSON, BARON DRUMALBYN (1908–1987)

Niall Macpherson was National Liberal MP for Dumfriesshire 1945–50, and National Liberal and Unionist MP for Dumfriesshire 1950–63. He was Joint Under-Secretary of State for Scotland June 1955–Oct 1960, Parliamentary Secretary, Board of Trade 1960–July 1962, Minister of Pensions and National Insurance 1962–Oct 1963, Minister of State, Board of Trade 1963–Oct 1964, and Minister without Portfolio Oct 1970–Jan 1974. He was created Baron Drumalbyn in 1963 and KBE in 1974.

Lord Drumalbyn's papers are in the care of his daughter, the Hon Mary Macpherson, who advised us that although she holds much of her father's correspondence, very little relates to his parliamentary career, or the National Liberal Party.

Drumalbyn's brother, Mr R. T. S. Macpherson, did not have any papers.

SIR ARTHUR HERBERT DRUMMOND RAMSAY STEEL-MAITLAND, 1st Bt (1876–1935)

Arthur Steel-Maitland (he assumed the additional surname Maitland on his marriage in 1901) was Conservative MP for Birmingham (East; Birmingham, Erdington from 1918) 1910–29 and Warwickshire (Tamworth) 1929–35. He was Parliamentary Under-Secretary of State for the Colonies May 1915–Sept 1917, Joint Parliamentary Under-Secretary of State for Foreign Affairs and Secretary to the Overseas Trade Department, Board of Trade 1917–April 1919, and Minister of Labour Nov 1924–June 1929. He was created a baronet in 1917.

A very large collection of Steel-Maitland family papers, including Sir Arthur's papers, was deposited in the SRO (GD 193) by Steel-Maitland's grand-daughter, Mrs R. M. Stafford. The papers are available for research on the condition that any proposed publication based on them is submitted for Mrs Stafford's approval prior to publication. A list of the papers has been compiled (NRA 34099).

As well as a large number of domestic papers, correspondence, and some university notebooks, most aspects of Steel-Maitland's career are represented in his papers. He was private secretary to C. T. Ritchie and Austen Chamberlain 1902–05 when they were successive Chancellors of the Exchequer. Treasury papers, for example on the budget, and on Chamberlain's 1905 Financial Statement, have survived. Steel-Maitland seems to have maintained a close relationship with Chamberlain, to which the large number of letters from Chamberlain in the collection bear witness. Steel-Maitland served as special commissioner on the Royal Commission on the Poor Law 1906–07; memoranda and correspondence concerning this work have survived. By that time he was prospective candidate for Rugby and a considerable number of papers have survived 1904–08.

A large amount of Birmingham constituency material has survived 1910–29: correspondence with constituents, with his agent, and arrangements for meetings. Steel-Maitland's work as Chairman of the Conservative Party is reflected by papers on party organisation and correspondence, for example, on the need in 1912 to purchase the *Daily Express* in order to preserve it for the Conservative cause. There are many papers on party organisation and administration 1923–35. There are also papers on contemporary political issues: Ireland; tariff reform; land taxation; women's suffrage; national insurance; reform of the House of Lords; and the empire.

Steel-Maitland's official career is well represented. There are papers concerning the work of the Colonial Office, including correspondence with Churchill, Leo Amery, and Austen Chamberlain. The Department of Overseas Trade is represented by papers on the organisation of the department, on the problems of inter-departmental rivalry, and on the reasons for Steel-Maitland's resignation in 1919 – a disagreement with Auckland Geddes. Steel-Maitland was also involved in the League of Nations' Union, an interest represented by pamphlets, minutes of meetings, correspondence, and a diary for the 1922 Geneva Assembly. Apart from travel diaries and a few fragments, this is the only diary in the collection, though there are notes and memoranda relating to other international conferences.

The Ministry of Labour papers include a considerable amount of material on the General Strike. There are Cabinet papers, memoranda on the origins of the 1926 coal strike, suggestions for settlement terms, notes of the course of negotiations, and notes concerning the Cabinet committee on the report of the royal commission on the coal industry. Correspondence for the 1920s includes a letter 1922 from Steel-Maitland to Austen Chamberlain expressing his doubts about the coalition and a reply rebuking him for splitting the Conservative Party over Ireland. There are several boxes of papers on Russia, and on the reform of trade union legislation. There are 30 boxes of speech notes 1906-29.

In July 1993, Sotheby's sold three letters between Churchill and Steel-Maitland – two were from Churchill to Steel-Maitland in 1925 and 1927, and a copy of one from Steel-Maitland to Churchill in 1927. Neither Mrs Stafford nor the SRO was able to advise of the provenance of these letters.

Adjusting to Democracy is a valuable guide to Steel-Maitland's work at the Ministry of Labour and to relevant PRO files.

(HENRY) DAVID (REGINALD) MARGESSON, 1st VISCOUNT MARGESSON (1890–1965)

David Margesson was Conservative MP for West Ham (Upton) 1922–23 and Warwickshire (Rugby) 1924–42. He was Parliamentary Secretary to the Treasury Nov 1931–Dec 1940, and Secretary of State for War 1940–Feb 1942. He was created Viscount Margesson in 1942.

A small collection of Margesson's papers was deposited in the Churchill Archives Centre by his daughter in March 1967 (MRGN). These papers are not generally available; applications to see them should be made to the Keeper of the Archives at the Churchill Archives Centre. A concise list is available (NRA 14618). They consist almost entirely of letters which have been arranged in chronological order 1924–50. The only exception to this arrangement is a ten-page 'candid portrait' of Neville Chamberlain written in 1939. This document is unsigned and its author is unknown.

Private Office papers for the Secretary of State for War are in the PRO at WO 259.

None of Margesson's papers as Chief Whip 1931–40 is known to exist in the possession of the Conservative Party.

Margesson's career is summarised by J. E. B. Hill in *DNB 1961–1970*, 722–4.

EDWARD MARJORIBANKS, 2nd Bt, 2nd BARON TWEEDMOUTH (1849–1909)

Edward Marjoribanks was Liberal MP for Berwickshire 1880–94. He was Parliamentary Secretary to the Treasury Aug 1892–March 1894, Lord Privy Seal and Chancellor of the Duchy of Lancaster 1894–July 1895, First Lord of the Admiralty Dec 1905–April 1908, and Lord President of the Council April-Oct 1908. He succeeded his father as 2nd Baron Tweedmouth and 2nd baronet in 1894, and was created KT in 1908.

According to his sister, Lady Aberdeen, Tweedmouth '... made it a rule never to keep any notes or journal of any kind, and he made it a point of honour to destroy all confidential communications between himself and Mr Gladstone and the many other politicians and public men with whom he corresponded' (*Edward Marjoribanks, Lord Tweedmouth K.T. 1849–1909. Notes and Recollections*, privately printed 1909, pp v-vi).

Nonetheless a small collection of Tweedmouth's papers is currently held by the Ministry of Defence Whitehall Library. There are eight volumes of printed or typed memoranda, and letters (three volumes for 1906, four for 1907, one for 1908), some of which are annotated. These volumes have been indexed. There are also three boxes of correspondence with members of the Cabinet, MPs, Admiralty officials, naval officers, and others. These include files on the 1907–08 and 1908–09 naval estimates, as well as routine business such as requests for help and for influence with appointments. The authors of this correspondence have been indexed. The location of this collection is currently under review, and potential readers are advised to check with the Ministry of Defence Library.

The much publicised letter from Emperor William II (Feb 1908), Tweedmouth's reply, and a commentary by Sir Vincent Baddeley, then Tweedmouth's private secretary, are to be found in the Bodleian Library (MS Eng Hist c 264).

(ALFRED) ERNEST MARPLES, BARON MARPLES (1907–1978)

Ernest Marples was Conservative MP for Wallasey 1945–74. He was Parliamentary Secretary, Ministry of Housing and Local Government Nov 1951–Oct 1954, Joint Parliamentary Secretary, Ministry of Pensions and National Insurance 1954–Dec 1955, Postmaster-General Jan 1957–

Oct 1959, and Minister of Transport 1959–Oct 1964. He was created Baron Marples (a life peerage) in 1974.

We have not been able to contact Lord Marples's widow.

There are a few letters 1935–45 between Marples and A. P. Wadsworth, editor of the *Manchester Guardian* in the *Guardian* Archive in the John Rylands University Library, University of Manchester (B/M192/1–10; NRA 18162).

Marples's work as Minister of Transport is only briefly discussed in William Plowden, *The Motor Car and Politics 1896–1970* (Bodley Head 1971). There are short summaries of Marples's career by Sir Kenneth P. Thompson in *DNB 1971–1980*, 548–9, and by Keith Robbins in *Blackwell*, p. 292.

HILARY ADAIR MARQUAND (1901–1972)

Hilary Marquand was Labour MP for Cardiff (East) 1945–50 and Middlesbrough (East) 1950–61. He was Secretary of the Department of Overseas Trade Aug 1945–March 1947, Paymaster-General 1947–July 1948, Minister of Pensions 1948–Jan 1951, and Minister of Health Jan-Oct 1951.

The small quantity of papers kept by Marquand were mostly destroyed during his last illness. The surviving papers, consisting of only a few press cuttings, are in the possession of his son, Professor David Marquand, Mansfield College, Oxford. Professor Marquand advised us that these press cuttings are of no great interest.

The NLW has acquired 65 letters written by Marquand to Graham F. Thomas 1945–61 (Graham F. Thomas Papers). The letters make reference to contemporary political events.

SIR FREDERICK JAMES MARQUIS, 1st EARL OF WOOLTON (1883–1964)

Frederick Marquis was knighted in 1935, and created Baron Woolton in 1939, Viscount Woolton in 1953, and Earl of Woolton in 1956. He was Minister of Food April 1940–Nov 1943, Minister of Reconstruction 1943–May 1945, Lord President of the Council May-July 1945 and Oct 1951–Nov 1952, Chancellor of the Duchy of Lancaster 1952–Dec 1955, and Minister of Materials Sept 1953–Aug 1954.

Three four-drawer filing cabinets of his papers were given by his daughter-in-law, Lady Forres (now Lady Lloyd George of Dwyfor), to the Bodleian Library in 1973 (MSS Woolton 1–118). They were catalogued during 1976–77. The papers have been listed and there is a name index of correspondents (NRA 21829). The papers are available for research. See Helen Langley, 'The Woolton Papers', *Bodleian Library Record*, XI, 5, 1984, 320–37.

A considerable number of papers survive from Woolton's tenure of the Ministry of Food, including many speeches and broadcasting notes such as 'The Kitchen in Wartime' Dec 1940. There are, for example, memoranda on the organisation of the ministry 1940, on agricultural prices, and aspects of rationing. There are also minutes to and from the Prime Minister, and diary notes Sept 1940–Jan 1944. A note on the envelope containing these says that a gap occurs from then till 1952 and then the notes were kept only spasmodically.

Woolton made notes on his feelings at becoming Minister of Reconstruction in Nov 1943. Several memoranda and some correspondence have survived including a note of a conversation with Erskine Hill in Nov 1943 on the future of the Conservative Party, and memoranda on the Beveridge report, on postwar Conservative policy, and on the position of 'political' and 'technical' ministers in the Cabinet.

From 1946 to 1955 Woolton was Chairman of the Conservative Party and some papers have survived from this work. They include correspondence with Churchill, particularly on party organisation, a reply by Conservative Central Office to allegations of inefficiency (Dec 1946), and papers on negotiations with the National Liberals in 1950 and much printed material including press cuttings and cartoons. (Several boxes of Woolton's papers are also to be found in the Conservative Party Archives in the Bodleian Library).

Some notes have survived from Woolton's terms of office as Lord President, his term as Chancellor of the Duchy, and from the Ministry of Materials.

In 1959 Woolton published his *Memoirs* (Cassell). Drafts and correspondence relating to the publication of this and other books and articles survive. There are also various memoranda, for example, on the machinery of government and Cabinet-making, on his first meeting with Churchill, and Woolton's assessment of Churchill. Fragments of correspondence survive, for example, with Anthony Eden, on Woolton's surprise at the admission by Sir Arthur Steel-Maitland, published in Lord Blake's biography of Bonar Law, that some peerages had resulted from contributions to party funds and the strong denial by Woolton that this had ever happened while he was in charge of the Conservative Party.

From 1908–14 Woolton worked for the Liverpool University Settlement. A few photos, some letters and some reflections on the significance of the work there are all that survive, apart from a draft obituary for Attlee in which Woolton contrasts the similarity of their early work with the dissimilarity of their later viewpoints. Many of Woolton's business papers have been destroyed, and all that remain from the earlier part of his life are papers from the various committees on which he served, such as the 1938 Cadman Committee on Civil Aviation.

Lord Woolton's grandson, Charles Sandeman-Allen, is preparing a biography of his grandfather. Mr Sandeman-Allen holds a collection of private family letters from Woolton's early life 1907–20. The 3rd Earl of Woolton has a small but valuable collection of Woolton's papers.

Some of Woolton's papers as Minister of Reconstruction and Lord President may be found in the PRO at CAB 124. There is also some correspondence with Sir William Jowitt 1940–45 in the PRO at CAB 127/160.

Dr Michael Kandiah's thesis, 'Lord Woolton's Chairmanship of the Conservative Party, 1946–55' (PhD thesis, University of Exeter 1993), utilised public papers as well as the private collections of the 3rd Earl and Charles Sandeman-Allen. A political biography by Dr Kandiah is scheduled to be published by the Scolar Press in 1997.

Woolton's career is authoritatively sketched by Lord Redcliffe-Maud in *DNB 1961–1970*, 728–31, and by John Ramsden in *Blackwell*, 292–3.

CHARLES FREDERICK GURNEY MASTERMAN (1873–1927)

Charles Masterman was Liberal MP for West Ham (North) 1906–11, Bethnal Green (South-West) 1911–14 and Manchester (Rusholme) 1923–24. He was Parliamentary Secretary to the Local Government Board April 1908–July 1909, Under-Secretary of State for Home Affairs 1909–Feb 1912, Financial Secretary to the Treasury 1912–Feb 1914, and Chancellor of the Duchy of Lancaster 1914–Feb 1915 (throughout his period in the Cabinet Masterman had no seat in the House of Commons and for this reason had to resign in 1915).

Papers relating to Masterman's wartime propaganda work at Wellington House were returned to the Foreign Office after the war. Masterman's remaining papers, formerly in the possession of his widow, Mrs Lucy Masterman, who died in 1977, are now held by the Birmingham University Library. There is a large collection, including official files, correspondence, press cuttings, and drafts of Mrs Masterman's life of her husband. The collection is currently not available for research while it is being relisted.

About 20 letters to Masterman from Churchill and Lloyd George were sold, mostly as single items, at Sotheby's on 19 Dec 1981. Copies of these are now part of the Birmingham University Library collection.

Lucy Masterman, *C. F. G. Masterman. A Biography* (Cass 1939, reprinted 1968) quotes fully from many letters and from her own contemporary diaries and notes which are also in the collection.

There is a useful outline of Masterman's life by George L. Bernstein in *MBR*, 3, 574–7. A longer biographical sketch drawing on a variety of sources other than the Masterman papers then in family possession, is Edward David, 'The New Liberalism of C. F. G. Masterman, 1873–

1927', in Kenneth D. Brown (ed), *Essays in Anti-Labour History: Responses to the Rise of Labour in Britain* (Macmillan 1974), 17–41, 245–9.

There are detailed studies of Masterman's role in wartime propaganda in M. L. Sanders and Philip M. Taylor, *British Propaganda during the First World War, 1914–1918* (Macmillan 1982), Nicholas Reeves, *Official British Film Propaganda During the First World War* (Croom Helm 1986), and Gary S. Messinger, *British propaganda and the state in the First World War* (Manchester UP 1992).

REGINALD MAUDLING (1917–1979)

Reggie Maudling was Conservative MP for Barnet 1950–74 and Chipping Barnet 1974–79. He was Economic Secretary to the Treasury Nov 1952–April 1955, Minister of Supply 1955–Jan 1957, Paymaster-General 1957–Oct 1959, President of the Board of Trade 1959–Oct 1961, Secretary of State for the Colonies 1961–July 1962, Chancellor of the Exchequer 1962–Oct 1964, and Home Secretary June 1970–July 1972.

In his *Memoirs* (Sidgwick and Jackson 1978 13–14), Maudling said 'I have never kept detailed records of my activities; it always seemed to me a rather cold-blooded activity to do so, and I much prefer to get on with the job and let the results speak for themselves'. Referring to a meeting in 1963 between himself, R. A. Butler, Lord Hailsham, and Lord Home at the time when Home was forming his government, Maudling wrote 'I kept a record of it, about the only detailed record I ever kept. Alas, I kept it in pencil and when I came to look at it a year or two later, it had faded beyond reading' (p. 130). Two previously unpublished documents are quoted in *Memoirs*: a letter from Reginald V. Brown about home brewing and a memo on incomes policy circulated to the Shadow Cabinet on 21 May 1976 (pp 265–7).

The papers which do survive have been deposited at Churchill Archives Centre (MLNG; NRA 18561). They consist of 28 boxes of constituency correspondence for the period 1971–79. The collection is subject to 30 year closure and the first files will not be available until 2002.

Papers relating to Budgets are in the PRO at T 171. There is an interview with Maudling on colonial problems in the Rhodes House Library (MSS Brit Emp s 484).

The Conservative Party Archives in the Bodleian Library should also be consulted. *Conservative Party Policy* is useful regarding the archives of the CRD.

Maudling is generously assessed by Julian Critchley in *Blackwell*, 297–9. His involvement in the Real Estate Fund of America and the subsequent investigations which led to his departure from office are documented from affidavits and other material on the public record in

Michael Gillard, *A Little Pot of Money: The Story of Reginald Maudling and the Real Estate Fund of America* (Private Eye with André Deutsch 1974).

SIR FREDERIC HERBERT MAUGHAM, 1st VISCOUNT MAUGHAM (1866–1958)

Frederic Maugham was knighted in 1928, created Baron Maugham (a judicial life peerage) in 1935, and Viscount Maugham in 1939. He was Lord Chancellor March 1938–Sept 1939.

The surviving papers of Lord Maugham, previously held by his son Robin, the 2nd Viscount Maugham, are now in the possession of his daughter, the Hon Mrs Diana Marr-Johnson, Flat 3, 14 Onslow Square, London SW7.

There is a small quantity of social correspondence (including letters from the Archbishop of Canterbury, Sir William Orpen, and an invitation to Chequers from Anne Chamberlain in Nov 1938); several family photo albums; programmes, invitations, and ephemera from the 1930s; letters of thanks from Lord Rothermere and Sir George Sutton following Maugham's conduct of a case on their behalf in 1926; and Maugham's notes on the privy council meeting after the death of King George V.

Kept with these papers is a bundle of letters from Lady Maugham to Robin Maugham in 1938–39, including one on 11 March 1939 about the events surrounding Maugham's appointment as Lord Chancellor.

Most of this material has been published in Robin Maugham's book, *Somerset and all the Maughams* (Longmans-Heinemann 1966). Lord Maugham's book quotes from a sketch of his father in an unpublished book by his sister, Kate Mary Bruce, entitled *Family Group*. Maugham himself published his memoirs, *At the End of the Day* (Heinemann 1954), but these contain almost no documentary material.

Copies of Mrs Marr-Johnson's own memoirs, *The Happiness Level*, are held by several members of the family. Written primarily as a record for her grandchildren, and insufficiently scandalous for publication, they give a daughter's view of her father.

Some of the papers quoted by R.F.V. Heuston in his brief biography in *Lord Chancellors 1*, 539–74, cannot now be found.

SIR PERCY HERBERT MILLS, Bt, 1st VISCOUNT MILLS (1890–1968)

Percy Mills was knighted in 1942, and created KBE in 1946, baronet in 1953, Baron Mills in 1957 and Viscount Mills in 1962. He was Minister of Power Jan 1957–Oct 1959, Paymaster-General 1959–Oct 1961, and Minister without Portfolio 1961–July 1962.

Mill's grandson, the 3rd Viscount, holds a small collection of his papers. These are available for research to *bona fide* researchers and scholars.

There are two files of miscellaneous speeches 1946–66 including many autobiographical reminiscences. There are five folders of ministerial speeches with chronological indexes and including texts of parliamentary questions and answers 1957–58 and 1960–61. One scrapbook contains press cuttings c.1939. There is a folder of letters relating to his political career and wartime administration, and a large folder of letters of congratulation from ministerial colleagues on Mills being created a Viscount. Other miscellaneous correspondents include Harold Macmillan, R. A. Butler, Sir Andrew Duncan, Lord Portal, and Iain Macleod.

There are also 190 pages of typescript diary notes on a 1930 cruise in Danish and Swedish coastal waters.

There is a brief sketch of Mills by the Earl of Halsbury in *DNB 1961–1970*, 755–6.

SIR ALFRED MILNER, VISCOUNT MILNER (1854–1925)

Alfred Milner was created KCB in 1895, Baron Milner in 1901, Viscount Milner in 1902, and KG in 1921. He was member of the War Cabinet and Minister without Portfolio Dec 1916–April 1918, Secretary of State for War 1918–Jan 1919, and Secretary of State for the Colonies 1919–Feb 1921.

Six hundred boxes of Milner's papers were bequeathed to New College, Oxford, but the papers are now housed in the Bodleian Library (MS Milner 1–684; NRA 14300). The papers have been catalogued and are available on microfilm. They have been arranged under the following main headings: general correspondence 1872–1925; diaries and notebooks 1875–1925; general papers 1886–1925; papers relating to South Africa 1892–1926; papers relating to the First World War 1913–19; papers as Secretary of State for the Colonies 1887–1923; personal papers 1885–1926; general printed material 1857–1939; family correspondence and papers 1824–1928.

Milner's notebooks cover a wide range of subjects from French and Arabic grammar, bimetallism, and economics. They include his lecture notes on political economy and on socialism, and notes about South Africa and Egypt. His diaries cover the years 1881–1925. There are also special diaries for Egypt 1919–10, Palestine 1922, and South Africa 1924–25.

Milner's general papers include papers relating to the National Service League 1900–18; Ireland 1886–1924; and agriculture 1903–25.

The South African papers include 61 volumes of bound official correspondence with the Secretary of State (Joseph Chamberlain), with the governors of the African colonies and, during the Boer War, with the military leaders. There is also a great deal of private correspondence (which includes some up to 1921) including private correspondence with Chamberlain. The correspondence includes copies of outgoing as well as incoming letters. Some of Milner's journals compiled during his various African journeys are included in this section. There are papers from the 1899 Bloemfontein Conference, from the peace negotiations, and even 'loot' from Bloemfontein – papers of Cape Ministers and telegrams.

The First World War papers contain both private and official documents which reflect Milner's active role in the war. There are many official papers, particularly on Russia, Siberia, and Persia 1917–18, minutes of the Eastern Committee of the War Cabinet March 1918–Jan 1919, papers on man-power and recruiting (including some on national service 1915–16), naval and military strategy, and on peace overtures. There are also private correspondence and miscellaneous War Office papers.

Milner's papers as Secretary of State for the Colonies include correspondence 1918–21, pamphlets, government printed papers relating to the colonies, and papers relating to Egypt 1881–1924.

His personal papers include pamphlets and articles about himself, copies of speeches and correspondence and papers, mainly financial, relating to the Rhodes Trust and papers concerning his election as Chancellor of Oxford University. The general printed material includes a collection of press cuttings 1872–1939 which cover all aspects of his career, as their bulk indicates. The printed papers are largely official papers, in particular command papers.

His personal correspondence and papers include many copies of outgoing letters as well as his own letters from Oxford to his mother, financial, and domestic papers.

There is also a collection of Lady Milner's papers 1900–55 and the papers of Cecil and Maurice Headlam 1931–40 relating to the publication of *The Milner Papers* (see below), including the typescript of an unfinished book on Milner.

A further collection of Milner's papers – two tin trunks and some box-files – was given to the Bodleian Library in 1973 by Mr Jan Milner (MSS Eng hist c 686–709; d 362; e 305–7). The papers have not yet been listed. Application to read them should be made to the Bodleian Library. These papers include much material from the 1890s but they are mainly from the last seven years of Milner's life and include War Office and Colonial Office files.

Some of Lady Milner's papers originally deposited by her daughter, Lady Hardinge of Penshurst, in the Kent Archives Office are now in the Bodleian Library. The collection includes a few items of Lord Milner's. A list is available (NRA 20659). In 1989 the Bodleian acquired a second tranche of Lady Milner's papers (MSS Violet Milner adds 1–25) which includes correspondence of and concerning Lord Milner and relating to *The Milner Papers*, 1931, 1933.

A further collection of Milner's papers has been deposited in the PRO (PRO 30/30; NRA 23395). It contains 25 boxes of papers for the period 1915–20 and includes papers on the 1915 military agreement between the allies and Italy, papers in defence of General Sir Hubert Gough, papers on the conflicting claims of the French and Arabs in Syria, on the 1919 campaign in Russia, papers of the 1919 Liquor Restrictions Committee, the 1919 India Reform Committee, and the 1920 Indian Disorders Committee. The collection also includes the agreement made between France and Britain which gave General Foch supreme command of the allied forces in France, and Milner's diary for 23–26 March 1918. This 1918 material was published in *The Times* 22 and 23 May 1928. The class list for these papers has been published by the List and Index Society, *Public Record Office, Gifts and Deposits. Supplementary Lists*, 70, 1971.

A further 27 volumes of papers concerning Milner's mission to Egypt 1919–20 are also available at the PRO (FO 848). The aim of the mission was to decide on future British policy in Egypt. The collection includes not only correspondence, memoranda, and minutes but also records of conversations in Egypt, notes of evidence taken, the Commissioner's reference books, and press cuttings.

The National Archives, Canada, holds microfilm copies of originals held at the Bodleian Library, including several letters from George Parkin 1893–96, as well as general correspondence, memoranda, and clippings (MG 27 II A 3).

A large number of Milner's papers have been published, in accordance with his own wishes; these only relate to South Africa: Cecil Headlam (ed), *The Milner Papers*, (2 vols, Cassell 1931–33). Alfred M. Gollin, *Proconsul in Politics: a study of Lord Milner in Opposition and in Power* (Anthony Blond 1964) quotes from the later papers. Sir John Evelyn Wrench's *Alfred, Lord Milner: the man of no illusions, 1854–1925* (Eyre & Spottiswoode 1958) quotes extensively from the Milner papers but is superseded by the more broadly based Terence H. O'Brien, *Milner: Viscount Milner of St James's and Cape Town 1854–1925* (Constable 1979).

ROBERT OFFLEY ASHBURTON CREWE-MILNES, 2nd BARON HOUGHTON, MARQUESS OF CREWE (1858–1945)

Robert Crewe-Milnes (he assumed the additional surname of Crewe in 1894 when he succeeded to his uncle's estates) succeeded his father as 2nd Baron Houghton in 1885. He was created Earl of Crewe in 1895, KG in 1908, and Marquess of Crewe in 1911. He was Lord President of the Council Dec 1905–April 1908 and May 1915–Dec 1916, Secretary of State for Colonial Affairs April 1908–Nov 1910, Lord Privy Seal Oct 1908–Oct 1911 and Feb 1912–May 1915, Secretary of State for India Nov 1910–March 1911 and May 1911–May 1915, President of the Board of Education Aug-Dec 1916, and Secretary of State for War Aug-Nov 1931. He was Liberal Leader in the House of Lords 1908–23 and 1936–44.

Many of Crewe's papers were accidentally destroyed during his lifetime in fires at his homes. Nevertheless, a very large collection – 150 boxes – of his papers was deposited in the Cambridge University Library by his widow in 1958 (Crewe Papers). Apart from a brief correspondence between Lord Stamfordham and Crewe in 1924 regarding honours, the entire collection is open for research. (The closed material will be available in 1999). The collection has been divided into five main groups: (C) 61 boxes of general correspondence; (P) four boxes of personal papers; (S) three boxes of speeches; (M) 21 boxes of miscellaneous papers; and (I) 21 boxes of India Office papers. A card index of correspondents has been compiled for most of the collection.

The general correspondence has been arranged alphabetically by name of correspondent; where more than one letter exists from an individual, the letters are in chronological order. Copies or drafts of Crewe's outgoing letters have been placed under their recipient's name. Amongst the longer series of correspondence are four volumes of letters from Lord Hardinge to Crewe 1910–15 and two volumes of Crewe's replies, a box of correspondence with Asquith 1908–27, two boxes of correspondence with John Morley 1892-1915, two boxes of letters from Lord Curzon (mainly 1908–25), and a box of letters from Ramsay MacDonald 1924. This section of the papers includes Crewe's letters to the various Indian governors.

The personal papers contain drafts, notes and final versions of Crewe's writings, including letters to the press, articles, and book reviews. There are letters of congratulation and of regret (for example, on his resignation as Secretary of State for India). In addition there is some family correspondence – letters from his father and to his sisters.

The speeches include notes and correspondence for speeches 1908–39. The miscellaneous section includes papers concerning various funds, such as the Florence Nightingale Memorial Fund 1910–16, political dinners for fellow peers, and the Imperial College of Science and Technology. It also includes papers concerning his term as Lord Lieutenant of Ireland 1892–95: there are papers concerning the Irish Land Commission and the Board of National Education. There are papers of the 1916 Reconstruction Committee, the Dardanelles Commission, and various Cabinet committees.

The India Office papers consist of a large number of subject files ranging from the Durbar, the appointment of various governors, the visit to India in 1912–13 of the Under-Secretary of State, Edwin Montagu, and the problems of Indians in South Africa, to correspondence about the need of the British Museum for a stuffed elephant.

The rest of the collection (some 40 boxes) consists of printed material: confidential prints, parliamentary bills, debates etc. A card index to this part of the collection, arranged in chronological order, has been compiled.

The National Archives, Canada, holds microfilm copies of some of the Cambridge University Library collection, including various letters and notes 1908–10 (MG 27 II A 4).

There is a small collection of letters from Crewe to Lord Curzon, Ramsay MacDonald, and Austen Chamberlain 1923–28 in the papers of Sir Eric Phipps in the Churchill Archives Centre (PHPP I/1/6–7).

A further small collection of papers is available in the PRO (FO 800/330). It consists of reports from the press attaché to Crewe when he was Ambassador to Paris. Eleven volumes of correspondence and papers 1929–36 relating to Crewe's biography of Lord Roseberg are in the NLS (MSS 10195–205; NRA 22490).

There is a thorough and detailed list of Crewe's correspondence, including stray letters in his correspondents' papers in David C. Sutton (ed), *Location Register of Twentieth-Century Literary Manuscripts and Letters* (2 vols, British Library 1988).

James Pope-Hennessy, *Lord Crewe 1858–1945. The Likeness of a Liberal* (Constable 1955), is based on the Crewe papers and frequently quotes from them.

(ARTHUR) HUGH (ELSDALE) MOLSON, BARON MOLSON (1903–1991)

Hugh Molson was Unionist MP for Doncaster 1931–35 and High Peak 1939–61. He was Parliamentary Secretary, Ministry of Works Nov 1951–Nov 1953, Joint Parliamentary Secretary, Ministry of Transport and Civil Aviation 1953–Jan 1957, and Minister of Works 1957–Oct 1959. He was created Baron Molson (a life peerage) in 1961.

Lord Molson advised us that he had retained no papers relating to his political career. His executors, Lee & Pembertons, London, confirmed that there were no papers.

Molson wrote a brief sketch of his career in his article 'Fifty-Four Years of Parliamentary Life', *Contemporary Review*, Aug 1985.

SIR WALTER TURNER MONCKTON, 1st VISCOUNT MONCKTON OF BRENCHLEY (1891–1965)

Walter Monckton was created KCVO in 1937, KCMG in 1945, and Viscount Monckton of Brenchley in 1957. He was Conservative MP for

Bristol West 1951–57. He was Solicitor-General May-July 1945, Minister of Labour and National Service Oct 1951–Dec 1955, Minister of Defence 1955–Oct 1956, and Paymaster-General 1956–Jan 1957.

Monckton's son, the 2nd Lord Monckton advised us that he and his sister gave all of their father's papers, except for a few family papers, to the Royal Archives and Balliol College, Oxford. Balliol College has deposited the papers in the Bodleian Library (MS Dep Monckton 1–63 and MSS Dep Monckton Trustees 1–89). There is a list available (NRA 20879).

The collection comprises 154 boxes of correspondence and papers. The major subject areas covered by the papers include: India 1928–60s; Hyderabad 1936–57; Ministry of Labour 1951–55; Suez crisis 1956–57; Central African Federation 1959–62; and the Monckton Commission 1959–60. There are also papers relating to the Ministry of Information 1939–42, and the Ministry of Defence 1955–56. There are various restrictions on some of the material. Correspondence with the royal family, in particular the Duke and Duchess of Windsor, is closed until 1999.

The Royal Archives has a small collection of Monckton's correspondence 1936–40 concerning the Duke of Windsor.

The PRO has identified papers relating to Monckton in the Defence Department 1955–56 (DEFE 13/25–70).

There are two biographies of Monckton: the 2nd Earl Birkenhead, *Walter Monckton: the life of Viscount Monckton of Brenchley* (Weidenfeld & Nicolson 1969), and H. Montgomery Hyde, *Walter Monckton* (Sinclair-Stevenson 1991). John Barnes's entry in *Blackwell*, 302–4, reflects recent scholarship.

Monckton's work at the Ministry of Labour is illuminated in Justin Davis Smith, *The Attlee and Churchill Administrations and Industrial Unrest 1945–55: A Study in Consensus* (Pinter Publishers 1990).

SIR ALFRED MORITZ MOND, 1st Bt, 1st BARON MELCHETT (1868–1930)

Alfred Mond was Liberal MP for Chester 1906–10, Swansea (Swansea West from 1918) 1910–23 and Carmarthenshire (Carmarthen) 1924–28. He joined the Conservative Party in 1926. He was First Commissioner of Works Dec 1916–April 1921, and Minister of Health 1921–Oct 1922. He was created a baronet in 1910, and Baron Melchett in 1928.

Mond's papers were used by Hector Bolitho for his biography, *Alfred Mond, First Lord Melchett* (Martin Secker 1933). Bolitho said in his foreword that Mond inherited a desk full of family papers from his father but never looked at them, either because he was too busy or because he was not interested. He also says that Mond never kept a diary or any souvenirs of his childhood. According to Bolitho anything of interest was used in the biography and the papers were returned to the family. Unfortunately these papers were destroyed by a fire during the Second World War.

The 4th Lord Melchett holds a small collection of Mond's papers. They are available to researchers, if his permission is obtained, at Courtyard Farm, Ringstead, Hunstanton, Norfolk PE36 5LQ. The papers have been catalogued and are divided into four files: biographical and personal (AB); government involvement (AG); politics (AP); and Zionism (AZ).

The AB file includes typed portions of Bolitho's biography; papers relating to Mond's various honours (including the Licence to bear Supporters' Arms 19 Nov 1910); documents relating to his swearing-in as Minister of Health 5 April 1921; and a notebook with quotations from his writings and sayings.

The AG file contains the few surviving documents relating to his time as Commissioner of Works and Minister of Health. Most of these surviving papers are Cabinet memoranda including several written by Mond on disability pensions and outdoor relief Nov 1921, on the Economy Bill May 1922, on the Increase of Rent Act, on the Local Authorities (Financial Provisions) Bill Oct 1922, on National Health Insurance May 1921–March 1922, and on Housing Aug 1922. There are also miscellaneous Cabinet papers 1921–22 relating to House of Lords reform, the Poplar Board of Guardians, unemployment and the National Health Insurance Bill 1922.

The AP file has been divided into 5 sections: free trade, with correspondence to Austen Chamberlain and Baldwin and others, press cuttings and speeches; constituency work, with correspondence with Lloyd George, Churchill, and Birkenhead, speeches and notes; private correspondence relating to politics, including correspondence with Lloyd George and Asquith Dec 1912–Aug 1914; general strike; and Liberal land policy, Mond's opposition and defection from the Liberal Party, with copies of speeches, notes, reports, and memoranda, mostly for 1925.

The AZ file includes correspondence with Lloyd George on the delay in settling the future of Palestine 1920; with Herbert Samuel on the need to lessen military expenditure so that the British taxpayer would be less concerned about the burden of Palestine 1921, and about the desirability of increasing Jewish immigration 1923; and with Lord Beaverbrook about the British presence in Palestine 1929. There are also addresses presented to Mond in Palestine.

There is much correspondence with Mond in the Weizmann Archives, Israel.

Papers relating to Mond's business interests survive among the archives of Imperial Chemical Industries. W. J. Reader in *Imperial Chemicals Industries. A History*, 1, *The Forerunners 1870–1926* (Oxford UP

1970), was given free access to all the documents available but he stated, in his bibliography: 'These archives are part of the working records of the business and the Company does not provide for general public access' (p. 524).

G. M. Bayliss, 'The Outsider: Aspects of the Political Career of Alfred Mond, 1st Lord Melchett (1868–1930)' (PhD thesis, University of Wales 1969), incorporates material from a wide range of sources; but it does not draw on the family papers or ICI archives.

The brief biography by Peter Morris in *DBB*, 4, 270–80, utilises ICI records but not family papers. The relevant chapters of Jean Goodman, *The Mond Legacy: A Family Saga* (Weidenfeld and Nicolson 1982) are based on the papers in Lord Melchett's possession as well as material in the ICI Millbank and Runcorn archives. A particularly controversial phase of Mond's ministerial career is recounted in Noreen Branson, *Poplarism, 1919–1925: George Lansbury and the Councillors' Revolt* (Lawrence and Wishart 1979).

SIR BOLTON MEREDITH EYRES-MONSELL, 1st VISCOUNT MONSELL (1881–1969)

Bolton Eyres-Monsell was Conservative MP for Worcestershire (South or Evesham) 1910–35. He was Civil Lord of the Admiralty April 1921–Oct 1922, Parliamentary and Financial Secretary to the Admiralty 1922–May 1923, Parliamentary Secretary to the Treasury July 1923–Jan 1924, Nov 1924–June 1929 and Sept-Nov 1931, and First Lord of the Admiralty 1931–June 1936. He was created GBE in 1929, and Viscount Monsell in 1935.

Seven boxes of Monsell's papers are in the possession of his widow, Lady Monsell. We have not been able to examine these papers which we understand are kept in Lady Monsell's bank.

Some correspondence 1932–34 with Sir Roger Keyes is in the PRO at ADM 230; NRA 32904.

THE HON EDWIN SAMUEL MONTAGU (1879–1924)

Edwin Montagu was Liberal MP for Cambridgeshire (Chesterton; Cambridgeshire from 1918) 1906–22. He was Parliamentary Under-Secretary of State for India Feb 1910–Feb 1914, Financial Secretary to the Treasury 1914–Feb 1915 and May 1915–July 1916, Chancellor of the Duchy of Lancaster Feb-May 1915 and Jan-July 1916, Minister of Munitions July-Dec 1916, and Secretary of State for India July 1917–March 1922.

Twenty-nine boxes of Montagu's papers have been deposited in the Trinity College Library, Cambridge (Montagu papers). They have been catalogued and indexed and are available for research.

Most of the papers in Trinity College relate to Montagu's work at the India Office 1910–14 and 1917–22. There is correspondence with the various governors in India 1913–14, with the Viceroy 1913, and with Lord Crewe 1913–14, and also about the organisation of the Secretary of State's Council 1911–13. Montagu made a tour of India in 1912–13 and both the manuscript and typed copy of the diary he kept then have survived. Extracts from this diary and a memoir were published by his nephew, Sir David Waley, in *Edwin Montagu: A memoir and an account of his visits to India* (Asia Printing House, Bombay 1964). From his term of office as Secretary of State several files have survived, especially on the post-war settlement with Turkey 1918–22. There is a file on the Amritsar massacre and on the problem of the Indians in Africa (including some correspondence with Churchill). There is correspondence with Lord Curzon 1917–22 and Austen Chamberlain 1917–20. A file of correspondence and press cuttings on Montagu's resignation has also survived. In 1917–18, after his announcement that the ultimate aim of British policy in India was the 'progressive realization of responsible government', Montagu made a second tour of India and again kept a diary which he dictated and sent to Lloyd George to give him some understanding of Indian problems. This diary has also survived; it was edited by Montagu's widow, the Hon Venetia Montagu, *An Indian Diary* (Heinemann 1930).

Some of Montagu's interest in non-Indian events is represented in this collection: there are papers from the Cabinet Committee on Food Supplies 1914–16, on Ireland 1914–21 (including a note by Montagu on the secret negotiations of June-July 1914), the problems of reconstruction March-July 1917, and correspondence with Lewis Harcourt and F. E. Smith on ministerial salaries 1915–16. There are memoranda and copies of letters sent to Lloyd George 1917–22 and a note by Montagu written 9 Dec 1916 on the fall of Asquith's government. Montagu was Asquith's parliamentary private secretary from 1906–10 and there is some correspondence with Asquith 1904–17, and notes for Asquith's 1908 Budget speech and various 1909 speeches. Montagu's own notes for the 1912 and 1913 Budgets have also survived.

The collection also includes miscellaneous correspondence 1904–22 arranged alphabetically, including correspondence with Lord Crewe 1911–19, and Sir Edward Grey 1909–16. There are eight files of letters from Montagu to his parents, mainly to his mother 1890s-1918. The minute book of the Cambridge University Liberal Club Nov 1886–Dec 1896 is to be found in the collection. There are also some of Venetia Montagu's papers: a diary kept on a tour of Russia and the Middle East, miscellaneous letters, and letters of condolence on Montagu's death.

The long series of letters 1910–15 from Asquith to Mrs Montagu, then Venetia Stanley, is in the possession of her granddaughter, Miss Anna Gendel. As a description both of Cabinet meetings and private discussions between Asquith and his colleagues (some of them were actually written during Cabinet meetings), the letters are an invaluable historical source. They are quoted frequently in Roy Jenkins, *Asquith* (Collins 1964) and published almost in their entirety in the second edition of Michael and Eleanor Brock (eds), *H. H. Asquith: Letters to Venetia Stanley* (Oxford UP 1982, 2nd ed 1985).

The Oriental and India Office Collections, British Library has a further collection of Montagu's papers – 44 volumes of correspondence during his period as Secretary of State for India – deposited by his sister in 1955 (MSS Eur D 523; NRA 20541). There are 11 volumes of correspondence 1917–21 between Montagu and Lord Chelmsford, the Viceroy from 1916–21, and three volumes 1921–22 between Montagu and Lord Reading, Chelmsford's successor. There are six volumes of correspondence 1917–22 between Montagu and Lord Willingdon, then Governor of Bombay and later of Madras, five volumes of correspondence 1918–22 with Lord Lloyd, Governor of Bombay, and six volumes of correspondence 1917–22 with the then Earl of Ronaldshay (later 2nd Marquess of Zetland), Governor of Bengal. In addition the material in the India Office Collection includes various addresses presented in India, three volumes of Montagu's diary for his 1912–13 visit to India, appendices to the diary for his 1918 visit, two scrapbooks from the 1918 visit, and a signed copy of the Montagu-Chelmsford Report.

Naomi B. Levine, *Politics, Religion and Love: The Story of H. H. Asquith, Venetia Stanley and Edwin Montagu* (New York UP 1991) examines Montagu's life. Professor Eugene C. Black of Brandeis University is writing a new biography.

JOHN MORLEY, VISCOUNT MORLEY OF BLACKBURN (1838–1923)

John Morley was Liberal MP for Newcastle-upon-Tyne 1883–95, and Montrose Burghs 1896–1908. He was Chief Secretary for Ireland Feb-Aug 1886 and Aug 1892–July 1895, Secretary of State for India Dec 1905–Nov 1910 and March-May 1911, and Lord President of the Council Nov 1910–Aug 1914. He was created Viscount Morley of Blackburn in 1908.

Sixty-seven volumes of Morley's papers are held in the Oriental and India Office Collections, British Library (MSS Eur D 573; NRA 10408) having been presented by his biographer F. W. Hirst at various dates between 1933 and 1947. They are almost entirely related to Morley's tenure of the India Office. They also include papers found at the National Liberal Club which were possibly left there by Hirst or Sir

Gilbert Jackson, and which were added to the India Office collection in 1960.

The papers mainly consist of bound volumes of correspondence between Morley and Lord Minto, the Viceroy. There are five volumes of letters from Morley to Minto 1905-10, and 19 volumes of letters from Minto to Morley for the same period. There are two volumes of correspondence March-May 1911 between Morley and Lord Hardinge, who succeeded Lord Minto. As well as correspondence, these volumes include notes of conversations and meetings, and various memoranda which were originally enclosed with the letters. In addition there are five volumes of telegrams exchanged between the Secretaries of State and the Viceroys 1903-10. There are many subject files on various topics of Morley's administration: for example, three files about reforms of the Indian Council 1907-09; a file on Mohammedan representation 1906-09; files on army administration; and files on the Kitchener-Curzon controversy. There is a file of papers relating to Lord Curzon, ranging from his views on Tibet, a 1906-09 Everest expedition, and on the Clive Memorial. There are eight volumes of correspondence between Morley and the Governor of Bombay, Sir George Clarke, later Lord Sydenham.

In addition to this Indian material, the collection contains a small amount of Morley's private correspondence. There are 18 letters from Lord Rosebery 1905-09, and copies of several letters from Andrew Carnegie (the originals were returned by Hirst to Mrs Carnegie in 1927; they are now in the Library of Congress, Washington, DC; a microfilm of the Carnegie-Morley correspondence 1883-1919 is available in the Bodleian Library, MS FILM 569). The collection also includes a few of Hirst's own papers – lectures on Morley, and letters collected by Hirst for his unfinished biography. There are also lists of speeches and correspondence that are no longer included in this collection.

It is known that Morley destroyed many of his papers. In discussing the fate of W. E. Gladstone's papers, Morley had told Lord Rendel in Jan 1888 that it was 'better all such papers should be destroyed. They cannot be published for thirty or forty years after death, and then can do no real good...'. Rendel recorded that Morley had 'made a codicil to his will ordering his own papers to be destroyed.' (F. E. Hamer, ed, *The Personal Papers of Lord Rendel*, Ernest Benn 1931, p. 180). In conversation with F. W. Hirst on 22 Sept 1899, Morley opined that he would probably write a better biography of Gladstone if all of the Gladstone papers were burnt. 'Yet the thought rather staggered him, and he said he would except his own diary from the flames!' (Frances W. Hirst *In the Golden Days*, Muller 1947, p. 189). Morley told Edwin Montagu in 1910: 'I have not a large collection of papers. Everything gets torn up in its turn' (Memo by Montagu, 3 Nov 1910, Montagu

MSS). Nevertheless, a fairly substantial collection of papers was burnt immediately after his death in 1923 by his sister Grace, in apparent accordance with his wishes, until Hirst intervened. This destruction may well have included most of his 20th century papers, which are now largely missing.

What survived was left to 'the full discretion' of his nephew, Guy Morley, with the proviso that his executors should neither help nor encourage any memoir, nor allow the papers to be used for any biography of Morley or his friends. Nonetheless, Morley expected that this proviso would be ignored, and was favourably disposed to the declared intention of F. W. Hirst to write a biography. Encouraged by the rest of his family, including Lady Morley, Guy Morley passed the papers on to Hirst, a longstanding friend and admirer, and these were the major source for his *Early Life and Letters of John Morley* (2 vols, Macmillan 1927), the first stage of an uncompleted and increasingly complicated study.

With the exception of the predominantly Indian material already cited, the papers concerning Morley's later life remained in Hirst's hands until his death in 1953. Unable to complete his intended biography in old age, he asked his godson, the late Lord Boyle, to undertake the task, with the proviso that the papers be left in the custody of Mr A. F. Thompson at Wadham College, Oxford, for eventual disposal in a major library, preferably the Bodleian. Because of other commitments, Lord Boyle was not able to complete the biography, and the process of retrieving (and adding to) the collection at Wadham has taken more than 25 years. It is not yet possible to provide access to the enlarged archive, but Mr Thompson is empowered to attempt to answer scholarly enquiries so far as he can from material still largely uncatalogued. In due course the archive will be transferred to the Bodleian, where it is possible that certain restrictions imposed both by Hirst and the Morley family will be put in place.

Apart from trivia, the collection at Wadham consists mainly of material relating to Morley's activities between the 1870s and the end of the century. There is extensive correspondence, notably with Joseph Chamberlain and Sir William Harcourt. More recently, a few sadly mutilated diaries, often cryptic on literary matters as well as political, have been recovered. The most useful of these have been published as Appendix I, 1892–94 in H. C. G. Matthew (ed), *The Gladstone Diaries* (Clarendon Press, Oxford 1994), vol 13. However, many gaps remain, and for the 20th century there is virtually nothing, apart from the India Office papers. It seems probable that Morley destroyed anything he regarded as sensitive concerning his later life and that on his death his sister Grace completed the process.

In 1972, one volume of papers was deposited in the Bodleian Library by the 2nd Viscount Harcourt (MS Harcourt dep 37; NRA 3679). The volume consists of miscellaneous papers and correspondence 1888–1904, including letters and memoranda relating to the Royal Grants Commission 1888–92, and letters from Earl Spencer 1895. A second batch of letters 1883–98 was acquired with the second acquisition of Harcourt papers in 1984 (MS Harcourt dep adds 14, fols 1–42).

The British Library purchased 36 letters to Morley from Churchill 1902–14 in 1979 (Add MS 60391AA). There are also papers relating to Morley's life of Gladstone in the British Library (Add MSS 56453). Notes relating to his life of Cobden are in the West Sussex RO (Cobden 307; NRA 10616).

Morley's library of c.11,000 volumes is held at Ashburne Hall, Manchester University. The collection includes a commonplace book containing quotations, extracts and thoughts on politics, literature, history, philosophy, etc. (1 volume). Trinity College Library, Dublin has a small collection of letters from Morley to John Dillon.

On 18 Dec 1986 Sotheby's offered for sale a collection of approximately 190 letters and memoranda from Edward Grey to Morley Dec 1905–June 1910. We do not know the provenance or fate of this collection.

There are some Foreign Office papers in the PRO at FO 800/628–61.

Many of Morley's papers were published both by Morley himself and later historians. His *Recollections* (2 vols, Macmillan 1917) include much of his correspondence with Lord Minto. Morley also arranged to publish posthumously his *Memorandum on Resignation: August 1914* (Macmillan 1928). Morley was a prolific correspondent and many of his letters can be found in other collections. A guide to the whereabouts of many of them is given in the bibliography of D. A. Hamer, *John Morley: Liberal Intellectual in Politics* (Clarendon Press, Oxford 1968). There is valuable commentary in F. W. Hirst, *In the Golden Days* (Frederick Muller 1947), and, for his literary activities, in John Gross, *The Rise and Fall of the Man of Letters* (Weidenfeld & Nicolson 1969).

There are useful monographs by Stephen E. Koss, *John Morley and the India Office 1905–1910* (Yale UP, New Haven 1969), and Stanley Wolpert, *Morley and India 1906–1910* (University of California Press, Berkeley and Los Angeles 1967). Sources relating to Morley's period as Secretary of State for India are usefully listed in Arnold P. Zaminsky, *The India Office, 1880–1910* (Greenwood Press, New York 1986).

HERBERT STANLEY MORRISON, BARON MORRISON OF LAMBETH (1888–1965)

Herbert Morrison was Labour MP for Hackney (South) 1923–24, 1929–31 and 1935–45, Lewisham (East) 1945–50 and Lewisham (South) 1950–

59. He was Minister of Transport June 1929–Aug 1931, Minister of Supply May-Oct 1940, Secretary of State for Home Affairs and Home Security 1940–May 1945, Lord President of the Council July 1945– March 1951, and Secretary of State for Foreign Affairs March-Oct 1951. He was created Baron Morrison of Lambeth (a life peerage) in 1959.

A small suitcase of papers formerly in the possession of Morrison's joint literary executor, Sir Norman Chester, is now in the Nuffield College Library. About 20 box-files of papers had been burned when Lord and Lady Morrison moved house in 1960.

The surviving collection has been sorted into five small boxes. It contains several typed draft chapters of Morrison's memoir, *Herbert Morrison: an Autobiography* (Odhams 1960) some of which contain manuscript amendments and all of which seem to contain much that was not used in the published volume. The drafts are entitled 'Personalities in Churchill's War Cabinet' (84pp), 'The Chamberlain Government' (24pp), 'On the Way to World War Again' (41pp), 'Ministry of Transport' (92pp), 'J. R. MacDonald' (93pp), and 'The General Strike' (54pp). There are press cuttings on reactions to the memoirs; about his appointment as President of the British Board of Film Censors May 1960; as well as other miscellaneous press cuttings 1951–64; and a file of cartoons collected 1949–50. There is also a small collection of photos.

The few pamphlets include Morrison's election addresses for the 1920 London County Council by-election (he was a member of the LCC 1922–45) and for the 1945 general election. There is also a transcript of an interview given to Derek Cooper in 1962 in which Morrison was asked biographical and political questions. In addition there is a small collection of correspondence including letters of congratulation for various speeches etc., from Churchill 1940–45. There is a memo of a discussion with Clement Attlee, Hugh Dalton, and Ernest Bevin on the post-war reorganisation of industry. There is correspondence with Attlee in 1947 on Morrison's illness and the resulting transfer of responsibility for economic affairs to Sir Stafford Cripps. There is also correspondence with Cripps on the desirability of Attlee's continuing as Prime Minister (summer 1947). There is a memo of a meeting with Attlee in April 1951 on Nye Bevan's resignation, and some correspondence on the timing of the 1951 general election. There is very little material for the period 1951–65. All of this material, as well as interviews with 300 people, was used for *Herbert Morrison: Portrait of a Politician* (Weidenfeld & Nicolson 1973) by Bernard Donoughue and G. W. Jones. The papers collected for this biography are now in the BLPES (NRA 30242).

Some Private Office papers as Lord President are available in the PRO at CAB 124. Roger Bullen and M. E. Pelly (eds), *Documents on*

British Policy Overseas (HMSO 1986), series II, vol I, draws on the Morrison papers as well as material in the relevant Foreign Office and Cabinet Office files.

A new biography by Dr John Rowett of Brasenose College, Oxford, is in preparation. It is foreshadowed in *Blackwell*, 310–14.

Morrison's period as Minister of Transport is the subject of Chapter 12 of William Plowden's *The Motor Car and Politics 1896–1970* (Bodley Head 1971). Lady Morrison recalls her life with Morrison in *Memories of a Marriage* (Frederick Muller 1977).

WILLIAM SHEPHERD MORRISON, 1st VISCOUNT DUNROSSIL (1893–1961)

William ('Shakes') Morrison was Conservative MP for Gloucestershire (Cirencester and Tewkesbury) 1929–59. He was Financial Secretary to the Treasury Nov 1935–Oct 1936, Minister of Agriculture and Fisheries 1936–Jan 1939, Chancellor of the Duchy of Lancaster 1939–April 1940, Minister of Food Sept 1939–April 1940, Postmaster-General 1940–Dec 1942, and Minister of Town and Country Planning 1942–Aug 1945. He was created GCMG in 1959, and Viscount Dunrossil in 1959.

Morrison's son, the 2nd Viscount Dunrossil, informed us that his father did not keep records for posterity, and that only personal or private papers, which are not available to researchers, have survived.

There are no Dunrossil papers relating to his term as Governor-General of Australia 1960–61 in the National Library of Australia or the Australian Archives. The Conservative Party Archives in the Bodleian Library should be consulted for earlier phases of his career. Private Office papers of the Minister of Food are in the PRO at MAF 286.

A brief biography of Morrison by Sir David Smith will appear in John Ritchie (ed), *Australian Dictionary of Biography*, 14 (Melbourne UP).

SIR OSWALD ERNALD MOSLEY, 6th Bt (1896–1980)

Oswald Mosley was Conservative MP for Middlesex (Harrow) 1918–22, Independent MP for Middlesex (Harrow) 1922–24, and Labour MP for Smethwick 1926–31. He was Chancellor of the Duchy of Lancaster June 1929–May 1930. He succeeded his father as 6th baronet in 1928.

In *My Life* (Nelson 1968) Sir Oswald said that most of his earlier papers were lost during the Second World War and that he wrote the book mostly from memory. There is a valuable bibliographical essay with details on the private and official papers then available in Robert

Skidelsky, *Oswald Mosley* (Macmillan 1975). Further details were provided in the second edition of Skidelsky's book in 1981.

Mosley's son, Lord Ravensdale (who writes under the name Nicholas Mosley), advised us that Mosley's surviving papers, previously in the possession of his widow, Lady (Diana) Mosley, have been deposited in the Birmingham University Library. They are not available for consultation while they are being listed.

In 1983, more than 100 Home Office files on Mosley and the British Union of Fascists were opened at the PRO (HO 45, 144, 283). The files, documenting the period 1934–38, deal with financial accounts, supporters, and alleged supporters (including Mussolini, and Lords Rothermere and Nuffield) and internal party documents. Material relating to the detention of Mosley in the Second World War is in HO 283. Richard Thurlow's book *Fascism in Britain: A History 1918–1985* (Basil Blackwell, Oxford 1987), which centres on Mosley and the BUF, makes use of these papers. The third edition (1990) of Skidelsky's biography also discusses the papers that were released in 1983.

There is a thorough examination of the documents in HO 144 in Paul Cohen, 'The Police, the Home Office and Surveillance of the British Union of Fascists', *Intelligence and National Security*, 1, 3, Sept 1986, 416–34, and in Stephen Cullen, 'Political Violence: The Case of the British Union of Fascists', *Journal of Contemporary History*, 28/2, April 1993, 245–67.

Selected documents from the PRO MEPO 2 collection consisting of Metropolitan Police files on political organisations, including the BUF, have been microfilmed, *Protest Movements, Civil Disorder and the Police in Inter-War Britain* (Harvester Microfilm, Brighton 1982). The files of the BUF form the bulk of the collection.

There is a very small collection of material relating to Mosley in the William Sabine and Christopher Temple Emmet Collections at the Hoover Institution on War, Revolution and Peace.

D. S. Lewis, *Illusions of Grandeur: Mosley, Fascism and British Society, 1931–81* (Manchester UP 1987) p. 270, refers to a collection of press cuttings and pamphlets with the Mosley Secretariat, London and to Mr J. Hamm 'in charge of the remnants of Mosley's post-war political party'. With the death of the secretary in May 1992, the Secretariat ceased to exist; and its papers passed into the care of the 'Friends of Oswald Mosley' which publishes a newsletter, *Comrade*, about the British Union of Fascists. It can be contacted through Mr John Christian at 101 Orwell Court, Pownall Rd, London E8 4PP.

Nicholas Mosley's *Rules of the Game: Sir Oswald and Lady Cynthia Mosley 1896–1933* (Secker & Warburg 1982) and *Beyond the Pale: Sir Oswald Mosley and Family 1933–1980* (Secker & Warburg 1983) used his father's papers placed at his disposal by his step-mother Lady Mosley. His autobiography, *Efforts at Truth* (Secker & Warburg 1994) reflects on his relationship with his father after 1945. Lady Mosley discussed her life in *A Life of Contrasts: The Autobiography of Diana Mosley* (Hamish Hamilton 1977). Her *Loved Ones: Pen Portraits* (Sidgwick and Jackson 1985) has a chapter on her husband.

A long unpublished manuscript on Mosley and fascism by Richard R. Bellamy (a former national inspector of the BUF) is in the Sheffield University Library (Bellamy MS). This is probably the same official history of the BUF written by Bellamy in 1939, a copy of which is held by the Friends of Oswald Mosley (Roger Griffen, *Fascism*, Oxford UP 1995, p. 178). Several other biographies written by supporters of Mosley include some useful information on him and the BUF: A. K. Chesterton, *Oswald Mosley: Portrait of a Leader* (Action Press 1937), and James Drennan (a pen-name for W. E. D. Allen, a former Conservative/Ulster Unionist MP), *BUF, Oswald Mosley and British Fascism* (Murray 1934).

The annotated bibliography by Philip Rees, *Fascism in Britain* (Harvester Press, Brighton 1979) remains useful.

ROBERT MUNRO, BARON ALNESS (1868–1955)

Robert Munro was Liberal MP for the Wick Burghs 1910–18, and Coalition Liberal MP for Roxburghshire and Selkirkshire 1918–22. He was Lord Advocate Oct 1913–Dec 1916, and Secretary for Scotland 1916–Oct 1922. He took the judicial title of Lord Alness in 1922, and was created Baron Alness in 1934, and GBE in 1946.

His widow knew of no papers relating to her husband's political career. His book, *Looking Back: Fugitive Writings and Sayings* (Thomas Nelson 1930), contains some articles previously printed elsewhere, his non-political speeches as Secretary for Scotland, and some of his speeches after he became a judge.

Private Office papers relating to Munro's period at the Scottish Office are dispersed through the files of the five main Scottish Office departments held at the SRO.

J. W. R. Mitchell, 'The emergence of Modern Scottish central administration 1885–1939 (DPhil, Oxford University 1987) has relevant material.

ANDREW GRAHAM MURRAY, VISCOUNT DUNEDIN (1849–1942)

Andrew Murray was Conservative MP for Bute 1891–1905. He was Solicitor-General for Scotland Oct 1891–Aug 1892 and July 1895–May 1896, Lord Advocate 1896–Oct 1903, and Secretary for Scotland 1903–Feb 1905. He was created Baron Dunedin in 1905, KCVO in 1908, GCVO in 1923, and Viscount Dunedin in 1926.

The bulk of Murray's estate was left by his second wife to his grand-daughter, Mrs G. R. Shaw, but she did not know of the existence of any papers. Mrs Shaw informed us that her grandfather was writing his memoirs but these could not be found. Murray's family had close ties with the Edinburgh law firm of Tods, Murray and Jamieson but they did not have any of his papers.

Twenty-two volumes of Murray's papers as Chairman of the Irish Free State Compensation Committee 1925–26 are available in the PRO (CO 905/17, 18). The papers include registers of claims for compensation as well as the committee's correspondence.

The NLS has some miscellaneous Murray papers in the collections of his friends, including six letters to Viscount Haldane 1915–29 (Haldane Papers); three letters and a note to the Library's first Librarian, W. K. Dickson 1924–34 (MS 9657); and single letters to Sir Henry Craik 1903 (MS 7175), and to his *DNB* biographer Lord Macmillan 1941 (MS 25265, Macmillan Papers).

Private Office papers relating to Murray's period at the Scottish Office are dispersed through the files of the five main Scottish Office departments held at the SRO.

Reference should be made to J. W. R. Mitchell, 'The emergence of Modern Scottish central administration 1885–1939' (DPhil, Oxford University 1987). There is a brief entry by Lord Macmillan in *DNB 1941–1950*, 609–11.

HARRY LOUIS NATHAN, 1st BARON NATHAN (1889–1963)

Colonel Harry Nathan was Liberal MP for Bethnal Green (North-East) 1929–35, and Labour MP for Wandsworth (Central) 1937–40. He was Parliamentary Under-Secretary of State for War Aug 1945–Oct 1946, and Minister of Civil Aviation 1946–May 1948. He was created Baron Nathan in 1940.

In our first edition we reported that Nathan's papers were in the possession of his son, the 2nd Lord Nathan, but were not available for research. The papers included several boxes of press cuttings 1924–39 and 1945–57, an album of Nathan's speeches and articles, a box of letters 1914–17 between Nathan and his parents, and seven boxes of correspondence. The papers were used by H. Montgomery Hyde in his biography of Nathan, *Strong for Service: the Life of Lord Nathan of Churt* (W. H. Allen 1968).

Lord Nathan now advises that he has no papers relating to his father. Nathan's daughter, Joyce, Lady Waley-Cohen, advised us that she does not know what happened to these papers.

MICHAEL ANTONY CRISTOBAL NOBLE, BARON GLENKINGLAS (1913–1984)

Michael Noble was Conservative MP for Argyllshire 1958–74. He was Secretary of State for Scotland July 1962–Oct 1964, President of the Board of Trade June-Oct 1970, and Minister for Trade 1970–Nov 1972. He was created Baron Glenkinglas (a life peerage) in 1974.

Noble's widow, Lady Glenkinglas, advised us that she did not have any papers relating to her husband's public life. His nephew, Sir Iain Noble Bt, also did not know of any papers.

Private Office papers relating to Noble's period at the Scottish Office are dispersed through the files of the five main Scottish Office departments held at the SRO.

Noble's brother, Sir Andrew Noble's family history, *History of the Nobles of Ardmore and of Ardkinglas* (privately printed 1971), covers 500 years, and only has generally available information on Noble.

There is a brief account of Noble's period at the Scottish Office in *Secretaries of State for Scotland*, 156–65.

SIR SYDNEY HALDANE OLIVIER, BARON OLIVIER (1859–1943)

Sydney Olivier was created KCMG in 1907, and Baron Olivier in 1924. He was Secretary of State for India Jan-Nov 1924.

A small collection of Olivier's papers is in the possession of his grandson, Dr R. B. O. Richards. These were used in Francis Lee, *Fabianism and Colonialism: The Life and Political Thought of Lord Sydney Olivier* (Defiant Books 1988). They are temporarily deposited at Rhodes House Library, but cannot at present normally be made available for research (NRA 14913).

The only papers to have survived concerning Olivier's official career, both as a civil servant and as Secretary of State for India, are the official letters of appointment and commission, some letters 1930–38 on trade unionism and the fixing of a minimum wage in the Colonies, and some printed official reports. However, the collection does reflect some of Olivier's activities in the Fabian Society (he was honorary secretary 1886–89, a very active member and a friend of George Bernard Shaw, Graham Wallas, and Sidney Webb). There is a note by Olivier on the origin and early history of the Society (written in 1889) and correspondence 1906–07 with Edward R. Pease, one of the founders of the society and secretary for 15 years. There are also copies of Fabian articles and pamphlets with which Olivier was concerned, and draft chapter headings 1939 for *The Dual Ethic in Empire*, a book which Olivier never completed. The collection also includes Olivier's account books

1909–38, some letters to his wife 1894–98, his wife's diaries and note-books 1908–13, 1929, 1931–33, 1935–39, and 1940–48, miscellaneous correspondence 1935–45 including letters from Graham Wallas and Leonard and Virginia Woolf, various photos, press cuttings, and some speech notes. Lady Olivier's diaries and her husband's letters to her have many observations on Olivier's civil service career, especially in British Honduras and the West Indies.

There are also several papers connected with the publication of Lady Olivier's memoir: Margaret Olivier, *Sydney Olivier: Letters and Selected Writings* (George Allen & Unwin 1948). The book includes a 20–page autobiographical fragment by Olivier covering his life to 1907, several articles by him, a short biography by his widow, and recollections by George Bernard Shaw. Lady Olivier's biography quotes from many letters, both from and to her husband. The manuscript collection includes these original letters or photocopies of them, the typescript of various sections of the book, and the proofs and correspondence about its publication.

There is also some Olivier material in the Charles Greenidge collection at Rhodes House Library (MSS Brit Emp s 285). Boxes 31–3 of this collection contain draft versions of *The Dual Ethic of Empire* which Lady Olivier had sent to Greenidge with a view to possible publication.

Printed copies of Olivier's correspondence with the Viceroy of India, Lord Reading, are in the Reading collection at the Oriental and India Office Collections, British Library (MSS Eur E 238/7). Typescript copies of his correspondence with Lord Lytton, Gover-nor of Bengal, are in the Lytton collection (MSS Eur F 160/8,11), and with the two Governors of Madras: Lord Willingdon in the Willingdon collection (MSS Eur F 93/5), and with Lord Goschen in the Goschen collection (MSS Eur D 595/2), also in the India Office Collection.

Sarah Howard provides a short, useful biography in *MBR*, 3, 622–6, and notes that other Olivier material can be found in the George Bernard Shaw Papers, British Library; the Sidney and Beatrice Webb (Passfield) Papers, London School of Economics Library; and the Fabian Society Archive, Nuffield College, Oxford. The entry on Olivier by John Saville in *DLB*, VIII, 181–7, provides a comprehen-sive list of Olivier's own writings as well as theses and other sources on him.

Brief reference to Olivier's role in Indian affairs is made in Robin Moore, *The Crisis of Indian Unity, 1917–1940* (Clarendon Press, Oxford 1974). There is a short sketch of Olivier's life to 1908, quoting from family papers, in the introduction to Pippa Harris (ed), *Song of Love: The Letters of Rupert Brooke and Noel Olivier 1909–1915* (Bloomsbury 1991).

RICHARD WILLIAM ALAN ONSLOW, 10th Bt, 5th EARL OF ONSLOW (1876–1945)

Richard Onslow was known as Viscount Cranley from 1876 until he succeeded his father as 5th Earl of Onslow and 10th baronet in 1911. He was created GBE in 1938. He was Civil Lord of the Admiralty Oct 1920–April 1921, Parliamentary Secretary to the Ministry of Agriculture April 1921, Parliamentary Secretary to the Ministry of Health April 1921–May 1923, Parliamentary Secretary to the Board of Education 1923–Jan 1924, Under-Secretary of State for War Nov 1924–Dec 1928, and Paymaster-General 1928–June 1929.

A small collection of Onslow's papers was deposited in the Guildford Muniment Room at the Surrey RO in 1972 by Jo, Dowager Countess of Onslow, widow of the 6th Earl (173; NRA 1088). There are six bound volumes of 'Private Papers' 1899–1913, 12 volumes of press cuttings, and a nine-volume typed history of the family. A further volume of reminiscences is still in the possession of the family but it is not available for research.

The 'Private Papers' are almost all from the period when Onslow was in the diplomatic service 1901–11, and when he was private secretary to Sir Edward Grey and to Sir Arthur Nicolson in the Foreign Office 1911–13. Possibly of greatest interest for the earlier period are Onslow's letters from his father Feb 1904–March 1906 describing the British political situation. From the Foreign Office period there are letters from British diplomats abroad and copies of Onslow's memoranda to Sir Arthur Nicolson on Foreign Office organisation. There are also several memoranda on whether Onslow should be allowed to vote in the House of Lords and still continue to work as a civil servant (he was allowed to vote but not to speak in debates).

The press cuttings, which are arranged chronologically, are very full; they cover national and political activities as well as social and personal events. There are two volumes of cuttings on the Boer War and one volume on the 4th Earl's death and funeral.

The nine volumes of family history were completed by Onslow with the help of several researchers in 1925. In the introduction he says that 'it embodies every scrap of information I can find relating to any member of the Onslow family'. It includes an unfinished biography of Onslow's father by Reginald Lucas. Three volumes describe in great detail Onslow's own life up to when he became a Civil Lord.

Some of these papers are quoted in Onslow's memoirs, *Sixty-three Years* (Hutchinson 1944).

The Codrington Library, All Souls College, Oxford, holds two volumes of correspondence between Onslow and Sir Dougal Malcolm 1903–13. The letters concentrate on political and international affairs.

WILLIAM HILLIER ONSLOW, 9th Bt, 4th EARL OF ONSLOW (1853–1911)

William Onslow succeeded his great-uncle as 4th Earl of Onslow and 9th baronet in 1870. He was created KCMG in 1887, and GCMG in 1889. He was Under-Secretary of State for the Colonies Feb 1887–Feb 1888 and Nov 1900–May 1903, Parliamentary Secretary to the Board of Trade Feb-Dec 1888, Under Secretary of State for India July 1895–Nov 1900, and President of the Board of Agriculture and Fisheries May 1903–March 1905.

Jo, Dowager Countess of Onslow, widow of the 6th Earl, deposited a small collection of Onslow's papers in the Guildford Muniment Room at the Surrey RO in 1972 (173). A list of the papers is available (NRA 1088).

There are 15 bound volumes entitled 'Private Papers' 1887–1911, 13 volumes of diaries, some travel journals, and three volumes of press cuttings 1889–1911. The latter, arranged chronologically, are very full; they range from political speeches to kennel records. The diaries cover the years 1869–92 (volumes for 1875–77, 1880–82, 1886–88 and 1890–91 are missing). They mainly record details of Onslow's travels and hunting; in some volumes there are only a few entries. The travel journals mainly date from the 1880s and cover Onslow's journeys in America, India, Switzerland, and elsewhere.

The volumes of 'Private Papers' include a large number of letters, as well as copies of bills, a few Cabinet memoranda, and some departmental papers. Onslow's early work at the Colonial Office is represented by papers on the Sugar Bounties Conference, and on proposals for an Australian federation. There is a gap in the papers between 1888–92, when Onslow was Governor of New Zealand. Only a copy of Onslow's letter to Queen Victoria on his return 14 Aug 1892 has survived. Throughout the volumes there is a great deal of material about smallholdings. There are several letters from Lord Salisbury, including some 1895–96 on Onslow's leadership of the Moderate Party on the London County Council. There are also many letters from Joseph Chamberlain both on Colonial Office business and on political affairs. At the time of the 1903 Cabinet split over Chamberlain's tariff reform proposals there are a good many letters from members of the Cabinet including one from Lord George Hamilton giving the reasons for his resignation. There are many departmental papers from Agriculture and Fisheries, e.g. on the North Sea fisheries. There is also a 15-page memo by Onslow on the political situation in St Petersburg and Berlin, written in Dec 1904, after a visit there.

Onslow was Chairman of Committees in the House of Lords 1905–10 and there are a number of papers on House of Lords' business, mainly of a routine and administrative nature, e.g. on the allocation of committee rooms. The three volumes for 1908–11 are particularly interesting for Onslow's part in the opposition to Lloyd George's 1909 Budget and to the 1911 Parliament Act. There are a great number of memoranda, minutes, drafts, and notes on reform of the House of Lords, including some papers of the House's own Select Committee (Feb-March 1908).

The papers of Onslow's son, the 5th Earl, also deposited in the Guildford Muniment Room (173) contain a nine-volume typed history of the family. Included in the history is an unfinished biography of Onslow by Reginald Lucas.

FRANCIS AUNGIER PAKENHAM, BARON PAKENHAM, 7th EARL OF LONGFORD (1905–)

Frank Pakenham was created Baron Pakenham in 1945, and KG in 1971. He succeeded his brother as 7th Earl of Longford in 1961. He was Parliamentary Under-Secretary of State for War Oct 1946–April 1947, Chancellor of the Duchy of Lancaster and Minister in Charge of the Administration of the British zone of Germany 1947–May 1948, Minister of Civil Aviation 1948–May 1951, First Lord of the Admiralty May-Oct 1951, Lord Privy Seal Oct 1964–Dec 1965 and April 1966–Jan 1968, and Secretary of State for the Colonies Dec 1965– April 1966.

Lord Longford informed us that the only papers he kept were his wife's letters to him. Lady Longford also kept her husband's letters to her, but none of these letters is available for research. They are used in *The Pebbled Shore: The Memoirs of Elizabeth Longford* (Weidenfeld & Nicolson 1986). Lady Longford refers to her diary, a collection of family photos, and the letters and papers of other family members and friends. Lady Longford also refers to the 'many letters' written to her by her husband but writes 'I must also thank him for having kept only a handful of mine ("I am not a man of property"), otherwise I should have been overwhelmed with material' (p. xii).

Twenty-two boxes of Lord Longford's papers and correspondence are in the possession of his son Thomas Pakenham, Tullynally Castle, Castlepollard, Co Westmeath, Northern Ireland. The papers 1970–85 principally concern penal reform. There is also correspondence, speech notes, articles, book reviews, and papers of a more general political nature, e.g. Criminal Justice Bills, nuclear disarmament, the Official Secrets Act, and the All-Party Penal Affairs Committee. There is also a typescript draft of Longford's *Diary of a Year* (1978). The collection has been listed by the PRONI (NRA 30594). Due to the confidential nature of much of the material, enquiries regarding access should be directed to Thomas Pakenham.

Records of the Leader of the House of Lords and Chief Whip 1945–94 are in the HLRO, but are subject to the 30 year rule (Longford was Leader of the House of Lords 1964–68).

According to Lord Longford, his three volumes of autobiography, *Born to Believe* (Jonathan Cape 1953), *Five Lives* (Hutchinson 1964), and *The Grain of Wheat* (Collins 1974), were written 'out of the top of my head' with no reference to any papers. *The Grain of Wheat* carries the story of his life forward from Oct 1964 to 1973 and quotes very occasionally from private correspondence. Lord Longford has recently produced a fourth volume of autobiography, *Avowed Intent* (Little, Brown 1994).

WILFRED PALING (1883–1971)

Wilfred Paling was Labour MP for West Riding of Yorkshire (Doncaster) 1922–31, West Riding of Yorkshire (Wentworth) 1933–50 and West Riding of Yorkshire (Dearne Valley) 1950–59. He was Parliamentary Secretary to the Ministry of Pensions Feb 1941–May 1945, Minister of Pensions Aug 1945–April 1947, and Postmaster-General 1947–Feb 1950.

Paling's brother, the late Mr W. T. Paling, informed us that shortly after Paling's death his family moved house and burnt what papers they found.

ROUNDELL CECIL PALMER, 3rd EARL OF SELBORNE (1887–1971)

Roundell Palmer was known as Viscount Wolmer 1895–1941. He was summoned to the House of Lords in 1941 in his father's barony of Selborne and succeeded his father as 3rd Earl of Selborne in 1942. He was Conservative MP for South-West Lancashire (Newton) 1910–18 and Hampshire (Aldershot) 1918–40. He was Parliamentary Secretary to the Board of Trade Oct 1922–Jan 1924, Assistant Postmaster-General Nov 1924–June 1929, and Minister of Economic Warfare Feb 1942–May 1945.

Selborne's political and ecclesiastical papers were deposited in the Bodleian Library in 1974 by his grandson, the 4th Earl of Selborne. They have been catalogued and listed (MSS Eng hist a 23–4; b 231–6; c 975–1026, 1030–1; d 442–57, 479–80; e 338; f 27-9; g 25–7). A further acquisition in 1979 was incorporated into the catalogue as well. The collection has been arranged by family correspondence and papers; general correspondence and papers; special correspondence and papers; correspondence and papers arranged by subject; and press cuttings.

Selborne's family correspondence includes many letters from his father 1901–41; his mother 1902–32; and his wife 1913–32. His special correspondence includes letters from Churchill 1911–55; Lord Eustace

Percy 1907–19; H. W. Dickinson 1906–10; and various members of the Cecil family.

As would be expected, there is a large amount of material relating to church affairs, especially the Anglican Church in India. The subject papers also include files on trade unions 1907–14; agricultural policy 1920s-30s; Post Office organisation 1926–32; and papers relating to the Ministry of Economic Warfare 1939–58. Selborne's general papers include notes and papers for a projected memoir (MS Eng hist c 1017). There are 16 volumes of press cuttings 1904–49.

Papers relating to Selborne's work at the Ministry of Economic Warfare, which are deposited with the Foreign and Common-wealth Office, form an integral part of the records of the Special Operations Executive and as such are closed indefinitely for research.

There is some of Selborne's correspondence in the Lambeth Palace Library (MS 2971).

Palmer family estate papers 1867–1983 are available at the Rural History Centre, Reading University (NRA 33526).

A biography of Selborne's brother Robert (who died of wounds received in action), *The Life of Robert Palmer, 1888–1916* (Hodder & Stoughton 1921), written by his aunt, Lady Laura Ridding, makes mention of Selborne.

WILLIAM WALDEGRAVE PALMER, 2nd EARL OF SELBORNE (1859–1942)

William Palmer was known as Viscount Wolmer from 1882 until he succeeded his father as 2nd Earl of Selborne in 1895. He was created GCMG in 1905 and KG in 1909. He was Liberal MP for Hampshire (East) 1885–86; in 1886 he became a Liberal Unionist and held the seat till 1892. He was Liberal Unionist MP for Edinburgh (West) 1892–95. He was Under-Secretary of State for the Colonies June 1895–Nov 1900, First Lord of the Admiralty 1900–March 1905, and President of the Board of Agriculture and Fisheries May 1915–July 1916.

Selborne's great-grandson, the 4th Earl of Selborne, gave his papers, including many family papers, to the Bodleian Library in 1970 (MSS Selborne 1–222). The collection has been listed and indexed (NRA 17810). Selborne's papers have been divided into nine main groups: special correspondence; correspondence and memoranda arranged by subject; general correspondence; family and personal correspondence; printed government papers; official papers arranged by subject; official papers arranged chronologically; non-official printed material; and miscellaneous papers.

Selborne's special correspondence fills 12 volumes and includes letters from A. J. Balfour, Lord Midleton, the Duke of Devonshire, the

Marquess of Salisbury, Lord Curzon, Lord Milner, and Joseph Chamberlain, under whom Selborne worked at the Colonial Office.

The correspondence arranged by subject has been subdivided by Selborne's main interests. His political correspondence 1885-95 includes the correspondence relating to his work as Liberal Unionist Chief Whip and his forecast of the results of the 1892 general election. There are two volumes of Colonial Office papers. They include notes of a conversation with Cecil Rhodes in 1897. The Admiralty correspondence includes correspondence with the royal family, Cabinet colleagues, and the Admiralty Board, as well as with various commanders. MSS Selborne 48-72 are papers related to Selborne's term of office as High Commissioner for South Africa 1905-10. They contain a good deal of correspondence with successive Colonial Secretaries, as well as with the royal family, other governors, and South African politicians; Selborne's correspondence on domestic politics 1900-14 ranges over tariff reform, the 1910-12 constitutional crisis (including papers concerning the Halsbury Club and minutes of some of its meetings), as well as Irish Home Rule. MSS Selborne 80-7 contain the papers related to Selborne's work as a member of the War Cabinet and his later political activities 1915-42. They include 'pen portraits' of his Cabinet colleagues after his resignation. MSS Selborne 88-91, Selborne's correspondence on ecclesiastical topics, ranges from Welsh disestablishment, and divorce reform, to the 1927-29 prayer book controversy.

The general correspondence, which covers the period 1883-1941, has been arranged in chronological order. Selborne's family and personal correspondence includes letters from his parents and family as well as letters to his parents about him. There are also nine volumes of correspondence with his wife 1900-39.

The printed official papers include white papers, bills, Cabinet memoranda, etc. and cover the years 1899-1905, and 1915-16. The official papers arranged by subject include a large number of Admiralty papers and papers on South Africa, particularly on the Union of South Africa Act. There are four volumes of official papers, chronologically arranged, relating to measures in which Selborne was particularly interested. The non-official papers, arranged by subject, fill ten volumes and include two volumes of press cuttings. The miscellaneous papers include three volumes of reminiscences written by Selborne in 1937.

Additional material was donated to the Bodleian in 1974 and 1975. These papers have been listed. Selborne's great-grandson donated a further collection of his papers in 1978 (MSS Selborne adds 1-37; NRA 22802). These include letters from his wife 1883-1939, and other members of his family. They also include a long series of correspondence with Edward VII 1901–05 (mainly in the hand of his secretaries), two volumes of general correspondence, and other miscellaneous papers.

In addition, the 4th Lord Selborne deposited the papers of Maud, Countess of Selborne, wife of the 2nd Earl (MSS Eng misc c 454–6, 685–9; d 422–31, 997; e 961–8; f 561–3). They include diaries 1871–74, and travel journals 1880–1930. Lady Selborne was daughter of the 3rd Marquess of Salisbury. Her correspondence includes many letters from the Cecil family as well as her husband's family and their children. There are also many letters from Herbert Baker 1911–40, Lionel Curtis 1914–35, and Philip Kerr 1909–16. There are three volumes of general correspondence. The papers of the 2nd Earl and his wife are described in the catalogue of the papers of the 3rd Earl.

A further small collection of papers was deposited by Selborne's sister, Lady Laura Ridding, in the Hampshire RO (9M68/95–1052; NRA 20787). The collection includes letters from Selborne to his son Jocelyn in 1909, letters from Lady Selborne to Jocelyn 1908–09 and to their daughter Mabel 1906–17, 1917–39. Possibly of greatest interest in the collection is a memo dated by Selborne 30 June 1916 giving his reasons for resigning from the Cabinet.

Additional papers relating to the Palmer family deposited in the Hampshire RO include papers relating to Selborne (19M75). The papers are divided into four categories: payment and account books; papers relating to various trusts; family correspondence; and miscellaneous.

Palmer family estate papers 1867–1983 are at the Rural History Centre, Reading University (NRA 33526).

Selborne's father, Roundell Palmer, the 1st Earl, published his autobiography *Memorials* (Macmillan 1898) detailing his personal and political memoirs. Selborne served as private secretary to his father when he was Lord Chancellor 1872–74.

A biography of Selborne's son Robert (who died of wounds received in action 1916), *The Life of Robert Palmer, 1888–1916* (Hodder & Stoughton 1921) was written by Lady Laura Ridding.

Selections from the papers in the Bodleian have been published in D. George Boyce (ed), *The Crisis of British Unionism: Lord Selborne's Domestic Political Papers, 1885–1922* (The Historians' Press 1987) (which also uses papers from 20 other collections), and D. George Boyce (ed), *The Crisis of British Power: The Imperial and Naval Papers of the Second Earl of Selborne, 1895–1910* (The Historians' Press 1990). L. Margaret Barnett, *British Food Policy During the First World War* (George Allen & Unwin, Boston 1985) devotes a chapter (pp. 48–68) to 'An Uphill Struggle. Lord Selborne at the Board of Agriculture'.

OSBERT PEAKE, 1st VISCOUNT INGLEBY (1897-1966)

Osbert Peake was Conservative MP for Leeds North 1929-55 and Leeds North-East May-Dec 1955. He was Parliamentary Under-Secretary of State, Home Office April 1939-Oct 1944, Financial Secretary to the Treasury 1944-Aug 1945, Minister of National Insurance Oct 1951-Sept 1953, and Minister of Pensions and National Insurance 1953-Dec 1955. He was created Viscount Ingleby in 1955.

Peake's son, the 2nd Viscount Ingleby, advised us that he has never had time to go through his father's papers, and consequently was not able to provide us with any details of surviving papers.

SIR WEETMAN DICKINSON PEARSON, 1st Bt, 1st VISCOUNT COWDRAY (1856-1927)

Weetman Pearson was created a baronet in 1894, Baron Cowdray in 1910, Viscount Cowdray in 1917, and GCVO in 1925. He was President of the Air Board Jan-Nov 1917.

A small collection of Pearson's papers is part of an extensive collection of the archive of S. Pearson and Son Ltd (later Whitehall Securities and currently Pearson plc) deposited in the Science Museum by his grandson, the 3rd Lord Cowdray (PEA papers). There is a comprehensive listing of the archives (NRA 28457).

Apart from Pearson's diaries of foreign tours and family financial papers, the collection includes a file of papers connected with his tenure of the Air Board. There is a letter from Lloyd George 2 Jan 1917, saying that Pearson's claim on behalf of the Mexican Eagle Oil Company against the Admiralty could stand over while Pearson was a minister; there is a file of papers concerning Pearson's resignation, including a cutting of Lord Northcliffe's letter to *The Times*, stencils of Pearson's letters to Lloyd George and his replies, letters of regret at his resignation, and a letter from Northcliffe 25 Jan 1918 saying that he thought Pearson was resigning because of affairs in Mexico. The collection also includes a bundle of Pearson's letters to his wife 1895-1927, though they are mainly for the period 1908-10. There are various personal financial papers and also some press cuttings from 1922 when Pearson proposed collaboration between Asquithian Liberals and Labour.

The archive of S. Pearson and Son Ltd records the business activities (especially in oil and civil engineering) of Pearson, particularly in Central and South America from 1889 onwards.

A further collection of papers was deposited in the Science Museum in 1985 (PEA COWD papers). A list is available. Although mostly consisting of company records, the collection includes some of Pearson's cash books, ledgers, and journals, estate papers, a volume of press cuttings relating to Pearson's art collections and interests, and a typescript copy of *Member for Mexico* (Cassell 1966) by Desmond Young. There is also a small collection of photos featuring Pearson.

The 3rd Lord Cowdray did not know of any other papers. Young's study, the short biography by R. K. Middlemas in *The Master Builders* (Hutchinson 1963) and J. A. Spender, *Weetman Pearson, First Viscount Cowdray* (Cassell 1930), are all based on and quote from Pearson's papers.

JOSEPH ALBERT PEASE, 1st BARON GAINFORD (1860–1943)

Jack Pease was Liberal MP for Northumberland (Tyneside) 1892–1900, Essex (Saffron Walden) 1901–10 and West Riding of Yorkshire (Rotherham) 1910–16. He was Chancellor of the Duchy of Lancaster Feb 1910–Oct 1911, President of the Board of Education 1911–May 1915, and Postmaster-General Jan-Dec 1916. He was created Baron Gainford in 1917.

Pease's grandson, the 3rd Lord Gainford, deposited a large collection (three bays) of his papers in the Nuffield College Library (Pease papers). The papers have been sorted but only a preliminary list has been made. Pease's papers have been divided into the following sections: diaries and scrap books; press cuttings; correspondence; business papers; domestic papers; political papers; official papers; claims commission papers; and BBC papers.

The main volumes of Pease's diary cover the period March 1908–May 1915. A volume covering the years 1908–10 has been edited by Cameron Hazlehurst and Christine Woodland, *A Liberal Chronicle: Journals and Papers of J. A. Pease, 1st Lord Gainford, 1908–1910* (The Historians' Press 1995). A second volume for 1911–15 is in preparation. Pease recorded in the diaries the course of discussions in Cabinet. Long selections from the diaries, as well as from the rest of his papers, are quoted in 23 draft chapters, entitled *War Reminiscences*, included in this division of the papers. There is also a diary of 10–11 Dec 1905, when Pease was offered a Junior Lordship of the Treasury. This section also includes scrap-book diaries 1892–1908 which Pease called his 'Political Diaries'. They mostly contain press cuttings of political events but they also include Pease's voting records and some comments by him on events.

There are 16 volumes of press cuttings 1881–1938, several of which overlap. They cover most aspects of Pease's life: his election campaigns, his official activities, as well as his social activities. There are 40 boxes of correspondence 1886–1943, arranged in a single chronological series. Pease's business papers cover a wide range of industries. There is a great deal of material about his family's ironstone collieries, and about the collapse of the family bank, J & J. W. Pease, in 1902. After the First

World War Pease was active in the electricity industry, as well as maintaining his mining interests. The domestic papers include the sale and purchase of various houses, domestic arrangements, insurance, etc.

The first part of Pease's political papers covers his election campaigns. There are press cuttings, posters, buttons, receipts, and election addresses for the various constituencies he held. There are drafts for several speeches and a collection of pamphlets and leaflets on the political interests of his day. For brief periods in 1906 and 1907 Pease reported to the King on the daily proceedings of the House of Commons. Copies of the telegrams he sent have survived.

Pease's official papers have been divided by the offices he held, with an additional section of miscellaneous Cabinet memoranda. As Chancellor of the Duchy, Pease was in charge of formulating various changes in the franchise and election laws. There are volumes of papers (memoranda, letters, notes of deputations, press cuttings, etc.) on this work, which aimed at the abolition of plural voting, and having general elections on the same day. There are also many papers on various aspects of women's suffrage. There are more bound volumes from Pease's tenure of the Education Office. These concern proposals for a new Education Bill 1912–14. The Post Office papers are mainly routine but they include Pease's papers on his inspection of the Dublin Post Office in 1916, with a collection of photos of the damage done during the rebellion.

After his exclusion from office in May 1915 Pease worked for the Claims Commission in France and Italy. His job was to assess damage done by the Allied troops and to arrange compensation. A few papers have survived for this period.

Pease was chairman of the British Broadcasting Company (before it became the Corporation) 1922–26. His papers include the company's first two minute books. There are many letters from John Reith and Mrs Snowden in the correspondence series. The papers were used by Asa Briggs in *The History of Broadcasting in the United Kingdom*, 1, *The Birth of Broadcasting*, 2, *The Golden Age of Broadcasting* (Oxford UP 1961–65), and Andrew Boyle, *Only the Wind Will Listen, Reith of the BBC* (Hutchinson 1972). Ian McIntyre, *The Expense of Glory: A Life of John Reith* (Harper Collins 1993) is also instructive on Pease's BBC period.

The collection includes not only Pease's own papers, but some of his father's and of other members of his family. The most important of these are the papers of his wife, Elsie. They include nine boxes of letters from Pease 1882–1941, many of which include important comments on the political situation.

M. W. Kirby, *Men of Business and Politics: The Rise and Fall of the Quaker Pease Dynasty of North-East England, 1700–1943* (George Allen & Unwin 1984) is authoritative on Pease's family business interests.

WILLIAM ROBERT WELLESLEY PEEL, 2nd VISCOUNT PEEL, 1st EARL PEEL (1867–1937)

William Peel was Conservative MP for Manchester (South) 1900–06 and Taunton 1909–12. He was Joint Parliamentary Secretary to the Ministry of National Service April 1918–Jan 1919, Under-Secretary of State for War and Air 1919–April 1921, Chancellor of the Duchy of Lancaster 1921–March 1922, Minister of Transport Nov 1921–March 1922, Secretary of State for India 1922–Jan 1924 and Oct 1928–June 1929, First Commissioner of Works Nov 1924–Oct 1928, and Lord Privy Seal Sept-Nov 1931. He succeeded his father as 2nd Viscount Peel in 1912, and was created GBE in 1919, Earl Peel in 1929, and GCSI in 1932.

Peel's grandson, the 3rd Earl Peel, informed us that when his mother moved to Scotland she destroyed all the papers concerning his grandfather's political career.

A small collection (22 ff) of papers 1928–33 is in the Oriental and India Office Collections, British Library (MSS Eur D 528). It consists of letters from Peel's second term as Secretary of State for India 1928–29; his opening speech as Chairman of the Burma Round Table Conference 1931; and his appointment and resignation (due to illness) as Chairman of the Joint Committee on Indian Constitutional Reform 1933.

The India Office Collection also holds correspondence from Peel with the various Viceroys of India, Governors of Bengal, and the Governor of Madras during his period as Secretary of State for India. The correspondence is scattered throughout various collections.

There is brief reference to Peel's role in Indian affairs in Robin Moore *The Crisis of Indian Unity, 1917–1940* (Clarendon Press, Oxford 1974), and in Carl Bridge *Holding India to the Empire: the British Conservative Party and the 1935 Constitution* (Sterling Publishers Private, New Delhi 1986).

EUSTACE SUTHERLAND CAMPBELL PERCY, BARON PERCY OF NEWCASTLE (1887–1958)

Eustace Percy (he was known as Lord Eustace Percy from 1899 when his father became the 7th Duke of Northumberland) was Conservative MP for Hastings 1921–37. He was Parliamentary Secretary to the Board of Education March-May 1923, Parliamentary Secretary to the Ministry of Health 1923–Jan 1924, President of the Board of Education Nov 1924–June 1929, and Minister without Portfolio June 1935–March 1936. He was created Baron Percy of Newcastle in 1953.

His widow, Lady Percy, informed us that he kept neither correspondence nor a diary and nothing survived. This is also stated in the preface to his own memoirs, *Some Memories* (Eyre & Spottiswoode 1958). The book includes a chapter on his ministerial and political career but it does not quote from any letters.

Dr J. R. Brooks's article, 'Lord Eustace Percy and the Abolition of the Compulsory, Elementary Curriculum in 1926', *Contemporary Record*, 7, 1, summer 1993, 86-102, makes use of scattered PRO files. Dr Brooks (of the School of History and Welsh History, University College of North Wales, Bangor) also plans a more substantial reappraisal of Percy's contribution to education, especially the priority he gave to technical education.

SIR ERNEST MURRAY POLLOCK, 1st Bt, 1st VISCOUNT HANWORTH (1861-1936)

Ernest Pollock was Unionist MP for Warwick and Leamington (Warwickshire, Warwick and Leamington from 1918) 1910-23. He was Solicitor-General Jan 1919-March 1922, and Attorney-General March-Oct 1922. He was created KBE in 1917, a baronet in 1922, Baron Hanworth in 1926, and Viscount Hanworth in 1936.

Twenty-five boxes of Pollock's papers were given to the Bodleian Library by his daughter, the Hon Lady Farrer in 1972 (Hanworth Papers, MSS Eng hist c 941-58, d 428-34; NRA 21155).

These papers throw an important light on the end of the Coalition Government in 1922, including a memo by Pollock entitled 'The Fall of the Coalition Government under Lloyd George in October 1922' (69 MS pp). It is not clear when this was written but a typed copy is marked 'Corrected by H. 14 Sept. 1931'. This memo is extensively quoted in *Lord Chancellors 1*, 387-91, 424-7, 460-2. It describes how Pollock and some Conservative junior ministers were so appalled by the honours scandal that they brought their own and the alleged feelings of the constituency parties before Austen Chamberlain at a meeting in June 1922. It goes on to describe a further meeting between Conservative Cabinet ministers and MPs on 3 Aug 1922, when Lord Birkenhead contemptuously dismissed the MPs' concern. Despite what Pollock calls misinterpretation and mishandling of the MPs' doubts, he voted to stay in the Coalition at the Carlton Club meeting. Having done so, he then felt obliged to refuse office in the new administration, despite a pressing offer by Bonar Law of the Lord Chancellorship, and great efforts in persuasion by Lord Beaverbrook through Pollock's cousin Guy Pollock. Some of the correspondence relating to these events survives with the memo.

There appear to be no surviving papers which relate either to Pollock's work as an MP or to his terms in office: only letters of congratulation on becoming Solicitor-General, Attorney-General, Master of the Rolls, and on being created a peer. There are, however, six volumes of press cuttings 1894–1935, though the major part of these is concerned with protection 1902–09. There are also seven volumes of miscellaneous letters 1881–1932. There do not seem to be any surviving papers relating to his work as Chairman of the Contraband Committee 1915–17, or as Controller of the Foreign Trade Department of the Foreign Office 1917–19. There is, however, a bundle of papers relating to his activities at the Peace Conference 1919, and a bundle concerning the prosecution of German war criminals 1918–22 and the German War Trials 1921–22. Of Pollock's later activities as Master of the Rolls 1923–35, and his concern for the preservation of historical documents, there remains only a bundle of notes, correspondence on a proposed bill to allow the British Museum to make loans to other museums 1931, and material on the proposed reduction in judges' salaries 1932. The collection includes 19th century Pollock family papers, including those of Sir Frederick Pollock (MSS Eng hist c 959–65, d 35–6). Some of these were used by Pollock in his biography of his grandfather, *Lord Chief Baron Pollock* (Murray 1929).

Pollock's role in relation to the punishment of war criminals is documented in James F. Willis, *Prologue to Nuremberg: The Politics and Diplomacy of Punishing War Criminals of the First World War* (Greenwood Press, Westport 1982).

ARTHUR AUGUSTUS WILLIAM HARRY PONSONBY, 1st BARON PONSONBY OF SHULBREDE (1871–1946)

Arthur Ponsonby was Liberal MP for Stirling Burghs 1908–18, and Labour MP for Sheffield (Brightside) 1922–30. He was Under-Secretary of State for Foreign Affairs Jan-Nov 1924, Under-Secretary of State for Dominion Affairs June-Dec 1929, Parliamentary Secretary to the Ministry of Transport 1929–March 1931, and Chancellor of the Duchy of Lancaster March-Aug 1931. He was created Baron Ponsonby of Shulbrede in 1930.

In a diary entry on 10 Aug 1916, Ponsonby records he was 'clearing up all my papers at Lincolns Inn Fields preparatory to leaving the flat...Turning out drawers of old papers and letters I came upon interesting correspondence but it is no good keeping it all so I made a high pile in the middle of the room for the paper pulper'. Fortunately a great deal survived the pulper, much more was accumulated; and an important collection of Ponsonby's papers was given to the Bodleian Library in 1971 (MSS Eng hist a 20; c 651–85; d 363) by his son, the 2nd Lord Ponsonby of Shulbrede. They do not include family papers or Ponsonby's diaries. The latter, now in the possession of the 3rd Lord Ponsonby of Shulbrede, include much material on personal affairs and for this reason they are closed to researchers.

The papers which are available in the Bodleian are mainly correspondence and press cuttings, with a few notes for speeches and memoranda. The letters begin in the 1890s while Ponsonby was in the Diplomatic Service. It is clear that by 1898 he was disillusioned with his official work and by the lack of work to be done. His memo written in 1900 entitled 'Suggestions for reform in the Diplomatic Service' survives. In the same year he wrote to John Hare describing the 'hopelessly unsatisfactory' situation in which he found himself and proposing to join an acting company. In Aug 1902 he actually resigned and there are many letters to him, and drafts of his own letters, which explain the circumstances. He wrote to Herbert Gladstone, the Liberal Chief Whip: 'I am a more faithful follower than ever of the Liberalism of which yourself & John Morley are the exponents. . .' and was offered a job working in the Liberal party organisation.

In 1906 he stood for Taunton but was defeated; a number of letters of sympathy from Taunton Liberals, an election poster, and an election address survive. He then became private secretary to Sir Henry Campbell-Bannerman, the new Prime Minister. There is a considerable amount of correspondence from this period: letters from Campbell-Bannerman; his Cabinet; the King's secretaries; letters from Vaughan Nash – a long series from the latter describes Campbell-Bannerman's last illness; and, equally important, a long series of letters from his brother Frederick (Fritz) Ponsonby, Assistant Private Secretary to the King. These cover a wide range of political topics, for example, a letter dated 26 March 1906 discusses Ireland, old age pensions, the Milner debate, and army reforms. There is also an exchange of letters in June 1908 when Ponsonby spoke against the King's intended visit to the Tsar. As well as correspondence related to his post as secretary to the Prime Minister, there is Ponsonby's own correspondence with leading Liberals and Radicals – Morley, C. F. G. Masterman, the Hammonds, and C. P. Trevelyan. The correspondence with Trevelyan and the Hammonds continued throughout Ponsonby's life and is an important source on their activities. There are also 'Leaves of a Diary begun in Downing St. Jan '06 but owing to pressure of work never gone on with' (Jan 1907).

Ponsonby's notes of impressions of Sir Henry Campbell-Bannerman are not included in the collection in the Bodleian. They are extensively quoted in F. W. Hirst, *In the Golden Days* (Frederick Muller 1947). Hirst says there that Ponsonby wrote about 20,000 words in 1920 for J. A. Spender, who was then writing his biography of Campbell-Bannerman. When Hirst used the notes, they were in the possession of Ponsonby's widow. The notes are not in the collection in the Bodleian, and the 2nd Lord Ponsonby was unable to find them.

When Campbell-Bannerman died, Ponsonby became Liberal MP

for Stirling Burghs, Sir Henry's constituency. Apart from a printed election address and letters of congratulations on being elected, the only constituency papers to survive are in a box of correspondence and papers (MS Eng hist c 666). There is some correspondence on the defeat of Ponsonby and others in the peace movement in the 1918 general election. No correspondence relating to the Brightside constituency seems to have survived.

Ponsonby's parliamentary career is vividly represented by his correspondence. There are letters about his exclusion from a Palace garden party in 1908, about the Liberal Foreign Affairs Committee 1910–14, about his publications and speeches, his stand against the war, and his association with members of the Union of Democratic Control. There is a great deal of material on his activities in the 1920s and 1930s: his vote against the 1926 service estimates; the 1927 Peace Letter Campaign; the various peace movements of the 1930s – the No More War Movement, the War Resisters International, the British Anti-War Movement, and the Peace Pledge Union. Ponsonby's correspondents for this period include Bertrand Russell, Albert Einstein, Aldous Huxley, George Lansbury, and Laurence Housman.

Little remains of his official activities. From the 1924 government there are only letters of congratulation on the conclusion of the Russian treaties and a few letters from Ramsay MacDonald. On his decision to become a peer there is an exchange of letters from friends giving advice, and a letter from his brother Fritz 2 Jan 1929:

> The King spoke very strongly about your peerage... How could anyone place any reliance on what Labour politicians said when you and Sidney Webb had to eat your words and tamely became Peers.
> I explained the whole thing to him and he then came round completely and finally ended by saying he saw your point of view and that no doubt you were quite right in accepting a peerage!

There is nothing from his periods of office at the Dominions Office and Transport; but a letter from Lord Passfield 4 Jan 1931 relates how MacDonald '...broke out into an admission that we were "too old a lot..."'. For the Duchy there are only congratulations on entering office and a few papers connected with a scheme to obtain portraits of all previous holders of the office. There is some correspondence in Aug 1931 on the end of the Labour government and an undated 'appreciation' of MacDonald expressing great disillusionment.

There is some correspondence on Ponsonby's activities in the Lords though little for his period as Leader of the Opposition. There is correspondence and press cuttings on his resignation as Leader, and referring to his numerous broadcasts, some of which were non-political, for example, on keeping a diary. There are no papers on his literary activities apart from reactions from friends in their letters.

Private Office papers relating to Ponsonby's period as a junior minister at the Foreign Office in 1924 are in the PRO at FO 800/227.

There is a biography by Raymond A. Jones, *Arthur Ponsonby: The Politics of Life* (Christopher Helm 1989) which draws on family papers now in the possession of the 3rd Lord Ponsonby of Shulbrede as well as the Bodleian collection, and a brief sketch by David E. Martin in *DLB*, VII, 192–7.

SIR WYNDHAM RAYMOND PORTAL, 3rd Bt, VISCOUNT PORTAL (1885–1949)

Wyndham Portal succeeded his father as 3rd baronet in 1931, and was created Baron Portal in 1935, Viscount Portal in 1945, and GCMG in 1949. He was Additional Parliamentary Secretary to the Ministry of Supply Sept 1940–Feb 1942, Minister of Works and Planning 1942–Feb 1943, and First Commissioner of Works 1943–Nov 1944.

There was no issue of Portal's marriage and he was succeeded as 4th baronet by his uncle. His cousin, the 5th baronet, did not know of the existence of any papers and added that Portal avoided putting pen to paper whenever possible.

Sir Jonathan Portal, the 6th baronet, confirmed that none of Portal's papers has since come to light.

There are some papers kept by Portal at the Ministry of Supply in the PRO at AVIA 11.

The entry on Portal by J. V. Sheffield in *DNB 1941–1950*, 685–6, is based on 'personal knowledge'.

(JOHN) ENOCH POWELL (1912–)

Enoch Powell was Conservative MP for Wolverhampton South West 1950–74, and Ulster Unionist MP for Down South 1974–83 and South Down 1983–87. He was Parliamentary Secretary, Ministry of Housing and Local Government Dec 1955–Jan 1957, Financial Secretary to the Treasury 1957–Jan 1958, and Minister of Health July 1960–Oct 1963.

Mr Powell has retained a fairly large collection of post-1945 papers. At his death a literary trust, created under his will, becomes operative and will be empowered, *inter alia*, to control access to 11 boxes of private and political correspondence and papers, including their eventual deposit.

Papers Mr Powell regards as being 'in the public domain', and which are made available at his discretion as a matter of convenience to serious researchers include 17 boxes of the texts of speeches delivered by him; five boxes of his published writings other than bound books; and 50 scrapbooks of press cuttings relating to him.

Papers relating to constituents in Down South and South Down are deposited with the PRONI, and consist of constituency correspondence 1974–87 and constituency subject files 1975–87 (D3107). Both of these are closed until his death. The PRONI also holds speeches or extracts from speeches 1974–93 made to political and other groups in or about Northern Ireland. These papers are open for research. The Library, University of St Andrews, holds a collection of speeches 1969–74.

Correspondence relating to constituents in Wolverhampton South West, general correspondence after Mr Powell's departure from Wolverhampton, and press cuttings from c.1984 to the present have been deposited in the Staffordshire RO, where they are closed until his death.

The materials 'in the public domain' have been partially used in 14 books on Powell's career and several other more general works on British politics.

Patrick Cosgrave, *The Lives of Enoch Powell* (Bodley Head 1989) draws on the texts of Powell's published speeches; and 'all the published material covering the period of his lifetime' were made available by Powell, plus two 'extended interviews'. Powell read the manuscript and drew attention to some – though not necessarily all! – errors of omission or fact (p. 5). Roy Lewis in *Enoch Powell: Principle in Politics* (Cassell 1979), states 'my grateful thanks are, however, due to Mr Powell for his careful and constructive reading of the manuscript and his readiness to answer almost all of my questions' (p. xi). Rex Collings (ed), *Reflections of a Statesman: The writings and speeches of Enoch Powell* (Bellew 1991) is confined to published or publicly spoken works.

Mr Powell recorded an interview for the British Oral Archives of Political and Administrative History in 1980 at the BLPES. Access to the transcript of the interview may be granted by Mr Powell or 'the Literary Trust under my will'. Access to a transcript of a 1980 interview between Powell and Mr A. L. Teasdale on the Conservative leadership contest Oct 1963 is available from Mr Teasdale, Nuffield College, Oxford OX1 1NF.

Michael Cockerell had access to Powell's papers in compiling the BBC portrait, 'Odd Man Out – A Film Portrait of Enoch Powell' (transmitted on BBC 2, Nov 1995).

Mr Powell contributed to the witness seminar on 'Conservative Government Difficulties 1961–1964' at the Institute of Contemporary British History.

The Conservative Party Archives in the Bodleian Library should be consulted. *Conservative Party Policy* is useful regarding the archives of the CRD.

ALBERT EDWARD HARRY MAYER ARCHIBALD
PRIMROSE, 6th EARL OF ROSEBERY (1882–1974)

Harry Primrose was known as Lord Dalmeny from birth until he succeeded his father as 6th Earl of Rosebery in 1929. He was created KT in 1947. He was Liberal MP for Edinburghshire 1906–10. He was Secretary of State for Scotland May–July 1945.

Lord Rosebery informed us that he never kept any papers because they did not seem of sufficient importance. Rosebery's daughter-in-law, Lady Rosebery, confirmed that there are none of the 6th Earl's papers at Dalmeny House.

The NLS does not have any of the 6th Earl's papers.

Private Office papers relating to Rosebery's period at the Scottish Office are dispersed through the files of the five main Scottish Office departments held at the SRO.

There is a candid but sparsely documented biography by Kenneth Young, *Harry, Lord Rosebery* (Hodder & Stoughton 1974).

JOHN DENNIS PROFUMO (1915–)

John Profumo was Conservative MP for Kettering 1940–45 and Stratford-on-Avon 1950–63. He was Parliamentary Secretary, Ministry of Transport and Civil Aviation Nov 1952–Jan 1957, Parliamentary Under-Secretary of State for the Colonies 1957–Nov 1958, Parliamentary Under-Secretary of State, Foreign Affairs 1958–Jan 1959, Minister of State for Foreign Affairs 1959–July 1960, and Secretary of State for War 1960–June 1963.

The report in Cook (*Sources*, 4, p. 116) of the existence of a fully catalogued collection of papers relating to Mr Profumo's political career appears to have been based on a misunderstanding.

Mr Profumo now advises that he has a personal scrapbook of pictures, letters, articles, etc., on his life but this is not available for research.

Profumo's recollections of his role as the Conservative Party's first head of broadcasting in the late 1940s and early 1950s are quoted in Michael Cockerell, *Live from Number 10: The Inside Story of Prime Ministers and Television* (Faber and Faber 1988). His participation in the Conservative Broadcasting Policy Committee and the 'Group' advocating commercial television is documented in H. H. Wilson, *Pressure Group: The Campaign for Commercial Television* (Secker & Warburg 1961).

Reference to Mr Profumo's association with Toynbee Hall may be found in Chapter V of Asa Briggs and Anne Macartney, *Toynbee Hall: The First Hundred Years* (Routledge & Kegan Paul 1984). There is an extended and well documented study of the 'Profumo affair' in Richard Lamb, *The Macmillan Years 1957–1963: The Emerging Truth* (John Murray 1995), 454–90.

ROWLAND EDMUND PROTHERO, BARON ERNLE (1851–1937)

Rowland Prothero was Conservative MP for Oxford University 1914–19. He was President of the Board of Agriculture and Fisheries Dec 1916–Aug 1919. He was created Baron Ernle in 1919.

Lord Ernle left 'all my manuscripts letters and papers and the copyright in all my books...' to his daughter Beatrice Hope, Mrs Victor Gilpin. She died in 1958 and left all her chattels to her two sons. The elder son, Mr T. E. Gilpin, informed us that all he had of his grandfather's papers were some scrapbooks of press cuttings from Prothero's electoral campaigns in North Bedford and some letters from eminent people 1919–37 which were 'of little consequence'. He knew nothing of the fate of any other papers which may have survived.

Prothero's *Whippingham to Westminster* (John Murray 1938) contains his reminiscences but gives few quotations from documents, however *The Land and its People: Chapters in Rural Life and History* (Hutchinson 1925) has chapters on 'The Food Campaign, 1916–18' and 'Women on the Land, 1917–19' recounting aspects of his work as President of the Board of Agriculture..

The bibliography of P. E. Dewey, *British Agriculture in the First World War* (Routledge 1989) should also be consulted.

SIR (PERCY) JOHN PYBUS, Bt (1880–1935)

John Pybus was Liberal MP for Essex (Harwich) 1929–31, and Liberal National MP 1931–35. He was Minister of Transport Sept 1931–Feb 1933. He was created a baronet in 1934.

In the first edition we reported that Pybus's brother, Mr Sydney J. Pybus, informed us that he had kept his brother's papers for many years but eventually destroyed them as no one had wanted to use them. Mr S. Pybus's son, Mr William M. Pybus confirmed that none of his uncle's papers has come to light since the first edition.

We have been unable to trace any papers belonging to Pybus's long-time companion, Miss L. E. Bowyer-Bailey.

The Phoenix Assurance Archives in the Cambridge University Library has one file on Pybus who was a director (PX2041). The file does not contain personal papers, but consists of formal correspondence, memoranda, and press cuttings about his various appointments within the company as well as a collection of obituary notices.

This file was used to compile the valuable entry on Pybus by R. P. T. Davenport-Hines in *DBB*, 4, 783–6.

HERWALD RAMSBOTHAM, 1st VISCOUNT SOULBURY (1887–1971)

Herwald Ramsbotham was Conservative MP for Lancashire (Lancaster) 1929–41. He was Parliamentary Secretary to the Board of Education Nov 1931–Nov 1935, Parliamentary Secretary to the Ministry of Agriculture and Fisheries 1935–July 1936, Minister of Pensions 1936–June 1939, First Commissioner of Works 1939–April 1940, and President of the Board of Education 1940–July 1941. He was created Baron Soulbury in 1941, GCMG in 1949, and Viscount Soulbury in 1954.

When our first edition was published, only a very small collection of Ramsbotham's papers was known to survive in the possession of his younger son, the Hon Sir Peter Ramsbotham. This collection was then in the care of Mr Nigel Middleton, Ulster College, The Northern Ireland Polytechnic. Mr Middleton was gathering material for a biography of Lord Soulbury. However, Sir Peter has not been able to contact Mr Middleton in recent years; and our own efforts to communicate with him have also been unsuccessful.

The papers which were lent to Mr Middleton consisted of five volumes of speeches made while Ramsbotham was at the Board of Education, two volumes of press cuttings, mainly covering 1920s election campaigns, and a small collection of miscellaneous papers.

There are accounts of Ramsbotham's period as President of the Board of Education in P. H. J. H. Gosden, *Education in the Second World War: A Study in Policy and Administration* (Methuen 1976); Nigel Middleton and Sophia Weitzman, *A Place for Everyone: A History of Education from the end of the 18th century to the 1970s* (Gollancz 1976), chapters seven and eight; and Joan Simon, 'Promoting educational reform on the home front: The T. E. S. and the Times 1940–1944', *History of Education*, 18, 3, 1989, 195–211.

JAMES EDWARD RAMSDEN (1923–)

James Ramsden was Conservative MP for Harrogate 1954–74. He was Under-Secretary and Financial Secretary, War Office Oct 1960–Oct 1963, Secretary of State for War 1963–April 1964, and Minister of Defence for the Army April-Oct 1964.

Mr Ramsden advised us that he has not kept many papers, only those which he thought 'might amuse somebody some day' (personal correspondence, 9 June 1994). These include Harold Macmillan's welcome 22 Oct 1960 on his appointment to the Under Secretaryship at the War Office: 'It will be nice to have a Minister again who is a Master of Foxhounds'.

SIR ROBERT THRESHIE REID, EARL LOREBURN (1846–1923)

Robert Reid was Liberal MP for Hereford 1880–85 and Dumfries 1886–1905. He was Solicitor-General May-Oct 1894, Attorney-General 1894–June 1895, and Lord Chancellor Dec 1905–June 1912. He was knighted in 1894, created GCMG in 1899, Baron Loreburn in 1906, and Earl Loreburn in 1911.

We were unable to find any of Lord Loreburn's papers when preparing the first edition. He died without leaving any issue. Loreburn's nephew, the late Dr R. C. Reid had a few early letters to his parents and family, but his widow was not able to find them. Loreburn's second wife, Violet Hicks Beach, was a niece of the 1st Earl St Aldwyn, but her family knew of no surviving papers.

Mr G. W. Monger informed us that he enquired without success of Lady Loreburn's executor (The Public Trustee), the solicitors acting for the estate (Messrs Trower, Still & Keeling), and Major W. W. Hicks Beach, Lady Loreburn's nephew. Mr Monger told the NRA in 1961 that Loreburn's papers were thought to have been destroyed in the Second World War. It may well be that Loreburn kept very few papers; he wrote to Arthur Ponsonby 23 April 1920: 'I have no papers. I never keep them...' (Ponsonby MSS).

The NLS has a number of small groups and single letters relating to Loreburn including: letters and a summary of his political views 1878–79 in the papers of John J. Reid, Scottish Liberal organiser (MS 19623); two single letters 1894 and 1895 (MS 9814); a letter to J. H. Balfour-Browne 1903 (MS 19609); a letter to the Hon Arthur R. D. Elliot (MS 19497); and three letters in the Haldane Papers 1912 (MS 5909).

There is a valuable short biography in *Lord Chancellors 1*. A brief biography by Robert Jordan is also available in *MBR*, 3, 689–93.

SIR JOHN CHARLES WALSHAM REITH, 1st BARON REITH (1889–1971)

John Reith was knighted in 1927, and created Baron Reith in 1940, and KT in 1969. He was Minister of Information Jan-May 1940, Minister of Transport May-Oct 1940, and Minister of Works (later Works and Planning) 1940–Feb 1942.

Reith's papers were transferred to the BBC Written Archives Centre in 1979 (S60; NRA 31050). The collection consists of 18 volumes of Reith's diaries 1911–71; correspondence 1940–71; enclosures 1889–1971; and press cuttings 1926–70. The papers, with some restrictions, are available to *bona fide* scholars.

Ian McIntyre, in his biography *The Expense of Glory: A Life of John Reith* (Harper Collins 1993), notes that at some time after April 1967, 'the diary entries for the period between January 1960 and February

1966 were severely edited and retyped'. Reith's secretary Miss Jo Stanley admitted to McIntyre that she had edited Reith's diaries, under his instructions, to remove all references to his former close friend Dawn Mackay (pp. 388–9). He also notes that passages from the diaries have been deleted for legal reasons (p. xv).

The Sun Alliance Group Personnel Department have a file on Reith from the Phoenix Assurance Company (McIntyre, p. xv).

Reith himself quoted frequently from the diaries in his memoirs, *Into the Wind* (Hodder & Stoughton 1949), and extensive selections from his First World War diary were published as *Wearing Spurs* (Hutchinson 1966). The first two volumes of the history of the BBC by Asa Briggs also drew on the diaries from the 1920s and 1930s: *The History of Broadcasting in the United Kingdom*, 1, *The Birth of Broadcasting*, 2, *The Golden Age of Broadcasting* (Oxford UP 1961–65). Charles Stuart edited a selection of the diaries in *The Reith Diaries* (Collins 1975). Andrew Boyle's biography of Reith, *Only the Wind Will Listen* (Hutchinson 1972) made no use of Reith's papers; but it quoted from a report on the diaries made for Lord Beaverbrook when he was considering buying them a few years before Reith's death.

SIR JOSEPH COMPTON-RICKETT (1847–1919)

Joseph Compton-Rickett (he assumed the additional surname of Compton in 1908) was Liberal MP for Scarborough 1895–1906 and West Riding of Yorkshire (Osgoldcross; Pontefract from 1918) 1906–19. He was Paymaster-General Dec 1916–Oct 1919. He was knighted in 1907.

For the first edition, we sought unsuccessfully to trace any of Compton-Rickett's heirs. His executors and trustees, to whom he left his copyright and his papers, were the Public Trustee, his son Arthur, Reginald Neale Spiers, and the Rev John Scott Lidgett. Compton-Rickett's widow died in 1933; her executors were R. N. Spiers and her son Arthur who died in 1937. His executors were R. N. Spiers and Reginald Denham. We were unable to trace Mr Spiers. Mr Denham could tell us nothing of Sir Joseph's papers; he had lost contact with the Compton-Rickett family in 1941 but believed that they had all died (Sir Joseph had four sons and four daughters). Arthur Compton-Rickett published several books, including *Joseph Compton-Rickett. A memoir* (Ernest Cooper, Bournemouth 1922), but his publishers were taken over and their successors were unable to put us into contact with the Compton-Rickett family. The memoir is a mixture of contributions from those who knew Compton-Rickett and selected passages from his own public writings.

Arthur Compton-Rickett left the copyright of his plays and some of his papers to Ella Cressee, who died in 1959. She left Arthur Compton-

Rickett's manuscripts to Miss Pamela Richardson. Miss Richardson, in her turn, passed the manuscripts to her nephew but she informed us that they consisted solely of Arthur Compton-Rickett's essays and short plays.

We recently contacted Professor Geoffrey Fletcher whose mother, Ursula Rickett, was a cousin of Compton-Rickett. Professor Fletcher's solicitors referred us to his cousin, Sir Denis Rickett, who did not know of any papers. Further enquiries of the Rickett family did not reveal any known surviving papers.

SIR MATTHEW WHITE RIDLEY, 5th Bt, 1st VISCOUNT RIDLEY (1842–1904)

Matthew Ridley was Conservative MP for Northumberland (North) 1868–85 and North Lancashire (Blackpool) 1886–1900. He was Under-Secretary of State for Home Affairs April 1878–April 1880, Financial Secretary to the Treasury Sept 1885–Jan 1886, and Secretary of State for Home Affairs July 1895–Nov 1900. He succeeded his father as 5th baronet in 1877, and was created Viscount Ridley in 1900.

A large collection of Ridley family papers, which includes a small number of Ridley's own papers, was deposited by the 4th Viscount Ridley in the Northumberland RO (Ridley [Blagdon] MSS). A list and index of the papers are available (NRA 4468).

The collection contains 100 letters to Ridley from politicians 1875–1903 arranged chronologically (ZRI.25.97). There are a few letters from Benjamin Disraeli, Sir Stafford Northcote, and Queen Victoria. The only other political papers are notes of Ridley's election expenses in 1868, 1880 and 1886, and his letter of appointment as a privy councillor in 1892. The other papers include a diary of a French tour 1873–74, letters from Harrow and Oxford about Ridley's scholarship, bank account books 1884–1901, game books 1864–1914, letters about his house and furniture, a copy of his will, and an album of letters of condolence to Lady Ridley in 1904.

(AUBREY) GEOFFREY (FREDERICK) RIPPON, BARON RIPPON OF HEXHAM (1924–)

Geoffrey Rippon was Conservative MP for Norwich South 1955–64 and Hexham 1966–87. He was Parliamentary Secretary, Ministry of Aviation Oct 1959–Oct 1961, Joint Parliamentary Secretary, Ministry of Housing and Local Government 1961–July 1962, Minister of Public Building and Works 1962–Oct 1964, Minister of Technology June-July 1970, Chancellor of the Duchy of Lancaster 1970–Nov 1972, and Secretary of State for the Environment 1972–March 1974. He was created Baron Rippon of Hexham (a life peerage) in 1987.

Lord Rippon advised us that he has not sorted out his surviving papers. He has no plans for an autobiography.

CHARLES THOMSON RITCHIE, 1st BARON RITCHIE OF DUNDEE (1838–1906)

Charles Ritchie was Conservative MP for Tower Hamlets 1874–85, Tower Hamlets (St George's) 1885–92 and Croydon 1895–1905. He was Financial Secretary to the Admiralty 1885–Aug 1886, President of the Local Government Board 1886–Aug 1892, President of the Board of Trade June 1895–Nov 1900, Secretary of State for Home Affairs 1900–Aug 1902, and Chancellor of the Exchequer 1902–Oct 1903. He was created Baron Ritchie of Dundee in 1905.

One volume of Ritchie's papers, all that appears to have survived, was given to the British Library by his grandson, the 3rd Lord Ritchie, in 1966 (Add MSS 53780). The letters and papers mostly concern Ritchie's resignation in 1903 on the tariff reform issue, but there are a few earlier letters relating to appointments, honours and retirement. There is a full list (NRA 10649). The British Library also holds a small collection of Ritchie's letters to Lord Avebury 1891–1900.

The Ritchie collection was extensively quoted in Alfred Gollin, *Balfour's Burden: Arthur Balfour and Imperial Preference* (Anthony Blond 1965). There is a useful biographical sketch based on a range of sources by Richard Jennings in *DNB 1901–1911*, 202–08.

ALFRED ROBENS, BARON ROBENS OF WOLDINGHAM (1910–)

Alfred Robens was Labour MP for Northumberland (Wansbeck) 1945–50 and Blyth 1950–60. He was Parliamentary Secretary to the Ministry of Fuel and Power Oct 1947–April 1951, and Minister of Labour and National Service April-Oct 1951. He was created Baron Robens of Woldingham (a life peerage) in 1961.

Lord Robens informed us that he never brought papers away from his various ministries, nor had he systematically kept papers; he added that the only diaries he kept were appointment diaries.

Lord Robens described his years as Chairman of the National Coal Board 1961–71 in *Ten Year Stint* (Cassell 1972).

FREDERICK OWEN ROBERTS (1876–1941)

Frederick Roberts was Labour MP for West Bromwich 1918–31 and 1935–41. He was Minister of Pensions Jan-Nov 1924 and June 1929–Aug 1931.

For the first edition, Roberts's son, Mr Reuben V. Roberts informed us that his mother destroyed most of his father's papers after his death, including a large volume of press cuttings and letters arranged in chronological order. All that remained in Mr Roberts's possession was a splendidly illuminated address of appreciation, presented to Roberts by the townspeople of Northampton in 1920, a file containing ballots for notices of motions, a lengthy correspondence about conditions in China in 1928, miscellaneous press cuttings including *Hansard*'s record of the announcement of the death of George V, a souvenir of the first airmail post between England and India, and the first minute book of the Group of Midland Branches of the Typographical Association 28 July 1917–27 Aug 1918. The minute book was particularly interesting because it traced the formulation of the Group's constitution and also contained press cuttings of the Group's activities and rough drafts of wages agreements.

We have not been able to determine the current location of this collection. The branch of the Suffolk RO at Bury St Edmunds (where Reuben Roberts was living in the 1970s) does not have the papers. They have not been deposited at the Northamptonshire RO either.

The National Museum of Labour History does not have any of Roberts's papers.

GEORGE HENRY ROBERTS (1868–1928)

George Roberts was Labour MP for Norwich 1906–18, and Coalition Labour then Independent MP for the same seat 1918–23. He was Parliamentary Secretary to the Board of Trade Dec 1916–Aug 1917, Minister of Labour 1917–Jan 1919, and Food Controller 1919–March 1920.

Roberts's daughter, Miss V. A. Roberts had a small collection of her father's papers. It included a note from Charles Bathurst 18 April 1914 congratulating Roberts on a speech about social reform: 'If you make many more of the same kind I shall feel bound to come across and sit on your benches'. There was a note from Lloyd George congratulating him on a speech 25 April 1917; the official notification of Roberts's being sworn as a Privy Councillor 22 Aug 1917; and a letter from John Wheatley in Aug 1924 asking Roberts to continue as chairman of an advisory committee on the welfare of the blind. There were also a few press cuttings, for example on Roberts's speech about Indian support for the British war effort Sept 1914, and on his work as Food Controller. We were not able to discover the fate of these papers.

Roberts was president and secretary of the Norwich branch of the Typographical Association, a paid TA organiser 1904–18, and a TA sponsored MP 1906–18. The archives of the Typographical Association have been deposited at the Modern Records Centre (MSS. 39/TA). Although there are no papers specifically relating to Roberts in the archive, his involvement in the TA may be traced through its minutes (MSS. 39/TA/1/26–41), and its journal *Typographical Circular* (MSS.

39/TA/4/1/33–47). The monthly journal includes reports from the organisers, including Roberts. He also reported on the Dec 1905 election results and thereafter wrote a monthly report, 'Labour in Parliament' (see A. E. Musson, *The Typographical Association*, Oxford UP 1954, for further details).

The National Museum of Labour History has some letters from Roberts to the Labour Representation Committee and the Labour Party. There were no Roberts papers at the Norfolk RO.

A brief biography by David E. Martin, drawing on the Labour Party archives and listing other sources, is in *DLB*, IV, 148–52. *Adjusting to Democracy* is a valuable guide to Roberts's work at the Ministry of Labour and to relevant PRO files.

GEORGE FREDERICK SAMUEL ROBINSON, 1st MARQUESS OF RIPON (1827–1909)

George Robinson was known as Viscount Goderich from 1833 until he succeeded his father as 2nd Earl of Ripon and his uncle as 3rd Earl de Grey in 1859. He was created KG in 1869, and Marquess of Ripon in 1871. He was Liberal MP for Hull 1852–53, Huddersfield 1853–57 and West Riding of Yorkshire 1857–59. He was Under-Secretary of State for War June 1859–Jan 1861 and July 1861–April 1863, Under-Secretary of State for India Jan-July 1861, Secretary of State for War April 1863– Feb 1866, Secretary of State for India Feb-June 1866, Lord President of the Council Dec 1868–Aug 1873, First Lord of the Admiralty Feb-Aug 1886, Secretary of State for the Colonies Aug 1892–June 1895, and Lord Privy Seal and Liberal Leader in the House of Lords Dec 1905–Oct 1908.

One hundred and thirty-five volumes of Ripon's papers were presented to the British Library in 1923 (Add MSS 43510–644). The papers have been arranged under the following headings: royal correspondence, special correspondence, correspondence about India, family correspondence, general correspondence, diaries, and miscellaneous.

Ripon's royal correspondence (two volumes) is arranged by individuals and includes letters from Queen Victoria and her secretaries 1869–95, and from King Edward VII 1864–1901. Ripon's special correspondents (53 volumes) – i.e. those from whom a considerable body of letters survive – include the 1st Earl Russell 1863–67, the 3rd Viscount Palmerston 1859–63, W. E. Gladstone (three volumes) 1863– 96, Lord Rosebery (one volume) 1886–1908, Sir H. Campbell-Bannerman 1888–1908, Asquith 1894–1908, John Morley (one volume) 1886–1909, and the 1st Earl of Kimberley (six volumes) 1864–1901. This series also includes six volumes of correspondence with colonial governors arranged by colony.

There are 55 volumes of correspondence concerning India. They include five volumes of correspondence 1859–1904 with the 8th Duke of Devonshire, mainly when he was Secretary of State for India, four volumes with Ripon's predecessor as Viceroy, the 1st Earl of Northbrook, volumes of correspondence with various Indian governors and Indian government officials and 14 volumes of printed official correspondence and papers with manuscript additions and corrections. Other copies of some of these printed volumes are available in the printed books department of the British Library.

There are 20 volumes of general correspondence 1849–1909 and three volumes of diary for 1878–80. The miscellaneous section includes notes for speeches and lectures and two political memoranda. Ripon's family correspondence consists of one volume of letters to his wife in 1880. His father's papers form a separate collection in the British Library.

The British Library also holds a collection of Ripon's letters to Lord Stanmore 1845–1908 (Add MSS 49233, 49238, 49240); Cabinet letters to Edward VII 1906 and 1908 (Add MSS 52512–13); letters to Sir S. H. Northcote 1871–72 (Add MSS 50038–9); letters to and from Lord Battersea 1893 (Add MS 47910).

The Buckinghamshire RO holds several items including reports from Colonel Burnaby on the French expeditionary force in Syria 1860, and letters from Lord Hobart, Governor of Madras 1873. The William R. Perkins Library at Duke University purchased 198 letters to Ripon in 1973. The letters deal with political, diplomatic, military, colonial, and ecclesiastical affairs for the period 1855–1907.

Lucien Wolf, *Life of the 1st Marquess of Ripon* (2 vols, John Murray 1921), quotes from many papers including a political memo by Ripon and his diary. Anthony Denholm, *Lord Ripon 1827–1909: A Political Biography* (Croom Helm 1982) draws on a wider range of sources.

SIR WILLIAM SNOWDON ROBSON, BARON ROBSON (1852–1918)

William Robson was Liberal MP for Tower Hamlets (Bow and Bromley) 1885–86 and South Shields 1895–1910. He was Solicitor-General Dec 1905–Jan 1908, and Attorney-General 1908–Oct 1910. He was knighted in 1905, and created Baron Robson (a judicial life peerage) in 1910, and GCMG in 1911.

In the first edition we advised that Robson's daughter-in-law, the Hon Mrs I. Robson, had only a few papers, including a 1906 election leaflet, a memo by Earl Grey on the Newfoundland Fisheries case (Robson presented the British Government's case to the International Court at the Hague 1910–11), a letter from Lewis Harcourt offering the GCMG as a reward for his efforts in that case Dec 1910, and correspondence relating to his resignation as a law lord in 1912. Mrs

Robson has since died, and her son Nigel's widow, Mrs Ann Robson, advised us that these papers are now longer to be found at the family home, Pinewood Hill.

Robson's grand-daughter, Mrs Rachel Maxwell-Hyslop, Water Lane House, Little Tew, Chipping Norton, Oxfordshire OX7 4JG, has a small collection of papers, consisting mostly of copies of speeches, photos, and press cuttings. She also has a copy of 'Philosophic Notes', the privately published religious tract which was previously thought to have been lost. Mrs Maxwell-Hyslop is hoping to write a biography of her grandfather.

Professor George W. Keeton, in his biography of Robson, *A Liberal Attorney General* (Nisbet 1949), quoted from the collection held by Mrs I. Robson, but added that Robson 'refused to keep any adequate record of his career and he had a distrust of "letters written for posterity"'. Professor Keeton states that 'Philosophic Notes' provides 'many important clues to the depths of Robson's character' (p. 233).

A further collection of some 300 letters and miscellaneous papers was found by Mr P. Audley-Miller in an old desk. They seemed to be an autograph collection; many of the letters were in envelopes headed 'signatures'. The letters were mainly from barristers, judges, civil servants and politicians, written when Robson was Solicitor-General and Attorney-General. They were in chronological order with undated letters at the end. There were 17 from the period 1891–1905 and 250 from 1906–20. There were 11 letters to Flood, Robson's clerk 1888–1910, and six letters to Sir Ryland Adkins 1913–19. There were also two writs summoning Robson to attend Parliament 1906 and 1910, and admission tickets to the Members' Gallery, the Official Gallery, and the Strangers' Gallery, and other miscellaneous papers. We have been unable to determine the present whereabouts of these papers.

WALTER RUNCIMAN, 1st VISCOUNT RUNCIMAN OF DOXFORD (1870–1949)

Walter Runciman was Liberal MP for Oldham 1899–1900, Dewsbury 1902–18, Swansea (West) 1924–29 and Cornwall (St Ives) 1929–37. He was a Liberal National from 1931. He was Parliamentary Secretary to the Local Government Board Dec 1905–Jan 1907, Financial Secretary to the Treasury 1907–April 1908, President of the Board of Education 1908–Oct 1911, President of the Board of Agriculture and Fisheries 1911–Aug 1914, President of the Board of Trade 1914–Dec 1916 and Nov 1931–May 1937, and Lord President of the Council Oct 1938–Sept 1939. He was created Viscount Runciman of Doxford in 1937.

The Runciman papers were deposited in the Robinson Library,

University of Newcastle upon Tyne, in 1969 (Runciman of Doxford papers). They comprise the papers of Runciman, together with some material relating to his wife Hilda, and to his father, the shipowner Baron Runciman of Shoreston. Some extra items were added in 1974 and 1984 and, at the end of 1989, further additions included Lady Runciman's diaries. The papers have been listed (NRA 73/173), and a catalogue, with both subject and correspondent indexes, is available for the main body of the collection (Alistair Elliot and Glenys Williams, *Catalogue of the Papers of Walter Runciman, 1st Viscount Runciman of Doxford (1870–1949)*, Newcastle University Library, 1973). There is a separate list of the 1989 additions, but other supplementary material has been added to the main catalogue. Researchers wishing to consult the papers should make written application to the Special Collections Librarian.

A large number of Cabinet papers from most of Runciman's offices appear to have survived in this collection. There are two volumes of Board of Education papers (bills, notes and correspondence) on the 1908 Education Bill; there is a complete set of memoranda circulated by Runciman as President of the Board of Trade Aug 1914–Sept 1915; and papers on the major problems of the day: the Committee of Imperial Defence; Ulster; Germany; the 1912 coal strike; the problems of blockade 1914–16. As well as these more formal papers, there is a collection of miscellaneous notes by Runciman, including some taken at Cabinet on the reform of the House of Lords.

The other political papers include material about Runciman's various elections, constituency matters, and the Liberal party (including files on the party's attitude to the General Strike and its financial problems 1926). There is also correspondence with Churchill, Herbert Samuel, and from Cabinet colleagues as well as papers on Runciman's mission to Czechoslovakia in 1938, and on his shipping and banking concerns. In addition there is a large collection of press cuttings and copies of, or notes for, speeches.

A further small collection (five volumes) relating to the mission to Czechoslovakia is available in the PRO (FO 800/304–8).

Runciman's early political views and his relationship with the Dewsbury constituency are the main theme of Martin D. Pugh, ' "Yorkshire and the New Liberalism"?', *Journal of Modern History*, 50, 3, Sept 1979, On Demand Supplement D1139–55.

A copy of a PhD thesis, 'The Runciman Mission to Czechoslovakia' by Karen Palmer (University of Belfast 1989) is available in The Robinson Library. Another PhD thesis, by Jonathan Wallace of the University of Newcastle upon Tyne, dealing with Runciman's political career, was in progress when we went to press.

HERBRAND EDWARD DUNDONALD BRASSEY SACKVILLE, 9th EARL DE LA WARR (1900–1976)

Herbrand Sackville ('Buck') was known as Lord Buckhurst until he succeeded his father as the 9th Earl De La Warr in 1915. He was created GBE in 1956. He was Parliamentary Under-Secretary of State for War June 1929–June 1930, Parliamentary Secretary to the Ministry of Agriculture and Fisheries 1930–Nov 1935, Parliamentary Under-Secretary to the Board of Education 1935–July 1936, Parliamentary Under-Secretary of State for the Colonies 1936–May 1937, Lord Privy Seal 1937–Oct 1938, President of the Board of Education 1938–April 1940, First Commissioner of Works April-May 1940, and Postmaster-General Nov 1951–April 1955.

Lord De La Warr informed us that he had no papers; he went through what papers he had and destroyed them because he did not think they would be of any interest.

His grandson, the 11th Earl De La Warr, did not know of any surviving papers of his grandfather.

The East Sussex RO holds a small collection of De La Warr's papers which was deposited in 1989 (A5411). The collection includes the transcript of a diary as a member of the British delegation to Ethiopia 1944; and political papers and speeches 1936–55. The collection also includes the diaries of Lady De La Warr on visits to Egypt 1937, America 1957, and Ceylon, Australia, and New Zealand 1959.

There is much from the perspective of 'independent television' on De La Warr's period as Postmaster-General in Bernard Sendall, *Independent Television in Britain*, 1, *Origin and Foundation, 1946–62* (Macmillan 1982).

SIR (JAMES) ARTHUR SALTER, BARON SALTER OF KIDLINGTON (1881–1975)

Arthur Salter was created KCB in 1922, GBE in 1944, and Baron Salter in 1953. He was Independent MP for Oxford University 1937–50, and Conservative MP for Lancashire (Ormskirk) 1951–53. He was Parliamentary Secretary to the Ministry of Shipping (War Transport from May 1941) Nov 1939–Feb 1942, Chancellor of the Duchy of Lancaster May-July 1945, Minister for Economic Affairs Oct 1951–Nov 1952, and Minister of Materials 1952–Sept 1953.

Lord Salter informed us that his papers were not available for research while his biography was being written by Dr Sidney Aster of the University of Toronto. When the biography is completed, Lord Salter's papers, along with Dr Aster's considerable working material and additional documentation, will be deposited at the Churchill Archives Centre.

The Salter papers originally filled two four-drawer filing cabinets. There are no papers before 1917 when he was a civil servant. A diary for 28 Nov-1 Dec 1917, notes and memoranda concerning convoys have survived from the International Conference on Shipping. The papers are particularly good for the period 1919–31 when Lord Salter worked for the League of Nations. There are memoranda by Lord Salter for the Reparations Commission 1919–30, notes on the organisation and administration of the League, correspondence with Lord Robert Cecil, for example on the entrance to the League of Germany in 1925, speeches, broadcast notes, and papers on particular topics such as the 1928 Kellogg Pact, and various proposals for a United States of Europe 1925–30.

Salter's papers reflect his diverse interests after his departure from the League in 1931. They cover his trips to India and China in 1931, and to China again in 1933, his work on economic problems, and his activities on such bodies as the BBC's Advisory Council and the All Souls' Foreign Affairs Group 1938–39. Correspondence about his nomination, election material, and press cuttings survive from his entry into Parliament in 1937. Salter was Gladstone Professor of Political Theory and Institutions at Oxford University 1934–44; his lifelong interest in Oxford is fully represented by his papers: agenda, minutes, and notes on college policy from All Souls, lecture notes, papers on the Oxford Preservation Trust and other Oxford bodies, including papers on various road schemes 1957–62. There are also papers relating to Salter's campaign 1937–39 for the storage of food and raw materials.

Salter's work at the Ministry of Shipping (later the Ministry of War Transport) is represented by both correspondence and memoranda. From Oct 1941 till 1943 Salter was Head of the British Merchant Shipping Mission to Washington DC. A large number of memoranda and correspondence has survived from this period including the official diary (that is, copies of all correspondence and telegrams) Oct 1941–June 1943. In 1944 Salter was Senior Deputy Director-General of the United Nations' Relief and Rehabilitation Administration; papers concerning his appointment and his work have survived, including papers relating to his visit to Germany in 1945. Only papers relating to his appointment and to the resignation of the government survive from Salter's tenure of the Duchy of Lancaster. There is some printed election material and lists of supporters from the 1945 general election. Election material and some correspondence with Churchill have survived from Salter's election for Ormskirk in 1951.

A considerable amount of material has survived from Salter's tenure of the Ministry for Economic Affairs and the Ministry of Materials. It includes correspondence, minutes, and memoranda largely on such economic issues as the balance of payments, inflation, and the Council of Europe. The correspondents in this group include Churchill and Leo Amery.

Several files of correspondence, draft speeches, memoranda, and extracts from *Hansard* reflect Salter's activities in the House of Lords. Subjects covered include the United Nations, Defence, Atomic Energy, and Rhodesia. In 1954 Salter was asked for economic advice by the government of Iraq. His resulting visits led to a considerable amount of correspondence, press cuttings, and a published report. A coup in Iraq prevented the implementation of his suggested reforms.

Salter published three volumes of memoirs: *Personality in Politics* (Faber & Faber 1948), *Memoirs of a Public Servant* (Faber & Faber 1961) and *Slave of the Lamp* (Weidenfeld & Nicolson 1967). Drafts, correspondence, and reviews of these and Salter's other publications are included in his papers.

Some of Salter's Private Office papers from the Ministry of War Transport are now available in the PRO (MT 62/95–123). The papers comprise correspondence files alphabetically arranged, with an original index. Salter's earlier career as a civil servant and subsequent ministerial appointments may also be traced in the surviving files of the ministries with which he was associated.

The League of Nations Archives (Section Files, Economic and Financial) contain 15 boxes (code numbers S104–S118) of Salter's papers 1922–31. Only one file is closed. (*Guide to the Archives of the League of Nations 1919–1946*, Geneva 1978).

SIR HERBERT LOUIS SAMUEL, 1st VISCOUNT SAMUEL (1870–1963)

Herbert Samuel was Liberal MP for North Riding of Yorkshire (Cleveland) 1902–18 and Lancashire (Darwen) 1929–35. He was Parliamentary Under-Secretary of State for Home Affairs Dec 1905–June 1909, Chancellor of the Duchy of Lancaster 1909–Feb 1910 and Nov 1915–Jan 1916, Postmaster-General Feb 1910–Feb 1914 and May 1915–Jan 1916, President of the Local Government Board Feb 1914–May 1915, and Secretary of State for Home Affairs Jan-Dec 1916 and Aug 1931–Sept 1932. He was Leader of the Liberal Party in the House of Commons Nov 1931–Nov 1935, and Leader in the House of Lords 1944–55. He was created GBE in 1920, GCB in 1926, and Viscount Samuel in 1937.

In his *Memoirs* (Cresset Press 1945) Samuel wrote that, although he had never kept a diary, he did keep notes of interesting conversations, in addition to a large collection of letters and political papers. Most of these papers were deposited in 1963 by his son, the late 2nd Viscount Samuel, in the HLRO (Samuel Papers; NRA 11187). The papers are available for research, but permission to quote from them must be obtained from Samuel's executors and from the Clerk of the Records,

HLRO. Samuel's grandson, the 3rd Viscount Samuel, has confirmed that there are no papers remaining in family hands.

Papers concerning Samuel's work in Palestine have been deposited in the Israel State Archives, Jerusalem. They are described in *Herbert Louis, First Viscount Samuel. A Register of His Papers at the State Archives*, by Elie Mizrachi (Jerusalem 1965). Most of this list is in Hebrew. Microfilm and other photographic copies of some of these papers are available at the HLRO and the Middle East Centre, St Antony's College, Oxford. They include 16 volumes of correspondence 1915–62, one volume of memoranda and minutes 1919–39, one volume of official papers 1920–44, and two volumes of press cuttings 1917–62.

The papers deposited in the HLRO are described briefly in M. F. Bond, *Guide to the Records of Parliament* (HMSO 1971), 283–4. Very detailed lists of the papers are contained in the HLRO, Memo 35, 1966, and Memo 41, 1969.

The papers in the HLRO have been divided into six main groups: political papers; personal papers; photos; press cuttings; literary, philosophical, and scientific papers; formal and ceremonial papers.

The political papers fill over 170 boxes; most of them are arranged in subject files. The earliest papers concern the conditions of employment of match box makers 1890–92. There are papers on Samuel's candidature for South Oxfordshire 1893–1900 and on his Cleveland constituency. There are a large number of papers concerning the Liberal party's organisation and administration. Samuel returned most of his Cabinet papers to the Cabinet Office but there are papers on some of the major political problems of his career: Ireland; reform of the House of Lords; the formation of the 1915 and 1916 Coalition governments and the 1931 National Government; India; Germany – including correspondence and notes of conversations with Neville Chamberlain, Lord Halifax, and others. There are also a few departmental papers including papers on the Marconi crisis (Samuel was then Postmaster-General), and the trial of Roger Casement (Samuel was at the Home Office). There are papers concerning the 1926 general strike and draft settlement terms by Samuel. Some of these papers were deposited in the HLRO in 1968 by Mr Frank Singleton who had borrowed them in 1939 for a projected biography of Samuel. Also included in the political papers are Samuel's letters to his mother 1881–1919, his wife 1898–1933, and his brother-in-law 1902–38, which include a great deal of political material. There are 13 volumes of general correspondence and papers 1888–1962.

Samuel's personal papers include his school papers, family correspondence, and some press cuttings. They also include some 50 letters from his wife 1925–52. His literary papers include drafts of his articles, pamphlets, and books and correspondence arising from them.

John Bowle, *Viscount Samuel* (Victor Gollancz 1957), was based on the papers and quotes extensively from them. It is superseded by Bernard Wasserstein, *Viscount Samuel: A Political Life* (Oxford UP 1992). Wasserstein had access to Samuel's correspondence with his sons Edwin (the 2nd Viscount Samuel) and Godfrey. He also reports the discovery of a complete list of books read by Samuel between 1889 and 1962 and Lady (Beatrice) Samuel's 'Dinner Books' 1904–33. Wasserstein's bibliography and footnotes are a comprehensive guide to relevant official files, private papers, archives, and theses.

SIR ROBERT ARTHUR SANDERS, Bt, BARON BAYFORD (1867–1940)

Robert Sanders was Conservative MP for Somerset (Bridgwater) 1910–23 and Somerset (Wells) 1924–29. He was Under-Secretary of State for War April 1921–Oct 1922, and Minister of Agriculture and Fisheries 1922–Jan 1924. He was created a baronet in 1920 and Baron Bayford in 1929.

Two notebooks (some 75,000 words) containing Sanders's diary for Feb 1910–21, and 1921–April 1935, previously held in the Conservative Research Department have been deposited in the Bodleian Library together with all that is known to survive from Sanders's correspondence (letters of 1911, 1914–18, 1920–21) formerly in the possession of his daughter, the Hon Mrs Vera Butler.

An edition of the diaries and letters has been published: John Ramsden (ed), *Real Old Tory Politics* (The Historians' Press 1984).

DUNCAN EDWIN SANDYS, BARON DUNCAN-SANDYS (1908–1987)

Duncan Sandys was Conservative MP for Lambeth (Norwood) 1935–45 and Wandsworth (Streatham) 1950–74. He was Financial Secretary to the War Office July 1941–Feb 1943, Parliamentary Secretary to the Ministry of Supply 1943–Nov 1944, Minister of Works 1944–Aug 1945, Minister of Supply Oct 1951–Oct 1954, Minister of Housing and Local Government 1954–Jan 1957, Minister of Defence 1957–Oct 1959, Minister of Aviation 1959–July 1960, Secretary of State for Commonwealth Relations 1960–Oct 1964, and Secretary of State for the Colonies July 1962–Oct 1964. He was created Baron Duncan-Sandys (a life peerage) in 1974.

Three hundred boxes of Lord Duncan-Sandys's papers have been deposited in the Churchill Archives Centre but are closed indefinitely (DSND; NRA 18561). However this situation may be reviewed in the future and interested readers should contact the Centre for further information.

The collection is grouped into 20 sections: pre-war papers 1930–39;

Second World War papers; Minister of Works 1943–46; Minister of Supply 1953–54; Minister of Housing and Local Government 1955–57 (including 65 files of press cuttings); Minister of Defence 1957–59; Minister of Aviation 1959–60; Secretary of State for Commonwealth Relations and the Colonies 1960–64; Europe 1947–72; civic trust 1957–69; world security trust 1965–72; capital punishment 1966–69; subject files 1966–73; countries 1964–72; correspondence 1941–73 (seven files of VIP correspondence and 52 files of general public correspondence); speeches 1944–74; official publications 1951–68; press cuttings 1941–70; personal papers 1917–51; photos 1901–67.

The PRO holds papers relating to Duncan-Sandys's period in Defence (DEFE 13/1–37) and Housing and Local Government (HLG 128/1).

For Duncan-Sandys's work at the Ministry of Defence see Colin Gordon, 'Duncan Sandys and the Independent Nuclear Deterrent' in Ian Beckett and John Gooch (eds), *Politicians and Defence: Studies in the Formulation of British Defence Policy 1845–1970* (Manchester UP 1981), 132–53. There is valuable guidance to publications, oral sources, and relevant public records in Simon J. Ball, 'Harold Macmillan and the Politics of Defence: The Market for Strategic Ideas during the Sandys Era Revisited', *Twentieth Century British History*, 6, 1, 1995, 79–100.

Biographies are being prepared by Dr John Barnes of the London School of Economics, and by Duncan-Sandys's son-in-law, Piers Dixon.

SIR JOHN SANKEY, VISCOUNT SANKEY (1866–1948)

John Sankey was knighted in 1914, and created GBE in 1917, Baron Sankey in 1929, and Viscount Sankey in 1932. He was Lord Chancellor June 1929–June 1935.

Sankey's papers have been given to the Bodleian Library (MSS Eng hist a 19; c 502–56, 558; d 313–40; e 242–303; f 21, 25), having been kept in solicitors' offices after the death of Sankey's sister in 1959. Some of the papers were destroyed in an effort to gain space, but it is thought that these were only press cuttings. Even so, some of the papers seen by Professor R.F.V. Heuston for his *Lord Chancellors 1* do not appear to have survived – for example, bar examination papers, and barrister's fee book. It should be pointed out that most of the papers now in the Bodleian were not produced for Professor Heuston because their existence had been forgotten.

More than two trunks of papers have survived. They seem to have been sorted by Sankey himself in 1940 and by his sister in 1948. The most important section of these papers is Sankey's diary covering the years, 1888, 1891–1947. The diary was written in small desk diaries and many of the entries are simply brief notes of appointments or activities. For example, while the Coal Commission of 1919 was sitting, the most informative entry about Sankey's attitude is for 13 March 1919: 'Owners' evidence. They are hopeless!' However, the diary is often kept in some detail, particularly after 1929, and is, for instance, very full on the events leading up to the formation of the National Government. Sankey himself described it as 'fairly copious'. In an entry on 16 Jan 1932 Sankey wrote 'Have torn up many old papers and documents this week. Referring to Coal Commission, Aliens, and Sinn Fein revolt'. He notes his continuing destruction of papers in his entries on 17–19 Jan 1932 (Bodleian Library MS Eng hist e 286, f 35).

The bulk of the papers is in the form of miscellaneous correspondence. This includes many letters of congratulation on Sankey's various appointments and honours, as well as more general correspondence for the 1930s and 1940s. There are also a great many press cuttings.

Sankey himself arranged his large collection of notes for speeches into what he described as 'volumes' or large bundles. The 13 'volumes' are indexed, giving the date, the occasion, and the place of each speech; each 'volume' has a list of contents.

Apart from the diaries, general correspondence, and press cuttings, Sankey's career is well represented by his papers. There is a minute book of the Home Office Advisory Committee on Enemy Aliens (16 April 1916–11 Dec 1918) of which Sankey was chairman and which usually records who was present or absent and occasionally gives details of the cases heard. There are some press cuttings, a small amount of correspondence, and minutes of evidence for 16 June 1919 of the 1919 Coal Commission.

There are also three seals and many papers derived from Sankey's tenure of the Woolsack. Papers concerning the Indian Round Table Conference predominate. For Dec 1930 there are drafts of the proposed Indian Constitution and comments by MacDonald and the former Viceroy, Lord Reading. For 1931 there are several printed reports and memoranda, often annotated by Sankey. There is also some correspondence: a nine-page typed letter from Sir Malcolm Hailey, Governor of the United Provinces 18 July 1931, and a seven-page letter from Lord Reading 28 Nov 1931, both on the state of affairs and future policy. There are notes by both Sankey 15 Sept 1931 (ten typed pp), and Lord Irwin (later Earl of Halifax) 25 Sept 1931 of their conversations with Gandhi. There is also a 15–page note by Sankey on the proceedings of the Federal Structure Committee. For 1932 there is a bundle of miscellaneous letters about the Round Table Conference, notes on a meeting of the Cabinet's Indian Committee 26 May 1932 which give the opinions of the various speakers, and notes for Sankey's speech at the close of the conference 24 Dec 1932. There are many memoranda and minutes of the Cabinet's Committee

1934–35; including what Sankey describes as the 'key document' – a 23–page memo by the Secretary of State for India, Sir Samuel Hoare, 27 Oct 1934 – and the report of the Committee to the Cabinet 29 Jan 1935.

As well as these papers on India there are many pages of notes by Sankey on Cabinet meetings: 22 July 1930; 15 June 1931; 21 and 22 Jan 1932; 26 May 1932; 28 and 30 Sept 1932. They cover various topics including agricultural policy, tariffs, the Ottawa Conference, and the resignation of Snowden, Samuel, and Sinclair. Sankey wrote a 26–page memo on the 1930 Imperial Conference, its proceedings, and its participants. There is also an exchange of correspondence with Mac-Donald 13 May 1931 on a speech by the Prince of Wales concerning protection, and whether it was an incursion into politics. Perhaps most interesting of all is a 12–page memo written by Sankey in June 1935 on the events leading up to his resignation. In it he says that MacDonald offered him the Lord Chancellorship in 1924 if Haldane would take Education. He goes on to claim that he nearly prevented the government's collapse in Aug 1931; he says that Arthur Henderson, the leader of the revolt against MacDonald, got cold feet at the last minute and that a reconciliation was only prevented by the intervention of Arthur Greenwood.

There is also a photo of a letter from Adolf Hitler to the 1st Viscount Rothermere dated 20 Dec 1935 with an English translation. Rothermere appears to have asked Hitler for his views on the current international situation and this letter sets these views out in some detail (eight typed pp).

SIR PHILIP ALBERT GUSTAVE DAVID SASSOON, 3rd Bt (1888–1939)

Philip Sassoon succeeded his father as 3rd baronet in 1912, and was created GBE in 1922. He was Conservative MP for Hythe 1912–39. He was Under-Secretary of State for Air Nov 1924–June 1929 and Sept 1931–May 1937, and First Commissioner of Works 1937–June 1939.

Sassoon died unmarried. For the first edition, Sassoon's sister, Sybil, Marchioness of Cholmondeley, informed us that several boxes of his papers were lost during the Second World War when his former house, Trent Park, was occupied by the War Office. The Marchioness added that her brother did not keep copies of letters or memoranda which he wrote. All that the Marchioness had was a small collection of approximately 40 letters. A large number of these were from Lord Esher during the period 1916–22 in which Lord Esher discusses the political situation. Sassoon's replies to these letters are to be found in Lord Esher's own papers, which have been deposited in the library of Churchill Archives Centre (ESHR).

This small collection is currently in the possession of the Marquess of Cholmondeley at Houghton, along with copies of correspondence between Sassoon and Lord Haig and other allied commanders during the First World War when Sassoon was aide-de-camp to Haig. The Marquess advised that he believes that much of Sassoon's correspondence was lost or destroyed after he died.

The draft text of Haig's Order of the Day 11 April 1918, the famous 'backs to the wall' message to British Forces in France, was bequeathed by Sassoon to the British Library (Add MS 45416).

There is a brief summary of Sassoon's career by Osbert Sitwell in *DNB 1931-1940*, 784-5.

JOHN EDWARD BERNARD SEELY, 1st BARON MOTTISTONE (1868-1947)

Jack Seely was Conservative MP for the Isle of Wight 1900-04, and Liberal MP for the same place 1904-06 and 1923-24, Liverpool (Abercromby) 1906-10 and Derbyshire (Ilkeston) 1910-22. He was Under-Secretary of State for the Colonies April 1908-March 1911, Under-Secretary of State for War 1911-June 1912, Secretary of State for War 1912-March 1914, Parliamentary Under-Secretary of State to the Ministry of Munitions June 1918-Jan 1919, and Under-Secretary of State for Air Jan-Dec 1919. He was created Baron Mottistone in 1933.

Seely's son, the 4th Lord Mottistone, deposited a small collection of his father's papers in the Nuffield College Library (Mottistone papers). The collection had been weeded by Seely's second wife. A further deposit in 1975 brought the collection to 42 boxes. The papers have been divided into five main groups: general correspondence; political papers; official papers; military papers; and literary papers and miscellaneous.

There are seven boxes of correspondence 1876-1947. The political papers include speeches, notes, correspondence, and press cuttings concerning Seely's non-official political life. There are many papers on the 1903-04 fiscal question, and on Chinese labour in South Africa, both controversies which contributed to Seely's becoming a Liberal in 1904. Seely's official papers are divided by his various terms of office at the Colonial Office, the War Office, and Munitions and Air. In addition there are two boxes of Committee of Imperial Defence papers 1910-14. These papers include many papers of the subcommittee on the transportation and distribution of food supplies in time of war 1910-11. Seely's War Office papers (six boxes) include notes and correspondence concerning his audiences with the King, and his 'Plot' dossier concerning the Curragh mutiny. There are also three boxes of Cabinet memoranda 1912-14. The military papers concern the administration of the Canadian Cavalry Brigade and include battle reports, reports on individual officers, speeches, and souvenirs of post-war reunions. Seely's literary papers consist of drafts or cuttings of his numerous newspaper articles. The last part of Seely's career is represented by a box of 'Invasion Papers 1940–45' and another on the 1944 Education Act. A personal name index of the collection has been compiled.

The 1975 deposit includes further Curragh papers; press reviews and miscellaneous correspondence relating to his literary works (see below); additional general correspondence 1920–53; additional 'Invasion Papers' 1940–45, and Education Bill Debate papers, as well as a collection of *Hansards* containing Seely's speeches May 1938–July 1946. There are also 12 boxes of press cuttings and photos 1897–1932.

An extensive collection of Mottistone estate papers is held by the Isle of Wight RO; a four volume indexed handlist is available.

Seely related some of the more adventurous exploits of his life and quoted from a few of his papers in *Adventure* (Heinemann 1930) and *Fear and Be Slain* (Hodder & Stoughton 1931).

THOMAS SHAW (1872–1938)

Tom Shaw was Labour MP for Preston 1918–31. He was Minister of Labour Jan-Nov 1924, and Secretary of State for War June 1929–Aug 1931.

Shaw's only surviving daughter, Mrs M. E. Halliwell, informed us that she had none of her father's papers, and that they were probably destroyed during the bombing of the Second World War. Shaw's widow had put most of her belongings into Harrods' furniture store and the store received a direct hit. Mrs Halliwell added that, in any case, her father never kept speech notes or press cuttings.

Adjusting to Democracy is a valuable guide to Shaw's work at the Ministry of Labour and to relevant PRO files.

SIR HARTLEY WILLIAM SHAWCROSS, BARON SHAWCROSS (1902–)

Hartley Shawcross was knighted in 1945, and created Baron Shawcross (a life peerage) in 1959. He was Labour MP for St Helens 1945–58. He was Attorney-General Aug 1945–April 1951, and President of the Board of Trade April-Oct 1951.

Lord Shawcross informed us that he has kept some press cuttings, copies of speeches, and a few personal letters; but none of these papers is at present available for research.

Lord Shawcross has produced an autobiography, *Life Sentence: The memoirs of Hartley Shawcross* (Constable 1995).

EMANUEL SHINWELL, BARON SHINWELL (1884–1986)

Manny Shinwell was Labour MP for Linlithgowshire 1922–24 and 1928–31, Durham (Seaham) 1935–50 and Durham (Easington) 1950–70. He was Parliamentary Secretary, Department of Mines at the Board of Trade Jan-Nov 1924 and June 1930–Aug 1931, Financial Secretary to the War Office June 1929–June 1930, Minister of Fuel and Power Aug 1945–Oct 1947, Secretary of State for War 1947–Feb 1950, and Minister of Defence 1950–Oct 1951. He was created Baron Shinwell (a life peerage) in 1970.

Lord Shinwell's papers were deposited at the BLPES between 1982 and 1986 (Shinwell papers). They have been listed and applications for use should be made to the Archivist.

Many of Lord Shinwell's papers were thrown away as he went along but he tried to keep letters which he felt would be of historical interest. No papers survive to document Shinwell's early trade union and Labour Party career and relatively few survive from his period of office in the 1945 Labour Government, the majority of the papers relating to Shinwell's later years as a backbench MP and a peer.

The collection has been divided into six sections: House of Commons' papers; House of Lords' papers; correspondence 1924–85; publications; family and miscellaneous papers; and photos 1900–74.

The House of Commons papers are mainly from his period as Minister of Fuel and Power, but also contain articles, speeches, cuttings, and correspondence on Labour Party discipline 1951–60 and 1964–68, including Shinwell's resignation as Chairman of the Labour Party. The House of Lords' material dates mostly from the 1980s and consists mainly of papers and correspondence on various bills.

The correspondence is divided into political and general correspondence. The political correspondents include many of Shinwell's political colleagues, while the general correspondence is mostly invitations and letters from Shinwell's supporters.

The section on publications contains articles, notes, and speeches from throughout Shinwell's career as well as material about his autobiographies, *I've Lived Through It All* (Gollancz 1973), and *Lead with the Left: My First 96 Years* (Cassell 1981). Shinwell's earlier autobiography *Conflict Without Malice* (Odhams 1955) remains useful.

The family papers include those of Shinwell's second wife, Dinah, as well as a large number of press cuttings collected by Shinwell, his family, and friends. The photos are mainly of Shinwell making official ministerial visits.

Peter Slowe's, *Manny Shinwell: An Authorised Biography* (Pluto Press 1993) makes use of the BLPES collection, as well as interviews with many of Shinwell's relatives and colleagues. J. S. Rowett applies a corrective to

Shinwell's 'entertaining but unreliable memoirs' in his short life in *Blackwell*, 372–4.

Colin Stafford is undertaking a PhD thesis, 'The Political Career of Emanuel Shinwell, 1884–1986', at the University of Newcastle.

EDWARD SHORTT (1862–1935)

Edward Shortt was Liberal MP for Newcastle-upon-Tyne (Newcastle-upon-Tyne, West from 1918) 1910–22. He was Chief Secretary for Ireland May 1918–Jan 1919, and Secretary of State for Home Affairs 1919–Oct 1922.

A very small collection of Shortt's papers which was in the possession of his daughter, Mrs A. D. Ingrams, is now held by her son, Mr David Ingrams, Bewley Down, Axminster, Devon EX13 7JM. For the first edition, Mrs Ingrams informed us that her father kept no diary and that she did not know of the existence of any other papers, and Mr Ingrams confirms that no further papers have been discovered. Transcripts of almost all the letters in this collection have been deposited in the Nuffield College Library (Shortt Papers).

The collection consists of two books of press cuttings and a few letters. The press cuttings are mainly of a biographical nature, but they cover the 1908 Newcastle by-election which Shortt fought and lost, as well as the Dec 1910 and the 1918 general elections. Shortt's election campaigns are also represented by photos, a letter of support from Asquith in 1908, and his election address in 1918. Nothing survives relating to his activities in support of the 1912 Home Rule Bill. A letter from Lloyd George 25 Nov 1915 thanks Shortt for his work in selecting munition workers to be withdrawn from military units. A very small amount of material survives from Shortt's tenure of the Irish Office including some very hostile letters to Mrs Shortt, as well as letters of regret when Shortt was transferred to the Home Office. Nothing survives from Shortt's tenure of the Home Office apart from letters of regret on his departure, including one from a policeman praising the minister's handling of the police strikes. An illuminated scroll was presented to Shortt from the Police Federation on 21 Nov 1922 as an appreciation of his work. There are several photos and letters of thanks from the royal family. The press cuttings include material on Shortt's activities as film censor from 1929 to 1935.

WILLIAM PHILIP SIDNEY, 1st VISCOUNT DE L'ISLE (1909–1991)

William Sidney was Conservative MP for Chelsea 1944–45. He was Parliamentary Secretary, Ministry of Pensions May–July 1945, and Secretary of State for Air Oct 1951–Dec 1955. He succeeded his father as 6th Baron De L'Isle and Dudley in 1945, and was created

Viscount De L'Isle in 1956, GCMG in 1961, GCVO in 1963, and KG in 1968.

De L'Isle's son, the 2nd Viscount De L'Isle, advised us that his family maintain a closed private archive which is not available for research.

Chris Cook, Jane Leonard, and Peter Leese, *Sources in Contemporary British History*, 2, *Individuals* (Longman 1994), notes information from the RAF Museum that this family archive includes papers as Secretary of State for Air including 'minutes to the Prime Minister, 1951–55; election speeches, 1955; and files relating to the Conservative Party and to the Commonwealth Parliamentary Association' (p. 95).

The National Library of Australia advised us that they do not hold or know of any original De L'Isle papers in Australia from his time as Governor-General of Australia 1961–65.

Mr Ronald T. Winch, 68 Vasey Crescent, Campbell, ACT 2601, Australia, possesses a small collection of unpublished research material based on several conversations with Lord De L'Isle 1985–87.

LEWIS SILKIN, 1st BARON SILKIN (1889–1972)

Lewis Silkin was Labour MP for Camberwell (Peckham) 1936–50. He was Minister of Town and Country Planning Aug 1945–Feb 1950. He was created Baron Silkin in 1950.

Lord Silkin told us, shortly before his death, that he had made it a practice never to keep any documents. His eldest son, Mr Arthur Silkin, confirmed that no papers have survived.

SIR JOHN ALLSEBROOK SIMON, 1st VISCOUNT SIMON (1873–1954)

John Simon was Liberal MP for Essex (South-West or Walthamstow) 1906–18 and West Riding of Yorkshire (Spen Valley) 1922–40; he was a Liberal National from 1931. He was Solicitor-General Oct 1910–Oct 1913, Attorney-General 1913–May 1915, Secretary of State for Home Affairs 1915–Jan 1916 and June 1935–May 1937, Secretary of State for Foreign Affairs Nov 1931–June 1935, Chancellor of the Exchequer May 1937–May 1940, and Lord Chancellor 1940–Aug 1945. He was knighted in 1910, and created GCSI in 1930, and Viscount Simon in 1940.

Simon's papers, formerly in the possession of his son, the 2nd Lord Simon, were deposited in the Bodleian Library in 1979 (MSS Simon 1–284). They are available for research and a detailed catalogue and index has been prepared (NRA 24981). The papers were used in Simon's own memoirs *Retrospect* (Hutchinson 1952), and in Edward B. Segal, 'Sir John Simon and British Foreign Policy: the Diplomacy of Disarmament in the Early 1930s' (PhD thesis, University of California, Berkeley 1969), which is available through University Microfilms Ltd (AAC 70–6219). Dr Segal says in his thesis that the biography of Simon by C. E. Bechhofer Roberts ('Ephesian'), *Sir John Simon* (Robert Hale 1938), is based to a large extent on memoranda provided by Simon, particularly on his period at the Foreign and Home Offices, and that Simon himself corrected and edited Roberts's manuscript.

The papers have been sorted into correspondence and papers relating to political and legal affairs; speeches, lectures, and broadcasts; printed papers, press cuttings, and photos. There are 16 volumes of diaries and notebooks 1907–53 and 30 volumes of appointment diaries 1918–53. The earlier volumes of diaries and notebooks appear to have been kept to help Simon with his speeches, and to keep him informed on particular subjects: there are notes and press cuttings on free trade and licensing. But the later volumes contain a fairly full narrative of events. There is a volume on the 1930–31 split of the Liberal Party, including a long report of a meeting of leading Liberals 20 Nov 1930 on proposals for 'a definite understanding with Labour'. Notes on Liberal Party organisation are in MSS Simon 234.

Correspondence and papers for 1931–35 include a large amount of material relating to allegations concerning Lord Simon's shares in Vickers and ICI and his libel suit against Rev J. Whitaker Bond Jan 1935.

The great bulk of the papers is formed by press cuttings 1903–21, and 1931–45. Some of the cuttings are arranged by subject, for example, India; successive general election campaigns; the 1938 Czechoslovakia crisis. There are some papers on the General Strike; the 1926–27 Liberal Party split; the 1931–32 activities of the Liberal Nationals; and India, particularly the work of the Statutory Commission 1927–30. The post-1940 papers mainly relate to Simon's legal judgements and opinions, for example, on capital punishment.

Additional material was acquired in 1986 (MSS Simon adds 1–5) concerning the Liberal National Party 1937–39; transcript memoranda relating to Bechhofer Roberts's biography, and material about Bretton Woods and Simon's memoirs.

Forty-nine boxes and 22 volumes of Simon's papers as Chairman of the Indian Statutory Commission 1927–30 – correspondence and evidence – presented by the 2nd Viscount Simon in 1955 and 1978, are in the Oriental and India Office Collections, British Library (MSS Eur F 77). There is a list of the papers.

Seven volumes of miscellaneous Foreign Office correspondence 1931–35 are available in the PRO (FO 800/285–91). A list has been compiled.

David Dutton, *Simon: A Political Biography of Sir John Simon* (Aurum Press 1992) uses the Bodleian collection as well as the official collections referred to above. R. F. V. Heuston's essay on Simon in *Lord Chancellors 2*, 37–62, is authoritative on legal matters.

GAVIN TURNBULL SIMONDS, 1st VISCOUNT SIMONDS (1881-1971)

Gavin Simonds was knighted in 1937, created Baron Simonds (a judicial life peerage) in 1944, Baron Simonds in 1952, and Viscount Simonds in 1954. He was Lord Chancellor Oct 1951-Oct 1954.

R. F. V. Heuston, *Lord Chancellors 2*, noted that Lord Simonds informed him of his intention to destroy all of his papers. It appears that Simonds did destroy his papers, and this is confirmed by his nephew Kenneth Simonds. Mr Simonds advised that the only surviving material is a manuscript of his uncle's memoirs ('Recollections') which has been deposited in the archives of Winchester College.

This unpaginated manuscript, which fills half a box-file, is open 'to bona fide scholars and researchers', with a rider that 'the passage of time could ease this inhibition'. Mr Simonds informed us that the manuscript is 'a gentle, personal, memoir' with few references to his uncle's political and legal career. There are quotations from it in Heuston's biographical essay. Copyright rests with Mr Simonds.

Intending readers should write in the first instance to the Archivist, Winchester College, to establish their credentials and arrange a convenient time for a visit.

There are copies of two long letters to Simonds (16 Oct and 26 Oct 1954) from the Australian Chief Justice, Sir Owen Dixon, in the Swinton Papers at the Churchill Archives Centre (SWIN 174/6/2).

SIR ARCHIBALD HENRY MACDONALD SINCLAIR, 4th Bt, 1st VISCOUNT THURSO (1890-1970)

Archibald Sinclair succeeded his grandfather as 4th baronet in 1912, and was created KT in 1941, and Viscount Thurso in 1952. He was Liberal MP for Caithness and Sutherland 1922-45. He was Secretary of State for Scotland Aug 1931-Sept 1932, and Secretary of State for Air May 1940-May 1945. He was Leader of the Liberal Party in the House of Commons Nov 1935-Aug 1945.

Many of Sinclair's papers were destroyed during the bombing of the Second World War and in a fire at his Caithness home but a large collection of papers was deposited by his son, the 2nd Viscount Thurso, in the Churchill Archives Centre (THRS). The papers were deposited in several stages, and in varying states of repair. The papers have been listed and most of them are available for research.

The largest section of the collection is Sinclair's general political correspondence 1922-38. The correspondence is arranged alphabetically within each year. There are several boxes of speeches 1925-51, and five boxes of the correspondence 1928-37 of Captain Keith, Sinclair's constituency and estate agent. Sinclair was Liberal Chief Whip 1930-31 and Leader of the Parliamentary Liberal Party. Thirteen boxes of Liberal organisation papers 1932–39 and six boxes of Scottish Liberal organisation papers 1932–38 are included in this collection. There are also several boxes of League of Nations Union papers 1936–39, boxes of papers on the 1929 electoral reform conference and the 1932 Ottawa conference, and two boxes of personal papers 1942–52. There are a large number of constituency papers. A further deposit of 23 boxes of papers covers politics 1945–51. Eight boxes of private correspondence 1915–22 include letters from Churchill, Edward Marsh, and Jack Seely. These papers, which were badly charred, have been repaired and listed and are available for research.

Sinclair's constituency papers, which were deposited with the NRA(S), have now been added to the collection at the Churchill Archives Centre. There are 23 files, almost all of them correspondence 1923–37 with the Scottish Office on particular cases arising in Sinclair's constituency though some issues of more general Scottish interest arise. There are two files from Sinclair's tenure of the Scottish Office, largely concerned with departmental work, but they include comments on Cabinet conclusions. There is also a file of correspondence 1934–36 between Sinclair and the Duke of Montrose on the possibility of cooperation between the Liberal party and the Scottish Nationalist Party. This correspondence includes much material about the votes and policies of the two parties.

Private Office papers relating to Sinclair's period at the Scottish Office are dispersed through the files of the five main Scottish Office departments held at the SRO.

Some – though not all – of Sinclair's papers as Secretary of State for Air are now available at the PRO (AIR 19/73–557). There are a great many departmental files on technical matters such as bomb sights and the defence of factories from aerial attack, but there are also many files of policy papers: correspondence with the Ministries of Aircraft Production and Economic Warfare on the division of responsibilities and cooperation between the three departments; papers on bombing policy over occupied countries and on German crops and forests. There are also drafts of some of the Prime Minister's speeches with Sinclair's comments, and Sinclair's own speeches.

A 20–page memo by Sinclair formerly in the Gladstone Library at the National Liberal Club is now to be found in the University of Bristol Library (DM785). It records a number of meetings between Sinclair and Neville Chamberlain 28 Aug, 2 and 3 Sept 1939, and meetings of Liberal leaders to consider those meetings. The document, a typed top copy, has manuscript amendments by Sinclair and is initialled by him. It is annotated 'Notes dictated to me by Sir Archibald Sinclair for sending to members of the Liberal Party Committee, T. D. Nudds 1939 August'. Nudds gave the document to the late Sydney Hope, whose executors gave it to the Gladstone Library.

There is also some material on Sinclair in the Sayer Archive.

There is a biography of Thurso by Dr Gerard De Groot, *Liberal Crusader: The Life of Sir Archibald Sinclair* (Hurst 1993). While writing the biography Dr De Groot held a large box of personal letters including correspondence between Thurso and his wife (particularly for 1918). He also had some files on post-1945 Liberal Party. Lord Thurso intends to deposit this material in the Churchill Archives Centre, with the rest of his father's papers.

The brief biographical chapter on Sinclair in *Secretaries of State for Scotland*, 46–53, draws on the Thurso papers. The papers are also used by Malcolm Baines, 'The survival of the British Liberal Party, 1933–59', in Anthony Gorst, Lewis Johnman, and W. Scott Lucas (eds), *Contemporary British History 1931–1961: Politics and the limits of policy* (Pinter Publishers, in assoc with The Institute of Contemporary British History 1991), 17–32. Reference should also be made to J. W. R. Mitchell, 'The emergence of Modern Scottish central administration 1885–1939' (DPhil, Oxford University 1987).

JOHN SINCLAIR, 1st BARON PENTLAND (1860–1925)

John Sinclair was Liberal MP for Dumbartonshire 1892–95 and Forfarshire 1897–1909. He was Secretary for Scotland Dec 1905–Feb 1912. He was created Baron Pentland in 1909, GCIE in 1912, and GCSI in 1918.

Lady Marjorie Pentland, Sinclair's wife, wrote *The Right Honourable John Sinclair, Lord Pentland, G.C.S.I. A Memoir* (Methuen 1928) and quoted from many letters and a diary. She said that the section of the book devoted to his governorship of Madras 1912–19 was longer than other sections because more material was available, partly because her husband had contemplated writing his memoirs of that period. It is believed that after Lady Pentland's death, her daughter, the Hon Margaret Sinclair, went through the papers in the house and burnt great quantities including, it is thought, Pentland's political papers. When the first edition was being prepared, Pentland's son, the 2nd Lord Pentland, did not know of any papers. A small collection of photos, correspondence, and cine-film had been sent to the 2nd Lord's daughter, the Hon Mary Rothenberg in the USA.

The SRO holds microfilm copies of some of this material, including Sinclair's commonplace book while Governor of Madras entitled 'J. S. – Journal', containing copies of notes and letters, and other notes dated 1912–19 on Indian politics and miscellaneous other matters, and a small folder containing letters from Florence Nightingale (RH4/97).

Other items, including two visitors' books from Government House,

Madras, a large bundle of letters c.1900–38, and letters from William Gladstone, do not appear to have been copied.

Sinclair was Sir Henry Campbell-Bannerman's executor, and the last two volumes of the latter's papers, deposited in the British Library (Add MSS 52520–1), contain letters, copies, and memoirs sent to Sinclair in response to his appeal for letters from Campbell-Bannerman.

The British Library has further correspondence and material relating to the biography of Campbell-Bannerman (Add MSS 41230, 41252).

Private Office papers relating to Sinclair's period at the Scottish Office are dispersed through the files of the five main Scottish Office departments held at the SRO.

Reference should be made to J. W. R. Mitchell, 'The Emergence of Modern Scottish central administration 1885–1939' (DPhil, Oxford University 1987).

SIR BEN SMITH (1879–1964)

Ben Smith was Labour MP for Bermondsey (Rotherhithe) 1923–31 and 1935–46. He was Parliamentary Secretary to the Ministry of Aircraft Production March 1942–Nov 1943, Minister Resident in Washington for Supply 1943–May 1945, and Minister of Food Aug 1945–May 1946. He was created KBE in 1945.

In the first edition, we noted that his widow, Lady Smith, had only a very small collection of papers which were not generally available. She informed us that many papers, including diaries, were destroyed in the bombing of the Second World War. All that she had were two volumes of press cuttings on Smith's work as Chairman of the West Midland district of the National Coal Board 1948–49 and 1946–50, and a volume of cuttings mostly about Smith's work at the Ministry of Food. The latter volume also included a collection of obituary notices. In addition to these volumes, Lady Smith had Smith's letter of appointment as a Privy Councillor 1944, a few social notes from Lord Beaverbrook, press cuttings on Smith's appointment to Washington, notes for a lecture on trade unionism given to Camberley Staff College 1934, and telegrams concerning the request of the Australian government for an official visit by Smith in 1945 (he was unable to go because of the 1945 general election). We have been unable to determine the current location of these papers.

The Southwark Local Studies Library holds a collection of press cuttings on Smith, as well as the records for the Bermondsey Borough Council (where Smith was an Alderman) and the Bermondsey Labour Party which includes material on Smith.

Private Office papers relating to Smith's period with the Ministry of Aircraft Production are in AVIA 9 at the PRO.

SIR FREDERICK EDWIN SMITH, 1st Bt, 1st EARL OF BIRKENHEAD (1872–1930)

F. E. Smith was Conservative MP for Liverpool (Walton) 1906–18 and Liverpool (West Derby) 1918–19. He was Solicitor-General June-Nov 1915, Attorney-General 1915–Jan 1919, Lord Chancellor 1919–Oct 1922, and Secretary of State for India Nov 1924–Oct 1928. He was knighted in 1915, and created baronet in 1918, Baron Birkenhead in 1919, Viscount Birkenhead in 1921, Earl of Birkenhead in 1922, and GCSI in 1928.

A small collection of papers was retained in the possession of Birkenhead's son, the 2nd Earl of Birkenhead, who stated that his father never kept a diary nor, on leaving office, did he take away any departmental papers. Of the few which now survive, many have either been quoted or paraphrased in the 2nd Earl's biography, the second edition of which includes additional material: *F. E. The Life of F. E. Smith First Earl of Birkenhead* by his son, the 2nd Earl of Birkenhead (Eyre & Spottiswoode 1959).

The surviving papers are now in the care of the 2nd Earl's daughter, Lady Juliet Townsend. They are not generally available for research. The papers have been arranged in a series of numbered box files which are labelled with the contents.

The earliest papers are letters. One which we previously noted from H. Hensley Henson, referring to Smith's appearance before Oxford magistrates following a demonstration during a visit to Oxford by the Prince of Wales in May 1897 can no longer be found. Smith's commission in the Oxfordshire Imperial Yeomanry is dated 9 Aug 1907. There are some early personal letters. Correspondents include Edward Carson 1913, Churchill 1908, 1911, 1913, Lord Fisher 1908, and Andrew Bonar Law 1912. There are a few letters relating to the 1906 election and some election addresses for Jan 1910.

A large portion of this collection covers Smith's wartime activities. There is correspondence concerning a dispute in 1916 over the calling-up of W. A. Pursey, the Attorney-General's second clerk, who was fit only for garrison duties. There is a letter from Lord Finlay 17 Jan 1917 in which he states his intention to adhere to Lord Buckmaster's decision not to create any silks for the duration of the war. There is correspondence concerning the organisation of a committee by J. H. Morgan to report on the 'breaches of the laws and customs of the war' by the Germans and their allies and on the degree of responsibility of the German General Staff or 'other highly placed individuals'. There is an Imperial War Cabinet Paper on 'Our Attitude towards the Ex-Kaiser' 28 Nov 1918.

At the end of 1917 Smith undertook a tour of Canada and the USA to encourage their war efforts. Correspondence concerning this tour and another made in 1923 survive. There are also papers dealing with allegations made by Ellis Powell in Nov 1918 concerning the Marconi case. There is a six-page typed introduction for the second edition of his book (written with J. W. B. Merewether), *The Indian Corps in France* (John Murray 1917).

There are letters of congratulations on his becoming Lord Chancellor and on becoming Secretary of State for India, and a collection of letters from friends and colleagues throughout the 1920s, including letters on his resignation in Oct 1928. There are letters and press cuttings referring to the 1921 Irish Treaty, and letters from successive Viceroys of India, Lord Reading and Lord Irwin. There is also a series of letters from Lord Rothermere March-April 1923 on the need for a new Conservative leader.

One box contains material relating to the second Earl's biography including letters giving information about his father's life, as well as the contract and correspondence relating to the publication of the book and reviews. There are press cuttings and photos of the unveiling of a bust of Lord Birkenhead at the Oxford Union on 4 Nov 1932.

Birkenhead's papers as Secretary of State for India are in the Oriental and India Office Collections, British Library (MSS Eur D 703). These papers have been divided into bound volumes of correspondence with the viceroy and governors, telegrams exchanged with the viceroy, 12 files of departmental papers, miscellaneous files, and miscellaneous files on English political questions. This last section includes papers on the 1926 General Strike, the 1927 Poor Law Amendment Act, and the 1928 parliamentary debates on the case of Major G. Bell Murray.

A collection of autograph notes made by Birkenhead (when he was Attorney-General) during the trial of Sir Roger Casement for treason in June 1916 was sold by Christie's in 1981 (Christie's catalogue, sale 4 Nov 1981). This collection is in the National Library of Ireland (MS 25, 057).

A biography by John Campbell, *F. E. Smith, First Earl of Birkenhead* (Jonathan Cape 1983) is based on the public and private collections noted above.

SIR REGINALD HUGH DORMAN-SMITH (1899–1977)

Colonel Reginald Dorman-Smith was Conservative MP for Hampshire (Petersfield) 1935–41. He was Minister of Agriculture and Fisheries Jan 1939–May 1940. He was knighted in 1937, and created GBE in 1941.

Sir Reginald informed us that, apart from what he deposited in the Oriental and India Office Collection, British Library, he kept no papers. He said that he left very little in the Ministry of Agriculture since he wrote his own speeches and did much of his own typing. Some papers he accumulated in Burma had to be destroyed before the Japanese could capture them though the Japanese did seize his red dispatch box which contained some papers. Enquiries to both the Japanese and American governments failed to produce any trace of the dispatch box or its contents.

There are 81 volumes and files of papers in the India Office Collection (MSS Eur E 215) deposited in 1955 and 1966 and almost entirely concerning Sir Reginald's governorship of Burma 1941–46. These papers are available for research. The collection includes the letters patent confirming his appointment, press cuttings, a draft chapter of memoirs on his appointment, daily reports 1941–42, letters and telegrams 1943–45, and personal letters and telegrams to the Secretary of State 1945–46. There is also some correspondence with the Burma and India Office 1946, correspondence with Burmese ministers, and a few official notes and drafts. Several papers concerning the invasion of Burma survive, including a report by Sir Reginald on the Burma campaign 1941–42 (written in 1943), correspondence and minutes on the return to civil administration in 1945, and an article written by Sir Reginald: 'Civil Government under Invasion Conditions'. There is some correspondence with Leo Amery. In addition the collection includes Lady Dorman-Smith's diaries for 1941–46, Sir Reginald's letters to her 1943–45, and hers to him 1941–46. There is some miscellaneous personal correspondence 1942–44 and press cuttings.

The IWM holds a folder of copies of telegrams sent in the period Dec 1941–May 1942 when Dorman-Smith was Governor of Burma (86/81/2). They provide an interesting picture of the daily changes in the military, political, and civil situation in Burma in the face of the Japanese attack and comments on morale, conditions in Rangoon, the evacuation of civilians and later the government, the attitude of the Burmese towards the war and the British, and his relations with the Chinese and American allies, together with a copy of the ISTD (SEAC) Report on Lower Burma Jan-April 1945.

Family papers, including photos and personal letters from Dorman-Smith to his brother Eric, are in the possession of Eric's son, Christopher Dorman-O'Gowan.

Dorman-Smith's papers were used by Maurice Collins, *Last and First in Burma 1941–1948* (Faber & Faber 1956), 'the materials for writing the present book have been provided in the first place by Sir Reginald Dorman-Smith himself' (p. 15); and in *Burma: the struggle for Independence 1944–1948* (2 vols, HMSO 1983–4), the editor Hugh Tinker states in Volume 1 (covering period 1944–46), 'for this volume, the papers of Sir Reginald Dorman-Smith ... are of paramount importance' (p. xiv).

There is a good deal of information regarding Dorman-Smith in the biography of his brother Eric by Lavinia Greacen, *Chink* (Macmillan 1990).

HASTINGS BERTRAND LEES-SMITH (1878–1941)

Hastings Lees-Smith was Liberal MP for Northampton 1910–18, and Labour MP for West Riding of Yorkshire (Keighley) 1922–23, 1924–31 and 1935–41. He was Postmaster-General June 1929–March 1931, and President of the Board of Education March-Aug 1931.

When we prepared the first edition we were unable to trace Lees-Smith's family. Lees-Smith's widow had remarried. Lady Uvedale, as she had become, told us after the first edition was published that her husband's papers had been burnt after his death. Subsequently Lees-Smith's son, Patrick Lees-Smith, advised us that his father's surviving papers were in the family's possession until 1983 when they were given to Dr Joyce Bellamy at Hull University. The papers were deposited in the Brynmor Jones Library at Hull University in 1990 (DLS; NRA 33413).

The papers are divided into five categories: correspondence, printed material and speeches, press cuttings, articles, and miscellaneous papers. There is a list available.

There are a few letters from parliamentary colleagues such as Arthur Ponsonby 1923, Ramsay MacDonald 1936, and Churchill 1941. There is some correspondence regarding Lees-Smith's appointment to the Committee of Privy Council on the coronation of Edward VIII 1936; and letters of appointment as Postmaster-General 1929 and President of the Board of Education 1931.

The small collection of speeches includes notes on Lees-Smith's maiden speech and his parliamentary election addresses for 1910 and 1931. There are also a few papers on the Joint Committee on the Sittings of Parliament 1923–24, and a few documents on the Savidge Inquiry of 1928. There are a number of articles written by Lees-Smith on education, politics, and America 1931–36.

There is a typescript of a thesis by Brenda Burns entitled 'H. B. Lees-Smith, M.A., M.P.: the life and career of one Labour M.P., 1878–1941' (July 1967).

Lees-Smith had 'declined to co-operate' with a Sept 1934 request by the Cabinet Office to return any Cabinet papers in his possession (report to Cabinet by Sir Maurice Hankey, 29 Nov 1935, PRO, CAB 24/257). But the collection in Hull does not include Cabinet papers.

A biography of Lees-Smith by David E. Martin may be found in *DLB*, IX, 175–81.

SIR DEREK COLCLOUGH WALKER-SMITH, Bt, BARON BROXBOURNE (1910–1992)

Derek Walker-Smith was Conservative MP for Hertford 1945–55 and Hertfordshire East 1955–83. He was Parliamentary Secretary to the Board of Trade Oct 1955–Nov 1956, Economic Secretary to the

Treasury 1956–Jan 1957, Minister of State, Board of Trade Jan-Sept 1957, and Minister of Health 1957–July 1960. He was created a baronet in 1960, and Baron Broxbourne (a life peerage) in 1983.

A small collection of Lord Broxbourne's papers are in the possession of his son, Sir Jonah Walker-Smith Bt, 32 Westbourne Park Villas, London W2 5EA. They are available for research.

Sir Jonah advised us that the most relevant material is a draft memoir which Broxbourne was writing before his final illness and death. The memoir, with the proposed title *Politics – Game or Art?*, remains unfinished and unpublished. Lord Broxbourne had planned 15 chapters, of which Sir Jonah has draft typescript copies of chapters 1–8 ('People and Politics', 'The Path to Westminster', 'The Ways and Workings of Parliament', 'Personal Life of Parliament', 'The Grass Roots – Members and their Constituents', 'The Nuts and Bolts – Secretaries and Others', 'The Corridors of Power', and 'The Greasy Pole') and chapter 15 ('"The Simple Great Ones"'). For chapters 9 and 12 ('Always a Bridesmaid – the Speakership and Allied Subjects' and 'Lawyers and Politics'), only notes survive, while nothing appears to have been written for chapters 10, 11, 13 and 14 ('Upper House – or Lethal Chamber?', 'The European Dimension', 'Members and Media', and 'Oratory – A Harlot in decline?').

JAN CHRISTIAN SMUTS (1870–1950)

Jan Christian Smuts was Minister without Portfolio and a member of the War Cabinet June 1917–Jan 1919. He was Prime Minister of South Africa 1919–24 and 1939–48.

An account of the papers found after Smuts's death, his wishes, and how they were interpreted, is to be found in the 1955 Creighton Lecture by Sir Keith Hancock, *The Smuts Papers*, 1956. The greater part of Smuts's early papers were destroyed during the Boer War but what survives includes some of Smuts's student notes, secret telegrams from President Kruger, some letters received by Smuts while on commando, letters from Boer generals and copies of Smuts's replies, some daily jottings, and Smuts's notes on the surrender, including notes of a meeting with Kitchener. An enormous collection of papers has survived from the post-Boer War period. Rather than break up this collection by returning official papers to the South African and British governments, it was decided to deposit the whole collection in the South African Government Archives, Pretoria (A.1) after it had been catalogued by the Smuts Archive Trustees. This was done in 1971.

The papers have been divided into public and private papers. The public papers were subdivided into British government papers (95 volumes) and South African papers (89 volumes). The British papers include 78 volumes 1916–19 and 17 volumes 1940–46. The South African papers have been subdivided as follows: six volumes of South African Republic papers 1897–1902; four volumes of Transvaal papers 1906–10; three volumes of National Convention papers 1908–1909; and 73 volumes of Union of South Africa papers 1910-48. This division also includes a volume of Anglo-Boer telegrams 1899–1900, and eight volumes of United Nations papers 1945–46. The papers are now all available for research.

The private papers have been subdivided into minor and major papers. There are 97 volumes of minor papers; these are mainly routine letters from secretaries, invitations, greetings, and so forth, but there are also parliamentary papers, the papers of the South African National Party 1912–34 and the papers of the United Party. The major papers, which mainly comprise Smuts's private correspondence, include 'out' letters copied from other collections. There are 108 volumes arranged chronologically, and alphabetically within each volume. A card index has been compiled. Microfilm copies of these papers and of the card index have been given to the University of Cape Town. The Cambridge University Library also has microfilm copies of the letters, but has an actual card index. The major papers at Cambridge also include Smuts's law notes, his philosophical writings, speeches and broadcasts 1902–50, political notes 1899–1950, and one box of papers concerning the South African National Party 1905–34 (vols 1–98 Microfilm 666–763, vols 100–1 Microfilm 765–6 [vols 99 and 102 have not been filmed]). There is also a large collection of press cuttings made by Smuts's wife (Microfilm 832–54). In 1962 five boxes of the papers of Mr and Mrs Arthur B. Gillett were added to the collection. They include letters from Smuts 1906–50 and the Gilletts' replies 1917–19. Typed copies of some of these letters had been put into the correspondence volumes. Ten reels of microfilm copies of these letters have been deposited in the Cambridge University Library (Microfilm 773–82).

In 1980, the IWM purchased a series of letters written by Smuts to G. N. Barnes in the 1920s and 1930s (Special Misc EE). The letters comment generally on world politics and on the uneasy peace between the two world wars.

A large number of the papers have been published in Sir W. Keith Hancock and Jean Van der Poel (eds), *Selections from the Smuts Papers, 1886–1950* (7 vols, Cambridge UP 1966–73). The entire collection was used for Sir W. Keith Hancock's biography: *Smuts: I. The Sanguine Years 1870–1919; II. The Fields of Force 1919–1950* (2 vols, Cambridge UP 1962–68). The biography by Smuts's son, Jan Christian Smuts Jr, *Jan Christian Smuts* (Cassell 1952) is meant to be only a memoir of his father but it does quote from Smuts's papers. *I Lived in his Shadow* (Bailey & Swinfen 1965) by Kathleen Mincher, his adopted daughter is based only on her reminiscences. Bernard Friedman, *Smuts: A Reappraisal*

(George Allen & Unwin 1975) is concerned with Smuts's role in South Africa, while Kenneth Ingham, *Jan Christian Smuts: The Conscience of a South African* (Weidenfeld and Nicolson 1986) is a reappraisal based on the archives.

PHILIP SNOWDEN, VISCOUNT SNOWDEN (1864–1937)

Philip Snowden was Labour MP for Blackburn 1906–18 and West Riding of Yorkshire (Colne Valley) 1922–31. He was Chancellor of the Exchequer Jan-Nov 1924 and June 1929–Nov 1931, and Lord Privy Seal 1931–Sept 1932. He was created Viscount Snowden in 1931.

In the introduction to *An Autobiography* (2 vols, Nicholson & Watson 1934) Snowden wrote that he never kept a diary but he did have full contemporaneous notes of various important events such as the formation of the first Labour government and the 1931 financial crisis. In the autobiography itself he appears to quote only from published speeches. After writing the autobiography he destroyed many of his papers. Colin Cross, author of *Philip Snowden* (Barrie & Rockliff 1966), discovered from a family source that what remained was destroyed after the death of Lady Snowden.

In correspondence with Frederick Jowett on 25 Sept 1934 regarding a request to return Cabinet documents to the Cabinet Office, Snowden commented 'personally I am rather glad to have the opportunity of getting rid of the enormous mass of documents I have. I have been rather worried about what would happen to them on my death. Most of them are of now of [sic] no importance and interest. Some of a personal nature I shall keep, but the bulk I shall return after I have carefully sifted them' (Bradford District Archives, DB39/Case 31/7).

Snowden's library and a collection of press cuttings and cartoons were given to the Keighley Public Library. The Leeds University Library has the draft of Snowden's radio speech on the 1931 budget.

Details of the Colne Valley constituency Labour Party records are in Cook, *Sources*, 1, p. 136. Speeches of Chancellors of the Exchequer are in the PRO at T 172/1520–9.

Keith Laybourn and David James (eds), *Philip Snowden: The First Labour Chancellor of the Exchequer* (Bradford Libraries and Information Service 1987), and Keith Laybourn, *Philip Snowden* (Temple Smith 1988), draw upon the Keighley Library collection, as well as letters to and from Snowden in other collections.

A useful guide to Snowden's publications is in Ralph H. Desmarais's article in *MBR*, 3, 771–5. There are brief sketches of Snowden's career by R. C. K. Ensor in *DNB 1931–1940*, 822–5; and by J. S. Rowett in *Blackwell*, 378–81.

SIR (ARTHUR) CHRISTOPHER JOHN SOAMES, BARON SOAMES (1920–1987)

Christopher Soames was Conservative MP for Bedford 1950–66. He was Parliamentary Under-Secretary of State, Air Ministry Dec 1955–Jan 1957, Parliamentary and Financial Secretary, Admiralty 1957–Jan 1958, Secretary of State for War 1958–July 1960, Minister of Agriculture, Fisheries and Food 1960–Oct 1964, and Lord President of the Council May 1979–Sept 1981. He was created GCMG and GCVO in 1972 and Baron Soames (a life peerage) in 1978.

The Churchill Archives Centre holds 94 boxes of papers which have not been catalogued (SOAM). They deal mostly with Soames's appointments as Ambassador in Paris 1968–72 and as Vice-President of Commission of the European Communities 1973–77. There are also papers dealing with his activities in the House of Lords 1978–86. These papers are closed indefinitely.

SIR DONALD BRADLEY SOMERVELL, BARON SOMERVELL OF HARROW (1889–1960)

Donald Somervell was Conservative MP for Cheshire (Crewe) 1931–45. He was Solicitor-General Sept 1933–March 1936, Attorney-General 1936–May 1945, and Home Secretary May-Aug 1945. He was knighted in 1933, and created Baron Somervell of Harrow (a judicial life peerage) in 1954.

Somervell had no children and bequeathed his estate including a small collection of papers to his nephew, Mr Robert Somervell. Mr Somervell gave these papers or photocopies of them to the Bodleian Library (Somervell Papers). The papers include a short political memoir, a journal for 1933–37, typed copies of letters sent to the King's Proctor concerning the divorce of Mrs Simpson, a memo written by the Parliamentary Counsel on the legislation needed if the King were to abdicate, two pages of diary for Oct 1945, and a transcript of a speech given by J. C. Smuts to the Other Club c.1942.

The political memoir consists of 84 typed pages which cover Somervell's political and official career. As well as comments on the role of the Attorney-General, it also contains recollections of the legal issues and political personalities of the day.

The journal begins with Somervell's reminiscences of his appointment as Solicitor-General; it is 88ff long and has a short summary of contents. It also contains details about the abdication of Edward VIII and for this reason parts of the journal and the file of copies letters were closed for research until the death of the Duchess of Windsor. Long extracts from the journal are published in H. Montgomery Hyde, *Baldwin. The Unexpected Prime Minister* (Hart-Davis MacGibbon 1973).

SIR FRANK SOSKICE, BARON STOW HILL (1902-1979)

Frank Soskice was knighted in 1945, and created Baron Stow Hill (a life peerage) in 1966. He was Labour MP for Birkenhead (East) 1945-50, Sheffield (Neepsend) 1950-55 and Newport 1956-66. He was Solicitor-General Aug 1945-April 1951, Attorney-General April-Oct 1951, Secretary of State for Home Affairs Oct 1964-Dec 1965, and Lord Privy Seal 1965-April 1966.

Lord Stow Hill's papers were listed by the Royal Commission on Historical Manuscripts, and deposited in the HLRO (Stow Hill papers; NRA 19657). Permission to consult the papers must first be obtained from the Hon Oliver Soskice, 18 New Square, Cambridge.

Lord Stow Hill destroyed many of his constituency and legal papers but a few fragments survive which reflect his political career. There are a few constituency papers 1960-63, largely routine, dealing with local issues. There are miscellaneous papers and letters, mostly from MPs and trade union officials asking for legal advice, but including a small amount of private social correspondence with parliamentary colleagues such as Clement Attlee and Hugh Gaitskell. There are in addition a few papers concerning Lord Stow Hill's work as a QC, particularly his appearance before the International Court at the Hague on behalf of the Indian and Thai governments.

JAMES RICHARD STANHOPE, 7th EARL STANHOPE, 13th EARL OF CHESTERFIELD (1880-1967)

James Stanhope was known as Viscount Mahon from 1880 until he succeeded his father as 7th Earl Stanhope in 1905. He was created KG in 1934, and succeeded his kinsman as 13th Earl of Chesterfield in 1952. He was Parliamentary Secretary to the War Office May 1918-Jan 1919, Civil Lord of the Admiralty Nov 1924-June 1929, Parliamentary and Financial Secretary to the Admiralty Sept-Nov 1931, Parliamentary Under-Secretary of State for War 1931-Jan 1934, Under-Secretary of State for Foreign Affairs 1934-June 1936, First Commissioner of Works 1936-May 1937, President of the Board of Education 1937-Oct 1938, First Lord of the Admiralty 1938-Sept 1939, and Lord President of the Council 1939-May 1940.

Most of the Stanhope family archives, known as the Chevening papers, and covering three centuries of the family's history, have been transferred to the Centre for Kentish Studies (U1590). The archives, which include some of the 7th Earl's papers, are extensive and cover 300 linear feet. They have been fully catalogued and there are no restrictions on access.

Stanhope's papers include his school reports; some papers concerning his military career including mentions in dispatches; pocket diaries 1902, 1912-14, and 1918-58; and journals of foreign tours. There is also some of his correspondence: general correspondence arranged alphabetically 1893–1960, which includes some congratulations on achieving his various offices, two letters about his appointment as First Lord from Churchill and Sir Andrew Cunningham, a few papers on his appointment as Lord President, and many letters from his mother 1905–22. His mother's papers include many letters from him, particularly concerning his foreign tours and his First World War experiences. There is also a typed memoir 'The War of 1914–1918'. No papers concerning Stanhope's official career are mentioned in the Royal Commission on Historical Manuscripts' list.

Aubrey N. Newman, *The Stanhopes of Chevening* (Macmillan 1969) includes a short biography of Stanhope. The book was based on the family archives and the chapter on Stanhope quotes frequently from memoirs compiled between 1945 and 1965.

SIR ALBERT (HENRY) STANLEY, BARON ASHFIELD (1874–1948)

Albert Stanley was knighted in 1914, and created Baron Ashfield in 1920. He was Conservative MP for Ashton-under-Lyne 1916–20. He was President of the Board of Trade Dec 1916–May 1919.

Neither of Lord Ashfield's two daughters had any papers relating to their father's life or career when inquiries were made for the first edition. They thought this may well have been because he himself was very averse to publicity and so kept nothing.

From 1919–33 Ashfield was Chairman of what became London Transport (he was largely responsible for the passage of the 1933 London Passenger Transport Act). T. C. Barker and Michael Robbins, *A History of London Transport* (2 vols, George Allen & Unwin 1963, 1974), 2, covers Ashfield's role in London transport and lists his published articles and speeches.

A list of relevant archives in the Greater London RO and London Transport archive accompanies Michael Robbins's biography of Ashfield in *DBB* , 5, 273–6.

EDWARD GEORGE VILLIERS STANLEY, 17th EARL OF DERBY (1865–1948)

Edward Stanley was Conservative MP for South-East Lancashire (Westhoughton) 1892–1906. He was Financial Secretary to the War Office Nov 1900–Oct 1903, Postmaster-General 1903–Dec 1905, Under Secretary of State for War July-Dec 1916, and Secretary of State for War 1916–April 1918 and Oct 1922–Jan 1924. He was known as Lord Stanley from 1893 until he succeeded his father as the 17th Earl of Derby in 1908. He was created KCVO in 1905, and KG in 1919.

A very large collection of his papers has been deposited on loan by his grandson, the 18th Earl of Derby, in the Liverpool City Library (920 DER [17]). The library also has deposits of 19th century Derby family papers. The papers have been given a preliminary sorting and an outline list of the papers is available; a complete list of the papers will not be available for some time. Lord Derby's permission must be obtained for photocopying, quotation, or reproduction of documents. The papers were used for, and are extensively quoted in, Randolph S. Churchill, *Lord Derby, King of Lancashire* (Heinemann 1959). Unfortunately, when this biography was being written, many of the letters were moved from the original files and not replaced; in some instances new subject files were created.

Derby's diaries were frequently quoted in Randolph Churchill's biography and also used in Robert Blake, *The Unknown Prime Minister: The Life and Times of Andrew Bonar Law 1858–1923* (Eyre & Spottiswoode 1955).

The diaries are only for the periods June 1918–Oct 1920 and May 1921–June 1927 and are not in volumes but take the form of carbon-copy typescripts in varying degrees of completeness. They cover much of the period in which Derby served as British Ambassador in Paris. The diaries for 1918–20 are written as daily diaries but are more in the nature of a political memoir giving accounts of conversations with politicians and diplomats, details of the international scene, information heard or received about statesmen, politicians, and international figures. The 1921–27 diaries include the period when he was Secretary of State for War and also take the form of political memoirs. The latter part of the diaries is very incomplete.

Derby is said to have written 40 letters a day and certainly this collection comprises an enormous correspondence of both in- and out-letters. There is only a small amount of pre-1918 material; Randolph Churchill stated that the papers for 1900–08 were missing when he was writing his biography. The papers have been divided into five main divisions: Liverpool papers; Lancashire papers; government offices; public life; and domestic.

The Liverpool and Lancashire papers reflect Derby's strong local ties and influence. There is correspondence on royal visits, with and about successive Lord Mayors, with Liverpool University, the Liverpool Chamber of Commerce, and with local politicians, including five files of correspondence with Sir Archibald Salvidge 1911–28 (1/29–33).

The papers arising from Derby's terms of public office have been divided by office. Only printed telegrams and reports by Lord Kitchener seem to have survived from his period as Financial Secretary to the War Office, and only draft bills and printed papers from the Post Office. Some correspondence from Derby's term as Director-General of Recruiting 1916 has survived. Derby's papers as Under-Secretary and later Secretary of State for War include much correspondence as well as Cabinet papers and official reports. For example there are files of correspondence with Lloyd George Sept 1916–April 1918, with Sir Douglas Haig and Sir Philip Sassoon Aug 1916–April 1918, and concerning the Supreme War Council 1918. Some correspondence has survived from Derby's second tenure of the War Office. Many papers have survived from his term as British Ambassador in Paris 1918–20. As well as various subject files, memoranda, and minutes, there are correspondence files with specific individuals such as Austen Chamberlain, Lord Robert Cecil, Churchill, and Sir Philip Sassoon.

The 'public life' division of papers covers a wide range of topics. There is correspondence with Americans or about America 1930–47, correspondence concerning various charities and other organisations, correspondence and papers connected with the Royal Commissions and Committees on which Derby served, such as the Royal Commissions on Divorce and Matrimonial Causes 1911, on Railways 1914, and on Indian Constitutional Reforms 1933–34. There is also Derby's correspondence with the War Office 1926–44 and with the Paris Embassy 1928–45. This division also includes Derby's correspondence with such politicians as Stanley Baldwin 1924–45, A. J. Balfour 1922, Lord Beaverbrook 1921–28, Lord Crewe 1923–28, Lord Curzon 1920–24, and with the King's successive secretaries 1914–15, 1924–41. There is also a file of correspondence about Derby's visit to Ireland 1921, and a file of memoranda on House of Lords' Reform 1911.

The 'domestic' division of papers includes family letters and a few typed extracts from Derby's diary, Dec 1923, Feb 1924, and Nov 1924, as well as papers concerning his houses, his furniture, his finances, and his various clubs.

A further collection of Derby's War Office papers 1922–24 is available for research at the PRO (WO 137). A wide range of subjects is represented – reparations, Egypt, India, and Ireland – as well as correspondence with the King's private secretaries and with the Prime Minister.

Papers relating to the estates of the Stanley family, including the 17th Earl of Derby, are held at the Lancashire RO. Details are given in R. Sharpe France, *Guide to the Lancashire Record Office*, Lancs County Council, Preston, 1985, 262–71.

EDWARD MONTAGU CAVENDISH STANLEY, LORD STANLEY (1894–1938)

Edward Stanley was known as Lord Stanley from 1908 when his father succeeded as the 17th Earl of Derby. He was Conservative MP for Liverpool (Abercromby) 1917–18 and Lancashire (Fylde Division) 1922–

38. He was Junior Lord of the Treasury Nov 1924–Nov 1927, Parliamentary and Financial Secretary, Admiralty Nov 1931–Nov 1935 and 1935–May 1937, Parliamentary Under Secretary, Dominions Office June-Nov 1935, Parliamentary Under Secretary of State, India Office and Burma Office May 1937–May 1938, and Secretary of State for the Dominions from May 1938 until his death in Oct 1938.

The only papers relating to Lord Stanley inherited by his son, the 18th Earl of Derby, were estate papers. Lord Derby's Librarian, Mrs Brenda Burgess, advised us that these papers will eventually go to the Lancashire RO.

The only Edward Stanley papers in the collection of his father's (the 17th Lord Derby) papers in the Liverpool City Library are in a folder of correspondence (920 DER (17) 42./8) written during the period 1916–38. Of these letters, only five were written by Lord Stanley, the remaining 23 are copies of letters to him from his father.

THE HON OLIVER FREDERICK GEORGE STANLEY (1896–1950)

Oliver Stanley was Conservative MP for Westmorland 1924–45 and Bristol (West) 1945–50. He was Parliamentary Under-Secretary of State for Home Affairs Sept 1931–Feb 1933, Minister of Transport 1933–June 1934, Minister of Labour 1934–June 1935, President of the Board of Education 1935–May 1937, President of the Board of Trade 1937–Jan 1940, Secretary of State for War Jan-May 1940, and Secretary of State for Colonial Affairs Nov 1942–Aug 1945.

Stanley's daughter, Dame Kathryn Dugdale, did not know of any surviving papers. She advised us that her father was 'a very private person and loathed writing letters'.

Private Office papers of the Secretary of State for War are in the PRO at WO 259.

Adjusting to Democracy is a valuable guide to Stanley's work at the Ministry of Labour and to relevant PRO files.

Stanley's work as Colonial Secretary is discussed (without reference to private papers) in David Goldsworthy, *Colonial Issues in British Politics 1945–1961* (Clarendon Press, Oxford 1971), and his period at the Ministry of Transport is covered in William Plowden, *The Motor Car and Politics 1896–1970* (Bodley Head 1971), especially at 270–9.

CHARLES STEWART VANE-TEMPEST-STEWART, 6th MARQUESS OF LONDONDERRY (1852–1915)

Charles Vane-Tempest-Stewart was known as Viscount Castlereagh from 1872 until he succeeded his father as 6th Marquess of Londonderry in 1884. He was created KG in 1888. He was Conservative MP for Down 1878–84. He was Postmaster-General April 1900–Aug 1902,

President of the Board of Education 1902–Dec 1905, and Lord President of the Council Oct 1903–Dec 1905.

Londonderry's great-grandson, the 9th Marquess of Londonderry, deposited his family archives in the Durham CRO (D/Lo). Handlists of the papers have been published: S. C. Newton, *The Londonderry Papers,* Durham 1966, and *The Londonderry Papers* (additional), Durham 1969 (NRA 11528 Pts 1 and 2). The collection includes only a small number of Londonderry's papers (D/Lo/F 517–75, 1085–122; D/Lo/C 628–30). The most important part of these papers is probably the extensive series of press cuttings 1886–1915 covering his political career. There are a few personal letters and invitations, some personal receipts and bills, and election expenses for the 1874 South Durham election. Many of the papers of Theresa, Marchioness of Londonderry (D/Lo/F 576–84; D/Lo/F 1123–44; D/Lo/C 631–91), are also in this collection and contain considerable material relating to political life, including correspondence with Walter Long, and the 2nd Lord Selborne. They are quoted in H. Montgomery Hyde, *The Londonderrys: A Family Portrait* (Hamish Hamilton 1979).

There are further Londonderry papers at the PRONI (D 2846), among them c.4600 documents and 15 volumes of Theresa Londonderry's correspondence and papers 1858–1919. This collection was chiefly deposited by Lady Mairi Bury, Londonderry's grand-daughter.

Londonderry's papers in his wife's collection include telegrams and press cuttings documenting his election as MP for Co Down in 1878, and letters to him 1886–1912 from correspondents including Queen Victoria, A. J. Balfour, J. Chamberlain, Lord Salisbury, and other colleagues and political opponents. Subjects covered include the major political offices held by him and Tory party politics, Home Rule, tactics in the House of Lords, etc.

Lady Londonderry's papers contain 158 letters from Sir Edward Carson 1903–19, many dealing with Ulster's opposition to the third Home Rule Bill, as well as other correspondence on Home Rule and Ulster Unionism including letters from Sir James Craig 1912–19 and Walter Long 1912–14.

There is extensive family correspondence including the Londonderrys' letters to each other 1874–1918. There are also many letters from the royal family, as well as a vast quantity of general correspondence 1890–1919, including regular correspondence with William Flavelle Monypenny, the biographer of Disraeli 1907–13. According to the PRONI: 'many important figures in literature, the arts, the army, the navy, the church and the law, and most important figures in politics (particularly Tory politics) and Society, during the period 1890–1919, feature among her correspondents'.

The PRONI also holds substantial quantities of papers relating to Londonderry's Irish estates (D 654).

The papers of H. Montgomery Hyde also at the PRONI (D 3084) include typescript copies of articles written by Lady Londonderry 1911–19 and approximately 200 pages of typescript notes by Lady Londonderry containing comments on the British coalition government, the Easter rising in Dublin, her impressions of Churchill, and her recollections of Tsar Nicholas II and his wife Alexandra 1914–19. There is also a typescript copy of Lady Londonderry's unpublished memoirs 'The Life of the Dowager Marchioness of Londonderry' (1915).

CHARLES STEWART HENRY VANE-TEMPEST-STEWART, 7th MARQUESS OF LONDONDERRY (1878–1949)

Charles Vane-Tempest-Stewart was known as Viscount Castlereagh from 1884 until he succeeded his father as 7th Marquess of Londonderry in 1915. He was created KG in 1919. He was Conservative MP for Maidstone 1906–15. He was Under-Secretary of State for Air April 1920–July 1921, First Commissioner of Works Oct 1928–June 1929 and Aug-Nov 1931, Secretary of State for Air 1931–June 1935, and Lord Privy Seal June-Nov 1935.

Londonderry's daughter, Lady Mairi Bury, deposited a large collection of family, political, official, and personal papers of Londonderry and his wife Edith in the PRONI (D 3099). The papers include Londonderry's private political correspondence 1899–1949, with various British and German politicians, and files relating to his terms as Minister of Education for Northern Ireland 1921–26, and in the Air Ministry 1919–21, 1931–35. There are papers concerning politics in north-east England and Ireland 1914–19. Londonderry's personal correspondence 1890–1949 includes letters from British and foreign royalty, and there are volumes of press cuttings 1860–1956 on social and political events.

Also included are the personal and political correspondence of Edith, Lady Londonderry 1886–1959, and personal correspondence between the Londonderrys and other members of the family. The collection also contains a number of papers on Londonderry's coal mines and the coal industry 1915–47; household papers 1885–86 and 1900–52; papers dealing with non-political organisations with which the Londonderrys were involved 1914–54 and Londonderry's Chancellorship of both the University of Durham and of Queen's University, Belfast 1930–48, and papers on functions and receptions held at the Londonderrys' houses 1920–59.

The papers of H. Montgomery Hyde also at the PRONI (D 3084) contain correspondence relating to his period as private secretary to Londonderry in the 1930s. There are letters, engagement lists, cuttings and booklets relating to Londonderry's period as Mayor of Durham and Chancellor of Durham University; correspondence and reviews concerning his book *Ourselves and Germany* (Penguin, Harmondsworth 1938); correspondence with newspapers and magazine editors; and some miscellaneous letters to Lady Londonderry. Montgomery Hyde used the family papers as well as the material then in his own possession in *The Londonderrys: A Family Portrait* (Hamish Hamilton 1979).

Londonderry's grandson, the 9th Marquess of Londonderry, deposited his family archives in the Durham CRO (D/Lo). Handlists of the papers have been published: S. C. Newton, *The Londonderry Papers*, Durham 1966, and *The Londonderry Papers* (additional), Durham 1969 (NRA 11528 Pts 1 and 2). The collection includes a small number of the 7th Marquess's papers (D/Lo/F585–613, 1145–6; D/Lo/C236–7).

There are four files of parliamentary speeches 1910 and 1921, and a file on his 1906 Maidstone election expenses and the petition to unseat him. There are ten files on the opening in 1921 of the Northern Ireland Parliament (Londonderry was Minister of Education and Leader of the Senate in the Government of Northern Ireland 1921–26). There are some personal accounts and miscellaneous sporting and social papers. There are some files of correspondence 1922–27 and 1932–38 arranged alphabetically, including correspondence with Sir Nevile Henderson, Leo Amery, Clement Attlee, and Herbert Morrison. The papers in the Durham CRO also include 356 letters from Londonderry to his wife 1895–1919.

In his autobiography, *Wings of Destiny* (Macmillan 1943), Londonderry quoted from his papers, especially letters from Ramsay MacDonald and Churchill.

RICHARD RAPIER STOKES (1897–1957)

Richard Stokes was Labour MP for Ipswich 1938–57. He was Minister of Works Feb 1950–April 1951, Lord Privy Seal April-Oct 1951, and Minister of Materials July-Oct 1951.

Approximately 42 boxes of Stokes's papers have been deposited by his family in the Bodleian Library (Stokes Papers). There is a list. Permission to read the papers must be obtained from Mr John Hull, 120 Cheapside, London EC2V 6DS.

Stokes's political and official careers are very sparsely represented in this collection; there are files on the 1935 election at Glasgow (Central) – including Stokes's election address, press cuttings, and a campaign diary – and on the 1938, 1945, 1950, and 1955 elections at Ipswich. There is a file of invitation cards and a list of letters of congratulations on his appointment as Minister of Works, a file of congratulations on his appointment as Lord Privy Seal, and a file of press cuttings on his attempt to settle the Persian Oil dispute in 1951. Nonetheless, the collection does enable the researcher to build up a picture of Stokes's career, particularly by the many volumes of press cuttings 1938–57, and his secretary's engagement diaries 1926–56. There is also an index of Stokes's speeches 1938–57 and many speech notes 1950–55.

One of Stokes's main interests was the Middle East. His interest began in the 1920s when he began to travel on behalf of his family firm, Ransomes and Rapiers. He kept a 'running diary' or 'running notes' of each of his tours, which were sent to his fellow-directors. Stokes continued the habit in politics and in office; for example, he sent notes to Lord Halifax of a conversation he had had with Von Papen in Turkey in 1940, and memoranda and notes of conversations made during a tour of the Middle East in 1947 to Clement Attlee and Ernest Bevin. Stokes's correspondence with Herbert Morrison 1952–57 and Hugh Gaitskell 1950–57 includes many assessments by Stokes of the political situation in the Near and Middle East. As well as his 'running notes' there are several files about Palestine 1938–47, and the Near East, including press cuttings, pamphlets, general correspondence, memoranda, correspondence about parliamentary questions, and letters by Stokes to the press.

Stokes seems to have arranged his correspondence alphabetically; but apart from the correspondence already noted, and some correspondence with Churchill, only the 'A's' have survived: correspondence with Attlee 1938–54, with the Aga Khan, and with the Ministry of Agriculture and Fisheries.

Stokes's activities during the Second World War are represented by files on the loss of HMS *Glorious* July 1940 including parliamentary questions, some press cuttings and publications of the Parliamentary Peace Aims Group 1939–41, and several files on the application of regulation 18B which allowed the detention of suspected persons during war time.

Shortly before his death Stokes had begun to read through his papers with a view to writing his memoirs. His notes, for example on Stalin and on his own Roman Catholicism, have survived.

About 100 letters from Stokes to various members of his family, mostly to his parents, June 1916–March 1919, have been deposited in the Department of Documents at the IWM (68/11/1). They were all written when Stokes was an officer in the Royal Field Artillery on the Western Front.

When the first edition of the Guide was published a further three boxes of papers demonstrating Stokes's great interest in a Land Value tax were in the care of the Secretary, The United Committee for the Taxation of Land Values Ltd (name now changed to the Centre for Incentive Taxation (LVT) Limited), 177 Vauxhall Bridge Road, London SW1V 1EU. The current Secretary advised us that these boxes cannot now be located. The three box-files almost all related to the activities of the Land Values Group within the Parliamentary Labour Party of which Stokes was secretary. The Group's activities were well represented; there were notices of meetings, extracts from speeches and articles, information sent to marginal constituencies 1953–54, distribution lists, and some correspondence files including A. W. Madsen 1950–51 and 1955–57, H. G. McGhee, MP 1951–52, and a file of correspondence with ministers about a rate on land values in 1948.

The PRO has papers relating to Stokes's interest in peace aims 1940–42 (INF 1/177B); and his Private Office papers as Minister of Materials are available in BT 172.

SIR EDWARD STRACHEY, 4th Bt, 1st BARON STRACHIE (1858–1936)

Edward Strachey was Liberal MP for Somersetshire (South) 1892–1911. He was Parliamentary Secretary to the Board of Agriculture and Fisheries Dec 1909–Oct 1911 (he had been spokesman for the Board from 1905), and Paymaster-General May 1912–May 1915. He succeeded his father as 4th baronet in 1901, and was created Baron Strachie in 1911.

Lord Strachie's only son, the late 2nd Baron Strachie, informed us that no papers had survived.

There are brief references to Strachie's life in Charles Richard Sanders, *The Strachey Family 1588–1932: Their Writings and Literary Associations* (Duke UP, Durham, NC 1953).

(EVELYN) JOHN ST LOE STRACHEY (1901–1963)

John Strachey was Labour MP for Birmingham (Aston) 1929–31, Dundee 1945–50 and Dundee (West) 1950–63. He was Under-Secretary of State for Air Aug 1945–May 1946, Minister of Food 1946–Feb 1950, and Secretary of State for War 1950–Oct 1951.

Strachey's papers are in the possession of his daughter Mrs Elizabeth Al Qadhi. A summary list is available at the National Register of Archives (NRA 34351). Applications to view the papers should be made to the Historical Manuscripts Commission.

The papers consist of 30 box-files covering the period 1920–63. The bulk of the papers come from the period after 1945 but there are a few earlier papers of considerable interest. There are no papers relating to Strachey's period at the Ministry of Food and very few relating to the War Office.

Possibly of greatest interest are the papers relating to the years 1931–40, when Strachey was one of the most prominent and possibly the most articulate exponent in Britain of communism. There are letters from R. Palme Dutt, Harry Pollitt, and other communist leaders on questions of party practice and policy. There is also an interesting collection of papers relating to the Left Book Club (Victor Gollancz, with Strachey and Harold Laski, organised the club and selected the books).

Strachey's later papers chiefly relate to his political writings. He was reconciled with the Labour Party and there are several letters from Hugh Gaitskell, Douglas Jay, and others.

The papers were used by Hugh Thomas in his biography, *John Strachey* (Eyre Methuen 1973) and by Michael Newman in *John Strachey* (Manchester UP 1989). Noel Thompson, *John Strachey: An Intellectual Biography* (Macmillan 1993) deals mostly with Strachey's political ideals.

GEORGE RUSSELL STRAUSS, BARON STRAUSS (1901–1993)

George Strauss was Labour MP for Lambeth (North) 1929–31 and 1934–50 and Lambeth (Vauxhall) 1950–79. He was Parliamentary Secretary to the Ministry of Transport Aug 1945–Oct 1947, and Minister of Supply 1947–Oct 1951. He was created Baron Strauss (a life peerage) in 1979.

Lord Strauss informed us that he had kept very few papers concerning his political career. Lady Strauss advised us that she had found little of political interest when she went through his papers.

The only item was a copy of his untitled autobiography, which was not commercially published. It has been deposited in the Churchill Archives Centre (STRS). The autobiography, which was probably written in the early 1990s, runs to 194 pages and covers the whole of Strauss's life. There are 18 chapters: Early Memories; Into Parliament; The House of Commons; The Soviet Union; Henry Moore, By-Election Songs and Waterloo Bridge; The Spanish Civil War; The Collapse of MacDonald's Government; Wartime; Post-War; Dalton and Gaitskell; The Steel Industry Battle; The Atomic Bomb and Soviet Spies; Slaugham (Strauss's country home); Bevan's Resignation; Theatre Censorship; Museum Charges and Clay Cross; Miscreants (on Nabarro, Stonehouse, and Maudling); The Lords. The early years of the memoir draw heavily on letters and appointment diaries still in the possession of Lady Strauss.

The papers of the North Lambeth Constituency Labour Party, deposited in the BLPES, include one box of Lord Strauss's constituency papers. The collection has been summarily listed, but contains nothing relating to Strauss's ministerial activities.

The transcript of the interview which Lord Strauss gave to the Nuffield Oral History Project (see Robert Skidelsky, *Politicians and the Slump. The Labour Government of 1929–1931*, Macmillan 1967, p. 186) is available to *bona fide* researchers on written application to the Librarian, Nuffield College.

JAMES GRAY STUART, 1st VISCOUNT STUART OF FINDHORN (1897–1971)

James Stuart was Unionist MP for Moray and Nairn 1923–59. He was Junior Lord of the Treasury May 1935–Jan 1941, Joint Parliamentary Secretary to the Treasury 1941–May 1945, Secretary of State for Scotland Oct 1951–Jan 1957. He was created Viscount Stuart of Findhorn in 1959.

Stuart advised the Keeper of the Records of Scotland in 1969 that he had five boxes containing papers of interest which were all destroyed in a fire. He also had some papers relating to Conservative Party organisation in Scotland. Cook in *Sources*, 4, p. 191, reported that neither his son, the 2nd Viscount Stuart of Findhorn, nor his nephew, the 20th Earl of Moray, knew of any surviving papers. Stuart's autobiography *Within the Fringe* (Bodley Head 1967) did not use unpublished sources.

A small collection of Stuart's papers is now known to be in the papers of the Earls of Moray in the possession of Stuart's nephew, the 20th Earl of Moray. The whole collection was listed by the NRA(S) in 1982. Stuart's papers form part five (NRA(S) 217; NRA 10983).

The Stuart papers consist of 19 bundles of material. The First World War papers include a personal diary kept while Stuart was serving in the Royal Scots 7 Jan-22 Feb 1915 and 12 May-23 Sept 1916, as well as 'Extracts from an Infantry Officer's diary' which includes engagements at the Somme and Arras 1916–17. There are two bundles of miscellaneous personal papers 1916–63 including a letter from his brother John regarding media coverage of the battle of Jutland 1916, letters to Mrs Read from Stuart while he was serving in the Royal Scots 1916–17, a letter of sympathy from King George VI on the death of Stuart's brother Francis in 1943, and a letter from Churchill on his retirement 1958.

The political papers include two files of miscellaneous correspondence and material on politically related matters, mostly political appointments 1933–56, and c.1930–42. They include a draft letter to Baldwin 26 Oct 1933 advising him that his optimism regarding the state of agriculture was not justified in Stuart's own constituency of Moray and Nairn; a note on Stafford Cripps's ambassadorship to Russia, and his subsequent career with a memo from the Prime Minister asking Stuart to call Lady Astor into order 5 April 1943; a letter from the Prime Minister to Stuart as Chief Whip March 1945 regarding political appointments; notes on 'the future of the party' 1945 and an undated paper 'the work in opposition'; and papers on the Suez crisis with a letter to Professor Roy Harrod on the health of the Prime Minister and on the American position Dec 1956; notes on the ministers of 1931; on ministerial appointments 1942; on appointments made in Chamberlain's and Churchill's governments of 1937 and 1940; and notes on discussions regarding the organisation of the Conservative Party 1944. Other political papers include papers 'for attention' 1942–64 containing letters and memoranda including particulars of possible candidates for the office of Secretary of State for the Colonies 1943; a file of notes, minutes of evidence, draft proposals and other papers relating to the Select Committee on Parliamentary procedure 1945; papers relating to Stuart's appointment as a privy councillor; and letters and cuttings regarding Stuart's retirement from the Scottish Office 1957, and other political appointments held by him, including a letter to Churchill offering his resignation as Chief Whip of the Conservative Party due to ill health 26 June 1948).

Other papers include a file of Stuart's unpublished writings 1968–70, including undated notes on 'Cabinet making' with particular reference to Churchill, and 'Off the Record', an account of Stuart's childhood written in May 1969. There are typescript and manuscript drafts of Stuart's autobiography (originally titled *No Regrets*); and a valuation by Sotheby's of Stuart's china, jewellery, furniture, and other property c.1939.

Private Office papers relating to Stuart's period at the Scottish Office are dispersed through the files of the five main Scottish Office departments held at the SRO. Stuart's period as Secretary of State for Scotland is briefly recounted by his private secretary, George Pottinger in *Secretaries of State for Scotland*, 130–45.

EDITH CLARA SUMMERSKILL, BARONESS SUMMERSKILL (1901–1980)

Dr Edith Summerskill was Labour MP for West Fulham 1938–55 and Warrington 1955–61. She was Parliamentary Under-Secretary to the Ministry of Food Aug 1945–Feb 1950, and Minister of National Insurance 1950–Oct 1951. She was created Baroness Summerskill (a life peerage) in 1961.

We were advised by the office of Lady Summerskill's son, the late Michael Summerskill, that a biography of Lady Summerskill is being written based on the surviving papers. It is likely that once the biography is completed the papers will be deposited in a public repository.

There are some press cuttings on Lady Summerskill in the National Museum of Labour History.

Lady Summerskill compiled her letters to her daughter, Dr Shirley Summerskill (also a Labour MP) in *Letters to My Daughter* (Heinemann 1957). She also wrote an autobiography, *A Woman's World* (Heinemann 1967) which quotes from only one document, the menu from a Chinese government banquet in 1954.

There is a brief entry on her in Olive Banks, *The Biographical Dictionary of British Feminists*, II: *A Supplement, 1900–1945* (New York UP 1990), 194–8.

SIR WILLIAM SUTHERLAND (1880–1949)

William Sutherland was Liberal MP for Argyll 1918–24. He was Chancellor of the Duchy of Lancaster April-Oct 1922. He was created KCB in 1919.

Sutherland had no children and the sole executrix and beneficiary of his will was his wife. She died two months before he did, having appointed him sole executor and main beneficiary of her own will. Their estate was divided between their respective families. We were unable to trace any of Sutherland's wife's brothers and sisters. Lord Beaverbrook was told by Sutherland's sister Mrs Ada Blair that there were no papers. The children of Sutherland's sisters knew of no papers, nor did the solicitor who acted for them. Enquiries made by the Barnsley Local History Library to the area headquarters of the National Coal Board (who took over George Fountain & Co, which Lady Sutherland partly owned), to the local Liberal Party, and at the Sutherlands' house, Birthwaite Hall, produced no clues to the whereabouts or fate of Sutherland's papers.

However, an article asking for information, which was published in *The Barnsley Chronicle* in 1993 drew two interesting responses to the editor, Sir Nicholas Hewitt, Bt. The first was from a man who wished to remain anonymous. He recounted that he had bought Sutherland's desk in the sale of his effects in the late 1940s. Finding that the drawer was sticking, he investigated and found a compartment which contained a hardback diary of 'jottings' belonging to Sutherland when he was Lloyd George's secretary, and £18,000 in bonds. The man gave the diary and bonds to Sutherland's secretary, James Sharp. Sharp's son, Dr Michael Sharp, was unable to shed any further light on this tantalising story.

The second response was from Harold Melling who had worked as a gardener at Sutherland's home in his youth during the period 1950–54. He recalled that Sutherland's old gardener, Arthur Senior, had once told him that during the period between Sutherland's death and the sale of his estate, there had been a bonfire which lasted for three days. The bonfire had been fuelled by some of Sutherland's books and papers.

HAROLD JOHN TENNANT (1865–1935)

Jack Tennant was Liberal MP for Berwickshire 1894–1918. He was Parliamentary Secretary to the Board of Trade Jan 1909–Oct 1911, Financial Secretary to the War Office 1911–June 1912, Under-Secretary of State for War 1912–July 1916, and Secretary for Scotland July-Dec 1916.

Tennant's daughter, Miss Alison Tennant, informed us for the first edition that no papers survived. Miss Tennant thought that many papers were destroyed early in the Second World War when her mother moved house. This was confirmed by her mother's former secretary, Mrs Hayesmore.

In *Kitchener: architect of victory* (William Kimber 1977), Professor George Cassar refers to Tennant papers in the possession of Mark Tennant. We were advised by Simon Blow, author of *Broken Blood: the rise and fall of the Tennant family* (Faber & Faber 1987), that Tennant's grandson, Mark Tennant, knows nothing of the whereabouts of any papers other than some correspondence between his grandparents relating to gardening and other domestic matters when they lived at Great Maythem. His stepmother has only a few scrapbooks.

Tennant published an annotated selection of his letters 1907–15 from Thomas Walker, his game-keeper: *Letters from a Lowland Keeper* (James Maclehose and Sons, Glasgow 1918). He also wrote a life of his father, *Sir Charles Tennant: His Forebears and Descendants*, which was privately published in 1932. Copies are held by various members of the Tennant family.

The biography of Tennant's second wife May by Violet R. Markham, *May Tennant: A Portrait* (The Falcon Press 1949) has useful references to her husband.

Private Office papers relating to Tennant's period at the Scottish Office are dispersed through the files of the five main Scottish Office departments held at the SRO.

Reference should be made to J. W. R. Mitchell, 'The Emergence of Modern Scottish central administration 1885–1939' (DPhil, Oxford University 1987).

FREDERIC JOHN NAPIER THESIGER, 1st VISCOUNT CHELMSFORD (1868–1933)

Frederic Thesiger succeeded his father as 3rd Baron Chelmsford in 1905, and was created KCMG in 1906, GCSI in 1916, and Viscount Chelmsford in 1921. He was First Lord of the Admiralty Jan–Nov 1924.

Chelmsford's daughter, the Hon Mrs Monck, had a volume of copied extracts from her father's letters to her mother 1914–15 (when he was on active service in India), and a collection of watercolours painted by her mother when she was vice-reine. These are now in the possession of her widower, Mr John Monck, Aldern Bridge House, Newbury, Berks RG15 8HQ. There are also five bound volumes of photos, mainly official, of the Chelmsfords in India which Mr Monck deposited in the Mary Evans Picture Library, 59 Tranquil Vale, Blackheath, London SE3 0BS.

Chelmsford's papers as Viceroy of India 1916–21 are held on permanent loan from his son, the 2nd Viscount Chelmsford, in the Oriental and India Office Collections, British Library (MSS Eur E 264; NRA

20538). The papers were bound up by the Viceroy's Private Office in India in the customary way: there is one volume of correspondence with the King 1916–21; five volumes of correspondence with the Secretary of State; eight volumes of telegrams exchanged with the Secretary of State; two volumes of correspondence with persons in England and abroad; ten volumes of correspondence with persons in India; and two volumes of speeches. In addition, there are ten volumes of dispatches exchanged between the Secretary of State and the Viceroy as Governor-General in Council; a volume of letters, memoranda, and minutes on various proposals for Indian self-government 1916–17; 25 volumes of reports on the Persian political situation 1916–21, compiled by the Government of India's Foreign and Political Department; and 16 volumes on the Afghan political situation 1916–21, and Afghan claims to representation at the Peace Conference.

Several letters and copies of letters between Lady Chelmsford and Colonel Sir Ralph Verney, Bt and his wife Nita concerning his appointment as Chelmsford's military secretary in India are with Col Verney's daughter, Mrs Jocelyn Thorne. They are quoted in *In Viceregal India, 1916–1921: The Life and Letters of Ralph Verney*, vol 2, edited by David Verney (Tabb House 1994).

Chelmsford's grandson, the 3rd Lord Chelmsford, was unable to find any of his grandfather's papers. Chelmsford's daughter, the late Anne, Lady Inchiquin, whose husband was her father's ADC when he was Viceroy of India, did not know of any papers.

There are no Chelmsford papers in the papers of his son-in-law Sir Alan Lascelles at the Churchill Archives Centre. All Souls College, Oxford, of which Chelmsford was Warden when he died, has none of his papers.

There is a brief biography by Stephen Gosling and John Saville in *DLB*, V, 213–16.

DAVID ALFRED THOMAS, VISCOUNT RHONDDA (1856–1918)

D. A. Thomas was Liberal MP for Merthyr Tydfil 1888–1910 and Cardiff 1910. He was President of the Local Government Board Dec 1916–June 1917, and Minister of Food Control 1917–July 1918. He was created Baron Rhondda in 1916, and Viscount Rhondda in 1918.

A collection of 350 of Thomas's letters was deposited by his daughter Viscountess Rhondda, in the NLW (D. A. Thomas Papers). The collection has been sorted but not catalogued. Most of the letters date from 1891–95 and concern Thomas's political and industrial activities. His correspondents include constituents, Welsh leaders, and leading members of the Liberal Party. Subjects include Disestablishment of the Church in Wales, Thomas's revolt (with Lloyd George,

Herbert Lewis, and Frank Edwards) against the government in 1894, the eight-hour day in the mines, and women's suffrage. The collection also includes some genealogical material, press cuttings, copies of the *Journals* published by the Food Ministry while Thomas was there, and political pamphlets and tracts.

The NLW also holds a collection of the papers of David Evans (David Evans Papers), a journalist who undertook much research into Thomas's life and who wrote *In Memory of Rt Hon Viscount Rhondda of Llanwern* (South Wales Printing and Publishing Company, Cardiff 1919). There is a draft typescript of an unpublished study of various aspects of Thomas's life completed in 1921. The typescript is divided into chapters headed 'His business life', 'His fight for output regulation', 'His conflicts with Labour', 'Industrial unrest and its remedy' and 'Achievement as industrial organizer'. Other papers include a small collection of press cuttings 1894-1900, copies of speeches and pamphlets and notes of conversations with Thomas 4 April 1913 and 21 Aug 1916.

D. A. Thomas: Viscount Rhondda by his daughter and others (Longmans, Green 1921) quotes from some of Thomas's letters and includes reminiscences of him by his daughter, by J. R. Clynes, and by the then Sir William Beveridge. J. Vyrnwy Morgan, *Life of Viscount Rhondda* (Allenson 1919), does not quote from unpublished material but was written with the help of Thomas's brother.

Thomas's career is discussed in Kenneth O. Morgan, 'D. A. Thomas: The Industrialist as Politician', *Glamorgan Historian*, III, Aug 1966, 33–51. Martin Daunton's contribution in *DBB*, 5, 473–80, is a useful guide to published and unpublished sources on Thomas's business career. Brinley Thomas provides a brief sketch of Rhondda's life and career in the *Dictionary of Welsh Biography* (The Honourable Society of Cymmrodorion 1959), 942–3.

JAMES HENRY THOMAS (1874–1949)

Jimmy Thomas was Labour MP for Derby 1910–36; he became a National Labour MP in 1931. He was Secretary of State for Colonial Affairs Jan-Nov 1924, Aug-Nov 1931 and Nov 1935–May 1936, Lord Privy Seal June 1929–June 1930, and Secretary of State for the Dominions 1930–Nov 1935.

A collection of Thomas's papers, formerly in the possession of his sons, was deposited in the Kent Archives Office, now the Centre for Kentish Studies (U 1625). A list of the papers is available (NRA 15918).

Thomas's *My Story* (Hutchinson 1937) quotes from a few letters, including correspondence with Ramsay MacDonald in Feb 1930 when Thomas offered to resign. But, according to W. G. Blaxland, in *J. H. Thomas: A Life for Unity* (Frederick Muller 1964), Thomas never kept a diary and wrote few letters. This seems to be borne out by the collection, of which a predominant feature is the very useful collection of press cuttings filling 33 volumes and covering the period 1919–34. Some 200 miscellaneous letters have survived. Thomas's correspondents include Raymond Asquith, the Prime Minister's eldest son, who was killed in 1916 and who was a prospective Liberal candidate in Derby (five letters). There are six letters from Lord Beaverbrook 1918–36, 12 from Lord Rothermere 1933–34, and 20 from MacDonald 1923–37. There are 16 drafts or notes for speeches.

A few fragments survive from Thomas's official career, including an offer (declined) from Lloyd George in Dec 1916 of the Ministry of Labour. From Thomas's periods in both the Colonial and Dominions Offices, correspondence with governors survive. There is also a copy of a declaration made by Violet Digby in 1924 relating to the publication of the Zinoviev letter. A circular letter to governors dated 7 Feb 1936 sets out the economic position and prospects for the colonies. As Lord Privy Seal Thomas had special responsibility for unemployment and a few papers concerning this survive, including papers connected with his dispute with Sir Oswald Mosley, during which Thomas offered to resign.

Very few papers in the collection relate to Thomas's trade union activities: a few letters concerning job applications, letters and memoranda on the refusal of the Irish railway men to carry troops because of intimidation in 1920, and papers connected with the National Union of Railwaymen's refusal to give Thomas a pension. There is also a report of the British Labour delegation to the USA 4 May-2 June 1917.

Thomas's career in the National Union of Railwaymen is reflected in the union's archive, which is held in the Modern Records Centre (MSS. 127) and in the archive of the International Transport Worker's Federation, also in the Modern Records Centre (MSS. 159). David Howell draws on this and other relevant material in '"I loved my Union and my Country": Jimmy Thomas and the Politics of Railway Trade Unionism', *Twentieth Century British History*, 6, 2, 1995, 145–73.

Reference should be made to two articles by Andrew Thorpe, 'J. H. Thomas and the Rise of Labour in Derby, 1880–1945', *Midland History*, 15, 1990, 111–28, and '"I am in the Cabinet": J. H. Thomas's Decision to Join the National Government in 1931', *Historical Research*, 64, 1991, 389–402.

JAMES PURDON LEWES THOMAS, VISCOUNT CILCENNIN (1903–1960)

James Thomas was Conservative MP for Hereford 1931–55. He was Junior Lord of the Treasury June 1940–Sept 1943, Financial Secretary to the Admiralty 1943–May 1945, and First Lord of the Admiralty Oct 1951–Sept 1956. He was created Viscount Cilcennin in 1955.

The Carmarthen RO holds a collection of Cilcennin papers which was deposited in 1980 (ACC 5605). The papers had originally been inherited by Cilcennin's sister, Miss Joan Thomas, and on her death went to the depositor, Mr H. R. P. Lloyd, by way of her trustee. There is a comprehensive chronological list available (NRA 24422). The introduction to the list notes that the trustee for Cilcennin's sister who inherited the papers 'signed the official secrets Act... the collection was weeded and many papers were destroyed though it is not known on what basis of selection'.

The collection spans the period c.1936–60 as well as some further correspondence regarding the papers up until 1980. The majority of the collection consists of personal correspondence with civil servants and politicians including Stanley Baldwin, Harold Macmillan, and a few notes from Prince Philip. There is regular correspondence from the late 1930s onwards with 'Bobbety' (Viscount Cranborne, later Lord Salisbury), Earl Mountbatten, and Anthony Eden, whose principal private secretary Thomas was 1937–37 and 1939–40. There is a group of congratulatory notes from political figures after Cilcennin's maiden speech in Parliament 1944, and many notes expressing regret at his resignation as First Lord of the Admiralty 1956. There are also notes commending Cilcennin for his loyalty to Eden in resigning with him from the Foreign Office in 1938. There are a host of papers on the Duke of Edinburgh's World Tour of 1956–57, on which Cilcennin was a guest.

Lord Avon utilised the Cilcennin papers when undertaking research for his own books, and his pencilled comments may be found on many of the papers. A diary which then existed is not now in the collection, nor is it to be found in the Avon collection at Birmingham University Library.

Surviving records of the Hereford Conservatives can be found in the Hereford RO.

CHRISTOPHER BIRDWOOD THOMSON, BARON THOMSON OF CARDINGTON (1875–1930)

Christopher Thomson was created Baron Thomson of Cardington in 1924. He was Secretary of State for Air Jan–Nov 1924 and June 1929–Oct 1930.

Thomson, who was unmarried, died in the R101 disaster. His brother, Colonel R. G. Thomson, advised us he did not know of the existence of any of his brother's papers. The late Sir Christopher Bullock, Thomson's principal private secretary at the time of his death, did not know of any papers; nor did the 2nd Lord Amwell, whose father was Under-Secretary of State for Air 1929–31 and a great friend of Thomson.

Princess Marthe Bibesco, in *Lord Thomson of Cardington: A memoir and some letters* (Jonathan Cape 1932), quoted from her own long correspondence with Thomson. She informed us that Thomson's mother permitted her to look at his correspondence. Some of these letters were quoted in Princess Bibesco's memoir but the fate of the originals is unknown. The British Library has some letters bought from Princess Bibesco in 1964.

Thomson's book, *Smaranda* (Jonathan Cape 1926), includes an account in diary form of his wartime service from March 1915 mainly in England, Romania, Russia, and the Middle East; and a few entries on his post-war work at the Paris Peace Conference and his earliest election campaigns. In the 'Compiler's Preface' Thomson wrote that 'General Y' (himself) 'was a profuse, discursive scribbler and notoriously indiscreet. Many entries in the diary have been entirely omitted and others rigorously expurgated...'. Maie Casey (Lady Casey) in her memoirs, *Tides and Eddies* (Michael Joseph 1966), p. 51, records that she was a neighbour and friend of Thomson at the time he was writing *Smaranda*. The book, she writes, was in 'diary form', and Thomson 'read to me from this material, altering passages as he read, ironing them out and polishing...'. Lady Casey informed us that the diary section of *Smaranda* 'was based on his diaries and was certainly *authentic* ... Any alterations he made through reading part one to me were not substantial, but only the minor revisions that any writer makes when he hears the sounds and rhythms of his written words'. Smaranda was the pseudonym for Princess Bibesco and for her country, Romania.

The second and third parts of *Smaranda* are semi-autobiographical stories based on Thomson's personal observation and experience.

Thomson's *Old Europe's Suicide* (T. Seltzer, New York 1922) is a narrative, partly in autobiographical form, of British policy in the Balkans 1912–19. It contains no quotations from contemporary documents.

In 1974, Thomson's nephew Commander R. W. D. Thomson presented to the IWM what was thought at first to be a diary 1918–19. The 'duplicate order book' is in fact part of the manuscript described by Lady Casey. It is not an original diary but a transcript of diary entries starting just before Thomson joined the staff of the Supreme War Council on 13 April 1918, including his mission to Mudros in Oct 1918 to negotiate peace terms with Turkey and the Paris Peace Conference. There are emendations consistent with Lady Casey's description of Thomson's working method. The 'diary' refers to Smaranda and the Smarandans and is actually a draft of pages 98–130 of the book *Smaranda* and includes instructions to the typist, a draft 'compiler's note', several passages struck out, and the draft 'Preface'. There is a long entry dated 13 Sept 1925 reflecting on the current political situation, particularly the crisis in the coal industry, which appears to be a draft speech or letter to constituents. There is also the draft of an article for *John Bull* on a visit to the USA. Some pages had apparently been removed from the book before it was given to the IWM.

The only other item deposited is a memo and covering note to the Secretary of State for War 25 March 1930 on 'the facts and probabilities of a war with France' particularly relating to the protection of a possible pipeline in Syria (IWM 74/39/1).

The PRO holds journals for the period 1918–21, and Private Office papers for his term as Secretary of State for Air which are available in AIR 19.

SIR WILLIAM LOWSON MITCHELL-THOMSON, 2nd Bt, 1st BARON SELSDON (1877–1938)

William Mitchell-Thomson was Conservative MP for Lanarkshire (North-West) 1906–10, Down (North) 1910–18, Glasgow (Maryhill) 1918–22 and Croydon (South) 1923–32. He was Parliamentary Secretary to the Ministry of Food April 1920–March 1921, Parliamentary Secretary to the Board of Trade 1921–Oct 1922, and Postmaster-General Nov 1924–June 1929. He succeeded his father as 2nd baronet in 1918, and was created KBE in 1918, and Baron Selsdon in 1932.

Mitchell-Thomson's grandson, the 3rd Lord Selsdon, informed us that he has little of interest relating to his grandfather's career: only letters of appointment; orders, certificates, and decorations; and cuttings of obituaries have survived.

(GEORGE EDWARD) PETER THORNEYCROFT, BARON THORNEYCROFT (1909–1994)

Peter Thorneycroft was Conservative MP for Stafford 1938–45 and Monmouth 1945–66. He was Parliamentary Secretary, Ministry of War Transport May–July 1945, President of the Board of Trade Oct 1951–Jan 1957, Chancellor of the Exchequer 1957–Jan 1958, Minister of Aviation July 1960–July 1962, Minister of Defence 1962–April 1964, and Secretary of State for Defence April–Oct 1964. He was created Baron Thorneycroft (a life peerage) in 1967.

Lord Thorneycroft informed us that he did not have any papers connected with his ministerial career, those he did have being destroyed by the Westminster Hall bomb in 1974.

The Conservative Party Archives in the Bodleian Library include a collection of papers from his time as Party Chairman 1975–81, which are not available for research at present.

The PRO has identified some papers relating to Thorneycroft's period at the Board of Trade (LAB 43/38) from 1951. Papers relating to Budgets are in T 171.

Thorneycroft's resignation as Chancellor of the Exchequer is examined in Rodney Lowe, 'Resignation at the Treasury: The Social Services Committee and the Failure to Reform the Welfare State 1955–57', *Journal of Social Policy*, 18, 1989, 505–26. Patrick Cosgrave outlines Thorneycroft's career in *Blackwell*, 400–2.

GEORGE TOMLINSON (1890–1952)

George Tomlinson was Labour MP for Lancashire (Farnworth) 1938–52. He was Joint Parliamentary Secretary to the Ministry of Labour and National Service Feb 1941–May 1945, Minister of Works Aug 1945–Feb 1947, and Minister of Education 1947–Oct 1951.

Tomlinson's only daughter, Mrs D. Hardman, did not know of the existence of any papers. Fred Blackburn's biography *George Tomlinson* (Heinemann 1954) was based largely on talks the author had with Tomlinson before his death. Mr Blackburn had no Tomlinson papers.

There is a small collection of press cuttings on Tomlinson in the National Museum of Labour History.

Tomlinson's work as Minister of Education is examined in D. W. Dean, 'Planning for a Post-War Generation: Ellen Wilkinson and George Tomlinson at the Ministry of Education 1945–51', *History of Education*, 15, 1986, 95–117.

SIR CHARLES PHILIPS TREVELYAN, 3rd Bt (1870–1958)

Charles Trevelyan was Liberal MP for West Riding of Yorkshire (Elland) 1899–1918, and Labour MP for Newcastle-upon-Tyne (Central) 1922–31. He was Parliamentary Secretary to the Board of Education Oct 1908–Aug 1914, and President of the Board of Education Jan-Nov 1924 and June 1929–March 1931. He succeeded his father as 3rd baronet in 1928.

The C. P. Trevelyan Collection, which forms part of a larger collection of family papers, was deposited by the Trevelyan family in the Library of the University of Newcastle upon Tyne in 1967. There is a main and an extra series of papers, which together comprise over 400 packets of material containing overall thousands of individual documents. The main series consists largely of personal and political correspondence, speech notes and press cuttings dating from throughout Trevelyan's life. Correspondents include Asquith, Attlee, Baldwin, Balfour, Churchill, Lloyd George, Ramsay MacDonald, Runciman, G. B. Shaw, Snowden, the Webbs and J. C. Wedgwood, amongst many others. The extra series contains Trevelyan's letters to his wife, as well as some political and other correspondence. A catalogue of the main series, with both correspondent and subject index, is available; the extra series has also been catalogued, but without a subject index. (Alistair Elliot and Glenys Williams, *Catalogue of the Papers of Sir Charles*

Philips Trevelyan, Bt (1870–1958), University Library, Newcastle upon Tyne 1973; *Catalogue of the Papers of Sir Charles Philips Trevelyan, 1870–1958, Extra Series*, University Library, Newcastle upon Tyne 1986). There is also a collection of purely family correspondence which has not yet been catalogued and cannot be seen without the permission of the Trevelyan family trustees.

Researchers wishing to consult these papers should make written application in advance to the Special Collections Librarian, University of Newcastle upon Tyne.

In *From Liberalism to Labour* (George Allen & Unwin 1921) Trevelyan explained how he made the transition between the two political parties. There is a biography based on the papers: A. J. A. Morris, *C. P. Trevelyan: Portrait of a Radical* (Blackstaff Press, Belfast 1977).

Trevelyan's letters home to his father and family during his travels in North America, New Zealand, and Australia March-Dec 1898 are in Charles Philips Trevelyan, *Letters from North America and the Pacific 1898* (Chatto & Windus 1969).

Material about Trevelyan's marriage to Mary (Molly) Bell is included in Pat Jalland's *Women, Marriage and Politics 1860–1914* (Clarendon Press, Oxford 1986).

GEORGE CLEMENT TRYON, 1st BARON TRYON (1871–1940)

George Tryon was Conservative MP for Brighton 1910–40. He was Under-Secretary of State for Air Dec 1919–April 1920, Parliamentary Secretary to the Ministry of Pensions 1920–Oct 1922 and Oct 1940–Feb 1941, Minister of Pensions 1922–Jan 1924, Nov 1924–June 1929 and Sept 1931–June 1935, Postmaster-General 1935–April 1940, Chancellor of the Duchy of Lancaster April-May 1940, and First Commissioner of Works May-Oct 1940. He was created Baron Tryon in 1940.

Neither of Tryon's two sons knew of the existence of any papers relating to their father's political career.

Tryon's grandson, the 3rd Lord Tryon, advised us that he held no relevant papers belonging to his grandfather, and believed that any papers were lost when the family moved out of their house at Great Durnford during the Second World War.

EDWARD TURNOUR, 6th EARL WINTERTON (1883–1962)

Edward Turnour was known as Viscount Winterton until he succeeded his father as 6th Earl Winterton (an Irish peerage) in 1907. He was created Baron Turnour (in the UK peerage) in 1952. He was Conservative MP for Sussex (Horsham) 1904–18, Sussex West (Horsham and Worthing) 1918–45 and Sussex West (Horsham) 1945–51. He was Under-Secretary of State for India March 1922–Jan 1924 and Nov

1924–June 1929, Chancellor of the Duchy of Lancaster May 1937–Jan 1939, and Paymaster-General Jan-Nov 1939.

Lord Winterton left all his papers to his literary executor and biographer, Mr Alan Houghton Brodrick. They have since been deposited in the Bodleian Library where a preliminary list has been prepared.

The collection includes Winterton's copious diaries which cover the period 1906–60 (with occasional gaps). There is miscellaneous correspondence and papers for the period 1916–60s, as well as literary and financial papers. There are letters to and from Viceroys and Governors in India 1922–28, 1925–29; and correspondence with political colleagues including Churchill, Baldwin, MacDonald, Selwyn Lloyd, Attlee, Halifax, Boothby, Neville Chamberlain, Hoare, Hore-Belisha, Beaverbrook, and Macmillan. The collection also contains press cuttings, photos, and family papers including Queen Alexandra's letters to Lady Winterton 1907 and 1909, the 5th Earl's diary, and transcripts of Turnour family letters 1599–1720.

There are quotations from the papers, including the diaries, in Winterton's *Pre-War* (Macmillan 1932), *Orders of the Day* (Cassell 1953), and *Fifty Tumultuous Years* (Hutchinson 1955), as well as in Alan Houghton Brodrick's *Near to Greatness. A Life of the 6th Earl Winterton* (Hutchinson 1961).

ROBERT HUGH TURTON, BARON TRANMIRE (1903–1994)

Robin Turton was Conservative MP for Thirsk and Malton 1929–74. He was Parliamentary Secretary, Ministry of National Insurance Nov 1951–Sept 1953, Parliamentary Secretary, Ministry of Pensions and National Insurance 1953–Oct 1954, Joint Parliamentary Under-Secretary of State for Foreign Affairs 1954–Dec 1955, and Minister of Health 1955–Jan 1957. He was created KBE in 1971, and Baron Tranmire (a life peerage) in 1974.

In *Sources*, Cook states that Lord Tranmire 'has retained a small collection of correspondence and press cuttings. The latter cover the years 1929–57'.

We were not able to make contact with Lord Tranmire or his family.

DENNIS FORWOOD VOSPER, BARON RUNCORN (1916–1968)

Dennis Vosper was Conservative MP for Runcorn 1950–64. He was Junior Lord of the Treasury Nov 1951–Oct 1954, Parliamentary Secretary, Ministry of Education 1954–Jan 1957, Minister of Health Jan-Sept 1957, Joint Parliamentary Under-Secretary of State, Home Office Oct 1959–Oct 1960, Minister of State, Home Office 1960–June 1961, and Secretary for Technical Co-operation 1961–May 1963. He was created Baron Runcorn (a life peerage) in 1964.

His widow, Mrs James Earle, who married Lord Runcorn in 1966, advised us that she had no official papers, only a few letters relating to Runcorn's departure from office.

PATRICK CHRESTIEN GORDON WALKER, BARON GORDON-WALKER (1907–1980)

Patrick Gordon Walker was Labour MP for Smethwick 1945–64 and Leyton 1966–74. He was Parliamentary Under-Secretary of State for Commonwealth Relations Oct 1947–Feb 1950, Secretary of State for Commonwealth Relations 1950–Oct 1951, Secretary of State for Foreign Affairs Oct 1964–Jan 1965, Minister without Portfolio Jan 1966–Aug 1967, and Secretary of State for Education and Science 1967–April 1968. He was created Baron Gordon-Walker (a life peerage) in 1974.

Gordon-Walker's papers were deposited by his son in the Churchill Archives Centre in 1981 (GNWR). A list is available (NRA 24835). There are diaries and associated correspondence from 1932 onwards. The rest of the collection has been divided partly by subject (Labour Party and Cabinet, international and Commonwealth affairs, Secretary of State for Education), and partly by category (writing and reviews, talks and broadcasts, press cuttings). Access to the papers is by written application to the Archivist, Churchill Archives Centre. Some of the diaries and correspondence are closed for specified periods.

Papers relating to his term as Secretary of State for Commonwealth Relations can be found in the PRO at CAB 127/296–325 (NRA 32409).

Gordon-Walker quoted from his papers, particularly from his diaries, in *The Cabinet* (Cape 1970, revised edition 1972). Selections from his diaries have been edited by Robert Pearce in *Patrick Gordon-Walker: Political Diaries 1932–1971* (The Historians' Press 1991).

Gordon-Walker's work as Secretary of State for Commonwealth Relations is discussed in David Goldsworthy, *Colonial Issues in British Politics 1945–1961* (Clarendon Press, Oxford 1971), which draws on the records of the Fabian Colonial Bureau, and R. D. Pearce, *The Turning Point in Africa: British Colonial Policy, 1938–48* (Frank Cass 1982). A. N. Porter's brief life of Gordon-Walker in *Blackwell*, 169–70, has a useful guide to further reading.

(DAVID) EUAN WALLACE (1892–1941)

Captain Euan Wallace was Conservative MP for Warwickshire (Rugby) 1922–23 and Hornsey 1924–41. He was Civil Lord of the Admiralty Nov 1931–June 1935, Under-Secretary of State for Home Affairs June-Nov 1935, Secretary for Overseas Trade at the Board of Trade 1935–May 1937, Parliamentary Secretary to the Board of Trade 1937–May 1938, Financial Secretary to the Treasury 1938–April 1939, and Minister of Transport 1939–May 1940.

Wallace's widow, Mrs Herbert Agar, gave his diary to the Bodleian Library (MS Eng hist c 495–8). The diary covers the period 22 Aug 1939–18 Oct 1940. It appears to have been dictated daily and contains a considerable amount of detail, for example, on the Cabinet meetings leading up to the declaration of war, and on the events leading up to the formation of Churchill's government in May 1940. At that time Wallace was offered the Office of Works on condition he took a peerage. He refused because he did not wish to preclude a further career in the House of Commons and instead accepted the post of Senior Regional Commissioner for Civil Defence in London, a post originally offered to, but refused by, Herbert Morrison. The diary stops in Oct 1940 when Wallace fell ill.

SIR WILLIAM HOOD WALROND, 2nd Bt, 1st BARON WALERAN (1849–1925)

William Walrond was Conservative MP for Devonshire (East) 1880–85 and Devonshire (Tiverton) 1885–1906. He was Chancellor of the Duchy of Lancaster Aug 1902–Dec 1905. He succeeded his father as 2nd baronet in 1889, and was created Baron Waleran in 1905.

Lady Waleran, widow of Walrond's grandson, the 2nd Lord Waleran, informed us that all his papers were destroyed during the First World War.

The Walrond Papers (Arthur L. Humphreys 1913) by Walrond's daughter-in-law, the Hon Charlotte M. L. Walrond, is a family history that prints many family documents but carries the story only as far as Walrond's father, the first baronet.

STEPHEN WALSH (1859–1929)

Stephen Walsh was Labour MP for South-West Lancashire (Ince; Lancashire, Ince from 1918) 1906–29. He was Parliamentary Secretary to the Ministry of National Service March-June 1917, Parliamentary Secretary to the Local Government Board 1917–Jan 1919, and Secretary of State for War Jan-Nov 1924.

When asked for the first edition, neither of Walsh's two sons nor his daughter knew of the existence of any papers; they believed that any papers that might have been kept were destroyed.

John Saville has contributed a brief biography and guide to sources in *DLB*, IV, 187–90.

SIR (JOHN) TUDOR WALTERS (1866–1933)

Tudor Walters was Liberal MP for Sheffield (Brightside) 1906–22 and Cornwall (Penryn and Falmouth) 1929–31. He was Paymaster-General Oct 1919–Oct 1922 and Sept-Nov 1931. He was knighted in 1912.

Walters's grand-daughter, Signora Ann Sangiovanni, Centro Residenziale, Colle Paradiso, Villino No Q4, 24, 00048 Nettuno (RM), Italy, has three albums of press cuttings including a volume of cuttings mainly for 1903–09 covering Walters's parliamentary and constituency activities. There are also several articles by Walters from *John Bull*, *The Spectator*, and *The Listener*, about post-war housing problems, and several obituary notices. Signora Sangiovanni advised us that these albums will be left to her son Anco Marzio Sangiovanni, who also lives in Italy.

Walters's only son and his son's wife are now dead. His only daughter, Mrs H. Lucey, had nothing other than a copy of her father's book *The Building of 12,000 Houses* (Ernest Benn 1927), a history of the Industrial Housing Association.

SIR JOHN LAWSON WALTON (1852–1908)

John Walton was Liberal MP for Leeds (South) 1892–1908. He was Attorney-General Dec 1905–Jan 1908. He was knighted in 1905.

When the first edition was compiled, a small collection of press cuttings was in the possession of Walton's grandson, Mr I. D. M. Reid. The collection consisted of two albums of obituary notices and a small file of press cuttings from Walton's political career in the 1890s. In addition there were some election cards, leaflets, election addresses, and election posters (including one in Hebrew). There were also several reprints of speeches by Walton and other Liberals, for example a lecture by Walton on Parliament, and a speech by Sir Henry Fowler on the Indian Frontier problem in 1894. We were not able to contact Mr Reid to confirm that he still had these papers.

No other members of the family had any papers relating to Walton's life and political career.

The brief biographical sketch by James Beresford Atlay in *DNB 1901–1911*, 586, is based only on published sources.

GEORGE REGINALD WARD, 1st VISCOUNT WARD OF WITLEY (1907–1988)

George Ward was Conservative MP for Worcester 1945–60. He was Parliamentary Under-Secretary of State, Air Ministry Feb 1952–Dec 1955, Parliamentary and Financial Secretary, Admiralty 1955–Jan 1957, and Secretary of State for Air 1957–Oct 1960. He was created Viscount Ward of Witley in 1960.

In *Sources*, Cook notes Viscount Ward's advice that he retained 'papers of personal interest only'.

We have not been able to contact Ward's only surviving child, the Hon Mrs P. C. H. Tritton who lives in Mexico. Ward's sister-in-law, the Hon Alethea Ward, did not know of any papers, nor did the son of Ward's second wife, Mr David Astor.

HAROLD ARTHUR WATKINSON, 1st VISCOUNT WATKINSON (1910–1995)

Harold Watkinson was Conservative MP for Woking 1950–64. He was Parliamentary Secretary, Ministry of Labour and National Service May 1952–Dec 1955, Minister of Transport and Civil Aviation 1955–Oct 1959, and Minister of Defence 1959–July 1962. He was created Viscount Watkinson in 1964.

Watkinson's autobiography *Turning Points: A Record of Our Times* (Michael Russell, Salisbury 1986) quotes from a few private letters and memoranda from senior military advisers and civil servants and from the Prime Ministers and other ministerial colleagues with whom he served, including Walter Monckton, Lord Mountbatten, Harold Macmillan, and Sir Francis Festing.

Watkinson records (p. 107) that as a result of 'the inept way in which ex-Ministers leaving office were dealt with at this time there was no opportunity of disposing of... rather a large collection' of policy papers which he kept for reference as Minister of Transport and Civil Aviation and Minister of Defence. 'These papers and the narrative that went with them were approved by Sir Burke Trend, as Secretary of the Cabinet, as being within the confines of security'.

They were deposited at Ashridge Management College of which Watkinson was then President where they are now available for research. They comprise nine box-files containing papers on the Ministry of Transport, Railway Disputes Dock Strike and Seaman's Strike 1951, general road and traffic policy, air policy for civil aircraft and shipping, defence, pay policy, exports participation, transport matters and budgets for 1976 and 1978 as well as various CBI magazines and journals for 1975 and 1976. These box-files correspond in content to particular chapters in Watkinson's autobiography.

Prospective researchers should contact the Chief Executive, Ashridge Management College, to arrange a mutually convenient time to visit the College. Photocopying facilities are available.

Watkinson also 'kept by me some documents and letters to which I felt I might wish to refer in describing some of the more significant turning points in the history of government in the fifties'. These additional papers, occasionally quoted in *Turning Points*, remained in Lord Watkinson's possession as did the 'Secret' and 'Top Secret' papers which were in his official strong box when it was reclaimed at the time of his dismissal as Minister of Defence (*Turning Points*, p. 163).

Official files relating to Watkinson's period as Minister of Defence are in the PRO at DEFE 13/1–6.

MAURICE WEBB (1904-1956)

Maurice Webb was Labour MP for Bradford (Central) 1945-55. He was Minister of Food Feb 1950-Oct 1951.

Webb left all his chattels to his widow, Mabel. She died in 1963 leaving her estate to Miss D. A. Williams. Miss Williams informed us that she did not know of the existence of any papers, though Webb was thought to have been writing a memoir at the time of his death. We were unable to contact Webb's brother, Harold.

SIDNEY JAMES WEBB, BARON PASSFIELD (1859-1947)

Sidney Webb was Labour MP for Durham (Seaham) 1922-29. He was President of the Board of Trade Jan-Nov 1924, Secretary of State for both Dominion and Colonial Affairs June 1929-June 1930, and for Colonial Affairs alone 1930-Aug 1931. He was created Baron Passfield in 1929.

A large collection of the papers of both Sidney and Beatrice Webb has been deposited in the BLPES. There are no restrictions on any of the papers, but written application to read them should be made in advance. The papers have been divided into two main collections, the Webb Trade Union Collection (Webb Trade Union) and private papers (Passfield).

The former, c.1814-c.1924 consists of 298 volumes of material collected for *The History of Trade Unionism* (Longmans, Green 1894), *Industrial Democracy* (Longmans, Green 1897) and other works. Section A consists of manuscript notes by the Webbs; section B of pamphlets and other printed material about trade unions; section C of trade union rule books; and Section D of trade union journals.

The private papers collection 1870-1947 represents 'the central collection for their personal and political life'. It has been divided into 13 sections, and a draft handlist is available. Section I, the most important, contains Beatrice Webb's diaries 1873-1943. The manuscript version fills 58 notebooks and includes some letters and photos. Beatrice Webb herself typed out many of her diaries and began editing them for publication. The following were the result: Beatrice Webb, *My Apprenticeship* (Longmans 1926); Margaret I. Cole and Barbara Drake (eds), *Our Partnership* (Longmans Green 1948); Margaret I. Cole (ed), *Beatrice Webb's Diaries 1912-1924* and *1924-1932* (Longmans Green 1952-56). See also George Feaver (ed), *The Webbs in Asia: The 1911-12 travel diary* (Macmillan 1992); David A. Shannon (ed), *Beatrice Webb's American Diary 1898* (University of Wisconsin Press, 1963); A.G. Austin (ed), *The Webbs' Australian Diary 1898* (Melbourne UP 1965); and Niraja Gopal Jayal (ed), *Sidney and Beatrice Webb: Indian Diary [1911]* (Oxford UP, Delhi 1987). A microfiche edition in 57 vols, with a printed index, was published in 1978. There is also a selection of extracts, *The Diary of*

Beatrice Webb, edited by Norman and Jeanne Mackenzie, published in four volumes (1982–85) by Virago Press in association with the LSE.

Section II consists of the Webbs' letters to each other, family and general correspondence; section III of legal and financial papers and photos; section IV of papers on their political activity; sections V, VI, VII, VIII, and XIIA of material concerning lectures and publications; section IX of their Fabian Society papers; section X of papers concerning the foundation, history, and administration of the London School of Economics (apart from his role in founding the LSE, Sidney Webb was Professor of Public Administration there 1912–27); section XI of their connection with the *New Statesman* (which the Webbs founded in 1913); section XII of the Potter family letters; and section XIII consists of Beatrice Webb's papers as a member of the Reconstruction Committee of the Ministry of Reconstruction 1916–18.

A number of small collections and individual items are listed separately. These miscellaneous collections include most importantly: Board of Trade papers mainly concerning labour exchanges, national insurance, overseas trade, and wartime administration 1911–43 (COLL MISC 0241); and the 'demi official' papers of Webb as Colonial Secretary concerning East Africa and the Joint Select Committee on East Africa 1929–31 (COLL MISC 0156). Other collections include: Sidney Webb's lectures on the civil service (COLL MISC 0243); papers concerning the taxation of ground rents 1893–1900 (COLL MISC 0190); a draft manuscript of 'Standard condition of employment' (COLL MISC 0282); manuscript articles written for the *Daily Despatch* on Sidney Webb in politics with corrections by Webb 1908 (COLL MISC 0280); and papers concerning wartime measures for the relief of distress 1914–15 (COLL MISC 0242).

The archives of the Fabian Society at Nuffield College, Oxford, also contain much Webb correspondence as do the Labour Party archives at the National Museum of Labour History (LP/ JSM, WNC, and WE).

Margaret Cole has written a memoir, *Beatrice Webb* (Longmans 1945). *Sidney and Beatrice Webb* by Mary A. Hamilton (Sampson Low 1932) is not based on any previously unpublished material. The biography written by Kitty Muggeridge (Beatrice Webb's niece) and Ruth Adam, *Beatrice Webb: A Life* (Secker & Warburg 1967), is based on Potter family papers as well as the Webb collection. See also Norman Mackenzie (ed), *Letters of Sidney and Beatrice Webb*, (3 vols, Cambridge UP 1978).

A compact joint biography of the Webbs with a comprehensive guide to sources was contributed by Margaret Cole to *DLB*, II, 376–96.

The contribution on Webb by Lonnie E. Maness in *MBR*, 3, 849–54, is also valuable on relevant published and unpublished sources.

SIR RICHARD EVERARD WEBSTER, Bt, VISCOUNT ALVERSTONE (1842-1915)

Richard Webster was Conservative MP for Launceston 1885 and the Isle of Wight 1885-1900. He was Attorney-General June 1885-Feb 1886, Aug 1886-Aug 1892 and July 1895-May 1900. He was knighted in 1885, and created GCMG in 1893, a baronet in 1900, Baron Alverstone in 1900, and Viscount Alverstone in 1913.

Webster's only son died before him; his widow, who became Mrs I. Ramsey, told us that all his papers were burnt during the Second World War. When the first edition was compiled, Webster's grand-children by his only daughter, Lady Durston and Miss Barbara Mellor, told us that they believed that Webster's papers were either destroyed at his death or later when their parents moved house. Webster's solicitors did not have any papers.

However, in 1980, a collection of general correspondence formerly in the possession of Miss Mellor was privately sold to a number of purchasers, including dealers. Details of the items are contained in the catalogue of a sale by Lawrence Fine Art of Crewkerne (19b Market St, Crewkerne, Somerset TA18 7JU) on 14 Feb 1980. The British Library purchased three volumes of letters written to Webster in the period 1865-1918 (Add MSS 61737-40) and the Bodleian Library has a small group of letters from Asquith (MSS Eng Lett E 159).

In *Recollections of Bar and Bench* (Edward Arnold 1914), described by F. D. Maurice in *DNB 1912-1921*, 562-3 as badly written and not interesting, Webster gave his reminiscences of his tenure of the Attorney-General's office and his period as Lord Chief Justice 1900-12, but quoted from no original documents.

JOSIAH CLEMENT WEDGWOOD, 1st BARON WEDGWOOD (1872-1943)

Josiah Wedgwood was Liberal MP for Newcastle-under-Lyme 1906-19, and Labour MP for the same constituency 1919-42. He was Chancellor of the Duchy of Lancaster Jan-Nov 1924. He was created Baron Wedgwood in 1942.

Wedgwood's eldest daughter and executrix, the Hon Mrs H. B. Pease, gathered her father's papers and bequeathed them to Keele University Library where they were placed by Wedgwood's grand-daughter Dr N. J. Pease in 1981.

The papers, almost all of which are letters, fill approximately 17 box-files. They have been weeded, and then divided into family and non-family letters, and arranged chronologically. The family letters naturally contain mainly family news but there are occasional comments on the political situation, particularly in Wedgwood's later letters to his children, who were themselves politically active. The non-family letters cover a wide range of topics but particularly reflect Wedgwood's interest in land value taxation, and East Africa. Mrs Pease informed us that she thought it probable that many papers relating to Wedgwood's support for Zionism and his work to help Jews fleeing Germany in the 1930s were destroyed in 1938–39 when he feared that England might be invaded.

Several papers survive from Wedgwood's activities in the First World War, in particular a five-page carbon copy of a letter from Wedgwood to Churchill 24 April 1915 describing the landings at Gallipoli. This is quoted in full in Wedgwood's *Memoirs of a Fighting Life* (Hutchinson 1940). Copies of this book are rare because the warehouse containing them was bombed just before they were distributed. The letter is also quoted in C. V. Wedgwood's biography of Wedgwood, *The Last of the Radicals* (Jonathan Cape 1951). In Wedgwood's early volume of memoirs, *Essays and Adventures of a Labour M.P.* (George Allen & Unwin 1924) he seems to be relying on memory, except when referring to his work on the Royal Commission on Mesopotamia and his minority report: he quotes from letters to Austen Chamberlain, Secretary of State for India, and to the Indian leaders, June-July 1917. There is further autobiographical content in *Testament to Democracy* (Hutchinson 1942).

There is a report by Wedgwood on his impression of the Western Front, including his assessment of various generals, and his views on conscription, a letter to Lloyd George 11 Oct 1916 expressing his horror at the fact that British losses in France were four times those of the French army, a memo Jan 1917 on the deplorable nature of British propaganda in the USA, and a memo on the effect of possible peace terms on East Africa. Wedgwood went to East Africa in 1916; typed notes of his conversations with the Governor, officials, and settlers survive. Wedgwood was sent to Siberia in 1918 to encourage the Russians to continue fighting and to persuade them of the worthlessness of German offers. His instructions have survived. He went to Siberia via the USA and his manuscript notes about that part of his voyage survive. Wedgwood's advice to the War Office (that they were wasting their money by helping the White Russians) was not well received and he was quickly recalled. On the way home he began to write an account for his grand-children of what he had done in the war; he never completed this.

No papers have survived from Wedgwood's tenure of the Duchy of Lancaster but there are carbon copies of letters he wrote in 1924 to J. H. Thomas about East Africa and to Lord Olivier about India. There are several long letters from Lajpat Rai concerning the course of Indian nationalism and also letters from the Viceroy, Lord Irwin (later the Earl of Halifax). There is a letter from Philip Snowden 24 Nov

(?1924) expressing strong disapproval of Ramsay MacDonald's fitness to continue as Leader of the Labour Party. There are two files of miscellaneous letters from the 1930s and early 1940s. Wedgwood's correspondents included Eden, Neville Chamberlain, Baldwin, Lord Beaverbrook, and Churchill; to the latter he sent frequent long letters on how to conduct the war. There are also letters about his memoirs and congratulations on his peerage.

There is a volume of press cuttings, mainly reviews of Wedgwood's various publications, and some leaflets on land reform.

Wedgwood papers as yet unlisted at Keele University include copies of family papers from the 17th and 18th centuries; 12 box-files of family letters 1881–1943; a box of diaries, field notes and letters on South Africa 1900–03 (copies held on microfilm at the National Army Museum); a box of press cuttings 1912–42; and a box of miscellaneous letters, papers and cuttings 1905–14.

Microfilm copies of the listed papers held at Keele University are available at the IWM (PP/MCR/104/JCW). In addition, the IWM has microfilm copies of several documents which were not included in the Keele University deposit in 1981 (JCW/2/1). The documents all relate to the Second World War and include correspondence with Halifax, Stanley, Attlee, and most notably a scathing letter to Churchill Oct 1941 telling him not to listen to advisors who have been proved wrong in the past, and a letter from Eden 6 Nov 1941 stating 'as to negotiation with Hitler – not only will I not do so but you may be sure that I could never resign myself to letting others do so any more than you could'.

The files collected by Wedgwood for his biographical research project on the history of Parliament are contained in 86 boxes held by the History of Parliament Trust at Wedgwood House, 15 Woburn Square, London WC1H 0NS. Confidential responses to Wedgwood's questionnaire to MPs in 1936–37 remain restricted. Box A-46 contains a range of correspondence unrelated to the Parliamentary history, including letters concerning Palestine.

Twenty-one volumes of press cuttings 1908–43 concerning Wedgwood's political career are in the Local Studies Collection in the Hanley Information Library, Stoke-on-Trent. They appear to have been compiled by or for Wedgwood and include miscellaneous pamphlets and election manifestos.

In addition to his volumes of memoirs, Wedgwood provided a brief self-portrait of his first 36 years in *A History of the Wedgwood Family* (St Catherine Press 1908). A recent specialist study is Joshua B. Stein *Our Great Solicitor: Josiah C. Wedgwood and the Jews* (Susquehanna UP, Selinsgrove 1992).

ANDREW WEIR, 1st BARON INVERFORTH (1865–1955)

Andrew Weir was created Baron Inverforth in 1919. He was Minister of Munitions (later Minister of Supply) Jan 1919–March 1921.

Only two files of papers was known to have survived in the possession of Weir's son, the 2nd Baron Inverforth. One file contained obituaries from local, national, and the shipping trade press. The other file included correspondence with Lloyd George 1919–21 on Weir's wish to resign ('As you know I am not a politician...'). There was also a collection of letters of appreciation when Weir did resign. Neither the 2nd Lord Inverforth's widow, Iris, Baroness Inverforth, nor his son, the Hon Vincent Weir, had any knowledge of these files.

Some of Weir's papers as Surveyor-General of the Army 1917–18, and Private Office papers have survived in the records of the Ministry of Munitions at the PRO (MUN/4/6467–644 and MUN/4/6651–868). They include correspondence on the supplies of such different items as boots, clothing, and airship fabric, notes for material for a speech to be made by Lord Curzon on the contribution of the Dominions and Allies July 1918, and notes of meetings and interviews held March-April 1917. There are also replies to letters of appreciation Feb 1919–Oct 1920, correspondence with Lloyd George on the need to reduce expenditure Aug-Sept 1920, and also papers relating to Weir's coat of arms and pedigree.

D. J. Rowe provides an overview of Weir's career in *DBB*, 5, 719–20.

SIR WILLIAM DOUGLAS WEIR, 1st VISCOUNT WEIR (1877–1959)

William Weir was knighted in 1917, and created Baron Weir in 1918, GCB in 1934, and Viscount Weir in 1938. He was President of the Air Board April 1918–Jan 1919.

Forty-two box-files of papers were deposited by his son, the 2nd Viscount Weir, in the Churchill Archives Centre. A list of the papers is available (WEIR; NRA 13671). The papers were used extensively by W. J. Reader in *Architect of Air Power: the Life of the First Viscount Weir of Eastwood* (Collins 1968) Reader says that Weir broke up his own files and only kept documents he thought historically important. Very few changes from Weir's own arrangement of the papers have been made by the Churchill Archives Centre: the papers are organised by subjects chronologically arranged; they form 24 sections. Most of the papers date from after 1918; it is possible that earlier papers were damaged by water and so destroyed. There are reports, 'impressions', and 'thoughts' as well as correspondence. No private correspondence is included in the collection.

Six boxes of papers relate to Weir's term of office at the Air Ministry.

They include notes on Lord Trenchard and ten items about the dismissal of the Hon Miss Violet Douglas-Pennant as Commandant of the WRAF. Weir's continued interest in air power is reflected by papers from the Civil Aviation Committee of which he was Chairman 1918–1920.

Papers also survive relating to his interest in the coal industry: correspondence, the evidence submitted by Weir to the Coal Industry Commission, press cuttings, memoranda, and pamphlets 1919–21, 1925–26, and 1930. Weir was a member of the Trade Boards Acts Committee 1921–22: correspondence, evidence, memoranda about the operation of the various boards, draft reports, and parliamentary debates have survived. Minutes, sub-committee papers and Weir's own notes to the Cabinet committee for the amalgamation of the forces' common services 1922–23 have also survived. There are minutes (and draft minutes), evidence, Weir's notes, and draft reports for the Cabinet committee on the reduction of national expenditure 1922–23. There are also papers from the Committee of Imperial Defence's Fleet Air Arm Committee 1923–24 including undated notes by Trenchard, papers concerning electricity supply 1923–33, railway electrification 1929–31, the merger of the Cunard and White Star Lines, the 1931 financial crisis (including a transcript of a meeting between the government and the National Confederation of Employers' Organisation, as well as Weir's own notes on the situation), papers about air disarmament 1932, the Ottawa Conference of 1932 (Weir was an industrial adviser), papers from the Cabinet Committee on Trade and Employment Panels 1932–34, the CID's Defence Policy Sub-Committee 1936–37, the Air Ministry 1935–38 (Weir was adviser to the Minister), and the Ministry of Supply 1939–41 (Weir was Director-General of Explosives at the Ministry).

There is also an extensive collection of Weir's papers at the Glasgow University Archives (DC96). The collection has been divided into 30 sections, and covers much of Weir's life, in particular his business interests. It was used in W. J. Reader, *The Weir Group: A Centenary History* (Weidenfeld & Nicolson 1971).

The collection includes Weir's letterbooks and general correspondence dating from 1899 until his death. The correspondence includes incoming and outgoing letters, which appear to have been kept chronologically up to 1928, and thereafter alphabetically. There are five envelopes containing correspondence extracted from this section during the writing of *The Weir Group*: public policy 1919–28; company policy 1919–28; housing 1919–28; company personnel and subsidiaries 1915–24; and business correspondence 1928–41.

There are drafts, press cuttings, research material and notes for Weir's speeches and letters to the press dating from 1901. Many of the speeches relate to employment and industrial matters.

Section DC 96/3 consists of personal, estate and miscellaneous papers, including letters of congratulations on his peerage and elevation to a viscountcy, and estate papers on Eastwood Park. There are also papers on Polnoon Estate.

Business papers include the cash books, journals, ledgers, and investment registers for Cathcart Investment Trust Ltd; papers and correspondence relating to Nickel and Mond Nickel, ICI, Cardonald Housing Corporation Ltd, and Animal Food Products Ltd; correspondence on the Association of Investment Trusts; various papers on income tax; and papers on Weir's particular interests, steel housing and the sugar beet industry. There are also files of papers relating to the British Standards Institution and the Federation of British Industry.

Section DC 96/17 relates to Weir's period at the Ministry of Munitions and Supply, while section DC 96/20 contains a small amount of material relating to the Air Ministry. Section DC 96/18, entitled 'Filing Cabinet' contains correspondence relating to the need for a government trade policy 1922–24, and correspondence with Ramsay MacDonald, Baldwin, and Churchill on the economy and trade improvement 1924–28. Section DC 96/22 contains government and political papers including correspondence with Baldwin 1919-35 and Neville Chamberlain 1925–38.

There is a substantial collection of reports on various matters of interest to Weir. The collection also includes Weir's desk diaries from 1919–24 and 1930–35 (not inclusive). There is a diary for the years 1921, 1923–24, and 1929, as well as a substantial collection of press cuttings 1917–56.

There is also a small collection of Lady Weir's papers, including correspondence with her son while he was at Cambridge.

Brief biographies of Weir are provided by Elizabeth Thompson in *DBB*, 5, 721–8, and Charles W. Munn in Anthony Slaven and Sydney Checkland (eds), *Dictionary of Scottish Business Biography 1860–1960* (Aberdeen UP 1986), 1, 197–200.

JOSEPH WESTWOOD (1884–1948)

Joseph Westwood was Labour MP for Midlothian and Peeblesshire (Peebles and Southern) 1922–31 and Stirling and Falkirk Burghs 1935–48. He was Parliamentary Under-Secretary of State for Scotland March-Aug 1931 and May 1940–May 1945, and Secretary of State for Scotland Aug 1945–Oct 1947.

Westwood's son, Councillor David Westwood, and other members of Westwood's family did not know of any surviving papers.

Private Office papers relating to Westwood's periods at the Scottish Office are dispersed through the files of the five main Scottish Office departments held at the SRO.

DLB, II, 402–3, has a brief entry on Westwood by Joyce Bellamy.

There is also a short survey of his political career in *Secretaries of State for Scotland*, 101–6.

JOHN WHEATLEY (1869–1930)

John Wheatley was Labour MP for Glasgow (Shettleston) 1922–30. He was Minister of Health Jan-Nov 1924.

In preparing the first edition of the Guide we were advised by Wheatley's daughter, Dr Elizabeth Wheatley, that she had none of her father's papers, but that her brother, Mr J. P. Wheatley, had a small collection of letters, ministerial papers, press cuttings, and pamphlets which were used by R.K. Middlemas in *The Clydesiders* (Hutchinson 1965). However, we were unable to contact Mr Wheatley to confirm the existence of this collection. Both Dr Wheatley and Mr Wheatley are now dead.

Wheatley's great-niece the Hon Mrs Kathleen Dalyell deposited a few papers in the NLS including a photocopy of a biographical sketch entitled 'Catholic Socialist' by Peter Kane 1969 (Acc 9368), and a microfilm of a family scrapbook containing cuttings and other material, mostly relating to Wheatley's death in 1930 but also including material 1910–30 (Acc 9369). There are also a few photos of his funeral.

Mrs Dalyell advised us that these papers belonged to her father, Lord Wheatley, and that they may have been part of a collection of papers on Wheatley which Dr Elizabeth Wheatley is believed to have owned. The fate of the remainder of Dr Wheatley's collection is not known.

The Strathclyde Regional Archives Mitchell Library has two original pen and ink political cartoons of Wheatley and James Maxton 23 April 1924 (prepared for *Punch* magazine) and 4 April 1925 (TD245, NRA(S) 0396). Also available is a pamphlet 'Eight-Pound Cottages for Glasgow Citizens' written by Wheatley and published by the Glasgow Labour Party in 1913 (TD488, NRA(S) 0396).

The Life of John Wheatley by John Hannan (Spokesman, Nottingham 1988) makes use of Cabinet papers, and the minutes of the Shettlestone Branch of the ILP, the Larnarkshire County Council, and the Glasgow Corporation. It is otherwise dependent on published sources. The essay on Wheatley in David Howell, *A Lost Left: Three Studies in Socialism and Nationalism* (Manchester UP 1986), 229–80, is based on published sources but refers to several specialist articles and to Samuel Cooper, 'John Wheatley, A Study in Labour History' (PhD thesis, University of Glasgow 1973). Ian Wood's political biography, *John Wheatley* (Manchester UP 1990) is a good guide to relevant trade union and party records. In the bibliography of this book Wood includes references to several other theses dealing with various aspects of Wheatley's life. Gerry C. Gunnin's doctoral study of *John Wheatley, Catholic Socialism, and Irish Labour in the West of Scotland, 1906–1924,* was published in 1987 by Garland, Hamden CT.

ELLEN CICELY WILKINSON (1891–1947)

Ellen Wilkinson was Labour MP for Middlesbrough (East) 1924–31 and Durham (Jarrow) 1935–47. She was Parliamentary Secretary to the Ministry of Pensions May-Oct 1940, Parliamentary Secretary to the Ministry of Home Security 1940–May 1945, and Minister of Education Aug 1945–Feb 1947.

Miss Wilkinson left all her estate to her sister Annie, who died in 1963. After Miss Annie Wilkinson's death, all Ellen Wilkinson's personal letters, etc., were destroyed in accordance with her sister's wishes. There is, however, some original material on Wilkinson scattered throughout a few small collections.

Her nephew, Dr Richard Wilkinson, has some original cartoons which are not available for research.

Betty D. Vernon, whose biography *Ellen Wilkinson 1891–1947* (Croom Helm 1982) makes use of a wide range of newspaper sources, interviews, letters from contemporaries, and some relevant documents in the PRO at ED/136 as well as Home Office files, has a small collection of photos and research material which will eventually be deposited in the Brynmor Jones Library at Hull University.

Mr T. D. W. Reid of Cheshire has a very small collection of material on Wilkinson, including a few original documents. This material is not available for research.

A few press cuttings, scrapbooks, and photos have been deposited in the National Museum of Labour History (LP/WI/1–8).

Wilkinson published a semi-autobiographical novel *Clash* (Harrap 1929; new edition Virago 1989) and contributed to Margot Asquith (ed), *Myself When Young* (Frederick Muller 1936). Beverly Parker Stobaugh's *Women and Parliament 1918–1970* (Exposition Press, New York 1978) has a brief essay on Wilkinson based primarily on the six scrapbooks in the Labour Party archives. There is also a short chapter on her in Kenneth O. Morgan, *Labour People: Leaders and Lieutenants from Hardie to Kinnock* (Oxford UP 1987), 101–6. See also David Rubinstein, 'Ellen Wilkinson Reconsidered', *History Workshop*, 7, Spring 1979.

Wilkinson's work as Minister of Education is examined in D. W. Dean, 'Planning for a Post-War Generation: Ellen Wilkinson and George Tomlinson at the Ministry of Education 1945–51', *History of Education*, 15, 1986, 95–117.

DAVID REES REES-WILLIAMS, 1st BARON OGMORE (1903–1976)

David Rees-Williams was Labour MP for Croydon (South) 1945–50. He was Parliamentary Under-Secretary of State for the Colonies Oct 1947–March 1950, Parliamentary Under-Secretary of State for Commonwealth Relations July 1950–June 1951, and Minister of Civil Aviation June–Oct 1951. He was created Baron Ogmore in 1950.

Lord Ogmore informed us that he preserved many papers concerning his personal, professional, and official life. These papers were selected and arranged by subject or by particular locations. They included many volumes of press cuttings, Ogmore's letters to his parents while he was practising as a solicitor in the Straits Settlement in the 1930s, and his diaries 1939–76.

His son, the 2nd Lord Ogmore, has retained many of his father's papers.

Others were deposited in 1989 in the NLW (C1989/55). A summary list is available. The papers have been divided into three sections: Liberal Party and Welsh Liberal Party (Ogmore joined the Liberal Party in 1959 and was its President 1963–64); Welsh affairs; and miscellaneous.

The Liberal Party and Welsh Liberal Party section comprises correspondence and papers 1959–74, including papers relating to the 1970 general election. Correspondents include Jeremy Thorpe, Jo Grimond, Frank Byers, and Emlyn Hooson. The Welsh Affairs section comprises correspondence and papers 1957–76, including papers relating to devolution in Wales 1967–75, and the Liberal Party's Government of Wales Bill 1967; the Commission on the Constitution 1967–74; and Wales and the European Economic Community 1970–72. Correspondents include George Thomas, John Morris, Douglas Jay, and Peter Bessell. The miscellaneous papers include papers relating to the Investiture Committee 1969; Liberal Party pamphlets and leaflets; and most notably, Ogmore's unpublished memoir 'The Dedication of a Prince' (1973).

SIR EDWARD JOHN WILLIAMS (1890–1963)

Ted Williams was Labour MP for Glamorganshire (Ogmore) 1931–46. He was Minister of Information Aug 1945–Feb 1946. He was created KCMG in 1952.

Lady Williams died in 1968. We were unable to contact either of Williams's daughters. There are none of Williams's papers in the Welsh Political Archive at the National Library of Wales, or in the Glamorgan RO.

Williams was British High Commissioner in Australia 1946–52, but the National Library of Australia has only a letter from Williams to Sir

Robert Menzies and his reply April 1953 in the Menzies Collection MS 4936, series 2, box 53).

Joyce Bellamy contributed the brief entry on Williams in *DLB*, III, 208–9.

THOMAS WILLIAMS, BARON WILLIAMS OF BARNBURGH (1888–1967)

Tom Williams was Labour MP for West Riding of Yorkshire (Don Valley) 1922–59. He was Parliamentary Secretary to the Ministry of Agriculture and Fisheries May 1940–May 1945, and Minister of Agriculture and Fisheries Aug 1945–Oct 1951. He was created Baron Williams of Barnburgh (a life peerage) in 1961.

Lord Williams's son, the Hon Horace Williams, had a very small collection of his father's papers. There were some notes for a speech on the 50th anniversary of the Parliamentary Labour Party in 1956, and outline notes on some of Williams's contemporaries: George Lansbury, Arthur Henderson, Ramsay MacDonald, James Maxton, Winston Churchill, Sir Austen Chamberlain, and Sir Anthony Eden. There were several letters from Clement Attlee: thanking Williams for his wartime work 26 May 1945; informing him that a general election is to be called 19 Sept 1951; commiserating with Williams's ill-health; and discussing the Labour MPs first elected in 1922 – they produced ten Cabinet ministers, four other ministers, seven under-secretaries, a chief whip, five junior whips, and one deputy chairman. There was a letter from B. Dais 14 June 1933 thanking Williams for his work for the release of political prisoners in India and for his work on behalf of the Congress party. There were also several letters on Williams's retirement from the House in 1959. The collection also included a few press cuttings: there were several articles from 1933 on Williams's work for the much-reduced Labour Opposition, and several from 1959 on Williams's retirement.

At the time of preparing the second edition, Mr Williams had recently died, and his widow, Mrs Margaret Williams, had not yet gone through his papers and was unable to confirm that the collection had survived.

There is correspondence to and from Williams in the CAB and MAF series at the PRO. Reference should be made to Roger Middleton, 'The Formulation and Implementation of British Agricultural Policy 1945–51' (PhD thesis, University of Bristol 1992), which makes extensive use of these PRO records.

Digging for Britain (Hutchinson 1965) is a volume of Williams's reminiscences which does not quote from unpublished sources. Joyce M. Bellamy and John Saville wrote the entry in *DLB*, II, 406–7.

SIR HENRY URMSTON WILLINK, 1st Bt (1894–1973)

Henry Willink was National Conservative MP for Croydon (North) 1940–48. He was Minister of Health Nov 1943–Aug 1945. He was created a baronet in 1957.

Willink destroyed many of his 'voluminous and meticulously preserved' papers on retirement. The small surviving collection was deposited in 1973 by his widow in the Churchill Archives Centre (WILL; NRA 18561). Applications for access should be made to the Archivist.

The papers mostly relate to Willink's family and university affairs, but there are a few papers relating to his political career: a draft election manifesto 1938; correspondence with W. S. Morrison about Czechoslovakia 1938; and his letter of appointment as Minister of Health 1943. The collection also includes a copy of an unpublished autobiography entitled 'As I Remember'. The 143-page autobiography does not quote directly from correspondence or other papers. But there are files of letters and press cuttings illustrating various chapters.

There is another small collection of papers at Magdalene College, Cambridge, where Willink was Master 1948–66 (C/HUW). The collection consists of one box, arranged into eight files, and relates mostly to College matters. However there is a file of 38 letters 1952–64 regarding the electric generating works and including correspondence with the then Minister of Fuel and Power, Geoffrey Lloyd.

Ronald Hyam has written a memoir of Willink in *Magdalene College Magazine and Record*, new series, 17, 1972–73.

JOHN WILMOT, BARON WILMOT OF SELMESTON (1895–1964)

John Wilmot was Labour MP for Fulham (East) 1933–35, Lambeth (Kennington) 1939–45 and Deptford 1945–50. He was Joint Parliamentary Secretary to the Ministry of Supply Nov 1944–May 1945, Minister of Aircraft Production Aug 1945–April 1946, and Minister of Supply Aug 1945–Oct 1947. He was created Baron Wilmot of Selmeston in 1950.

To save her executors the trouble of dealing with both her own and her husband's papers, Lady Wilmot burnt what papers she had.

Private Office papers are in AVIA 11 at the PRO.

Ben Pimlott utilised a wide range of sources for his brief essay on Wilmot in *DNB 1961–1970*, 1083–4.

SIR (JAMES) HAROLD WILSON, BARON WILSON OF RIEVAULX (1916–1995)

Harold Wilson was Labour MP for Lancashire (Ormskirk) 1945–50 and Lancashire (Huyton) 1950–83. He was Parliamentary Secretary to the Ministry of Works Aug 1945–March 1947, Secretary for the Overseas

Trade Department in the Board of Trade March-Oct 1947, President of the Board of Trade 1947–April 1951, Prime Minister Oct 1964–June 1970 and March 1974–April 1976, and Minister for the Civil Service Nov 1968–June 1970 and March 1974–April 1976. He was Leader of the Labour Party 1963–76. He was created KG in 1976, and Baron Wilson of Rievaulx (Life Peer) in 1983.

Lord Wilson informed us when the first edition was being prepared that until 1956 he destroyed most of his papers as he went along, so that very little material survived from his early political life. A series of robberies from various residences and offices resulted in the loss of an undisclosed number of papers, some of which were returned late in 1975. The substantial surviving collection, which was not available for research, consisted of a massive accumulation of constituency papers, and a series of papers concentrating on the period when Wilson was Prime Minister, in particular letters and memoranda to government colleagues and his letters and telegrams to foreign Prime Ministers and heads of state. Many letters and memoranda are cited in Wilson's *The Labour Government 1964–1970. A Personal Record* (Weidenfeld & Nicolson 1971) and in *Final Term, the Labour Government 1974–1976* (Weidenfeld & Nicolson 1979).

The papers were deposited in the Bodleian Library in late 1993.

A taped interview between Wilson and T. W. Scragg 1977 covering Wilson's career in relation to Merseyside is in the Huyton Central Library.

Philip Ziegler's authorised biography, *Wilson* (Weidenfeld & Nicolson 1993), was written with exclusive access to Wilson's private archive which Ziegler describes as 'some 200 boxes...arranged according to subject and period' and which included all of Wilson's official prime-ministerial papers (p. 571). Ziegler also refers to the papers relating to Wilson as a junior minister and President of the Board of Trade at the PRO. Ben Pimlott, *Harold Wilson* (Harper Collins 1992) and Austen Morgan, *Harold Wilson* (Pluto 1992) were written without access to these papers.

Wilson gave access to his papers, and provided information, to Michael Cockerell for *Live from Number 10: The Inside Story of Prime Ministers and Television* (Faber and Faber 1988).

SIR WALTER JAMES WOMERSLEY, 1st Bt (1878–1961)

Walter Womersley was Conservative MP for Grimsby 1924–45. He was Assistant Postmaster-General Dec 1935–June 1939, and Minister of Pensions 1939–Aug 1945. He was knighted in 1934, and created a baronet in 1945.

Womersley's daughter, Mrs Dorothy Moseley, 23 Burnmill Road, Market Harborough, Leicestershire LE16 7JF, has a small box of papers.

Most of these papers are photos or press cuttings. There are many photos of Womersley performing his various official duties. There are several articles by Womersley including a few of the weekly articles which he wrote for the *Grimsby Telegraph* on his parliamentary activities. There are also several biographical articles, obituaries, and tributes. There are some miscellaneous letters from Neville Chamberlain and Stanley Baldwin thanking Womersley for his support. There is also a long and interesting letter from Womersley to his wife describing the interview in which Churchill asked him to stay on as Minister of Pensions in May 1940.

The only papers surviving from Womersley's political campaigns are his election address for the Grimsby municipal elections of 1911 (Womersley was a Town Councillor 1911-23, Mayor 1922-23, and Alderman 1923-45), his election address for 1929, and a copy of the *Grimsby News* 8 June 1945 with the results of the 1945 general election. No ministerial papers have survived in this collection but there are a few letters of support from Nov 1942 when the Cabinet decision not to increase pensions was attacked. The correspondents include Sir John Anderson and James Stuart. The incident is referred to in Lord Winterton, *Orders of the Day* (Cassell 1953), 296-7. Womersley wrote to Lord Winterton after the publication of the book giving his own version; Lord Winterton's reply 23 April 1954, hoping that Womersley had not taken the criticism personally, survives.

Despite his defeat in 1945 Womersley remained politically active; this is demonstrated by a large bundle of notes for speeches given during the late forties and the 1950 and 1951 general elections. There is also a letter from Lord Woolton 2 Nov 1951 thanking him for his work and another from Lord Derby 28 Oct 1951 on the need to keep active Conservative groups in Labour strongholds. There is some correspondence on Womersley's various honours.

Such a small number of papers survived because Womersley lived at the Constitutional Club when in London; he had no room for storage there. His wife did not normally keep his letters.

Mrs Moseley informed us that upon her death, all of her father's effects would be in the care of her son, Walter Moseley, of 5 Church Close, Eton SL4 6AP.

Sir Peter Womersley, 2nd Bt, had no papers concerning his grandfather.

EDWARD FREDERICK LINDLEY WOOD, 1st EARL OF HALIFAX (1881-1959)

Edward Wood was Conservative MP for West Riding of Yorkshire (Ripon) 1910-25. He was Parliamentary Under-Secretary of State for the Colonies April 1921-Oct 1922, President of the Board of Education

1922–Jan 1924 and June 1932–June 1935, Minister of Agriculture and Fisheries Nov 1924–Nov 1925, Secretary of State for War June-Nov 1935, Lord Privy Seal 1935–May 1937, Lord President of the Council 1937–Feb 1938, and Secretary of State for Foreign Affairs 1938–Dec 1940. He was created Baron Irwin in 1925, GCSI in 1926, KG in 1931, and Earl of Halifax in 1944; he succeeded his father as 3rd Viscount Halifax in 1934.

Halifax's papers belong to his grandson, the 3rd Earl of Halifax, but were deposited on loan as part of a larger collection of the archives of the Halifax family in the Borthwick Institute of Historical Research in 1981 (A4.410). The papers have been listed (NRA 8128). A card index of names is being compiled. A microfilm of some of the papers, particularly those relating to the period 1938–39, and to Halifax's term as Ambassador in Washington 1941–46, has been deposited in the Churchill Archives Centre (HLFX microfilm).

Halifax's papers at the Borthwick Institute provide a comprehensive history of his political career. There is a large collection of speeches and lectures, many of which have manuscript annotations by Halifax. There are separate sections of papers relating to Halifax's appointments as Lord Privy Seal and as Foreign Secretary including trips to Germany 1937; and Ambassador to Washington. Papers relating to India include letters, memoranda, and drafts and notes on speeches, mostly dealing with his appointment as Viceroy of India 1926–31. Correspondents in the collection include many of Halifax's political colleagues, notably Baldwin, Neville Chamberlain, Churchill, Eden, and Macmillan. Other correspondents include King George VI, Queen Elizabeth, and President and Mrs Roosevelt. The collection also includes Halifax's diaries 1921–56 (A.7).

Halifax deposited a collection of his papers as Viceroy in the Oriental and India Office Collections, British Library in 1959 (MSS Eur C 152; NRA 27436). The collection consists of 38 volumes of correspondence, most of it printed and indexed. There is a volume of correspondence with the King 1926–31, five volumes of letters and five volumes of telegrams exchanged with the Secretary of State, and a further five volumes of departmental telegrams. There are also three volumes of letters and telegrams exchanged with people in England, and six volumes of letters and telegrams exchanged with people in India. There is a volume of correspondence with the Secretary of State concerning the Statutory Commission on India 1926–29, and another with Sir John Simon, the Commission's Chairman 1927–29. Another volume of correspondence covers a visit to England June-Oct 1929, when Irwin (as he was then) urged the establishment of the Round Table Conference; printed proposals for Indian reforms by Irwin and others 1930; and a volume of the proceedings of the Round Table Conference 1930–

31. There are also various notes, Legislative Assembly decisions, Orders in Council, and a volume of correspondence with his father.

Twenty volumes of Foreign Office miscellaneous general correspondence 1938-40 are to be found in the PRO (FO 800/309-28). Further volumes are being prepared for deposit in this class.

Many of Halifax's papers, including the diary, are quoted in the Earl of Birkenhead, *Halifax: the Life of Lord Halifax* (Hamish Hamilton 1965). Halifax himself quoted from his papers and gave his reminiscences in *Fulness of Days* (Collins 1957). There is a review of his early career in S. Gopal, *The Viceroyalty of Lord Irwin 1926-1931* (Oxford UP 1957).

Andrew Roberts, *The Holy Fox. A Biography of Lord Halifax* (Weidenfeld and Nicolson 1991) uses the principal family and official collections as well as papers of Halifax's contemporaries.

SIR (HOWARD) KINGSLEY WOOD (1881-1943)

Kingsley Wood was knighted in 1918. He was Conservative MP for Woolwich (West) 1918-43. He was Parliamentary Secretary to the Ministry of Health Nov 1924-June 1929, Parliamentary Secretary to the Board of Education Sept-Nov 1931, Postmaster-General 1931-June 1935, Minister of Health 1935-May 1938, Secretary of State for Air 1938-April 1940, Lord Privy Seal April-May 1940, and Chancellor of the Exchequer 1940-Sept 1943.

Wood's adopted daughter, Mrs Marjorie Brothers, informed us that she had no papers which belonged to her father. His estate was administered by his law firm, Messrs Kingsley Wood & Co. They deposited a small collection of press cuttings in the Templeman Library, University of Kent (Kingsley Wood papers). The collection, the result of a subscription to a press cutting agency, covers the period 1905-40. There are 15 quarto books for 1905-23, ten folio books for 1924-40, a volume on the 1918 Woolwich by-election, and a collection of unsorted cuttings for 1940.

Some of Wood's Air Ministry papers are now available at the PRO (AIR 19/25-72, 556). They include papers of the Air Defence Research Committee, correspondence with J. Moore-Brabazon, Sir Nevile Henderson, Churchill, Lord Londonderry, Sir Archibald Sinclair, Lord Trenchard, and others. There is also some correspondence 1938-39 with Conservative Central Office.

Helen M. Palmer's brief sketch of Wood in *DNB 1941-1950*, 971-3, is based mainly on published sources.

RICHARD FREDERICK WOOD, BARON HOLDERNESS (1920-)

Richard Wood was Conservative MP for Bridlington 1950-79. He was Joint Parliamentary Secretary, Ministry of Pensions and National

Insurance Dec 1955–April 1958, Joint Parliamentary Secretary, Ministry of Labour 1958–Oct 1959, Minister of Power 1959–Oct 1963, Minister of Pensions and National Insurance 1963–Oct 1964, Minister of Overseas Development June-Oct 1970, and Minister for Overseas Development, Foreign and Commonwealth Office 1970–March 1974. He was created Baron Holderness (a life peerage) in 1979.

Lord Holderness informed us that he held no official papers only some letters, photos, and press cuttings which cover 'in a very humble way' his entire political career from his adoption as a candidate in 1947. Lord Holderness has no objections to these papers being referred to, but has doubts as to their relevance and importance.

THOMAS McKINNON WOOD (1855–1927)

Thomas McKinnon Wood was Liberal MP for Glasgow (St Rollox) 1906–18. He was Parliamentary Secretary to the Board of Education April-Oct 1908, Parliamentary Under-Secretary of State for Foreign Affairs 1908–Oct 1911, Financial Secretary to the Treasury 1911–Feb 1912 and July-Dec 1916, Secretary for Scotland Feb 1912–July 1916, and Chancellor of the Duchy of Lancaster July-Dec 1916.

A small collection of his papers was given by his daughter-in-law, Mrs C. McKinnon Wood, to the Bodleian Library (MSS Eng hist c 499–500; d 311–12).

The papers comprise one box of correspondence, a collection of pamphlets, two volumes of press cuttings covering the years 1906–08, and a book of cuttings collected on McKinnon Wood's death. All the correspondence dates from the 20th century apart from papers concerning the burial of McKinnon Wood's parents. There is a letter from Harold Harmsworth 1901 on London County Council (LCC) and Liberal Party politics; a letter from John Sinclair 1902 about McKinnon Wood's candidature for the Orkneys; several letters 1906 asking McKinnon Wood to stay on the LCC; some notes for a speech to the LCC, and a solicitor's letter concerning a defamatory article in the *Standard* Jan 1907; a letter from Sir Henry Campbell-Bannerman 2 Nov 1907 offering a knighthood; letters of congratulation on McKinnon Wood's appointment to office at the Board of Education and the Foreign Office; several letters from Edward Grey on the conduct of Foreign Office business; a letter from McKinnon Wood to his Aunt Anne relating the circumstances of his appointment to the Treasury in 1911 and including a comment on his work by Grey: 'I have always felt quite safe all the time'. There is some correspondence in May 1915 with John Gulland and Asquith on the Cabinet reconstruction, and whether or not the Secretary for Scotland should be in the Cabinet. There is another long letter to Aunt Anne in 1916 explaining why he had accepted an apparent demotion in returning to the Financial Secretaryship at the Treasury.

The collection of 15 pamphlets consists of speeches and articles written by McKinnon Wood, mainly while he was a member of the LCC 1892–1907. They put the case of the Progressive Party, for example, *The London County Council: Three Years' Progressive Work* (1901); *The Progressive Party, Past and Present* (1904); and *Under Moderate Rule, First Year of 'Municipal Reform'* (1908). There is one pamphlet concerning McKinnon Wood's work at the Foreign Office: *British Commerce and the Declaration of London* (1911); and one reflecting his post-war views: *Government Extravagance makes the People Poor* (Cheltenham 1921).

Private Office papers relating to McKinnon Wood's period at the Scottish Office are dispersed through the files of the five main Scottish Office departments held at the SRO.

Reference should be made to J. W. R. Mitchell, 'The Emergence of Modern Scottish central administration 1885–1939' (DPhil, Oxford University 1987).

ARTHUR WOODBURN (1890–1978)

Arthur Woodburn was Labour MP for Stirlingshire and Clackmannanshire (Clackmannan and East Stirlingshire) 1939–70. He was Parliamentary Secretary to the Ministry of Supply Aug 1945–Oct 1947, and Secretary of State for Scotland 1947–Feb 1950.

Mr Woodburn informed us that he never kept any notes, diaries, or other papers relating to Cabinet business for fear that they might get into the wrong hands. However, during his lifetime he deposited five letters from Keir Hardie, Ramsay MacDonald, David Kirkwood, Robert Smillie, and Alexander Wilkie in the NLS (MS 7198, ff 125–9; NRA 29192) and also presented a small collection of papers relating to a parliamentary bill to facilitate the formation of a common European language 1962–66 to the Library in 1974 (Acc 6726).

Following Woodburn's death, his widow deposited a major collection of his papers in the NLS (Acc 7656; NRA 29172). A list is available. The papers, which were collected by Woodburn for a volume of reminiscences, have been arranged into 19 main groups: general correspondence; special correspondence and papers; autobiographical papers; personal and family correspondence and papers; secretaryship of state; parliamentary delegations and visits; Communist Party activities file; economics, finance, banking; education, Europe; elections; National Council of Labour Colleges; Scottish affairs, home rule, devolution; parliamentary speeches and questions; speeches and lectures, broadcasts, single articles; articles (collections); miscellaneous papers; press cuttings; invitations, photos; volumes (large), tapes, lantern slides.

Most important is the heavily corrected and amended draft typescript of 'Some Recollections', Woodburn's unpublished autobiography, which covers the period 1890–1950. There are also several autobiographical pieces on specific topics: 'The 1931 Crisis', 'Relations with Royalty', 'The Life of an M.P.', and others.

The library also has a list of articles by Woodburn written for the *Labour Standard* 1927–30 (MS Acc 3693). Woodburn was President of the National Council of Labour Colleges for over 30 years; the Council's papers are also in the NLS.

Relevant Private Office papers are in AVIA 9 at the PRO. Private Office papers relating to Woodburn's period at the Scottish Office are dispersed through the files of the five main Scottish Office departments held at the SRO.

Woodburn's ministerial career is briefly surveyed in *Secretaries of State for Scotland*, 106–16. W. W. Knox and A. MacKinlay, 'The Re-Making of Scottish Labour in the 1930s', *Twentieth Century British History*, 6, 2, 1995, 174–93, deals with Woodburn's period as secretary of the Scottish Labour Party, drawing on the Woodburn collection and the minutes of the Scottish Executive Committee of the Labour Party.

GEORGE WYNDHAM (1863–1913)

George Wyndham was Conservative MP for Dover 1889–1913. He was Under Secretary of State for War Oct 1898–Nov 1900, and Chief Secretary for Ireland 1900–March 1905.

The bulk of Wyndham's papers are in the possession of the Duke of Westminster, The Grosvenor Estate, Eaton Estate Office, Eccleston, Chester CH4 9ET. The papers form a part of the much larger collection of Wyndham's wife's papers (her first marriage was to the eldest son of the first Duke of Westminster). The papers have been partially arranged; they are not generally available.

Possibly the most interesting items in the collection are George Wyndham's letters to his wife. There are 21 files for the period 1887–1913; the letters have been arranged in chronological order and there is a brief note made by the Duke of Westminster's archivist on each file. Since no Private Office papers appear to have survived from Wyndham's term of office at the War Office and as Chief Secretary for Ireland, these letters form an important record of his activities and interests. Many of the letters, particularly from the earlier period, are purely personal; but there is some political comment, for example a description of Sir John Brunner as 'a bounder' who 'on account of his wealth' is 'somebody in the Radical Party', and a description of the formation of Arthur Balfour's government in 1902. Wyndham had been Balfour's private secretary 1887–89 and, from the letters to his wife, he seems to have remained a staunch supporter for the rest of his life. There are disappointingly few surviving letters from Balfour in this collection. Perhaps the major political event recorded by these letters is the passage of the Parliament Act in 1911.

Complementary to the series of letters from Wyndham to his wife are her own letters to him, as well as letters from his mother (ten files), his brother Guy, and his three sisters, Mary, Countess of Wemyss, Madeline, Mrs Adeane, and Pamela, Lady Glenconner, as well as some papers of Denis Hyde, one of Wyndham's private secretaries. The papers of another private secretary, George Fitzhardinge Berkeley, as well as those of Wyndham's Permanent Under-Secretary at the Irish Office, Sir Anthony (later Lord) MacDonnell, are in the Bodleian Library (MS Eng hist c 321 and MSS Eng hist a 11–12; b 206; c 350; d 235–8; e 215–18).

There is also a large box of unsorted constituency papers and a small amount of material relating to Wyndham's literary activities: five folders of poems, some articles, and correspondence with Hilaire Belloc.

As these papers were only discovered in 1969, they were not used by John Biggs-Davison in his biography, *George Wyndham: A Study in Toryism* (Hodder & Stoughton 1951); indeed he states that his 'supreme debt' is to the *Life and Letters of George Wyndham* by J. W. Mackail and Guy Wyndham (2 vols, Hutchinson 1924). These volumes include selections from letters from George Wyndham to his contemporaries, that is, letters which are now likely to be found in the papers of those individuals.

The two volumes of *Life and Letters* also drew on a more extensive, privately printed, edition of Wyndham's letters compiled by his brother Guy Wyndham: *Letters of George Wyndham 1877–1913* (2 vols, Constable, Edinburgh 1915). When editing the correspondence for this private publication (200 copies were printed), Guy Wyndham invited Wyndham's widow to put pencil brackets around 'intimate and private parts' which were not to be typed. Guy Wyndham himself proposed to 'further eliminate by brackets any parts on the typewritten copies that are not to be printed' as being too party political or personal (G. Wyndham to Lady Sibell Wyndham, 28 May 1914, Wyndham MSS, 11/2). In the preface to the volumes, the editor noted: 'criticism of the action of individuals in politics has been excluded...The letters to some were considered too personal for even private circulation; those to many – his colleagues – dealt with matters that must be left to the historian in the future...Nor have the letters to his wife been included...It is hoped that extracts from them may later be embodied in a supplementary volume' (pp. viii-ix). No supplementary volume was published.

Both the biography and the volumes of letters are available in the

British Library, the Bodleian Library, and elsewhere. Some of the originals of these letters are in the possession of Guy Wyndham's son, Mr Francis Wyndham. Mr Wyndham has nine volumes of letters, five of which contain George Wyndham's letters to his parents 1877–86, 1898–1905 (approximately 320 letters). There are also three albums of letters from all of the Wyndham children to their parents 1868–79, and an album compiled after George Wyndham's death, containing letters of sympathy, photos, and mementos. The album includes letters from A. J. Balfour and Mark Sykes, and an obituary of George Wyndham published by Sykes in the *Saturday Review* 14 June 1913.

Max Egremont, *The Cousins: The friendships, opinions and activities of Wilfrid Scawen Blunt and George Wyndham* (Collins 1977) draws on family papers. J. A. Thompson, 'George Wyndham: Toryism and Imperialism' in J. A. Thompson and Arthur Mejia (eds), *Edwardian Conservatism: Five Studies in Adaptation* (Croom Helm 1988), 105–28, is based on published sources. Wyndham's Chief Secretaryship is usefully summarised in Eunan O'Halpin, *The Decline of the Union: British Government in Ireland 1892–1920* (Gill and Macmillan, Dublin 1987), 24–51.

SIR EDWARD HILTON YOUNG, 1st BARON KENNET (1879–1960)

Edward Hilton Young was Liberal MP for Norwich 1915–23; re-elected as a Liberal in 1924 he crossed the floor in 1926 remaining as MP for Norwich until 1929. He was Conservative MP for Kent (Sevenoaks) 1929–35. He was Financial Secretary to the Treasury April 1921–Oct 1922, Parliamentary Secretary for the Department of Overseas Trade Sept-Nov 1931, and Minister of Health 1931–June 1935. He was created GBE in 1927, and Baron Kennet in 1935.

Young's papers, formerly in the possession of his son, the 2nd Lord Kennet, were deposited in Cambridge University Library in 1972 (Kennet papers). They have been listed in great detail by the National Register of Archives (NRA 12509). Written permission of Lord Kennet is required before access will be granted.

Young himself appears to have gone through his papers and his last arrangement has been maintained: an alphabetical arrangement by writer with the exception of some subject files. There are over 170 letters from his father 1882–1930 and over 70 from his mother. There are many letters from his political contemporaries though few from Lloyd George (Young was Chief Whip of the Lloyd George Liberals in 1922).

Young's subject files cover a wide range. Perhaps the most interesting to political historians is that concerning his resignation from the Liberal Party in 1926, because he felt Lloyd George's land proposals were too socialistic. The file contains correspondence with Lloyd George Feb 1926, and also a letter from Stanley Baldwin welcoming Young into the Conservative Party May 1926. There is a file of miscellaneous papers concerning the Department of Overseas Trade and two boxes of Cabinet memoranda, mainly on Health Ministry topics – rents, health insurance, maternity services, and town and country planning. On the latter subject there are notes of discussions with Lloyd George. There are files of speeches, broadcasts, and articles by Young, and volumes of press cuttings. There is also a draft autobiography 'In and Out', mainly written in 1959, and diaries for 1914–18.

Young's wife's papers, included in the same collection, are an important source of information about her husband as well as about her own distinguished life. There are a considerable number of his letters to her 1919–46, as well as her diaries for 1910–46 and her correspondence with the leading figures of her time, including two volumes of correspondence with Asquith 1912–26. Young edited selections from his wife's diaries: *Self-Portrait of an Artist* (John Murray 1949).

In *Ponsonby Remembers* (The Alden Press, Oxford 1965), Col Sir Charles Ponsonby Bt stated (p. 61) that Young, who was his predecessor as Member for Sevenoaks, gave him all of his constituency files. Sir Charles's son, Sir Ashley Ponsonby Bt advised us that these papers have not been preserved.

Ministers who were not in Cabinet 1900–1964

(* Ministers who obtained Cabinet positions *after* 1964)

Julian Amery, Lord Amery of
   Lustleigh
Sydney Arnold, Lord Arnold
Wilfrid Ashley, Lord Mount Temple
John Baird, 1st Viscount Stonehaven
Alfred Barnes
Frederick Bellenger
Reginald Bevins
Nigel Birch, Lord Rhyl
John Moore-Brabazon, 1st Lord
   Brabazon of Tara
George Brown, Lord George-Brown*
George Buchanan
Sir Archibald Boyd-Carpenter
Richard Causton, Lord Southwark
Charles Spencer-Churchill, 9th Duke
   of Marlborough
Robert Windsor-Clive, 1st Earl of
   Plymouth
Sir Ronald Cross
Savile Crossley, 1st Lord Somerleyton
Colin Davidson, 1st Viscount
   Davidson
Ness Edwards
Geoffrey Fitzclarence, 5th Earl of
   Munster
Reginald Fletcher, Lord Winster
Sir Hugh Fraser
Harry Gosling
George Sutherland-Leveson-Gower,
   5th Duke of Sutherland
Edward Grigg, 1st Lord Altrincham
Frederick Guest
Ivor Guest, 1st Viscount Wimborne
Harold Harmsworth, 1st Viscount
   Rothermere
Sir Patrick Hastings
Sir Lionel Heald
Arthur Henderson, Lord Rowley
Sir John Hobson

John Hope, Lord Glendevon
Henry Fitzalan-Howard, 15th Duke
   of Norfolk
Robert Hutchison, Lord Hutchison of
   Montrose
John Hynd
Albert Illingworth, Lord Illingworth
George Jellicoe, 2nd Earl Jellicoe*
Aubrey Jones
Sir Hudson Kearley, 1st Viscount
   Devonport
Frederick Kellaway
Philip Kerr, 11th Marquess of Lothian
Charles Key
Ernest Lamb, 1st Lord Rochester
Richard Law, Lord Coleraine
Thomas Legh, 2nd Lord Newton
John Llewellin, Lord Llewellin
George Lloyd, 1st Lord Lloyd
Charles McCurdy
Gordon Macdonald, 1st Lord
   Macdonald of Gwaenysgor
Joseph Maclay, 1st Lord Maclay
Niall Macpherson, Lord Drumalbyn
David Margesson, 1st Viscount
   Margesson
Hilary Marquand
Hugh Molson, Lord Molson
Sir Oswald Mosley
Harry Nathan, 1st Lord Nathan
Richard Onslow, 5th Earl of Onslow
Wilfred Paling
Roundell Palmer, 3rd Earl of
   Selborne
Weetman Pearson, 1st Viscount
   Cowdray
Ernest Pollock, 1st Viscount
   Hanworth
Arthur Ponsonby, 1st Lord Ponsonby
   of Shulbrede

Wyndham Portal, Viscount Portal
John Profumo
Sir John Pybus
James Ramsden
Sir Joseph Compton-Rickett
Frederick Roberts
William Robson, Lord Robson
Sir Philip Sassoon
William Sidney, 1st Viscount De L'Isle
Lewis Silkin, 1st Lord Silkin
Sir Ben Smith
Derek Walker-Smith, Lord
    Broxbourne
Frank Soskice, Lord Stow Hill*
Edward Strachey, 1st Lord Strachie
John Strachey
George Strauss, Lord Strauss
Sir William Sutherland
James Thomas, Viscount Cilcennin
William Mitchell-Thomson, 1st Lord
    Selsdon

George Tryon, 1st Lord Tryon
Robert Turton, Lord Tranmire
Dennis Vosper, Lord Runcorn
William Walrond, 1st Lord Waleran
Sir Tudor Walters
Sir John Walton
George Ward, 1st Viscount Ward of
    Witley
Maurice Webb
Richard Webster, Viscount
    Alverstone
Andrew Weir, 1st Lord Inverforth
William Weir, 1st Viscount Weir
David Rees-Williams, Lord
    Ogmore
Sir Edward Williams
Sir Henry Willink
John Wilmot, Lord Wilmot of
    Selmeston
Sir Walter Womersley
Richard Wood, Lord Holderness

Repositories

This list is arranged in alphabetical order. As in the main part of the *Guide*, collections are listed by the family name of each minister. As well as a list of the collections in each institution, we have given the address, and the officer to whom enquiries should be directed. Most of these details have been taken from the Royal Commission on Historical Manuscripts, *Record Repositories in Great Britain* (9th ed, 1991). Several institutions specify that researchers should make a written application and appointment, sometimes enclosing a character reference. Researchers are strongly advised to make such written application, even where it is not specified: collections are sometimes kept in outside stores and are not immediately accessible. Advance warning is particularly necessary for unlisted collections, so that the library can try to arrange for the member of its staff who knows most about such collections to be at hand. An asterisk (*) next to the name of a minister indicates that there are future plans to deposit this minister's papers in the repository – they are not necessarily available there currently.

ABERDEEN UNIVERSITY LIBRARY, Department of Special Collections and Archives, King's College, Aberdeen AB9 2UB
Head of Special Collections, University Archivist
Baird

ASHRIDGE MANAGEMENT COLLEGE, Berkhamsted, Hertfordshire HP4 1NS
Archivist
Watkinson

AUSTRALIAN WAR MEMORIAL, GPO Box 345, Canberra ACT 2601, Australia
Manager, Information Services
Casey; Munro-Ferguson

BATTERSEA LIBRARY, 265 Lavender Hill, London SW11 1JB
Local History Librarian
Burns

BBC WRITTEN ARCHIVES CENTRE, Caversham Park, Reading RG4 8TZ
Written Archivist
Chuter Ede; Hill; Reith

BEDFORDSHIRE COUNTY RECORD OFFICE, County Hall, Cauldwell St, Bedford MK42 9AP
County Archivist
Burgin

BIRMINGHAM UNIVERSITY LIBRARY, Special Collections Department, Edgbaston, Birmingham B15 2TT
Sub-Librarian (Special Collections)
AN Chamberlain; J Chamberlain; JA Chamberlain; Eden; Masterman; Mosley

BODLEIAN LIBRARY, Department of Western Manuscripts, Broad Street, Oxford OX1 3BG
Keeper of Western Manuscripts
Addison; Asquith; Attlee; AJ Balfour; Birrell; Griffith-Boscawen; Lennox-Boyd; GA Brown; Bryce; J Boyd-Carpenter*; Wynn-Carrington; J Chamberlain; Crookshank; Davidson; Duke; Worthington-Evans; HAL Fisher; Goschen; Greenwood; Grey; EMW Grigg; Harcourt; Key; Mackenzie; Maclean; MH Macmillan; JI Macpherson; Marjoribanks; Marquis; Milner; Monckton; Morley; RC Palmer; WW Palmer; Pollock; Ponsonby; Sanders; Sankey; Simon; Somervell; Stokes; Turnour; Wallace; Webster; Wilson; TM Wood; Wyndham

BORTHWICK INSTITUTE OF HISTORICAL RESEARCH, York University, St Anthony's Hall, York YO1 2PW
Director
Lansbury; EFL Wood

BRADFORD DISTRICT ARCHIVES, 15 Canal Road, Bradford BD1 4AT
District Archivist
Jowett

BRITISH LIBRARY, Manuscript Collections, Great Russell Street, London WC1B 3DG
Director of Special Collections
Addison; Asquith; AJ Balfour; Campbell-Bannerman; Birrell; Brodrick; Burns; Cave; EAR Gascoyne-Cecil; Duff Cooper; RA Cross; Chuter Ede; HCK Petty-Fitzmaurice; Arnold-Forster; Giffard; Gladstone; Ormsby-Gore; Hobhouse; Kitchener; Long; HP Macmillan; MH Macmillan; Morley; Ritchie; Robinson; Sassoon; J Sinclair; Thomson; Webster; Wyndham

BRITISH LIBRARY OF POLITICAL AND ECONOMIC SCIENCE, 10 Portugal Street, London WC2A 2HD
Archivist
Amory; Boyle; Brooke; Butler; J Chamberlain; Dalton; Goschen; Douglas-Home;

Lansbury; JR MacDonald; JS Maclay; HS Morrison; Powell; Shinwell; Strauss; Webb

BROTHERTON COLLECTION, LEEDS UNIVERSITY LIBRARY, Leeds LS2 9JT
Sub-Librarian
Boyle; Snowden

BRYNMOR JONES LIBRARY, UNIVERSITY OF HULL, Cottingham Road, Hull HU6 7RX
Archivist
Hall; Lees-Smith; Wilkinson *

BUCKINGHAMSHIRE RECORD OFFICE, County Hall, Aylesbury HP20 1UA
County Archivist
Robinson

CAERNARFON AREA RECORD OFFICE, Victoria Dock, Caernarfon County Archivist and Museums Officer
D Lloyd George

CALIFORNIA STATE UNIVERSITY, NORTHRIDGE, Delmar T Oviatt University Library, 18111 Nordhoff St, PO Box 1289, Northridge California 91328–1289, USA
Curator, Special Collections/Archives
Burns

CAMBRIDGE UNIVERSITY LIBRARY, Dept of Manuscripts and University Archives, West Road, Cambridge CB3 9DR
Keeper of Manuscripts and University Archives
Baldwin; Bridgeman; Dalton; Grey; Hoare; Crewe-Milnes; Pybus; Smuts; Young

CAMBRIDGESHIRE RECORD OFFICE, HUNTINGDON, Grammar School Walk, Huntingdon PE18 6LF
Deputy County Archivist
Fellowes

CARMARTHENSHIRE AREA RECORD OFFICE, County Hall, Carmarthen SA31 1JP
County Archivist
Campbell; JPL Thomas

CENTRE FOR KENTISH STUDIES, County Hall, Maidstone ME14 1XQ
Head, Heritage Services
Akers-Douglas; Stanhope; JH Thomas

CHURCHILL ARCHIVES CENTRE, Churchill College, Cambridge CB3 0DS
Keeper
AV Alexander; Asquith; Attlee; Noel-Baker; Hore-Belisha; Bevin; Bracken; Bridgeman; Carson; WL Spencer-Churchill; Duff Cooper; Maxwell-Fyfe; AC Geddes; PJ Grigg; Haldane; Hankey; Buchan-Hepburn; DM Hogg; QM Hogg; Horsbrugh; Hynd; Inskip; Jones; Cunliffe-Lister; GA Lloyd; S Lloyd; A Lyttelton; O Lyttelton; McKenna; Margesson; Maudling; Crewe-Milnes; Salter *; Sandys; Sassoon; Simonds; AH Sinclair; Soames; Strauss; Gordon-Walker; W Weir; Willink; EFL Wood

CLWYD RECORD OFFICE, The Old Rectory, Hawarden, Deeside, Clwyd CH5 3NR
County Archivist
Gladstone

CODRINGTON LIBRARY, ALL SOULS COLLEGE, Oxford OX1 4AL
Librarian
RWA Onslow

COLEG HARLECH, Harlech, Wales
Librarian
Griffiths

CONSERVATIVE PARTY ARCHIVES, Bodleian Library, Broad Street, Oxford OX1 3BG
Archivist
Baldwin; Barber; Butler; AN Chamberlain; WL Spencer-Churchill; Eden; EWM Grigg; JH Hare; Heath; DM Hogg; QM Hogg; Joseph; S Lloyd; Macleod; Marquis; Maudling; WS Morrison; Powell; Thorneycroft

COURTAULD INSTITUTE OF ART, Somerset House, Strand, London WC2R 0RN
Librarian
Lee

DUKE UNIVERSITY (see WILLIAM R PERKINS LIBRARY)

DURHAM COUNTY RECORD OFFICE, County Hall, Durham
DH1 5UL
County Archivist
Chaplin; CS Vane-Tempest-Stewart; CSH Vane-Tempest-Stewart

DURHAM UNIVERSITY LIBRARY, Archives and Special Col-
lections, 5 The College, Durham DH1 3EQ
Senior Assistant Keeper
Lawson; MJ MacDonald

EAST SUSSEX RECORD OFFICE, The Maltings, Castle Precincts,
Lewes BN7 1YT
County Archivist
Sackville

EPSOM LIBRARY, 12 Waterloo Road, Epsom
Surrey KT19 8BN
Chuter Ede

FAWCETT LIBRARY, LONDON GUILDHALL UNIVERSITY, Old
Castle Street, London E1 7NT
Reference Librarian
Emmott

GLAMORGAN RECORD OFFICE, County Hall, Cathays Park,
Cardiff CF1 3NE
Archivist
Windsor-Clive

GLASGOW UNIVERSITY ARCHIVES, The University, Glasgow
G12 8QQ
University Archivist
Collins; Horne; JS Maclay; WD Weir

GLOUCESTERSHIRE RECORD OFFICE, Clarence Row, Alvin
Street, Gloucester GL1 3DW
County Archivist
Hicks Beach

GREATER LONDON RECORD OFFICE AND HISTORY
LIBRARY, 40 Northampton Road, London EC1R 0HB
Head Archivist
Burns; AH Stanley

GUILDFORD MUNIMENT ROOM, Castle Arch, Guildford GU 3SX
Archivist in charge
Brodrick; RWA Onslow; WH Onslow

HALLWARD LIBRARY, UNIVERSITY OF NOTTINGHAM
Manuscripts Department, University Park, Nottingham NG7 2RD
Keeper of the Manuscripts
Betterton

HAMPSHIRE RECORD OFFICE, Sussex St, Winchester SO23 8TH
County Archivist
WW Palmer

HANLEY INFORMATION LIBRARY, Bethesda Street, Hanley
Stoke-on-Trent ST1 3RS
County Librarian
Wedgwood

HARRIET IRVING LIBRARY, UNIVERSITY OF NEW BRUNS
WICK, Archives and Special Collections, BOX 7500, Fredericton N
E3B 5H5, Canada
Manager
Aitken

HARTLEY LIBRARY, UNIVERSITY OF SOUTHAMPTON, High
field, Southampton SO9 5NH
Archivist
Ashley

HEREFORD AND WORCESTER RECORD OFFICE, County Hal
Spetchley Road, Worcester WR5 2NP
County Archivist
Windsor-Clive; James; JPL Thomas

HOOVER INSTITUTE ON WAR, REVOLUTION AND PEACE
Stanford, California 94305–6010, USA
Assistant Archivist for Reference
Clynes; Mosley

HOUSE OF LORDS RECORD OFFICE, House of Lords, Londo
SW1A 0PW
Clerk of the Records
Addison; Aitken; Benn; Cadogan; Carington; RAJ Gascoyne-Cecil; Davidsor

Emmott; Fellowes; Gibson; Douglas-Home; QM Hogg; Jellicoe; Bonar Law; S Lloyd; D Lloyd George; Macleod; Pakenham; Samuel; Soskice

HULL, UNIVERSITY OF (see BRYNMOR JONES LIBRARY)

IMPERIAL WAR MUSEUM, Department of Documents, Lambeth Road, London SE1 6HZ
Keeper of the Department of Documents
HH Alexander; GN Barnes; Hore-Belisha; Bellenger; Birch; JA Chamberlain; RH Cross; French; Kitchener; GW Lloyd; Dorman Smith; Smuts; Stokes; Thomson; Wedgwood

INSTITUTE OF CONTEMPORARY BRITISH HISTORY, 34 Tavistock Square, London WC1H 9EZ
Director
J Amery; Gaitskell; Douglas-Hamilton; Powell

INTELLIGENCE CORPS ASSOCIATION, Templer Barracks, Ashford, Kent TN23 3HH
Secretary
Baird

ISLE OF WIGHT COUNTY RECORD OFFICE, 26 Hillside, Newport PO30 2EB
County Archivist
Seely

JOHN RYLANDS UNIVERSITY LIBRARY, UNIVERSITY OF MANCHESTER, Deansgate, Manchester M3 3EH
Administrator
JR MacDonald; Marples

KEELE UNIVERSITY LIBRARY, Keele ST5 5BG
Archives and Special Collections
Wedgwood

KEIGHLEY PUBLIC LIBRARY, Reference Library, North Street, Keighley, West Yorks BD21 3SX
Reference Librarian
Snowden

KENT ARCHIVES OFFICE (see CENTRE FOR KENTISH STUDIES)

KENT, UNIVERSITY OF (see TEMPLEMAN LIBRARY)

LANCASHIRE RECORD OFFICE, Bow Lane, Preston PR1 2RE
County Archivist
RA Cross; EGV Stanley; EMC Stanley

LEAGUE OF NATIONS ARCHIVES, Geneva, Switzerland
Archivist
Salter

LEEDS DISTRICT ARCHIVES, Chapeltown Road, Sheepscar, Leeds
LS7 3AP
Senior Archivist
Gaitskell

LEEDS, UNIVERSITY OF (see BROTHERTON COLLECTION)

LIDDELL HART CENTRE FOR MILITARY ARCHIVES, The
Library, King's College London, Strand, London WC2R 2LS
College Archivist
HH Alexander; Hore-Belisha; A Geddes; Haldane; Ismay

LINCOLNSHIRE ARCHIVES, St Rumbold Street, Lincoln LN2 5AB
Principal Archivist
Chaplin; Crookshank

LIVERPOOL RECORD OFFICE AND LOCAL HISTORY
DEPARTMENT, City Libraries, William Brown Street, Liverpool L3
8EW
Principal Archives Officer
EGV Stanley; EMC Stanley

LIVERPOOL UNIVERSITY LIBRARY, PO Box 123, Liverpool L69
3DA
Curator of Special Collections
AJ Balfour; Birrell; Lindsay

LONDON GUILDHALL UNIVERSITY (see FAWCETT LIBRARY)

MAGDALENE COLLEGE, Cambridge CB3 0AG
Librarian
Willink

MANCHESTER, UNIVERSITY OF (see JOHN RYLANDS UNIVERSITY LIBRARY)

McGILL UNIVERSITY (see McLENNAN LIBRARY)

McLENNAN LIBRARY, McGILL UNIVERSITY 3459 McTavish Street, Montreal PQ H3A 1Y1, Canada
Curator of Manuscripts
N Buxton

MIDDLE EAST CENTRE, St Antony's College, Oxford OX2 6JF
GA Lloyd; Samuel

MINISTRY OF DEFENCE WHITEHALL LIBRARY, 3–5 Great Scotland Yard, London SW1A 2HW
Head, Reader Services
Campbell; Marjoribanks

MITCHELL LIBRARY, GLASGOW, 201 North Street, Glasgow G3 7DN
Departmental Librarian, Rare Books and Manuscripts
Johnston; Wheatley

MITCHELL LIBRARY, State Library of New South Wales, Macquarie Street, Sydney NSW 2000, Australia
Librarian
Wynn-Carrington; Lygon

MODERN RECORDS CENTRE, University Library, Warwick University, Coventry CV4 7AL
Archivist
Bevin; Hodge; GH Roberts; JH Thomas

NATIONAL LIBRARY OF AUSTRALIA, Canberra ACT 2600, Australia
Manuscript Librarian, Collections and Reader Services
Baird; Wynn-Carrington; Casey; Munro-Ferguson; JAL Hope; EJ Williams

NATIONAL LIBRARY OF IRELAND, Kildare St, Dublin 2, Ireland
Librarian
FE Smith

NATIONAL LIBRARY OF SCOTLAND, Department of Manuscripts, George IV Bridge, Edinburgh EH1 1EW
Keeper of Manuscripts, Maps and Music
Adamson; Campbell-Bannerman; Elliot; GG Sutherland-Leveson-Gower; Graham; Haldane; Horne; Johnston; Lindsay; JR MacDonald; HP Macmillan; Crewe-Milnes; Murray; Reid; Wheatley; Woodburn

NATIONAL LIBRARY OF WALES, Department of Manuscripts and Records, Aberystwyth SY23 3BU
Keeper of Manuscripts and Records
Baldwin; Windsor-Clive; Ormsby-Gore; Griffiths; Hartshorn; Bonar Law; D Lloyd George; Marquand; DA Thomas; Rees-Williams

NATIONAL MARITIME MUSEUM, Manuscripts Section, Romney Road, Greenwich, London SE10 9NF
Chatfield

NATIONAL MUSEUM OF LABOUR HISTORY, 103 Princess Street, Manchester M1 6DD
Archivist
AJ Barnes; GN Barnes; A Bevan*; Bondfield; Clynes; Gosling; Hartshorn; A Henderson; Hodge; Jowett; JR MacDonald; GH Roberts; Summerskill; Tomlinson; Webb; Wilkinson

NATIONAL REGISTER OF ARCHIVES (SCOTLAND), West Register House, Charlotte Square, Edinburgh EH2 4DF
Registrar
GW Balfour; AH Bruce; Munro-Ferguson; JAL Hope; JP Maclay

NEW BRUNSWICK, UNIVERSITY OF (see HARRIET IRVING LIBRARY)

NEWCASTLE UPON TYNE, UNIVERSITY OF (see ROBINSON LIBRARY)

NEW COLLEGE LIBRARY, Oxford OX1 3BN
Archivist
HAL Fisher

NORFOLK RECORD OFFICE, (Due to fire, enquiries to:) Gildengate House, Anglia Square, Norwich NR3 1EB
County Archivist
Fellowes

NORTHUMBERLAND RECORD OFFICE, Melton Park, North Gosforth, Newcastle upon Tyne NE3 5QX
Heritage Centre Officer
Ridley

NORTH YORKSHIRE COUNTY RECORD OFFICE, Malpas Road, Northallerton DL7 8TB
County Archivist
Dundas

NOTTINGHAMSHIRE ARCHIVES, Castle Meadow Road, Nottingham NG2 1AG
Principal Archivist
Betterton

NOTTINGHAM, UNIVERSITY OF (see HALLWARD LIBRARY)

NUFFIELD COLLEGE LIBRARY, Oxford OX1 1NF
Archivist
RS Cripps; Emmott; Gaitskell*; Creech Jones; Lindemann; HS Morrison; Pease; Seely; Shortt; Strauss; Webb

OLDHAM ARCHIVES SERVICE, Local Studies Library, 84 Union Street, Oldham OL1 1DN
Archives Officer
Emmott

OPEN UNIVERSITY, Walton Hall, Milton Keynes
A Bevan*

ORIENTAL AND INDIA OFFICE COLLECTIONS, BRITISH LIBRARY, 197 Blackfriars Road, London SE1 8NG
Director of Special Collections
Anderson; Benn; Brodrick; VA Bruce; Casey; SC Cavendish; RAT Gascoyne-Cecil; S Cripps; RA Cross; Curzon; Dundas; HCK Petty-Fitzmaurice; Fowler; GF Hamilton; WF Hare; Hoare; RD Isaacs; Kitchener; Pethick-Lawrence; Montagu; Morley; Olivier; Peel; Simon; FE Smith; Dorman Smith; Thesiger; EFL Wood

OXFORD, UNIVERSITY OF (see BODLEIAN LIBRARY)

PUBLIC RECORD OFFICE, Ruskin Avenue, Kew, Richmond TW9 4DU
Keeper of Public Records
Aitken; HH Alexander; J Amery; Amory; Anderson; Ashley; Attlee; Noel-Baker;

Baldwin; AJ Balfour; GW Balfour; Barber; Montague-Barlow; AJ Barnes; Benn; Bevin; Lennox-Boyd; Moore-Brabazon; Brodrick; Bryce; Burgin; Butler; EAR Gascoyne-Cecil; RAJ Gascoyne-Cecil; AN Chamberlain; J Chamberlain; JA Chamberlain; WL Spencer-Churchill; Duff Cooper; S Cripps; Curzon; Dalton; Dugdale; Chuter Ede; Eden; Worthington-Evans; HCK Petty-Fitzmaurice; Gaitskell; AC Geddes; E Geddes; A Greenwood; Grey; Hankey; Head; A Henderson; A Henderson (Rowley); Hoare; QM Hogg; Horsbrugh; Hudson; RD Isaacs; Ismay; Kearley; Kerr; Kitchener; Lansbury; Bonar Law; Law; Leathers; Cunliffe-Lister; Llewellin; GW Lloyd; S Lloyd; D Lloyd George; Long; O Lyttelton; JR MacDonald; M MacDonald; Macleod; MH Macmillan; McNeill; Maudling; Milner; Crewe-Milnes; Monckton; Monsell; Morley; H Morrison; Mosley; Murray; Ponsonby; Portal; Runciman; Salter; Sandys; Simon; A Sinclair; B Smith; Snowden; EGV Stanley; Stokes; CB Thomson; Thorneycroft; Watkinson; A Weir; Wilkinson; T Williams; Wilmot; EFL Wood; K Wood; Woodburn

PUBLIC RECORD OFFICE OF NORTHERN IRELAND, 66 Balmoral Avenue, Belfast BT9 6NY
Director
Carson; Chaplin; Gibson; GF Hamilton; McNeill; Powell; CS Vane-Tempest-Stewart; CSH Vane-Tempest-Stewart

QUEEN'S UNIVERSITY ARCHIVES, Kathleen Ryan Hall, Kingston K7L 3N6, Canada
Archivist (Public Service)
VA Bruce; E Grigg

READING UNIVERSITY LIBRARY, PO Box 223, Whiteknights, Reading RG6 2AE
Keeper of Archives and Manuscripts
MH Macmillan

RHODES HOUSE LIBRARY, South Parks Road, Oxford OX1 3RG
Librarian
Montague-Barlow; Lennox-Boyd; Ormsby-Gore; Creech Jones; Maudling; Olivier

ROBINSON LIBRARY, UNIVERSITY OF NEWCASTLE UPON TYNE, Newcastle upon Tyne NE2 4HQ
Special Collections Librarians
Runciman; Trevelyan

ROYAL AIR FORCE MUSEUM, Department of Aviation Records, Grahame Park Way, Hendon, London NW9 5LL
Keeper of Aviation Records
Moore-Brabazon

ROYAL ARCHIVES, Windsor Castle, Berkshire SL4 1NJ
Registrar
Monckton

ROYAL COMMONWEALTH SOCIETY LIBRARY, 18 Nor-
thumberland Avenue, London WC2N 5BJ
Librarian
MJ MacDonald

RURAL HISTORY CENTRE, University of Reading, PO Box 229,
Whiteknights, Reading RG6 2AG
Archivist
RC Palmer; WW Palmer

ST DEINIOL'S LIBRARY, HAWARDEN, Clwyd Record Office,
Hawarden Branch, The Old Rectory, Hawarden, Deeside CH5 3NR
County Archivist
Gladstone

SAYER ARCHIVE, 68 Staines Road, Hounslow, Middlesex TW3 3LF
Archivist
Aitken; GN Barnes; AN Chamberlain; Eden; D Lloyd George; A Sinclair

SCIENCE MUSEUM, South Kensington, London SW7 5NH
Archivist
Pearson

SCOTTISH RECORD OFFICE, HM General Register House, Edin-
burgh EH1 3YY
Keeper of Records of Scotland
*Adamson; AJ Balfour; GW Balfour; AE Brown; AH Bruce; Collins; Colville;
Dundas; Elliott; Munro-Ferguson; Gilmour; Ormsby-Gore; JAL Hope; Johnston;
Kerr; JS Maclay; McNeil; Steel-Maitland; Munro; Murray; Noble; Primrose;
AHM Sinclair; J Sinclair; Stuart; Tennant; Westwood; TM Wood; Woodburn*

SHEFFIELD ARCHIVES, 52 Shoreham Street, Sheffield S1 4SP
Principal Archivist
AV Alexander

SHEFFIELD UNIVERSITY LIBRARY, Western Bank, Sheffield S10
2TN
Archivist
Mosley

SHROPSHIRE RECORD OFFICE, Castle Gates, Shrewbury SY1 2AQ
Head of Records and Research
Bridgeman; Windsor-Clive; GG Sutherland-Leveson-Gower

SOUTH AFRICAN GOVERNMENT ARCHIVES, Central Archives Depot, Department of National Education, Private Bag X236, Pretoria 0001, South Africa
Archivist
Smuts

SOUTHAMPTON, UNIVERSITY OF (see HARTLEY LIBRARY)

SOUTHPORT PUBLIC LIBRARY, Lord Street, Southport, Merseyside PR8 1DJ
Librarian
Curzon

SOUTH WALES COALFIELD ARCHIVES, The Library, University of Wales, Swansea, Singleton Park, Swansea SA2 8PP
The Archivist
A Bevan; Edwards; Griffiths

SOUTHWARK LOCAL STUDIES LIBRARY, 211 Borough High Street, London SE1 1JA
Local Studies Librarian
Causton; GA Isaacs; B Smith

STAFFORDSHIRE RECORD OFFICE, County Buildings, Eastgate Street, Stafford ST16 2LZ
County Archivist
Chaplin; Powell

SURREY RECORD OFFICE, County Hall, Penrhyn Road, Kingston upon Thames KT1 2DN
County Archivist
Chuter Ede

TEMPLEMAN LIBRARY, University of Kent, Canterbury, Kent CT2 7NU
Librarian
K Wood

TOWER HAMLETS LOCAL HISTORY LIBRARY AND ARCHIVES, Central Library, 277 Bancroft Road, London E1 4DQ
Archivist
S Buxton; Lansbury

TRADES UNION CONGRESS, Congress House, Great Russell St, London WC1B 3LS
Librarian
Burns

TRINITY COLLEGE LIBRARY, Trinity College, Cambridge CB1 1TQ
Archivist
Butler; Pethick-Lawrence; Montagu

TRINITY COLLEGE LIBRARY, College Street, Dublin 2, Ireland
Assistant Librarian, Manuscripts Department
Hicks Beach; Birrell; Carson; Arnold-Forster; Goschen; Morley

UNIVERSITY COLLEGE LONDON LIBRARY, Manuscripts Room, Gower Street, London WC1E 6BT
Archivist
Gaitskell

UNIVERSITY OF BRISTOL LIBRARY, Tyndall Avenue, Bristol BS8 1TJ
Librarian
AH Sinclair

UNIVERSITY OF ST ANDREW'S LIBRARY, North Street, St Andrews, Fife KY16 9TR
Librarian
Powell

VASSAR COLLEGE LIBRARY, Poughkeepsie, New York 12601, USA
Curator of Rare Books and Manuscripts
Bondfield

WANDSWORTH MUSEUM, PUTNEY LIBRARY, Disraeli Road, London SW15
Burns

WARWICK, UNIVERSITY OF (see MODERN RECORDS CENTRE)

WARWICKSHIRE COUNTY RECORD OFFICE, Priory Park, Cape Road, Warwick CV34 4JS
County Archivist
Hobson

WEIZMANN ARCHIVES, Rehovot, Israel
Curator
Bracken; Mond

WELSH POLITICAL ARCHIVE (see NATIONAL LIBRARY OF WALES)

WICHITA STATE UNIVERSITY, Wichita, Kansas 67208–1595, USA
Special Collections
N Buxton

WILLIAM R PERKINS LIBRARY, DUKE UNIVERSITY, Durham, North Carolina 27708–0185, USA
Asquith; AJ Balfour; Brodrick; N Buxton; Robinson

WILTSHIRE RECORD OFFICE, County Hall, Trowbridge BA14 8JG
County Archivist
Eccles; Arnold-Forster; Long

WINCHESTER COLLEGE, Winchester, Hants SO23 9NA
Archivist
Simonds

YORK, UNIVERSITY OF (see BORTHWICK INSTITUTE OF HISTORICAL RESEARCH)

Index of Ministers

ROYAL HISTORICAL SOCIETY

GUIDES AND HANDBOOKS No. 19

A Guide to the Papers of British Cabinet Ministers 1900–1964 is the revised and expanded edition of a volume first published by The Royal Historical Society in 1974. While much of the information is drawn from the 1974 text, a great deal comes from subsequent new research. Its aim is to provide up-to-date information on the papers of 323 ministers in the first edition and include all Cabinet ministers (or those who held positions included in a Cabinet) until the resignation of Sir Alec Douglas-Home as Prime Minister in 1964. Thus the scope of this edition has increased from the 323 ministers in the first *Guide* to 384, and therefore incorporates those who held relevant positions in the Churchill, Eden, Macmillan and Home governments. Information is provided on 60 'new' ministers and the previously omitted Lord Stanley. This *Guide* therefore is a major research tool and a source of information on personal papers, often in private hands, of people who played major roles in twentieth-century political life.

CAMERON HAZLEHURST is Head of the School of Humanities at Queensland University of Technology.
SALLY WHITEHEAD is Senior Research Assistant in the School of Humanities at Queensland University of Technology.

CAMBRIDGE
UNIVERSITY PRESS

ISBN 0-521-58743-3

9 780521 587433 >